An Actor's Work

Stanislavski's 'system' has dominated actor-training in the West since his writings were first translated into English in the 1920s and 30s. His systematic attempt to outline a psycho-physical technique for acting single-handedly revolutionized standards of acting in the theatre.

Until now, readers and students have had to contend with inaccurate, misleading and difficult-to-read English-language versions. Some of the mistranslations have resulted in profound distortions in the way his system has been interpreted and taught. At last, Jean Benedetti has succeeded in translating Stanislavski's huge manual into a lively, fascinating and accurate text in English. He has remained faithful to the author's original intentions, putting the two books previously known as *An Actor Prepares* and *Building a Character* back together into one volume, and in a colloquial and readable style for today's actors.

The result is a major contribution to the theatre, and a service to one of the great innovators of the twentieth century.

Konstantin
Stanislavski

An Actor's Work

A Student's Diary

Translated and edited by Jean Benedetti

Routledge
Taylor & Francis Group

LONDON AND NEW YORK

First published 2008 by Routledge
First published in paperback 2010
by Routledge
2 Park Square, Milton Park, Abingdon, Oxon, OX14 4RN

Simultaneously published in the USA and Canada
by Routledge
711 Third Ave, New York, NY 10017
Routledge is an imprint of the Taylor & Francis Group, an informa business

Translation, text and Afterword © 2008; 2010 Routledge

Translator's Foreword and editorial matter © 2008; 2010 Jean Benedetti

Introduction © 2008; 2010 Declan Donnellan

Typeset in Joanna by RefineCatch Limited, Bungay, Suffolk

British Library Cataloguing in Publication Data
A catalogue record for this book is available from the British Library

Library of Congress Cataloging-in-Publication Data
Stanislavsky, Konstantin, 1863–1938.
   [Rabota aktera nad soboi. English]
   An actor's work : a student's diary / Konstantin Stanislavski ;
translated and edited by Jean Benedetti.
         p. cm.
Includes bibliographical references and index.
   1. Method (Acting)   I. Benedetti, Jean.   II. Title.
   PN2062.S7613 2008
   792.02′8–dc22

                                                                  2007045357
ISBN10: 0–415–42223–X (hbk)
ISBN10: 0–415–55120–X (pbk)
ISBN10: 0–203–93615–9 (ebk)

ISBN13: 978–0–415–42223–9 (hbk)
ISBN13: 978–0–415–55120–5 (pbk)
ISBN13: 978–0–203–93615–3 (ebk)

Printed and bound in the United States of America
By Edwards Brothers Malloy on sustainably sourced paper.

To Maria Petrovna Lilina, who has shared my labours, my best teacher, beloved actress, ever devoted help-meet in all my theatrical endeavours, this book is dedicated.

CONTENTS

YEAR TWO: EMBODIMENT

INTRODUCTION

Declan Donnellan

The best Stanislavski story I know isn't about an actor at all but about a dog. An actor had a dog. This dog used to come to rehearsals and, being rather lazy, would sleep in the corner all day long. Strangely, every evening, just before the actors were to finish, the dog would already be at the door, leash in mouth, waiting to be taken home. What astounded Stanislavski was that the dog would wearily haul himself to his feet several minutes before his master called him. Regular as clockwork, come the end of every rehearsal, the dog would trot to the door and wait there patiently. Now how could a dog possibly know that the rehearsal was over before anyone moved to the door? Finally Stanislavski figured it out. The dog could hear when the actors started talking like normal human beings again. The difference between the fake and the living was just as sharp as Pavlov's bell.

Stanislavski was obsessed with life. When he uses the word 'art' it often reads as a code for 'life'. This fusion is clear even in the title of his autobiography *My Life in Art*. His absolute priority was that the stage should flow with life. He hated empty effects and loved genuine vitality. He abhorred hollow gestures that pretend to breathe. He sought that curious mixture of discipline and spontaneity that characterises all good art.

Presumably this is why he continues to inspire us. His own inspiration he drew from many sources. As a young man he was particularly impressed by the ensemble style of a German company on tour in Moscow, and also by Eleanora Duse, the great Italian star who seemed to efface her virtuosity in a struggle for the living moment. But of course he drew most of his inspiration from the life he saw ebbing and flowing around him.

In the first place, Stanislavski had a vision of a living theatre, a theatre that was not only a building or even a company, but a whole attitude to theatre itself.

Then the question he had to ask was: 'How can I do this? How can I make life flow on stage?'

This is normally the moment when we all speed on to find out how he answered the question. 'What do I need to do, what exercises can I practice, to become a successful actor? Just show me the steps and I'll follow the plan!' But it is precisely here that we need to slow right down. We need to remember what it is that Stanislavski first saw. Stanislavski saw, or had a vision of, a form of acting that brimmed with life. To his consternation he realised that the line between the sham and the authentic can be very narrow. Yes we can immediately see the gulf that seems to separate the terrible old ham from the sophisticated naturalism of the modern film star. But the sham often seems very real and the most perfectly natural performance can also be perfectly fake. In fact separating appearance from reality is one of our toughest struggles and being clever can make it harder. Sometimes it takes a dog to tell the difference.

Stanislavski saw that it is easier to give the audience a clever ride than a real experience. But his fundamental intuition was that acting is more than seeming to be real. Above all, he knew that acting and pretending are utterly different and that the distinction is both subtle and crucial. In a way, all his work helps to explain that difference.

And somehow that first intuition of Stanislavski can get squashed in our acceleration to learn the techniques and devices that he invented (and frequently discarded). The first step is not to ask 'How can I be a successful actor?' The first question must always be 'What is good acting?' And the answer will remain the same: 'When it is alive'. Strangely we need to keep returning to this point of departure, otherwise we are forever lost.

A few days ago a foreigner approached me in the street and inquired in precise English: 'Excuse me please, but which way is Belsize Park?' When I answered he looked at me carefully and asked with great emphasis: 'But how will I recognise it when I get there?' It was a very good question. Learning to recognise when we get there is of vital importance in every field.

Learning to recognise things is of great importance to Stanislavski, for example, the actor must learn to see the constraints imposed on the character. Stanislavski gives great importance to the 'Given Circumstances'. The idea seems so obvious and yet it is so subtle. He understands that life is only possible within a context. That character and action are all dependent on the 'Given Circumstances', that we need to see the tiny realities that make up the world we live in. Our species is painfully learning that its very survival depends on the health of the planet. We cannot exist in a vacuum.

Unfortunately Stanislavski has become a myth and this has done him a disservice. Like many great thinkers, Stanislavski articulates some of the eternal conflicts with such deceptive simplicity that we tend to imagine ourselves reflected back. Perhaps that is why he is so easily appropriated.

For example he understands that theatre will always be stretched between two poles – one of form, the other of content. Now although Stanislavski was fascinated by the inner workings of the actor, he was no theatre puritan. He adored his make up, wanted to parade Tuzenbach's body around the stage at the end of *Three Sisters*, and developed such a fad for sound effects that Chekhov threatened to begin his next play with the line, *'Isn't it incredible, such a hot summer and you can't hear a cicada anywhere!'* It wasn't theatrical gestures that Stanislavski hated – it was empty theatrical gestures.

A main theme of his early work does seem to be an escape from 'superficial' theatre into something more 'true'. This becomes counterbalanced by the understanding that in fact theatre needs both of these extremities to have any life. We need to be playful to live, but excessive playfulness starts to look like hysteria. Like many great artists, Stanislavski navigates between these eternal poles, profane and sacred, rough and holy, earth and clouds, showbiz and sacrament. Ignoring one pole may help us feel more comfortable in the short term, but ultimately leads to artistic suicide. To live fully we need to negotiate the narrow rim between order and chaos.

So Stanislavski is not one thing. Like any great thinker he is a bundle of contradictions. For example, he was an amateur who yearned to be truly 'professional'. Although contemporaries agreed that he was a gifted actor, somewhere in his heart he always felt untrained. Certainly his writings erupt with this struggle, which was not just to train his student actors, but also to become 'professional' in himself. It is this humility that makes Stanislavski truly remarkable. He was wise precisely because he knew that he didn't know.

As a director Stanislavski saw a group of actors acting. And he understood that his job as director was to help the actors to act together and to bring the acting level of the weakest actor up to that of the strongest. Throughout his life he invented exercises to help actors act better. Nothing more than that – and nothing less than that. He had no grandiose plan. He knew that he was permanently reacting to the circumstances that surrounded him – his own 'Given Circumstances'. And all given circumstances change, apart from the one that says that everything must change. That is one reason why his body of theatre writing is the most systematic, enduring and revolutionary, precisely because he knew that any fail-proof system is doomed to failure.

He often changed his mind and had a whim of steel. Prey to enthusiasms and fads, like Toad of Toad Hall, suddenly all his students would have to be equipped with a certain notebook to write down observations and then, just as suddenly, all this would be forgotten.

Over the years, and particularly after the revolution, his students separated, each of them bearing a memory of their teacher's thinking. But these memories rarely amounted to more than a snapshot – a photograph of Konstantin Sergeevich's thinking at any given time, the temporary truce in his conflicting thoughts. That is why so many of his disciples have so seriously disagreed. Konstantin Sergeevich would probably have agreed with most of them! But he is unlikely to have agreed with any of the disciples who claimed that their way was the only true way.

The last century saw forces within both superpowers convert Stanislavski to their own ideological uses. Of course first they both had to erase his inconvenient humanity of proportion. The Soviet Union dreaded the ambivalence of metaphor, so certain apparatchiks contorted his theories into a loudspeaker for the dreariest Stalinist naturalism. But across the planet another fate befell him. One of Stanislavski's enduring tenets was that actors had to be present in the moment enabling them to adapt and react spontaneously with their partners. But in the United States some prised him away from this essentially ensemble context and forced him to testify for the individualist star who prepares the great role well away from the prying eyes of colleagues. Thus for much of the last century Stanislavski was communised and capitalised to taste.

Rising fundamentalism of the present century threatens to rival the totalitarian horrors of the last. And Stanislavski is threatened by fundamentalism too. Great spiritual leaders stress that when there is a conflict between the letter of the law and the spirit of the law, then, without exception, it is the spirit that must prevail. The problem with all fundamentalists is that they are never quite fundamental enough. A scripture which was written to help people can easily be used as an instrument to control or even to punish them.

Konstantin Sergeevich Stanislavski never intended his words to become scripture. He never sought to create a 'system'. Unlike Freud he never wanted to invent a science. Above all he would be at pains to say that where there is true life on stage, leave well alone!

The growing desire of students to acquire skills may be fair enough, but sometimes it is important to remember that there is more to learning than a stashing of qualifications and information. It is also important to be open to a teacher's spirit, which cannot be quantified, or even described. Some of us are lucky enough to have great teachers, but they are great not because they have access to secret information, or because they are clever at getting their point across, but because they imbue their pupils with confidence. They fill their pupils with a passion for their subject and infuse them with a sense that they *can*, rather than with a sense that they *cannot*. They empower their pupils to go on after them. Ultimately they can even enable their pupils to disagree with them and to break free.

Meyerhold was a pupil of Stanislavski. Stanislavski enabled the young man to start his own studio. The two disagreed, sometimes quite violently. Meyerhold is occasionally held up as some sort of antidote to his teacher, as if they were the Danton and Robespierre of theatrical theory. But Meyerhold took the spirit of Stanislavski and converted it – just as Stanislavski, years before, was struck by the ensemble spirit of the touring German company, breathed in that spirit and breathed it out again, transformed. Indeed Stanislavski said that he regarded Meyerhold as his true heir and was the last person to give him a job directing before his pupil was murdered in the Lyubyanka. Clearly Meyerhold absorbed a lot more from Stanislavski than a few exercises – his system of biomechanics is utterly infused with his teacher's insatiable thirst for life.

But the current consumerist tendency in education which prizes only the acquisition of visible skills is not as worrying as the increasing clamour for certainty. We want to know how to be a success, we want results fast – and no frills. Now it would be great if there existed a step-by-step fail-proof process to act well or make good theatre, but there simply isn't – just as no religion with a first-you-do-this-then-you-do-that system can guarantee redemption. Sure there are exercises that can help. Sure there are procedures that may help life flow. But sometimes they don't work, and Stanislavski was at pains to point this out. His frustration often boils over.

Why does he continue to inspire so many actors and theatre makers, including those who seem to be so far from his tradition? Because life is all he wanted. Life is what he struggled to let flow through the actors, between the actors, between the actors and the audience. His words are a fascinating and moving account of this struggle. His writing is important because it helps us come into contact with his great spirit. He was revolutionary because he helped us to see that there is more to acting than mere pretending, to sense that beyond the trivial there is something toweringly alive that is worth the struggle.

Declan Donnellan

October 2007

Declan Donnellan is joint artistic director of Cheek by Jowl and associate director of the Royal National Theatre. In 1999, with his partner Nick Ormerod, he formed an ensemble of actors in Moscow. His book, The Actor and the Target, originally published in Russian, has since been translated into several languages.

www.cheekbyjowl.com

Translator's Foreword

Jean Benedetti

This book is neither a literal nor an academic translation but rather an attempt to follow Stanislavski's original intention: to provide an accessible account of the 'system' for actors in training without abstract theorizing. Hence the form he chose: a diary kept by a young student in which he describes the acting classes given by Tortsov (Stanislavski) and his own struggle, alongside his classmates, to master a new method.

An Actor's Work has always presented problems both to Russian- and non-Russian-speaking readers. First it is a work that is only half written. In 1888 when he was in his mid-twenties Stanislavski conceived the idea of a 'grammar' of acting. His first attempt, *A Draft Manual* dates from 1906 when the 'system' began. Thereafter he attempted formal exposition in the form of lectures and classes but came to the conclusion that actors did not respond to this kind of approach. He gave a series of talks at the Bolshoi school between 1919 and 1921, which represent the first tentative account of the 'system' but he never attempted to publish them. He then experimented with the novel form, *The Story of a Role, The Story of Production* both of which he abandoned. Finally, in the late 1920s, he decided upon a diary form, a journal kept by a student as he goes through the process of training, *An Actor's Work on Himself*.

He began work after his heart attack of 1928 which put an end to his acting career, drawing heavily on earlier incomplete articles and his Notebooks, so that much of the material dates from before the Revolution. Intended as a single volume, it outlined a two-year course of training in which the student first learns the process by which the inner life of a character is created and then how this is expressed in physical and technical terms. The result is a unified, coherent psycho-physical technique.

The accidents of history, which I have discussed elsewhere, caused the two aspects of training to be separated out. A single volume to become two so that some thirteen years separate the Russian edition of Part One (1938) and Part Two (1953). Thus the unity of the psycho-physical technique was lost. Even Elizabeth Hapgood, Stanislavski's first translator, thought they were separate books and that Part Two represented a revision of the ideas contained in Part One. From the very beginning, Stanislavski had serious misgivings about dividing the book. He feared that the first volume, dealing with the psychological aspects of acting would be identified as the total 'system' itself, which would be identified as a form of 'ultranaturalism'. His fears were justified. Directors have seen the 'system' as purely 'psychological'. They are unaware of the enormous emphasis Stanislavski placed on physical and vocal technique and on a detailed analysis of the script. I have, therefore, attempted to restore the unity of Stanislavski's teaching concept by recreating a single volume as was originally intended.

One of the difficulties of presenting a readable account of Stanislavski's ideas is his style, which is at considerable variance with his other writings. He was haunted by the possibility that he would be misunderstood, as had so often been the case in the past, even by close associates. In consequence his tendency was to overwrite and over-explain, using several words where one or two would do, and repeating definitions like a mantra. His style all too often obscured his meaning. When his life-long friend and theatre historian, Lyubov Gurievich, saw Stanislavski's first draft chapters in 1929 she understood the problem. They were repetitive and verbose. She suggested to Stanislavski that he should complete the book and that then the two of them should edit and cut it into readable form.

Stanislavski had two other collaborators on the book, Norman and Elizabeth Hapgood. Mrs Hapgood spoke fluent Russian and had been Stanislavski's interpreter at a White House reception in 1923, while her husband, Norman, was an experienced publisher and editor.

In 1929 Stanislavski renewed his acquaintance with Mrs Hapgood in Nice, where he was convalescing after his heart attacks. They agreed to collaborate on an American translation. The first thing Norman Hapgood did was to take his blue pencil and edit down Stanislavski's partial draft while Elizabeth Hapgood suggested certain revisions that were then translated back into Russian. When Stanislavski returned to Russia, the book was still unfinished. Mrs Hapgood took the completed chapters back with her to America but did not receive the remaining chapters until 1935.

Stanislavski's task on his return to Moscow was to prepare the Soviet edition,[1] working once again with Mrs Gurievich. It is with this edition that we are now concerned. This edition was to differ substantially from the edition given to Mrs Hapgood; the reasons for this were two-fold.

First, Stanislavski would endlessly rewrite, whilst Mrs Gurievich used her 'blue pencil'. She would carefully edit his drafts and introduce an element of order. Unfortunately he would then revise and rewrite, re-introducing chaos. Finally, in despair, Mrs Gurievich had to give up the unequal struggle so that the final chapters of Part One are Stanislavski's alone and the deterioration in the writing is all too evident. Even after the proofs had been returned to the printers, he continued to draft sections for a possible second edition. Thus, even the Russian edition of 1938 was, in his mind, 'provisional'.

Second, he was locked in a bitter battle with pseudo-Marxist Soviet psychology, which was Behaviourist and did not recognize the existence either of the subconscious or of the Mind. Consequently, he substantially rewrote whole passages in an attempt to appease the authorities. Nowhere are the differences between the two editions more marked than in Chapters 14, 15 and 16.

The reasons for the difficulties of Stanislavski's style go deeper than his personal foibles. His was a pioneering effort. He was attempting to define the actor's processes (mental, physical, intellectual and emotional) in a comprehensive way that had never been undertaken before. His problem was that there was no available language or terminology to which he could turn. Many concepts which we now take for granted such as non-verbal communication or body language did not exist. Even the notion of comprehensive, systematic training did not exist. Teaching in drama schools consisted mainly in students preparing scenes that were then reworked by the tutor. Sometimes a student would only prepare one or two scenes throughout his entire studies and would merely learn to copy his master's tricks. He had no coherent process, no 'grammar' of his own. Stanislavski wanted to develop the actor-creator. He was driven, therefore, to cobble together a 'jargon' that was unknown outside the Art Theatre. His experience of teaching the 'system' in the early years had made him wary of formal lecturing or of using scientific terminology. Actors either shied away from it or bandied technical terms about to give the impression that they understood, when in reality, they did not.

---

[1] For a full account of the writing, translating, editing and publication of the work and on the differences between the American 1936 edition and the Soviet 1938 edition see my *Stanislavski his Life and Art*, 3rd edition, 1999.

Stanislavski's 'jargon' is made up of disparate elements. Where possible he used ordinary, everyday words, what he called his 'home-grown' vocabulary. Thus when analyzing a play he did not talk about dividing it up into its component parts or sections, but of cutting it up into 'Bits' or pieces, as you would carve a lump of meat.[2] In defining their course of action, actors set themselves 'goals', gave themselves simple, practical direct 'Tasks', not high-flown philosophical or emotional purposes. For the rest, he took what he could where he could. When he came to discuss non-verbal communication, he drew on concepts drawn from yoga which he had studied in the early 1900s. Where there were technical, scientific definitions such as intellect, feeling and will, he used them. Sometimes he would adapt words to suit his own purpose. This is the case with his decision to use the French word mise-en-scène/mises-en-scène to denote the outer stage action which literally 'puts on stage' the inner action of the play either as a whole or at individual moments.[3] The most significant example, perhaps, is his use of the key term experiencing (perezhivanie) which denotes the process by which an actor engages actively with the situation in each and every performance. He was sometimes obliged, particularly when dealing with the subconscious to create his own terms and definitions which are often highly convoluted and confusing. The reader has to come to terms with the 'jargon' just as the students do in the book. Indeed that is the book's purpose: for the reader to experience the students' learning process. As an aid, I have, as in previous books, given the major terms of 'system' initial capital letters to indicate their transformation from everyday words to technical definitions.

THE USA AND RUSSIA: A HISTORY OF PUBLICATION

An Actor Prepares

For commercial reasons, Part One, An Actor Prepares was reduced by Mrs Hapgood and Edith Isaacs, managing editor of Theatre Arts Books, to almost half its length. It loses its essential form as the diary of a first-year student, and becomes a straight narrative. Many of the lively classroom discussions where ideas are hammered out, not to mention the humour, disappeared. There is, in the original, no Director- enunciating principles in the abstract, but a rigorous and sympathetic teacher who guides students through a process of trial and error. Mrs Hapgood also decided not

[2] See Chapter 7.
[3] See Glossary.

to use Stanislavski's home-grown terms but to replace them with rather more abstract words. Thus, 'Bit' becomes 'unit'.

Building A Character

Part Two, *Building a Character* again in the translation by Elizabeth Hapgood, presents much more serious editorial problems. Stanislavski did not live to complete Part Two. At his death in 1938 only one or two chapters, such as that on Speech existed in draft, although the overall contents of the book were clear. There were, in addition, a number of fragments of varying length that would have provided the basis for the completed manuscript.

Three versions of Part Two are available. The first, translated by Elizabeth Hapgood, which appeared in 1950, was based on material supplied by Stanislavski's son, Igor. Mrs Hapgood believed that this material represented Stanislavski's final thoughts. In 1955, Part Two appeared as Volume 3 in the 8-volume Soviet edition of Stanislavski's *Collected Works*. It included material from the archives unavailable to Mrs Hapgood. It was presented as a reconstruction. In 1990, a further expanded version appeared as Volume 3 of the new 9-volume edition of the *Selected Works* and was clearly marked *Material for a Book*.

Although the 1955 and 1990 editions were fully annotated, no editorial work was done on the body of the text. Close examination of the published Russian texts reveals how rough a state the material is in. Much of it is drawn, as internal evidence indicates, from earlier periods of Stanislavski's life, not from the mid-1930s. Many passages are variant versions of material that had already been used in Part One. Other material is repeated in more than one section. Even in apparently complete chapters there are repetitions. In the chapter on Speech, for example, punctuation, stress and pauses are discussed twice with slightly different examples. Some material in the section The General Creative State may well have been intended for Chapter 15 of Part One.

This is of interest to specialists and scholars, but if an attempt is to be made to produce a book which, in accordance with Stanislavski's wishes is to be of practical use in actor training, to be used in conjunction with Part One, a degree of editorial work is necessary.

I have removed as far as possible redundant passages or material which has been used in Part One. I have also removed the sections in the chapter on Speech which discuss the correct pronunciation of Russian consonants and which have little meaning for non-Russian speakers. Technical training in voice and body have advanced considerably in theatre schools and conservatoires since the 1930s so that some of Stanislavski's ideas, which were pioneering at the time, are now of only historic interest. I have, therefore, edited and conflated two original chapters, Singing and Diction and Speech and its Laws into one, Voice and Speech. In the final chapters, Basics of the System and How to use the System, I have omitted almost entirely since they are fragmentary and largely summarize material from earlier sections. The revisions to Part One which he intended for a second edition appear as Appendices at the end of the book, as do the practical exercises he suggested.

I have included Stanislavski's original draft Preface, which has never been translated before. It was reconstructed by the editors of the current 9-volume from entries in Stanislavski's *Notebooks* of the early 1930s. The original drafts set out his intentions much more clearly. The Preface to the 1938 Russian edition is essentially a political statement, a defence against criticisms he had received. I have also included in the Appendices the drafts Stanislavski made after the book had gone to the printer for a possible second edition.

THE 'SYSTEM' AND THE METHOD

One major obstacle to the proper understanding of Stanislavski's teaching has been the widespread confusion between the 'system' and the Method as defined by Lee Strasberg at the Actors' Studio in New York. Strasberg was perfectly aware of the differences between his teaching and Stanislavski's, which centred on the role of Emotion Memory.[4] In the 'system' the primary emphasis is on action, interaction and the dramatic situation which result in feeling with Emotion Memory as a secondary, ancillary technique. In the Method, Emotion Memory is placed at the very centre; the actor consciously evokes personal feelings that correspond to the character, a technique which Stanislavski expressly rejected. Whereas in the 'system' each section of the play contains something an actor has to *do*, in the Method it contains something he has to *feel*. Strasberg's main concern was to enable the actor to unblock his emotions. There is little or no textual or dramaturgical analysis.

In the early 1950s, Strasberg took charge of the Actors' Studio. The original founders, Elia Kazan, Robert Lewis and Stella Adler were generally proponents of the 'system' in its late form. Adler spent six weeks in Paris in 1934 working with Stanislavski on the Method of Physical Action, which Strasberg categorically and angrily rejected when she explained it to him. A bitter dispute broke out among the teachers at the Studio.

[4] See Chapter 9.

Strasberg was initially engaged exclusively as a teacher of theatre history and was not allowed to take acting classes since he was not trusted. It was with the departure of Elia Kazan to Hollywood that an opportunity arose for him to take over. He then refashioned the Studio in his own image. Indeed, he became the Studio; its teachings were his. It was in fact thanks to the impact of the films of Elia Kazan, and a series of commanding performances by actors such as Marlon Brando (taught by Stella Adler not Strasberg) that the Method achieved worldwide fame and was identified with the 'system'. This was made possible because most actors and directors, as Stanislavski had feared, thought that *An Actor Prepares*, a cut version of half a book, was the complete 'system'. The 'system' meant subjectivity and emotion.[5] To compound the confusion, the term *perezhivanie* (experiencing) was commonly translated as 'emotional identification'.

In the 1950s only one or two schools in the UK taught the 'system' as laid down by Stanislavski himself. Again the 'system' was identified with the Method, which was generally derided by successful professionals. Only Michael Redgrave, among the leading actors of his time had any real understanding of Stanislavski. It is only in the last thirty years that Stanislavski's authentic teachings have become known in university drama departments and theatre schools. Yet even comparatively well-informed people still confuse the 'system' and the Method, hence the importance of reaffirming the integrity of Stanislavski's thought.

THE CHARACTERS IN THE BOOK

A note should be added about the names of the characters in the book. Stanislavski followed a tradition by which characters were given names that reflected the essential nature of their personalities. Stanislavski becomes Tortsov, which derives from the word for creator. Tortsov is a combination of the mature Stanislavski and his mentor, the leading tenor of the Bolshoi, Fydor Komissarzhevski. The student keeping the diary is Nazvanov, meaning the chosen one. He is a combination of the young Stanislavski, with the same first name Kostya (Konstantin) and Stanislavski's favourite pupil, Vakhtangov, who first came to Stanislavski's attention as a stenographer. Other students are called Brainy, Fatty, Prettyface, Big-mouth, Youngster, Happy, Showy. These linguistic niceties are lost on non-Russian speakers. Indeed, the simple pronunciation of Russian names presents difficulties which can be a barrier to understanding.

[5] For a detailed analysis of the problem, see Richard Horby, *The End of Acting*, Applause Books, 2000.

Mrs Hapgood wisely, and probably with Stanislavski's agreement, gave each of the students first names and I, like translators into other languages, have followed her example.

The pupils

Darya Dymkova
Grisha Govorkov
Marya Maloletkova
Konstantin (Kostya) Nazvanov
Leo Pushchin
Pavel (Pasha) Shustov
Nikolai Umnovikh
Varya Veliaminova
Igor Veselovski
Ivan (Vanya) Viuntsov

The teachers

Ivan Rakhmanov
Arkady Tortsov

ACKNOWLEDGEMENT

I would like to express my profound gratitude to Katya Kamotskaia, a professional actress and director, and graduate of the Vakhtangov School in Moscow, for going through the draft translation and making many invaluable suggestions as to meaning and nuance. Our joint study of Stanislavski's often convoluted and opaque text revealed the difficulties his style presents even for native Russian speakers when attempting to decipher his meaning. The final translation is the result of many hours of detailed discussion.

Jean Benedetti
October 2007

PUBLISHER'S ACKNOWLEDGEMENTS

The publishers would like to acknowledge the support and contribution of the following:

Louise Jeffreys and Sarah Shaw at the Barbican Centre; Paul Fryer and Andrew Eglington at Rose Bruford College; Bella Merlin; Anne Meyer; Declan Donnellan and Jacqui Honess-Martin of Cheek by Jowl; Maxime Mardoukhaev and Olga Alexeev, Paris; Laurence Senelick, Tufts University, Boston; Anatoly Smeliansky, Moscow Art Theatre Studio-School; The National Theatre, London; Marie Christine Autant-Mathieu at CNRS, Paris

Russian Language Consultant: Katya Kamotskaia
Publisher: Talia Rodgers
Marketing: Tom Church and Chris Bowers
Production Manager: Andrew Watts
Cover Designer: Jamie Keenan
Copy-Editor: Sandra Stafford
Proof-Reader: Carol Fellingham-Webb

An Actor's Work

ORIGINAL DRAFT PREFACE

[EXTRACTS]

My book has no pretensions to be scientific. Although I take the view that art should be on good terms with science, I am alarmed by the kind of scientific sophistries actors use at moments when they are creating intuitively, and it is that with which this book is mainly concerned. Acting is above all intuitive, because it is based on subconscious feelings, on an actor's instincts. That, of course, does not mean that an actor should be an ignoramus, that he has no need of knowledge. Quite the contrary, he needs it more than anyone, because it provides him with material with which to be creative. But there is a time and a place for everything. Actors should educate themselves, build up a store of learning and real-life experiences, but onstage, while they are acting, they should forget what they have learned and be intuitive.

Intuition must be the bedrock of our work, because our constant concern is the living human spirit, the life of the human soul. You cannot create or come to know a living spirit through your brain, you do it, first and foremost, through feeling. That awareness is created and sensed by the actor's own living spirit.

In the theatre, knowing means feeling.

If my book influences future generations and attracts some attention, it will be subject to rigorous criticism both scientific and non-scientific. That is to be welcomed because criticism by intelligent professionals can clarify many misunderstandings and gaps in our technique. It will reveal and explain the deficiencies of my book. I will be proud and happy to have been the cause of such debates and studies which will be directed towards the true nature of our work and not towards attempts to provide surrogates for it, as has been the case in recent times. It is also certain that a number of opinions will be expressed by people who understand neither the theatre nor scientific studies of it. Perhaps, too, those people who consider themselves experts will speak out, as will people who fear real art in the theatre, or who batten down on to it so they can exploit it. They will take refuge in fine-sounding phrases, essays, learned words which have no meaning and are harmful to our professional practice and fill the heads of actors and audiences alike with irrelevancies.

As a defence against these philistines and outsiders, I hasten to alert actors and other professionals as to what they can expect from my endeavours.

They should expect practical benefit, real help from the advice my book tries to give. If there is no practical benefit, my book is useless. Therefore, whenever I speak of creative work or art I will be guided by the theatre itself, that is, feeling. I will speak of art and creative work exclusively on the basis of my feelings, and the things I have learned in a lifetime of experience, during which I have listened keenly both to myself as an artist, while I was active, and to others, as director and teacher.

Only this material and the conclusions I have drawn from my experiments, my own work, my observations and my practice, are of any interest either to professionals, i.e., actors, directors and others active in the arts or, possibly, men of science, if they want living material, drawn from day-to-day experience for their research into theatre practice. In a word, whatever scientists may wish to make of my book, and whichever way they proceed, its import is purely practical.

When studying any system, method, or practical advice, one thing becomes apparent. Those who study any of them have one distinguishing feature – impatience. They want a quick return from their reading. And so they launch themselves furiously on books on different systems but are soon disappointed and throw them away. The practical suggestions I make suffer this common fate more than any others. It is easy to fall in love with them but, because they do not at first produce benefit but rather a temporary set-back, disenchantment sets in as fast as enchantment did earlier.

I fear the impatience which is so very characteristic of actors (not true actors) and so I would like to remind you of one elementary truth which is easy to forget. Any system has to become so familiar that you forget about it. Only after it has become part of your flesh and blood and heart can you begin, unconsciously, to derive real benefit from it.

You must absorb and filter any system through yourself, make it your own, retain its essentials and develop it in your own way.

The essence of my book is access to the subconscious through the conscious. I try to use the conscious methods in an actor's work to study and stimulate subconscious creativity — inspiration. I maintain, on the basis of long practice, that this is possible, with, of course, this one proviso, that all creative initiative be given to nature, the only true creator, which is capable of creating, forming what is truly beautiful, inscrutable, unattainable, inaccessible to any form of consciousness, i.e., which has a living spirit within it. The conscious mind can only help her.

Acting is above all inward, psychological, subconscious. The best thing is when creation occurs spontaneously, intuitively, through inspiration.

But what if that doesn't happen?

Then there is nothing for it but to stimulate subconscious creation through the conscious means, by our technique.

My system is intended for those who are creative. My system is for those who have talent.

It is said talented people don't need a system, that they create unconsciously. That is what most, almost all people say. But strangely enough, highly talented people do not, geniuses do not.

However, before attaining the beguiling heights of inspiration, we have to deal with the conscious technique for achieving it.

We are faced not only with the actor's invisible, creative mind but also his visible, palpable body. That is real, material, and to work on it you need the 'drudgery' without which no art is produced at all.

We need this prosaic daily grind as singers need to place the voice and the breath, as musicians need to develop their hands and fingers, as dancers need exercises for their legs. The only difference is that straight actors need this preparatory work to a much higher degree. Singers only have to deal with the voice, breathing and diction, pianists only have to deal with their hands but we have to deal both with these and also with the body, the face, with our psychology and physiology — with everything at once.

We only realize the need for this grind in preparing our mechanism, it only becomes easy and pleasurable, when it is directed towards some compelling, ultimate goal from the start — the subconscious, ever-inspiring creative power of nature herself.

It is not enough to write a book about the feelings associated with our own creative process. You must educate people capable of reading the book. I am doing my best to do that. But one has to recognize that there are already, and there will be yet more, false disciples . . . Avoid these people like the plague. They are dangerous because they approach the system superficially, as form, passing from high-point to high-point. Their understanding of it is extraordinarily simplistic. Simplistic thinking is dangerous. It springs from narrowness of mind, lack of talent, obtuseness in understanding the human soul and one of the most complex processes of its inner life. Stupid people do all the external exercises for their own sake, forgetting that they are not what matters. It is what they produce mentally. But this inner world is not for the dull-witted, and so they reject it. What use is the whole system in that case? It is of use to their career, for money, for the status of these artistically boring, talentless people. They will give themselves out to be my pupils. Don't believe them. They are the worst enemies of art.

Systems of all kinds have become 'the fashion' in the theatre. It is essential for every actor on the way up, for his status, his career, his popularity, to create his own system and his own studio to boot. These 'systems' do not, by any means, pay 'dividends' so what use are they? In reality there is only one, unique 'system' which belongs to our own creative nature as artists and human beings. We must study it from every angle and base our laws on it. But we must be careful. You can complicate nature's creative laws to such an extent it becomes impossible to apply them. On the other hand, you can strip them down to such bare essentials they lose all meaning.

We are forever reading clever articles and criticisms on the art of the theatre and actors' performances. They demonstrate great erudition and philosophical ability in the writer but what practical contribution do they make? None, or almost none and in many cases they are simply confusing.

We know clever directors who do the same.

Similarly, we know eminent, 'simplistic' teachers. Their approach to art and creative work is extraordinarily facile. You have hardly mentioned the results of some interesting test or experiment and they have written down what they need and the very next day, in the numerous institutions in which they teach, are proclaiming the latest findings in psychotechnique which have not yet been fully tested by the people actually doing the research.

They have developed an extraordinary capacity for avoiding what's necessary, what's difficult in art and for clinging on to what is irrelevant but easily accessible. For example, it is easy to do the exercises but difficult to use them to develop a psychotechnique.

The actor Leonidov says: 'There is truth and "truth".' My students, the ones I have spoken of, have revealed many 'truths' which they mistakenly give out as the 'system' but they say nothing of its real truths which are so dear to me.

These 'simplistic' people end their study of, their acquaintance with, the 'system', put a stop where the 'system' genuinely starts to reveal what it really is, i.e., at the point where the crucial part of the creative act emerges – the work of nature and the subconscious.

They very often underrate the complex, difficult part and overrate the easier, more available part, the first, preparatory part. People who approach art in this simplistic manner prove to be the 'system's' most dangerous enemies. No less dangerous are our 'unintelligible' disciples. Mostly they are honourable men of science, literature, theoreticians with no feeling for the actor's art, for the human essence of theatre and of our psychotechnique.

There are 'admirers' who only think of the end-product, of a performance being correctly interpreted and staged. They focus all their attention on it, forgetting the actors who alone can give life to a performance – soul.

Every word of this book has been verified in practice. There is no place for speculation. I have taken the facts of my own experience and only hidden behind another name (Tortsov) for convenience.

This close proximity of the so-called 'Stanislavski system' to the actor as a human being, a creative organism is its most important teaching, especially now when everyone is getting as far away from it as they can, in a search for the new, whatever the cost.

While not denying the constant need to keep up with the times, I consider it dangerous to force any aspect of our subtle, capricious, complex creative nature. It takes pitiless revenge on what we see in contemporary acting. Our tasks change but creative nature and its laws do not.

The content, tasks, forms of the things we create may change, but they must not infringe the laws of nature and cause forcing. Where forcing steps in, creative work ends and so does art itself. Forcing is our most dangerous enemy.

There is one aspect of our art which is apparent to every actor, to whatever school he belongs. The realist, the naturalist, the impressionist, the cubist take food into the mouth, chew it, swallow it down the throat to the stomach. Exactly the same thing is true of the subject matter we perceive in art, the way we assimilate it, develop it, embody it, ways nature has established once and for all, and which are not susceptible of change under any circumstances.

So actors and others working in the theatre should create what and how they please but on one essential condition: that their creative process should not run counter to nature and her laws. If you want to sing the communist 'Internationale' or the Tsarist anthem you need a well-placed voice, and technique. It is of this placing and of this technique that this book speaks and nothing else. It is written in defence of the laws of nature.

Year One

EXPERIENCING

МОСКОВСКИЙ
ХУДОЖЕСТВЕННЫЙ
ТЕАТР

AN ACTOR'S WORK

INTRODUCTION

. . . In February 19. . in the town of N,[1] where I was working, a friend and I, who was also, like me, a stenographer, were invited to take down a public lecture given by the well-known actor, director and teacher Arkadi Tortsov. That lecture decided my future and my fate: I felt irresistibly drawn to the stage and have already enrolled at the theatre school and will soon start working with him and his assistant, Ivan Rakhmanov.

I am infinitely happy to have finished with my old life and to have set out in a new direction.

But there is one thing from that past that will come in useful, my shorthand.

What if I were systematically to take down all the classes as far as possible verbatim? In that way I could make a whole textbook! It would help me go over the things we had done. And later, when I had become an actor, these notes would serve as a compass at difficult moments in my work.

I've decided. I will keep my notes in the form of a diary.

1

AMATEURISM

.. .. 19..

Today we waited for our first class with Arkadi Tortsov, not a little scared.
But all he did was come in and make an astonishing announcement. He
has arranged a showing for us in which we are to present extracts from
plays of our own choice. This is to take place on the main stage before an
audience consisting of the company and the management. He wants to see
us in performance, on stage, in a set, in full make-up, costume and lighting.
Only a presentation of this kind, so he said, can give a clear picture of how
stageworthy we are.

The students froze, bewildered. Appear on that stage in our theatre? That
was artistic sacrilege! I felt like going to Tortsov and asking him to transfer
the show to some other less imposing venue, but he was gone before
I could get to him.

The class was cancelled and we were given the free time to choose our
extracts.

Tortsov's proposal sparked off a lively discussion. At first only a few
were in favour. Particularly warm support came from a well-built young
fellow named Grisha Govorkov, who, so I heard, had already played in
some minor theatre or other, from a tall, ample, beautiful blonde, Sonya
Velyaminova, and from the small, boisterous Vanya Vyuntsov.

But the rest of us gradually came round to the idea. We could see the
glare of the footlights in our imagination. Very soon the showing seemed
attractive, useful, almost vital. Our hearts beat faster at the thought of it.

At first Paul Shustov, Leo Pushchin and I were very moderate in our ambitions. We thought of short sketches and frothy little comedies. We thought that was all we could handle. But all round us the names of great Russian writers – Gogol, Ostrovski, Chekhov – and then of masters of world literature were being bandied about more and more confidently, so that almost before we knew it, moderation was far behind us. Now we hankered after the Romantics, something in costume and verse. I was tempted by the role of Mozart in Pushkin's *Mozart and Salieri* and Leo by Salieri. Pasha thought he might try Schiller's Don Carlos. Then we started talking about Shakespeare and I opted for Othello.[1] I settled for him because I didn't have a copy of Pushkin at home, but I did have a Shakespeare. I was gripped with such a fever for work, such a need to get busy right away, I couldn't waste time looking for a book. Pasha said he would play Iago.

Today we were also told that the first rehearsal had been fixed for tomorrow.

As soon as I got home, I shut myself in my room, settled back on the sofa, opened my book reverentially and began to read. But by page two I felt I just had to start acting. I couldn't help myself. My legs, my hands, my face began to move of their own accord. I had to declaim the lines. And suddenly, there, in my hands, was a large ivory paper-knife which I stuck in my belt to look like a dagger. A towel was transformed into a turban and the multi-coloured cord from the window-curtains served as a baldric. I fashioned a robe and a mantle out of sheets and a blanket. An umbrella became a scimitar. But I didn't have a shield. Then I remembered that next door, in the dining room, behind the cupboard there was a large tray that could serve me as a shield. The moment for battle had come.

Thus armed, I felt like a proud, majestic, handsome warrior. But I looked modern, smooth and polished. But Othello is African! There has to be something of the tiger about him. I went through a whole series of exercises to try and discover the characteristic movement of a tiger. I prowled around the room, skilfully with slinking steps, between the gaps in the furniture, hiding behind the cupboard, stalking my prey. In a single bound, I sprang from cover to fall upon my imaginary enemy, represented by a large cushion. I smothered it 'like a tiger' and crushed it beneath me. Then the cushion became my Desdemona. I embraced her passionately, kissed her hand, which I had fashioned out of a corner of the cushion, then contemptuously flung her away, embraced her again, then strangled her and wept over her corpse. Some moments weren't at all bad.

I worked for five hours without noticing. That's not something you do because you're forced to! In moments of artistic inspiration, hours seem like minutes. This was clear proof that the mood I had experienced was indeed genuine inspiration!

Before taking off my costume, I took advantage of the fact that everyone in the apartment was asleep and slipped out into the empty hall where there was a large mirror. I switched on the light and took a look at myself. What I saw was not at all what I had expected. The poses and gestures I had worked out didn't look at all like what I had imagined in my head. The mirror revealed an angularity and an ugliness of line in my body that I never knew I had. I was so disappointed my energy evaporated.

.. .. 19.. .

I woke up much later than usual, dressed as fast as I could and ran to school. As I entered the rehearsal room, I found everyone waiting for me. I was so embarrassed that, instead of apologizing, I came out with a stupid, trite phrase:

'I think I'm a bit late.'

Rakhmanov gave me a long reproving look and finally said:

'They've all been sitting here, waiting, getting nervous and impatient, and you think you're a bit late! They all came here keyed up for work, but because of you I have lost all interest in teaching you. It is very difficult to rouse the urge to create and extremely easy to kill it. What right do you have to hold up the entire group? I have far too much respect for our work to tolerate such sloppiness, and that is why I feel I have to apply a military kind of discipline when it comes to what we do together. The actor, like the soldier, needs iron discipline. This first time I will let it pass with a simple reprimand, without entering it into the day book. But you must apologize at once to everyone, and in future make it a rule to arrive at rehearsal a quarter of an hour early and not after it has started.'

I stammered my apologies and promised not to be late again. However, Rakhmanov no longer wanted to start work. The first rehearsal, he said, is a special event in an actor's life, and he should always have happy memories of it. Because of me, today's rehearsal had been ruined. So, let this, our most important rehearsal, take place tomorrow, and replace today's fiasco. Rakhmanov then left the room.

But that wasn't the end of it. Another 'roasting' was in store for me from my classmates, led by Grisha. That 'roasting' was even hotter than the first. I won't forget today's fiasco in a hurry.

I planned to go to bed early, because after today's commotion and last evening's disappointment I was afraid to try and work on the role. Then suddenly I caught sight of a bar of chocolate. I started to mix it with some butter. The result was a brown blob. It spread easily on my face and turned me into a Moor. My teeth seemed whiter in contrast to my dark skin.

Sitting at the mirror, I spent a long time admiring how white they were, learning to flash them and roll the whites of my eyes.

I needed to try on the costume to see how successful the make-up was, and once it was on I wanted to perform. But I didn't find anything new, just repeated what I had done the previous evening and that had already had lost its edge. Still I did manage to see what my Othello is going to look like on the outside. That's important.

....19..

Today was our first rehearsal, and I put in an appearance well before the start. Rakhmanov invited us to set up the space and arrange the furniture ourselves. Fortunately Pasha agreed to all my suggestions, as he was not interested in externals. It was especially important to me to arrange the furniture so that I could move through it as I had in my room. Otherwise, inspiration would not come. However, I couldn't do what I wanted. I tried very hard to believe I was in my own room, but I couldn't. In fact, it was more of a hindrance to my acting.

Pasha already knew his lines, but I had either to use the book or to convey the rough meaning of whatever I could remember using my own words. To my surprise, rather than helping me, the actual lines got in my way. I would have been happy to do without them, or to have cut them by half. Not only the words but also the author's thoughts, which were not mine, as well as the actions he indicated, limited the freedom I had enjoyed when studying at home.

Even more unsettling was the fact that I didn't recognize my own voice. In fact neither the mise-en-scène[2] nor the idea of the character I had worked out at home had anything to do with Shakespeare's play at all. How, for example, was I to use the flashing teeth, the rolling eyes, the 'tigerish' movements, which were my way into the part, in the comparatively quiet opening scene between Iago and Othello?

Yet I couldn't get away from my tricks or my mise-en-scène because I had nothing else to put in its place. On the one hand, I spoke the lines in an artificial way and, on the other, I played my own savage in an artificial way with no relation whatsoever between the two. The words got in the way of the acting, and the acting got in the way of the words. A general feeling of discordance all round.

Once again, I found nothing new working at home, I just repeated the old things which I was unhappy with. What does repeating the same feelings, doing the same things mean? Do they belong to me or to my savage Moor? Why is yesterday's acting like today's, and why will tomorrow's acting be like today's? Has my imagination dried up? Or don't I have the material I need in my memory for the role? Why did work go so quickly at the start, and why have I come to a dead end?

While I was mulling this over in my mind, my landlord and his wife were sitting down for evening tea next door. I had to go to another part of the room and to say my lines as quietly as possible so as not to draw attention to myself. To my surprise these tiny little changes gave me new life, and made me somehow relate to my work and, indeed, the role itself in a new way.

That was the secret. You mustn't stick too long to one thing and endlessly repeat something which has gone stale.

I have decided. At tomorrow's rehearsal, I'll improvise everything – mise-en-scène, interpretation, my whole approach.

.. .. 19..

Today I improvised everything from the start. Instead of moving, I sat. I decided to act without any gestures or movement, or pulling faces. And what happened? I was in trouble from the moment I opened my mouth. I forgot the lines, the proper inflections, and I stopped dead. I had to get back fast to the mises-en-scène I had set. It was obvious I couldn't play my savage except by using the ways I knew. But I wasn't in control of them, they were in control of me. What was this? Slavery?

.. .. 19..

On the whole today's rehearsal felt better. I am getting used to the place where we work and the people we work with. Most of all, opposites are beginning to come together. My previous way of portraying a savage had nothing to do with Shakespeare. In the early rehearsals I felt contrived when I tried to force African features into the role, but now it's as though I had injected something into what I am doing. At least I feel less at war with the author.

.. .. 19..

We rehearsed on the main stage today. I had counted on magic and inspiration backstage. And what did I find? Instead of the glare of the footlights, a mess. The sets I had expected to see were stacked up in piles. It was all gloom and silence, with not a soul in sight. The vast stage was empty and barren. Down by the footlights there were a few bentwood chairs marking out a new set and, on the right, a stand with three lighted bulbs.

As soon as I stepped onto the acting area I was confronted by the gaping hole of the proscenium arch and beyond it a boundless, deep, dark void. I was seeing the auditorium from the stage for the first time, with the curtain up, empty, with no one present. Somewhere out there – a long way off it seemed to me – a bulb glowed under a lamp-shade. Its light fell on a sheaf of papers on a table. Hands were preparing to note down all our faults 'with no quarter given' . . . I felt as though I was being swallowed by the void.

Then someone called out, 'Begin.' I was being asked to go into Othello's imaginary room, marked out by the chairs, and take my place. I sat down, but not on the chair I was supposed to according to my plan. The designer couldn't recognize the layout of his own room! Someone else had to explain to me which chair represented what. It was a long time before I could fit into the tiny acting area marked out by the chairs and focus on what was going on around me. It was difficult for me to make myself look at Pasha, who was at my side. At moments my mind was drawn towards the auditorium, then towards the rooms adjoining the stage, technicians' rooms where life went on despite us. People came and went, carrying this or that, sawing, hammering and arguing.

In spite of all this, I carried on speaking and moving automatically. If all the work I had done at home had not driven my little tricks, the lines, and inflexions into me, I would have come to a stop as soon as I opened my mouth. But that's what finally happened. It was the prompter's fault. I realized at once that this 'gentleman' was the worst kind of conspirator, and no friend to the actor. In my opinion a good prompter is someone who can keep silent for a whole evening and then, at the critical moment, give you the one word which has slipped your memory. But our prompter kept whispering away the whole time and was a terrible nuisance.[3] You don't know where to stand or how to get away from this over-zealous man who, in his desire to help, seems to worm his way through your ear into your very soul. Finally he won. I was thrown, I stopped, and I asked him to leave me alone.

.. .. 19..

Our second rehearsal was in the main theatre. I arrived very early and decided to do my preparatory work onstage in front of all the others rather than alone in my dressing room. Work was in full swing. They were putting up the set and arranging the props for our rehearsal. I started to get ready.

It would have been absurd, given all the chaos around me, to try and find the cosiness I had known when working at home. The most import-ant thing was for me to fit in to my new surroundings. So I marched downstage and stared at the ominous black hole so as to get used to it and free myself from the draw of the auditorium. But the more I tried to ignore it, the more I thought about it, the greater the draw from the ominous blackness beyond the picture-frame became. At that moment a stagehand who had come up beside me dropped some nails. I started to help him pick them up. And suddenly I felt fine, almost at home on the vast stage. But once the nails had all been picked up, and my good-natured companion had gone, once again I felt threatened by the hole, and once again I felt as though I was being sucked into it. I had felt so wonderful just a moment before! But that was understandable. While I was picking up the nails I wasn't thinking about the black hole. I hurriedly left the stage and sat in the front rows.

The rehearsal of the other excerpts began, but I didn't see what was going on. I waited my turn, a bundle of nerves.

There is a positive side to the agony of waiting. It brings you to the point where all you want, whatever they're afraid of, is to have it over and done with as soon as possible. That was how I felt today.

When the time finally came for my scene, I went up onstage. The set, that had been cobbled together from various bits of flats, wings and rostrums etc., was up. Some of the pieces were placed back to front. The furniture, too, was a jumble. Still, the overall look under the lights was pleasing, and Othello's room, as they had set it up for us, seemed secure. With a great effort of imagination I should be able to find something that reminded me of my own room.

But as soon as the curtains opened and the auditorium gaped wide before me, I fell completely under its power. And I experienced a novel, and for me unexpected, sensation. The set and its ceiling cut the actor off from the vast backstage area, the huge dark void above, the rooms next to the stage and the scene-docks. Such isolation is, of course, welcome. The trouble is that it acts as a kind of reflector, concentrating all the actor's attention on the auditorium, much as a concert platform acts as a shell to direct sound towards the listeners. Something else was new. In my panic, I felt the need to keep the audience amused lest – God forbid! – they should get bored. That made me over-anxious and prevented me from concentrating properly on what I was doing and saying. So the words and moves raced ahead of my thoughts and feelings. The result was gabble and rush. This was true of both action and gesture. I flew through the text until I was breathless, but couldn't alter the tempo. Even my favourite moments whizzed by like telegraph poles seen from a train. A fraction of a pause and disaster struck. I frequently looked imploringly at the prompter, but he studiously wound his watch as though nothing were happening. His revenge for yesterday, no doubt.

I got to the theatre earlier than usual for the dress rehearsal because we had costume and make-up. I was given a beautiful dressing room. They had taken the oriental robe of the Prince of Morocco from *The Merchant of Venice* out of stock. All this boded well for my performance. I sat at the dressing table on which a number of wigs, beards, and all sorts of make-up and props were laid out.

Where was I to begin? . . . I put some brown on one of the brushes, but it was so hard that I had great difficulty in getting even a small speck onto it, and not a trace stayed on my skin. I swapped the little brush for a stick of colour. The result was the same. I smeared some of it on my fingers and started to apply it to my skin and, this time, managed to colour it slightly. I tried out the other colours, but only one of them, blue, stayed on properly. But blue isn't exactly the colour you need for a Moor. I tried to put some spirit-gum on my cheek and stick a small strand of hair to it. The spirit-gum stung me and the hair wouldn't lie flat . . . I tried on one wig, a second, a third without the slightest idea where was the front and where the back. All three, set above an unmade-up face, revealed their 'wiggery'. I wanted to remove the little make-up I had managed to put on my face, but how was I to do it?

At that moment a tall, very lean man in glasses and a white smock, a pointed moustache, and a long imperial beard came in. This 'Don Quixote' bent over and without further ado began to work on my face. He used Vaseline to remove everything I had daubed on and, first having greased my brushes, started applying colour all over again. The colours went onto the greasy skin easily and evenly. 'Don Quixote' painted my face the colour of a deep suntan, which is right for a Moor. But I was sorry to lose the earlier, darker colour the chocolate had given me: the whites of my eyes and my teeth had shone brighter then.

When my make-up was complete and my costume was on, I inspected myself in the mirror and was genuinely amazed at 'Don Quixote's' art. I was lost in self-admiration. The angularity of my body disappeared beneath the folds of the robe, and the wild expressions I had worked out matched the overall impression very well.

Pasha and some other classmates came in. They too were enthusiastic about my appearance and unanimous in their praise without a trace of envy. They gave me heart and restored my self-confidence. Onstage I was thrown by the unexpected lay-out of the furniture. One of the armchairs had been moved, strangely, away from the wall almost to centre stage, the table had been moved far too near the prompter's box, right downstage as though it were on display. I was so nervous I wandered endlessly around the stage and kept catching the edges of my robe and my scimitar on the furniture and the corners of the set. But that didn't stop me from mechanically babbling my lines and aimlessly roaming about. I think I just about managed to get to the end of the scene. But when I came to the climax, a thought flashed through my mind, 'I'm going to forget my lines.' Panic seized me, I stopped speaking, I was lost, and saw empty white circles before my eyes . . . I myself don't know how or what caused me to go into automatic mode, but once again this saved me from disaster.

After that I gave up. I had only one thought, to get it over with as quickly as possible, take off my make-up, and run out of the theatre.

So here I am at home. Alone. At the moment I turn out to be my own worst company. I'm sick at heart. I thought I'd go and visit friends and take my mind off things, but I didn't. I am sure everyone has heard of my disgrace and are pointing the finger at me.

Fortunately dear old Leo came. He had noticed me in the audience and wanted to know what I had thought of his Salieri. But I couldn't tell him anything. Although I'd seen his performance from the wings, I was in such a state of nerves waiting to go on that I hadn't watched what was happening onstage. I didn't ask him about myself. I was afraid of criticism which might destroy what little self-confidence I had left.

Leo spoke eloquently about Shakespeare's play and the role of Othello. But he pointed to demands in it which I can't meet. He spoke very well about the bitterness, the amazement, the shock that the Moor feels when he is convinced that hideous vice lies beneath Desdemona's mask of beauty. That makes her all the more terrible in Othello's eyes.

After my friend had gone I tried to go over one or two passages in the role in the light of what he had said – and I wept, such was my pity for the Moor.

.. .. 19..

Today was the day for our show. I knew exactly how it would go. I would get to the theatre, sit down to be made up, 'Don Quixote' would make his appearance, and bend down over me. But even if I liked myself in the make-up and wanted to act, nothing would come of it. I had a feeling of complete indifference to it all. But that mood only lasted until I got to my dressing room. Then my heart began to beat so hard it was difficult to breathe. I had a feeling of nausea, of terrible exhaustion. I thought I was ill. Fine. Illness would explain away my failure in my first appearance as an actor.

What confused me more than anything onstage was the solemn hush, the order. When I stepped out of the darkness of the wings into the full glare of the footlights, the overhead spotlights, and the flood-lights from the wings, I was stunned and blinded. The lighting was so brilliant that it formed a curtain of brightness between me and the auditorium. I felt protected from the crowd and could breathe freely. But my eyes soon became accustomed to the lights and then the blackness of the auditorium became even more frightening, and the pull of the audience even stronger. It seemed to me that the theatre was full of people, and that thousands of eyes and opera glasses were being trained on me alone. It was as though they were transfixing their prey. I felt I was the slave of that huge crowd and became servile, lacking in all principle, ready for any kind of compromise. I was ready to turn myself inside out, to lick their boots, to give them more than I genuinely had or was capable of. But inside I was emptier as ever before.

After a superhuman effort to squeeze feelings out of myself and my incapacity to achieve the impossible, tension invaded my entire body, ending as cramp which gripped my face, my hands, the whole of me, paralysing all movement, all motion. All my strength went into this meaningless, fruitless tension. I had to use my voice to help my numb body and feelings, and I raised it to shriek. But even there tension did its work. My throat was constricted, I couldn't catch my breath, my pitch went up right into the top register, and I couldn't bring it down. As a result I went hoarse.

I had to do more physically. But I was no longer in a fit state to control my hands, legs, my gabbling, and all this was heightened by my overall tension. I was ashamed of every word I uttered, of every gesture I made and immediately found wanting. I went red in the face, my fingers and toes went stiff, and I pressed myself with all my might against the back of the armchair. Suddenly my helplessness and embarrassment drove me into a fury. I don't know exactly against whom, myself or the audience, but as a result I felt free of everything around me for a few minutes and I became spontaneous and bold. The famous line, 'Blood, Iago, blood!' burst from me without conscious effort. This was the cry of a man really in torment. How it came out I don't know. Perhaps I felt the injured soul of a trusting man in these words and instinctively felt sorry for him. There was also the memory of the interpretation of Othello which Leo had recently given me, which surfaced with great clarity and stirred my feelings.

I had the impression that the audience pricked up its ears for a moment, and that a rustle went through it like wind through treetops.

As soon as I sensed their approval such energy boiled up inside me that I didn't know what to do with it. I was carried away by it. I don't remember how I played the end of the scene. I only remember that my awareness of the lights and the big black hole vanished, that I was free from any kind of fear, and that a new, mysterious, exhilarating life had been created for me. I know no greater delight than those few minutes I experienced. I saw that Pasha was surprised by my new lease of life. It sparked him off and he began to play with great verve.

The curtains closed and there was applause. I had happiness and joy in my heart. Suddenly my belief in my own talent increased. I had a new assurance. When I returned, triumphant, from the stage to my dressing room, I had the impression that everyone was looking at me with enthusiasm.

After I had changed, I went into the auditorium during one of the intervals, full of myself, with the dignified air that befits a provincial 'star' and with what seems to me now a clumsily assumed indifference. To my surprise I found neither the festive atmosphere nor the full lighting which is normal in a 'proper' performance. Instead of a packed house I saw all of twenty people in the stalls. For whom had I exerted all that effort? However, I quickly consoled myself, 'The audience for today's showing may be small,' I said to myself, 'but they are connoisseurs – Tortsov, Rakhmanov, the greatest actors in our theatre. Those are the people who applauded me. I wouldn't swap their meagre applause for a standing ovation from thousands.'

Choosing a place in the front rows where I could readily be seen by Tortsov and Rakhmanov, I sat down in the hope that they would call me over and say something nice.

The lights came up. The curtains opened and immediately Marya Maloletkova, another student, simply flew down a flight of stairs that had been added to the set. She fell to the floor in a heap and cried, 'Save me!' with such a heart-rending cry that I went cold all over. Then she started to say something, but so quickly you couldn't understand a word. Then suddenly she forgot her lines, stopped mid-word, covered her face with her hands and ran into the wings where you could hear the sound of muffled voices approving and consoling her. The curtains closed but her cry of 'Save me!' was still ringing in my ears. That's real talent! One entrance, one word, and you feel it.

Tortsov was absolutely electrified, or so it seemed to me. 'The same thing happened to me as to Marya,' I reflected, 'one phrase, "Blood, Iago, blood!", and the audience was in my grip.'

Now, as I write, I have no doubts about my future. However, this confidence doesn't prevent me from being aware that I didn't quite have the great success I imagined. And yet, somewhere in my heart of hearts, I hear trumpets sounding victory.

2

THE STAGE AS ART AND STOCK-IN-TRADE

Today we assembled so that Tortsov could give us his notes on our performances.

He said:

'In art we need, above all, to find and understand what is beautiful. And so, let us first remember the positive moments in what you gave us. There were only two, the first when Marya ran down the stairs with the desperate cry, "Save me!", and the second was Kostya's "Blood, Iago, blood!" In both instances you, the players, like us the audience, surrendered totally to what was happening. We were stunned and fired by the same common emotion.

'These moments of success, which we can abstract from the whole, can be termed the *art of experiencing* which we cultivate here in our theatre and study in our school.'

'What is the art of experiencing?' I asked, curious.

'You know what it is because it happened to you. Try and tell us what you were aware of, physically, while you were being genuinely creative.'

'I don't know, I don't understand a thing about it,' I said, stupefied by Tortsov's praise. 'All I know is that they were unforgettable moments, and that's the only way I want to act, and I am ready to give myself body and soul to that kind of acting . . .'

I had to stop, otherwise I would have burst into tears.

'What?! You don't remember your agony as you searched for

something terrible? You don't remember how your hands, your eyes and your whole being darted here and there, looking for somewhere to go and something to hold on to? You don't remember how you bit your lip and could hardly hold back your tears?' Tortsov enquired.

'Yes, now that you tell me, I think I am beginning to remember how I felt,' I admitted.

'But you couldn't have remembered without me?'

'No, I couldn't.'

'That means, you were behaving subconsciously?'

'I don't know, maybe. Is that good or bad?'

'Good, if the subconscious led you along the right path, and bad if it didn't. But, in the show, it didn't let you down, yet what you gave us in those few successful moments was better than anything you could have hoped for.'

'Really?' I asked, breathless with pleasure.

'Yes, because it is always best when an actor is completely taken over by the play. Then, independent of his will, he lives the role, without noticing *how* he is feeling, not thinking about *what* he is doing, and so everything comes out spontaneously, subconsciously. But, unfortunately, this is not always within our power to control.

'That puts us in an impossible situation. We are supposed to create on inspiration, but only the subconscious can do that, and we can't control it.'

'Would you mind telling us, please, the way out of this?' asked a perplexed Grisha, with a hint of irony.

'Fortunately there is one,' Tortsov stopped him. 'It is the *indirect*, not the *direct* influence of the conscious on the subconscious mind. Certain aspects of the human psyche obey the conscious mind and the will, which have the capacity to influence our involuntary processes.

'True, this demands long, complex creative work, which only proceeds partially under the direct guidance and influence of the conscious mind. It is, for the most part, subconscious and involuntary. Only one artist has the power to do it, the most discriminating, the most ingenious, the most subtle, the most elusive, the most miraculous of artists – nature. Not even the most refined technique can be compared to her. She holds the key! This attitude, this relationship to nature absolutely typifies the art of experiencing,' said Tortsov heatedly.

'But what if nature plays tricks?' someone asked.

'You have to learn how to stimulate and control her. There are special methods for that, our psychotechnique, which you are about to study. Its purpose is to arouse and involve the creative subconscious by indirect, conscious means. It is no accident that one of the fundamentals of our art of experiencing is expressed in the principle: *subconscious creation through the actor's conscious psychotechnique.* (The subconscious through the conscious, the involuntary through the voluntary.) Let us leave the subconscious to nature, the magician, and apply ourselves to what is available to us — *the conscious approach to creative activity and our psychotechnique.* What they teach us, in the main, is that once the subconscious starts working we must try not to get in its way.'

'How strange that the subconscious should need the conscious,' I said in amazement.

'That seems perfectly normal to me,' said Tortsov. 'Electricity, wind, water and other forces of nature require a knowledgeable and intelligent engineer to control them so people can use them. In the same way, our subconscious creative forces cannot be controlled without their own kind of engineer, without a conscious psychotechnique. Only when the actor understands and feels that his inner and outer life onstage, with all the conventions that this implies, is proceeding naturally and normally, even to the point of being totally naturalistic in accord with all the laws of human nature, can the deep secrets of the subconscious make a cautious appearance. From them feelings which we cannot always understand emerge. They take us over, for a brief or even a lengthy period of time, moving in directions dictated by something within our inner selves. Having no control over this driving force, being unable to study it, we simply call it 'nature' in our terminology.

'But if we transgress the workings of life as a human organism, we stop creating believably onstage. Immediately the subconscious, which is apprehensive, fears it will be attacked and takes refuge once more in its secret depths.

'So psychological realism, or even naturalism, is essential for him to stimulate the work of the subconscious and produce a burst of inspiration.'

'In other words, in our art we need uninterrupted, subconscious creation,' I added in conclusion.

'You can't work the whole time subconsciously and on inspiration,' remarked Tortsov. 'Such geniuses don't exist. And so our art requires us to prepare the soil for this kind of genuine, subconscious creation.'

'How can that be done?'

'Above all you must create consciously and believably. That will prepare the best soil for the subconscious and for inspiration to burgeon.'

'Why?' I said, not understanding.

'Because what is conscious and credible gives birth to truth, and truth evokes belief, and if nature believes in what is happening inside you, then she, too, becomes involved. And in her wake comes the subconscious, and, just possibly, inspiration may then follow.'

'What does it mean to play "credibly"?' I asked.

'That means thinking, wanting, striving, behaving truthfully, in logical sequence in a human way, within the character, and in complete parallel to it. As soon as the actor has done that, he will come close to the role and will begin to feel as one with it.

'Here we call that *experiencing a role*. This process and the term which defines it take on a quite exceptional importance. They are crucial to the art of acting as we profess it.

'Experiencing helps the actor to fulfil his basic goal, which is *the creation of the life of the human spirit in a role and the communication of that life onstage in an artistic form*.

'As you can see, our prime task is not only to portray the life of a role externally, but above all to create the inner life of the character and of the whole play, bringing our own individual feelings to it, endowing it with all the features of our own personality.

'Always remember that this principle, this basic purpose, must be your guide at every moment of your creative life. That is why we think first and foremost of the inner aspect of a role, that is of its psychological life which we create by using the process of experiencing. It is the most important feature of creative work and must be the actor's first concern. You must experience a role, that is experience feelings analogous to it each and every time you do it.

' "Every great actor should feel, really feel what he is portraying," said Tommaso Salvini, the finest representative of this school of acting. "I even consider that he is not only required to feel this emotion once or twice, while studying the role, but more or less at every performance, be it the first or the thousandth" ' – Tortsov was quoting from an essay by Tommaso Salvini (his reply to Coquelin) which Ivan Rakhmanov had passed to him.[1] 'That is also how our theatre understands the art of the actor.'

.. .. 19..

After long arguments with Pasha, I took the first favourable opportunity to say to Tortsov:

'I don't understand how you can teach someone to experience and to feel in the right way if he himself doesn't "feel" or "experience" it!'

'So, what do you say? Can you teach yourself or someone else how to get into a role and find its deepest meaning?' asked Tortsov.

'Let's say . . . yes, though it isn't easy,' I replied.

'Can you select interesting and important things to aim for in the role, discover the right approach to it, can you arouse truthful intentions and perform the right actions?'

'Yes, I can,' I agreed once more.

'So, see if you can do that with absolute honesty, meticulously, while at the same time remaining cold and indifferent. You can't. You will become personally involved, and start to feel that you are in the same situation as the character in the play. You will experience your own feelings, as being parallel to his. Work through the whole part in this way, and you will then see that every moment of your life onstage will evoke corresponding personal experiences. An unbroken sequence of such moments creates continuous experiencing, living "the life of the human spirit". This state of total consciousness where there is genuine inner truth, is the best for arousing feeling, and the most favourable soil for stimulating the sub-conscious to work, short- or long-term, or for flashes of inspiration.'

Pasha attempted to sum up:

'So, from everything you have said, I gather that the study of acting comes down to mastering the psychotechnique of experiencing. Experiencing helps us fulfil the basic purpose of creative work, which is to create "the life of the human spirit" of a role.'

'Our purpose is not only to create "the life of the human spirit in a role", but also to communicate it outwardly in an artistic form,' Tortsov corrected him. 'So the actor must not only experience the role inwardly, he must embody that inner experience physically. Outer communication relies very strongly on inner experiencing in our school of acting. To be able to reflect a life which is subtle and often subconscious, you must possess an exceptionally responsive and outstandingly well-trained voice and body, which must be able to convey hidden, almost imperceptible inner feelings instantly in a distinct and accurate manner. This is why an actor of our school, much more so than of other schools, must be concerned not only with his mental apparatus that facilitates the process of experiencing, but even more with his physical apparatus, his body, which conveys his inner feelings in a believable manner — their outer form, their embodiment.

'The subconscious exerts a strong influence here. The subtlest tech-nique cannot compare to the subconscious when it comes to physical embodiment, although it lays arrogant claims to superiority.

'I have alluded in the last two classes in very broad outline to what makes up the art of experiencing,' concluded Tortsov.

'We firmly believe and know from our working practice, that only this kind of theatre, enriched with the actor's own experiences as a living organism, as a human being, can communicate all the elusive nuances, the hidden depths of a role. Only acting of this kind can fully capture an audience and bring them to a point where they not only comprehend but, more importantly, experience everything done onstage, and so enrich their own inner lives, leaving a mark that time will not erase. But more than that – and this is extremely important – the fundamentals of the creative act and the organic laws of nature on which our kind of acting is founded protect the actor from being thrown completely out of joint. Who knows what kind of directors or what kind of theatres you will have to work in? Not all directors and all theatres work in accordance with the laws of nature – far from it. In the majority of cases they blatantly flout them, and that can always throw an actor. If you know where true art begins and ends, and the creative laws of nature, you won't go astray. You will understand your mistakes, and so be able to correct them. Without the firm foundations that the art of experiencing can provide, and which are laid down by nature, you will get yourself into a mess, and lose your standards. That is why I consider it indispensable for all actors, of whatever school, to study the fundamentals of the art of experiencing. Every actor should begin his work at school this way.'

'Yes, yes, that's what I'm after with all my heart!' I exclaimed. I felt inspired. 'And I'm so happy that I was able, in part at least, to achieve our main purpose by experiencing.'

'Don't get carried away too soon,' said Tortsov, dampening my ardour, 'otherwise you will experience bitter disappointment later on. Don't confuse the true art of experiencing with what you displayed throughout the scene.'

'What did I display then?' I asked, like a criminal brought before a judge.

'I've already told you that, in the whole performance there were only one or two good moments of real experiencing, which brought you anywhere near our kind of acting. I use them as examples to illustrate to you and the other students the fundamentals of that kind of art, our concern at this moment. As far as the whole scene between Othello and Iago is concerned, it certainly cannot be called the art of experiencing.'

'What do you call it?'

'We call it *playing on gut instinct*,' stated Tortsov.

'And what is that?' I asked, feeling the ground disappear from under my feet.

'In a performance of that kind,' Tortsov continued, 'isolated moments suddenly, unexpectedly rise to great artistic heights which stun the audience. The actor experiences or creates on inspiration, in a kind of improvisation. But do you feel you are gifted and strong enough, mentally and physically, to play all five acts of *Othello* with the same exaltation that you played – accidentally – one short line, "Blood, Iago, blood!"?'

'I don't know . . .'

'Well I do. It is beyond an actor even of exceptional emotional power, and enormous physical strength!' replied Tortsov. 'Nature needs the support of a well-developed psychotechnique. But you have not acquired that yet, any more than those instinctive actors, who see no need for technique at all. They, like you, believe in inspiration alone. And if that should fail, they, and you, have nothing with which to fill the gaps, the dead spots in the acting, the places which have not been experienced. This results in long periods of low nervous energy, total artistic impotence and naive, amateurish playacting. At those moments your performance, as with any instinctive actor, became lifeless, stilted and laboured. So during your first tottering steps, moments of exaltation, alternated with playacting. That is the kind of theatrical performance which we call playing on instinct.'

Tortsov's criticisms of my failings made a great impression on me. They not only distressed me, they frightened me. I lapsed into a kind of stupor and didn't hear anything he said after that.

.. .. 19..

Once again we heard Tortsov's comments on the show.

First he turned to Pasha.

'You also gave us some interesting moments, which were genuine art, only it wasn't the art of experiencing but, strange as it may appear, the art of representation.'

'Representation?!' exclaimed Pasha, in great surprise.

'What kind of art is that?' the students asked.

'It is the second school of acting and its nature can best be explained by the person who demonstrated it in one or two successful moments in the show.

'Pasha! Remember your Iago!' Tortsov said, turning to him once more.

'I knew something from my uncle about our approach, so I went straight to the inner content of the role and spent a long time delving into it,' said Pasha by way of justification.

'Your uncle helped you?' enquired Tortsov.

'A little. At home I thought I achieved genuine experiencing. Sometimes in rehearsal I felt individual moments in the role, too. That's why I don't understand how the art of representation comes into it,' Pasha went on, still trying to justify himself.

'In this kind of acting you also experience your role once or twice – at home or in rehearsal. The fact that this highly important process is present means we can consider this second school as real acting.'

'How do you experience the role in this kind of acting? The same way as we do in ours?' I asked.

'In exactly the same way, but the goal is different. You can experience the role every time, as we do, or you can experience it once or twice, so as to register the outward form a feeling takes. Having noted the form, you then learn to repeat it mechanically with the help of trained muscles. That is the representation, the reproduction of a role.

'So, in this school of acting, the process of experiencing is not the most important creative factor, but only one of the preparatory stages. The work that follows is the search for an artistic outward form, one which gives clear, visual expression to the inner content. Here, the actor relies above all on himself and tries fully to feel, to experience the life of his character. But, I repeat, he does not do that during performance, in front of an audience, but only at home or in rehearsal.'

'But Pasha did do it during the show! That means it was the art of experiencing,' I said in his defence.

Someone else supported me, saying that while Pasha had overplayed the role because of nerves, there had been a few moments of real experiencing, worthy of what we call acting.

'No,' countered Tortsov. 'In our kind of acting, which means experiencing every moment in the role, that experiencing must be felt anew and physically embodied anew.

'Improvisation on an imaginary theme can be a great help. It lends freshness and spontaneity to a performance. This was the case in a few successful moments in Kostya's playing. But I could not detect this freshness, this improvisation in Pasha's way of feeling the role. But he did carry me along with him here and there by his precision and artistry. But . . . in all his playing there was a coldness which led me to suspect that his performance was fixed once and for all, leaving no room for improvisation, thus denying it freshness and spontaneity. Nonetheless, I felt the whole time that the original, on which he skilfully based his reproduction, was good, believable, and that he was speaking about a genuine and vital "life of the human spirit" of the role. This echo of an earlier process of experiencing, at certain moments, turned reproduction into genuine art.'

'But where did I, the nephew of the actor Shustov, learn the art of representation?'

'Let's look into that. Tell us more about how you worked on Iago,' Tortsov continued.

'I used a mirror to see how my experiences were being conveyed externally,' Pasha recalled.

'That is dangerous and yet typical of the art of representation.

Remember, a mirror must be used with caution. It leads an actor to observe not what is inside but what is outside.'

'Nonetheless, the mirror helped me to understand how my exterior expressed my feelings,' said Pasha in self-justification.

'Your own feelings, or the feelings created by the role?'

'My own, but right for Iago, too.'

'And so, when you were working with the mirror what concerned you was not so much the outside, the manner, but more importantly how you were able physically to reflect the inner feelings you had experienced, "the life of the human spirit"?' asked Tortsov, pressing him further.

'Yes, exactly.'

'That, too, is typical of the art of representation. And precisely because it is art, it requires a form, which conveys not only the outside of a role but, chiefly, its inside – "the life of the human spirit".'

'I remember I was pleased with certain moments when I saw a faithful reflection of what I was feeling,' Pasha continued.

'And you set, once and for all, technical ways of expressing those feelings?'

'They did it themselves, through constant repetition.'

'So, finally, you found a set form for the successful moments in your performance, and you were able technically to embody them?'

'It would appear so.'

'And you used these forms every time you repeated what you did at home or in rehearsal?'

'I must have done, out of habit,' Pasha acknowledged.

'So, tell us then, did the set forms emerge each time of their own accord, as a result of inner experiencing, or, having seen the light of day, and having been fixed once and for all, were they repeated mechanically without your feelings being involved?'

'It seems to me I experienced them every time.'

'No, that didn't come over to the audience in the first showing. In the art of representation people do what you did, they try to arouse and observe typical human traits in themselves that convey the inner life of a role. Having created, once and for all, the best form they can find for them, they learn how to give natural embodiment to them, without their feelings being in any way involved. This is achieved by trained muscles, by the voice, through all the virtuoso techniques and devices proper to any art, and through endless repetition. The art of representation develops muscular memory to the highest degree.

'Once he is accustomed to reproducing a role mechanically, the actor repeats it without any expense of nervous or mental energy. He not only

considers this quite unnecessary but even damaging to a public performance, as every emotional disturbance upsets his control and alters the
shape and form of something that has been permanently set. Imprecision
of form and uncertainty as to how it is to convey it damage its effect.

'All this is true, to a greater or lesser extent, of certain passages in your
performance as Iago.

'So, remember what happened in the future.'

'I wasn't happy with other places in the role or in the character of Iago
himself. But I found the answer by using a mirror,' Pasha recalled. 'Ran-
sacking my memory for a suitable model, I remembered an acquaintance
of mine, who bore no relation to the role, but who, I thought, was the
very personification of cunning, evil, and deviousness.'

'So you observed him and tried to adapt yourself to him?'

'Yes.'

'How did you use your memories of him?'

'To tell the truth I only copied his mannerisms,' Pasha admitted. 'I saw
him standing at my side. He moved, stood still, sat, and I glanced at him
and repeated everything he did.'

'That was a great mistake! At that moment you betrayed the art of representation and lapsed into mimicry, copying, imitation, which has nothing
to do with real creative work.'

'What should I have done so as to absorb the image of Iago I had
acquired fortuitously from the outside?'

'You should have let the new material filter through you, and given it
life by using your imagination, as we do in the school of experiencing.

'Once this living material has become part of you, and the character has
been created in your mind, you must go a stage further. One of the best
representatives of the school of representation, Coquelin the Elder, has
written about this graphically.

' "The actor creates a model in his imagination, then like a painter,
captures every trait and transfers it not onto canvas but onto himself," '
Tortsov read, quoting from Coquelin's little book which Rakhmanov had
handed to him.[2] ' "Then, like the painter, he captures all its features and
puts them not on canvas, but on himself. He endows his Two with every
aspect of this person. He sees Tartuffe in a particular costume. He puts it
on. He sees a certain way of walking and copies it. He forces his own face,
and, as it were, like a tailor cuts and sews his own flesh until the critic
inside his One is happy and says that this indeed looks like Tartuffe. But the
matter does not end there, for there would only be a superficial resemblance, the outside of a character, not the character itself. He must make
Tartuffe speak with the voice he thinks should be his and should make him

walk and talk, think and listen with the very soul he thinks to be Tartuffe's to shape the entire performance. Only then is the portrait ready. It can be put on the easel, the stage and the audience will say, 'That's Tartuffe' or 'the actor played badly . . .' "'

'But that's terribly hard, very complicated,' I said most distressed.

'Yes. Coquelin himself acknowledged as much. He said: "The actor does not live but plays. He remains cold towards the object of his acting, but his artistry must be perfect."

'And indeed,' added Tortsov, 'the art of representation demands perfection if it is to remain art.'

'Then isn't it simpler to trust nature, real creative work, and genuine experiencing?' I asked.

'Coquelin confidently declares, "Art is not real life, nor even its reflection. Art is itself a creator. It creates its own life, outside time and space, beautiful in its own abstraction."

'Of course we cannot agree with such an arrogant challenge to the one true, perfect, unattainable artist – creative nature.'

'Can they really believe that their technique is more powerful than nature herself? What nonsense!' I said unable to control myself.

'They believe that the stage life they create is better. Not the genuine, human life we actually know, but another which has been enhanced.

'That is why actors of the school of representation live each role truthfully, humanly only at the beginning, in the preparatory stages, but at the moment of actual performance, they switch to a convention-based life. To justify this approach they argue that theatre, performances are conventions, that the stage does not have adequate means to convey an illusion of real life. The theatre, therefore, should not only accept conventions, but take them to its heart.

'This kind of acting has beauty but no depth. It is effective rather than deep. Form is more interesting than content. It acts on the eyes and ears rather than on the heart and, in consequence, more readily delights than disturbs.

'True, acting of this kind can make a considerable impression, one which grips you while you are watching and leaves you with beautiful memories, but these impressions don't warm your heart or go very deep. Its effect is acute but transitory. You marvel, but you don't believe. And so there are some things it cannot do. This kind of acting can manage to provide whatever is designed to startle, surprise, it can give you the theatrically beautiful, or picture-postcard feelings. But when it comes to the expression of deep passions, it is either too showy or too superficial. The subtlety and depth of human feelings will not yield to mere technique.

They need the direct support of nature itself at the moment when experiencing naturally occurs and is embodied. Nonetheless, the representation of a role, which arises from a process of genuine experiencing, must be recognized as creative work, as art.'

.. .. 19..

In today's class Grisha declared with great enthusiasm that he is an actor of the school of representation, that its fundamentals are dear to his heart, that they are what his artistic nature demands, and that he bows before them, that this and this alone is what he understands by art. Tortsov questioned the validity of his views, reminding him that experiencing is an essential part of the art of representation, and that he was by no means convinced that Grisha was capable of controlling that process whether onstage or at home. However our argumentative friend declared that he always feels and experiences what he does onstage very strongly.

'Every single person feels and experiences something at every moment of his life,' said Tortsov. 'If we felt nothing, we would be dead. Only the dead feel nothing. What is important for you is to experience your own feelings which are parallel to the role or something else which bears no relation to it?

'Very often even the most experienced actors bring to the stage something which they worked out at home, but which is not in any way relevant to the role or the stage as art. That's what happened to all of you. Some of you showed off your voices, your meaningful inflexions, your technique. Others delighted the audience by trotting around in a lively manner, by balletic leaps, by desperate playacting, or you tried to tempt us with beautiful gestures and poses. In short, you brought things that were quite unnecessary for the characters you were portraying.

'And you, Grisha, did not approach your role by starting with its inner content, or by experiencing it, or by reproducing it. You came at it quite differently. You think you created something that can be qualified as art. But where there is no awareness of living feelings that are parallel to the character's, there can be no talk of a genuine act of creation.

'So don't delude yourself, but try to dig deeper and understand where genuine art begins and ends. Then you will realize that your acting bears no relation to it at all.'

'What was it then?'

'Stock-in-trade. True, it wasn't bad as a commentary on the role, a convention-based illustration of it, with fairly efficient artifice.'

I'll skip over the long argument Grisha started and pass on directly to

Tortsov's explanation of the dividing line between real art and stock-in-trade.

'There is no genuine art where there is no experiencing. It begins where feeling comes into its own.'

'And stock-in-trade?' Grisha asked.

'That, in turn, begins where creative experiencing, or the artistic reproduction that results from it, ends.

'Whereas in the arts of experiencing and of representation experiencing is indispensable, in stock-in-trade it is an accident. Actors of this kind aren't able to create each role individually. They aren't able to experience and give natural physical embodiment to what they have experienced. The stock-in-trade actor can only speak his lines as though he were reporting them, and accompany his report with theatrical tricks that have been worked out once-and-for-all. That greatly simplifies the tasks with which stock-in-trade acting has to deal.'

'What does this simplification consist of?' I asked.

'You will understand that better, when you know where the tricks of the trade come from, things we, here, call *actors' clichés*, how they were created and how they were developed.

'If you want to convey the feelings in a role, you have to understand them. And to do that you must undergo similar experiences. You cannot ape feeling, you can only fake its outward consequences. But stock-in-trade actors aren't capable of experiencing a role, and so they can never understand what the outward consequences of this creative process are.

'How can that be? How can you find an outer form without the prompting of inner feelings? How are you to convey, through voice and movement, the external results of a non-existent inner life? There's nothing for it but to resort to simple, convention-based theatrics. This is an extremely primitive, formal, outward portrayal of feelings, which the actor has never known or experienced. This is mere imitation.

'Using mimicry, voice, and movement the stock-in-trade actor only presents the audience with external clichés, as though they expressed "the life of the human spirit" of a role, a dead mask for non-existent feelings. There is a large, ready-made battery of tricks, which ostensibly convey by outward means all the possible feelings you can encounter in the course of your career for this kind of playacting. There is no actual feeling in them. There is only imitation, a resemblance to its supposed outer results. There is no psychological content. There are only the technical tricks which are supposed to express it.

'Some of these tricks which have been fixed for all time, have been preserved by the stock-in-trade tradition, which our predecessors have passed on to us, such as, for example, clasping the palms of one's hands to the heart during a declaration of love, or tearing at one's collar to represent death. Others are taken over ready-made from our talented contemporaries (such as stroking one's forehead with the back of one's hand, as Vera Komissarzhevskaya[3] did in tragic moments). A third kind of trick may be invented by the actors themselves.

'There is a special, stock-in-trade manner of merely delivering a role, that involves the voice, diction, long speeches (exaggerated top and bottom registers at climaxes with a specific actor's vibrato, or with special declamatory, vocal flourishes). There are tricks for walking (stock-in-trade actors don't walk across the stage, they strut), for movements and actions, for shaping the body and external acting (these are especially acute in stock-in-trade actors and are not based on beauty but on mere prettiness). There are formal tricks for displaying all possible human feelings and passions (flashing one's teeth, rolling one's eyes to suggest jealousy, as Kostya did, covering one's face and eyes with one's hands instead of weeping, tearing one's hair to suggest despair). There are tricks for imitating whole characters and types from different strata of society (peasants spit on the ground and wipe their nose with the hem of their smock, soldiers have clinking spurs, aristocrats play with their monocles). There are tricks for historical periods (operatic gestures for the Middle Ages, movements learned from dancing masters for the 18th century). There are tricks for specific plays and roles (the Mayor in The Inspector General[4]), a special way of bending the body towards the audience during asides, with the hand held in front of the mouth. All these actors' habits have, with time, become traditional.

'Thus, a generalized actors' diction, as well as a particular way of delivering a role with pre-established effects, with a particular theatrical gait, and picturesque poses and gestures, was developed once and for all.

'Ready-made mechanical tricks are easily reproduced by stock-in-trade actors with trained muscles. They become a habit, second nature, which replaces real nature.

'This fixed mask of feeling soon wears out, loses its fleeting resemblance to life, and turns into a mere cliché, a trick-of-the-trade, or a conventional, external sign. A string of these clichés constitutes a kind of ritual by which an actor illustrates every role, and goes hand in hand with a conventional delivery of the lines. Stock-in-trade actors want to exchange vital, genuine experiencing and creative acting for these tricks. But nothing can compare with real feeling, which will not allow itself to be communicated by the mechanical tricks of the stock-in-trade actor.

'A few of these clichés retain a certain theatrical effectiveness, but the overwhelming majority of them are in such bad taste they are offensive.

They astound you by their lack of understanding of human feeling, their simplistic relationship to it, or merely by their stupidity.

'But time and custom have made the ugly and senseless familiar and dear to us. For example, the grimaces of the comic in an operetta, or the comic old woman trying to look young, or the doors of a box set which open and close automatically when the hero or a touring star makes an entrance or an exit, have been hallowed by time and are considered by some to be perfectly normal.

'That is why even unnatural clichés have become part of the stock-in-trade and are now included in the actor's ritual; other clichés have degenerated to such an extent that no one can tell whence they came. Actors' tricks, which have lost the inner meaning that gave rise to them, have become mere theatrical conventions. They have nothing in common with real life, and block out the actor's true humanity. There is an abundance of such conventional clichés in opera, ballet, and especially neo-classical tragedy, in which people try to express the heroes' most complex and sublime experiences with conventional, stock-in-trade tricks (for example, by looking picturesque, by exaggerated moving of the body, "tearing" at one's heart in moments of despair, shaking one fists in fury, or wringing one's hands in supplication).

'Stock-in-trade actors are convinced that this diction and these movements, which they all have in common – for example, a sickly sweet voice for lyrical passages, monotony for epic poetry, stridency for hatred, a false sob in the voice for grief – apparently elevate an actor's voice and body, make them beautiful, theatrically more effective, more visually powerful. But, unfortunately, nobility is not always properly understood. There are many ways to represent beauty but they are often merely dictated by bad taste. And there is a great deal more bad taste in the world than good. That is why we have bombast instead of nobility, the pretty-pretty instead of beauty, and theatrical effect instead of expressiveness. And all this, from conventional speech and diction to an actor's walk and gesture, benefits the ostentatious side of theatre, which is too crude to be art.

'The actor's stock-in-trade speech and bodily expression have degenerated into displays of effect, bombastic nobility, out of which a special kind of theatrical prettiness is created.

'Clichés cannot replace experiencing.

'The pity is, too, that all sorts of clichés have stuck. They eat an actor away, like rust. Once they have found an opening they dig in deeper, spawn, and try to take over every moment in a role, every aspect of an actor's technique. They fill every blank hole. Frequently, they jump in before any feelings have been aroused, blocking their path. And so, the actor must be vigilant and ward off these intruders.

'Everything I have said also applies to the gifted actor who is capable of real creative work. It can be said of typical stock-in-trade actors, that almost everything they do consists of an adroit selection and combination of clichés. A few of these have their own kind of charm, and unsophisticated audiences don't realize that they amount to no more than mere mechanics.

'But no matter how perfect actors' clichés may be, they cannot move an audience. For that you need additional stimuli, special tricks which we call *actors' emotion*. Actors' emotion isn't genuine emotion, or genuine, artistic experiencing. It is an artificial stimulation of the periphery of the body.

'For example, if you clench your fist and contract the muscles of your body or start to pant, that can lead to considerable physical tension which, from the auditorium, can often be taken for the appearance of a powerful personality aroused by passion. You can storm and rage externally, mechanically, with complete sang-froid, for no reason at all, in general. This creates a faint likeness of physical frenzy.

'Actors who are more highly strung induce actors' emotion by artificially stimulating their nerves. The result is their own kind of theatrical frenzy, hysterics, as empty of inward meaning as is artificial physical frenzy. In both cases, we are dealing not with acting as an art but with playacting, not with the living feelings of the human being/actor which have been shaped to the role, but with actors' emotion. Yet, this emoting can reach its goal, can bear a faint resemblance to life, and make a certain impression, since the artistically naive don't question it, and are satisfied with crude imitation. Actors of this type are often convinced they serve genuine art. They don't realize that what they do is mere theatrical stock-in-trade.'

.. .. 19..

Tortsov continued his analysis in today's class.

It was mainly poor Vanya who got the worst of it. Tortsov didn't even consider his acting as stock-in-trade.

'What was it then?' I interposed.

'The most appalling ham-acting.'

'Which I didn't do?' I asked, just in case.

'Yes, you did!'

'When was that?!' I exclaimed, horrified. 'You told me I acted instinctively.'

'And as I explained to you, that kind of acting is composed of moments of genuine creative work which alternate with moments . . .'

'Of stock-in-trade? . . .' The question burst from me.

'There was no way you could achieve stock-in-trade because it requires long hard work, as with Grisha, and you haven't had time for that. That is why you imitated a savage using extremely amateur clichés in which one could discern no technique at all. And without technique, not only is there no art but no stock-in trade either.'

'How could I have used clichés when it was my first time onstage?'

'I know young schoolgirls who have never been to a theatre, or a performance, or even a rehearsal, and yet they perform tragedies using the most inveterate and vulgar clichés.'

'That's to say, not even stock-in-trade but mere, amateur ham-acting?'

'Yes! Only ham, fortunately.'

'Why "fortunately"?'

'Because it is easier to fight against amateur ham than professional ham, when it's deeply ingrained. Beginners, like you, if they are gifted, can accidentally and momentarily feel a role properly, but they cannot communicate it as a whole in a consistent, artistic form, and therefore always take refuge in ham-acting. In the early stages this is comparatively harmless, but you must remember that in ham-acting there is a very great hidden danger against which you must fight right from the start, lest you develop the sort of habits that cripple an actor and distort his natural gifts. Try to understand where stock-in-trade and mere ham begin and end.'

'Where does it begin?'

'I will use you as an example. You are an intelligent person. So why, apart from one or two moments, was what you did during the show so absurd? Can you actually believe that Moors, renowned for their culture in their time, behaved like wild animals, prowling round their cages? The savage you portrayed snarled, flashed his teeth, and rolled his eyes even during a quiet conversation with his aide-de-camp. Where did such an approach come from? Explain to us how you could possibly arrive at this absurdity. Isn't it because, for an actor who has gone astray, any kind of idiocy is possible?'

I recounted the work I had done at home in almost as much detail as I had put in my diary. I was able to illustrate some of it in action. To make things clearer I set out the chairs in the same way the furniture is arranged in my room.

Tortsov laughed a great deal at some of the things I did.

'That is how you create the worst kind of stock-in-trade,' he said when I had finished. 'That is what mostly happens when you take on something which is beyond you, something you neither know nor feel.

'My impression, during the show, was that your main intention was to astonish, to shake the audience. With what? With real feelings, rooted in your own nature, which matched the character you were to portray? You had none of that. Nor did you have a complete, living image from which to make an external copy. What was there left for you to do? Grab at the first available feature that happened to cross your mind. Like every human being, you have quite a store of them to suit every occasion. You see, every impression we receive is preserved in one form or another in our memory which, when necessary, we express as an image. In the case of such fortuitous, fleeting general images, we pay little attention to whether what we are communicating corresponds to the real world. We are content with any sort of trait, any sign. Day-to-day living has even provided us with stereotypes or with tokens, with which we give physical embodiment to these images. Say to any one of us, "Play a savage, without thinking about it, right now." I'll wager you that most people will do just what you did during the show, because prowling about, baring one's teeth, rolling the whites of one's eyes have been associated in our imagination since time immemorial with a false representation of the savage.

'These tricks "in general" are present in every human being to convey jealousy, rage, agitation, joy, desperation or whatever. And these tricks are set in motion irrespective of when, how and under what circumstances a person experiences them. This kind of "playing" or more precisely "play-acting" is ridiculously elementary. In order to convey a strength which has no real existence, you shout yourself hoarse, you force your facial expression to the point where it becomes a grimace, you exaggerate your movements and actions, shake your fists, clasp your head in your hands and so on. All these tricks are there inside you but, fortunately they are not legion. And so it is not surprising that you used them all in the space of one hour's work. Tricks such as these appear quickly, spontaneously, but soon become wearisome.

'In sharp contrast, real, artistic forms that are meant to convey the inner life of a role, are difficult to find and are created slowly, and never become wearisome. They are self-renewing, they grow continually, and invariably thrill both actor and audience. That is why a role based on natural forms flourishes, while one based on playacting and amateur ham-acting soon becomes lifeless and mechanical.

'All these, so to speak, "common human clichés" are, like obliging fools, more dangerous than enemies. These clichés are there inside you, as they are in every human being and you used them onstage in the absence of the ready-made, carefully elaborated technique of the stock-in-trade actor.

'As you can see, ham-acting, like stock-in-trade, starts where experiencing ends. But stock-in-trade is suitably organized to replace feelings with mere artifice and uses practised clichés, while ham-acting does not have even these at its disposal and indiscriminately sets in motion the first available "common" or "traditional" clichés which have neither been polished nor adapted for the stage.

'What happened to you is understandable and excusable in beginners. But be careful in future. Amateur ham and "common clichés" can, in the long term, result in the worst kind of stock-in trade. Don't give it a chance to develop.

'You can do that first by fighting unremittingly against clichés and, second, by studying how to experience a role not only in isolated moments in a performance, as you did with Othello, but the whole time you are performing. In that way you will be able to leave acting on instinct behind and enter into the art of experiencing.'

.. .. 19..

Tortsov's words made an enormous impression on me. There were moments when I came to the conclusion that I really ought to leave the school.

That was why today, when I met Tortsov in class I renewed my questions. I wanted to draw a general conclusion from everything that had been said in the previous classes. Finally I reached the conclusion that my acting had been a mixture of the best in our business, i.e., moments of inspiration, and the worst, i.e., ham.

'It wasn't quite the worst,' Tortsov reassured me. 'What some of the others did was even worse. Your amateurism can be cured, but the mistakes made by others arose out of a conscious principle, which is not always possible to alter or eradicate.'

'What is that?'

'The exploitation of art.'

'What is that?' the students asked.

'Take what Varya did, for example.'

'Me?!' Varya jumped out of her seat in surprise. 'What did I do?'

'You were giving us a display of your little arms and legs, in fact the whole of you, since people can get a better view onstage.'

'Me? My little arms and legs?' our poor young beauty said in some perplexity.

'Yes, indeed, your little arms and legs.'

'That's awful, terrible, terrible,' Varya repeated, 'I did it without even knowing it.'

'That's the way it always is when bad habits have taken hold of you.'

'Then why did I get so much applause?'

'Because you've got very nice little arms and legs.'

'And what's wrong with that?'

'What's wrong is that you were flirting with the audience, not playing Kate. Shakespeare didn't write *The Taming of the Shrew* so that a student called Varya could show off her little arms and legs and flirt with her admirers. Shakespeare had something else in view, something quite foreign to you and a mystery to us.

'Unfortunately our art is often exploited for purposes quite alien to it. You, because you wanted to show how beautiful you are, others to gain popularity, to have outward success or to advance their careers. This happens all the time in our business, and I am giving you a timely warning about it. Take careful note of what I am about to say to you. The theatre, because it is public, because of the element of display in it, is a double-edged sword. On the one hand it has an important social mission, but, on the other, it attracts people who want to exploit it to make a career for themselves. These people profit from the ignorance of some and the depraved tastes of others, they resort to favouritism, to scheming and other means that have nothing to do with creative work. Deeds of that kind are the most pernicious enemies of art. You must fight them as hard as possible, and, if that does not work, then they must be driven off the stage. And so,' he turned to Varya once more, 'make up your mind once and for all. Did you come here to serve art and make sacrifices for it or to exploit it for your own personal ends?

'However,' he proceeded, turning back to all of us, 'it is only in theory that art can be divided into separate categories. Reality and practice are not interested in labelling things. They mix all manner of schools together. In fact, we often see how great artists, out of human weakness, fall into stock-in-trade, while stock-in-trade actors, at moments, rise to the level of genuine art.

'The same thing occurs in the performance of every role in every play. Alongside moments of real experiencing, there are moments of mere representation, stock-in-trade, ham and exploitation. So, the more essential it is for an actor to know where art ends, and the more important it is for the stock-in-trade actor to understand the line where art begins.

'So, in our business there are two basic schools of thought, *the art of experiencing and the art of representation*. The common background against which they shine is stock-in-trade theatre be it good or bad. It must be acknowledged that in moments of excitement, flashes of genuine creative work can break through the tedious clichés and playacting. We must equally protect our art against exploitation as this iniquity can slip in unnoticed.

'As far as amateurism is concerned, it is helpful and harmful in equal measure, depending on which path it travels.'

'How are we to defend ourselves against all the dangers that threaten us?' I enquired.

'There is only one way, as I have already told you: ceaselessly to fulfil the basic goal of our art, and that consists in the creation of *the life of the human spirit of a role in a play and in giving that life physical embodiment in an aesthetic, theatrical* form. The ideal of the genuine artist is contained within these words.'

It became clear to me from this discussion with Tortsov that it was too soon for us to appear onstage and that the show we students had given had done more harm than good.

'It did you some good,' replied Tortsov when I expressed my thoughts to him. 'It demonstrated to you what you must never do onstage, and what you must avoid in the future.'

At the end of our discussion, as we were beginning to disperse, Tortsov announced that tomorrow we will begin classes to develop our voice and body, i.e., lessons in singing, diction, gymnastics, rhythm, expressive movement, dance, fencing, acrobatics. These classes will take place every day as the muscles of the human body demand systematic, unremitting, lengthy exercise if they are to develop.

3

ACTION, 'IF', 'GIVEN CIRCUMSTANCES'

.. .. 19..

Today we assembled in the school theatre, which is small but fully equipped.

Tortsov came in, looked at us intently and said:

'Marya, go up onstage.'

I couldn't begin to describe the terror which gripped the poor girl. She started rushing about the place, her feet slipping on the polished parquet floor like a young puppy. Finally we caught hold of her and carried her to Tortsov who was laughing like a schoolboy. She covered her face with her hands and babbled over and over again:

'My little darlings, please, I can't! My dears, I'm scared, I'm scared!'

'Calm down and let's play. This is what our play is about,' said Tortsov, paying no more attention to her distress. 'The curtains open and there you are, sitting onstage. Alone. You sit, just sit, and go on sitting. Then the curtains close. That's all. Nothing could be easier. Right?'

Marya didn't answer. Then, without a word, Tortsov took her by the arm and led her onto the stage. The students roared with laughter.

Tortsov whirled round.

'My dear young friends,' he said, 'you are in class. And Marya is experiencing a most important moment in her life as an actress. You must learn when and where it is right to laugh.'

Marya and Tortsov went up onstage. Then we all sat down in silence, expectantly. The atmosphere was hushed, as before the start of a performance.

Finally the curtains slowly opened. Marya was sitting downstage centre. She had, as before, covered her face with her hands as she was afraid of seeing the audience. Silence reigned and that led us to expect something special from her. The pause was riveting.

Marya doubtless felt this too and realized that she ought to do something. Cautiously, she removed first one hand from her face, then the other, but at the same time hung her head so low that all we could see was the parting in her hair. There was another agonizing pause.

Finally, sensing the general mood of expectancy, she looked out into the auditorium, but instantly turned away as though blinded by the bright lights. She began to fidget, sitting first this way, then that, adopting ridiculous poses, leaning backwards, sideways, pulling at her short skirt, staring fixedly at something on the floor.

Finally, Tortsov took pity on her, gave the signal, and the curtains closed.

I rushed up to Tortsov and asked him to repeat the exercise with me.

They sat me down in the centre of the stage.

I won't lie. I wasn't frightened. After all, this wasn't a performance. Nonetheless, I felt ill at ease. I was split down the middle by conflicting demands. The stage by its very nature put me on display, while the human feelings I was looking for needed solitude. There was one person inside me who wanted me to entertain the audience, and another who told me to pay no attention to them. And though my legs, hands, head, and torso obeyed me, at the same time, despite myself, they added a certain something of their own, over and above what was needed. A simple movement of the hand or foot turned into something mannered. The result was a kind of photographic pose.

Strange! I'd been onstage only once. The rest of the time I'd lived a normal human life. Yet it was far, far easier for me to sit onstage in a theatrical rather than a human way – unnaturally. Up there onstage, theatrical falsehood was more congenial to me than natural truth. I was told that my face looked stupid, guilty, apologetic. I didn't know what to do or where to look. Still Tortsov didn't let up, but let me go on stewing.

After me other students tried the exercise.

'Now let's move on,' said Tortsov. 'In time we shall come back to this exercise and learn how to sit onstage.'

'Learn just to sit?' the students cried in amazement. 'But we did sit . . .'

'No,' Tortsov declared firmly, 'you didn't just sit.'

'How should we have sat?'

Instead of answering, Tortsov got up and walked in a business-like way onto the stage. There he sank heavily into an armchair, just as if he were at home.

He didn't do anything or try to do anything, but nonetheless the simple way he sat captured our attention. We wanted to watch him and understand what was going on inside his head. He smiled and we smiled too. He became thoughtful and we wanted to know what he was thinking about. He glanced at something and we just had to know what had attracted his attention.

In life we wouldn't have been interested in watching Tortsov just sit there. But when it happens onstage, for some reason, you watch with particular attention and even take a degree of pleasure in what you see. That was not the case when the students were onstage. No one felt like watching them, or was interested in knowing what was going through their minds. They amused us by their helplessness and their desire to please, but Tortsov paid no attention to us while we, on our side, were drawn to him. What was the secret? Tortsov revealed it to us:

'Everything that happens onstage must occur for *some reason or other*. When you sit there, you must also sit for a reason and not merely to show yourself off to the audience. But this is not easy, and you have to learn how to do it.'

'What was your reason for sitting there just now?' asked Vanya.

'To take a rest from you and the rehearsal I've just had at the theatre.'

'Now come with me and let's act another play,' he said to Marya. 'I'll act with you, too.'

'You?!' she exclaimed and rushed onto the stage.

Once again she was made to sit centre stage and once again she tried very hard to change her position. Tortsov stood beside her and concentrated on looking for something in his notebook. Meanwhile, Marya gradually settled down and finally stopped moving completely, fixing her gaze attentively on Tortsov. She was afraid of disturbing him and patiently waited for further instructions from her teacher. Her pose became natural. The stage brought out her good points as an actress, and I was quite taken with her.

A considerable period of time elapsed in this way. Then the curtains closed.

'How did you feel?' Tortsov asked her after they had both returned to the auditorium.

'Me?' she asked in confusion. 'Were we acting then?'

'Of course.'

'But I thought I was just sitting and waiting until you found what you wanted in your notebook and told me what you wanted me to do. I didn't act anything at all!'

'That's just what was good about it, that you were sitting there for a reason and weren't playacting,' said Tortsov, picking up her words. 'Which do you think is best,' he said, addressing all of us, 'sitting onstage and showing off your legs, like Sonya, or the whole of yourself, like Grisha, or sitting and actually doing something, however insignificant? It may not be very interesting, but it creates life onstage, whereas showing oneself off in one way or another simply leads us beyond the confines of true art.

'Acting is action. *The basis of theatre is doing, dynamism.* The word "drama" itself in Ancient Greek means "an action being performed". In Latin the corresponding word is *actio*, and the root of this same word has passed into our vocabulary, "action", "actor", "act". So, drama is an action we can see being performed, and, when he comes on, the actor becomes an agent in that action.'

'Look, please, I'm sorry,' Grisha said suddenly. 'You're trying to tell us that theatre is action. But, if I may ask, in what way was your sitting in the armchair action? To me it was total and absolute inaction.'

'I don't know whether it was action or not,' I said with some heat, 'but his "inaction" was far more interesting than your "action".'

'If someone sits motionless onstage it doesn't mean he's being passive,' Tortsov explained. 'You can be motionless and nonetheless fully active, not outwardly, physically, but inwardly, mentally. Besides which, quite often, physical stillness is the result of intense inner action, and that is especially important and interesting in creative work. The value of art can be defined by its inner content. So I will modify my formula and say: *acting is action – mental and physical.*

'In this way one of the most basic principles of our art is satisfied, that is the dynamic, active nature of our creative work in the theatre and of our art.'

.. .. 19..

'Let's do another play,' said Tortsov, turning to Marya. 'Here's the plot. Your mother has lost her job. She hasn't anything left to sell to cover your drama school fees, so tomorrow you will be thrown out for non-payment. But a friend has come to the rescue. Since she has no money, she has brought a brooch with a precious stone in it, the only thing of value she could find. This generous gesture on your friend's part has taken you aback and moved you. How can you accept such a sacrifice? You can't bring yourself to do it, and so you refuse. Then your friend pins the brooch on the curtain, and goes out into the corridor. You follow. There is a long scene while she tries to persuade you. You say no again, you weep, you express your gratitude. Finally you accept her sacrifice, your friend leaves, and you come back into the room to get the brooch. But . . . where is it? Could someone have come and taken it? There are many tenants in the apartment, so it's possible. A tense and thorough search begins.

'Go up onstage. I will pin the brooch up, and you will return to look for it in one of the folds of the curtain.'

Marya went into the wings. Tortsov didn't bother to pin up the brooch but, after a few moments, asked her to come back. She catapulted from the wings, ran to the proscenium arch, immediately recoiled, clasped both hands to her head in a spasm of horror . . . then rushed to the opposite side, grabbed the curtain, tore at it desperately, then buried her head in its folds. That was meant to represent the search for the brooch. When she couldn't find it, she rushed back into the wings with her hands convulsively clutched against her breast, which, evidently, was meant to express the tragic aspect of the situation.

Those of us sitting in the front rows could scarcely contain our laughter.

Marya flew down from the stage to the auditorium in evident triumph. Her eyes were shining and her cheeks were flushed.

'How did you feel?' asked Tortsov.

'Oh, my darlings! So wonderful! I can't tell you how wonderful . . . I can't, I really can't say any more. I'm so happy!' she exclaimed, sitting down, then jumping up, clutching her head. 'I felt it, I really felt it!'

'Fine,' said Tortsov approvingly. 'And where's the brooch?'

'Oh, yes! I forgot about it . . .'

'Strange,' said Tortsov, 'you did all that looking for it and . . . forgot about it.'

Quick as a flash Marya was up onstage again, starting to finger the folds of the curtain.

'Remember,' Tortsov reminded her, 'if you find the brooch you are saved, and can continue coming to school. If you don't, then you're done for. You'll be thrown out.'

With that Marya's face turned grave. She fixed her eyes upon the curtain and began to examine every fold of the material attentively, systematically.

This time the search proceeded in a different incomparably slower tempo, and we could all believe that Marya was not wasting a moment, that she was sincerely worried and anxious.

'Dear God! Where is it? It's lost! . . . ' she repeated under her breath. 'No!' she exclaimed in despair and bewilderment after she had inspected all the folds in the curtain.

Her face expressed alarm. She stood there dumbfounded, her eyes staring. We watched her with bated breath.

'She's very responsive,' said Tortsov under his breath to Rakhmanov.

'How did you feel when you looked the second time?' he asked Marya.

'How did I feel?' she repeated the question listlessly. 'I don't know, I was busy looking,' she said, after a pause for thought.

'That's right. This time you were busy looking. But what did you do the first time?'

'Oh! The first time! I was so emotional! I experienced such terror. I can't! I can't! . . . ' She recalled it with rapture and pride, flushing with excitement.

'Which of the two states of mind did you like better? When you rushed about and tore at the curtain, or when you examined it more calmly?'

'Well, when I was looking for it the first time, of course!'

'No. Don't try to convince us you were looking for the brooch the first time,' said Tortsov. 'You didn't give the brooch a moment's thought. You just wanted to suffer – for suffering's sake. Now, the second time you were really looking. We could all see that very clearly, we understood, we believed that your bewilderment and dismay were well-founded. And so, the first time you looked you achieved nothing. It was run-of-the-mill theatrical posturing. The way you looked the second time was perfectly right.'

This verdict stunned Marya.

'We don't need mindless rushing about onstage,' Tortsov continued. 'There should be neither rushing about for rushing about's sake, nor suffering for suffering's sake. Onstage you shouldn't perform actions "in general" for actions' sake. You should perform them *in a way which is well-founded, apt and productive.*'

'And be genuine,' I added.

'Genuine action is well-founded and apt,' Tortsov stated. 'So,' he continued, 'as you should do things genuinely onstage, all of you go up onstage and . . . start doing things.'

Up we went, but for a long time didn't know where to begin.

Whatever you do onstage must be done in such a way as to make an impression. But I couldn't find actions interesting enough to hold the audience's attention, and so I began to repeat my Othello but soon realized that I was posturing, just as I had in the show, and stopped.

Leo portrayed a general and then a peasant. Pasha sat in a chair in a Hamlet-like pose and portrayed first grief then disillusion. Sonya flirted, while Grisha made her a declaration of love in the traditional manner, as it is done on stages all over the world.

Then I glanced over at the far corner of the stage, where Nikolai and

Darya had taken refuge. I nearly exclaimed out loud, seeing their pale, drawn faces, their staring eyes and rigid bodies. It seems they were playing the 'scene with the swaddling clothes' from Ibsen's *Brand*.[1]

'Now let's analyse what you showed us,' said Tortsov. 'I'll start with you,' he said, turning to me, 'and with you and you,' he said to Marya and Pasha. 'All of you, sit where I can see you and start feeling the same things you portrayed just now, you – jealousy, you – suffering, you – melancholy.'

We sat down and tried to summon up the necessary feelings, but nothing happened. While I was moving about the stage like a savage, I wasn't aware of the absurdity of my actions when I had nothing inside. But when I was forced to sit quite still, with no external posturing, the senselessness, the futility, the impossibility of the task I had been set became crystal clear.

'How, in your opinion,' asked Tortsov, 'can you sit on a chair and will yourself to be jealous, furious, or sad without a why or wherefore? Can you summon up "creative action"? You've just tried to do it and nothing happened, no feelings sprang to life and so you had to start playacting, using your face to demonstrate non-existent experiences. You can't squeeze feelings out of yourself, you can't be jealous, love, suffer for the sake of being jealous, loving, or suffering. You can't force feelings. That only leads to the most repulsive kind of ham acting. So, when choosing an action, leave your feelings alone. They will appear of their own accord as a result of something which has gone before, that evokes jealousy, love, or suffering. Think hard about what has gone before and re-create it. Don't be concerned with the result. Playing at passion, as Kostya, Marya and Pasha did, playacting stereotypes, as Leo and Vanya did, mechanical acting like Igor's and Grisha's are widespread faults in our profession. They are the besetting sins of those who are accustomed to presenting theatrical stereotypes and posing onstage. The true actor should not ape the outward manifestations of passion, or copy outward form, or indulge in mechanical playacting according to some ham ritual or other, but perform actions in a genuine human fashion. You must not play passions and characters but react under the influence of passion, in character.'

'How can you do anything on a bare stage floor with just a few chairs?' the students asked in their own defence.

'Dear God, word of honour, if we had some scenery to work in, with furniture and a fireplace and ashtrays and all the trappings, then we could perform actions well enough!' Vanya assured him.

'Fine!' said Tortsov and left the room.

.. .. 19..

Today's class was scheduled for the school theatre, but the main door to the auditorium was locked. However, at the appointed time, another door was opened for us, which led directly onto the stage. When we got there, to our general astonishment, we found ourselves in an entrance hall. Beyond it was a comfortably furnished sitting room. In the sitting room were two doors, one of which led to a small dining room and a bedroom, while through the other we reached a corridor which had a brightly lit room on the left. The whole apartment was partitioned off partly by canvas, partly by flats from various sets. The furniture and props had likewise been drawn from plays that were in the repertoire. The curtains were closed and blocked by furniture so that it was difficult to tell where the footlights and the proscenium arch were.

'Here you have a whole apartment in which you can not only do things, but live,' Tortsov explained.

Because we couldn't feel the stage boards beneath our feet we behaved as though we were at home, as in everyday life. We started by looking over the room. Then each of us found a comfortable corner for ourselves, took a partner, and began a conversation. Tortsov reminded us that we had gathered there not for a chat but for study.

'What do we have to do?' we asked.

'The same as in the last class,' Tortsov explained. 'You must do whatever you do in a genuine, well-founded, way that is apt.'

But we went on standing there, motionless.

'I don't know, honestly . . . how we can . . . suddenly do things in a apt way without a why or wherefore?' Pasha ventured.

'If you can't manage to do things without a why or wherefore, then do them for a reason. Can't you motivate something here, in this real-life setting? If I were to ask you, Vanya, to go to that door and shut it, would you refuse?'

'Shut the door?! With pleasure,' he answered in his usual affected manner.

Quick as a flash he slammed the door and returned to his place.

'That's not what I call shutting a door,' commented Tortsov. 'That's called slamming a door so as to be left in peace. The words "to shut the door" imply shutting it so that there won't be a gust of air, as there is now, or to prevent what we are saying from being heard in the hall.'

'But it won't stay shut! Honestly! There's no way!'

To prove his point he demonstrated how the door just opened.

'Then you will need to put more time and effort into doing what I ask.'

Vanya went again, fiddled with the door for a long time and finally shut it.

'There we are, a genuine action,' said Tortsov to him encouragingly.

'Tell me to do something too,' I badgered Tortsov.

'Can't you think of something for yourself? There's a fireplace and firewood. Go and light a fire.'

I did as he said, put the wood in the fireplace, and then noticed I had no matches. I had to badger Tortsov once more.

'What do you want matches for?' he said in amazement.

'What do you mean, what for? To light the wood.'

'Heaven help us! It's a prop fireplace, made out of papier mâché. Do you want to send the theatre up in smoke?!'

'Not light it for real, but pretend to,' I explained.

'To "pretend" to light it, you only need "pretend" matches. Here take them.'

He gave me his empty hand.

'As though striking a match mattered! What you need is something else. It's essential to believe that, if there were real matches in your hand, then you would do just what you are doing now, with nothing in them. One day when you play Hamlet, once you have been through all the complexities of his mind, you will reach the moment when you kill the king. Will everything really depend on whether you have a really sharp sword in your hand? Will you really be unable to finish the play if you haven't got one? No, you can kill the king without a sword, and light a fire without matches. You should kindle your imagination instead.'

I went back to lighting the fire and vaguely heard Tortsov giving everyone something to do. He sent Vanya and Marya into the hall to think up various games. He told Nikolai, as a former draughtsman, to make a plan of the apartment and measure it by pacing it out. He took a letter from Sonya, and told her to find it in one of the five rooms, and then told Grisha that he had actually given Sonya's letter to Leo with a request to hide it somewhere very secret. That forced Grisha to follow Leo around. In a word, Tortsov got us all moving and, for a short while, made us perform real actions.

For my part I went on pretending to light the fire. My imaginary match 'pretended' to go out several times. I tried all the while to see it and feel it between my fingers. But without much success. I also tried to see the fire in the grate and sense its warmth, but that didn't work either. I'd soon had enough of lighting the fire. I had to find something new to do. I started rearranging the furniture and other objects, but as these tasks were contrived and had no real foundation I carried them out mechanically.

Tortsov drew my attention to the fact that mechanical, unfounded actions are performed extraordinarily quickly onstage, much more quickly than conscious, well-founded ones.

'And it isn't surprising,' he explained, 'that when your actions are mechanical, when you have no real purpose in mind, you have nothing on which to focus. It really doesn't take long to move a few chairs around. But if you have to place them in a certain order, for a definite purpose, for example to seat the important and not so important guests at the dinner table, then you can move these same chairs around several times, for hours.'

But my imagination had dried up. I couldn't think anything up. I buried my head in an illustrated magazine and looked at the pictures.

Seeing that the others had gone quiet, too, Tortsov gathered us all together in the sitting room.

'Aren't you ashamed of yourselves?' he appealed to us. 'What kind of actors are you, if you can't get your imagination working? Bring me a dozen children and let me tell them that this is a new apartment, and you would be amazed by their imagination. They would think up a game that would never end. So be like children!'

'It's easy to say "be like children"!' sighed Pasha. 'It's their nature to play, they want to, but we have to force ourselves.'

'Well, of course, if you don't "want to" there's no point in talking about it,' Tortsov replied. 'But in that case, I have to ask whether you are really actors?'

'Look, please, I'm sorry! Open the curtain, give us an audience then we'll feel like it,' Grisha explained.

'No. If you are actors, you'll do things, you won't need them. Tell me honestly, what's stopping you from getting into the game?' Tortsov insisted.

I started to explain my situation. I could light a fire and move furniture but all these small actions were of interest to no one. They are too short. I lit the fire, I shut the door – bang! It's done. But if a second action were to stem from the first and lead to a third, that would be another matter.

'So,' Tortsov summed up, 'what you need are not small, external, semi-mechanical actions but broad, deep, complex ones with great potential.'

'No, that's too much, too difficult. That's not what we have in mind. Give us something simple but interesting,' I explained.

'That depends on you, not me,' Tortsov said. 'You can perform an action in an interesting or in a boring way, make it short or long. Is it really a matter of external goals, or of inner, motivating causes, circumstances under which and for the sake of which an action is performed? Take a simple thing like opening or shutting a door. What could be more senseless than such a mechanical task? But suppose that here, in this apartment, where Marya is giving a house-warming, a man once lived, who is now a raving lunatic. He has been taken to a mental institution . . .

What if it turned out he had escaped and was there, outside the door, what would you do?'

Once the question had been put in this way our attitude – or as Tortsov then put it, 'our inner aim' – suddenly changed. We stopped thinking about ways we could prolong the game, and worried not about what would result from it outwardly, in terms of show, but inwardly, and wondered whether this or that action was right in terms of the problem we had been set. Our eyes began to measure out the distance to the door and to look for safe ways to get to it. We examined our surroundings so as to adapt to them, we tried to see where we would run if the madman broke into the room. The instinct of self-preservation made us anticipate possible dangers and suggested ways of dealing with them.

You can judge our mood at that moment from the following quite minor incident. Vanya, either deliberately or quite spontaneously, leaped back from the door and we all did the same, as one, colliding with each other in the process. The women began to scream and ran into the next room. I found myself under the table with a heavy bronze ashtray in my hand. We didn't stop, even when the door was tight shut. As there was no key, we started barricading it with tables and chairs. Then we had to telephone the psychiatric hospital so that they could take every possible measure to recapture their violent patient.

I was in a state of high excitement and as soon as the acting exercise was over I turned to Tortsov and shouted:

'Make me light a damp fire. It'll bore me to death. If we can manage to bring that exercise to life I'll be the most enthusiastic proponent of the "system".'

Without a moment's hesitation Tortsov told us that today Marya was giving a house-warming to which she had invited her friends and acquaintances from the school. One of these, who knew the star actors, Moskvin, Kachalov and Leonidov,[2] very well, had promised to bring one of them along to the party. He wanted to make the students happy. The only problem was that the apartment was cold. The double windows hadn't been put in for the winter, there was no firewood left and now, as if for spite, there'd been a sudden frost so that every room was icy, and there was no way we could receive important guests. What were we to do? We got wood from a neighbour, lit a fire in the sitting room, but it began to smoke. We had to douse the fire and go to the janitor. While he was dawdling about, it became quite dark. Now we could light the fire, but the wood was damp and wouldn't ignite. And our guests would be here any minute.

'Now, tell me, what would you do if the story I have just invented were really true?'

It was a tightly woven web of circumstances. We had once again to summon up all our natural ingenuity to unravel it and get out of a difficult situation.

One of the most worrying circumstances was the expected arrival of Moskvin, Kachalov and Leonidov. The shame we would feel would be particularly acute. We were fully aware that if such an embarrassing situation were to occur in reality, we would be in for an uncomfortable time. We all did our best to help, tried to devise a plan of action, suggested it to our friends, and then tried to carry it out.

'This time,' Tortsov stated, 'I can say what you did was genuine, that is productive and apt.

'But what led you to that point? One tiny word: if.'

The students were in raptures.

It seemed as though an 'Open Sesame' had been revealed to us, that we could use it to gain access to the whole of art, and that if a role or an exercise wasn't working, all we had to do was pronounce the word 'if' and everything would go like clockwork.

'So,' said Tortsov, summing up, 'today's class has taught you that *stage action must be inwardly well-founded, in proper, logical sequence and possible in the real world.*'

.. .. 19..

Everyone is mad about the word 'if'. They talk about it whenever they can, they sing its praises. Today's class was practically one long eulogy to it.

Tortsov barely had time to get through the door and take his place before the students clustered round him to express their enthusiasm and excitement.

'A successful experiment enabled you to understand and experience for yourselves, how inner and outer actions arise out of nature and the human organism, of their own accord, through the use of "if".

'So let us take this living example and re-examine the function of every stimulus, every factor in our experiment.

'Let's start with "if".

'Its significance lies, above all, in the fact that it initiates every creative act,' Tortsov explained. 'For actors, "if" is the lever which lifts us out of the world of reality into the only world where we can be creative.

'There are "ifs" which merely spur us on towards longer term, step-by-step, logical developments. For example.'

Tortsov held out his hand to Pasha and waited for something to happen. The men looked at one other blankly.

'As you can see,' said Tortsov, 'nothing happened between us. So, I will introduce "if" and say: if I had offered you not my empty hand but a letter, what would you have done?'

'I would have taken it and looked to see who it was addressed to. If it had been addressed to me, then I would have asked you to excuse me, opened the letter and started reading it. But since it's private, and since I might show my feelings while reading it . . .'

'And *since* it would be more sensible to go somewhere else to avoid that,' Tortsov prompted.

'. . . then I would go into another room and read it there.'

'You see how many conscious thoughts in proper sequence, how many logical steps – if, *then, since* – how many different actions this little word "if" can call up. That is generally the case.

'But there are times when "if" does its work alone, quickly, without the need of outside assistance. For example . . .'

With one hand Tortsov gave Marya a metal ashtray and with the other passed Sonya a glove of chamois leather, saying:

'A cold little frog for you and a soft little mouse for you.'

The words were scarcely out of his mouth before the two women recoiled in disgust.

'Darya, drink some water,' Tortsov ordered.

She raised the glass to her lips.

'It's poisoned,' he warned her.

Darya froze instinctively.

'You see!' said Tortsov triumphantly. 'These were not simple but "magic ifs", provoking instantaneous, instinctive actions. You achieved the same results, albeit not so sharp-edged and effective, as in the acting exercise about the madman. In that instance the assumption that something abnormal was going on immediately produced a strong state of real agitation and dynamic action. An "if" of that kind can also be considered "magic".

'In any further examination of the qualities and attributes of "if" we should turn our attention to the fact that there exist, so to speak, *single-storey* and *multi-storey* "ifs". For example, just now in the experiment with the ashtray and the glove, we dealt with a single-storey "if". All we had to say was, what if the ashtray were a frog and the glove a mouse, and the immediate response was an action.

'But in complex plays, there are a huge number of possible "ifs", created by the author and others, so as to justify this or that line of behaviour in the leading characters. There, we are dealing not with single-storey but with multi-storey "ifs", that is, with a considerable number of hypotheses and the ideas complement them, all of which are cleverly intertwined.

There, the author says: if the action takes place in such and such a period, in such and such a country, in such and such a place or house, if such and such people live there, with such and such a cast of mind, with such and such ideas and feelings, if they come into conflict in such and such circumstances, and so on.

'The director complements the author's ideas with his own "ifs" and says: if there were such and such relationships among the characters, if their particular habits were such and such, if they lived in such a setting and so on, how would the actor react if he were placed in these circumstances?

'In their turn, the designer, the lighting man and other members of the production team will add their own artistic ideas to the play.

'You should also appreciate a certain hidden quality in the word "if" – a certain power you experienced during the exercise with the madman. This quality, this power caused an instantaneous shift, a step forward.'

'Yes, that's it, a shift, a step forward!' I agreed, feeling that this was the right definition for my own experience.

'Thanks to which,' Tortsov continued, 'as in *The Bluebird*, when the magic diamond[3] is rotated, something happens which makes the eye see differently, the ear hear differently, the mind to understand the things around it differently. What we have here is a device, a creative idea which, through the operation of nature itself, produces an action that is apt, a real action, one which is essential if we are to achieve the goal we have set ourselves.'

'And it seems to happen unawares!' I said enthusiastically. 'After all, why should the property fireplace matter to me? But once it became subject to "if", once I had accepted the idea that famous actors were coming and that the impossible fireplace would make us all look stupid, it became a thing of great importance to me. I really hated that piece of cardboard scenery, I cursed the cold snap and I simply didn't have time to do all the things my imagination suggested once it had been prompted.'

'The same thing happened in the acting exercise with the madman,' said Pasha. 'There again, the door, which was the starting-point for the exercise, turned into a means of defence. The basic goal, the focus of our attention was the instinct of self-preservation. This all happened naturally, spontaneously . . .'

'And why did it?' Tortsov broke in passionately. 'Because the prospect of danger always excites us. Like yeast, it always produces ferment. As far as the door and the fireplace are concerned, they only affect us in so far as they are linked to other, much more crucial matters.

'The secret of "if", as a stimulus, lies in the fact that it doesn't speak about actual facts, of what is, but of what might be . . . "if" . . . This word is not a statement, it's a question to be answered. The actor must try to answer it.

'That is why the step forward and the solution occurred without forcing or deception on my part. The fact is I didn't actually tell you for certain there was a madman outside the door. I didn't lie. On the contrary, the very use of the word "if" was an overt recognition that I was merely introducing a hypothesis and that, in reality, there was no one outside the door. I just wanted you to tell me, honestly, what you would do if the story about the madman proved to be true. I didn't ask you to have delusions. I didn't foist my own feelings on you, but gave you absolute freedom to experience whatever each of you would naturally "experience" on your own. And you, for your part, didn't force yourselves to accept my story about the madman as actual or real, but took it as a hypothesis. I didn't force you to believe in the truth of this fictitious madman, you yourselves freely accepted the possibility that such a thing might exist in real life.'

'Yes, and the good thing is that "if" is truthful and above-board, it does things openly. That removes the feeling of having been cheated we often feel in performances,' I said enthusiastically.

'But what would have happened if, instead of an obvious story, I had sworn that there was a genuine, "bona fide" madman outside the door?'

'I wouldn't have believed such a blatant lie, I wouldn't have budged,' I said. 'And it's good, too, that "if" creates a mood which precludes any forcing. Only in such circumstances can you seriously consider something which doesn't exist but could occur in the real world,' I continued, getting quite carried away.

'That is another characteristic of "if",' Tortsov reminded me. 'It arouses an artist's dynamism, which is mental rather than physical, but does so without forcing, through nature itself. The word "if" is a spur, a stimulus to inner and outer creative dynamism. All you have to do is say "What would I do, how would I handle it if the story of the madman turned out to be actually true?" and immediately you are dynamic and alive. You didn't just give a simple answer to a question which had been put to you. Your nature, as an actor, became an urgent call to action. The pressure was such that you didn't hesitate but started to deal with the issue facing you. The real, human instinct of self-preservation governed your actions just as though they had occurred in life itself . . .

'This is by far the most important attribute of the word "if", which links it to one of the fundamentals of our school of acting, which is that *creative work and art are dynamic and active.*'

'But it would seem that "if" doesn't always operate freely,' I objected. 'For example, although my step forward seemed sudden, in fact it took a long time. The moment the wonderful "if" was introduced I believed it right away and the step forward happened. But a moment later I began to have doubts, I said to myself, "What is it you're after? You know all these 'ifs' are made up, games, not real life." But then another voice disagreed, "I don't dispute that, the 'ifs' are made up, games, but absolutely possible, feasible in the real world. No one's forcing you. All you have to do is ask, "What would I have done if I had been at Marya's that evening and found myself in the same circumstances as her guests?"

'Having experienced the fiction as fact, I was able to take it seriously and think what I would do about the fireplace and how I would handle the visiting celebrities.'

.. .. 19..

'So the "magic" or simple "if" triggers off creative work. It provides the first impetus for the further development of the creative process in a role.

'As to the way in which this process develops let Pushkin speak in my place!

'In his article "On National-Popular Drama and on the play 'Martha the Seneschal's Wife' " Pushkin says:

' "Truth of the passions, feelings that seem true in the supposed circumstances, that is what our intellect requires of a dramatist."[4]

'For my part I will add that this is precisely what our intellect requires of an actor, with this difference, that the circumstances which for the dramatist are supposed for us actors are imposed, they are a given. And so we have created the term Given Circumstances and that is what we use.'

'Given Circumstances . . . in the. . . .', said a worried Vanya.

'Think hard about this remarkable dictum and afterwards I will give you an example of how our beloved "if" can help us fulfil Pushkin's magisterial injunction.'

'Truth of the passions, feelings that seem true in the hypothetical circumstances, that is what our intellect requires of a dramatist,' I recited in all manner of tones, as I read the dictum I had written down.

'It's useless for you to keep on repeating this masterly phrase,' said Tortsov stopping me, 'that won't reveal its inner meaning. When you can't grasp an idea all at once, break it down into its logical parts.'

'What we need to understand most of all is what we mean by the words Given Circumstances, don't we?' asked Pasha.

'They mean the plot, the facts, the incidents, the period, the time and place of the action, the way of life, how we as actors and directors understand the play, the contributions we ourselves make, the mise-en-scène, the sets and costumes, the props, the stage dressing, the sound effects etc., etc., everything which is a given for the actors as they rehearse. The Given Circumstances, just like "if", are suppositions, "products of the imagination". They have a single origin: the Given Circumstances. They are the same as "if" and "if" is the same as the Given Circumstances. One is a hypothesis ("if"), the other is a corollary to it (the Given Circumstances). "If" always launches the creative act and the Given Circumstances develop it further. One can't exist without the other, or acquire the strength they need. But their functions are somewhat different. "If" is a spur to a dormant imagination, and the Given Circumstances provide the substance for it. Together and separately they help bring about the step forward.'

'But what's "truth of the passions"?' asked Vanya.

'The truth of the passions is the truth of the passions, i.e., genuine, living, human passions, feelings, the actor's own personal experiences.'

'And what are "feelings that seem true"?' Vanya persisted.

'Not genuine passions, feelings or experiences, but a hint of them, a mood closely related to them, seeming like truth and therefore true-seeing. This is a way of conveying the passions, not directly, spontaneously, subconsciously but, so to speak, prompted by our feelings.

'As far as Pushkin's dictum as a whole is concerned, it will be easier for you to understand it, if you turn the words in the phrase around and say:

'Given Circumstances, truth of the passions. In other words: first establish the Given Circumstances, genuinely believe in them, and then "truth of the passions" will arise of its own accord.'

'In the Gi-ven Cir-cum-stan-ces,' said Vanya trying desperately to understand. Tortsov came to his rescue.

'In practical terms you are faced roughly with the following sequence of events. First, you must have a clear, personal view of all the Given Circumstances which you have brought together from the play itself, the direction, and your own creative imagination. This gives you an overall picture of the character and his circumstances ... You must sincerely believe that such a life is possible in the real world. You must become so used to it that it becomes an intimate part of you. If you can do that, then the truth of the passions or feelings that seem true will arise of their own accord.'

'I'd like a rather more concrete, practical technique,' I said.

'Take your beloved "if" and bring it face to face with all of the Given Circumstances you have brought together. Say to yourself: if there were a madman trying to break in, if the students were at Marya's house-warming, if the door were broken and couldn't be locked, if we had to barricade it, etc., what would I do, and how would I do it?

'This question immediately arouses your dynamism. Respond to it through action, say: "That's what I would do!" And do the thing you want, whatever you are drawn to do, without thinking about it.

'Then you will feel inwardly – either subconsciously or consciously – what Pushkin calls "the truth of the passions" or, at least, feelings that seem true. The secret of this process is, don't force your feelings, leave them alone, don't think about "the truth of the passions" because these "passions" don't depend on us, but emerge of their own accord. They will not be coerced.

'The actors should concentrate on the Given Circumstances. Start living them and then "the truth of the passions" will arise of itself.'

When Tortsov explained that all the possible Given Circumstances and 'ifs', provided by the author, the actor, the director, the lighting designer and the other members of the production team, create a theatrical atmosphere, similar to life as we live it, Grisha got indignant and 'stood up' for the actor.

'Look here, please, I'm sorry,' he protested, 'what is left for an actor if everything is done by other people? A few trifles?'

'What do you mean, trifles?' Tortsov turned on him. 'To believe in another person's thoughts and genuinely live them – you call that a trifle? Don't you know that creating on someone else's idea is infinitely more difficult than making up a story of your own? We know of cases where a bad play has achieved world renown thanks to its being reworked by a great actor. We know that Shakespeare reworked other people's stories. And we rework dramatists' creations. We discover what is hidden beneath their words. We invest someone else's text with our own subtext. We establish our relationship to people and the circumstances of their lives. We filter all the material the author and the director have given us through our own personalities. We reshape it, give it life, fill it with our own imagination. We become bound to it, we live in it psychologically and physically. We produce "the truth of the passions" in ourselves. The end result is genuinely productive action, closely connected with the ideas at the heart of the play. We create living, typical images through the passions and feelings of the characters we portray. This is a mammoth task – "trifles" indeed! No, this is creative work on a vast scale, genuine art!' said Tortsov in conclusion.

.. .. 19..

When he arrived, Tortsov told us the plan for today's class:

'After "if" and the Given Circumstances, today we will talk about inner and outer action.

'Have you any idea how important this is in acting, which by its very nature is based on dynamism?

'This reveals itself in actions, and actions convey the essence of a part, the actor's own experiencing, and the inner world of the play itself. We judge the people being portrayed, we understand who they are, through their deeds and actions.

'This is what action gives us and what the audience expects to get from it.

'But what do they get from us in the vast majority of cases? Mostly a great deal of fussiness, a plethora of uncontrolled gestures, nervous, mechanical movements. We are much more lavish with them in the theatre than we are in real life.

'But all these histrionics are quite different from human actions in real life. Let me demonstrate the difference. When someone needs to delve deep into his innermost, secret thoughts and experiences (as in "To be or not to be" in Hamlet), he turns in upon himself and tries to express what he is thinking and feeling in words.

'Onstage actors behave quite differently. At moments of intimacy, they come right downstage, look at the audience, and declaim their non-existent experiences in a loud, flashy emotional way.'

'What does that mean, excuse me, "declaim their non-existent experiences"?'

'That means doing what you do, when you want to fill your inner emptiness with an external display of ham acting.

'It's more advantageous to present a role you don't inwardly feel to an audience "effectively", to rounds of applause. But a serious actor hardly wants a lot of theatrical hubbub in passages that convey his most cherished thoughts, feelings and the innermost secrets of his being. For deep inside those passages are the actor's own personal feelings, parallel to the role. He wants to convey them not to the sound of vulgar bursts of applause, but, quite the opposite, to heartfelt silence, in great intimacy. If the actor sacrifices these things, and has no compunction about debasing this solemn moment, then he demonstrates that for him the words he is articulating are empty, that he has not invested them with anything precious or private. You cannot have an uplifting relationship with empty words. You need them only as sounds through which you can show off your voice, your diction, your vocal technique, your actorish, animal energy. As to the thoughts and feelings the play was written to express, they can only be communicated "in general", sadness "in general", joy "in general", tragedy, despair, etc. This is dead, mere outward form, stock-in-trade.

'The same thing occurs with outer as with inner action (in speech). When the actor, as a human being, has no need to do what he is doing, when the role and his acting are not directed towards the purpose they should be serving, then those actions are empty, not experienced, they communicate nothing essential. Then nothing remains but to do things "in general". When the actor suffers for suffering's sake, when he loves for loving's sake, when he is jealous or asks forgiveness for its own sake, when all these things are done because they are written, and not because they are experienced in the heart and life of the role, then the actor has nowhere to go, and then "playing in general" is the only way out for him.

'How terrible the expression "in general" is!

'How much slovenliness, muddle, frivolity, chaos it implies.

'Would you care to eat something "in general"? Would you care to speak, read "in general"? Would you care to have a good time "in general"?

'What gales of boredom and emptiness blow through statements like that!

'When the expression "in general" is used to judge an actor's performance, for example: "Such and such an actor played Hamlet pretty well in general" – such a judgement is an insult to the performer.

'Play love, jealousy, hate "in general" for me!

'What does this mean? Playing a mish-mash of these passions and their constituent parts? And it's just this mish-mash of passions, feelings, thoughts, logical action, images which actors serve up to us onstage "in general".

'Most amusing of all, they are genuinely moved and feel their playing "in general" very strongly. You won't convince them that they have neither passion, nor personal experience, nor thought, but just a mish-mash inside. These actors sweat, are moved, carried away by their own performance, and yet have no idea what it is that moves and excites them. This is the "actor's emotion", the hysteria I spoke of earlier. This is being moved "in general".

'Real acting and playing "in general" are incompatible. One destroys the other. Art loves order and harmony, but "in general" means disorder and chaos.

'How am I to protect you from our sworn enemy "in general"?!

'You fight it by introducing a foreign body into this messy playing, which will destroy it.

' "In general" is superficial and trivial. And so introduce a greater element of planning into your acting and a more serious attitude to what you are doing. That will destroy the superficiality and the frivolousness.

' "In general" is chaotic and senseless. Introduce logic and sequence into a role, and that will oust the bad habit of playing "in general".

' "In general" starts everything and finishes nothing. Make sure your work is complete.

'That is what we shall be doing throughout our study of the "system", so that we don't end up with acting "in general", but will develop once and for all genuine, productive, purposeful, human action in our work.

'It is that alone which I acknowledge as art, that alone which I support and develop.

'Why am I so scathing about "in general"? Here's why.

'How many performances are there, daily, across the world, which are acted according to their inner truth as real art requires? About ten.

'How many performances are there, daily, across the world which are acted not with regard to the inner truth but "in general"? Tens of thousands. And so, don't be surprised if I tell you that throughout the entire world, daily, hundreds of thousands of actors wreak havoc on themselves by systematically developing wrong, harmful, theatrical habits. It is all the more appalling because, on the one hand, the theatre itself and its demands drive the actor towards these dangerous habits. On the other hand, actors themselves, looking for the line of least resistance, wrongly make use of the stock-in-trade "in general".

'So, one way or another, ignoramuses gradually, systematically drag the art of the actor towards its ruin, i.e. towards the destruction of the creative act, for the sake of a shoddy, conventional external playing "in general".

'So you see we have got to fight the whole world, the conditions in which we appear in public, routine methods of rehearsing, and especially the received wisdom about acting, which is erroneous.

'Given all the obstacles that are put in our way, if we wish to achieve success we must have the courage to acknowledge that, for many reasons when we make an entrance, before a packed house, when we must be creative art in public, we lose our sense of real life completely. We forget everything, how we walk, how we sit, eat, drink, sleep, talk, look, listen – in a word, how we act internally and externally. We have to learn all this anew, on the stage itself, precisely in the same way a child learns to talk, look and listen.

'I will often have occasion to remind you of this unexpected and important conclusion in the course of our studies. For the moment, we are trying to understand how we can learn to do things onstage, not in a histrionic way – "in general" – but in a human way – simply, with the truth of a living organism, freely, not in the way the conventions of the theatre demand, but as the laws of a living, natural organism demand.'

'In short, you mean, learn to banish the theatre from the theatre,' Grisha said.

'Absolutely. How to banish the Theatre (capital T) from the theatre (small t). You can't cope with such a task all at once, but you can gradually, as part of the process of growing artistically and of developing your psychotechnique.

'Now, Vanya,' said Tortsov turning to Rakhmanov, 'I'm going to ask you to see that, when onstage, the students are always genuine, productive, apt in what they do never merely give the appearance of doing. So the moment you notice them veering into playacting or – even worse – into hamming, stop them at once. Once your classes are under way (and I'm anxious for that to happen) develop special exercises which will oblige them always to perform actions onstage. Do these exercises more often, longer, from one day to the next, so that you train them gradually, methodically in genuine, productive, purposeful action onstage.

'The human capacity for action must become inseparable in their minds from the mood they feel onstage in front of an audience. They should experience the same mood in public as they do in class, without an audience. As you train them day by day to be active in a human way onstage, instil the proper habit of being normal people and not stuffed dummies.'

'What kind of exercises? What kind do you mean?'

'Set up the classes in a serious, rigorous manner, so as to keep the players on their toes, as in a performance. You can do that.'

'Of course!' Rakhmanov concurred.

'Call them up onstage one by one and give them something to do.'

'What?'

'Well, for example, looking through a newspaper and saying what's in it.'

'That takes too long for such a large class. You would have to look at everything.'

'Does that really mean you have to know the contents of the entire newspaper? The important thing is to achieve genuine, productive, purposeful action. When you see that a situation has been created in which the student is actually involved in what he is doing, and he is not put off by the fact that the class is public, then call on another student and let the first one go off somewhere upstage. While there, he can continue his exercise and ram home the habit of living, human action onstage. To develop that habit and root it once and for all in oneself, you need to spend "x" amount of time onstage in genuine, productive, apt action. You must help them acquire this "x" amount of time.'

As the class was ending Tortsov explained to us:

' "If", the Given Circumstances, inner and outer action – are important factors in our work. But they are not the only ones. We need very many special skills, qualities and gifts (imagination, concentration, a sense of truth, tasks, dramatic potential etc., etc.).

'Let us confine ourselves, for the sake of brevity and convenience to calling them by one name, Elements.'

'Elements of what?' someone asked.

'I'm not going to answer that question for the moment. It will become clear in its own good time. The art of controlling these Elements, the ability to combine them, to bring them together and unite them, requires considerable practice and experience and, consequently, time and in the first rank among them stand "if", the Given Circumstances, inner and outer action. We shall be patient and, for the moment, devote all our efforts to studying and developing each of these Elements. This will be the primary, the principal goal of our studies this year.'

4

IMAGINATION

Today, as Tortsov was ill, the class was held in his apartment. He settled us comfortably in his study.

'You now know', he said, 'that our work begins by introducing the magic "if" into the play and role, and this lifts the actor out of everyday life into the world of the *imagination*. The play, the role, are stories, a series of magic and other "ifs", Given Circumstances which the author has made up. Genuine "facts", the normal world, do not exist onstage. The normal world is not art. This by its very nature, needs inventiveness. And that, in the first instance, is manifest in the work the author has produced. The actor's task is to use his creative skills to transform the story of the play into *theatrical fact*. Our imagination has an enormous role to play here. So we ought to spend a little longer on it and become familiar with its creative function.'

Tortsov pointed to the walls which were covered with all manner of set designs.

'These are all pictures by my favourite young designer, now dead. He was very eccentric. He would make sketches for plays that had not yet been written. Here, for instance, is a sketch for the last act of a unwritten play by Chekhov, which he conceived not long before his death. An expedition is ice-bound in the terrifying, bleak arctic. A large steamship is hemmed in by floating blocks of ice. The soot-black funnels stand out in sinister fashion against the white background. Hard frost. An icy wind stirs up gusts of snow. As they whirl upwards they take the form of women in shrouds. And here we see the figures of a husband and his wife's lover, clutching each other. Both have fled from life and gone on this expedition so they could forget their heart-rending drama.

'Who could believe that this sketch was made by someone who had never been outside Moscow? He created an arctic landscape using his observations of nature during winter here, what he knew from stories, from descriptions in literature and in scientific books, and from photographs. The picture was created out of all the material he had collected. The dominant role in this work fell to his imagination.'

Tortsov then took us over to another wall on which a series of landscapes was hanging. In fact they were repetitions of the same theme: some kind of holiday resort, modified each time by the artist's imagination. The same row of beautiful houses in a pine forest at different times of the year and the day – in the blazing sun, during storms. Further along, there was the same landscape but with the forest chopped down, replaced by artificial ponds, with newly planted trees of different kinds. The artist amused himself by playing with nature and with people's lives. In his sketches he built houses and towns, knocked them down, and replanned whole districts and razed mountains.

'Look, how beautiful! The Kremlin on the seashore!' someone exclaimed.

'The artist's imagination created all this, too.'

'And here we have sketches for a non-existent play about interplanetary life,' said Tortsov, leading us to another series of drawings and water-colours. 'Here we see a station for machines of some kind which maintain interplanetary communications. See, there's a huge metal box with large balconies and figures of beautiful alien beings. It's the terminus. It hangs in space. Humans can be seen at its windows, passengers from Earth. A string of similar termini going up and down, can be seen extending into infinite space. They are held in a state of equilibrium by the countervailing attraction of huge magnets. On the horizon are several suns and moons. Their light creates fantastic effects, not visible from earth. To be able to paint such a picture you need to have not just imagination, but also a good sense of fantasy.'

'What's the difference between them?' someone asked.

'Imagination creates what is, what exists, what we know, but fantasy creates what isn't, what we don't know, what never was and never will be. But perhaps it could be. Who can tell? When popular fantasy created the magic carpet in fairy-tales, who would have thought that people would soar through the air someday in airplanes? Fantasy knows everything and can do anything. Fantasy, like imagination, is essential to a painter.'

'And the actor?' asked Pasha.

'Why do you think that an actor would need imagination?' countered Tortsov.

'How do you mean, why? To create the magic "if", the Given Circumstances,' replied Pasha.

'But the author has created them already without any help from us. His play is fiction.'

Pasha fell silent.

'Does the dramatist provide everything the actor needs to know?' asked Tortsov. 'Can you reveal the lives of all the characters in full in a hundred pages or so? Or is there a great deal left unsaid? For example, does the author always tell us in enough detail what happened before the play begins? Do we get an exhaustive account of what will happen after it is over, or what goes on in the wings from which the characters come and go? The dramatist is sparing with that kind of commentary. In the script you get *Enter Petrov* or *Petrov exits*. But we cannot enter from a mysterious void and exit into it without considering the purpose of such movements. Such actions have no credibility. We know the other kind of stage directions the dramatist provides: *stands, walks about animatedly, smiles, dies*. We are given cryptic descriptions of character, such as: *a young man of pleasing appearance. Smokes a lot.*

'But is that sufficient to create fully what a character looks like, his mannerisms, his walk, his personal habits? And what about the dialogue? Are we supposed to learn it by heart and speak it parrot-fashion?

'And what about all the author's stage directions, the director's demands, the moves, the mises-en-scène and the whole production? Is it really enough to remember them and carry them out as a formal pattern?

'Can that really portray the character, determine all the nuances of his thoughts, feelings, aspirations, and actions?

'No, all this has to be filled out and given depth by the actor. Only then can everything given us by the author and the rest of the production team stir the innermost recesses of the heart, in actors and audience alike, to life. Only then can the actor begin to live the inner life of the character, behave in the way the author, the director, and his own living feelings prescribe.

'Our most immediate source of help here is our imagination, with its magic "if" and Given Circumstances. It not only tells us what the author, the director, and the others have not, but it gives life to everything that has been done by the production team, whose creative work reaches the audience primarily through the actors' success.

'Now, do you understand how important it is for actors to possess a vivid, clear imagination. We need it at every moment of our artistic life, be it while studying or performing.

'The imagination takes the initiative in the creative process, drawing the actor along behind it.'

The class was interrupted by an unexpected visit by a well-known tragedian U . . . who is on tour in Moscow at the moment. The celebrity talked about his successes and Tortsov translated his account into Russian.

When Tortsov had seen our fascinating guest to the door and returned, he said, laughing:

'Of course, he was exaggerating, but, as you can see, he's a fascinating man who sincerely believes the things he concocts. We actors are so used to embellishing facts with details from our own imagination that we carry these habits over from the stage to real life. There, of course, they are superfluous but in the theatre they are essential.

'Do you think it's easy to concoct stories in such a way that people will listen to you with bated breath? That's creative work, too, stemming from the magic "if", the Given Circumstances, and a well-developed imagination.

'When it comes to men of genius one can't say they are lying. They look at the real world, not as we do, but with different eyes. They don't see life as we mortals do. Can you condemn them because imagination gives them sometimes grey-, sometimes blue-, sometimes green-, sometimes dark-, sometimes rose-coloured glasses to see through? And would it be of any benefit artistically, if these people were to take off their glasses, and learn to see reality and works of art with nothing to screen their eyes, seeing quite soberly only what the daily round provides?

'I confess that there are occasions when I too tell lies, if, as an actor or director, I have to work on a role or a play which I don't find particularly engaging. Then, I dry up, my creative faculties are paralysed. A prod is needed. So I start assuring everybody that I am keen on the new play, I praise it. To do that, I have to think about what's missing. And the need to do that spurs the imagination on. I wouldn't do such a thing in private, but when other people are there you begin to justify your lie, willy-nilly, and get things going. Then, very often, you take the material you have invented and introduce it into the play.'

'If the imagination plays such an important role for actors, what can people do if they haven't any?' Pasha asked shyly.

'Develop it, or give up the stage. Otherwise you will fall victim to directors who will replace your imperfect imagination with their own. Then you will stop being an independent artist and become a mere pawn. Wouldn't it be better to try and develop your own imagination?'

'But that must be very difficult,' I sighed.

'That depends on what kind of imagination you have in mind! There is the kind of imagination which takes the initiative, which works on its own. It develops on its own, without special effort. It works constantly, tirelessly, waking or sleeping. There is also the kind of imagination which lacks initiative but which readily accepts anything suggested to it and then develops it independently. That kind of imagination is comparatively easy to develop. However, if the imagination just accepts what has been suggested to it, and doesn't develop it, then there are problems. There are people who neither create on their own nor accept what is given them. If they can only latch onto the externals of what has been demonstrated to them, they have no imagination and without imagination you cannot be an actor.'

'Take the initiative or not?'

'To accept and develop, or not to accept?'

These questions give me no peace. After evening tea, when quiet fell, I locked myself away in my room, settled comfortably on the sofa, surrounded myself with cushions, closed my eyes and, although I was tired, began to let my imagination wander. But from the very first moment my attention was distracted by circles of light, multi-coloured dots which filled the darkness before my eyelids.

I put out the lamp, supposing that was the reason.

'What shall I imagine?' I wondered. But my imagination did not fail me. It drew a picture of treetops in a pine forest, swaying rhythmically in a gentle breeze.

That was pleasant.

There seemed to be a scent of fresh air.

From somewhere . . . in the silence . . . came the sound of a clock ticking.

....

I had drifted off.

'Of course,' I concluded, rousing myself. 'You can't just let the imagination wander without taking the initiative. I'll fly in an airplane. Above the treetops. Here I am flying over them, over the fields, the rivers, towns, villages . . . over . . . the treetops . . . They are slowly, slowly swaying . . . There's the scent of fresh air . . . of pines . . . A clock ticking . . .

....

'Who's that snoring? Not me, surely? Did I fall asleep? . . . For how long?'

They're sweeping the floor in the dining room . . . shifting furniture about . . . The morning light is piercing through the curtains. The clock strikes eight . . . in . . . i . . . tia . . . tive . . .

I was so disconcerted by my failures at home that I couldn't contain myself and told Tortsov everything at today's class, which took place in 'Marya's apartment'.

'Your experiment failed because you committed a series of errors,' he told me in response. 'First you forced your imagination, instead of coaxing it. Second you let your imagination wander at random, wherever and however chance drove you. Just as you should not do something for the sake of doing something (act for the sake of the action itself), so you must not let your imagination wander for the sake of letting it wander. There was no sense, no purpose in the work your imagination was doing, and that is essential during the creative work. Third, your ideas weren't active, weren't dynamic. The dynamic quality of the imagination has a very special significance for actors. Their imagination must incite first inner then outer action.'

'But I was performing actions, because mentally I was flying over the woods at a furious pace.'

'And when you are stretched out in an express train, travelling along at a furious pace, are you also performing actions?' asked Tortsov. 'The locomotive, the driver, they are working, but the passenger is passive. If, while the train is in motion, you are engaged in a business discussion, arguing, or drafting a report, then that would be another thing, and we could talk about work or action. The same applies to your flight in an airplane. The pilot was working, but you weren't engaged in any activity. If you had been navigating or if you had been taking photographs of various areas below, we could talk about activity. We need an active not a passive imagination.'

'How do you make yourself active?' Pasha enquired.

'Let me tell you about my six-year-old niece's favourite game. It is called "and what if?" and is played this way. The little girl asks me, "What are you doing?" "I'm drinking tea," I answer. "But if it weren't tea but castor oil, how would you drink it?" I have to remember what the medicine tastes like. And when I do and make a face, the child floods the whole room with laughter. Then comes another question: "Where are you sitting?" "On a chair," I answer. "But if it were a hotplate, what would you do?" Mentally I have to sit on a hotplate and make incredible efforts not to get burned. When I get it right, the little girl starts to feel sorry for me. She waves her hands and shouts, "I don't want to play any more!" And should you continue with the game, it all ends in tears. So, think up a game like this for yourselves, one that might provoke dynamic actions.'

'That seems a primitive, crude approach to me,' I remarked. 'I'd like to find something more subtle.'

'Don't rush things! You've got time! For the moment, be content with simple, elementary daydreaming. Don't try to fly too high. Live with the rest of us here on earth, among the things around you in the real world. Make this furniture, the objects which you can feel and see part of your work. Take, for example, the improvisation with the madman. There our own ideas were incorporated into the real life around us. The room in which we found ourselves, the furniture with which we barricaded the door – in a word the world of objects – underwent no change. We only introduced the idea of an imaginary madman. In other respects the scene depended on something real not something left hanging in the air.

'Let's try and perform a similar experiment. We are now in a classroom, working. That is real. Let it, its furnishings, the class, all the students and their teachers look and be the same as they are now. With the help of "if" I will transport myself into an imaginary life and, to do that, I will change only the time of day and say to myself, "Now it isn't three in the afternoon, but three in the morning." Use your imagination to justify the fact that the class has dragged on so long. It's not difficult. Let's say that tomorrow you have an examination, and there's a great deal still to do, so we've stayed behind in the theatre. We now have new circumstances and new concerns. Your families at home are getting anxious. You've not been able to tell them you are still working because there is no telephone. One of you has missed a party he had been invited to. Another of you lives very far away, and doesn't know how he is to get home when the trolley-car isn't running, etc. This new idea produces many other thoughts, feelings and moods, all of which influence the general atmosphere which gives a tone to everything that follows. This is one of the preliminary stages in the process of experiencing. So, with the aid of our new ideas we prepared the ground, the Given Circumstances for a scene which we could develop and call "Night Class".

'Let's try and do one more experiment. Let's incorporate another new "if" into our real world – that is this room and the class now in progress. Let the time of day remain the same – three o'clock in the afternoon – but let's change the time of year. Instead of winter and minus fifteen degrees Celsius outside, let it be spring when we have wonderful warm weather. You see, your mood has already changed. You are already smiling at the prospect of a walk through the town after class. Decide what you will do, find something to justify it, and the result will be a new exercise that will develop your imagination.

'I will give you one more "if". The time of day, year, this room, our school, the class stay as they are, but we have all been transported from Moscow to the Crimea, that is, we have changed the place of the action that lies beyond the confines of this room. Instead of the street outside, there's the sea in which you will swim after class. Ask yourselves how you came to be in the south. Justify this given circumstance with any idea you like. Perhaps we are on tour in the Crimea, but have not interrupted our regular school work while here? Justify various moments of this imaginary life, respecting the "if" we have introduced, and you will get a new given of reasons for exercising your imagination.

'I will introduce yet another "if" and transport us to the arctic at that time of year when it stays light twenty-four hours a day. How are we to justify this change of place? Perhaps we've gone there to shoot a film. We need to be true to life and simple, for anything wrong ruins the shot. Not all of us are able to get through without playacting and I, as the director, am obliged to take charge of your studies. Having accepted all these new ideas with the help of "if", and believing in them, now ask yourself, "What would I do first in the given conditions?" By resolving this question you will automatically get your imagination working.

'And now, in a new exercise, we will invent all the Given Circumstances. We will retain only this room, nothing else of the world around us, but we will greatly transform it in our minds. Let's suppose that we are all members of a scientific expedition and have set out on a long journey by air. As we are flying over an unexplored region, disaster strikes. The engine cuts out and we have to land in a mountain valley. The engine has to be repaired. This holds up the expedition for a long time. The good thing is that we have supplies. However, they are not particularly plentiful. We have to get food by hunting. Besides that we have to build some kind of shelter, organize the cooking, keep a look out for a sudden attack by natives or wild animals. So, in our minds, we have put together a life full of fears and dangers. Every moment of that life demands essential, purposeful actions which are planned in logical sequence in our imagination. We must believe they are essential. Otherwise the story loses meaning and attraction for us.

'However, actors' work doesn't consist only in using their imagination, but also in the physical expression of what they have imagined. Transform the imaginary into reality, and play an episode in the life of the members of this expedition for me.'

'Where? Here? In "Marya's apartment"?' we asked in amazement.

'Where else? Don't go and order a special set for us! Because in this instance we have our own designer, who will fulfil all our demands in one second for free. It is no problem for him to transform the sitting room, the corridor, the hall into whatever we think fit. This designer is our imagination. Tell it what you want. Decide what you would first do after the airplane landed, if this apartment were a mountain valley and this table a large stone, the lamp with its shade a tropical plant, the crystal chandelier a branch laden with tropical fruit, the fireplace an abandoned forge.'

'What will the corridor be?' asked Pasha with interest.

'A ravine.'

'Right!' said the ebullient young man with delight. 'And the dining room?'

'A cavern in which, it would appear, some sort of primitive people once lived.'

'And the entrance hall?'

'That is an open space with a broad horizon and a wonderful view. Look, the bright walls of this room create the illusion of outdoors. And so you can take off in your airplane from this flat space.'

'And the auditorium?' Pasha persisted.

'A bottomless abyss. You need expect no danger from there, from natives or wild beasts, any more than from the terrace and the sea. So you must set watch by the door to the corridor, which represents the ravine.'

'And what does the sitting room itself represent?'

'You have to use that for repairing the airplane.'

'And where's the airplane?'

'Here it is,' said Tortsov, pointing to the sofa. 'The seat is the passenger compartment. The window curtains are the wings. Open them as wide as possible. The table is the engine. First of all you have to examine the motor. The damage to it is significant. At the same time other members of the expedition can settle themselves for the night. Here's a blanket.'

'Where?'

'The tablecloth.'

'Here are some tins and a barrel of wine.' Tortsov pointed to some large books in the bookcase and to a big vase. 'Examine the room more closely, and you will discover objects that are essential for your new life.'

Work was soon in full swing, and we began to live the bleak life of an expedition stranded in the mountains in the cosy sitting room. We found our bearings and adapted to them.

I can't say I believed in the transformation. No, I simply didn't notice what I didn't need to see. We had no time to notice. We were too busy. The artificiality of the story was concealed by the truth of our feelings, our physical actions and our belief in them.

After we had played the improvisation we had been given successfully enough, Tortsov said:

'In this improvisation the world of the imagination became part of the real world even more strongly. The story of a disaster in a mountain spot was squeezed into the sitting room. This is just one of innumerable examples of how, with the help of the imagination, we are able, inwardly, to give a new life to the world of inanimate objects. You must not reject it. On the contrary you must assimilate it into the life your imagination has created.

'This happens continuously in our rehearsals. With a few cane chairs we can create anything the author's and the director's imagination can conceive: houses, squares, ships, forests. At the same time, while we may not believe that the chair is a genuine tree or rock, we do believe in the genuineness of our relationship to these artificial substitutes and treat them as if they were trees or rocks.'

.. .. 19..

Class began with a brief introduction. Tortsov said:

'So far our exercises on the imagination have, to a greater or lesser extent, been connected with the world of objects around us (the room, the fireplace, the door) and with real life (our class). Now I am going to move out of the world of objects and into the world of the imagination. There our actions will be just as dynamic, but performed in the mind. We will abandon the here and now and move elsewhere, to individual settings, familiar to each of you, and there we will each do whatever our imagination suggests to us. Decide where you want to be in your mind,' said Tortsov to me. 'Where and when does the action take place?'

'In my room, in the evening,' I declared.

'Splendid,' Tortsov approved. 'I don't know how it is with you, but to feel as if I were in an imaginary apartment I would first have to go up the steps, ring at the front door, in a word complete a series of logically connected actions. Think about the doorknob, how the door opens and how you go into your room. What do you see in front of you?'

'Straight ahead, the wardrobe, the washstand . . .'

'And on the left?'

'The sofa, the table . . .'

'Try to go round the room and live in it a little. Why are you frowning?'

'I've found a letter on the table. I remember that I haven't answered it, and that makes me feel ashamed.'

'Good. Clearly you are now able to say "I am being" in my room?'

'What does that mean, "I am being"?' the students asked.

'In our vocabulary, "I am being" refers to the fact that I have put myself in the centre of a situation I have invented, that I feel I am really inside it, that I really exist at its very heart, in a world of imaginary objects, and that I am beginning to act as me, with full responsibility for myself. Now, tell me, what do you want to do?'

'That depends on what the time is right now.'

'That's logical. Let's presume it's eleven o'clock at night.'

'That's the time the apartment starts to quieten down,' I observed.

'What do you want to do now that it's quiet?' asked Tortsov encouragingly.

'Convince myself that I'm not a comic but a tragic actor.'

'What a pity you want to waste time in such an unproductive way. And how are you going to convince yourself?'

'I'll play some tragic role or other just for me,' I said, thus revealing my secret ambitions.

'Which one? Othello?'

'Oh, no. I can't work on Othello in my room any more. Every nook and cranny there pushes me into doing things I've done many times before.'

'So what will you play then?'

I didn't reply as I hadn't yet found an answer.

'What are you doing now?'

'I'm examining the room. Isn't there some object or other that could suggest an interesting subject for me to work on? . . . Here, for example, I remember there's a dark corner behind the wardrobe. It's not exactly gloomy in itself, but it appears so in the evening light. Instead of a hanger, there's a hook sticking out, as though inviting me to use it to hang myself. So, if I really wanted to hang myself what would I do first?'

'So, what would you?'

'First of all, of course, I would have to find a rope or a belt, so I go through the things on my shelves and in my drawers.'

'Do you find something?'

'Yes . . . But the hook is too low. My feet touch the floor.'

'That's a pity. Find another hook.'

'There isn't one.'

'In that case the best thing you can do is go on living.'

'I don't know, I'm all confused, my imagination's dried up,' I confessed.

'Because the story you invented wasn't logical. In nature everything is logical and sequential (with one or two exceptions) and your make-believe must be the same. It is no wonder that your imagination refused to follow a line that had no logical premise and led to an idiotic conclusion.

'Nonetheless your experiment with an imaginary suicide gave you what I hoped it would. It clearly demonstrated a new aspect of the way we make-believe. Here the actor's imagination is freed from the world around him (in this particular case from this room) and is transported to an imaginary one (that is to your apartment). In this imaginary setting everything was familiar to you, so your material was still drawn from life. That made it easier for you to search your memory. But what if you were dealing with a life that was not familiar to you? This gives us another aspect of the imagination.

'To understand what it is, step aside once more from the world of the here and now, and in your mind move to other worlds, which do not actually exist at the moment, but might. For example, probably no one here has made a trip around the globe. But this is as possible in reality as it is in the imagination. You mustn't implement your ideas "anyhow", "in general", "approximately" (they are all intolerable in art) but in all the detail with which a major undertaking is prepared.

'You will have to deal with all sorts of situations on your journey – the daily life, the customs of strange countries and peoples. You're unlikely to be able to find all the information you need in your own memory. So you will have to get it from books, maps, photographs and other sources which either provide direct knowledge or reproduce other people's impressions. Using this information you can sort out which places you will visit in your mind, what time of year, what month, where, in your mind, you will sail to in a steamship, in which cities you will need to stop over. You will also get information about the conditions and customs of this or that country, city, etc. All these important data give your work a firmer foundation, make it less flimsy, something which always occurs when you make-believe "in general". It leads the actor into play-acting and stock-in-trade. After a great deal of preparatory work, you can fix your itinerary and set out on your way. Only don't forget that at all times you must be in touch with what is logical and sequential. That will enable you to bring wavering, unstable fantasies nearer to unwavering, stable reality.

'Moving on to a new aspect of daydreaming, I bear in mind that it has wider possibilities than reality itself. So, the imagination pictures what does not exist in real life. For example, in dreams we can be transported to others planets and abduct fairy-tale princesses. We can fight and vanquish non-existent monsters, we can plunge into the depths of the sea and marry the Empress of the Deeps. Try and do that in the real world. You're not likely to find the material you need for these stories ready-made. Science, literature, painting, folk-tales provide us with hints, nudges, starting-off points for these mental excursions into these non-existent realms. Thus, the most important creative work falls to our sense of make-believe. In which case, we need, more than ever, ways to draw the world of fable and the world of fact closer together. I have spoken of the importance of sequence and logic. They bring the impossible and the probable together. So, when creating the fabulous and the fantastical, be logical and orderly.

'Now,' said Tortsov after a short reflection, 'I want to explain to you how the exercises you have already done can be used in various combinations. For instance, you can tell yourself: "Say I am looking at the way my fellow students, with Tortsov and Rakhmanov at their head, are getting on with their school studies in the Crimea or the arctic. I'll just take a look at how they are getting on with their expedition in an airplane." When you do that, you step aside mentally and watch how your friends are roasting in the Crimean sun, or freezing in the north, how they are repairing the damaged airplane in the mountain valley, or preparing to defend themselves against wild beasts. In that instance, you are a mere spectator of the picture your imagination has painted, and you play no role whatsoever in this imaginary life.

'But now you feel you want to be a part of the imaginary expedition or in the classes down on the southern shore of the Crimea. "What would I look like in these circumstances?" you ask yourself, and once more you step aside and see your fellow students, only now with yourself among them, in class in the Crimea or on the expedition. This time, too, you are a passive observer in your daydream, you are your own audience, an audience of one.

'Finally you get tired of watching yourself, and want to be active. To do that, you imagine you are there, you study in the Crimea or in the arctic, and then you repair the airplane or guard the camp. But now, as a character in an imaginary life, you don't see yourself but the things around you and respond inwardly to everything that is happening as a genuine participant. At that moment, when you are imagining actively, the mood which we call "I am being" is created in you.'

.. .. 19..

'Take a look inside yourselves, and tell me what happens in your minds when you think about our school work in the Crimea, as you did in the last class,' Tortsov asked Pasha at the beginning of today's class.

'What happens in my mind?' mused Pasha. 'For some reason I have a picture of a small, shabby hotel room with an window open onto the sea, warmth, many students in the room and someone doing exercises to develop the imagination.'

'And what happens to you,' asked Tortsov turning to Darya, 'when you think of that group of students mentally transported to the arctic?'

'I have a picture of glaciers, a campfire, a tent, and all of us dressed in furs.'

'So,' Tortsov concluded, 'all I have to do is set a theme for you and you begin to see pictures with what we call your mind's eye. In our actors' jargon we call these *mental images, the inner eye.*

'Judging from personal experience, to imagine, fantasize means above all to see the things one is thinking about with the mind's eye.

'And what happened when, in your mind, you were preparing to hang yourself in the dark corner of your room?' Tortsov asked, turning to me.

'When, in my mind, I saw the familiar setting once again, the doubts I know all too well, and which I am used to dealing with when alone, came alive in me once more. I felt an aching sadness in my heart and the desire to free myself from the doubts gnawing at me. And so, in my mind, out of impatience and weakness of character, I sought a way out through suicide,' I explained, a little agitated.

'So,' Tortsov summed up, 'all you had to do was see the familiar setting in your mind's eye, feel its atmosphere, and immediately familiar thoughts connected with the place where the action occurred came alive in you. Thoughts produce feelings and experiences, and then the impulse to action.

'And what do you see with your mind's eye when you remember the scene with the madman?' Tortsov asked, turning to all the students.

'I see "Marya's apartment", many young people, dancing in the hall, supper in the dining room. It's light, warm, happy! And there, on the stairs, at the front door a huge, emaciated fellow with a shaggy beard, in hospital slippers, in a robe, chilled to the bone and hungry,' said Pasha.

'Do you really see only the beginning of the scene?' Tortsov asked Pasha, who had fallen silent.

'No, I have a picture of the wardrobe which we moved to barricade the door. I also remember how in my mind I talked on the telephone to the hospital the madman had escaped from.'

'And what else do you see?'

'To tell the truth, nothing more.'

'Not good! Because with a small, scrappy supply of material like that you can't create a continuous series of mental images for the whole scene. What are we to do?'

'You have to think up, make up what's not there,' Pasha suggested.

'Yes, precisely, make it up! That's what you always have to do in situations when the author, the director and the rest of the production team have not provided everything the actor needs to know when he is being creative.

'First we need a continuous line of Given Circumstances through which the scene can proceed, and secondly, I repeat, we need an unbroken series of inner images linked to these Given Circumstances. Put briefly *we need an unbroken line not of plain, simple Given Circumstances but ones that we have coloured in full.* So remember this well, forever: every moment you are onstage, every moment in the outer and inner progress of the play, the actor must see what is going on around him (i.e. the external Given Circumstances, created by the director, the designer and the rest of the production team) or what is going on inside, in his own imagination, i.e. those images which depict the Given Circumstances in full colour. A continuous line of fleeting images is formed, both inside and outside us, like a film. It lasts as long as the creative process lasts, projecting the Given Circumstances which the actor has fully coloured, onto the screen of his mind's eye, so that he now lives his own life entirely.

'These images create a corresponding mood inside, which then acts upon your mind and evokes matching experiences.

'Constantly watching the film of your mental images will, on the one hand, make sure you stay within the play, and, on the other, unfailingly and faithfully guide your creative work.

'Now, concerning mental images, is it correct to say that we really see them within us? We have the capacity to visualize things which do not exist in actual fact, but which we merely picture to ourselves. It is not difficult to verify this capacity of ours. Take the chandelier. It is outside me. It is, it exists in the material world. I look at it and feel, as it were, that I am extending "my ocular antennae" towards it. But now I take my eyes off the chandelier, close them, and want to see it again in my mind's eye, "from memory". To do that, I have to withdraw my "ocular antennae", so to speak, and then direct them from inside myself, not outward towards a real article, but at some sort of imaginary "screen in our mind's eye" as we call it in our jargon.

'Where is this screen to be found, or, rather, where do I take it to be, inside or outside myself? My own feeling is that it is somewhere outside me, in the empty space before me. The film itself is running inside me, but I see it projected outside me.

'To make sure you understand me completely, I will talk about it in other terms.

'Mental images arise in our imagination, our memory, and, thereafter, our minds, as it were, project them outside ourselves, so we can see them.

But we see these imaginary objects from the inside out, so to speak, not from the outside in, with our mind's eye.

'The same thing happens with hearing. We hear imaginary sounds not with outer but with our inner ears, but we identify the source of these sounds, in most cases, as not inside but outside ourselves.

'I would say, turning this statement on its head, that imaginary objects and images take shape outside ourselves but nonetheless arise, in the first instance, inside ourselves, in our imagination and our memory. Let us test this by using an example.

'Kostya!' said Tortsov, addressing me. 'Do you remember my lecture in the town of . . . ? Can you see the platform on which we both were sitting? At this moment, are those images inside or outside yourself?'

'I feel them outside myself as I actually did then,' I answered without needing to think.

'And with what eyes are you now looking at the imaginary platform, with inner or outer eyes?'

'Inner.'

'Only by resolving such questions can we understand the term "inner eye".'

'Create mental images at every moment in a long play! That's terribly complicated and difficult!' I exclaimed.

'Complicated and difficult? As a punishment for saying that try to tell me the complete story of your life from the first moment you can remember,' Tortsov unexpectedly proposed.

I began.

'My father used to say, childhood is remembered in decades, youth in years, middle-age in months and old age in weeks.

'That's how I perceive my past. And indeed much of what is engraved on my memory is visible in the minutest detail. For instance, the first moment of my life that I can remember is the garden swing. It frightened me. I can see other episodes of my life as a child equally clearly, my mother's room, granny, the courtyard, the street. A new phase, adolescence, is engraved on my memory particularly clearly, because it coincided with my starting school. After that my mental images illustrate shorter but more numerous bits of my life. Thus, long phases and individual episodes stretch back from the present into the past in a long, long line.'

'Can you see it?'

'See what?'

'The unbroken line of phases and episodes which stretch right back through your past.'

'I can see it but there are gaps,' I admitted.

'You hear!' exclaimed Tortsov triumphantly. 'In a few minutes Kostya has made a film of his entire life, yet he can't do the same thing for the life of a role which takes a mere three hours to convey in a performance!'

'But surely I didn't recall my entire life? Just a few moments of it.'

'You lived through your entire life and memories of the most important moments remained. Live through the entire life of a role and let the most essential landmarks in it also remain. Why do you think this so difficult to do?'

'Because life makes a film out of mental images by natural means, but the imaginary life of a role has to be created by the actor, and that is very difficult, very complex!'

'You will soon be convinced that this isn't actually so very difficult. If I were to suggest that in the mind's eye you draw a line made, not out of mental images, but out of your own innermost feelings and experiences, that would seem not only "complex" and "difficult" but impossible to achieve.'

'Why?' said the students.

'Because our feelings and experiences are elusive, capricious, mutable and cannot be pinned down or, as we say in our actors' jargon, "fixed". Sight is more amenable. The things we see are more freely, more deeply engraved on our visual memory and are resurrected anew in our representations of them.

'Besides, the things we see in dreams, despite their illusory character, are nonetheless more real, more tangible, more "material", if one can speak thus about a dream, than are representations of feelings our emotion memory vaguely suggests to us. So let the more accessible, the more amenable mental images help us revive and pin down the less accessible, the less stable, innermost feelings.

'Let the film of your mental images sustain moods, which are in keeping with the play, inside us. Let them, as they open out within us, evoke corresponding experiences, impulses, intentions and actions themselves.

'That is why in every role we need not plain but illustrated Given Circumstances,' concluded Tortsov.

'That means,' I said, wanting to talk it through, 'that if I create a film inside me, composed of the mental images I have for each moment of Othello's life, and project that film onto the screen of my mind's eye . . .'

'And if', Tortsov interjected, 'they truly reflect the play's Given Circumstances and magic "if", and if they evoke in you moods and feelings parallel to the role itself then, truly, you will find your mental images take possession of you each time, and you will truthfully experience Othello's feelings every time you view the film inside you.'

'Once the film has been made, it's not difficult to project it. The whole question is, how to make it,' I said, unwilling to yield.

'Of that, more next time,' said Tortsov as he got up and left the class.

.. .. 19..

'Let us use our imagination to make a film,' Tortsov proposed.

'About what?' the students asked.

'I deliberately choose an inactive theme, because an active one can automatically arouse your dynamism without any prior help from the imagination. However, a subject with little action in it necessitates hard preparatory work by the imagination. For the time being I am not interested in dynamism itself but in preparing for it. That's why I am choosing the least active theme. I propose that you live the life of a tree with deep roots in the earth.'

'Fine! I am a tree, an oak a hundred years old,' Pasha decided. 'But even though I say this, I don't believe it can possibly be so.'

'In that case, say to yourself, this is me, but if I were an oak, if around me and within me the circumstances were such and such, what would I do?' said Tortsov to help him.

'Yes but,' said Pasha thoughtfully, 'how can I be active in a state of inaction, standing motionless on the spot?'

'Yes, of course, you can't move from one spot to another, you can't walk. But there are other actions apart from this. To stimulate them, don't you first need to decide where you are? In a forest? In the middle of a field, on a mountain peak? Choose the place you find the most exciting.'

Pasha thought he was an oak growing in a mountain clearing, somewhere in the Alps. On the left, far off, a castle, around him, a wide-open space, far off, the silvery gleam of a chain of snowy mountains and, nearer, endless little hills which, seen from above, look like petrified ocean waves. Here and there, scattered villages.

'Now, tell me, what do you see close by?'

'I see my own dense crown of foliage which is making a great deal of noise because my branches are swaying.'

'Yes! Up there, where you are, there's a strong wind.'

'In my branches I can see birds' nests of some kind.'

'That's good, given your solitude.'

'No, there's nothing good about it. Life with these birds is difficult. They make noise with their wings, sharpen their beaks on my trunk and sometimes squabble and fight. That's annoying . . . Beside me, there's a flowing stream, my best friend, someone I can talk to. It keeps me from drying up,' said Pasha, broadening out his fantasy.

Tortsov made him spell out every detail of his imaginary life.

Then Tortsov turned to Leo, who without any recourse to his imagination chose something highly commonplace, something very familiar, that was easy to revive in his memory. His imagination is rather poor. He pictured a dacha with a garden in Petrovski Park.

'What do you see?' Tortsov asked.

'Petrovski Park.'

'You cannot take in the whole of Petrovski Park at a glance. Choose some definite spot for your villa. What do you see in front of you?'

'A fence with railings.'

'What kind?'

Leo said nothing.

'What is this fence made of?'

'What is it made of? Wrought iron.'

'What's the design? Draw it for me.'

Leo ran his finger tip over the tabletop for a long time, and it was evident that he was thinking about what he had been talking about for the very first time.

'I don't understand. Draw it more clearly,' said Tortsov, pushing him to the limits of his visual memory. 'So, fine . . . let's say you can see this . . . Now, tell me, what lies beyond the fence?'

'A road.'

'Who is walking, driving along it?'

'Summer tourists.'

'And?'

'Coachmen.'

'And?'

'Carters.'

'And who else is going along it?'

'Riders.'

'On bicycles perhaps?'

'That's it. That's it! Bicycles, cars . . .'

It was clear that Leo was not making the slightest effort to stimulate his imagination. What is the use of such a passive imagination, when the teacher does all the work for the student?

I expressed my perplexity to Tortsov.

'There are one or two points in my method of stimulating the imagination which are worth noting,' he replied. 'When the student's imagination is inactive, I ask a simple question. You can't help but respond when someone asks you something. Sometimes the student replies without thinking, just to get himself off the hook. But I don't accept that kind of answer, and I demonstrate its inadequacy. If he is to give a more satisfactory answer, the student either has to stir his imagination immediately, make himself see the things he has been asked about in his mind's eye, or tackle the question by using his intelligence, through a series of logical appraisals. The work of the imagination is quite often prepared for and guided by this kind of conscious, mental activity. So, the student finally sees something from his memory or his imagination. Before him stand well-defined, visual images. The imagination has worked for a brief moment. After that I repeat the process, with the help of another question. Then a second brief moment of insight occurs, then a third. In this way, I maintain and extend his imagination and evoke a whole series of living moments, the sum total of which provides a picture for his imaginary life. Let's admit, the picture still may not be very interesting, but the fact that it has been created out of the student's own mental images is enough. Once his imagination has been roused he can see it twice, thrice, many times. Repeating the picture engraves it more firmly in his memory and he feels at home with it. However, the imagination can be lazy and does not always respond to a simple question. Then all the teacher can do is prompt an answer to the question. If what the teacher has suggested satisfies the student, then, while he accepts another's image as his own, at least he begins to see something. If the opposite is the case, then the student modifies what has been suggested according to his own taste, and that also obliges him to look and see with his mind's eye. In the end, for this once, some semblance of an imaginary life has been created, created in part out of his own material . . . I see you are not very happy with this result. Still, even such forced moments of imagination produce something.'

'What precisely?'

'Maybe, but prior to this there were no images or pictures with which to create a life. Everything was vague and fuzzy. But after working like this something takes shape and form. The soil into which the teacher and the director can sow new seeds has been created. This is the invisible priming on which a picture can be painted. Moreover, with my approach, students copy the teacher's techniques of stimulating their imagination and learn to arouse it with questions prompted by their own intelligence. They create the habit of fighting consciously against the passivity and sluggishness of their imagination. And that is quite a lot.'

.. .. 19..

Today Tortsov continued the exercises to develop the imagination.

'In the last class,' he said to Pasha, 'you told me *who* you were, *where* you were in your dream, what you *saw* around you . . . Now tell me what you *hear* with your inner ear as an ancient oak.'

At first Pasha could hear nothing. Tortsov reminded him of the racket the birds make as they build their nests in the oak's branches and added:

'So, what do you hear around you in your mountain clearing?'

Now Pasha could hear the bleating of sheep, the lowing of cows, the tinkling of little bells, the sound of shepherds' pipes, women talking as they rested under the oak from their heavy labour in the fields.

'Now tell me *when* the things you can see and hear in your imagination are happening. In which period? In which century?'

Pasha chose the feudal period.

'Good. In that case, what sort of noises do you hear which are characteristic of those times, as an old oak?'

After a pause, Pasha said he could hear the song of a wandering minstrel, wending his way to a feast at the next castle: here, under the oak, by the stream, he rests, washes, changes into his finery and prepares for his performance. Here he tunes his harp and has a last rehearsal of his new song which is about spring, love and the sorrows of the heart. At night the oak hears a courtier make a declaration of love to a married lady and then their long kisses. Then the violent oaths of two sworn enemies ring out, the clash of arms and the dying cries of a wounded man. At dawn the anxious voices of people who are looking for the dead man can be heard, then, when they have found him, general commotion and individual, sharp cries fill the air. They lift the body, and heavy, regular steps can be heard as they carry it away.

There was scarcely time for Pasha to catch his breath before Tortsov put another question to him:

'Why?'

'What do you mean, why?' we asked in amazement.

'Why is Pasha an oak? Why is he growing in the Middle Ages, in the mountains?'

Tortsov attributed great significance to this question. According to him, by answering it, it's possible to elicit the past of this imaginary life.

'Why do you grow all alone in that clearing?'

Pasha thought up this possible story about the ancient oak's past. Once upon a time the whole mountain area had been covered by a dense forest. But the Baron, who was lord of the castle that could be seen not far off, on this side of the valley, had to be continuously on the alert against attacks from the neighbouring lord. The forest could conceal the enemy army's movements and be used for an ambush. So he cut it down. Only the mighty oak remained because, just beneath it, in its shadow, a spring welled up through the earth. If the spring dried up, then the stream, which provided water for the Baron's flock, would also disappear.

Another of Tortsov's questions, *for what reason?*, also stumped us.

'I can understand your difficulty since, in this case, we are talking about a tree. But generally speaking, the question, "for what reason?" is of considerable importance. It obliges us to clarify what we are aiming for and this, and goal defines the future, and impels us to positive action. The tree, of course, cannot establish aims for itself, but it can serve some sort of purpose, not unlike real activity, and that is useful in some way.'

Pasha found the following answer. The oak was the highest spot in this place. So it could be used as a splendid watch-tower from which to observe the hostile neighbour. The tree was considered to have done great service in this respect in the past. No wonder then, that it was held in exceptional esteem by the inhabitants of the castle and the nearby villages. A special festival was arranged in its honour, every spring. The Baron himself appeared at it and drank a huge cup of wine as a toast. People bedecked the oak with flowers, sang songs, and danced round it.

'Now that the Given Circumstances have taken shape in our imagination,' said Tortsov, 'and have been brought to life one by one, let us compare what we had at the beginning and what we have now. Before, when all we knew was that you were in a mountain clearing, your inner vision was general, fuzzy, like an underdeveloped roll of film. Now, with the help of the work we have done, your image has become much clearer. You have come to understand *when, where, why, for what reason* you are there. You can already distinguish the outlines of a new life, previously unknown to you. You can feel the ground beneath your feet. You have lived in your mind. But this is not enough. The stage demands action. You must evoke it by setting tasks and intentions towards them. To do that you need new "Given Circumstances" and the magic "if", new ideas to stimulate you.'

But Pasha couldn't find them.

'Ask yourself and answer this question sincerely. What event, what imaginary disaster could jerk you out of your mood of indifference, rouse you, frighten you, delight you? Feel yourself in the mountain clearing, create the "I am being" and answer only after you have done that,' Tortsov advised.

Pasha tried to do what he was bid but couldn't think of anything.

'In that case, let's approach the problem indirectly. So, first, tell me what you are most sensitive to in life. What most often excites you, frightens you, delights you? My question is quite unrelated to the subject of our make-believe. Yet, once we know your own natural inclinations, we can easily bring the ideas you have closer into line with them. So, tell me about one of your typical features or interests.'

'Any kind of quarrel excites me. Does that seem strange to you, given my rather meek appearance?' said Pasha, after some reflection.

'All right! In that case, there's a raid! The enemy duke's forces are advancing to occupy your lands, and are already coming up the hill where you stand. Their lances glitter in the sun, catapults and battering-rams are on the move. The enemy know that look-outs often climb up into your top branches to observe them. They will cut you down and burn you!' said Tortsov threateningly.

'They won't succeed!' was Pasha's vehement response. 'I won't be abandoned. I'm needed. Our men aren't asleep. They're already running here. The knights are galloping on their steeds. The look-outs are sending messengers to them every minute . . .'

'Now, the battle grows all round you. Cross-bows rain a hail of arrows down on you and your look-outs, some of whom are covered in burning tow and coated with pitch. Stop and decide, before it's too late, what you would do in the circumstances I have given you, if this were happening in real life.'

It was clear that Pasha was casting about in his mind to find some way out of the magic 'if' Tortsov had introduced.

'What can a tree do to save itself when its roots are buried in the earth and it has no capacity to move?' he exclaimed, frustrated by the hopelessness of the situation.

'Your frustration is quite enough for me,' said Tortsov approvingly. 'The problem is insoluble, and it's not your fault if you have been given an imaginary subject which is devoid of action.'

'Why did you give it then?' we asked, perplexed.

'To show you that even when you are faced with an inactive subject, the imagination can produce a mental breakthrough, evoke a vital impulse to action. But most of all our exercises should show you how to create the material, the mental images, and the film for a role, and that this process is by no means as difficult and complicated as it appears.'

.. .. 19..

All Tortsov could do in today's class was explain to us that the actor needs imagination not only when creating but also when renewing what has already been created and is now getting jaded. This is effected by introducing a new idea, or revitalizing individual details.

'A practical example will show you. Let us take, say, a scene which you have already exhausted, although you didn't do it completely. I am talking about the "madman" improvisation. Breathe new life into it as a whole or in part by inventing something new.'

But nothing new occurred to any of us.

'Listen,' asked Tortsov, 'how did you learn there was someone, a starving madman, outside the door? Did Marya tell you? Yes, she opened the door onto the staircase and saw the former tenant. They say he was carried off to the psychiatric hospital in a fit of violent madness . . . But while you were barricading the door, Grisha ran to the telephone to communicate with the hospital and they replied that madness had nothing to do with it, that the patient had a simple case of delirium tremens. He is an alcoholic. But now he is well again, has been discharged, and has returned home. But who knows, perhaps the information is wrong, perhaps the doctors were mistaken.

'What would you do if all this really happened?'

'Marya ought to go out and ask him why he has come back,' said Leo.

'How terrifying! My dear friends, I couldn't, I couldn't! I'm scared, I'm scared!' Marya exclaimed with a frightened face.

'Leo will go with you. He's strong and healthy,' said Tortsov encouragingly. 'One, two, three, begin!' he commanded turning to all of us. 'Focus on the new circumstances, obey your impulses and go.'

We played the exercise through with enthusiasm, with genuine excitement, and won the approval of Tortsov and of Rakhmanov who was taking part in the class. The new version had produced its effect and revitalized us.

At the end of class Tortsov summed up our work on developing the creative imagination, and, having recalled the specific stages of this work, he ended with these words:

'Every idea you have must be precisely substantiated and strictly determined. The questions – who, when, where, why, for what reason, how – which we asked so as to stir our imagination, helped us create a picture of our imaginary, illusory life with greater and greater definition. There are, of course, cases when the picture draws itself without the aid of conscious, mental activity, without leading questions, just intuitively. But you yourselves can see that you can't rely on the dynamic energy of the imagination, and leave it to fend for itself. That is out of the question when you have been given a precise theme for your make-believe. Imagining "in general" without a well-defined, solidly based theme, is fruitless.

'However, when we invent using our reason, we often get no more than pallid reflections of the life we have imagined. And that is not enough for creative acting which demands that the human being/actor, his personality, should be in ferment, that he should surrender to the role not only psychologically but physically. What are we to do? Put another familiar question to yourselves: "What would I do if my fiction became fact?" You know from your own experience that we are drawn to respond to this question through action by our very nature as artists. This question proves an excellent stimulus, urging our imagination on. For the moment don't give this action physical form, but let it remain an impulse. It is important only that this impulse be aroused and experienced by us not only psychologically but physically. Experiencing it this way fixes the story we have created.

'It is important to recognize that imagination, while devoid of flesh and blood, has the ability to summon genuine actions from flesh and blood – from our bodies. This capability plays a large role in psychotechnique.

'Listen carefully to what I am about to tell you: *every one of our movements onstage, every word must be the result of a truthful imagination.*

'If you speak a word, or do something mechanically onstage, not knowing who you are, where you have come from, why, what you need, where you are going, or what you will do there, you will be acting without imagination, and this fragment of your existence onstage, however long or short, will hold no truth for you. You will perform like a machine that's been wound up, an automaton.

'If I ask you, right now, the simplest question: "Is it cold or hot today?" before you can answer "cold" or "hot" or "didn't notice", you need to go to the street in your mind, remember how you walked or rode here, check your body, remember how the passers-by muffled themselves up or turned up their collars, how the snow crunched under your feet and only then will you pronounce the one word we need.

'All these pictures perhaps will flash through your mind in an instant, and from the outside it might seem that you answered almost without thinking. But the pictures were there, your body sensations were there, the process of verification was there, and you only answered as a result of the complex workings of your imagination.

'So, not a single scene, not one single step onstage must be performed mechanically, without an inner reason, that is without the imagination.

'If you hold fast to this rule all your exercises in school, to whichever section of our programme they belong, will develop and strengthen your imagination.

'Conversely, everything you do onstage coldly ("in a frigid way") will be your undoing as it will inculcate the habit of doing things automatically, without imagination.

'Creating a role, transforming of the dramatist's world into theatrical fact, everything from first to last, proceeds in cooperation with the imagination.

'What can warm us, excite us so much as our own imagination? If it is to respond to all the demands we make on it, it must be mobile, dynamic, responsive and properly developed.

'So, pay particular attention to developing your imagination. Develop it in every possible way – through those exercises with which you are already familiar, that is, direct work on the imagination as such, as well as indirect work. Make it a rule never to do anything onstage mechanically, as mere outward form.'

5

CONCENTRATION AND ATTENTION

The class took place in 'Marya's apartment', in other words, in the set with the curtains closed.

We continued working on the exercises with the madman and the damp fireplace.

Thanks to Tortsov's promptings our performance turned out well. It was so enjoyable that we asked to do both scenes over again.

While we were waiting, I sat with my back resting against the wall.

Then something quite unexpected happened. To my amazement, for no apparent reason, the two chairs next to me toppled over onto the floor. No one had touched them, but they fell all the same. I picked them up and managed to right two others that were tilting badly. While I was doing this my eyes were caught by a long, narrow, vertical crack in the wall. It grew bigger and bigger and finally, as I watched, reached its whole height. Then I realized why the chairs had fallen. Someone was opening the curtain, one of the 'walls' of our room, and this was pushing objects away and toppling them over. Someone had opened the curtain.

And there was the black hole with Tortsov and Rakhmanov standing in silhouette in the semi-darkness.

As the curtain opened I felt totally different inside. What shall I compare it to?

Imagine me and my wife (if I had one) in a hotel room. We talk heart to heart, we undress and go to bed. We are free and uninhibited. Then suddenly we see that a huge door, to which we had paid no attention, has opened and there, in the shadows, there are strange people, our neighbours, watching us. How many they are we can't tell. In the darkness there appear to be a lot of them. We grab our clothes quickly, comb our hair and try to behave with proper restraint as though we were guests.

Suddenly, I felt taut as a violin string, and whereas a moment ago I had felt at home, now I found myself in company in nothing but my nightshirt.

It is amazing how the feeling of intimacy can be shattered by the black hole. While we were in a nice sitting room, we were unaware that there was an important side and an unimportant side. Wherever we stood, whichever way we turned, it didn't matter. When the fourth wall opened, the black hole became the side that mattered, and we had to adjust to it, because it was from there that we were being watched. It didn't matter whether the person you were in communication with, or the person speaking, felt comfortable onstage, what mattered was that you could be seen and heard by people who were not present in the room with you but sitting, invisible, on the other side of the footlights, in the darkness.

And Tortsov and Rakhmanov, who had been in the room with us a moment ago and had seemed familiar and ordinary, were now in the darkness, beyond the proscenium arch, and became quite different in our eyes – rigorous, demanding.

The same change happened to other students. Only Grisha was the same with the curtain open or shut. Need I say that our acting turned into mere display, and was a failure.

'No, until we have learned to ignore the black hole we won't make any progress, that's for sure,' I inwardly resolved.

I talked to Pasha about it, but he thought that if we were given a completely new exercise with a useful commentary by Tortsov to inspire us, it would take our minds off the auditorium.

When I spoke to Tortsov about Pasha's suggestion he said:

'Fine, let's try it. Here's a riveting tragedy that will, I hope, stop you thinking about the audience:

'It takes place in Marya's apartment as before. She has just married Kostya who has been taken on as a cashier in some charity or other. They have an enchanting new-born baby. The mother leaves the room to bathe it. The husband sorts out papers and counts the money, note this – the charity's money. Because of the late hour he has not been able to return it to the place where he works. Bundles of old, greasy banknotes are piled up on the table.

'Opposite Kostya is Marya's younger brother, who is retarded, a hunchback. He observes Kostya tearing off the strips of bright paper – the bands – from the bundles and throwing them into the fireplace where they burn brightly. He likes the way they blaze.

'All the money has been counted. Over 10,000 of it.

'Taking advantage of the fact that her husband has finished his work, Marya calls him to go and enjoy the baby whom she is bathing in the next room. Kostya goes out and the hunchback imitates him, throwing the bits of paper into the fire. When there are no more coloured bands left, he starts to throw in the money. This, in fact, burns even more brightly, more cheerfully than the coloured paper. Excited by this game, the hunchback throws all the money into the fire, the charity's entire capital, along with the accounts and the invoices.

'Kostya returns just at the moment when the last bundle is starting to burn. Realizing what has happened he loses control and hurls himself at the hunchback, pushing him away with all his might. The idiot falls, striking his temple against the fender. The panic-stricken Kostya grabs the last charred bundle and lets out a cry of despair. His wife rushes in and sees her brother stretched out by the fireplace. She runs over to him, tries to lift him but cannot. Seeing blood on his face, she yells to her husband to fetch some water, but Kostya doesn't take it in. He is in a daze. Then his wife rushes to get the water, and no sooner has she left the room than her screams ring out. The joy of her life, the enchanting new-born baby has drowned in the bath.

'If this tragedy does not take your mind off the black hole, it means you have hearts of stone.'

The new exercise excited us by its melodramatic, its startling character . . . but we proved to have hearts of stone indeed, because we couldn't play it.

Tortsov suggested that, as usual, we should start with 'if' and the Given Circumstances. We started by telling each other stories, but this wasn't the free play of the imagination but contrivance, ideas we squeezed out of ourselves and which, of course, were incapable of stimulating us creatively.

The draw of the auditorium proved stronger than the tragic horrors onstage.

'In that case,' Tortsov decided, 'let us cut ourselves off once more and play these "horrors" with the curtain closed.'

The curtain was closed and our nice sitting room was cosy once more. Tortsov and Rakhmanov came back from the auditorium and became friendly and well-disposed once more. We started the scene. We brought off the quiet parts, but when it came to the drama I was not satisfied with what I had done. I wanted to give so much more, but I didn't have the necessary feeling and energy. Without realizing it, I had gone right off the track and fallen victim to 'playacting'.

Tortsov's impressions confirmed my own feelings. He said:

'At the beginning what you did was right, but, at the end, you were putting on a show of action. You were squeezing feelings out of yourself or, as Hamlet puts it "tearing a passion to tatters". So it's no use complaining about the black hole. It was not only that which prevented you from living truly onstage since the results were the same as with the curtain closed.'

'If it was the auditorium that was the trouble when the curtain was open,' I confessed, 'then, when it was closed, to be frank, the trouble was you and Ivan Rakhmanov.'

'So that's it!' Tortsov exclaimed with great good humour. 'Ivan, that's the last straw. We're a black hole! Let's take umbrage and leave! Let them play all on their own!'

Tortsov and Rakhmanov exited tragicomically. The rest followed. We were alone and tried to play the exercise without anyone watching, that is, with nothing in the way.

Strange as it seems, when we were alone things got even worse. My attention still wandered to my fellow actor. I observed his acting intensely, criticized it and, do what I might, became an audience. In their turn my fellow actors observed me attentively. I felt that I was at one and the same time a spectator and an actor under scrutiny. At the end of the day, it's stupid, boring and most of all pointless to play for each other.

But then, by chance, I glanced at the mirror, liked what I saw, felt heartened and remembered the work I had done at home on Othello when, as today, I had to perform for myself, looking in the mirror. I enjoyed being 'my own audience'. My confidence rose and so I agreed to Pasha's proposal that we should call Tortsov and Rakhmanov back and show them the results of our work.

As it turned out we didn't need to send for them as they had been watching what we had been presenting on our own through a crack in the door.

We gathered from what they said that our performance was worse than when the curtain was open. Then it had been bad but modest and restrained, now it was just as bad, but self-assured and carefree.

When Tortsov summed up today's work, what emerged was that when the curtain was open we were inhibited by the audience sitting out there in the darkness, beyond the footlights. When the curtain was closed, Tortsov and Rakhmanov sitting in the same room inhibited us. When we were alone our fellow actors inhibited us by turning into an audience, and, when I played just for myself alone, I became my own audience and inhibited myself as an actor. So, whichever way you look at it, the audience is the obstacle. But, even so, it is boring playing without one.

'Worse than little children,' said Tortsov to our shame.

'There's nothing for it,' he decided after a short pause, 'we shall have to set aside our exercises for the time being and work on objects of attention. They are the principal culprits in what happened and we shall start on them next time.'

.. .. 19..

Today there was a large notice hanging up in the auditorium:

CREATIVE CONCENTRATION AND ATTENTION

The curtain representing the fourth wall of the cosy sitting room was open and the chairs, which were usually set against it, had been removed. Our comfortable room, with one wall missing, now stood open to the gaze of the auditorium. It had been transformed into a normal stage set and had lost its snug feeling.

Electric cables with lightbulbs were placed at various points on the set walls.

We were lined up along the footlights. There was a pregnant silence.

'Who has a heel missing?' Tortsov suddenly asked us.

The students began looking at their own and other people's footwear giving the matter their full attention.

Tortsov put another question:

'What happened in the auditorium just now?'

We didn't know what to answer.

'You mean you didn't notice my secretary? He's a very busy, noisy sort of person. He brought me some papers to sign.'

The fact was we hadn't seen him.

'Amazing!' exclaimed Tortsov. 'How could that happen? And with the curtain open, too! Weren't you told that the auditorium irresistibly drew you to it?'

'I was busy with my heel,' I said by way of justification.

'Really!!' said Tortsov still more amazed. 'An insignificant little heel proved to be stronger than the big black hole! That means it's not so difficult to divert your attention from it. The secret is very simple: *to divert your attention from the auditorium you must become engrossed in what is happening onstage.*'

'So, in fact,' I thought to myself, 'all I had to do was get interested for a minute in what was happening on this side of the footlights and I involuntarily stopped thinking about what was happening on the other.'

Then I recalled the occasion when the nails spilled onto the stage and the conversation I'd had with the stagehand, and when I became so engrossed in the nails that I forgot about the yawning black hole.

'Now, I hope you understand,' said Tortsov, summing up, 'that the actor needs an object on which to focus his attention, only not in the auditorium, but on the stage, and the more compelling that object is, the more it can command attention.

'There is not one single moment in a man's life when his attention is not engaged by some object or other.

'And the more compelling the object, the greater its power over the actor's attention. To draw it away from the auditorium one must be clever and sneak in some object up here, onstage. You know how a mother distracts a child with a toy. In the same way an actor must be able to sneak in a similar sort of toy for himself, to take his mind off the auditorium.'

'Yet,' I thought to myself, 'why go to the trouble of sneaking in an object when there are plenty of them onstage anyway?

'If I am the *subject* then everything outside me is *object*. And the whole world is outside me . . . There are so many, there are all kinds of objects! Why create them?'

But Tortsov countered this by saying that's how things happen in life. Objects do arise and attract attention spontaneously, in a natural way. We know perfectly well *what* to look at and *how* to look at it, at every moment of our existence.

But in the theatre this is not so, in the theatre there is an auditorium which prevents the actor from living normally.

I should know that better than anyone, according to Tortsov, after the performance of *Othello*. Besides, on our side of the footlights there is a wealth of objects far more interesting than the black hole. Only you must be well and truly able to see the things that are found there. You must use regular exercises to help you hold your concentration. You must develop a special technique which will help you focus on an object in such a way that the onstage object will distract you from what is offstage. In a nutshell, according to Tortsov, we have to learn to look and see.

Instead of a lecture on which objects exist in life and consequently in the theatre, Tortsov told us he would give us a graphic illustration of them onstage.

'The points and pools of light which you are about to see illustrate various aspects of objects with which you are familiar in life and, therefore, essential in the theatre.'

There was total blackout in the auditorium and onstage. After a few seconds, close to, on the table around which we were sitting, a small electric lamp, concealed in a box, suddenly came to life. Amid the general gloom the point of light became the only clear, noticeable attraction. Nothing else drew our attention.

'This little lamp, shining in the darkness,' explained Tortsov, 'illustrates the immediate object, the immediate focal point. We use it at those moments when we have to concentrate and not allow our attention to fly off in other directions.'

When the lights came back on Tortsov turned to the students:

'Concentrating on a point of light in the darkness is comparatively easy for you. Now we shall try and repeat the exercise only this time in the light.'

Tortsov asked one of the students to observe the back of an armchair closely, and me the fake property enamel on the table, to a third he assigned a knick-knack, to a fourth a pencil, to a fifth a rope, to a sixth a match and so on.

Pasha started to unravel the rope but I stopped him, saying that the exercise we had been given was not about action but about concentration and so we could only observe the article and think about it. But Pasha didn't agree and insisted on doing it his way. We had to turn to Tortsov to settle the dispute. He said:

'Concentrating on an object produces a natural need to do something with it. Action concentrates the attention even more closely on the object. So, concentration plus action creates a close bond with the object.'

When, once again, I started to look at the tabletop with its fake enamel I had a desire to trace the outline of the design with any pointed object that came to hand.

Doing so actually obliged me to observe, to examine the design even more attentively. Meanwhile Pasha was concentrating on unravelling the rope and doing it with great gusto. Other students became absorbed in some action or other or in attentively observing an object.

Finally Tortsov stated:

'The immediate focal point becomes totally absorbing for you not only in the dark but in the light, too. That's good!'

Then, first in total blackout, then in the light, he demonstrated the mid and distant focal points to us. As in the first example with the immediate focal point, to maintain concentration for as long a time as possible, we had to provide a firm foundation for what we were doing in our imagination.

We easily succeeded in doing the new exercises in the dark.

The lights came up full.

'Now, look closely at the things about you and select from among them some mid or distant focal point or other and concentrate all your attention on it,' Tortsov suggested.

There were so many immediate, mid and distant things about us that for a minute our eyes wandered aimlessly.

Instead of a single focal point, a dozen things leaped to one's eyes, which, if I were inclined to play on words I would call not points but a row of omission points. Finally my eye was caught by a small statuette, way off, on the fireplace but I couldn't maintain it as the centre of my attention for very long since everything round it distracted me and the statuette was soon lost among a hundred other items.

'Ah-ha!' exclaimed Tortsov. 'Evidently before we can establish mid and distant focal points in the light we have to learn how to look and see onstage.'

'What is there to learn?' someone asked.

'How's that? It's a difficult thing to do with other people present and with the black hole in front of you. For example, one of my nieces loves to eat, get up to mischief, run about and chatter. Up until recently she used to eat on her own, in the nursery. Now they have put her at the family table and she has forgotten how to eat, chatter and get up to mischief. "Why don't you eat and talk to us?" they asked her. "And what are you staring at me for?" the child answers in return. How are we to teach her to eat and chatter and get up to mischief once more, in front of other people?

'The same is true of you. In life you know how to walk and speak and sit and look but in the theatre you lose this ability, and say to yourself, when you feel the closeness of the crowd, "What are they staring at me for?" You have to be taught everything from scratch – onstage and in front of people.

'Remember now, all, even the simplest, most elementary actions which we know perfectly well in life fall apart when someone makes an entrance onstage, in the glare of the footlights, in front of a packed house. That is why we have to learn to walk, move, sit, lie down all over again. I mentioned this to you in our first classes. Today, as regards the question of concentration, I have already stated that you must learn to look and see, listen and hear onstage, too.'

.. .. 19..

'Choose something,' said Tortsov when the students had settled down onstage with the curtain open. 'An object, perhaps that towel hanging on the wall with its bright, eye-catching design.'

Everyone started looking diligently at the towel.

'No!' said Tortsov, stopping us. 'That's not looking, that's staring glassy-eyed.'

We stopped straining but that didn't convince Tortsov that we were seeing what our eyes were focused on.

'Pay closer attention!' Tortsov commanded.

Everyone leaned forward.

'There was still very little concentration and a deal of mechanical staring.'

We knitted our brows and tried to appear to be concentrating.

'Concentrating and seeming to be concentrating are not the same thing. Check for yourselves what fake and genuine observation are.'

After much trial and error we settled down, tried not to tense up and looked at the towel.

Suddenly Tortsov burst out laughing and turned to me and said:

'If only I could take a photograph of you, you wouldn't believe that strain could reduce a human being to the absurd state you were in just now. Your eyes were literally popping out of your head. Do you really need to strain so much just to observe? Do less, less! Much, much less! Free yourself from tension. Cut down by 95%! Go on . . . go on . . . Why are you stretching out towards the object, why are you leaning so far towards it? Ease back. Less, less! Go on, go on! Go on, much, much less!' Tortsov went on at me.

The more persistently he reiterated 'go on, go on', the less the tension which had prevented me from 'observing and seeing' became. The excess tension had been enormous, unbelievable. You've no idea how great it is as you stand, hunched, before the black hole. Tortsov is right when he speaks of 95% excess tension when an actor observes anything onstage.

'How simple it is, how little we need to observe and see!' I exclaimed ecstatically. 'It's extraordinarily easy compared with what I have been doing up until now. Why didn't I realize that you don't see anything with your eyes popping and your body so tense but that when there's no tension or strain I can see everything in detail. But that's difficult, too, just doing nothing onstage.'

'Well, yes,' said Tortsov in reply. 'Because every minute of the time all you were thinking was, "Why did the audience pay good money if I'm not trying to present something to them. I must earn my salary as an actor, I must entertain the audience"!'

What a happy state to be in, to sit onstage without being tense and quietly look and see. To have that right when faced with the wide-open jaws of the proscenium arch. When you feel the right to be out there onstage, then nothing frightens you. Onstage today I took pleasure in simple, natural, human observation and seeing, and remembered how Tortsov sat in simple manner in our first class. I am familiar with that state in life. There it gives me no pleasure. I am too used to it. But I knew it onstage for the first time and that was entirely thanks to Tortsov.

'Well done!' he shouted at me. 'That's called looking and seeing. And how easy it is for us to look and see nothing onstage. What can be more appalling than an actor's vacant eyes! They are convincing witnesses to the fact that the mind of the person playing the role is half-asleep or that his concentration is somewhere out there, beyond the confines of the theatre and the life being depicted onstage, that the actor is living something else which has nothing to do with the role.

'A wagging tongue, hands and feet moving like an automaton cannot replace thoughtful eyes that give life to everything. Not for nothing are the eyes called "the mirror of the soul".

'An actor's eyes that look and see attract the audience's attention and at the same time they direct it to the object they should properly be looking at. Contrariwise, an actor's vacant eyes direct the audience's attention away from the stage.'

After this explanation Tortsov said:

'I showed you lightbulbs illustrating immediate, mid and distant focal points, which are essential for every sighted creature and consequently for every theatrical creation and the person performing it.

'The bulbs I have indicated so far have represented objects onstage as they should be viewed by the actor. That is what should happen in the theatre but rarely does.

'Now I will show you what should never happen onstage but which, unfortunately, almost always does with the vast majority of actors. I will show you what almost always occupies actors' attention when they are out there onstage.'

Following this introduction little beams of light suddenly darted about. They filled the entire stage and auditorium, illustrating the actor's concentration when it is unfocused.

Then the beams disappeared and in their place on one of the orchestra seats a strong, 100-watt lamp started to burn.

'What's that?' a voice asked.

'A ferocious critic,' Tortsov answered. 'A great deal of attention is paid to him when an actor is performing.'

The beams darted about once more and vanished once more and finally another large bulb lit up.

'That's the director.'

This lamp had scarcely been extinguished before a tiny, dim, barely noticeable little bulb began to flicker.

'That's your poor fellow actor. He doesn't get much attention,' Tortsov remarked ironically.

The dim little bulb went out and we were then dazzled by a spotlight right downstage.

'That's the prompter.'

Then the ubiquitous beams darted about once more. They flickered and went out. While this was happening I remembered my state of mind during the Othello presentation.

'Do you now understand how important it is for an actor to be able to look and see onstage?' said Tortsov as the class ended. 'That is the difficult art you have to learn!'

.. .. 19..

To our general disappointment, instead of Tortsov, Rakhmanov turned up at the class alone and explained that, on Tortsov's orders, he was going to work with us.

So, today was Rakhmanov's first class.

What's he like as a teacher?

Of course he is quite different from Tortsov. But none of us could have anticipated he would turn out to be the man we got to know today.

In life, because of his admiration for Tortsov, he is quiet, reserved and taciturn but when Tortsov's not there he is energetic, decisive and rigorous.

'Concentrate! Don't let your attention wander!' he ordered in a powerful, confident tone. 'Here's the exercise. I will indicate an object for each of you to observe. You will note its form, outline, colour, detail and special characteristics. You will have to do all this while I count to thirty. Thirty!! I say. After that I will ask for a blackout so you can't see the objects and will get you to talk about them. In the blackout you will describe what your visual memory can recall. I will verify and compare what you say with the object. I will bring the lights up again for that purpose. Pay attention! I will begin. Marya, the mirror.'

'Oh, my little darlings!' she said, pointing at the mirror in a great fluster. 'This one?'

'No need for useless questions. There's only one mirror in the room, no other. No other! An actor should think fast.

'Leo, the picture. Grisha, the chandelier. Varya, the album.'

'The plush one?' she queried in honeyed tones.

'I've told you. I don't say things twice. An actor should catch things on the wing. Kostya, the carpet.'

'There are several. Which one?'

'When there's a doubt, decide for yourself. Make mistakes, but don't have doubts and don't keep asking questions. An actor must be resourceful. Resourceful, got it?!'

'Vanya, the vase. Nikolai, the window. Darya, the cushion. Leo, the piano. 1, 2, 3, 4, 5 . . .' Rakhmanov counted slowly up to thirty and ordered:

'Blackout!'

After the blackout he called on me and told me to give an account of what I had seen:

'You gave me a carpet,' I said and started a detailed explanation. 'I didn't choose which one right away and so lost time.'

'Get to the point,' Rakhmanov ordered. 'The point!'

'It's a Persian carpet. The overall background is reddish-brown. There's a broad border round the edge.' I went on describing it until Rakhmanov shouted:

'Lights! You've not remembered correctly, my lad! Failed. You've been asleep! Blackout! Leo!'

'I didn't grasp the subject of the picture because of my short-sightedness and my distance from it. I only saw a yellow patch on a red background.'

'Lights!' ordered Rakhmanov. 'There's no yellow or red in the picture.'

'I was asleep. I failed,' said Leo in a deep voice.

'Grisha!' called Rakhmanov.

'Well that gold chandelier is flea-market stuff with bits of glass.'

'Lights!' ordered Rakhmanov. 'The chandelier is a genuine antique, dating from the time of Alexander I.[1] Failed!

'Blackout! Kostya, describe the carpet again.'

'I didn't know I'd have to do it again, I'm sorry. I wasn't thinking,' I confessed, taken unawares.

'Then think another time. Correct your mistakes and don't for one second sit twiddling your thumbs, doing nothing. You might as well all know, I'll question you twice, four times until I get an exact description of your impressions. Leo.'

'I failed. Twice, I failed.'

Finally Rakhmanov got us to see and describe the item he had given us down to the smallest detail. To do that he had to call on me five times. The nerve-racking work I have described here went on for half an hour at top speed. The eyes got tired and concentration was strained. We couldn't go on working at that intensity for long. Rakhmanov knew it and so split his class into two parts of half an hour each.

We stopped the exercises temporarily and went off to our dance class.

After that it was Rakhmanov's class once again, when we did just what we had done in the first half only with the count down to twenty.

Rakhmanov promised he would get the exercise down to 3–5 seconds.

'That's the way to sharpen concentration,' he declared.

Now, as I record today's class with Rakhmanov in my diary, I am beginning to have doubts. Should I, is it worth writing down what happens in Rakhmanov's classes in detail, verbatim? Or would it be better to write down the exercises in another notebook? These notes could form a guide of practical exercises, or a kind of manual of 'training and drill' as Rakhmanov calls his classes. These notes would come in useful to me for my daily practical exercises and, in time, for my directing and teaching work . . .

Decision.

Henceforward I will keep two notebooks. In one I will continue my diary and will write down the *theory* of art proper, as taught us by Tortsov, in the other I will transcribe the *practical* exercises Rakhmanov does with us. That will be a manual on the 'system' based on the classes in 'training and drill'.

.. .. 19..

Today, Tortsov continued illustrating objects of attention, using lights. He said:

'So far we have been dealing with points of light as objects. Now I am going to show you what we call *the circle of attention*. It represents not a single point but a definite small area with many different objects in it. The eye can jump from one to another but never crosses the circumference of the circle.'

After Tortsov's introduction there was a blackout and, a second later, a large lamp, standing on the table beside which I was sitting, came on. It cast a pool of light onto my head and hands. Its happy glow lit the centre of the table which was covered with knick-knacks. The rest of the stage and the auditorium were lost in an awesome gloom. I felt much more at ease in the pool of light, which, as it were, focused my entire concentration into its circle, beyond which was darkness.

'This pool of light on the table illustrates the *small circle of attention*. You, or rather, your head and hands which are in the lit area, are at its centre. This circle is like the small diaphragm of a camera which shows the tiniest part of an object in detail.'

Tortsov was right: all the knick-knacks on the table drew attention to themselves spontaneously.

You only have to be in a circle of light, in the dark, and you immediately feel cut off from everything. There, in the circle of light, as in your own home, there is no one to fear and nothing to be ashamed of. There you can forget the fact that in the darkness, on every side, many strange eyes are watching you living. I feel even more at home in the small circle of light than I do in my own apartment. There the nosey landlady peeps through the key-hole whereas in the small circle the black walls of darkness seem impenetrable. In such a narrow circle of light, with one's attention focused, it is easy to observe things in precise detail and live one's most intimate feelings and thoughts and perform the most complex actions. You can resolve difficult problems. You can relate to other people, entrust your most intimate ideas to them, evoke memories of the past and dream about the future.

Tortsov understood my state of mind. He came right up to the footlights and said with some animation:

'Note this: the state of mind you are now in we call *"public solitude"*. It is called public because we are all here with you. It is solitude because you are cut off from us by a small circle of attention. In a performance, with a thousand eyes on you, you can always retreat into your solitude, like a snail in its shell.

'Now I will show you the *medium circle of attention*.'

Blackout.

Then a fairly large space with a collection of furniture in it was lit up: a table, chairs and the corner of a piano, a fireplace with large armchairs in front of it. I found myself in the centre of this circle.

It was impossible for the eyes to take in all this space at once. I had to examine it bit by bit. Each thing in the circle emerged as a separate, independent focal point. The only drawback was that with the area of light enlarged, half-tones were created. These half-tones fell outside the confines of the circle, and as a result the walls seemed less solid. Moreover, my area of solitude was now too big. If the small circle can be compared to a bachelor flat, the medium circle could be likened to a family apartment. Since it is bleak to live alone in an empty, cold mansion with a dozen rooms, all I wanted was to get back to my nice little circle of attention.

But I only felt like that while I was alone. When Pasha, Leo, Marya, Vanya and others joined me in the circle of light we could hardly squeeze ourselves inside it. We formed a group that spread over armchairs, chairs and the sofa.

A large area provides scope for broader action. In a large space it's easier to talk about general not personal, intimate matters. For that reason it was simple to create a lively, youthful, impassioned crowd scene in the medium circle. That's something you can't repeat to order. Like the small circle, the medium circle made me experience what the actor's state of mind is when the area of attention expands.

An interesting detail here: all through today's class I never gave a single thought to my hated enemy onstage, the black hole. That's amazing!

'Now, here's the *large circle* for you!' said Tortsov when the whole sitting room was flooded with bright light. The other rooms still remained in darkness but our concentration had already started to be lost in the large space.

'And here's the *largest circle* for you,' cried Tortsov when all the other rooms were bathed in light.

I was swallowed up by the large space.

'The dimensions of the largest circle depend on how far you can see. Here, in the room, I opened out the field of vision as much as possible. But if we were not in the theatre but in the open plains, or at sea, the dimensions of the circle of attention would be determined by the horizon. Onstage the vanishing point is the one the designer paints on the backdrop.

'Now,' Tortsov announced after a short pause, 'I will repeat the same exercise but in the light.

'Now, with the footlights and the overhead spots full up, create the small circle of attention and public solitude, then the medium and large circles.'

To help the students Tortsov demonstrated devices for maintaining concentration which can fly off in all directions when the lights are at full.

'To prevent that, you must restrict the circle of concentration by using the shapes of the objects in the room. For example, the round table with all manner of things on it. Its surface area defines the small circle attention with the lights up. And the fairly large carpet on the floor with the furniture on it is the medium circle.

'Another, even larger carpet clearly outlines the large circle with the lights up.'

Where the floor was uncarpeted Tortsov calculated the amount of space he required by using the parquet squares which have left their mark on the stage-cloth. True, it's more difficult to fix the outline of the circle and keep one's concentration within it but the squares help.

'And there you have the whole apartment, the largest circle of attention.

'And all this with the lights at full.'

The more the area expanded, to my despair, the more the black hole seemed to take over the stage and overwhelmed my powers of concentration. As a result all the exercises we had done earlier and which had given me hope, went for nothing. Once again I felt helpless.

Seeing the state I was in, Tortsov said:

'I'll tell you about another technique which will help you focus your attention. It's this. As the circle, with the lights at full, grows bigger, the area on which you have to concentrate grows larger. However, this can only continue as long as you are able, mentally, to hold onto the circumference firmly. As soon as it begins to waver and dissolve, you must quickly reduce the circle to dimensions you can cope with.

'But it's just at that moment, very often that disaster strikes. Our concentration slips out of control and dissolves into space. We have to pull it back together again and focus it. To do that, use a focal point quickly, maybe, for example from this little bulb in the box on the table which has lit up again. No matter if it doesn't seem as bright as it did earlier in the darkness that will not prevent it from drawing your attention to it.

'Now, once you have latched onto it for a minute, first establish a small circle with the lights full up and with the bulb at its centre. Then select a medium circle of attention with the lights full up and a number of small circles within it.'

We did everything we'd been told. When the area of attention was extended to the limit I once again dissolved into the huge space of the stage.

On the round table the bulb in the box came alight again.

'Look quickly at the focal point,' Tortsov shouted at us.

I fixed my eyes on the lighted bulb with the lights full up, and hardly noticed that everything around it had been plunged into darkness, and a medium circle had been formed out of a large one.

Then the medium circle was narrowed down to a small one. That's even better! It's my favourite and I can control it freely.

After that Tortsov made the transition he had already shown us from the small to the big circle and back again from the big to the small and once again from the small to the big and back again.

This was repeated a dozen times and finally became, to some extent, a habit.

But then, after repeating it a dozen times, in the largest circle with the whole stage lit up, Tortsov cried:

'Find the medium circle with the lights full up, and let your gaze wander freely within it.

'Stop! Your concentration's gone! Latch onto your lifesaver, the bulb. That's why it's alight. Yes! Good!

'Now, again, with the lights up, create the small circle. That's not difficult with the bulb burning at its centre.'

Then we went back, in reverse order, to the large circle, clutching hold, in moments of danger, of the glowing bulb, the focal point. This was also done several times.

'If you get lost in the large circle,' Tortsov repeated to us the whole time, 'then aim at the focal point. Keep hold of it, create the small circle, then the medium one.'

Tortsov was trying to develop the reflex of making the transition from the small circle to the large one and vice versa, subconscious and automatic, without our losing concentration in the process.

I haven't yet developed this reflex but nonetheless have understood that the technique of retreating into public solitude when the circle is expanding can become a real necessity onstage.

When I mentioned this to Tortsov he remarked:

'You will only appreciate the full value of this technique when you find yourself on a vast concert platform. An actor feels helpless there, as in a void. Then you'll understand that to save yourself you must have complete control over the medium and small circles of attention.

'In moments of panic and confusion, you must remember that the wider and emptier the large circle, the narrower and firmer must be the medium and small circles within it, and the more your public solitude must shut things out.'

After a short pause Tortsov went on to demonstrate, using lights, other groups of small, medium and large circles outside us.

Up to that point we had always been at the centre of all these circles of attention but now we found ourselves in the darkness, outside the pool of light.

All the lights faded and then, suddenly the bulb hanging over the table in the next room came up. The circle of light fell on the white cloth on the dining table.

'There you have a small circle of attention outside yourselves.'

Then this circle expanded to the size of a medium circle, outside us. It lit the whole area of the neighbouring room, then took over all the other areas except the room in which we found ourselves.

'There you have the large circle, outside us.'

It was comfortable, from the darkness of the sitting room, to observe what was going on around us right up to the most distant point in our field of vision. I could choose to observe individual focal points and the small, medium and large circles of attention outside ourselves.

These exercises with circles of attention of all dimensions outside ourselves, were performed with the lights full up. This time the sitting room and all the other rooms were lit. We had to choose to narrow and extend the circles of attention outside us as we had done earlier when we were the centre of our own circle.

At the beginning of today's class, in a burst of enthusiasm, I exclaimed:

'If only one could always stay in the small circle!'

'You can! It's up to you!' Tortsov answered.

'But I can't carry the bulb and its shade around with me everywhere as though it were an umbrella.'

'That's not what I'm suggesting, of course not. But you can take the small circle of attention everywhere with you, not only onstage but in life itself.'

'How can that be?'

'You'll see right now. Go up onstage and behave as you would at home: stand, walk, sit here, there.'

I went up. There was a blackout during which a circular pool of light appeared from somewhere and started moving along with me.

I went into the room and the circle followed.

Then something incomprehensible happened. I sat down at the piano and played a tune from *The Demon*,[2] the only one I am able to play.

This extraordinary fact can only be fully appreciated if I explain a little. The fact is I am no musician and play at home secretly, when I am completely alone. It's a disaster if someone hears me tinkling and comes into my room while I'm playing. Then I slam the lid shut, turn bright red and in a word behave like a schoolboy who's been caught smoking. But today I made a public appearance as a pianist and felt no inhibitions at all, played without stumbling and not without pleasure. Unbelievable! Marvellous! How can we explain it?! Perhaps the circle of attention defends us more stoutly onstage than it does in life, and the performer feels more secure there than in the real world. Or does the circle of attention possess a quality unknown to me?

Of all the secrets of the creative process imparted to us during our short time at the school, the small, mobile circle of attention has been of the most essential, practical value to me. The mobile circle of attention and public solitude, these henceforth are my bulwarks against anything squalid on stage.

The better to explain their value to us, Tortsov told us a Hindu folk-tale. Here's how it went:

'A Maharajah was choosing his chief minister. He would choose any man who could walk round the walls of the city with a jar filled to the brim with milk and not spill a drop. Many tried and on the way they were shouted at, threatened, had their attention distracted and thus spilled the milk.

' "These men are not ministers," said the Maharajah.

'But then a certain man came. No shouts, nor threats nor stratagems could distract his eyes from the brimming jar.

' "Shoot!" said the sovereign.

'They shot, but that didn't work.

' "Now that's a minister," said the Maharajah.

' "Did you hear the shouting?" he asked him.

' "No!"

' "Did you see them threatening you?"

' "No, I was watching the milk."

' "You heard them shooting?"

' "No, sire. I was watching the milk."

'That is what is called being in the circle. That is real concentration and, moreover, not in a blackout but in the light,' said Tortsov in conclusion to the story.

'So, try the experiment in the full glare of the footlights.'

Alas, it became clear we couldn't count on getting the job as the Maharajah's minister. With the lights up I couldn't shut myself inside the mobile circle and create public solitude.

Then Rakhmanov came to our aid with a new idea. He handed us cane hoops, the kind riders jump through at the circus. Some were large, others a little smaller. If you put this hoop over your head and hold it so that you are at its centre, then you are in the circle and the rim of the hoop enables you to maintain the shape of the circle within clearly fixed limits. As you pace about the room you can see and physically feel the mobile circle of attention which you have to carry about with you mentally.

Rakhmanov's idea was a help to some, Leo for example.

The fat fellow said:

'I feel like Diogenes . . . in his barrel.[3] Cramped because of my pot belly but tolerating it for the sake of my solitude and my art.'

As for me, I adapted in my own way to the difficult problem posed by the mobile circle.

I made my own discoveries today in the street.

It was strange. It was easier for me, in the street, amid the crowds of pedestrians, the moving trolley-cars and automobiles, to trace the line of an imaginary circle of concentration and walk with it than it had been onstage.

I did it quite easily in the Arbat[4] in the most crowded spot, after saying to myself:

'This is the circumference of the circle which I define as the limits to which my own elbows jut out from under my briefcase and the furthest point my feet and legs reach as they step out before me. This is the line beyond which my attention must not stray.' To my amazement I was able to maintain it within the prescribed limits. However, to be so occupied in a crowded place did not turn out to be entirely convenient and almost had dire consequences. I trod on someone's foot, almost knocked over a street-vendor and his stand, and failed to greet an acquaintance. That obliged me to enlarge the circle to a medium one, pushing it out quite far beyond the limits of my own body.

This proved safer but made concentration more difficult as the people coming towards me and following behind darted through the broader circle as though it were a courtyard. Had there been no circle, in a large space I would hardly have noticed them but within the narrow limits I had set for the purposes of observation, strangers of little interest to me, became, against my will, more conspicuous than I would have wished. They drew my attention to them – as with the small circle of a magnifying glass or a microscope, when every minor detail leaps to the eye. Here's what happened in my mobile circle. My concentration was sharpened, and seized avidly on everything that fell within its field of vision.

I tried experimenting in expanding and contracting the circle of attention, but I had to call a halt when I almost failed to count the number of steps leading down to a basement.

Walking through Arbat Square I selected the largest circle of attention which I could visually hold and suddenly all the lines in it became a blur. Then I heard a desperate honking and a driver swearing and saw the snub nose of a car which had almost run me over.

'If you get lost in the large circle reduce it at once to a small circle,' I recalled Tortsov's words. That's what I did.

'Strange,' I debated with myself. 'Why is it easier to create solitude in Arbat Square, which is huge, and in a crowded street, than onstage? Isn't it because no one cares about me there, whereas onstage everyone is supposed to watch an actor? That's an inescapable condition of the theatre. That's why he exists, for people to look at, and at the public solitude of the character.'

That same evening chance provided me with an even more instructive lesson. This is what happened. I went to a lecture by Professor X . . ., was too late for the beginning and arrived in a rush in the packed hall just as the lecturer in a quiet voice was setting out the thesis and basic premise of his talk.

'Sh . . . quiet! Let us listen!' people shouted at me from all sides.

Feeling myself the general centre of attention I lost my head and in a flash my concentration went, as it did during *Othello* at the first show. But immediately, machine-like, I limited my circle of attention to the confines of the mobile circle, and all the focal points within it became so precise that it was possible for me to find the number of my seat. That calmed me down so much that then and there, in public, without hurrying, I began doing exercises on expanding and contracting the circle of attention from large to small and vice versa, from small to large. While I was doing this I felt that my composure, my lack of haste, my self-confidence impressed the whole assembly and their shouting ceased. Even the lecturer stopped and took a pause. And I enjoyed holding everyone's attention and feeling I had them in the palm of my hand.

Today I understood, that is, felt, not in theory but in practice, the usefulness of the mobile circle of attention.

.. .. 19..

Tortsov said:

'So far we have been turning our attention outwards, towards objects that were dead, inanimate, that had not been given life by "if", the Given Circumstances, our own ideas. We needed attention for attention's sake, objects for the objects' sake. Now we must turn our attention inwards, towards objects that are imaginary, in our minds.

'What kind of objects are these? Some people think that if you look into the mind you can see its constituent parts, intellect and feeling, the power of concentration itself and the imagination. So now, Vanya, look into your mind and try to find the power of concentration and imagination.'

'Where am I to look for them?'

'Why can't I see Rakhmanov. Where is he?' Tortsov asked suddenly.

Everyone looked around and then began to think.

'Where has your concentration gone to?' Tortsov asked Vanya.

'Going through the theatre looking for Rakhmanov . . . and I dropped in at his home.'

'And where is your imagination?' asked Tortsov.

'In the same place as my concentration, looking,' decided Vanya very pleased with himself.

'Now remember the taste of fresh caviare.'

'I remember,' I answered.

'Where is the object of your attention?'

'First of all I imagined a large plate of caviare on the table with the hors d'oeuvres.'

'That means that in your mind the object was outside you.'

'But immediately the image evoked its taste in my mouth,' I remembered.

'That is, inside you,' commented Tortsov, 'that's where your concentration was focused.

'Pasha! Remember the smell of salmon.'

'I remember.'

'Where is the object?'

'In the beginning it, too, was on the table with the hors d'oeuvres,' Pasha remembered.

'That is, outside you.'

'And then, somewhere here, in my mouth, my nose, in a word, inside me.'

'Now remember Chopin's *Marche Funèbre*.[5] Where is the object?'

'Initially outside me, in the funeral procession. But I hear the sound of the orchestra somewhere deep in my ears, that is, inside me,' Pasha explained.

'And that's where your concentration is focused?'

'Yes.'

'So, we first inwardly create visual representations – Rakhmanov's residence, a table full of hors d'oeuvres or a funeral procession and then, through these representations, we inwardly stimulate one of our five senses and finally focus on the result. So, in our imagination, our concentration does not approach the object directly, but indirectly, via another, so to speak, secondary object. That is what happens with our five senses.

'Varya, what do you feel when you're just about to go onstage?'

Our young beauty hesitated. 'I don't honestly know how to put it.'

'What are your concentrating on right now?'

'I honestly don't know . . . the dressing room . . . backstage . . . our theatre . . . before the show begins . . . our first show.'

'And what are you doing in the dressing room?'

'I don't know how to express it . . . Worrying about my costume.'

'And not about the role of Kate?'

'About Kate too.'

'And what are you feeling?'

'I'm in a hurry, I keep dropping everything . . . I won't be on time . . . there's the bell . . . and somewhere here, there, too . . . it's like a vice . . . I feel weak, as though I were ill . . . Ooh! My head is really spinning.'

Varya leaned back in her chair and covered her eyes with her beautiful hands.

'As you can see, the same thing happened again this time. You had a picture, a representation of life backstage just prior to your entrance. It produced a response, past experiences were revived which, if they had gone any further, who knows, might have made you actually faint.

'The objects of our attention are liberally strewn around us both in our real world and – especially – in our imagination. The imagination paints not only things which actually exist but also fantastic worlds which could not actually be. A fairy-story cannot happen in real life, but it lives in our imaginary world. This is a world in which there is an incomparably greater diversity of objects.

'You can appreciate how inexhaustible the material available to us is when we concentrate inwardly.

'The difficulty, however, is that the objects of our imagination are unstable and often elusive. If the material world demands well-trained powers of concentration, these demands are increased many times when it comes to unstable imaginary objects.'

'How can you make imaginary objects stable?' I asked.

'In exactly the same way as you do with real objects. Everything you know about them applies in equal measure to inner objects and inward concentration.'

'Does that mean that in our imagination we can make use of immediate, mid and distant focal points, and small, medium and large immobile and mobile circles of attention?' I asked Tortsov urgently.

'Surely you feel them inside, don't you? That means they exist and you must use them.'

Pursuing his comparison between outer and inner objects of attention, Tortsov said:

'You remember how, time and again, the black hole distracted you from what was happening onstage?'

'Of course I remember,' I exclaimed.

'So remember this, inward concentration can momentarily be diverted from the role by an actor's thoughts about his own personal life. And so, there is a permanent struggle between the right and wrong, the helpful and harmful kinds of concentration.

'The wrong kind of concentration deflects us from the line we should be following, and draws us to the other side of the footlights, to the auditorium, or beyond the confines of the theatre.'

'So, to develop inward concentration, we must mentally perform the same exercises which you once showed us for outer concentration?' I said, trying define the question more precisely.

'Yes,' Tortsov confirmed, 'then as now, you first need exercises which will help you to take your mind off things you shouldn't be looking at or thinking about and, second, exercises so you can concentrate inwardly on the things the role needs. Only then can our concentration become strong, keen, precise, firm outside as well as in. That requires long, systematic work.

'Of course, concentrating inwardly comes first because the major part of an actor's life is lived in the imagination and the given circumstances we have devised. All this is present, invisibly, in the actor's mind and is available only when he concentrates inwardly.

'Having to create in public, as we do, is distracting, and it is difficult, standing before a packed house, to bring all our concentration to bear on an unstable inner object. It isn't easy to learn to observe it onstage with the mind's eye. But habit and hard work overcome all obstacles.'

'There must, of course, be special exercises for that?' I asked.

'There will be more than enough of them in the course of your school and, later, your stage work! Like the creative process itself, it requires your outward and more particularly inward concentration to be continuously active. If the student or actor understands this and is consciously concerned with his chosen profession at home, in school and onstage, if he is sufficiently disciplined in this respect and is always inwardly self-possessed then the rest is easy. His power of concentration is receiving the training it needs even without special exercises.

'But conscientious daily work of this kind demands great strength of will, steadfastness and self-control and not everyone is so endowed. So, apart from actual stage work, it is possible to train one's power of concentration in private life. With this end in view, do the same exercises you did to develop the imagination. They are equally effective for developing concentration.

'When you've gone to bed and put out the light try, each night, to go over in your mind your whole life during the day just ended, remembering it exactly, in the very last detail. For example, if you think about lunch or morning tea then try to remember and see not only the food you ate but the dishes on which the courses were served and how the table was set. Remember the thoughts and inner feelings stirred by lunchtime con versation, the taste of what you ate. At other times, instead of remembering the day you've just spent, recall more distant moments in your life.

'In your mind observe in even greater detail, the apartments, the rooms, the places where you once lived and walked, then, as you remember individual things, use them mentally. This will take you back to a once familiar sequence of actions and the line that day in your past followed. Go over them in detail using your inward concentration.

'Try and remember your nearest and dearest, living or dead, as clearly as possible. A major role when doing this is assigned to your powers of concentration which is provided with a basis for further exercises.'

.... 19 ..

Today Tortsov continued the unfinished class. He said:

'Concentration and objects must, as you know, be extremely stable in acting. We don't need the kind of concentration which superficially skims the surface. Acting demands the co-ordination of the entire organism.

How can we achieve the stability of the object and of concentration? You know how. So let us test it out in practice. Kostya! Go onstage and look at the bulb in the box on the round table.'

I went onstage. The lights dimmed with the exception of the one bulb which became my sole object. But after a minute I came to hate it. I felt like throwing it on the floor I had come to hate it so much.

When I mentioned this to Tortsov he reminded me:

'You know, it's not the object itself, the bulb, that causes us to concentrate, but an idea your imagination suggests. This idea gives it new life and, aided by the given circumstances, makes the object interesting. Create a wonderful and exciting story round it. Then this detestable bulb will be transformed and become a stimulus to creative activity.'

There was a long pause during which I looked at the bulb but could think of nothing that might provide a reason for my looking.

Finally Tortsov took pity on me.

'I will help you. Say this little bulb is the half-open eye of a slumbering fairy-tale monster. Its gigantic trunk is invisible in the profound gloom. In that way it will appear all the more terrifying to you. Say to yourself, "If fiction became fact, what would I do?" Some fairy-tale prince might have thought about just the same question before engaging the monster in combat. Answer the question using simple, human logic – from which side is it better to attack, his snout which is turned towards you, or his tail which is a long way behind? Perhaps you devise a poor plan of attack, perhaps the fairy-tale hero does it better, still, all the same, you think of something and focus your attention on the object and beyond that to your thoughts about it. As a result your imagination is aroused. It takes hold of you and an impulse to action results. And if you take action that means you have accepted the object, you believe in it, you have formed a link with it. That is, your goal has become clear, and your attention has been distracted from anything which is not onstage. But that is only the beginning of the process of giving new life to the object of attention.'

The task facing me seemed difficult. But I remembered that 'if' does not coerce or squeeze out feelings but only requires an answer 'in terms of human logic', as Tortsov puts it. For the moment all I needed to decide was from which side it was better to fall on the monster. After that I started to reason logically and in sequence: 'What is that light in the darkness?' I asked myself. 'That is the half-open eye of the slumbering dragon. If that is so, it is looking directly at me. I must hide from it.' But I was afraid to stir. What was to be done? The more I thought about it, the more I went into detail, the more important the object of attention became for me. And the more preoccupied I became with it the more it mesmerized me.

Suddenly the bulb flickered and I started. Then it began to glow more strongly. It blinded me and at the same time alarmed and frightened me. I recoiled as it seemed to me the monster had spotted me and was on the move. I told Tortsov about this.

'You have finally managed to fix a chosen object! It ceased to exist in its initial form. and disappeared, as it were, to emerge in another, stronger form, fortified by your imagination (it was a little bulb, it became an eye). The transformed object creates an emotional reaction. Concentration of this kind involves not merely the object, it sets the whole of an actor's creative apparatus to work, and uses it to prolong its own creative activity.

'You must be able to revitalize the object and beyond that the power of concentration itself, turning it from something cold, intellectual, rational into something warm, *sensory*. This terminology has been taken into our actors' jargon. On the other hand the term "sensory concentration" is not ours but belongs to I.I. Lapshin who first applied it in his book *Artistic Creation*.[6]

'In conclusion I must tell you that sensory concentration is particularly necessary and particularly valuable to us when establishing the "life of the human spirit in a role", that is, when fulfilling the basic goal of our art. From this you can judge the significance of sensory concentration in our creative work.'

After he had finished with me Tortsov summoned Pasha, Leo and Igor to the stage and performed similar experiments with them.

I won't note them down, so as not to repeat myself.

.. .. 19..

My uncle is ill. I was late for class. I was called to the telephone several times while we were working. Finally I had to leave before the end of the class. If, to these interruptions, you add my own abstracted state of mind, which prevented me from listening to what Tortsov was saying then the scrappy, fragmentary nature of my notes on today's class is understandable.

I arrived in class when a heated argument with Leo was in progress. He, evidently, had been saying that he found it difficult, not to say impossible, to be concerned simultaneously with the role, technique, the audience (which cannot be ignored), his lines, his partner's lines, the prompter and sometimes several objects at once.

'That needs a lot of concentration!' he exclaimed.

'You may not think you can do it, and yet a juggler on horseback in a circus copes with a far more difficult task and risks his life doing it. He has to balance his legs and body on the back of a horse, keep an eye on the stick placed on his forehead with a large rotating plate on top of it and, apart from that, he has to juggle with three or four balls. He has many objects at the same time. But he also finds it possible to call out jauntily to the horse.

'The juggler can do all this because human beings possess multi-level concentration and one level does not interfere with another.

'It is only difficult initially. Fortunately many of our habits become reflex. And concentration can be one of them. Of course, if up till now you thought that, provided he has ability, an actor works on instinct, you will have to change your opinion. Ability without work is only raw, unprocessed material.'

How the argument ended I don't know as I was called to the telephone and had to go to the doctor.

On my return to the theatre and to the class I found Grisha standing downstage with his eyes popping out of his head while Tortsov was hotly trying to convince him of something.

'What's happening? What are they arguing about?' I asked the fellow next to me.

'Grisha said you mustn't take your eyes off the audience,' he laughed.

'We're out there in front of a crowd of people,' the argumentative young man exclaimed.

But Tortsov disagreed and said, 'You must.'

I won't linger over the dispute but will merely note the conditions in which, in Tortsov's view, one can direct one's eyes towards the auditorium.

'Let us assume you are looking at the imaginary wall which should separate the actor from the auditorium. What position should the eyes be in when they are directed towards some immediate focal point on the imaginary wall? They have to squint almost as hard as when you are looking at the end of your nose. But what does the actor do in the vast majority of cases? By ingrained habit, he looks at the wall with his eyes directed towards the stalls where the director, or a critic, or some female admirer is sitting. In which case his eyes are not looking at the angle nature requires when we are looking at a nearby object. Do you think the actor, his fellow actor and the audience don't notice a physiological error like that? Do you really hope to deceive your experience and ours, as people, with such unnatural behaviour?

'I'll give you another example. You have to look into the distance, to the furthest line of the horizon at sea where departing ships can be seen.

'Remember the position the eyes are in when looking into the distance.

'They look straight ahead so that both lines of vision are almost parallel with each other. To achieve this position of the eyes you have, as it were, to bore through the wall at the back of the stalls and in your mind discover the most distant imaginary point and concentrate your attention on it.

'But what do actors do instead? Once again, as always, they direct their gaze toward the director, the critic or the lady admirer in the stalls.

'Do you really think you can deceive yourself and the audience in such cases?

'Once you have learned, technically, to set the object in its proper place and concentrate your attention on it, once you have grasped the importance of space for the angle of vision onstage, then you can look at the audience as though you were looking through and beyond them or, conversely, as though your gaze fell short of them. Until then break the habit of telling physical lies. That throws concentration out of joint when you are young and technically insecure.'

'Just where do you think we should look then for the meantime?' asked Grisha.

'For the meantime, look to the left or the right of the top of the proscenium arch. Don't worry, the audience will see your eyes. When necessary they will turn towards the imaginary object which is supposedly found on this side of the footlights. This just happens, instinctively, as it should. But if you don't have this inner, subconscious need, avoid looking straight ahead at the non-existent wall or into the distance until you have developed the requisite psychotechnique.'

I was called away again and didn't get back to the class.

.. .. 19..

In today's class Tortsov said:

'To appreciate how an actor's power of concentration works more fully, we must discuss it as a potential source of creative material.

'An actor must concentrate not only onstage but in life. He must concentrate his whole being on anything which catches his attention. He musn't see things like some half-attentive ignoramus but penetrate to the heart of the thing he is observing.

'Without that our creative method would be one-sided, at one remove from other people's truth in life, from contemporary events, and would have no connection with them.

'There are people who are observant by nature. They notice and register everything that goes on around them firmly in their memory with no effort of will. They are able to select what is most important, interesting, typical and colourful in what they have observed. When you listen to these people you see and understand things which escape those who are less observant, who don't know how to look, see in life or speak vividly about what they have seen.

'Unfortunately not everyone is endowed with this power of concentration, which is so essential for an actor, and which reveals what is quintessential and characteristic in life.

'Very often people are incapable of doing this even in their own basic self-interest. They are even more incapable of seeing and hearing closely so as to learn the truth of life or develop a sensitive and caring approach to others, or to create in a truthful, artistic manner. That is given to one in a million. How painful the spectacle of human blindness is. It turns people who are kindly by nature into the innocent tormentors of their nearest and dearest and wise men into fools, who do not realize what is being done before their very eyes.

'People can't tell the state of mind of the person they are talking to from the face, the look in the eye, the timbre of the voice. They are incapable of looking actively and seeing the complex truth of life, they are incapable of listening attentively and hearing in a genuine way. If they could do that, their creative work would be infinitely richer, subtler, deeper. But you cannot condemn a man for what nature has not given him, rather you must try to develop and supplement the little he has.

'Work on concentration demands enormous effort, the will to do it and systematic exercises.

'How can you teach people who are not observant to notice and see the things nature and life provide? First you must explain to them how to look and see, listen and hear not only what is bad but above all what is beautiful. The beautiful elevates the soul and stirs its finest feelings, leaving indelible, deep tracks in emotion and other kinds of memory. The most beautiful thing of all is nature itself. Observe her as closely as possible. For a start, take a flower, or a leaf, or a cobweb, or the pattern the frost makes on the window-pane and so on. All these are works of the supreme artist, Nature. Try to define, verbally, what pleases you about them. That will focus your attention more firmly on the object you are observing, make you relate to it more consciously, so you can appreciate it and investigate its essence more profoundly. Don't be squeamish about the dark side of nature. And don't forget either, that there are positive things hidden among negative phenomena, that there is an element of beauty in what is most ugly, just as the beautiful contains things which are not beautiful. But the truly beautiful does not fear what is ugly. Very often the latter only serves to set off the beauty of the former.

'Seek out both, define them verbally, know them and be able to see them. If you don't, your concept of beauty will become one-sided, cloying, prettified, sentimental and that is a great danger for art.

'Then, turn to the study of works of art themselves – literature, music, exhibits in museums, objets d'art and so on, anything and everything you happen to catch sight of, which will help you develop good taste and a love of the beautiful.

'But don't do it with the cold eye of the analyst, pencil in hand. The genuine actor is set on fire by what is happening around him, he is carried away by life, which then becomes the object of his study and his passion. He greedily devours everything he sees and tries to record what he has registered, not like a statistician, but like an artist, not just in a notebook but in his heart. For what he digs out isn't empty, but living, pulsating, creative raw material. In a word, in art you cannot use a cold approach. We need a certain degree of inner fire, we need sensory concentration. This also applies to the search for raw material to use in the creative process. For example, when a sculptor finds a block of marble and looks at it so he can create a statue of Venus from it, it excites him. He has a premonition, an intuition of the body, the work he will create in this or that nicety in the stone, this or that vein. And so it is with us, actors. Basic to any process in which we dig for creative material is a store of enthusiasm. That, of course, does not exclude the massive work the intellect does. But should our thoughts not be ardent, not cold? Quite often in life chance helps to stir the imagination naturally and powerfully. I will tell you about something that happened to me as an example.

'I was visiting a well-known author, a favourite of mine, on business. When I was shown into his study I was immediately struck dumb with astonishment. His desk was strewn with manuscripts, papers and books, testimony to the fact that he had recently been at work. Next to the table was a large bass drum, kettle-drums, a huge trombone and music stands which couldn't be fitted into the sitting room next door. They spilled out into the study through wide, sliding double doors. Chaos reigned next-door: furniture had been moved against the walls higgeldy-piggeldy and music stands set up in the space that had been cleared.

' "Can the author really do his work here, in a situation like this, with the noise of the bass drum, the kettle-drums and the trombone playing away?" I thought. "Isn't this a surprising discovery, one that could attract the attention of even the most unobservant individual and force him to do everything he could to understand and explain this mystery?" It's no wonder my own concentration was fully stretched and working with all its might.

'Oh, if only actors could be as interested in the life of the play and the role as I was at that moment in the things in the house of my favourite writer! If only they would always investigate what was going on around them in real life with that degree of concentration! How rich in creative material we would be! In that case the process of research would be accomplished as it should by a genuine actor.

'However, we must not forget that it is not difficult to be observant when what surrounds us immediately engages our interest. Then everything happens of itself, by natural means. But what happens when nothing rouses our curiosity, excites us, impels us to ask questions, to speculate, to explore what we see?

'For example, imagine that I had dropped in at the apartment of this famous writer not on the day when an orchestral rehearsal was happening, but at an ordinary time, when the music stands had been cleared away and all the furniture was in its proper place. I would have seen the apartment of my favourite writer as the most commonplace, almost petit-bourgeois setting, one that, at first glance, would not speak to my feelings, would in no way characterize the famous man who lived there, would not titillate my attention, my curiosity and imagination, would not impel me to ask questions, to speculate, to observe or investigate.

'In that case you would have needed quite exceptional natural curiosity, acute powers of observation to help you detect the barely perceptible but typical signs and hints of people's lives, or you would have needed technical help, a jolt, a back-up method to help arouse your dormant powers of concentration.

'But exceptional natural gifts are not ours to bestow. As far as technique is concerned you have first to find, recognize, study and learn to master it. For the moment use the things you have already experimented with in practice and which you know well. I am talking about ways of giving the imagination a jolt, which would help you stir it when it is inactive. This technique arouses your powers of concentration, it leads you away from the position of coolly observing someone else's life and raises your creative temperature a degree or two.

'As before, ask yourself questions and answer them honestly, sincerely: the *who, what, when, where, why, wherefore* of what you observe happening. Define, in words, what you find beautiful, typical in the apartment, in the room, in the things which interest you, what best of all characterizes the owners. Define the purpose of the room, the articles in it. Ask yourself and answer, why is the furniture arranged this way and not some other way, the things too. What hints they give us about the owners' habits. For example, using the chance visit I mentioned to my favourite author ask yourself, "Why are a bow, a Turkish shawl and a tambourine lying on the sofa? Who is interested in dancing and music? Is it the head of the house or someone else?" To answer these questions you will have to find out who this unknown "someone" is. How will you find him or her? By these questions, enquiries, speculation? You can deduce the presence of a woman from the woman's hat lying on the floor. This is confirmed by the portrait on the desk and the framed pictures in the corner which have still not been hung on the wall after a recent move into the apartment. Take a look at the albums lying around on tables. You will find many photographs of the same woman. In some of the snapshots she is beautiful, in others deliciously plain but always unique. This will reveal the secret to you, the caprices which govern the life of this house, who it is who is interested in dancing, painting and who conducts an orchestra. You will learn a great deal from this imaginative speculation, the questions, the rumours which have grown up around a famous man. From them you know that a well-known writer fell in love with the woman he uses as the heroine of all his plays, novels and stories. Perhaps you are frightened that these speculations and ideas which you have to accept willy-nilly may distort the material you have drawn from life? Have no fear! Very often the personal things you add (if you believe them) enhance it.

'I'll confirm this by giving you the following incident as an example. As I was watching the people passing along the boulevard I saw a large, dumpy old woman pushing a small baby carriage in which there was a canary in a cage instead of a child. Most probably the woman passing by me had simply placed her burden in the baby carriage rather than have to carry it in her hand. But I decided to take a different view, and I decided that the old woman had lost all her children and her grandchildren and that there was only one single creature she loved in the entire world – the canary in the cage. And now she was pushing it along the boulevard just as once, not long ago, she had pushed her last beloved grandchild. This version of things is sharper, more theatrical than reality itself. Why should I not record it in my memory in precisely that form? You see, I'm not a statistician who needs the data he has gathered to be exact, I'm an actor who needs creative emotions.

'The picture I've described from life, embellished by my imagination, lives to this day in my memory and lends itself to the stage.

'Once you have learned to look at the life around you and to discover creative material in it, you will need to study material which is even more important to you and on which your creative work will mainly be based. I am talking about the emotions that arise from personal, direct communication, from mind to mind, from living objects, that is, from people.

'Material drawn from the emotions is particularly precious. From it is formed "the life of the human spirit in a role" which is our fundamental goal of our art. It is difficult to dig this material out because it is invisible, intangible, indefinable and only inwardly sensed by our intuition.

'True, many invisible, deeply felt experiences are reflected in one's facial expressions, in the eyes, the voice, one's speech, one's movements and in one's physical apparatus. This makes the task of observation easier, but even then it is not easy to understand who people really are because they rarely open up and reveal themselves as they really are. In the majority of cases they hide their experiences, and an outward mask serves as a barrier. This doesn't help the observer, who finds it even more difficult to divine feelings which have been deliberately hidden.

'Our psychotechnique has yet to develop methods for all the processes I have described, and so all I can do is limit myself to some practical advice which may at least provide a little help. My advice is not new and is this, when the inner world of the person we are observing is revealed through his actions, thoughts, impulses which are shaped by his condition in life, observe them attentively and ask yourself: "Why did this person do it this way and not some other way, what was in his mind?" Draw the appropriate conclusions from all this, define your attitude towards the object you are observing and use all this to help you understand the shape of his personality.

'When success comes after long, penetrating observation and investigation then the actor has obtained workable, raw creative material.

'But there are times when another person's inner life will not yield to our own conscious mind, when it is accessible only to intuition. Then we have to delve into its innermost recesses, and seek creative material using what we might call the probes of our own feelings.

'In this process we are dealing with the most subtle kind of concentration and observation, which are subconscious in origin. Our normal powers of concentration are not sensitive enough fully to search out material in other, living, human souls.

'If I were to try and convince you that our psychotechnique is capable of dong this, I would be telling a lie and that would get us nowhere

'All we can rely on in this complex process, when we are seeking out this resistant, subtle, creative emotional material, is our worldly wisdom, our human experience, our sensitivity and our intuition. We shall wait for science to help us discover practical, legitimate approaches to another man's mind. We shall study ways of investigating the logic, the order and sequence of its feelings, its psychology and characteriology. Perhaps this will help us develop methods by which to search for subconscious, creative material not only in our environment but in people's inner lives.'

6

MUSCULAR RELEASE

Here's what happened.

Tortsov came into class and called Marya, Vanya and me up onstage and made us repeat the 'burning money'. We began.

At first, everything went well. But as we approached the moment of tragedy I felt something give, I seized up, I felt tight . . . here . . . there. I got angry. 'I won't give in,' I said doggedly and, as a help, squeezed something hard — as it turned out, a glass ashtray. The harder I gripped it the more I seized up, and the more I seized up the tighter I gripped. Suddenly something crunched. I felt a searing pain and my hand was wet and warm. A sheet of white paper on the table was bright red. My cuffs were red. Blood was spurting from my hand.

I was scared. I could feel my head spin, I felt sick. I don't know whether I fainted or not. I remember the hubbub. I remember Rakhmanov and Tortsov. One of them gripped my arm painfully while the other tied a ligature around it. I was first led, then carried. Grisha was panting heavily in my ear from the weight of his burden. I was touched by his attitude towards me. I have a hazy recollection of the doctor and the pain he caused me. Then increasing weakness . . . faintness . . . Evidently, I passed out.

There's a temporary lull in my life in the theatre. Naturally, my notebook entries have also stopped. There's no place in them for my private life, the more so as there's nothing so dreary as lying in bed.

.. .. 19..

Leo came and gave a very graphic account of events at school.

It appears that my sorry accident has had its repercussions on our studies. They have had to jump ahead and work on the body.

Tortsov said:

'We shall have to interrupt the strict, systematic, theoretical sequence of our programme and talk, earlier than we had intended, about one of the most important elements in our work, the process of *muscular release*.

'The proper place to deal with this question would be when we talk about external technique, that is, about work on the body. But the facts indicate, with some urgency, that it would be more appropriate to address this question now, early in the programme, when we are talking about our psychotechnique.

'You cannot imagine how damaging muscular tension and physical tightness can be to the creative process. When they occur in the vocal organs, people who are born with beautiful voices become hoarse, wheezy, or even lose their voices altogether. When there is tightness in the legs, an actor walks as though paralysed, when there is tightness in the arms, they go rigid, like poles at a railway crossing. The same tightness and all it implies, is to be found in the spinal column, the neck, the shoulders. In every instance it deforms the actor and prevents him from acting. But the worst of all is when tightness takes over the face and distorts it, freezing its power of expression, petrifying it. Then the eyes are wide and staring, cramped muscles give an unpleasant look to it so that it does not correspond to what the actor is experiencing. Tightness can occur in the diaphragm and in the other muscles, which form part of the respiratory process, and disrupt its proper working and cause breathlessness. All this cannot but be harmful to the process of experiencing, to the external, physical embodiment of what is being experienced and to the actor's overall mental state.

'Can I persuade you that physical tension paralyses our whole capacity for action, our dynamism, how muscular tension is connected to our minds? Let's do an experiment. Up onstage there's a piano, try and lift it.'

The students, in turn, with considerable physical tension, lifted a corner of the piano.

'Multiply 37 by 9, quickly, while holding up the piano,' Tortsov ordered a student. 'You can't? Well then, remember all the shops in our street from the corner of the lane onwards. You can't do that either? Well, sing the cavatina from *Faust*.[1] Nothing? Try and sense the taste of kidney soup or recall the feel of touching silk plush or the smell of burning.'

To do what Tortsov had asked, the student had to put down the corner of the piano he had been holding up with considerable tension then, after a pause for breath, in an instant, remembered all the questions, understood them, and answered them in order, summoning up all the physical sensations that were required.

'So,' concluded Tortsov, 'to answer my questions you had to put the piano down and relax your muscles and only then could you could get on with remembering.

'Doesn't this demonstrate how muscular tension impedes our thinking, and the process of experiencing even more? There can be no question of true, subtle feeling or of the normal psychological life of a role while physical tension is present. So, before we start creative work we must get our muscles into proper working order, lest they shackle our freedom of action. If we don't, then we encounter the things that are talked about in My Life in Art. In that book there is an account of how an actor, as a result of tension, clenched his fist and dug his nails into the palm of his hand or squeezed his toes and put the whole weight of his body on them.

'And here we have a new, even more convincing example – the terrible accident Kostya had! He suffered because he infringed the laws of nature. Let us wish the poor fellow a speedy recovery, and let the mishap which befell him serve him and all the rest of you as a warning. There are things you should never do onstage. Get rid of them, once and for all.'

'But is it possible to get free of physical constriction permanently? What did Tortsov say about that?'

'Tortsov again recalled something in My Life in Art about an actor who suffered from acute muscular tension. He developed the habit of regular, automatic self-monitoring. As soon as he walked out onstage his muscles just relaxed, they were free of excess tension. The same thing happened when he was in difficulty.'

'That's amazing,' I said. I envied his good fortune.

'But it's not only acute muscular tensions which distort an actor's work. Even the most insignificant tension anywhere, which you can't detect, can paralyse the whole creative process,' Pasha continued, recalling what Tortsov had said. 'Here's a practical example, to confirm it. One particular highly gifted actress with a powerful personality, couldn't always display it to its best advantage. She only managed to do so in rare, chance moments. Very often feeling was replaced by mere physical tension (or, as we put it, "straining"). They worked a great deal with her to free the muscles and achieved a great deal but it was only partially helpful. They happened to notice that in dramatic passages her right eyebrow was lightly tensed. I suggested that when moving towards a difficult passage, she train herself to rid her face of tension until she had made it completely free. When she had done that, all the tension in her body was released, of its own accord. She became a new person, her body became buoyant, expressive and her face mobile, clearly conveying how she was experiencing the role. Feeling found its way out from the secret recesses of her subconscious, just as if it had emerged from a prison cell. Once this freedom had been achieved, she joyously poured out everything that was in her heart, and this inspired her.'

.. .. 19..

Nikolai, who visited me today, is sure that Tortsov said that you musn't release excess bodily tension altogether. That would not only be impossible, but unnecessary. But Pasha is equally convinced, from what Tortsov says, that releasing the muscles is essential, and must also be continuous both onstage and in life. If not, constrictions and contractions can become extreme and stifle the embryo of living feeling when we are trying to be creative.

But how are we to reconcile these opposites? Is total release of the muscles impossible or essential?

Pasha, who visited me after Nikolai left, had roughly the following to say on the matter:

'In people of nervous disposition muscular tensions are unavoidable at no matter what moment of their lives.

'They will always occur in an actor, in so far as he is human, whenever he makes a public appearance. If you reduce tension in the spine it will crop up in the shoulders, get rid of it there and, lo and behold, it shifts to the diaphragm. And so tensions appear here and there the whole time. You must therefore wage a constant battle against this defect. You cannot eradicate evil altogether, but you can fight it. And you do that by developing an observer or monitor in yourself.

'The role of the monitor is a difficult one. It must, in life as onstage, be tirelessly on the lookout lest excess tension, muscular constrictions appear. The monitor should eliminate these tensions as they emerge. This process of self-monitoring must be brought to the point where it becomes a reflex. But more than that, it must be transformed into a daily habit, a natural requirement not only for quiet moments in a role but, most importantly, in moments of high nervous and physical excitement.'

'What?!' I said. 'Not go tense when you are all worked up?'

'Not only that but, on the contrary, relax the muscles as much as you can,' Pasha affirmed.

'Tortsov said,' Pasha continued, 'that in moments of great excitement actors tense up even more because they do too much. We know what effect that has on the creative process. And so, to stop yourself straining in moments of great excitement you must pay special attention to freeing the muscles, absolutely, totally, from tension. The habit of continuous self-monitoring, of fighting against tension must be the actor's normal state onstage. This must be achieved through lengthy exercises and systematic training. You must behave in such a way that at moments of great excitement the habit of relaxing the muscles becomes more normal than the urge to go tense,' said Pasha.

'And is that possible?!'

'Tortsov is convinced it is. "Let tension arise," he says, "if it can't be avoided. But let the monitor follow close behind and check on it."

'Of course until this becomes a habit, you have to give a great deal of conscious thought to the monitor, and direct it, and this distracts you from your attempts to be creative. But, afterwards, releasing the muscles or at least the effort to do so in highly dramatic moments becomes a normal occurrence. You should work daily, systematically to develop this habit, not only in class and the exercises you do at home but in real life, offstage, which means while you sleep, get up, eat, walk, work, rest, in a word at every moment of your existence. You must make muscular control part of your physical being, make it second nature. Only in this way can the muscular monitor be of help to us when we are acting. If we only work on muscular release during class, we shall not achieve the desired result because the time we have to do exercises is limited, and doesn't allow us to develop a habit to the point where it becomes an unconscious reflex.'

When I doubted whether this could be done, Pasha quoted Tortsov himself as an example. It seems that in the early years of his career he used to be in a such a high state of nerves that muscular tension nearly caused him to go into spasm. But, thereafter, he developed an automatic internal monitor, he created the impulse, at moments of great nervousness, not to tense, but, on the contrary to relax his muscles.

Good old Rakhmanov also came to see me today. He brought greetings from Tortsov and said that he had given him the job of demonstrating some exercises to me.

'Kostya can't do much while he's in bed,' Tortsov had said, 'but let him try this. That's the best assignment for him.'

The exercise consisted of lying on my back on a flat, hard surface (for example, the floor) and in identifying those groups of muscles which were unnecessarily tense.

And, to become more aware of your impressions while in this posture, you should define those places where constriction is to be found, 'There is constriction in my shoulders, my neck and my waist.'

Tensions, once noted, must immediately be released, one by one, searching all the while for new ones.

With Rakhmanov watching me, I tried to do a few exercises flat on my back, not on a hard floor, but on a soft bed.

Having released the muscles and retained only the necessary tension to support the weight of my body I named these places: both shoulder-blades and the pelvis.

But Rakhmanov would have none of it:

'Hindus, my lad, learn to lie like small children or animals. Like animals!' he repeated to make sure I understood. 'You'd better believe it!'

Then he explained why this was necessary. It would appear that when you lay a baby or a cat on the sand and make it keep still or let it fall asleep and then carefully lift it up, the imprint of its whole body will remain. If you conduct the same experiment with an adult, all that remains are strong traces of the shoulder blades and the pelvis, the other parts of the body only come into slight communication with the sand and leave no imprint in it because of constant, chronic, muscular tension.

To become like a child when you are lying down and to be able to leave the form of your body in soft soil, you must free yourself from all muscular tension. The body achieves maximum rest in that state. Rest of that kind will revitalize you in half an hour or so in a way that, under other circumstances, is impossible to achieve in a whole night. Caravan drivers do this, and not without reason. They can't linger in the desert, they have to limit their sleep to the minimum. A long sleep is replaced by releasing the body from all muscular tension, and that refreshes a tired body.

Rakhmanov does this every day between his day-time and evening work. After ten minutes' rest he feels completely on form. Without this respite he couldn't do the work he has to do, day after day.

As soon as Rakhmanov left I called the cat into the room and laid it on one of the softest cushions on the sofa in which its form was clearly visible. I decided it would teach me how to lie down and rest with my muscles relaxed.

I recalled Tortsov saying, that the actor, like a babe in arms, must learn everything from scratch, to see, to walk, to talk and so on. We all know now to do this in life. The trouble is that in the overwhelming majority of cases we do it badly, and not according to nature. Onstage we need to see, walk, speak differently – better, more normally than in life, more closely to nature. First, because our defects are all too visible, all too glaring in the footlights. Second, because these defects influence our state of mind.

These words obviously relate to the business of lying down. That is why I am now lying on the sofa with the cat. I observe it sleeping and try to imitate it. But it's not easy, lying down so that not a single muscle is tense and all the parts of the body are touching the cushions. I'm not saying it is difficult to detect and define this or that tense muscle. Releasing it is no great mystery either. The thing is that once you have freed yourself from one tension another immediately appears, and a third and so on ad infinitum. The more attention you pay to constrictions and cramps the more you create. In this way you also learn to spot sensations you never noticed before. This helps you discover more and more constrictions and the more you do so the more new ones you discover. In a short time I was able to release tensions in the back and the neck. I can't say I felt physically renewed as a result but it did become clear to me how much excess, useless, harmful muscular tension we suffer from and had never suspected. When you remember the story of the tenseness in the eyebrow, you develop a serious fear of muscular constriction. Although I didn't achieve total release of all my muscles, I had a foretaste of the pleasure which, in time, I will experience once I have achieved full muscular freedom.

The main problem is I can't tell one muscle from another. I can't tell where my hands and head are.

How tired I am from today's exercises!

There's not much rest lying down like that!

. . . Just now, while lying down, I managed to release the major tensions and limited my circle of attention to the end of my nose. As a result my head became fuddled as it does when you start to get dizzy and I fell asleep just as my Mr Kat does. It would appear that a slackening of the muscles, together with a reduction of the circle of attention is a good remedy for insomnia.

.. .. 19..

Leo was here today and told me about the classes in training and drill. Rakhmanov, on Tortsov's orders, made the students adopt a great variety of positions both horizontal and vertical, i.e., sitting, half-sitting, standing, kneeling, alone or in groups, with chairs, tables and other pieces of furniture. In all these positions, as when lying down, they had to locate muscles where there was excess tension and name them. It goes without saying that a certain tension in a few muscles was essential for each position, but only in them, and not in the contiguous muscles, which must remain at rest. It must be remembered that there are different kinds of tension. You may contract the right muscles just as much as you need for a given position, but you can push the contraction to the verge of spasm, cramp. This kind of excess is harmful both to the position and to the creative process.

Having told me in detail about the classes, good old Leo suggested that we do the same exercises together. Of course I agreed despite my weakness and the danger of opening an unhealed wound. There then ensued a scene worthy of the pen of Jerome K. Jerome.[2] Great big Leo, red in the face and sweating from the strain, panting and puffing, lay on the floor and assumed the most bizarre poses. And lying next to him there was me, long, lean, weak, with a bandaged hand and in striped pyjamas like a circus clown. The number of somersaults we turned, my dear fat friend and I! We lay down, apart and then together and assumed positions like wrestling gladiators; we stood apart and then together like effigies on a monument. Sometimes I stood and Leo lay down, thrown into the dust, then he stood upright and I was on my knees, then we both adopted a praying position or stood to attention like two grenadiers.

All these positions required the constant release of this or that group of muscles and an increase in the control exercised by the monitor. For that we needed well-trained powers of concentration, which would quickly find their way around, distinguish our physical sensations and investigate them. It was much more difficult to distinguish between necessary and unnecessary tensions in complex positions than when lying down. It isn't easy to pin down those that are necessary and eliminate those that aren't. We need to understand what is governing what.

No sooner had Leo left than I turned, as the first order of business, to the cat. From whom can one learn softness and freedom of movement if not from him?

And he really is inimitable! Beyond anything I can do!

The number of positions I dreamed up for him – upside down, on his side, on his back! He hung from each paw individually and then from all four, then the tail. And in each of these positions you could observe him tense for the first second and immediately relaxing with extraordinary ease, get rid of the unnecessary and fix the necessary tension. Having understood what was required of him, my Mr Kat adapted to the position and gave it just the amount of support that was needed. Then he settled down, ready to stay in the approved position as long as he was required. What extraordinary adaptability! During my sessions with Mr Kat something unexpected happened . . .

Who do you think it was?! How can one explain such a miracle?!

It was Grisha!!!

How glad I was to see him!

Even when I was semi-conscious, lying in his arms streaming with blood and he was carrying me and groaning in my ear, I was vaguely aware how warm-hearted he can be. Today I had this feeling again. I saw him differently, not the way we usually see him. He even talked about Tortsov quite differently from usual and provided an interesting detail about the class.

When talking about relaxation and the tensions necessary to maintain a specific position, Tortsov recalled an incident in his own life. In Rome, he happened to attend a demonstration by an American woman in a private home. She restored the statues of classical antiquity. They have come down to us in various forms, with no arms, no legs, no head, with broken torsos of which only the parts remained. She tried to guess the pose of the statue from the surviving parts. To do this she was obliged to study the laws of equilibrium in the human body and learn from her own experience how to determine the centre of gravity in every position she adopted. She developed a quite exceptional skill in locating the centre of gravity instantly and it was impossible to throw her off balance. They pushed her, threw her, made her stumble, had her adopt positions in which, apparently, it was impossible to keep one's balance but she always emerged victorious. And more than that, small and frail as she was, she could knock quite a hefty man over with a light shove. That was also achieved thanks to a knowledge of the laws of equilibrium. She could tell her opponent's weak spots, where to push him so as to throw him off balance and make him stumble without any great use of force.

Tortsov never discovered the secret of her art. But, as a result of a series of examples she gave, he learned the importance of finding the centre of gravity. He saw the degree to which it was possible to develop the agility, flexibility and adaptability of his body, in which the muscles only do the work indicated by a highly developed sense of equilibrium. Tortsov charged us to study this skill.

Who should I study if not Mr Kat? So, when Grisha had gone I started a new game with the animal: I pushed him, threw him, turned him upside down, tried to knock him off his feet but it was impossible. He only fell when he wanted to.

.. .. 19..

Leo was here and told me how Tortsov had checked on the work on training and drill. It seems some important additions were introduced today. Tortsov demanded that each stance should not only be checked by our individual monitors for the automatic release of tension, but should also be substantiated by our own powers of invention, the Given Circumstances and 'if'. From that moment it ceases to be a mere stance, it acquires an active Task, it becomes action. So, let us suppose I raise my arm and say to myself:

'If I were standing like this, and above me there was a peach on a tall branch, what would I have to do to pick it?

'All I have to do is believe this story, and immediately, because I have a true-to-life task – picking the peach – a dead position becomes a living, genuine action. Just feel the truth inherent in this action and nature itself will immediately come to your aid. Excess tension will be released, but necessary tension will be retained, and this will occur without the intervention of conscious technique.

'There can be no groundless, unsubstantiated posing onstage. There is no place for theatrical conventions in genuinely creative work or serious art. If a convention is necessary for some reason, it must be given proper grounds, it must serve inner meaning and not just look good.'

Leo went on to tell me that in today's class there was a demonstration of test exercises which he then illustrated for me. He lay on the sofa, very comically, and took the first position that occurred to him. He hung down from the sofa with his face near the floor and his arm stretched out. The result was a ludicrous, meaningless position. You could feel he was uncomfortable and that he didn't know which muscles to tense and which to relax. He set the monitor in motion and he indicated which tensions were necessary and which were superfluous. But he couldn't find a free, natural position in which all his muscles were working correctly.

Suddenly he exclaimed: 'There's a great big cockroach! Bang it on the head with a stick, quick!'

At that instant he stretched out towards some focal point – the imaginary cockroach – to crush it and immediately all his muscles fell into place and started to work properly. The position had been substantiated, it was credible – the outstretched arms, the body half hanging down, the legs resting on the back of the sofa. Leo froze, squashing the imaginary cockroach and it was clear that his bodily apparatus had fulfilled the task correctly.

Nature is a better guide to a living organism than the conscious mind and well-known famous 'acting' techniques.

All the exercises Tortsov did today were designed to make students conscious of the fact that onstage, in whatever stance or bodily position you adopt, there are three stages.

The first – excess tension, which is inevitable in every new pose and with the excitement produced by appearing in public.

The second – automatic release of excess tension using the monitor.

The third – substantiation or justification of the pose if it does not, of itself, produce belief.

Tension, release, justification. 'Tension, release, justification,' Leo repeated as he took his leave.

He went. With the cat's help I casually tried out the exercises I had just been shown and tried to understand their meaning.

Here's what happened. To get into my teacher's good graces I set him beside me on the sofa and began to fondle and stroke him.

But instead of lying down he jumped out of my hands onto the floor, pointed and softly, silently began to steal towards a corner of the room where, apparently, he had detected his prey.

I couldn't take my eyes off him. I kept a close watch on each of his movements. So as not to lose sight of him I had to bend double like the 'contortionist' at the circus. It was far from an easy pose, what with my bandaged hand. I immediately used it as a test case and let my new-fledged monitor go over my entire body to look for muscular tensions. At first things couldn't have been better. There was tension only in those places where there should be. That was understandable. I had a living Task and nature itself was performing the action. But as soon as I transferred my attention from the cat to myself, everything suddenly changed. My concentration went, muscular constrictions appeared here and there and necessary tension increased inordinately, almost to the point of muscular spasm. Contiguous muscles also started to work unnecessarily. The living task and the action were gone and the usual actor's cramps were there in full force.

Meanwhile one of my slippers fell off, I bent over to put it back on and fasten the buckle. Once again the result was a difficult, tense pose because of my injured, bandaged hand.

I checked this too, using my monitor.

And what do you think? While my attention was focused on the action itself everything was fine. The groups of muscles needed for the pose contracted strongly but no excess tension was apparent in the free muscles. But as soon as I switched my attention from the action itself and lost sight of the Task, as soon as I became absorbed in observing myself physically, unnecessary tension arose and necessary tension turned into constriction.

Here's another good example which appeared to happen on purpose but which was actually quite fortuitous. While I was washing the soap slipped through my fingers and rolled between the washstand and the wardrobe. I had to reach out after it with my good hand and leave the bad one dangling. Once again the result was a difficult bodily position. My monitor wasn't asleep. It checked the tension of the muscles of itself. Everything was fine, only the necessary, operative muscles were tense.

'Let's repeat the same position to order,' I said to myself. I did so. But the soap was already in my hand and there was no real need to assume the position any more. The living Task had gone. What remained was dead. When I monitored my muscles, the more consciously I related to them, the more unwanted tensions were created, and the more difficult it became to tell them apart and locate the necessary ones.

But then my attention was caught by a dark strip in roughly the same place that the soap had been earlier. I reached out to touch it and figure out what it was. It turned out to be a crack in the floor. But that wasn't the point. The point was that my muscles and their natural state of tension were once more in proper working order. After all these tests it was clear to me that living tasks and genuine action (a real or imaginary life, well substantiated by the Given Circumstances in which an actor sincerely believes) draws nature itself into play as a matter of course. Only she can fully guide the muscles and tense or release them correctly.

.. .. 19..

I curled up on the sofa just now.

Something disturbed me while I was half asleep. There was something I had to do . . . Send a letter? To whom? . . . Then I realized that was yesterday and today . . . today I am ill and have to see to my bandages.

No, it's not the bandages . . . but . . . Leo came and told me something . . . but I didn't write it down . . . it's very important. Yes, I remember: tomorrow there's a dress-rehearsal . . . Othello . . . I'm not lying comfortably . . . I understand, it's all clear now.

Both shoulders were raised because of strain. There were muscles which were severely tensed so that I couldn't unwind . . . But the monitor, scanning the whole body, woke me up. Thank God I've unwound. I've found another centre of gravity and now I'm fine, comfortable, much better . . . I've snuggled deeper into the soft sofa on which I'm lying . . . But once again I've forgotten something. Now I've remembered why I forgot it.

Yes . . . I understand, it's my monitor again, or rather, the inspector. The inspector of muscles . . . That's more impressive. Once again I woke for a second and realized there was tension in my back . . . Not only in my back but in my shoulders as well . . . and the toes of my left foot were clenched.

And so the whole time I was dozing the monitor and I were looking for tensions. They are still there even as I write.

Now I remember that I had the same vague unease yesterday, when Leo was here. And the day before when the doctor came I had to sit down because of discomfort in my spine. When I sat down, it went.

What does it all mean? New tensions occur all the time? Continuously? Why wasn't it so before? Why didn't I notice and why didn't I have a monitor inside? Does that mean it has come alive and is there inside me?

Or rather, because it is active I am discovering more and more tensions, which I didn't notice before. Or rather, they are old, chronic tensions of which I have only just started to be consciously aware. Who can tell?

One thing is certain, something new is happening to me . . . which wasn't happening before.

.. .. 19..

Pasha told me that Tortsov moved on from static positions to gesture, and also how he got the students to this point and what conclusion he drew.

The class took place in the auditorium.

All the students were lined up, as though for an inspection. Tortsov ordered them to raise their right arms and they obeyed him as one.

They raised their arms slowly and heavily, like barriers at a level-crossing. At the same time Tortsov and Rakhmanov felt their shoulder muscles, and said: 'The neck and back aren't relaxed. The whole arm is tense' . . . etc.

'You don't know how to raise your arms,' Tortsov decided.

The task we had been given was quite simple yet no one was able to fulfil it. What was required of us students was, so to speak, the 'isolated' action of the single group of muscles which controls the movement of the shoulders while all the remaining muscles – neck, back, and especially the waist – were to remain free from tension of any kind. The waist, as we know, very often, turns the whole body in the opposite direction to the arm being raised so as to help its movement.

These excess, contiguous muscular tensions remind Tortsov of the keys of a bad piano, which stick together when you strike them. So, with the note 'C' you also hear the adjacent 'B' and 'C#'. Fine music you get from an instrument like that! The music of our own movements would be equally 'fine' if these muscles worked like bad piano keys. It's not surprising if under these circumstances our movements are not precise, clean but like a badly oiled machine. The movements we make must be distinct like the clear-sounding notes of a piano. Otherwise the contours of a particular role will be unclear and the communication of its inner and outer life vague and lacking in artistry. The more subtle the feelings, the more precision, clarity, flexibility they require when they are physically embodied.

'My impression of today's class', Pasha continued, 'is that Tortsov unscrewed us, stripped us down into all our parts, the small bones, the individual joints and muscles, like a mechanic, then washed, cleaned and oiled them and put everything back together again as it was and screwed it all back in place. I feel more flexible, more agile, more expressive now.'

'And what else was there?' I asked, interested by what Pasha was saying.

'He demanded,' he recalled, 'that when moving each individual, "isolated" group of muscles – shoulders, arms, back, legs – all the other muscles should be without tension of any kind. So, for example, when we raise our arm using the shoulder muscles and tensing them in the correct way, the elbow, the hand and the fingers and finger-joints should hang down and all the corresponding groups of muscles should be totally released, slack and tension-free.'

'And did you manage to do it?' I said, interested.

'To be honest, no,' he admitted, 'we just had an inkling of what will happen in time.'

'Was what you were asked to do really all that difficult?' I asked rather puzzled.

'At first glance it was easy. But none of us could do what was asked as we should. They require special preparation. What is the answer? We would have to remake ourselves completely, body and soul, from head to foot and adapt to the demands of our art, or rather, to the demands of nature. For art is in harmony with her. Life and the bad habits that have been grafted onto her mar our nature. Shortcomings which slip by unnoticed in life became obvious in the glare of the footlights and stick out like a sore thumb to an audience.

'On the other hand, this much is clear. Onstage, life is shown within the confined space of the picture-frame stage, as in the diaphragm of a camera. People view this life, crammed within the proscenium arch, through binoculars. They examine it like a miniature under a magnifying glass. So nothing escapes the audience's attention, not a single detail, not the slightest thing. If arms which stick out like a level-crossing are just about tolerable in life they are unbearable onstage. They make a human being look as though he's made of wood, they transform him into a dummy. Such actors seem to have hearts just like their arms – made of wood. If to that you add a ram-rod back then the result is a "block-head" in full meaning of the word and not a human being. What can this "block of wood" express? What kind of experiences?'

According to Pasha, in today's class, no one managed to do the simplest tasks – raising one's arm using the appropriate group of shoulder muscles. The same exercise was done flexing their elbows, then their wrists, then the first, second and third finger-joints etc., with the same lack of success. This time the whole arm tried to join in. And when Tortsov suggested doing all the movements he had described for flexing the arm in orderly succession, from the shoulder to the fingers and back again from the fingers to the shoulder, the outcome was even more of a flop. That's understandable. If you can't manage each of the flexions separately, then it's even harder to perform them in logical sequence.

However, Tortsov didn't show the exercises with the notion we would be able to do them quickly. He told Rakhmanov to do them regularly in our class on training and drill. These same exercises were done with the neck rotated in all directions, with the spinal column and with the waist, the legs and particularly with the wrists which Tortsov calls the eyes of the body.

Leo came. He was kind enough to demonstrate everything Pasha had explained in words. His gymnastics were extremely funny. Especially the bending and unbending of the vertebrae of the spinal column one by one, starting with the highest, at the occiput, and ending with the lowest, at the pelvis. Because of dear old Leo's tubby body the fat rolled from place to place, giving an impression of fluidity of movement. I doubt whether he was able to find the vertebrae and feel them individually. That's not as simple as it seems. We have twenty-four points of flexion in all. It is not as easy as it looks. I was only able to find three vertebrae, that is three places in the spinal column. But we have thirty-four of them.

Pasha and Leo left. It was Mr Kat's turn again.

I started a game with him and observed his highly distinct, incredible, indescribable poses.

Such harmony of movement, such bodily development which you find in an animal, is not within the grasp of humans!

No technique can attain the same perfect mastery of the muscles. Only nature is capable of unconsciously achieving such virtuosity, lightness, precision, such unconstrained movements, such flexibility. When this handsome cat leaps, frisks or darts to trap my finger which I have pushed through a crack, it passes instantly from complete rest to lightning movement which it is difficult to see. How sparing he is in his use of energy! The way he distributes it. As he prepares to move or leap, the cat doesn't waste strength pointlessly on excess tensions. They don't exist. He gathers up his strength so that, at the right moment, he can immediately direct it to the motor centre he requires at a given moment. That's why his movements are so precise, sure and strong. Confidence combined with lightness, agility and freedom of the muscles creates the quite exceptional flexibility of movement for which felines are justly famous.

To test and measure myself against the cat, I went round the room in my 'tigerish' walk as Othello. With the very first step, despite myself, all my muscles tensed and I clearly recalled my physical sensations at the first show, and understood what my mistake had been. Someone whose body is in the grip of cramps cannot feel free and really live a life onstage. If it is difficult to do multiplication sums when you are tense from holding up a piano, how can you master the finest, inner feelings in a complex role like Othello and the subtleties of its psychology! Tortsov provided me with a lesson for life in that presentation – and a good one. He obliged me to do, with great arrogance, things one should never do onstage.

It was a very wise and persuasive proof by contradiction.

7

BITS AND TASKS

Today's class took place in the auditorium. As we entered we saw a large placard with the inscription:

BITS AND TASKS

Tortsov congratulated us on having reached a new, extremely important phase in our studies and began to explain what Bits were and how a play or a role can be divided into its constituent parts.

What he had to say was, as ever, clear and interesting. But nonetheless, first I'll write down not what happened in Tortsov's class but what happened after it was over, something which helped me understand Tortsov's explanation.

Today, for the first time I went to the house of the famous actor, Pasha – my friend Pasha's uncle.

At lunch the great actor asked his nephew what had been happening at school. He is interested in our work. Pasha told him we had reached a new phase – 'Bits and Tasks'.

'Do you know Shpondya?' the old man asked.

It seems that one of Pasha's children is taking acting lessons from a young teacher with the curious name of Shpondya who is an ardent devotee of Tortsov. Consequently all the children and young people have learned our terminology. The magic 'if', 'creative ideas', 'genuine action' and other terms I was still not familiar with cropped up in their youthful talk.

'Shpondya teaches all day every day,' joked the great actor, who, at that moment, had a huge turkey set before him. 'He was at our house once. A dish was served like this one. My finger hurt. I asked him to carve and share it out.'

'Children!' Shpondya said to my crocodiles. 'Imagine that this is not a turkey but a full-length, five-act play, *The Inspector General*, for instance. Can you take it all in, in one go? Remember, not only can't a turkey be taken in all in one go, a five-act play can't either. So we have to cut it up into very big bits. Like so . . . like so . . .'

With these words Uncle Pasha carved the legs, the wings and the breast and set them on a plate.

'Here are your first big bits,' Shpondya announced. Well, of course, all my crocodiles bared their teeth and wanted to gulp down the lot immediately. However, we managed to restrain the gluttons. Shpondya used this example and said: 'Remember, you can't manage a big bit all at once. So slice it into smaller parts. Like so . . . like so . . . like so . . .' said Pasha dividing the legs and the wings at the joints.

'Give me your plate, crocodile,' he said turning to the elder son. 'Here's a big bit for you. That's scene one.'

' "I have invited you, gentlemen, to inform you of some disagreeable news," ' the young man quoted, returning his plate clumsily trying to assume a bass voice.

'Eugene Onegin, take the second bit with the postmaster,' said the great actor to his young son, 'Prince Igor and Tsar Fydor, here's the scene with the two landlords, Bobchinski and Dobchinski for you, Tatyana Repin and Katya Kabanova, take the scene between Marya and Anna,' said Uncle Pasha as he distributed the bits on the children's plates.[1]

'Eat it all up at once!' ordered Shpondya. Uncle continued. 'And what happened? My starving crocodiles fell on it and wanted to gulp it down in one go.

'You can't imagine how fast they crammed the huge bits into their mouths, one choked . . . the other gasped for breath. But . . . no harm was done.'

'Remember,' said Shpondya, 'if you can't cope with a large bit all at once, cut it up into smaller and smaller and if necessary into even smaller.' 'Right! You've cut it up, put it in your mouth and you're chewing it,' said Uncle Pasha, describing what he himself was doing.

'Mother! It's tough and dry,' he suddenly said to his wife with a pained expression, in a quite different, so to speak, domestic tone.

'If it's dry,' the children explained using Shpondya's words, 'spice it up with the beauty of your imagination, your own ideas.'

'Here you are, papa, a magic "if" sauce,' quipped Eugene Onegin handing his father a herb sauce. 'This comes from the poet, the "given circumstances".'

'And this, papa, is from the director,' quipped Tatyana Repina, giving him some horseradish from the sauce-boat.

'Here's something from the actor; it's spicier,' joked Prince Igor, offering a sprinkling of pepper.

'Wouldn't you like some mustard, from a "leftist"[2] artist, to add more piquancy?' suggested Katya Kabanova to her father.

Uncle Shustov mixed everything he had been given with a fork, cut the turkey into small bits and started to steep them in the sauce he had created. He kneaded, pressed, turned the bits so that they were soaked in the liquid.

'Ivan the Terrible, repeat after me,' said the impish Eugene Onegin, 'Bits' . . .

'Biss,' said the child doing his best, to general amusement.

'The bits are marinated in an "imaginary" sauce.'

Ivan the Terrible came out with such gibberish that everyone present, and he too, burst out laughing and took a long time to recover.

'You know this "imaginary" sauce is rather tasty,' said old Shustov, turning the finely cut up bits in the liquid. 'It makes you want to lick your fingers. Even this shoe-leather is made edible, you'd think it was meat,' he said to the embarrassment of his wife. 'That's just how the bits of a role must be soaked more and more deeply in the Given Circumstances. The drier they are, the more sauce you need. The more the one the more the other.

'Now, gather up the tiny bits soaked in the sauce as best you can in one big one and . . .'

He shoved them into mouth and chewed a long time with a ridiculously blissful face.

'That's the "truth of the passions",' joked the children in theatrical jargon.

I came away from Shustov's house full of thoughts about Bits. It was as though my whole life was divided into them, reduced to them.

Once your mind has been pointed in this direction, it involuntarily looks for bits in life itself and in the actions you perform. For example, as I was taking my leave I said, one bit. As I was going down the steps, at the fifth step the thought came to me, how shall I count going down, – as one bit or should each step be counted as a separate bit!? What would be the result? Uncle Shustov lives on the third floor and there are at least sixty steps up to his apartment . . . so, is that sixty Bits? In that case, would every step along the pavement have to be counted as a bit? Too many to cope with!

'No,' I decided, 'coming down stairs is one bit, the way home, another. But what about the main entrance? Is that one or several Bits? Better let it be several. For this once don't let's be stingy as I made a lot of savings earlier.'

So, I came down stairs –
>two Bits

Grasped the door-handle –
>three Bits

Pressed it –
>four Bits

Opened one half of the door –
>five Bits

Crossed the threshold –
>six Bits

Closed the door –
>seven

Released the handle –
>eight

Went home –
>nine

Bumped into a passer-by . . .

No, that's not a Bit but an accident.

I stopped at a shop window. What should be done in this instance? Consider the reading of each book title as an individual bit or subsume looking at the entire display under one Bit?

I subsumed it under one.
>ten.

Having returned home, undressed, gone over to the washstand, reached out for the soap I calculated:
>two hundred and seven

Lathered my hands –
>two hundred and eight

Put the soap down –
>two hundred and nine

Washed the soap off –
>two hundred and ten

- Do the work beforehand → THEN
let go & let it live in you
- Emotion ⇒ energy in motion

BITS AND TASKS 139

Finally I got into bed and pulled the blanket over me –
                    two hundred and sixteen.

And then what? All sorts of ideas were popping up in my head. Did I really have to count each one of them as a new Bit? I had to leave the question unanswered but here were my thoughts on the matter:

'If you go on counting this way in a five-act tragedy, like *Othello*, then, of course, you'll reach over several thousand Bits. Will you really be able to remember all of them? You'd go crazy! You'd get them all mixed up. You'll have to keep the number down. How? With what?

.. .. 19..

I took the first available opportunity today to ask Tortsov to resolve my dilemma concerning the vast number of Bits. This was his answer:

'A ship's pilot was asked: "How can you remember all the twists in the banks, the shoals, the reefs on a long journey?"

' "I don't bother with them," the pilot answered, "I go by the fairway."

'The actor also, in his role, must go not by the small Bits which are numberless and which cannot all be remembered, but by the large, most important Bits, through which the creative path passes. These large Bits may be likened to the areas through which the fairway passes.

'Based on what was said, if you had to describe your departure from Shustov's apartment as a film what would you need to ask yourself first:

' "What am I doing?"

' "I'm going home."

'That means going home is the first large, important Bit.

'But there were stops along the way, when you were window-shopping. In those moments you weren't on the move but standing still and doing something else. So we will count the window-shopping as a new, independent Bit. After that you once again went on your way, that is you returned to your first Bit.

'Finally you went into your room and started to undress. That was the beginning of a new Bit in your day. And when you went to bed and started to let your mind wander, that was a new Bit. So, instead of your two hundred Bits we have counted, in all, four. These are the fairway.

'Taken all together, these few Bits form one important, large Bit, that is, going home.

'Now let us say that when you convey this first Bit – going back home – you walk and walk and walk and nothing else. To convey the second Bit – window-shopping – you stand, and stand and stand, that's all. In portraying the third Bit you wash and wash and for the fourth you lie and lie and lie in your bed. Of course, that kind of acting is boring, monotonous and the director insists you develop each Bit in detail. That obliges you to divide all the individual Bits into their smaller, constituent parts, to develop them and convey each of them clearly, in every detail.

'If these new Bits prove monotonous then you will have to break them down again into medium, and tiny parts and repeat the same work with them until your passage down the street displays all the details which characterize this action: meeting people you know, greeting them, observing what is going on around you, bumping into people and so on. Having eliminated what is superfluous and merged the small Bits into very large ones you create "the fairway" (or plan).'

Then Tortsov went on to explain the same things that Uncle Shustov had explained during lunch. He and I exchanged glances and laughed remembering how the famous actor had cut the large bits of turkey into small portions and soaked them in a 'marinade of creative ideas', how he then gathered all the small bits with his fork into something large, how he crammed it into his mouth and chewed with relish.

'So,' said Tortsov in conclusion, 'from the largest to the medium-size, from the medium-size to the small, from the small to the tiniest Bits so that you can once more combine them and return to the largest.

'Dividing a play and a role into small Bits is only permissible as an interim measure,' Tortsov warned. 'The play and the role cannot be left in such a fragmentary form for very long. Broken statues, pictures that have been ripped to shreds are not works of art, however beautiful the fragments are. With small Bits we are dealing rather with preparatory work but, when acting, they are combined into large Bits, and we ensure they are maximal in size and minimal in number. The larger the Bits, the fewer the number and the more they help us grasp the play and the role as a whole.'

I understand the process of dividing a play into small parts so as to analyse and study them but it is not clear how I then reconstruct them into large Bits.

When I spoke to Tortsov about this, he explained:

'Let's say you had broken down an exercise we did in class into one hundred Bits, that you were completely wrapped up in them and that you had lost sight of the whole and you were playing each of the Bits quite well in isolation. But you musn't imagine that a simple student exercise is so complex and profound that you can divide it into a hundred, basic, independent Bits. Obviously many of them recur and are inter-connected. When you have examined each Bit in terms of its essentials, you will realize, let us say, that the first and fifth Bits and Bits 10–15, the twenty-first Bit etc., are all about one thing and, let's say, Bits 2–4, 6–9, 11–14 etc., are organically related to one another. The consequence is that instead of a hundred Bits we have two large, meaningful Bits which are easy to manipulate. In this way a difficult, messy scene turns into something simple, easy and accessible. In brief, large Bits, which have been well thought out, are easy for actors to master. Bits like that, that are laid out during the length of the play, serve us as a fairway which shows us the right course to follow, and leads us through the dangerous shoals, reefs and the complex threads of the play, where we can easily get lost.

'Unfortunately many actors get by without it. They don't know how to dissect a play, examine it and so are forced to deal with a huge number of vacuous, fragmented Bits. There are so many of them that the actor gets into a muddle and loses all sense of the whole.

'Don't take these actors as a model, don't break the play up unnecessarily, in performance don't use the small Bits but just follow the fairway through the large Bits, which have been properly worked out and brought to life in all of their constituent parts.

'The technique of dividing into Bits is quite simple. Just ask yourself, "What is the one essential thing in the play?" and then start to recall the main stages, without going into detail. Let's say we are dealing with Gogol's *The Inspector General*. What is the one indispensable thing in it?'

'Khlestakov, the Inspector,' Vanya answered.

'Or, better still, the whole episode with Khlestakov,' said Pasha.

'Agreed,' acknowledged Tortsov. 'But it's not just Khlestakov we're dealing with. We need the right atmosphere for the tragicomic incident which Gogol described. It's scoundrels like the Mayor, the cheats, the liars, the scandal mongers like Zemlianki, Lyapkin-Tyapkin, Dobchinski and Bobchinski and the rest who create it. From this it follows that not only could the play *The Inspector General* not exist without Khlestakov, neither could it exist without the naive inhabitants of a town "out of which you could ride for three years and not reach any other country".'

'And what else can't the play do without?'

'Stupid romanticism, provincial flirts like Marya Antonovna thanks to whom the betrothal and the whole commotion in the town occurs,' someone said.

'And what else can't the play do without?'

'The nosey Postmaster, the prudent Osip, the bribery, the letter, the arrival of the real inspector,' the students kept interrupting each other as they remembered.

'We've now taken a bird's eye view of the whole play in its major episodes and have thus divided the play into its constituent parts. These are the important, largest Bits out of which the play is composed.

'Precisely the same division into parts, for analytical purposes, occurs in each of the medium-size and small Bits, which then form the largest Bits.

'There are instances when you have to introduce your own personal actor's or director's Bits into a play which a bad author hasn't properly worked out. Only pressing need can justify this kind of licence. But there are people who are in love with their own ideas who do the same thing with great, monolithic indivisible, classical works which do not need additions of any kind. All isn't lost if these Bits have some natural affinity with the play. Mostly this isn't the case. Then a canker grows within the living organism of this beautiful play and that kills the particular Bit or the whole play.'

At the end of the class, reviewing everything that had been done today Tortsov said:

'In time you will learn the practical meaning of Bits for an actor. What torment to go onstage with a role that has been poorly analysed, badly worked out, that hasn't been divided into clear-cut Bits. How burdensome to act in such a performance, how wearisome it is for the actor, how long drawn out it is, how huge and frightening it seems. You feel quite different in a role that has been properly analysed and studied. As you make up you only think of the very first Bit, in relation, of course, to the entire play and its ultimate goal. You play the first Bit and move on to the second and so on. A performance like that seems easy. When I think of that kind of performance, I am reminded of a schoolboy on his way home from his lessons. If the way is long and the distance frightens him, do you know what he does? He takes a stone and throws it as far as he can in front of him and . . . then he gets worried: "What if I can't find it?" But he does find it and is glad and throws the stone even further with renewed zeal and then gets worried again as he looks for it. By dividing a long walk into sections with the agreeable prospect of taking things easy at home the schoolboy stops thinking about the distance and doesn't even notice it.

'So, in your roles or your acting exercises go from one large Bit to the next without losing sight of the final goal. Then even a five-act tragedy which starts at eight and finishes after midnight will seem short to you.'

.. .. 19..

'You need to divide the play into Bits not only so that you can analyse and study the work but for another, more important reason, which is hidden deep within each Bit,' Tortsov explained in today's class.

'There is a creative Task stored in each Bit. The Task arises organically out of its own Bit, or, vice versa, gives birth to it.

'We have already stated that you must not force extraneous, unrelated

Bits into the play, and you mustn't do that with Tasks either. Like Bits they must flow in logical sequence from one to the other.

'Because of the organic connection between them, everything that was said earlier about Bits is applicable to Tasks.'

'If this is the case then we have large, medium-size and small, primary and secondary Tasks which can be merged into each other. It means that Tasks also create a fairway,' I said recalling what I knew about Bits.

'Tasks are the lights which show where the fairway is and stop you losing your way in any given segment of your course. These are the basic stages in a role which guide the actor during the performance.'

'Tasks?!' said Vanya with much thought, 'There are Tasks, or problems, in arithmetic! We have the same kinds of problems – Tasks – here! No way to understand it! To play well, that's our Task – and our problem!' he decided.

'Yes, that is a major Task, one that will last us a lifetime!' Tortsov confirmed. 'And how many things we have to do?! Just consider, we have to get through the first, second, third and fourth years of the course. Aren't these Tasks? True, but not quite as big as how to become a great actor! . . .

'And to get through each year, think of the number of times you'll have to come to school, attend classes, understand what they're about, the number of exercises you'll have to do! Aren't these Tasks? True, less important than getting through each year. And to get to school each day, the number of times you'll have to wake up on time, get up on time, wash, dress, run down the street. These are Tasks, too, but even smaller ones.'

'And to wash yourself, how many times you have to pick up the soap and scrub your hands and face,' Vanya was reminded. 'And the number of times you'll have to put on your trousers, jacket and do up the buttons!'

'These are all Tasks, too, but the tiniest ones,' Tortsov explained.

'Life, people, circumstance and we ourselves endlessly set up a whole series of obstacles one after the other and we fight our way through them, as through bushes. Each of these obstacles creates a Task and the action to overcome it.

'A human being wants something, fights for something, wins something every moment of his life. Yet, frequently, if his goal is of any great importance, he will not achieve it in his lifetime.

'Universal human problems cannot be solved by one man, but by several generations, over centuries.

'Onstage these universal human Tasks are fulfilled by poets of genius, like Shakespeare and great actors, like Mochalov and Tommaso Salvini.[3]

'Theatre consists in staging major human Tasks and the genuine, productive and purposeful actions necessary to fulfil them. As to the results, they take care of themselves if everything that has been done beforehand is right.

'The mistake most actors make is that they think not about the action but the result. They bypass the action and go straight for the result. What you get then is ham, playing the result, forcing, stock-in-trade.

'Learn not to play the result onstage but to fulfil the Task genuinely, pro-ductively, and aptly through action all the time you are performing. You must love the Tasks you have, find dynamic actions for them. For example: think of a Task now and fulfil it,' Tortsov suggested to us.

While Marya and I were deep in thought Leo came up to us with the following idea:

'Suppose we were both in love with Marya and had both proposed to her? What would be the first thing we would do if that had really happened?'

First of all the three of us chose a complicated series of Given Circum-stances and divided them into Bits and Tasks which gave rise to actions. When the action flagged we introduced new 'ifs' and Given Circumstances which gave rise to their own problems. We then had to solve them. Because of the way we constantly spurred ourselves onward we were kept busy the whole time and didn't even notice when the curtain rose. It revealed an empty stage with the scenery ready stacked against the walls for an eventual evening performance.

Tortsov suggested we go up onstage and continue our experiment, which we did. When it was over Tortsov said:

'Do you remember one of our first classes when I suggested you go up on an empty stage and do something? At that time you couldn't do it and wandered helplessly about, playacting characters and feeling. Today, despite the fact that you were once again onstage without a set of any kind, or furniture or props, many of you felt free and at ease. What was it that helped you?'

'Inner, active Tasks,' Pasha and I decided.

'Yes,' Tortsov confirmed, 'they guide the actor along the proper path and stop him playacting. Tasks make an actor conscious of his right to go onstage, and live his own life, one parallel to the role.

'It's a shame that today's experiment didn't convince everyone, as for some students even today the Tasks were not used to produce action but were Tasks for Tasks' sake. And so they soon degenerated into hammy, showy "gimmicks". That's what happened to Igor. With others, Varya for instance, once again the Task was purely external, almost narcissistic. With Grisha, as usual, the Task was reduced to making his technique shine. All this cannot give good results but merely creates the desire to play at doing actions rather than actually performing them. With Leo, the Task was not bad but too rational, too literary. Literature is a fine thing but it is not everything in acting.'

.. .. 19..

Today Tortsov said:

'There are many varieties of Tasks. But not all of them are necessary or useful. Many are harmful. So it is important for an actor to be able to judge the quality of the Tasks so he can reject those that are unnecessary and decide on those that are.'

'What are the signs by which to recognize them?' I asked.

'By "necessary Tasks" I mean:

'1. Tasks that exist on our side of the footlights and not on the other. In other words, Tasks which are related to the play, directed towards the other actors, and not to the audience in the front rows.

'2. Tasks which are right for the actor as a person, and are in keeping with the role.

'3. Creative and aesthetic Tasks, that is, ones which are conducive to the basic goal of acting, the creation of "the life of the human spirit of a role" and to communicating it artistically.

'4. Genuine, living, dynamic, human Tasks which drive the role forward, and not histrionic, conventional, dead ones which bear no relation to the character but which are there to amuse the audience.

'5. Tasks in which the actor, his fellow actors and the audience can believe.

'6. Fascinating, exciting Tasks which are capable of stimulating experiencing.

'7. Apposite Tasks, that is, ones which are typical of a role and precisely, not approximately related to the meaning of the play.

'8. Tasks which are rich and correspond to the deeper meaning of the role, not ones that are shallow, and skim the surface of the play.

'It only remains for me to warn you against Tasks which are very widespread in our profession and extremely dangerous, automatic, motor, actorish Tasks which lead straight to stock-in-trade acting.'

'So,' I said, in summary, 'you say there are inner and outer Tasks, that is physical and psychological ones.'

'And basically psychological ones,' Tortsov added.

'What kind of Tasks are those?' I questioned.

'Imagine. You come into a room, nod your head to say hallo, and shake my hand. These are everyday Tasks. Psychology has nothing to do with them.'

'What! Does that mean that onstage we can't greet each other?' said Vanya in amazement.

Tortsov lost no time reassuring him.

'You can greet each other, but you can't mechanically feel love, passion, hate and fulfil living, human Tasks with motor skills, without feeling anything, as you are so fond of doing.

'On another occasion,' Tortsov continued, 'you stretch out your hand and take mine and at the same time try to express, in your eyes, feelings of love, respect and gratitude. This is a Task we perform every day, but there is an element of the psychological in it. In our vocabulary we call these Tasks basically psychological.

'And here's a third instance. Let's suppose there was a disgraceful scene yesterday. I insulted you publicly. And today, when we meet, I want to go to you, offer you my hand and ask your pardon, say it was all my fault and ask you to forget what happened. To offer one's hand to yesterday's enemy is not simple by any means, and needs a lot of forethought and feeling. There's a lot of resistance to overcome before you can do it.

'A Task of that kind can be qualified as psychological, and is quite complicated.'

In the second half of the class Tortsov said:

'However true the Task, its main, its most important quality is its fascination for the actor himself. It has to be pleasing, draw him, make him want to do it. Like a magnet it attracts his will to create.

'We call these Tasks *creative Tasks*. Moreover it is important that these Tasks be feasible, accessible, achievable. If the opposite is the case they force the actor's nature. For example, what was your Task in your favourite scene, the "abandoned child" in *Brand?*'

'To save humankind,' answered Nikolai.

'You see! Is such a gigantic Task within the capabilities of the average person? Take a slightly easier Task to begin with – something physical, but attractive.'

'Is a physical Task . . . interesting?' said Nikolai shyly turning to him with a gentle smile.

'Interesting to whom?' Tortsov asked him.

'The audience,' our bashful psychologist answered.

'Don't worry about them. Think about yourself,' answered Tortsov. 'If you're interested in it the audience will go along with you.'

'It doesn't interest me though. I'd like a psychological Task better.'

'All in good time. It's premature for you to plunge into psychology and into other Tasks. You'll get to them later. For the moment limit yourself to the simplest Task, a physical Task. Every Task can become attractive.'

'There's no way to separate the . . . mind from the body. It's easy to mix things up, to get it wrong . . . that's what I'm afraid of,' Nikolai admitted, confused.

'Yes, yes! That's what I'm saying,' Tortsov agreed. 'In every physical, in every psychological Task and its fulfilment there's a great deal of the other. There's no way you can separate them. Let's suppose you have to play Salieri in Pushkin's play *Mozart and Salieri*. Salieri's psychology, once he has decided to murder Mozart, is complex. It is a difficult decision to make, to take the goblet, fill it with wine, add the poison in and offer it to his friend, the genius whose music enraptures people. These are physical actions. Yet how much psychology there is in them. Or, more accurately, all these are complex psychological actions but how physical they are! Here's a simple bodily action for you. Go up to someone and slap him. To be able to do that genuinely, how many complex, psychological experiences you have to live through beforehand! Perform a series of physical actions with a goblet of wine, with a box on the ear, justify them internally with Given Circumstances and "if" and then decide where the body ends and the mind begins. You'll see that it's something that's not at all easy to decide. It's easy to mix them up. But don't be afraid of mixing them up. Use the ambiguity of the borderline between physical and psychological Tasks. When selecting a Task don't define the borderline between your physical and mental sides too precisely. Do it approximately, as it were, using your feelings as a rough guide, but with a constant bias towards the physical. I won't hold it against you if you make a mistake. It can only be useful at the creative moment.'

'How can a glaring mistake be useful?' we said in amazement.

'Because it will stop you frightening your own feelings, because a mistake insures you against forcing mentally. Carrying out a physical Task truthfully helps you create the right psychological state. It transforms a physical Task into a psychological one. As I have already told you, any physical Task can be given a psychological base.

'Let's agree for the moment to deal with physical Tasks. They are easier, more accessible, easier to achieve. There's less risk of careering off into playacting. We'll talk about psychological Tasks all in good time but for the moment I advise you to look for physical Tasks in all your exercises, excerpts and roles.'

.. .. 19..

Important questions came next, namely, how to derive Tasks from Bits. The psychotechnique of this process consists of devising an appropriate name for the Bit under examination, preferably one which characterizes its meaning.

'What's the point of this "baptism"?' said Grisha sarcastically.

To this Tortsov replied:

'Do you know what a well chosen name represents, one which defines the meaning of a Bit?

'It is its quintessence. To obtain it, you must "distil" the Bit, like a liqueur, squeeze out its essence, crystallize it and find an appropriate name for the resulting "crystal". While the actor is looking for this word, he is at the same time probing, studying the Bit, crystallizing and synthesizing it. In selecting the name you find the Task itself. The correct title, which defines the essence of the Bit, reveals the Task lodged inside it.

'To understand this in practice, let's try it, say, in the "abandoned child" section from Brand,' said Tortsov. 'Let's take the first two Bits, two episodes. I will remind you of their content.

'Agnes, the wife of Pastor Brand, has lost her only son. In her grief she is sorting through the baby linen, the petticoats, the toys he has left behind, all sorts of things – relics. Every item is soaked in a grieving mother's tears. Her memories are heart-rending. The tragedy occurred because they live in a damp, unhealthy area. When the child fell ill the mother entreated her husband to leave the parish. But Brand, a dedicated fanatic, did not wish to forsake his duty as a pastor for the sake of his family. This cost them their son.

'Let me remind you of the content of the second Bit or episode. Brand enters. He suffers too, and he suffers for Agnes. But his fanatical sense of duty drives him into cruelty, and he persuades his wife to give away the things and toys the dead child has left behind to a gypsy woman, because they prevent Agnes from dedicating herself to God and realizing the basic idea of their lives – service to one's fellow man.

'Now, distil the essence of both Bits and find appropriate names for them.'

'What is there to think about? It's all obvious. The name for the first Task is mother-love and the name for the second Task is, if you will allow me, a fanatic's sense of duty,' Grisha explained.

'Good, so be it,' Tortsov agreed. 'I don't propose to go into details over how to crystallize the Bit. We'll deal with that when we come to work on the role and the play.

'For the moment I advise you never to define a Task by a noun. Reserve that for a Bit, *a Task must invariably be defined by a verb.*'

'Why?' we asked in amazement.

'I'll help you answer that question, but on condition that you first try and fulfil the Tasks that have just been defined by nouns, namely 1) mother-love, 2) a fanatic's sense of duty.'

Vanya and Varya went to it. He made an angry face, stared goggle-eyed, straightened his back until it was rigid. He pounded the floor, stomping his heels, spoke in a bass voice, strutted, hoping to achieve firmness, strength, decisiveness in the expression of a sense of duty 'in general'. Varya also postured, trying to express tenderness and love 'in general'.

'Don't you find', said Tortsov having watched them, 'that the nouns with which you defined your Tasks drove one of you to play the image of an apparently powerful man and the other to play emotions, a mother's love. You presented people of power and affection but you weren't them. And that was because a noun is a representation, it expresses a certain state, an image, a simple occurrence.

'You see, nouns only express these representations figuratively or in terms of form, with no attempt to suggest dynamism or action. Yet every Task must inevitably be active.'

'Look here, I'm sorry, but a noun can illustrate, represent, define and that, with all respect, is also action!' Grisha contended.

'Yes, it's action, only not the genuine, productive, fit for purpose action, but stagey "representational" action, a reproduction, which we do not recognize and are doing our best to drive out of the theatre.

'Now let's look at what happens if we change the Task from a noun to a corresponding verb,' Tortsov continued.

'How can that be done?' we asked to know.

'Very simply,' said Tortsov. 'Before you choose the verb place the words "I want" in front of the noun you are going to transform: "I want to do . . . what?"

'I'll try and demonstrate this by an example. Let's suppose we are conducting an experiment with the word "power". Place "I want" in front of it. You get, "I want power". A want like that is too general, unreal. To give it life introduce a more concrete goal. If you find that tempting, then the desire and the impulse to action so as to attain it will rise in you. That is what you should define with a precise name, one that expresses its meaning. That will be a verb, defining a living, dynamic Task and not an inactive representation, a concept which a noun creates.'

'How are we to find this word?' I asked, not understanding.

'Say to yourself: "I want to do . . . what . . . to achieve power?" Answer the question and you will realize what you have to do.'

'I want to be powerful, and not have to wait,' decided Vanya, without hesitation.

'The word *be* defines a static state. It does not have the necessary dynamism for an active Task,' Tortsov commented.

'I want to acquire power,' Varya corrected him.

'That's getting a little more dynamic but still too generalized and impossible to achieve at once. Look, sit on this chair and try to want to acquire power "in general". You need a more concrete, immediate, real, achievable Task. As you see not all verbs are useful, not all words drive you to dynamic, productive action. You must know which names to choose for your Tasks.'

'I want power so I can make the whole of humankind happy,' someone suggested.

'That's a beautiful phrase but in reality it's difficult to believe it can be achieved,' objected Tortsov.

'I want power so I can enjoy life, live joyfully, stand in good esteem, gratify my wishes, satisfy my pride,' Leo corrected.

'That want is more real, and easier to satisfy, but to achieve it you must first resolve a whole series of subsidiary problems. A goal of that kind cannot be achieved in one go; you have to go about it step by step, like going up a staircase to the upper floor. You don't get up there in one. Take each step leading to your Task and count it.'

'I want to appear business-like, clever, to create self-confidence. I want to stand out, gain favour, attract attention and so forth.'

After this Tortsov returned to the scene with the 'abandoned child' in Brand and came up with the following suggestion to involve all the students:

'Let all the men put themselves in Brand's situation and find names for his Tasks. They must really understand his psychology. As for the women, let them be Agnes. The subtleties of a woman's and a mother's love are more accessible to them.

'One, two, three! The contest between the men's half and the women's half of the class begins!'

'I want to gain power over Agnes to force her to make a sacrifice, to save her and have command over her.'

I couldn't get a word out before all the women rushed at me and bombarded me with their wants.

'I want to remember the dead child!'

'I want to be near him! I want to talk to him!'

'I want to nurse and cuddle him, look after him!'

'I want to bring him back to life. – I want to follow him in death! – I want to sense him near me! – I want to feel him with his things! – I want to call him back from the grave! I want to bring him back to me! – I want to forget his death! – I want to deaden my pain!'

Marya, shouted one single phrase, louder than the rest,

'I want to take hold of them and never let them go!'

'In that case,' the men stated in their turn, 'let's fight it out!' – 'I want to prepare Agnes, win her over to me!' – 'I want to hold her to me!' – 'I want to make her feel how much I understand her sorrow!' – 'I want to paint the delight and joy of having done one's duty for her!' – 'I want to explain man's great Tasks to her!'

'In that case,' the women cried in reply, 'I want to move my husband to pity with my pain.' – 'I want him to see my tears!'

'I want to hold him even more closely and not let him go!' cried Marya.

In reply the men said: 'I want to frighten her with her responsibility to mankind!' – 'I want to threaten her with punishment and separation!' – 'I want to express my despair at our inability to understand each other!'

More and more thoughts and feelings were produced the whole time this battle lasted and they needed appropriate verbs to define them, and the verbs, in their turn, evoked impulses to action.

In my efforts to convince the women I struggled with them and when all the Tasks my intelligence, my feelings and my will had suggested were exhausted I had the sensation that we had now really played the scene. That gave me satisfaction.

'Each one of the Tasks you selected was true in itself and to one degree or another produced action,' Tortsov said. 'For those with a more dynamic nature the Task, "I want to remember the dead child" said little to their feelings; they needed another Task, "I want to take hold of them and not let go." Of what? Things, memories, thoughts about the dead child. But if you suggest these same Tasks to someone else they will leave him cold. It is important that every Task should appeal to you, and excite you.

'Now, it seems to me that I have made you answer the question "Why should a Task be defined not by a noun but by a verb", for yourselves.

'For the moment that's all I can tell you about Bits and Tasks. The rest I will tell you in time when you know more about our way of acting and our psychotechnique, and when we have plays and roles which can be divided into Bits and Tasks.'

8

BELIEF AND THE SENSE
OF TRUTH

There was a placard for the class. On it was written:

BELIEF AND THE SENSE OF TRUTH

Before class started the students were onstage looking for something Marya regularly loses, her handbag.

All at once Tortsov's voice unexpectedly rang out. He had been watching us from the orchestra stalls for some time.

'The picture-frame stage and the glare of the footlights reveal what is happening so well. You were really experiencing what you were doing while you were looking. Everything was truthful, we could believe everything. The small physical tasks were performed with precision, they had definition and clarity, attention was sharp. The Elements we need for creative work were functioning properly and harmoniously ... In a word, a real work of art was being created onstage,' was the unexpected conclusion he made.

'No ... How could it be art? It was reality, genuine truth, a "commonplace event" as you call it,' the students objected.

'Repeat this "event".'

We put the handbag where it had been before and started to look for something that had already been found and no longer needed to be looked for. Of course, we didn't get what we were after.

'No, this time I didn't feel either Task or action or genuine truth,' was Tortsov's criticism. 'Why can't you repeat something you have just experienced in reality? You don't need to be actors to do that but just people.'

The students explained to Tortsov that the first time they had to look but the second time there was no necessity for that so they were only pretending to look. The first time it was genuine but the second time it was a counterfeit, a representation, a lie.

'Then play looking for the handbag without lies, just with truth,' Tortsov proposed.

'But,' we hesitated, 'that's not so simple. We have to prepare, to rehearse, to experience it.'

'How do you mean, experience it? Weren't you experiencing it, when you were looking for the handbag?'

'That was reality, now we have to create and experience something fictitious.'

'You mean onstage you have to experience things differently from in life?' said Tortsov uncomprehendingly.

Word by word, by dint of fresh questions and explanations, Tortsov brought us to the realization that in the real world, genuine truth and belief create themselves. For example, just now when the students were onstage looking for a lost object, genuine truth and belief were created. But that happened because then there was no acting but reality.

But when there is no reality onstage and you have acting, then the creation of truth and belief needs to be prepared in advance. That means that truth and belief first arise in the imagination, as an artistic fiction, which is then translated onto the stage.

'So, to arouse genuine truth in oneself and replicate the search for the handbag, you have first, as it were, to pull some lever in yourself and transfer the life of the imagination onto the stage,' Tortsov explained. 'There you create a fictitious event of your own, similar to reality. In this process the magic "if" and Given Circumstances, when they are properly understood, help you to feel and to create theatrical truth and belief onstage. So, in life there is truth, what is, what exists, what people really know. Onstage we call truth that which does not exist in reality but which could happen.'

'Look, please, I'm sorry,' Grisha asked, 'how can you talk about truth in the theatre when you know that everything there is fiction, a lie, from the plays of Shakespeare to the papier mâché dagger Othello is stabbed with?'

'If you're troubled by the fact that his dagger is papier mâché and not steel,' Tortsov retorted to Grisha, 'if you really call this crude, fake prop a lie, and if you stigmatize the whole of art along with it and stop believing life onstage is genuine, then set your mind at rest. In the theatre what is important is not whether Othello's dagger is papier mâché or metal, but whether the actor's inner feeling truly, genuinely, justifies Othello's suicide. The important thing is that the actor/human being should behave as though the circumstances and conditions of Othello's life were genuine and the dagger with which he stabs himself was real.

'Decide what is more interesting, more important to you, what it is you want to believe, that the material world of facts and events exists in the theatre and in the play, or that it is the feeling which is born in the actor's heart, stirred by a fiction, that is genuine and true?

'That is the truth of feeling we talk about in the theatre. That is the theatrical truth the actor needs in performance. There is no genuine art without truth and belief. And the more real surroundings are onstage, the nearer to nature the actor's experiencing should be.

'But often what we see is something quite different. A realistic setting is created, decor, props, everything about them is true, but the truth of the feelings and experiencing in the acting is forgotten. This contradiction between the truth of objects and the falsity of feeling only serves to underline all the more strongly the absence of genuine life in the performance.

'To prevent this from happening, always try and justify what you do onstage with your own "if" and Given Circumstances. Only by creative work of this kind can you satisfy your sense of truth and your belief in the genuineness of your experiencing.

'This process we call the process of justification.'

I wanted to understand the important things Tortsov had been saying fully, and asked him to summarize in a few words what is truth in the theatre. This is what he had to say:

'Truth onstage is what we sincerely believe in our own and in our partners' hearts.

'Truth is inseparable from belief, and belief from truth. They cannot exist without each other and without both there can be no experiencing or creative work.

'Everything onstage must be convincing for the actor himself, for his fellow actors and for the audience. Everything should inspire belief in the possible existence in real life of feelings analogous to the actor's own. Every moment onstage must be endorsed by belief in the truth of the feelings being experienced and in the truth of the action taking place.

'That's the kind of inner truth and naive belief which is essential for the actor,' said Tortsov in conclusion.

.. .. 19..

I was at the theatre today working on sound effects. During the interval Tortsov came to the Green Room and talked to the actors and us students. He turned to me and Pasha and said casually:

'What a pity you didn't see today's rehearsal. It would have shown you very clearly what genuine truth and belief are. It just so happens we are rehearsing an old French play at the moment, which starts with a young girl running into the room and declaring that her doll has a tummy ache. One of the characters suggests giving the doll medicine. The little girl runs off. After a few moments she returns and explains that the sick doll is better. That is the scene, and, later, the tragedy of "illegitimate parents" is built on it.

'There wasn't a doll in the theatre props. In its place we took a piece of wood, wrapped it in a piece of beautiful light material and gave it to the little girl. The child immediately accepted the piece of wood as her daughter and gave it her love. The trouble was that the doll's young mother did not agree with the author of the play and his method of treating indigestion. She would have nothing to do with medicines but preferred irrigation. With that in mind the actress decided to make changes in the script and substituted her own words for the lines. She produced solid arguments for this, drawn from her own experience which had taught her that irrigation was more effective and more pleasant than laxatives.

'At the end of the rehearsal she would not be separated from her daughter for anything. The props master was willing to give her the piece of wood but not the piece of material which was needed for that evening's performance. A childhood tragedy ensued with wailing and weeping. This only stopped when it was suggested to the child that she change the beautiful, light material for a cheap, rough but warm cloth used for dusting. The child discovered that warmth was more useful for an upset stomach than the beauty and brightness of the material she already had, and willingly agreed to the swap.

'That is belief and truth!

'That's who we should learn acting from!' exclaimed Tortsov.

'I am reminded of another instance,' he continued. 'One day I called my niece a frog because she was hopping about and for a whole week she took on this role and would not move about except on all fours. She spent several days under tables, behind chairs and in the corners of the rooms, hiding from people and her nanny.

'On another occasion she was praised for behaving like a grown-up at lunch and immediately this naughty child became very prim and proper and started teaching her own governess good manners. That was a very quiet week for the people in the house, since the little girl was not to be heard. Just think, to hold one's natural bent in check, for a whole week, of one's own free will, for a game, and find pleasure in the sacrifice. Doesn't that demonstrate the suppleness of the imagination and the compliancy, the modesty of the child in choosing a theme for her game? Isn't that belief in the genuineness and truth of one's own ideas?

'It is quite amazing how long children can concentrate on one object or one action. They like to stay in the same mood in their favourite character. The illusion of real life which children establish in their play is so strong that it is difficult for them to get back to reality. They create pleasure out of anything that comes to hand. All they have to say to themselves is, "what if" and what they have invented is alive in them.

'The child's "what if" is much stronger than our magic "if".

'Children have one quality we should try to copy. They know what they can believe and what they can ignore. And the little girl I was telling you about just now treasured her maternal feelings and managed to ignore the piece of wood.

'The actor must become involved with the things he can believe in and take no account of things which are a hindrance to him. That will help him forget the black hole and the condition of appearing in public.

'So, once you approach acting with the truth and belief of children at play, you will then be able to become great actors.'

.. .. 19..

Tortsov said:

'I outlined the meaning and function of truth in the creative process for you in highly general terms. Now let us talk a little about lies onstage.

'It's good to possess a sense of truth but you also need to have a sense of lies.

'You are surprised that I separate these two notions and make them opposites. I do so because life itself requires it.

'There are many theatre managers, actors, audiences, critics who only love conventions, the theatrical and wrong onstage.

'In some this can be explained by rank, bad taste and in others because they are surfeited. Like overfed gourmets, they demand something with a tang, something piquant. They like a touch of spice in the staging and the acting. They want something "special" that doesn't exist in life. The real world bores them, and they don't want to have to face it onstage. "Anything rather than real life," they say and, to avoid it, they look for as much distortion as possible.

'They justify all this by learned words, essays, lectures, elaborate, fashionable theories apparently prompted by their researches into the finer points of art. "The theatre needs beauty!" they say. "We want to relax, enjoy ourselves, laugh while at a play! We don't want to suffer and weep." "There's enough misery in life itself," others say.

'At the opposite end are the many theatre managers, actors, audiences, critics who love and acknowledge only the slice of life, naturalism, realism onstage – the truth. These people want normal and healthy fare, good "meat" without spicy, harmful "sauces". They aren't afraid of strong impressions, which purge the soul. They want to have a good cry, a good laugh, to experience, to participate indirectly in the life of the play. They want a reflection of the genuine "life of the human spirit" onstage.

'Add to this the fact that, in both cases, there is an element of exaggeration, when spiciness and contortion are taken to such extremes it verges on deformity and when simplicity and naturalness verge on ultra-naturalism.

'Both these two extremes border on the worst kind of playacting.

'Everything I have said forces me to divide truth from lies and to speak of them separately.

'But loving them and hating them is one thing. It is another . . .' Tortsov was suddenly lost in thought and after a pause, without finishing his sentence, he turned to Darya and Nikolai:

'Play your favourite scene with the "abandoned child" from Brand for us.'

They did what they were told with a seriousness which was moving but with the usual toil and 'sweat'.

'Tell me,' said Tortsov to Darya, 'why were you both so tentative just now, like unconvincing amateurs?'

Darya said nothing, all huddled up with downcast eyes.

'What got in the way?'

'I don't know! I don't act what I am feeling. You say something and then you want to take it back.'

'Why is that so?' Tortsov pressed her, until finally she acknowledged her panic-stricken fear of being wrong and playacting.

'Ah!' said Tortsov seizing on these words. 'You were afraid of playacting?'

'Yes,' acknowledged Darya.

'And you, Nikolai? Why was there so much effort, strain, ponderousness, so many tedious pauses?' Tortsov demanded.

'I wanted to dig deeper, get to the bottom of it, capture the living feeling in myself . . . to be a person . . . for there to be struggle, fear in the heart . . . you have to persuade, convince people . . .'

'You searched for genuine truth, feeling, experience, the subtext behind the words? Is that it?'

'Exactly! Exactly!'

'Here you have the representatives of two different types of actor,' Tortsov said to the students. 'Both of them hate lying onstage, but each in their own way. For example, Darya is panic-stricken by it and so concentrates only on lies. That's all she thinks about. She doesn't give a thought to truth, she can't give herself time to think about it, as her fear of lying has her completely in its grip. That is total slavery in which there can be no question of creative work.

'With Nikolai we find the same servitude caused not by fear of lies but, on the contrary, by a passionate love of truth. He gives no thought to the first as he is completely taken up with the second. Need I tell you that the struggle against lying, just like the love of truth for truth's sake, cannot lead to anything except overacting.

'You can't go onstage and be creative if you have one obsession, "how not to be wrong". You can't go on with the sole thought of creating truth come what may. Only greater lies will come of that.'

'How can we guard against it?' poor Darya asked almost in tears.

'By asking two questions which sharpen our creative powers, as a whetstone does a razor. When you are obsessed by lying, check on yourself by asking, as you stand in the glare of the footlights:

' "Am I doing what I should, or struggling against lies?"

'We go onstage not to struggle against our defects but to perform actions which are genuine, productive and fit for purpose. If they achieve their goal that means the lie has been conquered. To check whether your actions are truthful or not ask yourself another question:

' "For whom am I doing what I do, for myself or for the audience, or for the living person standing in front of me, that is, for my fellow actor?"

'You know that the actor is not his own judge in performance. Neither is the audience. It draws its conclusions at home. The judge is your fellow actor. If you have an effect on your fellow actor, if you oblige him to believe in the truth of your own feelings and there is communication, that means you have achieved your creative goal, and lies have been conquered.

'The actor who doesn't reproduce, doesn't playact but continuously performs actions which are genuine, productive, appropriate purpose, the actor who communicates not with the audience but with his fellow actor, is one who keeps inside the play and the role, with living truth, belief, the "I am being". He is living the truth onstage.

'There is another way to combat lies,' said Tortsov to console the weeping Darya. 'Uproot them.

'But what guarantee is there that another lie will not take over the place you have cleared?

'You must go about things differently and plant a seed of truth under the new lie as it appears. The seed will supplant the lie as a new tooth pushes out a milk tooth. Properly justified "ifs", Given Circumstances, compelling tasks, truthful actions will push out clichés, playacting and lies.

'If you knew how important, how essential it is to be aware of truth and to throw out lies. This process, which we call the eradication of lies and clichés, must occur unnoticed, as a matter of habit, constantly monitoring every step we take onstage.

'Everything I have just been saying about the cultivation of truth is applicable not only to Darya but to you as well, Nikolai,' Tortsov commented, turning to our 'draughtsman'.

'I have one piece of advice which you should bear closely in mind. Never exaggerate the striving for truth or the significance of lies. A passion for the first leads to playacting truth for truth's sake. That is the worst of all lies. As far as extreme fear of lies in concerned that creates an unnatural caution which is also one of the biggest theatrical "lies". You must relate to this last, as to truth onstage, calmly, equitably, without nit-picking. Truth is needed in the theatre in so far as it can sincerely be believed, in so far as it helps convince you and your fellow actor, and enables you to fulfil your appointed creative tasks confidently.

'You can derive benefit from lies too if you approach them intelligently.

'A lie is a tuning fork for what the actor has no need to do.

'It's no great disaster if momentarily we make a mistake, and hit the wrong note. The important thing is to use this as a tuning fork to define the limits of the credible, that is, of truth, so that at the very moment we go wrong it sets us back on the right path. Under these circumstances a momentary upset, a wrong note are of advantage to the actor, showing him the limits beyond which he should not go.

'This process of self-monitoring is essential during creative work, and it must be constant, permanent.

'When he is excited, because he is creating publicly onstage, the actor always wants to give more feeling than he actually has. But where is he to get it? We don't have reserve stores of emotions to keep our experiencing in the theatre consistent. You can underplay or overplay an action, make more effort than is necessary, in an apparent expression of feeling. But that doesn't strengthen feeling, it destroys it. It is external playacting, exaggeration.

'The protests made by one's sense of truth prove to be a better regulator at such moments. These protests should be heeded even at moments when the actor is inwardly living the role as he should. At such moments, not infrequently, because of nerves, his external, expressive apparatus makes excessive efforts and unconsciously starts to playact. This inevitably leads to lies.'

At the end of the class Tortsov talked about an actor who possessed a very subtle sense of truth when he was sitting in the auditorium watching other people acting. But when he went onstage and became a character in a play, he lost his sense of truth.

'It is difficult to believe', said Tortsov, 'that one and the same person who had just been condemning the falsity and playacting of his colleagues with such subtle understanding, once up onstage made even greater mistakes than those he had just been criticizing.

'In such actors, and others like them, the sense of truth as a member of the audience and as an actor in a performance are different.'

.. .. 19..

In class Tortsov said:

'The best thing for an actor is when truth and belief in the reality of what he is doing arise spontaneously.

'But what about when that doesn't happen?

'Then you have to search for and create this truth and belief yourselves using your psychotechnique.

'You can't create something you yourselves don't believe or consider to be untrue.

'Where are you to search, and how are you to create truth and belief within yourselves? Won't it be in your inner feelings and actions, that is in your mind, as an actor and a human? But feelings are too complex, elusive, capricious, they are difficult to pin down. Truth and belief either arise spontaneously in the mind or are created by the complex working of our psychotechnique. The easiest thing of all is to find and stimulate truth and belief in the body, with the tiniest, simplest physical Tasks and actions. They are accessible, stable, visible, tangible, they submit to the conscious mind and to orders. And they are also easy to pin down. That is why we turn to them in the first instance so that with their help we can start creating the role.

'Let's do an experiment'.

.. .. 19..

'Kostya, Vanya! Go onstage and play the exercise in which you were least successful. I think it was the "burning money".

'You can't get a grip on it mainly because you want to believe, all in one go, in all the terrible things I thought up for the story. "In one go" led you to acting "in general". Try to overcome a difficult exercise in parts, starting with the simplest physical actions, but of course in full accord with the whole. If each, tiny, subsidiary action is related to the truth, then the whole will flow properly and you will believe it is genuine.'

'Please give me some prop money,' I said to the stagehand standing in the wings.

'You don't need it. Use emptiness. Mime it,' ordered Tortsov.

I started counting non-existent money.

'I don't believe you!' said Tortsov stopping me as soon as I stretched out to take the imaginary packet.

'What is it you don't believe?'

'You didn't even look at what you were touching.'

I looked at where the imaginary packet was, saw nothing, stretched out my hand and pulled it back again.

'You might at least have the courtesy to press your fingers together to so you don't drop the packet. Don't throw it down, put it down. It only takes a second. Don't skimp it if you want to justify and physically believe in what you are doing. Who would untie it that way? Find the end of the piece of string which tied the packet together. Not like that! You can't do it in one go. In the majority of cases the ends are tied and tucked under the string so that the packet can't come undone. It's not so easy to straighten out the ends. That's it,' Tortsov said approvingly. 'Now count each packet.

'Oof! How quickly you did all that. Not even the most highly experienced cashier alive could count old, crumpled notes that fast.

'You see into what realistic detail, into what small truths we have to go to convince our own nature physically of what we are doing onstage.'

Action by action, second by second, logically, in sequence, Tortsov guided what I was doing physically. While I was counting the imaginary money I gradually remembered how, in what order, in what sequence this is done in life.

As a result of all the logical actions Tortsov suggested to me I developed a new attitude towards working with 'nothing'. It exactly filled the role of the imaginary money, or rather, enabled me to focus on an object which in reality did not exist. They are not the same thing at all – waving one's fingers meaninglessly and counting the dirty, used rouble notes which, in my mind, I was looking at.

As soon as I felt the truth of physical action I felt at home on the stage.

And at the same time, spontaneously, impromptu actions occurred. I meticulously untied the string and put it on the table beside me. This tiny action encouraged my sense of truth, and produced a whole series of fresh impromptu actions after it. For example, before counting the packets I tapped them on the table for a long time to make sure the edges were even, to make them tidy. Vanya, who was beside me while I was doing this, understood my action and laughed.

'What is it?' I asked him.

'That came off very well,' he explained.

'That's what we call a total and thoroughly justified physical action in which the actor, as a human being, can believe!' Tortsov shouted from the stalls.

After a short pause Tortsov began talking:

'This summer, after a long break, I was staying near Serpukhov[1] again, in a villa in which I had spent my summer holidays several years earlier. The small house, in which I rented a room, was some way from the station. But if you went in a straight line, through the gully, the apiary and the woods you cut the distance several fold. At one time, because I had passed that way so often, I had beaten a path which, during the years I had been absent, had become overgrown with tall grass. I had to blaze the trail anew with my own feet. It was difficult at first. I was always straying from the right direction and ending up on the road which was full of ruts and potholes because of the heavy traffic. This road led in the opposite direction to the station. I had to turn back, retrace my steps and follow the path further. I was guided by the familiar pattern of trees and stumps, the rise and fall of the land. My memory of them was intact and guided me.

'Finally a long line of flattened grass appeared and I walked along it to the station and back.

'My frequent trips to town caused me to take this way almost daily and so a path was very soon made.'

After another pause Tortsov continued:

'In "burning money" with Kostya today we plotted a line of physical actions and gave life to it. That line is, in its way, a kind of "path". You know it well enough in real life but onstage you have to beat it anew.

'Alongside this, the right line, Kostya has another, wrong line, ingrained by habit. It is made up of clichés and conventions. He turned off along it momentarily against his will. This wrong line can be compared to a country road pitted with ruts. The road led Kostya momentarily away from the right direction and into mere stock-in-trade. To avoid this, Kostya, like me in the woods, has to discover and lay down once again the right line of physical actions. This can be compared to the trampled grass in the wood. Now Kostya has to "tread it down" further until it has become a "path" which someday will fix the right path for the role once and for all.

'The secret of my method is clear. It's not a matter of the physical actions as such, but the truth and belief these actions help us to arouse and feel.

'Like small, medium-size, big and bigger Bits, actions and so on, in our business there are small, big and bigger truths and moments of belief. If you can't grasp the truth of a large-scale action at one go, then you will have to divide it into parts and try at least to believe in the smallest of them.

'That's what I did when I beat my path through the gully and the wood. There I was guided by the smallest signs, memories of the right path (tree stumps, ditches, knolls). Likewise, with Kostya, I proceeded not by the biggest but by the smallest physical actions, discovering small truths and moments of belief. One gave rise to another, both of them produced a third, a fourth, etc. Does that seem a small thing to you? You're wrong, it's enormous. Do you know that often by getting the feel of one small truth and one moment of belief in the genuineness of the action, an actor can suddenly see things clearly, can feel himself in the role and believe in the greater truth of the whole play. A moment of living truth suggests the right tone for the entire role.

'I could give you so many examples of this kind from my own experience. Something unexpected happens while an actor is giving a routine performance. A chair falls over, or an actress drops her handkerchief and he has to pick it up, or the setting has changed and unexpectedly he has to move the furniture round. Just as a breath of fresh air freshens a stuffy room, so an accident, breaking through from real life onto the convention-ridden stage gives life to dead, clichéd acting.

'The actor has to pick up the handkerchief or the chair impromptu as it was unrehearsed. An unexpected action of that kind is performed not in a theatrical but in a human fashion, and creates a genuine, life-like truth in which you have to believe. Truth of that kind is acutely different from convention-based, theatrical "acting". It produces living action onstage, drawn from the real world from which the actor has strayed. Often such a moment is enough to set you in the right direction or to produce a new creative impetus, a breakthrough. A revitalizing current flows through the whole scene and perhaps through the whole act or the whole play. It depends on the actor, whether to accept an accidental moment, that has burst in from the real world, and include it in the role, or deny it and step outside of the role.

'In other words, the actor can handle the accident as the character in the play and incorporate it for this once into the role. But he can also step outside his role for a second, remove the accident which occurred against his will (i.e. picking up the handkerchief or the chair) and then resume his convention-based onstage life which had been interrupted.

'If one small truth and moment of belief can put an actor in a creative state then a whole series of such moments, in logical succession, and in sequence, can create a very big truth and a whole, long period of belief. They will support and reinforce each other.

'Don't neglect small physical actions but learn to use them for the sake of truth and your belief in the genuineness of what you are doing.'

.. .. 19..

Tortsov said:

'You know that small physical actions, small physical truths and moments of belief assume great importance not only in simple passages, but also in very intense, climactic moments when you are experiencing tragedy and drama. For example, what do you do when you are playing the second, dramatic half of the "burning money"?' said Tortsov to me. 'You hurl yourself at the fireplace, you snatch the packet of money from the blaze, then you bring the hunchback round, try to save the little child, etc. These are the successive phases of physical action through which the physical life of the role develops naturally and in sequence during the most tragic part of the exercise.

'Here's another example:

'What do a close friend or the wife of a dying man do? They make sure the sick man is quiet, carry out the doctor's orders, take his temperature, apply compresses and plasters. All these small actions acquire a distinct importance in the life of the sick man, and so they are carried out as though they were sacred, you put all your heart into them. And not surprisingly, for when fighting with death, carelessness is a crime, it could kill the patient.

'And here's a third example:

'What is Lady Macbeth doing at the climax of the tragedy? A simple physical action, washing drops of blood off her hands.'

'Look, please, I'm sorry,' said Grisha hurriedly intervening on Shakespeare's behalf. 'Do you really mean to say that a great writer created his masterpiece so that she could wash her hands or do other naturalistic actions?'

'Such a disappointment, isn't it?' said Tortsov ironically. 'Not to think about the "tragic", to abandon the kind of tension, the kind of histrionics you're so fond of, "sentimentality", "inspiration". Forget about the audience and the effect you're having on them and instead of trying to charm them, confine yourself to small, physical, realistic actions, small physical truths and a sincere belief in their genuineness!

'In time you will understand that this has to be done not for the sake of naturalism but for truth of feeling, so as to believe it is genuine, and that in life itself experiences of a high order are very often revealed in the most ordinary, little, naturalistic actions.

'We actors need to make full use of the fact that these physical actions acquire great force within the context of the Given Circumstances. Then there is an interaction between mind and body, action and feeling, thanks to which the outer helps the inner, while the inner stimulates the outer. Washing the blood off helps Lady Macbeth fulfil her ambitious thoughts and her ambitious thoughts oblige her to wash off the blood. It is no accident that in her soliloquy Lady Macbeth alternates between washing her hands and remembering individual moments of Banquo's[2] murder. The small, real, physical action of washing off the drops acquires great significance in Lady Macbeth's subsequent life and powerful intentions (ambitious thoughts) need the help of small, physical actions.

'But there is another, simpler, practical reason why the truth of physical action acquires great significance in moments of tragic climax. The fact is that, in moments of intense tragedy, the actor has to reach the highest point of creative tension. That is difficult. Indeed, an enormous effort is needed to reach a state of abandon when you have no natural urges to drive you on! Is it easy, against your will, to reach that sublime state which only occurs when you are completely carried away by the thing you are creating? Such an approach goes against nature, and it is all too easy to jump the track and come up with mere stock-in-trade, histrionics and playacting, when you have muscular tension in place of genuine feeling. Playacting is easy, it's familiar, you're so used to it that it's become mechanical, a habit. It's the line of least resistance.

'To avoid making this mistake, you need to take hold of something real, stable, organic, tangible. For that we need some clear, clean, exciting but easily doable physical action that typifies the moment we are experiencing. This sets us on the right path naturally, automatically and doesn't let us veer off on wrong paths at moments when creation is difficult.

'It is precisely in moments when we experience tragedy and drama in a heightened manner that truthful, simple physical actions become very important. The simpler, more accessible, more doable they are, the easier they are to hold on to in difficult moments. The right Task leads to the right goal. This prevents the actor from taking the line of least resistance, that is of clichés and stock-in-trade.

'There is another important circumstance which gives even greater force and meaning to simple, physical actions.

'It is this: tell an actor that his role, his Task, his actions are psychological, profound, tragic and he will immediately tense up and playact passion, "tear it to tatters" or rummage around in his soul and press some feeling or other into service to no purpose whatsoever.

'But if you give the actor the simplest, physical Task within interesting, exciting Given Circumstances, then he will start performing it, without scaring himself, and without thinking whether there is psychology, tragedy and drama in what he is doing.

'Then the feeling of truth comes into its own and that is one of the most important moments in the creative act, which an actor's psychotechnique leads up to. Thanks to this kind of approach, feeling is not forced and develops naturally and fully.

'With major authors even the smallest physical tasks occur within highly significant Given Circumstances that contain tempting stimuli for emotion.

'So, in tragedy, as you can see, you must do the opposite to what Nikolai did, namely, don't drag feelings out of yourself but think how to perform all the physical actions within the Given Circumstances throughout the play as you should.

'Tragic moments must be approached not only without strain and forcing, like Nikolai, but also without being twitchy and jumpy, like Darya, and not in one go either, as with the majority of actors, but gradually, in sequence, logically, sensing every small or large truth of physical action in turn and believing in them.

'When you have mastered this technique of approaching feeling, you will develop a completely different, a proper attitude towards tragic and dramatic climax. They will no longer scare you.

'Often the difference between drama, tragedy, farce and comedy only consists in the Given Circumstances in which the actions occur. In all other respects physical life remains the same. People sit, walk, eat in tragedy and farce alike.

'But perhaps that's of no interest to us? The important thing is why it is done. The important things are the Given Circumstances, the "if". They bring an action alive, justify it. An action acquires a quite different meaning when it occurs in tragic or other circumstances in the play. In the first case it is transformed into a great event, an exploit. Of course this happens with the approval of truth and belief. We like small and large physical actions because of their clear, tangible truth. They create the life of our body and that is half the life of the role.

'We like physical actions because they lead us easily and imperceptibly to the very life of the role, to the feelings it contains. We like physical actions, too, because they help us fix our concentration on the stage, the play, the role and focus on the line of the role we have firmly established.'

.. .. 19..

Tortsov told Vanya and me to repeat the 'burning money' from the previous class. I was in luck, I was able to recall what I had done comparatively quickly and performed all the physical actions.

It's so good to feel the truth onstage not only in your mind but in your body as well! You can feel the ground under your feet, you can stand firm on it and be sure that no one will knock you over!

'What a joy it is to believe in yourself onstage and to feel that others believe you too!' I exclaimed when we had finished playing.

'And what helped you find that truth?' Tortsov asked.

'An imaginary object! Emptiness.'

'Or, rather, physical actions, using emptiness, mime,' Tortsov corrected me. 'That's an important factor and we shall have to speak of it many times more. Consider this, your attention, which had been scattered all over the theatre, is riveted by a non-existent object. This object is onstage, at the centre of the play, it cuts the actor off from the audience, and from everything not on the stage. Miming an object focuses the actor's concentration first on himself then on physical actions and obliges him to observe them.

'Miming also helped you to break down large physical actions into their constituent parts and study each of them separately. Once, in your very early childhood, when you were learning how to look, hear, walk, paying great attention, you studied every small, constituent act. You will have to do the same thing onstage. In your artistic childhood you have to learn everything from scratch as well.

'And what else helped you achieve the truth in the "burning money",' Tortsov enquired.

I was silent. I couldn't immediately think what it was.

'You were helped by the logic and sequence of the actions which I got out of you. That is also a most important factor which we must spend quite some time on.

'Logic and sequence are also part of physical actions. They give them order, stability, meaning and help stimulate action which is genuine, productive and purposeful.

'In real life we don't think about it. It all happens spontaneously. When we are given money at the post office or the bank we don't count it as Kostya did in the scene before I corrected him. At the bank we count money as Kostya did after I had worked with him.'

'Yes! At the bank you can miscount a hundred-rouble note or a two-hundred, and everyone's afraid of doing that, but counting up a non-existent object isn't frightening. There's no real harm done onstage,' the students reasoned.

'In life, because the same working actions are frequently repeated you get what I might call an "automatic" logic and sequence of physical and other actions,' Tortsov explained. 'The subconscious vigilance exercised by our powers of concentration, the instinctive self-monitoring we require appear spontaneously, and invisibly guide us.'

'The logic and se . . . quence of ac . . . tions . . . vi . . . gi . . . lance self- . . . mon . . . itoring,' repeated Vanya, drumming these curious words into his head.

'I'll explain to you what "the logic and sequence of actions" means, their "automatic nature" and other terms which frighten you. Listen to me:

'If you have to write a letter you don't start by sealing the envelope. Isn't that so? You prepare paper, pen, ink, think what it is you want to say and commit your ideas to paper. Only after all that do you take an envelope, address it and seal it. Why do you do it that way? Because you are being logical and sequential in your actions.

'But have you seen the way actors write letters onstage? They rush to the table, twiddle the pen wildly in the air over the first scrap of paper that comes to hand, somehow cram the barely folded paper into an envelope, touch the letter to their lips and . . . that's it.

'Actors who behave in that way have neither logic nor sequence in their actions. Do you understand?'

'I understand,' said Vanya, satisfied.

'Now let's talk about the automatic nature of logic and sequence in physical actions. While you are eating you don't rack your brains over every detail, how to hold your knife and fork, what to do with them, how to chew and swallow. You have eaten thousands of times in your life and everything has become so routine it is automatic and so happens of itself. You understand instinctively that if they had no logical sequence, your actions would not enable you to eat, and satisfy your hunger. Who watches over the logic and the automatic actions? Your subconscious, your ever vigilant power of concentration, your instinctive self-monitoring. Understand?'

'Yes, sir! I understand!'

'That's what happens in real life. But onstage it's another matter. Up there, as you know, we perform actions not because they are part of our daily lives and are biologically necessary to us, but because the author and the director have told us to.

'The biological necessity for physical action disappears onstage, and "automatic" logic and sequence with it, together with the subconscious vigilance and instinctive self-monitoring which are so natural in life.

'How are we to get by without them?

'We have to replace automatic reflexes with a conscious, logical, chronological monitoring of each moment of physical action. In time, thanks to frequent repetition, a habit is created.

'You need to understand how urgent it is for this awareness of the logic and sequence of physical actions, their truth, for belief in this truth, to become a habit as soon as possible.

'You can't imagine how fast we will develop this awareness and the need for it, if only we do the right exercises.

'That's not all. The need for logic and sequence, for truth and belief carries over, of itself, into all other fields: thoughts, desires, feelings, words, into all these Elements. Logic and sequence give them discipline – especially concentration. They teach you to keep the object of your attention onstage, or inside yourself, to watch over the way you perform the small constituent parts not only of physical but also of inner, mental actions.

'Having felt inner and outer truth and believing in it, an impulse to action automatically arises, and then action itself.

'If all aspects of an actor's nature, as a human being, are working logically, sequentially, with genuine truth and belief, then the process of experiencing is complete.

'Training actors logically, sequentially, who relate to everything that is going on in the play and the role with genuine truth and belief, is an enormous undertaking!'

Unfortunately the class was interrupted by Darya fainting. We had to carry her out and summon a doctor.

.. .. 19..

'I can tell from Kostya's questioning look what it is he's waiting for,' said Tortsov as he came into class. 'He needs to know as soon as he possibly can how to master the technique by which small physical actions influence feelings. The work we did on "action without objects" will to a large degree help you in this.

'You saw what we did and know how it can help.

'Remember, at the beginning, when he was doing the "burning money", Kostya was performing actions with "nothing", without any kind of purpose, without a guide, not knowing what he was up to, because all his vigilance, his monitoring, his automatic logic had disappeared. I took on the role of Kostya's consciousness, tried to make him understand the purpose and the links between the constituent parts of a large action (counting money), the logical, sequential way they develop. I taught Kostya to establish conscious control over each, small, subsidiary action.

'You saw what that led to. Kostya remembered, recognized, felt the truth, the life of his actions and began to perform them genuinely, productively and purposefully. Today he remembered them all without any special effort.

'Kostya can repeat what we have structured ten, a hundred times and an automatic process will be created within the logical, sequential actions.'

'It could be, if I may say so, that we would get so used to working with "nothing" that then when they give us "something" we won't be able cope with it and will get into a mess,' said Grisha provocatively.

'So why don't we rehearse with real things from the start?' someone asked.

'How many do we need to get our imagination going?' observed Pasha.

'Not so long ago, for example, we built a house and dragged beams and bricks about,' I remembered.

'There are other, more important reasons. Grisha will show you by a practical example,' observed Tortsov. 'Grisha! Go onstage and write a letter with the real things that are lying on the round table.'

Grisha went up onstage and did as he was told. When he had finished Tortsov asked the students:

'Were you able to see all his actions and believe in them?'

'No,' declared the students almost as one.

'What did you miss, and what seemed wrong to you?'

'First of all I didn't see where the paper and pen came from,' someone said.

'Ask Grisha who he was writing to and what he wrote. He won't be able to tell you because he doesn't know himself,' observed another.

'You couldn't even write a simple note in so short a time,' criticized a third.

'Yet I can remember in every last detail how Duse, when she was playing Marguerite Gautier (in Dumas' La Dame aux Camélias), wrote her letter to Armand.[3] Decades have passed since I saw it but I can still savour every minute detail of her physical action, that of writing a letter to the man she loved,' Tortsov observed.

Then he turned once more to Grisha:

'Now do the same exercise in mime.'

It took a lot of time and trouble before it was possible to guide him, remind him, step by step, logically in chronological sequence, of all the small constituent parts of a large action. When Grisha had recalled them and put them in orderly sequence Tortsov asked the students:

'Now do you believe he was writing a letter?'

'Yes.'

'Did you see, can you recall where he got the paper, pen and ink from?'

'Yes.'

'Did you feel that before he wrote the letter, Grisha went through what was in his mind and then put it down, logically, step by step on paper?'

'Yes.'

'What conclusion do you draw?'

We were silent as none of us knew what to answer.

'The conclusion is this,' said Tortsov. 'The audience, as it watches the player's actions, must also automatically feel the "automatic" process, the logic and sequence of actions with which we are familiar in life. Otherwise they will not believe in what is happening onstage. So give them that logic and sequence in every action. Initially give it consciously and then, with time and use, it will become automatic.'

'There's another conclusion,' affirmed Grisha. 'You know that even using real things, you have to work on each physical action.'

'You're right, but work with real things early in your career proves more difficult than work with "nothing",' Tortsov observed.

'Yes, but do you know why?'

'Because with real things you rush through many actions instinctively, automatically as in daily life, so that as an actor you can't keep track of them. It is difficult to catch hold of these fleeting actions but, if you botch them, the result is gaps in the logic and sequence of actions which ruin them. In its turn, this botched logic destroys truth, and without truth there is no belief and no experiencing, either for the actor or for the audience.

'With mime it is otherwise. With that, willy-nilly, you have to focus your attention on each, minute constituent part of a large action. If you don't do that you cannot recall nor carry out all the subsidiary parts of the whole and, without them, you can't be aware of the large action as a whole.

'You must first think about, then carry out the action. In this way, thanks to the logic and sequence of what you do, you approach truth by a natural path and from truth you go to belief and thence to genuine experiencing.

'Now you can understand why in the early stages, I recommend you to start with "action without objects" and for the moment deny you real objects.

' "Nothing" forces you to investigate the nature of physical actions more attentively, more profoundly and study them.

'Hold on to this technique and these exercises with all the passion you can muster, and, with their help, achieve organic truth.'

'Look, please, I'm sorry,' Grisha objected, 'can you really say that miming is genuine, physical action?'

Pasha backed him up. He also found that actions with real objects and actions with imaginary objects (emptiness) were by nature different.

'For example, let's take drinking water. It calls, as you know, for a whole series of real, physical actions and natural processes, such as raising the liquid to one's mouth, sensations of taste, swallowing . . .'

'Yes, yes!' Tortsov interrupted him. 'You have to repeat all these finer points even when miming, as without them you wouldn't swallow.'

'But look, what are we to do it with when there's nothing in the mouth?'

'Swallow your saliva, air, it's all the same!' Tortsov suggested. 'You'll tell me it's not the same thing as swallowing a tasty wine. I agree. There's a difference. But even so there are still many moments of physical truth which are sufficient for our ends.'

'Look, excuse me, but doing that distracts you from the important things, the meaning of a role. In life, you know, drinking just happens, it requires no concentration,' Grisha insisted.

'No, but when you taste what you are drinking, that requires concentration,' Tortsov objected.

'But when you're not tasting it, you're not thinking about it.'

'The same thing happens with miming. As I've told you, do something a hundred times over, understand, recall every single moment and your body, by its nature, will recognize an action you already know and will help you repeat it.'

After class, while the students were saying goodbye, Tortsov gave some instructions to Rakhmanov. I could hear them as Tortsov was speaking loudly:

'Here's what you must do with the students. In the early stages, assume the role of their consciousness, point out the mistakes they have made in the small, constituent actions.

'Let each student in turn understand that they must know the constituent parts of major actions and their logical development. The students must continuously train their powers of concentration to see to it that the demands nature makes are precisely fulfilled. The students must always feel the logic and sequence of physical action so that it becomes a necessity for them, part of their normal state of mind, they must cherish each small component of large actions, as a musician loves every note of the melody he is playing.

'Up till now you have always seen to it that the students behaved productively, purposefully, and didn't just represent characters. That's fine!

Carry on with this in the classes on "training and drill". As previously, write letters, set the dining table, prepare every possible kind of dish, drink imaginary tea, sew clothing, build a house, etc., etc. Only from now on do all these physical actions without objects, with "nothing", remembering that these exercises are essential for us to establish genuine, organic truth and belief through physical action in an actor.

'Kostya now knows how miming forced him to investigate each moment of the physical action, counting the money. Bring this work on concentration to the highest possible degree of technical perfection. It is extremely important. After this, place the same physical action in a number of different Given Circumstances and "ifs". For example, the student knows perfectly how to get dressed. Ask him: "How do you get dressed on your free day when you don't have to rush to school?"

'He should remember and get dressed just as he would on his free day.

' "How do you dress on a school day when you have time to spare before work begins?"

'And, when he is late for school.

'And when there's an emergency or a fire in the house.

'And when he's not at home but a guest somewhere, etc.

'In all such moments people get dressed physically in the same way. They pull on their trousers, knot their tie, do up their buttons, etc., in precisely the same way each time. The logic and sequence of all these physical actions doesn't change whatever the circumstances. This logic and sequence must be mastered once and for all, developed to perfection in every given physical action. The Given Circumstances, the magic or other "ifs" in which the same physical action occurs change. The setting we are in influences the action, but we needn't worry about that. Nature, our experience of life, habit, the subconscious itself take care of that for us. They do everything we need. What we have to think about is whether the physical action is being carried out properly, logically and sequentially in the Given Circumstances.

'You are helped in studying and correcting actions by mime exercises through which you come to recognize the truth. That is why I invest these exercises with such special significance and ask you once more to bring your attention to bear on them.'

'Aye, aye!' Rakhmanov responded, sailor fashion.

.. .. 19..

The logic and sequence of physical actions is now firmly fixed in our minds. That's what we concentrate on during our exercises, our training and drill, etc.

We're devising every conceivable experiment in class and onstage. A concern for the logic and sequence of physical actions has, indeed, become part of our real lives. We've created a sort of game in which we watch each other to detect a lack of logic and sequence in our physical actions.

Today, for example, because they were late cleaning the school stage, we had to wait for Tortsov's class in the corridor next to the school theatre. Suddenly Marya squealed:

'Oh my darlings! It's awful. I've lost the key to my room!'

We all started looking for it.

'That wasn't logical,' Grisha objected to Marya. 'The first thing you did was bend down, and it was only then you thought about where you were going to look. From that I conclude that your physical actions were not carried out to look for the key but so you could flirt with us, the audience.'

'My darlings, what a pest he is!' said Marya heatedly.

Meanwhile Vanya was hot on Sonya's heels.

'There! That's that! You lose! No sequence! Don't believe you! You've been fumbling the sofa with your hand and looking at me. So you lose!' nagged Vanya.

Add Leo's, Igor's, Pasha's and, in part, my own comments and it's clear that the people searching were in a hopeless situation.

'Stupid children! Stop tying yourselves in knots!' thundered Tortsov's voice.

The students froze, in their shock.

'Sit down on the bench all of you and you, Marya and Sonya, walk up and down the corridor,' Tortsov ordered in a voice that seemed unusually severe to us.

'Not that way! Do people really walk like that? Heels in, toes out! Why don't you bend your knees? Why is there so little movement in your hips? Watch your centre of gravity! Otherwise there's no sense, no logic in our movements! I don't believe you! Don't you know how to walk? Where's the truth and belief in what you are doing? Why are you wobbling as though you were drunk? Look where you're going!'

The longer, the harder Tortsov found fault with them, the more nit-picking he became, the more the two tormented students lost confidence. Tortsov plugged away at them to such a degree that they lost any sense of where their knees, heels and feet were. Looking for the groups of motor muscles which Tortsov called into play, the poor, lost women set in motion muscles that were not necessary. That drew more nit-picking from the tutor.

It ended with them muddling up their legs and Sonya came to a dead stop in the middle of the corridor, with her mouth wide open and her eyes full of tears, afraid to move.

When I looked at Tortsov to my amazement I saw that he and Rakhmanov were hiding their mouths with their handkerchiefs, shaking with laughter.

The joke was quickly explained.

'Don't you understand,' said Tortsov, 'that your silly game destroyed the meaning of my technique. Is establishing the logic and sequence of the constituent parts of a large action purely physically really what's at stake? It's not them I need, I need truth of feeling and sincere belief from the actor.

'Without truth and belief everything that is done onstage, all logical and sequential physical actions, become mere convention, that is they produce lies in which it is impossible to believe.

'The most dangerous thing for my method, for the whole "system" and its psychotechnique, indeed for the whole of art, is a formal approach to the complexity of creative work, a narrow, primitive understanding of what it is. Learning to break down a large physical action into its constituent parts, establishing the logic and sequence among them in a formal way, devising appropriate exercises for that purpose, doing them with students but with no concern for what is most important, bringing physical action to the point of genuine truth and belief, isn't hard and it's profitable!

'What a temptation for those who exploit the "system". There is nothing more senseless or dangerous to art than a system for a system's sake. You must not make it a goal in itself, you must not convert its means into its meaning. That's the biggest lie of all.

'That was precisely the lie you were creating just now, while you were looking for something you had lost, when I walked in here. You picked holes in every small, physical action not so that you could discover its truth and establish belief in it, but so that you could realize, in a purely external way, the logic and sequence of physical actions as such. That's a senseless and dangerous game which bears no relation to art.

'Let me also give you a piece of friendly advice. Never allow your art, your creative work, your methods, your psychotechnique and so on turn you into exaggerated, nit-picking critics. That can deprive an actor of his common sense, or induce a state of paralysis or stupor. Why should you want to develop these things in yourselves and in others using a senseless game. Give it up, otherwise in a very short time an excess of caution, nit-picking and a panicky fear of lies will paralyse you. Look for the lie in so far as it helps you discover the truth. And don't forget that the nit-picker and the critic create untruth more often than not, just as the actor who is the object of this nit-picking involuntarily stops performing the active task he has selected and starts playacting truth instead. The biggest lie of all is concealed in playacting. To the devil with the nit-picker both outside and inside you – in the audience and even more in you yourselves. The critic is all too happy to find a home in the actor's ever doubting mind.

'Develop a healthy, calm, judicious, understanding, true critic in your-self – the actor's best friend. He doesn't drain the life out of actions but makes them vital, he helps you perform them not as mere form but in a genuine way. The true critic can look and see the beautiful while the wrong, petty-minded, nit-picking critic only sees what's bad while what's good passes him by unseen.

'I give the same advice to those among you who are watching other students' work. Those who are monitoring other people's work should confine themselves to serving as a mirror and to saying honestly, without nit-picking, whether or not you believe what you are seeing and hearing and to indicating those moments which convince you. That's all that's demanded of you.

'If the members of the audience were as demanding and as nit-picking as regards truth in the theatre as you are in life, we poor actors wouldn't dare show ourselves onstage.'

'And isn't the audience demanding when it comes to truth?' someone asked.

'It is exacting, but not nit-picking like you. On the contrary. What a good audience wants most of all is to believe everything, it wants to be convinced by a story and that sometimes leads to naiveté of legendary proportions.

'I'll tell you about something unusual that happened to me recently.

'I was at a party with some acquaintances where old Pasha performed a conjuring trick to amuse the young people. Before our very eyes he removed the shirt from one of the guests without touching his jacket or waistcoat only after undoing his tie and shirt buttons.

'I knew the secret of the trick because by chance I had seen him rehearse it and had heard what he said to his assistant. But I forgot all that while I was actually watching the trick and was carried away by old Pasha in his new role.

'After the trick was over everyone was amazed and discussed how it had been done, and I discussed it with them forgetting, or rather, not wanting to remember, what I knew. I wanted to forget so as not to deprive myself of the pleasure of believing and being taken in by it. I have no other explan-ation for this incomprehensible lapse of memory and for my naiveté.

'The audience in a theatre also wants to be "taken in", it likes believing in theatrical truth and forgetting that it's all play and not real life.

'Win over the audience with the genuine truth and belief in what you are doing.'

.. .. 19..

'Today we'll work on the second part of the "burning money" in the same way as we did with the first a few days ago,' Tortsov explained as he came into class.

'That's a more difficult task and we may not be up to it, you know,' I commented as I went onstage with Marya and Vanya.

'No matter,' said Tortsov trying to calm me, 'I'm really not giving you this exercise so you can be certain of getting the better of it, but so that you will better understand what it is you lack and what you have to learn when engaged in a difficult Task. For the moment do what you can. If you can't master everything all in one go just give me part of it, just establish the line of the outer physical actions. Feel the truth in it.

'For example, can you stop what you are doing for a moment and go into the dining room when your wife calls and see how she is bathing the baby?'

'Yes, I can, that's not difficult!'

I got up and went towards the next room.

'Oh, no!' said Tortsov stopping me hurriedly. 'You can't even seem to do that properly. Still, entering a room and exiting from it into the wings is no easy matter. So it is no wonder you had so little logic or sequence.

'Check for yourself how many small, scarcely perceptible but essential physical actions and truths you left out. For example, before your exit you were dealing not just with trivia but with important things, like putting company papers in order and checking the cash. Why did you suddenly push your work to one side, why didn't you walk, why did you run out of the room as though the roof were falling in? Nothing terrible had happened, your wife had called you, that's all. Besides which, in life would you really go and see a babe-in-arms with a lighted cigarette in your mouth? The poor child would cough because of the smoke. And your wife would hardly allow someone smoking into a room where a newborn baby was being bathed. So, first of all, find somewhere to put the cigarette, leave it here, in this room and then go out. Each of these small, secondary actions is easy to perform.'

That's what I did. I put the cigarette down in the drawing room and went into the wings and waited for my entrance.

'So, now you have done each of these small physical actions separately and formed them into one big action, an exit to the dining room. It was easy to believe.'

My return to the drawing room was likewise subjected to many modifications, only this time because I was not performing actions simply. I was relishing every detail, playing them for all they were worth – and more. That, too, is a source of lies onstage.

Finally, we approached the moment of high drama. On my re-entrance, as I was going back to the table where I had left the papers, I saw that Vanya had set light to them and was taking an idiot's delight in his game.

Scenting the moment of tragedy, I lunged forward like a warhorse that has heard the signal for the attack. My nature ran away with me, making me playact – I couldn't stop myself.

'Stop! You've lost your head! You've gone right off the track! You're following a wrong line!' said Tortsov stopping me. 'Go over what you have just done while the trail is fresh.'

'I was representing tragedy,' I confessed.

'And what should you have done?'

What I should have done was simply go over to the fireplace and pluck the burning packet of money from the flames. But to do that I would first have to clear a path, shoving the hunchback out of the way. That's what I did. But Tortsov found that, given the weakness of my shove, there could be no question of a catastrophe or death.

'How can we provoke and justify a more violent action?'

'Here, look,' said Tortsov, 'I'll set light to this piece of paper and throw it here, into this big ashtray and you stand a little further off and, as soon as you see the flames, run to save the bits which are not burning.'

No sooner had Tortsov done what he said than I dashed towards the burning paper, bumped into Vanya and nearly broke his arm.

'You see,' said Tortsov, catching hold of me, 'is what you just did really anything like what you did before? This time a catastrophe might have occurred whereas earlier all we had was playacting.

'Of course, you shouldn't conclude that I recommend breaking actors' arms and crippling people onstage. All that emerges from this is that you didn't take one important circumstance into account, namely that money burns instantly and so, to save it, you have to take action instantly as well. You didn't do that and so violated the truth and our belief in it. Now let's go on.'

'What? . . . Is that all?' I said in real bewilderment.

'What more should there be? You saved what you could and the rest got burned.'

'And the murder?'

'There wasn't any murder.'

'How wasn't there any murder?'

'Look. For the character you were playing there just wasn't any murder. You were depressed because you'd lost the money. You didn't even notice that you knocked the idiot over. If you had realized what had happened you wouldn't just have stood there rooted to the spot but rushed to get help for the dying boy.'

'Perhaps so . . . but we have to do something here. It's a dramatic moment you know!'

'I understand. To put it bluntly, you want to do the full tragedy. But it's better not to. Let's get on.'

We went on to another and for me difficult moment: I had to stand stock still, or in Tortsov's expression, in 'tragic inaction'.

I froze and . . . felt for myself that I was overdoing it.

'There they are, my dear friends! The old, old clichés our grannies and grandpas knew. How stubborn these inveterate, horny-handed clichés are,' Tortsov teased me.

'What do they look like?'

'Horror-struck staring eyes, tragic rubbing of your brow, holding your head in your hands, running your fingers through your hair, clutching your hand to your heart. All these clichés are three hundred years old.

'Now let's clear away all this trash!' he ordered. 'Away with all clichés. All this acting with your brow, your heart, your hair – out! In their place give me even the smallest but genuine, productive, purposeful action, truth and belief.'

'And how can I give an action in a moment of dramatic inaction?' I wondered.

'How can there be action in a moment of dramatic inaction? If it exists, tell me what it is.'

We had to trawl through a host of memories to recall what a man does in a moment of dramatic inaction. Tortsov recounted the following incident:

'An unfortunate woman was told of her husband's untimely death. After long and careful preparation the sorrowful messenger finally pronounced the fatal words. The poor woman froze. But there was no hint of tragedy on her face (unlike the stage where actors like to play moments like these full out). This stillness, this total absence of expression, was terrible. He had to stand quite still for a few moments, so as not to intrude prematurely on her thoughts. Finally he had to move and this brought her out of her stupor. She emerged . . . and fell senseless.

'After a considerable lapse of time, when it was possible to talk to her about the past, she was asked what she was thinking about in the moment of her "tragic inaction".

'It transpired that five minutes before she received the news of her husband's death she was getting ready to go out to buy one or two things for him . . . But as he was dead she would now have to do something else. But what? Start a new life? Say goodbye to the old one? She relived the whole of her past life in an instant, stood face to face with the future and could not see what it meant, couldn't find the equanimity she needed for life to go on and so . . . fainted because of the helplessness she felt. You will agree that several minutes of dramatic inaction were quite dynamic. In effect, reliving all one's life, a long one, in such a brief period and considering its value! Isn't that action?'

'Yes but it's not physical, it's purely psychological.'

'Yes, agreed. It's not physical but another kind of action. Let's not split hairs about what we call it and try to be precise. In every physical action there's something psychological, and there is something physical in every psychological action.

'One distinguished scientist says that if you try to write down your feelings you get a discussion of physical action.

'For my own part I would say that the nearer action is to being physical the less risk you take of forcing your feelings.

'But . . . fine, so be it, let's talk about the psychological, let's deal not with outer but with inner action, not with the logic and sequence of outward physical actions but with the logic and sequence of feelings. The most difficult and important thing is understanding what it is we have to do. You can't do something you don't understand without the risk of falling into acting "in general". You need a clear plan and a line of inner action. To establish that you need to know the nature, logic and sequence of feelings. Up till now we've been dealing with the logic and sequence of physical actions which are palpable, visible, accessible to us. Now we've encountered the problem of the logic and sequence of elusive, invisible, inaccessible, unstable inner feelings. This area, this new task which confronts you is notoriously complex.

'It's an easy thing to say – nature, the logic and sequence of feelings. These are all extremely complex, psychological questions which science has still analysed very little, and so can provide us with no practical indicators or basic principles.

'There's nothing for it but to find a way out of our difficult situation with the help of our own, so to speak, home-grown means. We'll talk about them next time.'

'How then are we to resolve the highly complex question of "the logic and sequence of feeling" without which we cannot bring the pause, "tragic inaction", to life?

'We are actors, not scientists. Our sphere is action. We are guided by our practice, our human experience, our memories of daily life, logic and sequence, truth and belief in what we are doing onstage. That is the angle from which I approach the question.'

After a short pause Tortsov continued:

'Practical experience has taught me a method which is absurdly simple. It consists in asking myself, "What would I do in real life if I fell into 'tragic inaction'?" Just answer this question in a natural, human way and no more.

'As you see, I turn to simple physical action for help with feeling.'

'If you don't mind I can't agree with that, because, you know, there are no physical actions in the realm of feeling. They're psychological,' said Grisha.

'No, you're mistaken. Before taking a decision people's imagination is highly active. With their inner eye they see what and how things might happen and mentally go through the actions they plan. Actors physically feel the things they are thinking about and can hardly restrain their own inner impulse to action, its struggle to find outward expression.

'Mental images of actions stimulate the most important thing of all – inner dynamism, the impulse to external action,' Tortsov insisted. 'And you should note that this entire process takes place in the world in which we normally create. An actor's work is done not in real life, but in an imaginary life that does not, but could, exist. To us actors it appears to be reality itself.

'Therefore, I maintain that when we speak of an imaginary life and imaginary actions, we should relate to them as we would to genuine, real, physical acts. So, the technique of learning the logic and sequence of feelings through the logic and sequence of physical actions is fully justified in practice.'

As always, when I have a complicated job to do I get everything muddled in my head. I have to remember, bring together and evaluate every fact, every Given Circumstance in the acting exercise one by one: happiness, the family, my obligations to it and to the public company I serve, my responsibilities as treasurer, the importance of the invoices; my love, my strong feelings towards my wife and my son; the idiot, the hunchback who is always stuck under my nose, the forthcoming audit and shareholders' meeting; the catastrophe, the appalling sight of the burning money and the documents, the instinctive urge to save them, my state of numbness, madness, exhaustion. All this was created in my representation of events, in my mental images, and was reflected in my feelings. Having put the facts in place, I then had to understand where they led, what awaited me in the future, what bits of evidence there were against me.

First there was the big, fine apartment. It was a sign I was living beyond my means, spending too much. The total absence of money in the cash-box, the fact that the invoices had been half burned, the death of the idiot boy and the fact that there was not a single witness to my innocence, my son's drowning. This was a new piece of evidence to indicate I had been planning to run away and that a babe-in-arms and a idiot would have been great obstacles. The judge would say, 'That is why in the first instance this criminal put an end to them both.'

The death of my son involved not only me but my wife in the crime. Moreover, there would inevitably be difficulties in our relationship as a result of the murder of her brother. And so I couldn't expect her to defend me.

All the facts, 'ifs', and Given Circumstances confused and muddled me so that at first I couldn't see any way out except to run away and hide.

But after a second my hasty decision was undermined by doubts.

'Where can I run to?' I asked myself. 'Is the life of a fugitive any better than prison, and wouldn't running away in itself be a strong piece of evidence against me? No, I won't flee from justice but tell everything just as it was. What have I to fear? I'm not guilty. Not guilty? . . . Yes, but prove it!'

When I explained all my thoughts and doubts to Tortsov he said:

'Write down all your ideas on paper then translate them into action, because those are just what is of interest to you in answering the question, "What would I do in real life if I were suddenly to find myself in a state of 'tragic inaction'?" '

'How can you translate ideas into action?' asked the students who had not understood.

'Very simply. Let's assume that you have a list of your ideas in front of you. Read it through. Good apartment, no money, burned documents, two dead persons, etc.

'What would you do once you had written down and read these lines? You would recall, select, evaluate the facts which could serve you as evidence. That's the first of your ideas that has been turned into action. Read further down the list. Having come to the conclusion that there is no way out of your situation you decide to run away. What will your action be?'

'Change the earlier plan and make a new one,' I decided.

'That's your second action. Continue on down the list.'

'Farther on I criticize the plan I have just made and tear it up.'

'That's your third action. On!'

'Further on I decide to make a clean breast of what happened.'

'That's your fourth action. Now all that remains is to carry out everything you have planned. If this is done, not in an histrionic fashion – as form, "in general" – but in a human fashion – genuinely, productively, purposefully, then a living, human state, similar to the state of your character you are portraying, will be created not only in your head, but in your total being, in all your inner Elements.

'Every time you repeat a pause of "tragic inaction", the moment you perform it, go over your ideas once again. They will come to you, each day, in a slightly different form. No matter – for better or worse it is important that they should belong to today, that they should be new. Only if this is so can you avoid repeating what you have already learned, or inflicting clichés on yourself and resolve the same problem anew, a little better each time, more profoundly, more fully, with greater logic and order. Only under these conditions can you preserve genuine truth, belief, and action which is productive and apposite in this scene. That will help you sincerely experience it in a human way and not present it in a conventional theatrical way.

'So, you respond to the question, "What would I do if I were in a state of tragic inaction?", i.e., in a highly complex psychological state, not in scientific terms but through a series of highly logical, sequential actions.

'As you see, in our homegrown way, imperceptibly, practically, we resolve the problem of the logic and sequence of feelings in the small-scale way we need for the moment so that we can get on with things.

'The secret of this technique is that since we cannot cope with the complex problem of the logic of feelings, we leave it aside and turn our enquiries to something which is more accessible to us – the logic of action.

'Then we answer the question not in an academic but in a totally practical way, through our knowledge of the world, with the help of our own human nature, our daily experience, our instinct, flair, logic, sequence and the subconscious itself.

'Having created a logical sequence of physical actions, we are aware, if we pay attention, that another line is being created inside us, parallel to it: the logic and sequence of our feelings. That is understandable. Without our noticing it, inner feelings give rise to actions, they are indissolubly linked to the life of those actions.

'This is yet another convincing example of how the logic and sequence of physical and psychological actions, when justified, leads to truth and belief of feelings.'

Today, Tortsov once again made me, Vanya and Marya play 'the burning money'.

At first, in the scene of counting the money, something went wrong. Tortsov, like the first time, had to guide my efforts step by step. Once I had felt the truth of the physical actions and believed they were genuine, I was on fire: things became easier, my imagination was working.

While I was counting the money I happened to look at the hunchback – Vanya – and for the first time I came face to face with the question, of who he was and why was he always under my nose? I couldn't go on until I had clarified my relationship to the hunchback.

'You see!' exclaimed Tortsov when I told him about it. 'Small truths demand ever greater truths.'

Here is the story I made up with Tortsov's help to justify my relationship with my fellow actor.

My wife's beauty and health were bought at the cost of deforming her brother, the idiot. They were twins. When they came into the world their mother's life was in danger. The obstetrician had to operate and risk the life of one of the children to save the life of the other and of the mother herself. Both lived, but the boy was born an idiot and a hunchback. It seemed to the healthy people that some kind of guilt lay on the family and it felt constant self-reproach.

This story produced a breakthrough in my mind. It altered my attitude to this poor hunchback. I felt full of genuine kindness for him, I began to see his deformity with different eyes and even felt something akin to pangs of guilt for the past.

The whole scene of counting the money came alive in the presence of the poor freak who found delight in the burning papers. I was ready to play any kind of game with him, out of pity: banging the packets on the table, funny movements and faces, silly gestures when throwing the papers in the fire and things that came into my head. Vanya entered into the spirit of what I was doing and reacted well to it. His enthusiasm spurred me on to invent new things. A whole, different scene was created: cosy, living, warm, happy. It drew a response from the auditorium at every moment. That also spurred me on. Then the moment came when I had to go into the dining room. To whom? To my wife? Who was she? Another question sprang up.

Here again, it was impossible to do anything until I had settled the question, who my wife was. I made up an extremely sentimental story which I'd rather not write down. Still, it got me going, and made me believe that if things were as my imagination pictured them, then my wife and my son were infinitely dear to me. I would work for them joyfully, without respite.

Now that the exercise had come to life, my previous playacting seemed offensive.

It was so easy to go and see my son in the bath. This time I didn't have to remember the cigarette, I carefully left it behind in the sitting room. My tenderness and concern for the child demanded it.

The reason why I had to come back to the table and the papers was now clear. I was working for my wife, my son, for the hunchback!

Now that I knew my past, the burning of the company's money took on a different meaning. Now I had to say to myself, 'What would I do if this happened in reality?' and straight away my heart began to beat faster from a feeling of impotence. How awful my immediate future looked as it bore down on me. I had to open the curtain onto the future. To do that I had to be perfectly still, and 'tragic inaction' turned out to be extremely active. Both were necessary for me to concentrate all my energy and strength on the work my imagination and mind were doing.

The later section with the attempt to save the dying hunchback went off naturally, spontaneously. That was understandable given my new, affectionate attitude towards him. He had become my relative and dear to me.

'One truth reveals and gives rise to other truths logically, one after the other,' said Tortsov, when I told him of my experiences. 'First you discovered the small truths in "counting the money" and were happy when you managed to recall, down to the smallest detail, the actual physical process of counting money in real life. Having felt that truth onstage when you were counting the money, you wanted to achieve the same, trueness to life in the other moments, in your encounters with the other characters – your wife and the hunchback. You wanted to know why the hunchback was always there in front of you. With the help of everyday logic and sequence you created a story which was probable and easy to believe in. The sum of all this forced you to live truthfully onstage, according to the laws of nature.'

Now I started to look at the exercise I had been sick of with different eyes and it evoked living feelings in response. I had to acknowledge that Tortsov's method was outstanding. But it seemed to me that its success was based on the action of the magic 'if' and the Given Circumstances. It was they which had produced the breakthrough in me and not the creation of physical and imaginary actions. So why not start with them earlier? Why waste time on physical actions?

I spoke to Tortsov about this.

'Of course!' he agreed. 'I suggested starting with that . . . a few months ago, when you first did the exercise.'

'Then it was difficult for me to get my imagination started. It was dead,' I remembered.

'Yes, and now it's alive and it's easy for you not only to make up stories but also to live them in your mind, to feel their truth and to believe in it. Why has this change taken place? Because previously you sowed the seeds of your imagination on stony ground and they perished. You sensed the truth but didn't believe in what you were doing. Posturing, physical tension, wrongness in the body make ungrateful soil for the creation of truth and experiencing of feeling. But now not only your psychological but also your physical life are in good order. Everything in them is truth. You believe in them not with your intelligence but with the things your own nature as an organism senses. It is not surprising then if, under those conditions, your imaginative ideas put out roots and bring forth fruit. Now your imaginings are not idle, as before, in a void, not "in general" but have a considerably stronger base. Now what you imagine has not abstract but concrete meaning. They inwardly justify outward action. The truth of physical actions and belief in them stimulates our minds.

'But the most important thing you have learned today is this – just now you were not onstage in "Marya's apartment", you weren't playing, you *were*. You genuinely lived with your imaginary family. That is what we call, in our terminology, the state of "I *am being*". Its secret is the fact that the orderly logic of physical actions and feelings led you to the truth, the truth evoked belief and together they created "I am being". And what is "I am being"? That means, I am, I live, I feel, I think as one with the role.

'In other words "I am being" leads to emotion, to feeling, to experiencing.

' "I am being" is distilled, almost absolute truth onstage.

'Today's performance was also remarkable in that it vividly illustrated a new, important quality truth has. And that is the fact that small truths evoke bigger truths, bigger and bigger, the very biggest, etc.

'All you had to do was to consciously direct your small physical actions and genuinely believe in them. But it was not enough for you just to count the money, you had to know who you were doing it for, who you were trying to amuse and so on.

' "I am being" onstage is the result of wanting ever bigger truths, even absolute truth itself.

'Where truth, belief and "I am being" are, inevitably you have genuine, human (and not theatrical) experiencing. These are the strongest "lures" for our feeling.'

Coming into class Tortsov stated:

'Now you know what truth and belief are onstage. It remains to be proved if all of you have them. And so I am going to conduct an individual review of your feeling of truth and belief in it with each of you.'

Grisha was the first to be called onstage. Tortsov told him to play something.

Of course our king of representation needed his permanent partner, Varya.

As usual they played some sort of rubbish full out.

This is what Tortsov said at the end:

'For a skilful mechanic like you, who is only interested in the technique of representation, what you did today seemed right to you, and you were enamoured of your own technical mastery.

'But I did not share your feelings because what I look for in acting is the innate, creative power of nature itself, which imbues a dead role with genuine human life.

'Your sham truth helps you represent "characters and passions". My truth helps us create the characters and the passions themselves. Between your art and mine there is the same gulf fixed as between the words "seem" and "be". I need genuine truth, you are satisfied with the truth-like. I need belief, you limit yourself to the belief the audience has in you. When they see you, they can rest assured that everything will be done exactly in conformity with the traditional tricks they know. They have faith in your technical proficiency, just as they have faith a gymnast won't fall off the trapeze. In your kind of acting an audience is an audience. In my kind it becomes an involuntary witness of and a participant in the creative process. It is drawn into the very heart of the life being enacted.'

Instead of answering what Tortsov had said, Grisha, somewhat venomously, stated that Leo held another view of truth from Tortsov. To support his view on truth in acting Grisha quoted Pushkin's lines, ones we all recall on such occasions:

> Far dearer than the darkness of base truth
> I find the all-uplifting lie.[4]

'I agree with you – and Pushkin too. It's demonstrated by the lines you have quoted in which the poet speaks of the lie we believe in. It's because we believe it that the lie uplifts us. If we had no belief, would the lie have any beneficial, uplifting effect on us? Imagine that some people come to see you on the first of April, when we enjoy fooling each other, and try to persuade you that the government has decided to put up a statue to you in recognition of your artistry. Would you be uplifted by such a lie?'

'I'm not an idiot, you know, I wouldn't believe a stupid joke like that!' Grisha responded

'So, to be uplifted you would have to "believe a stupid joke",' said Tortsov reminding him of his own words. 'Pushkin expresses almost the same opinion in some other lines:

And shed hot tears upon a tale.[5]

'You don't shed tears over something you don't believe in. So long live the lies and stories we believe in, since they can uplift the actor as well as the audience! Such lies become truth for the people who believe them. And this is even stronger confirmation of the fact that onstage everything must become truth in the actor's imaginary life. And I don't see that in your playing.'

Tortsov spent the second half of the class putting the little scene that Grisha and Varya had just played right. Tortsov checked over the small physical actions in their acting and went after truth in just the same way as he had with me in the 'burning money'.

But . . . an incident occurred, which I must write down, as it provoked a rebuke from Tortsov which I found highly instructive. This is what happened:

Grisha unexpectedly broke off what he was doing, stopped acting and stood silent with a nervous, angry look on his face. His hands and lips were trembling.

'I can't keep quiet any longer! I've got, I mean . . . to come out with it!' he began after a short silence in which he struggled with his emotion. 'Either I don't understand a thing, in which case I'd better quit the theatre or, I'm sorry, but what you're teaching us here is poison and we should have none of it.

'For the last six months you've had us move chairs, close doors, light fires. Soon you'll be asking us to pick our noses for the sake of realism, with small or large physical truth. But, I'm sorry, moving chairs about onstage isn't art. Truth isn't demonstrating some naturalistic garbage. To hell with that kind of truth, it makes me sick!

' "Physical action"? No, look, I'm sorry. The theatre isn't a circus. There, yes, physical action – catching the trapeze, jumping onto a horse's back – is extremely important, the acrobat's life depends on it.

'But the great writers of the world don't create works of genius so that their heroes can use physical actions as a kind of exercise. You know?! And that's all we're made to do. We're suffocating.

'Don't grind us into the dust! Don't clip our wings! Let us take wing, fly high, close to the eternal . . . the otherworldly, the universal, up there in the highest spheres! Art is free! It needs space, not small truths. It needs scope, you see, to fly high, not crawl along the ground like tiny insects. We want something beautiful, noble, inspiring! Don't cloud our sky!'

'Tortsov's right not to let Grisha soar among the clouds. It doesn't suit him,' I thought to myself. 'What? Grisha, our king of representation, wants to fly up to heaven?! "Do acting" instead of doing exercises?!'

When Grisha had finished Tortsov said:

'Your protest surprises me. Up till now we have thought of you as an external, technical actor, since that is the area in which you have distinguished yourself. Now, quite unexpectedly, we learn that your real vocation lies in the spheres beyond the clouds, that you need the eternal, the universal, an area in which you haven't exactly distinguished yourself in any way at all.

'So where do your artistic intentions fly exactly? Out here, towards us, in the auditorium, to which you display yourself, for which you always represent characters, or there, to that side of the of the footlights, i.e., the stage, the author, the actors, the art you serve, towards "the life of the human spirit of a role" which you are experiencing? I gather from what you said it's the latter. Fine! So show your innermost self to us as soon as you can, throw away your beloved technique and its so-called elevated style, which audiences with poor taste seem to need.

'Conventions and lies have no wings. It is not given to the body to fly. At best it can jump three feet off the ground or stand on tiptoe and so stretch a little higher.

'The imagination, feelings, thoughts can fly. Only they possess invisible wings that have no substance, no flesh. We can only speak of them when we dream, as you put it, of the "otherworldly". In them lie hidden the living recollections of our memory, that "life of the human spirit" which is our dream.

'It is this that can drive not only "upwards" but considerably further, into those worlds which nature has not yet created but which live in an actor's unbounded fantasy. But in fact your feelings, thoughts, imagination fly no further than the auditorium whose slave you are. And so they should shout your own words back at you: "Don't grind us into the dust! We are suffocating! Don't clip our wings! Let us take wing, fly high, close to the eternal . . . the universal! Give us something uplifting and not threadbare, theatrical clichés!" '

Tortsov wickedly imitated the vulgarity of Grisha's histrionic emoting and declamatory style.

'If the tempest of your inspiration does not lift your wings and bear you up in the whirlwind, you, more than anyone, need the line of physical actions, their truth and belief to be able to take off.

'But you're afraid of it, you find it humiliating to do exercises which are compulsory for all actors. Why do you expect to be the exception to the general rule?

'Dancers sweat and pant every morning during their exercises before flying "en pointe" in the evening. Singers vocalize every morning, extend their range, develop the diaphragm, find the resonators in the head and nose so that in the evening they pour their soul into their singing. Artists of all kinds take care not to neglect their bodies or fail to do the physical exercises which their technique demands.

'Why do you want to be the exception? At a time when we are aiming for a close, direct link between our bodies and our minds so that one may influence the other, you are trying to keep them apart. And that's not all. You're even trying to cut yourself off completely (in words only, of course) from one half of your nature – the physical. But nature has played a joke on you, she hasn't given you the thing you prize, elevation of feeling and experiencing. She has merely granted you the physical technique of an exhibitionist, instead.

'You more than anyone are intoxicated by outward, stock-in-trade tricks, declamation, emoting and all the usual old clichés.

'Which of us is nearer to the sublime, you who rise a little on tiptoe and, in words only, soar into "the wide blue yonder" while you are in fact entirely in the power of the audience or I, who need technique and physical actions so that, with the help of truth and belief, I can convey complex human experiences? Make up your mind, which of us is nearer the ground?'

Grisha said nothing.

'It's quite incomprehensible!' Tortsov exclaimed after a pause. 'The people who talk most about the sublime are those who have the least gift for it, people who lack invisible wings with which to fly. They talk about acting and creative work in an artificial, bombastic, incomprehensible and pretentious way. Real actors, on the other hand, talk about their art in a simple, comprehensible way.

'Aren't you to be numbered among the first of these?

'Think about it, and also about the fact that in roles for which you are suited, you could become a fine, useful actor.'

After Grisha, Varya presented her scene. To my amazement she did all the simple exercises quite well and in my view justified them.

Tortsov praised her and then suggested she take the paper knife from the table and stab herself with it.

At the first whiff of tragedy Varya immediately became bombastic and began 'to tear a passion to tatters' appallingly, and when it came to the climax she suddenly let out such an unexpected 'bellow' that we couldn't contain ourselves and burst out laughing.

Tortsov said:

'I had an aunt who married an aristocrat and proved a superlative "lady". She walked the knife edge with consummate art and pursued her high society "politics" brilliantly, so that she always came out on top whatever the circumstance. Everyone believed her. However, once she had to win over the relatives of a man who had just died and whose burial service was taking place in a packed church. My aunt approached the bier, struck an operatic pose, looked at the dead man's face, held an effective pause and declaimed to the entire church, "Farewell, friend! Thank you for everything!" But her sense of truth betrayed her. She went wide of the mark and nobody believed her grief. More or less the same thing happened to you just now. In comic passages you wove the role into a pattern of lace, and I believed you. But in the strong dramatic passage you missed the mark, too. You evidently have a one-sided feeling for truth, which is right for comedy but out of joint in drama. Like Grisha you must find your real place in the theatre. To understand one's "type" in time is important in our art.'

. . . . 19. .

Tortsov went on with his review of the feeling of truth and belief in it and first called on Vanya.

He played the 'burning money' with me and Marya. I maintain that Vanya experienced the first half superbly, as never before. He astonished me this time with his sense of proportion and convinced me anew that he was genuinely gifted.

Tortsov praised him but then expressed a reservation:

'But why in the death scene did you playact the sort of "truth" we never want to see, spasms in the stomach, nausea, retching, terrible grimaces, twitches throughout the entire body . . .?

'In that passage you offered naturalism for naturalism's sake. You needed the truth of dying for the truth of dying's sake. You weren't living memories of the last minutes of "the life of the human soul" but were interested in the audience's memories of the way the body expires physically.

'That was wrong.

'In Hauptmann's play *Hannele*,[6] naturalism can be tolerated. But we use it so as to bring out the meaning of the play more clearly. It's a technique we can accept. But why, when we don't need it, should we take things from life which we should reject as unnecessary dross? Tasks and truth of this kind are anti-artistic and so is the impression they leave behind. The repulsive doesn't create the beautiful, the crow cannot give birth to a dove, the nettle cannot bear a rose.

'So, not all the truths we know in life are good for the theatre.

'Truth in the theatre must be genuine, not glamorized. It must be purged of unnecessary, mundane details. It must be true in a realistic sense but made poetic by creative ideas.

'Let truth onstage be realistic, but let it be artistic, let it uplift us.'

'But what does this kind of artistic truth consist of?' Grisha asked with a touch of venom.

'I know what you're after, a discussion about the loftiness of art. I can tell you, for example, that there is the same difference between artistic and unartistic truth as there is between a portrait and a photograph. The latter gives you everything, the former only the essential. You need the talent of the artist to put what is essential onto canvas. As regards Vanya's playing in the "burning money", it should be noted that for the audience the important thing was for the hunchback to die, not for that death to be accompanied by that physical display. They are photographic details which are harmful to a picture. We want a single, essential feature or other, which characterizes a man dying, and not by any means all the symptoms he gave us. Otherwise the important thing, the death, the departure of someone dear, is pushed into the background, and secondary symptoms stand out, and the audience will feel sickened at the very moment when they should be weeping.

'I am well aware of what I am expected to say here, but I won't! Why? Because certain undemanding people are all too easily satisfied. A few words of explanation and they think they know everything there is to know about what is art. For me, such a state of mind is harmful. It tells us nothing and at the same time lulls our sense of curiosity and the spirit of enquiry which are so essential to an actor.

'If I refuse to answer then you will be worried, intrigued, disturbed, it will put you on your guard and force you to examine yourself and seek the reply to an unanswered question.

'That's why I make it clear to you that I have no intention of defining, or finding forms of words for what is art in Art. I am a practitioner and I can help you to understand, that is feel, the nature of artistic truth, but not in words, in action. If this is to happen, you will need to arm yourselves with a great deal of patience, because it will take a year, or rather, it will automatically become clear when you have been through the whole "system". Then you will be able to chart the birth, refining and crystallization of simple, everyday, human truth in art for yourselves. That won't happen all at once, but while the role is shaping and growing. By taking what is most essential into ourselves, endowing it with the beauty of form and expression appropriate to the stage, by paring away what is superfluous, with the help of our subconscious, our artistry, our talent, our flair and our taste, we turn the role into something poetic, beautiful, harmonious, simple, comprehensible, ennobling and purifying for the audience. These qualities help what we create onstage not only to be truthful and truth-bearing but artistic as well.

'This essential sensory awareness of beauty, of the artistic, cannot be defined by dead formulae. It demands feeling, practice, experiment, the right kind of curiosity and time.'

After Vanya, Marya played the scene with the 'abandoned child'. The content of the scene is as follows: Marya was returning home and on the way found an abandoned baby. The exhausted, abandoned child quickly expired in her arms. At first she showed her joy at finding the child with extraordinary sincerity and treated it as though it were a real baby. She jumped and ran with it, swaddled it, kissed it, adored it, forgetting that she was dealing with a piece of wood wrapped in a tablecloth.

But suddenly the young child stopped reacting to her games. Marya looked at it a long time trying hard to understand the reason. The expression on her face changed. The more her bewilderment and terror were reflected in it, the more she concentrated. She laid the young thing carefully on the sofa and drew back. When she was a certain distance away, she froze in tragic bewilderment. That was all. Nothing more. But how much truth, belief, naiveté, youth, charm, womanliness, taste, genuine drama, there was in it. How beautifully she contrasted the death of a newborn babe with the thirst for life of a young woman! How delicately she felt the first encounter with death by a young, vital being, the first glimpse of a place where there is no life.

'There you have artistic truth!' Tortsov exclaimed enthusiastically when Marya went offstage. 'You could believe everything she did, as it was all experienced and taken from genuine life as lived, not wholesale, but with discrimination, using only what was necessary. No more, no less. Marya knows how to observe, she can descry the beautiful and has a sense of proportion. That's an important quality.'

'How is it a young beginner, a student, can show such perfection?' some wondered enviously.

'Through natural talent and, most importantly, an exceptionally fine feeling for truth. Whatever is subtle, truthful, is invariably of high artistic quality. What could be better than untouched, unspoiled natural truth?'

At the end of the class Tortsov explained to us:

'It would appear I have told you all I can about the feeling of truth, lies and belief onstage for the present.

'The time has come to start thinking about how to develop and test out this important gift of nature.

'Occasions and pretexts for such work arise plentifully, as the feeling of truth and belief appear with every step we take when we are being creative, be it at home, onstage, in rehearsal or in performance. Everything the actor does and the audience sees must be imbued with the feeling of truth and sanctioned by it.

'Every exercise, even the most insignificant, connected with the inner and the outer line of action, needs to be monitored and sanctioned by the feeling of truth.

'It is clear from all I have said that every moment of our work in school, in the theatre or at home can serve to further its development.

'Our sole remaining concern is that all these moments should serve us for good and not for ill, that they should help us develop and fortify that feeling of truth and not lies, wronghood and playacting.

'It is a difficult task since it is easier to cheat and falsify than to speak and act in a truthful manner.

'Enormous concentration is required, as is constant monitoring from the tutors so that the students may grow stronger in the feeling of truth in the right way.

'Forget about things which are still beyond you, and which run counter to our nature, logic and common sense! Such things produce disturbance, forcing, playacting, lies. The more often they are allowed onstage the worse it is for the feeling of truth, which is demoralized and thrown out of joint by what is wrong.

'Beware of making lies and wrongness a habit onstage, do not allow bad seeds to put out roots in you. Tear them out ruthlessly. Otherwise weeds will grow and choke the small, precious, essential shoots of truth in you.'

9

EMOTION MEMORY

The class began with Tortsov suggesting we go back to the 'madman' and the 'damp fireplace', which we had not done for some time. The students greeted his suggestion with enthusiasm. They missed the exercises. Besides, it was good to repeat something we were sure of and which had been successful.

We played with even greater energy. That was hardly surprising. Each of us knew what he had to do and how. We were so sure of ourselves we showed off rather. Once again, as before, seeing Vanya's fright we rushed about in all directions.

Only today his fright was no surprise to us, we had time to prepare, to think who was going to run where. As a result the general rush was more clearly defined, better rehearsed and therefore considerably stronger than before. We shouted our heads off.

As for me, I ended up under the table, as before, only I didn't find an ashtray so grabbed hold of a large album. The same thing can be said of the others. Sonya, for example: the first time she accidentally knocked a cushion down when she collided with Darya. There was no collision today, but she still knocked the cushion down so that she could pick it up as she had the last time.

What then was our surprise, that when the exercise was over Tortsov and Rakhmanov told us that while our earlier efforts had been direct, sincere, fresh and true, what we had done today was wrong, insincere and contrived? All we could do was throw up our hands in despair.

'But we were feeling it, experiencing it!' the students said.

'Everybody inevitably feels and experiences something at every moment of his life,' Tortsov replied. 'If he were not feeling or experiencing anything, he wouldn't be a person but a corpse. Only the dead feel nothing. The whole question is what precisely you were "feeling" and "experiencing".

'Let's take a look at it and compare what happened previously with what you did today when you repeated the exercise.

'There can be no doubt, the mise-en-scène, the moves, their sequence, the tiniest details of the grouping were retained with astonishing precision. Just look at the piled up furniture blocking the door. It's almost as though you'd taken a photograph of the way everything had been arranged and had built the barricade using it as a blueprint.

'The whole external, factual side was repeated with quite astonishing precision, clear evidence of the fact that you possess a keen memory for the stage picture, grouping, physical action, movements, moves, etc. So much for the external side. But is it really so important where you were standing and how you were grouped? I, as the audience, am much more interested in knowing how you were responding internally, what you were feeling. It is your own individual experiences, which you bring to the role from the real world that give it life. But you didn't give me these feelings. If the external action, the mises-en-scène, the grouping are not substantiated from within, they are mere form, dry, and unnecessary for us onstage. And that is what makes the difference between today's performance and the one you did earlier.

'The first time I suggested the idea of the mad, uninvited guest, you all, as one, started thinking about the vital problem of self-preservation. All of you weighed up the circumstances, and only when you had done that, did you begin to do anything. That was a logical, truthful approach, genuine experiencing physically embodied.

'Today, on the other hand, you were enjoying a favourite game and instantly, without a moment's thought, without weighing the Given Circumstances, you started copying the external actions you had known previously. That was wrong. The first time everything was quiet as the grave, today it was all bubble and excitement. You all rushed to get things in the right place: Sonya – a cushion, Vanya – a lampshade, Kostya – an album instead of an ashtray.'

'The props man forgot to set it,' I said in self-justification.

'And you arranged it in advance the first time, did you? Perhaps you knew that Vanya would shout and frighten you?' said Tortsov ironically. 'Strange! How could you foresee that today you would need an album? Apparently it was supposed to come to hand by chance. What a shame none of these chance events was repeated today! And here's another detail. The first time you had your eyes glued to the door behind which the imaginary madman was supposed to be. But today you weren't concerned with him but with us, your audience, Rakhmanov and me. You wanted to know what impression you were making. Instead of hiding from the madman you were showing yourselves off. If, the first time, your actions were prompted by your feelings, your intuition, your everyday experience, today you followed a well-beaten track blindly, almost mechanically. You repeated the first, successful version, and didn't create a genuine, new life belonging solely to today. You drew your material not from everyday life but from theatrical memories of "acting". The things which sprang to life inside you, spontaneously, and were naturally reflected in action the first time round, today were artificially inflated, exaggerated to produce a greater effect on the audience. In a word what happened to you was what once happened to a young man who went to see Vasili Samoilov[1] to ask if he should go on the stage.

' "Go out and then come in again and say what you have just said," the famous actor suggested.

'The young man repeated his first entrance externally but couldn't recapture the experience he had felt, coming in for the first time. He didn't justify and give inner life to his outer actions.

'However, neither the comparison I made with the young man nor today's failure should trouble you – it's all in the order of things and I will tell you why. The fact is that the best stimulus to creative activity is often the element of surprise, the freshness of a creative theme. This element of surprise was present the first time you performed the exercise. My suggestion that there might be a madman outside the door genuinely disturbed you. Today the element of surprise had gone, because you knew everything in advance. It was old history, patently clear, up to and including the form your actions would take. In that case, why bother to think again, or justify what you were doing using your own experience of life, your feelings, the things you have lived through in the real world? What's the point of doing this if everything has already been set up and approved by me and Rakhmanov. Ready-made forms are a great temptation for an actor. Hardly surprising then that you, who have hardly ever been onstage before, were tempted by the ready-made and in so doing displayed an excellent memory for externals. But as for memory of feelings, that was not evident today.'

'Memory of feelings?' I said, trying to be clear what he meant.

'Yes. Or as we will call it *Emotion Memory*. Formerly, following Ribot,[2] we called it "affective memory". That term has now been abandoned but has not been generally replaced by another. But we need a word of some kind to define it so we have agreed to call the memory of feelings, Emotion Memory.'

The students asked for a clearer explanation of what these words implied.

'You'll understand it from this example which Ribot provides:

'Two travellers were cut off on a cliff by the tide. They escaped and afterwards recounted their impressions. One of them remembered every single one of his actions, how, where, why he had gone there, where he came down, how he placed his feet, where he jumped. The other remembered almost nothing of all that but only remembered the feelings he lived through, first excitement, then wariness, alarm, hope, doubt and, finally, a state of panic.

'These feelings had been retained in his Emotion Memory.

'If today, by simply thinking about the exercise, all the feelings you had experienced the first time returned as with the second traveller, if you had lived them and started afresh in a way which was genuine, productive and purposeful, if all this had happened spontaneously, with no effort of will, I'd say you had a first class, quite exceptional Emotion Memory.

'But, unfortunately, that's a very rare phenomenon. So I'll scale down my demands and say, if you had begun the exercise, guided only by the moves you had set, and this had then reminded you of the feelings you had experienced, and if you had surrendered to these emotion memories, you would have carried out the exercise with them in command. In that instance I would say you didn't have an exceptional or a superlative Emotion Memory, but a good one.

'I'm prepared to relax my demands still further and accept the fact that you started the exercise in an external way, as outward form, that the familiar moves and physical actions did not breathe life into the feelings associated with them, that you showed no sign of needing to weigh up the Given Circumstances within which you were supposed to react, as you did the first time. In such cases you can help yourself by using your psychotechnique, that is, by introducing new "ifs" and Given Circumstances, weigh them up thoroughly and arouse your slumbering powers of concentration, your imagination, your sense of truth, belief, thoughts and through them your feeling.

'If you had managed to do that, I would acknowledge you had Emotion Memory.

'But you didn't give evidence of any of this today. Today, like the first traveller, you repeated the line of the external actions with exceptional clarity but didn't make them glow with inner experience. Today you were concerned only with results. That's why I say, you didn't give evidence of Emotion Memory.'

'Does that mean we haven't got any?' I asked desperately.

'No. You're drawing a wrong conclusion. But we'll test it out in the next class,' Tortsov answered calmly.

.. .. 19..

Today's class began with a check on my Emotion Memory.

'Do you remember,' said Tortsov, 'when in the green room you told me about the great impression Moskvin made on you when he was on tour in ***? Can you remember his performances so vividly that you are carried away by them just as you were five or six years ago?'

'Perhaps not as acutely as then, but my memories still stir me greatly.'

'Strong enough for your heart to beat faster when you think about them?'

'Well, if I really let them.'

'And what do you feel, mentally or physically when you remember the tragic death of your friend, which you also told me about in the green room?'

'I chase such painful memories away, they're depressing.'

'That's the kind of memory which helps you relive all the feelings you experienced earlier during Moskvin's tour or when your friend died — that's Emotion Memory.

'Just as your visual memory resurrects long forgotten things, a landscape or the image of a person, before your inner eye, so feelings you once experienced are resurrected in your Emotion Memory. You thought they were completely forgotten but suddenly a hint, a thought, a familiar shape, and once again you are in the grip of past feelings, which are sometimes weaker than the first time, sometimes stronger, sometimes in the same or slightly modified form.

'Once you can blench or blush simply by recalling something that happened to you, once you are afraid to think about a past misfortune, you have a memory for feelings, or Emotion Memory. Only it is not sufficiently developed for you to fight, all on your own, against the problems inherent in public performance.

'So, tell me,' said Tortsov turning to Pasha, 'do you like the scent of lily of the valley?'

'Yes, I do,' Pasha answered.

'And the taste of mustard?'

'Separately, no, but with beef, yes.'

'And stroking a cat's fur or fine velvet, you like that?'

'Yes.'

'And do you recall what it feels like?'

'I do.'

'And do you like music?'

'I like that too.'

'Do you have favourite melodies?'

'Of course.'

'Which, for example?'

'Many of Tchaikovski's songs, Grieg, Musorgski.'

'Can you recall them?'

'Yes. I have a good ear.'

'An ear and aural memory,' Tortsov added. 'I hear you like painting?'

'Very much.'

'Do you have favourite pictures?'

'I have.'

'Can you recall them, too?'

'Very well.'

'And you like nature?'

'Who could fail to?'

'Have you a good memory for landscapes, the layout of a room, the shape of things?'

'I have.'

'For faces, too?'

'Yes, for those that make an impression on me.'

'Give me an example of a face you remember clearly.'

'Kachalov for example. I saw him close to and he made a great impression on me.'

'That means you have visual memory.

'These are all recurrent impressions produced by memory stirred by the five senses. They do not belong to the category of experiences in our Emotion Memory, they are independent of it.

'Nonetheless, sometimes I will speak of the five senses in parallel with Emotion Memory. It's more convenient.

'Do actors need the impressions made on our five senses, and to what extent do they need them?

'To answer that question let us look at each of the senses.

'Of all the five senses sight is the most receptive to impressions.

'Hearing is also very acute.

'That is why it is easiest to act upon our feelings through our sight and hearing.

'It is a well-known fact that certain painters have such a sharp inner eye that they can paint a portrait of someone who is not present.

'Some musicians have an ear that is so perfect that they can play through a symphony they have just heard in their minds, recalling all the details of the performance, and the most insignificant departures from the score. Theatre artists, like painters and musicians, possess visual and auditory recall which enable them to imprint and revive visual and aural images, of a person's face and its expression, of the line of his body, his walk, mannerisms, movements, voice, the intonations of the people they meet, their clothing, details, even the most mundane, nature, landscapes and so on. Moreover, a person and even more so an actor can remember and reproduce not only the things he sees and hears in real life but also things which are created unseen and unheard in his imagination. Actors of the visual type like to be shown what is required of them and then it is easy for them to understand the feelings being discussed. Actors of the auditory type, on the other hand, want to hear the sound of the voice, the speech or the intonations of the character they portray as soon as possible. For them it is their auditory recall which provides the initial impetus towards feelings.'

'And the other senses. Do we need them, too?' I asked with interest.

'Of course!'

'If we do, how can we make use of them, to what end?'

'Imagine', Tortsov explained, 'that you are playing the first scene of Act Three of Chekhov's *Ivanov*. Or imagine that one of you is going to play the Cavaliere di Ripafratti in Goldoni's *La Locandiera*, and that he is supposed to go into ecstasies over the papier mâché, prop ragout which Mirandolina has supposedly prepared with such mastery. You have to play this scene in such a way that you make your own and the audience's mouths water. To do that, as you are performing the scene, you must reproduce something like the taste, if not of a genuine ragout then of some other tasty dish, otherwise you will simply playact and not experience the taste and pleasure of eating.'

'But what about touch? In which play would you need that?'

'Perhaps in *Oedipus* in the scene with his children, when Oedipus, who has gouged out his eyes, touches them.'

'In that case you need a well-developed sense of touch.'

'But, look here, I'm sorry, but a good actor will express all that without worrying about feeling but just through technique,' said Grisha.

'Beware of such assertions of self-sufficiency. The most perfect technique cannot compare with the unattainable, unachievably subtle art of nature itself. In my time I have seen many famous actors, technical virtuosi of all schools and nationalities, and I maintain that not one of them could attain the heights the actor's genuine subconscious can reach when invisibly prompted by nature herself. You must never forget that many aspects of our nature are complex and will not submit to being consciously directed. Only nature has power over those parts of us which are inaccessible to us. Without her aid we can only partially, not fully, master the highly complex, creative apparatus we need for experiencing and physically embodying a role.

'Recollections of taste, touch and smell may have little application for us in our acting, nonetheless sometimes they assume great importance, but their role is only secondary.'

'What does it consist of?' I pressed him.

'I'll give you an example,' said Tortsov. 'I'll tell you something which I happened to see not long ago. Two young men had spent a night on the town and were trying to remember the tune of a cheap polka they had heard somewhere but didn't know where.

' "It was . . . Where was it though? . . . We were sitting by a pillar or a column," one of them painfully recalled.

' "What's a column got to do with it?" said the other angrily.

' "You were sitting on the left and on the right . . . who was sitting on the right?" said the first reveller, straining to see in his mind.

' "No one was sitting there and there wasn't any column. And we were eating stuffed fish, Jewish style, that's true enough and . . ."

' "There was a reek of cheap eau de cologne," the other reminded him.

' "Yes, yes", the second man agreed, "the reek of cheap Eau de Cologne, and the stuffed fish smelled disgusting, I'll never forget it!"

'These impressions helped them remember a woman who had been sitting with them eating crayfish.

'Then they saw the table with the food on it, the column by which they actually had been sitting. Then one of the revellers suddenly sang a trill a flute had played and showed how the musician had played it. He also remembered the leader of the band.

'So, gradually, memories of taste, touch and smell were revived and, with them, the visual and auditory impressions received during the course of that evening.

'Finally one of the revellers remembered a few bars of the cheap polka. The other, in his turn, added a few bars more and the two of them sang the tune which had been revived in their memory, and conducted it like the bandleader.

'But that wasn't the end of it. The revellers remembered they had exchanged some insults while they were in a drunk state, and started arguing hotly again and as a result started abusing each other again.

'You can see clearly from this example the tight relationship and inter-action of our five senses and their influence on the things which Emotion Memory recalls. So, as you see, the actor needs not only Emotion Memory but sensory memory.'

.. .. 19..

As Tortsov is out of Moscow on tour our studies have been curtailed for a while. We had to make do with 'training and drill', dance, gymnastics, placing the voice (singing) and scientific subjects. As classes were tempor-arily interrupted so, too, were the entries in my notebook.

But an incident occurred recently in my private life which made me understand something very important for our acting and for Emotion Memory in particular. This is what happened.

Not long ago I was going back home with Pasha. Our way was blocked in the Arbat by a large crowd. I love to watch things that happen in the street and pushed my way to the front. There I was confronted by an appalling sight. Near me lay an old beggar in a pool of blood, with a fractured jaw and both hands and half of one foot severed. The dead man's face was terrible, the lower jaw was shattered and his rotten old teeth had been knocked out and were lodged in his bloody whiskers. The hands were lying there separate from the body. It looked as though he had stretched them right out before him begging for mercy. One finger was raised as though to threaten someone. The toe of his boot with bones and flesh in it had also rolled to one side. The trolley-car which was standing near its victim seemed huge and terrible. It was baring its teeth and hissing like an animal. The driver was repairing something in the engine probably to show that it had been responsible and clear himself. A man was bending over the corpse, looking intently at its face and stuffing a dirty handkerchief into its nose. Nearby children were playing with water and blood. They liked it when the rivulets of melted snow mingled with the red blood and formed a new rose-coloured stream. One woman was weeping, the rest stood staring in curiosity, horror, or distaste. They were waiting for the authorities, the doctor and the ambulance, etc.

This realistic-naturalistic picture produced a terrifying, shattering impression on me. It was in sharp contrast to the sunny day, the blue, clear, happy, cloudless sky.

I came away very depressed and could not rid myself of the terrifying impression it had made for a long time. The memory of the scene I have described brought on a painful mood which did not leave me all day.

I woke in the night, recalled the picture imprinted on my mind, shaking even harder, it seemed terrible to be alive. The tragic accident seemed more awful in memory that it had been in reality, perhaps because it was night and everything seems worse in the dark. But I attributed my state to Emotion Memory which had made the impression all the stronger. I was even happy to be terrified as it indicated that I had a very good memory for feelings.

A day or two after the incident I have described I was once again walking through the Arbat near the place where the accident had occurred and involuntarily stopped, thinking over what had recently happened. Everything terrible had gone, there was only one less human life in the world. The cleaners calmly swept the street, as though removing the last traces of the tragic accident, the trolley-cars happily ran past the fateful spot, stained with human blood. Today the cars didn't bare their teeth or hiss as they did then but on the contrary rang their bells jauntily so they could roll along more merrily.

The memory of the recent, terrible accident was reborn, linked to my thoughts about the brevity of human life. But what had been crudely natu-ralistic – the fractured jaw, the amputated hands, part of the foot, the raised finger, the children playing in the bloody puddles – although it shook me no less than it had then, shook me in quite a different way. The feeling of repulsion vanished and indignation took its place. I would define what happened in my mind this way: on the day of the tragic accident, marked by what I had seen, I could have written a caustic newspaper account like a street reporter but on the day of which I speak I would have been able to put together a passionate article about the cruelty of life. When I recall the accident, I am not stirred by the naturalistic details, but by a feeling of pity, tenderness for the victim. Today I thought with particular warmth of the woman who was bitterly weeping.

It's amazing how great an influence time exerts on the growth of our recalled emotions.

This morning, that is, a week after the accident, going to school, I once again passed by the fateful spot and remembered what had happened there. There was the snow, white today as it had been then. That was life. The black figure lying on the ground, stretching out towards something. That was death. The streaming blood was the passions that flow out of people. All round, as in sharp contrast, once again there was the sky, the sun, the snow, nature. That was eternity. The crammed trolley-cars driving past me seemed to me like the transitory generations of man moving towards eter-nity. And the whole picture that a short while back had appeared repulsive, then terrifying, now became majestic. If, the first day, I wanted to write a newspaper report and then was drawn towards a feature article of philo-sophical character, today I was inclined to poetry, verses, celebratory lyrics.

Still affected by the changes in my feelings and emotion memories, I fell to thinking about an incident that Leo told us about not long ago. Our dear good fellow had taken up with a simple country girl. They got on well together but she had three unbearable faults. First, she never stopped talking. Since she was not very well educated, her talk was stupid. Second she had bad breath and third she snored terribly all night. Leo left her and her faults were a major cause of their separation.

Quite some time passed and he started to dream once more of his Dulcinea.[3] Her bad side seemed unimportant to him, it had dimmed with time and her good side emerged more clearly. A chance meeting occurred. Dulcinea was in domestic service in an apartment into which he had purposely moved. In a short time everything was back as it had been.

Now, when his recollected emotions have become reality, Leo dreams of separation again.

.. .. 19..

How strange. Now, after a short passage of time, when I recall the accident in the Arbat, it is mostly the trolley-car that I see in my mind. Not the one I saw then, but another, which had been stored in my memory after an accident that happened quite some time earlier.

Last autumn, late in the evening I was riding back to Moscow from Streshnovo[4] on the last trolley. The car went off the rails before it managed to reach the deserted clearing. It required the combined strengths of the few passengers to put it back on the rails again. How huge and mighty the car then seemed to me and how insignificant and pitiful the people were by comparison.

The question I would like to answer is, why are these feelings from the distant past more strongly imprinted on my Emotion Memory than the things I experienced recently in the Arbat? . . .

And here's another strange, quite similar thing. Remembering the beggar stretched out on the ground and the unknown man bending over him, I thought not of the tragic accident in the Arbat but of another incident. Some time ago I came across a Serb crouching over a monkey that was dying on the pavement. The poor man, with eyes full of tears, was trying to stick a dirty piece of sugarplum into the animal's mouth. This scene evidently moved me more than the death of the beggar. It stuck deeper in my memory. That is why now the dead monkey and not the beggar, the Serb and not the unknown man come to mind when I think of the recent accident. If I had to stage this scene I wouldn't draw on the emotions associated with it from my memory but on something else, registered quite some time earlier, in different circumstances and with totally different characters, i.e. the Serb and the monkey. Why should this be?

.. .. 19..

Tortsov returned from his travels and took today's class. I told him of the way things had gone after the tragic accident. Tortsov praised my powers of observation.

'What happened to you', he said, 'illustrates very well the process of crystallization which takes place in our Emotion Memory. Everybody, in their time, sees not one but many tragic accidents. They are stored in the memory but not every detail, only the features which have made the most impact. All these traces of similar experiences and feelings are distilled into a single, wider, deeper memory. There is nothing superfluous in it, only what is most essential. This is a synthesis of all like feelings. It is related not to the small, individual parts of the incident but to all similar cases. That is memory on the grand scale. It is clearer, deeper, denser, richer in content and sharper than reality itself.

'For example, when I compare my impressions of my recent travels with earlier tours, I see that though the one I have just finished has left a very good impression on me, that impression is nonetheless marred by a number of minor, irritating, disagreeable moments that clouded everyone's pleasure.

'I don't recall anything similar from my earlier travels. Emotion Memory has purified them in the melting pot of time. That's good. Were it not so, minor details would overwhelm what was important, and what was important would be lost in a welter of trivia. Time is a wonderful filter, a powerful purifier of memories, of feelings one has had. Moreover time is a great artist. It not only purifies, it lends poetry to memory.

'Thanks to this quality, even dismal, real and crudely naturalistic experiences become more beautiful and artistic with time. It makes them irresistibly attractive.

'But it will be said that great poets and artists write and paint from nature!

'That may be so, but they don't photograph it, they are inspired by it, they filter the model through their own personality, and enrich it with living material from their own Emotion Memory.

'If it were otherwise, and authors wrote their villains photographically, from nature, in all the realistic detail they saw and felt in the living model, their creations would be repulsive.'

After that I told Tortsov how the memory of the beggar was replaced in my memory by the recollection of the monkey and one trolley-car by the other.

'There's nothing surprising in that,' said Tortsov. 'Using a rather commonplace comparison, I can tell you that we can't put the recollections of our feelings in order the way we do the books in our library.

'Do you know what Emotion Memory is? Imagine a large number of houses and a large number of rooms in them, and in them a countless number of cupboards and chests with many drawers, boxes, large and small, including a very tiny one with a bead in. It's easy to find the house, the room, the cupboard, the shelf, it's more difficult to find the large and small boxes. But where is the sharp eye that can find the bead that fell on the floor this morning, glinted for a moment and then was gone for ever? You can only come across it again by accident.

'It's the same thing with the archives of our memory. It has its cupboards, chests, large and small boxes. Some are accessible, others less so. How, among them, are you going to find the "little bead" of recollected emotion that first glinted and then was gone forever, as a meteor flares for an instant and then vanishes forever? When they appear and blaze within you (like the image of the Serb and his monkey), thank heaven for granting them to you. But don't for a moment imagine you can retrieve a feeling that has gone forever. Tomorrow, instead of the Serb, you will remember something else. Don't imagine you can return to yesterday's memory, be content with today's. Learn to accept memories that have come to life afresh. Then your heart will respond with renewed energy to anything that no longer excites you in a play that you've played too often. You will take fire and then, perhaps, inspiration will appear.

'But give up the idea of hunting old beads – they are beyond recall, like yesterday, like childhood joys, like first love. Try to let each day bring forth new, fresher inspiration in you, one sufficient unto the day. No matter if it is weaker than yesterday's. The good thing is that it is today's, it is natural, it appeared spontaneously for an instant out of its hiding place to fire your creative efforts. Besides, who can say for sure which of the flashes of genuine inspiration is better or worse. They are all beautiful in their own way if only because they are – inspiration.

.. .. 19..

At the beginning of the class I asked Tortsov to shed some light on something that puzzled me:

'Does it mean,' I said, 'it is we who hold these beads of inspiration and they don't fall into our minds from without, don't wing their way from above, from heaven? Does it mean they are, so to speak, recurrent, not spontaneous, first time ever?'

'I don't know,' said Tortsov, avoiding a straight answer. 'Questions about the subconscious are not intellectually my business. Besides, let's not destroy the mystery and awe with which we surround moments of inspiration. Mystery is beautiful and is a spur to creation.'

'Yes but is everything we experience onstage a repeat? Do we have any first-time experiences? What I would like to know is, is it a good thing or not when feelings which we have never experienced in real life are aroused for the first time onstage?' I insisted.

'It depends which kind they are,' said Tortsov. 'For example, let's suppose you are playing Hamlet and, in the last act, you hurl yourself, sword in hand, at Pasha who is playing the king, and that for the first time in your life you have an irresistible lust for blood you have never known before. Let's also suppose that the sword is blunt, a prop, and that the whole affair passes without blood being drawn, yet there could still be a very nasty fight, which would mean bringing the curtain down early and an investigation. Does it do the show any good if the actor indulges in first-time feeling and is "inspired"?'

'Does that mean spur-of-the-moment feelings are undesirable?' I insisted.

'On the contrary, they're highly desirable,' said Tortsov to calm me. 'They are direct, strong, vivid but they don't occur onstage in the way you imagine, that is, for long periods, or for an entire act. They burst through, here and there, but only as discrete moments. In that sense they are desirable in the highest degree and I welcome them with all my heart. May they visit us more often and intensify the truth of our emotions, which we prize more than anything in performance. Because they are unexpected, first-time feelings provide an irresistible stimulus for an actor.

'One word of warning. We aren't masters of spur-of-the-moment experiences, they master us. And so all we can do is leave it to nature, and say to ourselves, if spontaneous feelings do arise, then let them appear when they are needed, lest they run counter to the play and the role.'

'That means we are powerless when it comes to the subconscious and inspiration,' I cried in a horrified voice.

'Are our acting, our technique merely reduced to first-time feelings? They are rare not only onstage but in life itself,' said Tortsov to console me. 'We have the repeated, the recurrent feelings which our Emotion Memory prompts. Learn, first and foremost, to use them. They are more accessible to us.

'Of course, an unexpected, subconscious "find" is attractive. This is our dream, the aspect of creative work we like most. But it doesn't follow that we should belittle the importance of the conscious recollections of our Emotion Memory. You should, on the contrary, cherish them, as it is only through them that you can exert some degree of influence on inspiration.

'We must remember the basic principle of our school of acting: "*the subconscious through the conscious*".

'We must also cherish our store of memories because the actor brings to the role not the first memories that come to mind, but others that have been carefully chosen and are the most dear to him, memories of feelings he has experienced in his own life. The life of the character he is portraying, fashioned out of material drawn from his Emotion Memory, is often dearer to him than his own everyday life. Isn't that good soil for inspiration? The actor carefully transfers his best qualities onto the stage. The form and setting will vary according to the play, but the actor's human emotions, which run parallel to the feelings of the role, must remain alive. They must not be faked, or replaced by something else, some convoluted actor's trick.'

'What?' said Grisha in amazement. 'You mean in all roles – Hamlet, Arkashka, Nestchastlichev,[5] Bread and Sugar in *The Blue Bird*, do you really mean we should make use of our own personal feelings?'

'How could it be otherwise?' said Tortsov puzzled in his turn. 'An actor can only experience his own emotions. Or do you want the actor to get new set of feelings, a new heart and mind for every role he plays? Do you think that's possible? How many hearts is he supposed to have room for? You can't pluck your own heart out and rent another, more suitable for the role. Where would you find one? From a dead role you haven't brought to life yet? The role is waiting for you to give it a heart. We can borrow clothes or a watch, but you can't borrow feelings from another person or a role. Someone please tell me how that's done? My feelings are an inseparable part of myself, as yours are of you. We can understand, feel a role, put ourselves in its place and start behaving as the character would. That evokes experiences which are similar to the role in us. But these feelings belong not to the character the author has written, but to the actor himself.

'Whatever dreams you may have, whatever you may have experienced in reality or in your imagination, you are always yourself. Never lose communication with yourself onstage. Act from your own personality as an actor/ human being. You can never run away from yourself. If you deny your "me", then you cut the ground from under your feet, and that is the most terrible thing that can happen. The moment when you lose communication with yourself onstage is the moment when experiencing ends and playacting begins. So, however many performances you give, whoever it is you are portraying, you must use your own feelings, always. Infringement of this law is tantamount to the actor murdering the character he is playing, depriving it of the pulsating, living, human soul which alone gives life to a dead role.'

'You mean you play yourself your whole life?' said Grisha in astonishment.

'That's just what I mean,' Tortsov said. 'Always play yourself onstage but always with different combinations of Tasks, Given Circumstances, which you have nurtured, in the crucible of your own emotion memories. They are the best and only material for inner creative work. Make good use of them and don't depend on borrowing things from others.'

'But look here, I'm sorry,' Grisha argued, 'I haven't room inside for all the feelings of all the roles in all the plays in the world.'

'You will never be able to play the roles you can't properly find room for. They are not your repertoire. Actors should not be divided up according to type but according to their personality.'[6]

'How can one person be Arkashka and Hamlet?' we said in wonder.

'First and foremost an actor is neither one thing nor the other. He either has a well or poorly developed personality, both mentally and physically. You won't find Arkashka's chicanery and Hamlet's nobility in any one given actor, yet the germ, the seeds of almost all human virtues and vices lie within him.

'An actor's art and inner technique must be directed towards finding a natural way to discover the seeds of innate human virtues and vices in himself, and thereafter to nurture and develop them for whatever role he happens to be playing.

'So, the character is put together by the actor out of the living Elements of his own self, out of his Emotion Memories and so on.'

My head was bursting with all the things Tortsov had revealed to me and I told him so.

'How many notes are there in music?' he asked me. 'Only seven,' he said, answering his own question. 'And yet the combinations of these seven notes are far from being exhausted. And how many psychological Elements are there in a person – states, moods, feelings? Personally I've never counted them but I have no doubt there are more of them than there are notes in music. So you can rest easy, there's enough to last your artistic lifetime. So, make it your business to learn, first, the means and techniques whereby to draw emotional material from your inner self and, secondly, the ways and means whereby to create infinite combinations of human souls, characters, feelings and passions for your roles.'

'What are these ways and means?' I pressed him.

'First and foremost, learning how to activate our Emotion Memory,' Tortsov explained.

'How do you activate it?' I insisted.

'You know, it can be done by a number of internal stimuli. But there are external stimuli. We'll talk about that next time, as it's a complex question.'

.. .. 19..

Today we worked with the curtain closed, in 'Marya's apartment'. But we didn't recognize it. The dining room was where the living room had been, the dining room had turned into a bedroom and the hall had been made into several small rooms, partitioned off by cupboards. There was cheap, jerry-built furniture everywhere. It was as though some stingy landlady had come into our quarters and transformed the nice apartment we once had into cheap, furnished, money-making one-night rooms.

'Happy house-warming!' Rakhmanov greeted us.

Once they had recovered from their surprise the students asked in chorus to return to the comfort of 'Marya's apartment'. They felt awful in the new quarters and wouldn't be able to work properly.

'There's nothing we can do,' was Tortsov's negative response. 'The theatre needs what we had earlier for its current productions. They've given us what they can in exchange, and set things up as best they could. If you don't like it, change things round so you feel comfortable with them.'

A great hustle and bustle ensued, work went with a will. Soon there was total chaos.

'Stop!' Tortsov cried. 'What came from your Emotion Memory, what recurrent feelings did you have when you were creating this chaos?'

'In Armavir . . . when . . . there was . . . an earthquake . . . the furniture . . . moved . . . like this,' our draughtsman and surveyor Nikolai muttered.

'I don't know how to put it. It was like having people in to polish the floors before a special occasion,' Sonya recalled.

'It's a shame, my dears. My heart just sank,' Marya complained.

As we were moving the furniture an argument took place. Some were looking for one mood, others for another, depending on how they felt, and their Emotion Memories when they saw the furniture arranged in this way or that. Finally the furniture was placed tolerably well. We accepted the way it was arranged, but asked for more light. At that point a demonstration of lighting and sound effects began.

First of all there was bright sunlight and we all felt good. At the same time onstage a whole symphony of sounds started – cars, trolley-cars, bells, factory sirens and train whistles in the distance indicated that the working day was in full swing.

Then, gradually, half-light set in. We were sitting in the twilight. It was cosy, quiet and a little sad. We felt inclined to dream, our eyelids grew heavy. Then a strong wind sprang up, almost a storm. The window panes rattled, the wind howled in the chimney. There was rain then snow at the window. With the fading light everything quietened down. The noises from the street ceased. The clock struck in the next room. Then someone started playing the piano, loudly at first, then quietly and sadly. The chimney howled and our hearts grew heavy. Evening began to invade the room, the lamps were lit, the piano stopped. Then outside the windows, somewhere afar, the clock tower struck twelve. Midnight. Silence reigned. A mouse scratched in the cellar. From time to time a car honked its horn or a locomotive whistled briefly. Finally it all died away and darkness set in and it was silent as the grave. After a short while the grey light of dawn appeared. When the first rays of the sun burst into the room I felt as though I had been born again.

Vanya was the most enthusiastic.

'Better than in real life,' he assured us.

'In life you don't notice the influence of light over a full twenty-four hour period,' said Pasha, explaining his impressions, 'but when everything lasts only a few minutes, as it did just then, and all the changing shades of day and night flash by, you feel the power it has over you.'

'Feelings change with light and sound – at one moment sadness, then alarm, then coming to life,' I said, conveying my own impressions. 'At times you'd think there was a sick man in the house who'd asked you to talk quietly, at others that people live peacefully together and then it's not so bad to be alive. Then you feel good and want to talk loudly.'

'As you can see,' Tortsov hastened to tell us, 'the things around us influence the way we feel. And that happens not only in real life but on the stage, too. Here we have our lives, our personality, we have woods, mountains, seas, towns, villages, castles and cellars. They live, reflected, on the painter's canvas. In the hands of a talented director all the production values, the theatrical effects no longer seem like crude forgeries, but become a work of art. When they relate to the inner feelings of the characters, they become much more meaningful than in real life. The mood they evoke, if it matches the play, focuses attention marvellously on a character's inner life, and influences the actor's mind and feeling. So, the externals of the setting and the mood they create is a stimulus for us. And so, when an actress is playing Marguerita,[7] being tempted by Mephistopheles as she is praying, the director must provide her with the appropriate church-like atmosphere. It helps her feel the role.

'The director must also create the right mood of enforced isolation for Egmont[8] in the dungeon scene.

'He will be grateful, because mood guides feeling.

'The production team must help us with everything they have at their disposal. Their skills are hidden stimuli for our Emotion Memory and recurrent feelings.'

'But what happens when a director creates a beautiful setting, that doesn't go very deeply into the meaning of the play?' Pasha asked.

'Unfortunately that happens all too often, and always ends in trouble, because the director's mistakes steer the actors in the wrong direction and create a wall between them and their role.'

'And what if the director's whole production is just plain bad?' someone asked.

'That's even worse! The work of the director and the production team will lead to diametrically opposite results. Instead of focusing the actor on the stage and the role, a bad set will draw him away from the action and put him in the power of the full house, beyond the footlights.'

'And if the director gives us the kind of vulgar, theatrical, tasteless production I saw last night at the N . . . Theatre?' I asked.

'In that case the poison will work its way into the actor and he will follow in the director's footsteps. Some people find very powerful "stimuli" in theatrical vulgarity. So, as you can see, the externals of a production can be a double-edged sword in a director's hands. They can do good or harm.

'In their turn, actors must learn to look, see, understand the things around them, and surrender to the illusion without reserve. When an actor has that ability, those skills, he can make full use of all the latent stimuli in the externals of the production.

'Now, a question for you,' Tortsov continued. 'Is a fine set a help to an actor, does it stimulate his Emotion Memory? Imagine beautiful backdrops painted by a famous artist with a wonderful command of colour, line and perspective. See them from the auditorium and they draw you towards the stage. But go up on stage yourself and you are disappointed, you want to leave. Wherein lies the secret? If the sets are only intended as paintings, and the actor's needs have been forgotten, then they are no good for the stage. In designs like that, just as in a picture, the painter has been dealing merely with two and not three dimensions, with width and height. As far as depth, or, in other words, theatrical space, is concerned, it is empty and dead.

'You know from your own experience what a bare, flat, empty stage is, how difficult it is to concentrate, to find your true self even in a simple little exercise or scene.

'But try out a space like a concert platform, go right down front and communicate the whole of the "life of the human spirit" of Hamlet, Othello or Macbeth. How hard it is to do that without help from the director, with no mises-en-scène, no props and furniture which you can lean on, sit on, rest on, group yourselves around. After all, every one of these helps you live onstage, and give physical expression to your inner mood. That is easier to achieve with a production which is full of ideas than with an actor standing down by the footlights like a block of wood. We need the third dimension, space, which is moulded, through which we move and in which we live and behave. We need the third dimension more than the first two. What use is it to us actors to have a backdrop by the hand of an artist of genius hanging behind us. Very often we don't see it since we have our backs to it. It merely incites us to effective playacting, so as to match the background. It doesn't help us because that was all the designer was concerned with while he was creating it. He wanted to show himself off, forgetting all about the actor.

'And where are those geniuses, those technical actors who can stand in front of the prompter's box and convey the whole content of the play and the role with no outside help from the production team, the director, and the designer?

'Until such time as our acting has reached such heights of perfection that it can ensure the actor, singlehanded, is equal to his creative tasks, we shall require the services of the director and the production team who have all the stimuli that décor, layout, lighting, sound, etc., can provide at their disposal.'

.. .. 19..

'What are you hiding in a corner for?' said Tortsov to Marya.

'I am trying to hide! I just can't go on!' she said in great agitation, pushing herself even deeper into the corner, hiding from a dismayed Vanya.

'And why are you all sitting so cosily together?' said Tortsov to a group of students, who were grouped on the sofa by the table in the cosiest corner, awaiting his arrival.

'We're listening . . . to jokes!' Nikolai, the draughtsman, answered.

'And what are the two of you, you and Grisha, doing by the lamp?' said Tortsov to Sonya.

'I . . . I . . . don't know what to say . . .,' she said, embarrassed. 'We're reading a letter . . . because . . . I really don't know why . . .'

'And why are you walking up and down with Pasha?' Tortsov questioned me.

'We're talking something over,' I replied.

'In short,' Tortsov concluded, 'each of you selected the most suitable spot, created the appropriate grouping, and used them for your own purposes, according to your mood, whatever you were experiencing and doing or, alternatively, the moves suggested what you had to do, your Task.'

Tortsov sat by the fireplace with us facing him. Several people pulled up their chairs so as to be nearer to him and hear better. I settled myself at the table with the lamp so it would be easier to write. Grisha and Sonya found seats together further off, so they could whisper to each other.

'Now, why are you sitting here, you there and you at the table?' said Tortsov, once more demanding an explanation.

We once again answered for our actions and Tortsov again concluded that each of us, in his own way, had made use of the mise-en-scène, according to the setting, our mood and experiences.

Then Tortsov led us to different corners of the room. The furniture was arranged differently in each of them and he asked us to define what moods, emotion memories, recurrent experiences they provoked in our minds. We had to define the circumstances and the manner in which we would use the given mise-en-scène.

After that, Tortsov arranged us in a series of different groupings, as he thought best, and we had to recall and define in what mental state, what conditions, what mood or given circumstances it would be comfortable for us to sit in the way he told us. In other words, if, previously, we had grouped ourselves according to our mood, as we had felt the task within the action, Tortsov was now doing that for us and all we had to do was justify someone else's layout, try and find the corresponding experiences and actions and discover the corresponding mood within them.

As Tortsov said, just as an actor often encounters the first two cases, when he has to create his own mises-en-scène, so, in his working practice, he meets a third, when he has to justify someone else's. So we need to have control over them.

Later on we did an experiment, 'proof through opposites'. Tortsov and Rakhmanov sat down as though they were going to start the class. We settled ourselves to suit the 'matter in hand and the mood'. But Tortsov changed the layout until it was unrecognizable. He deliberately seated the students awkwardly, counter to the mood and the things we were supposed to be doing. Some seemed to be a long way off while others, although they were near the tutor, had their backs to him.

The disparity between the mises-en-scène and the mood and the business in hand threw us.

This example was a concrete demonstration of how important the link between the staging and the actor's mental state is, and what a sin it is to break it.

Tortsov then ordered all the furniture to be placed against the walls, sat all the students along them and placed one single armchair in the middle of the empty floor.

Then, he called on each of us in turn and asked us to exhaust every possible position for this chair our imagination could devise. All these positions must, of course, be inwardly justified – by our imagination, Given Circumstances and feelings. We all did everything in turn, defining what personal experiences the staging, grouping and positions pushed us towards or, vice versa, what moods occurred spontaneously. This made us appreciate the value of fine helpful, rewarding staging, that exists not for its own sake but for the feelings which it evokes and then fixes.

'So,' said Tortsov, summing up, 'on the one hand the actor looks for a setting that matches the mood, the matter in hand, the immediate Task, and on the other hand the mood, the Task, the matter in hand themselves create the setting. They, too, are stimuli to our Emotion Memory.

'People usually think that when we use detailed sets and stage dressing, lighting, sound and other directorial delights our first concern is to dazzle the audience. Not so. We use these stimuli not only for the audience, but for the actors, too. We try to help them focus on what's onstage and make them ignore what's off it. If the mood we create on our side of the footlights matches the play, then we establish a creative atmosphere, one which correctly stimulates Emotion Memory and experiencing.

'Now, after a series of experiments and demonstrations, are you convinced that all the means and effects we employ – the staging, the sets, the layout, the lighting, the sound and other things – to create a mood onstage are wonderful external stimuli to our feelings?' Tortsov asked.

The students, Grisha excepted, agreed with this proposition.

'But there are a few actors', Tortsov continued, 'who don't know how to look and see onstage. Whatever set they are in, however that set is lit, whatever sounds fill it, whatever illusion has been created, they aren't interested in it, only what's out front. Not only can't you interest them in the setting, you can't even interest them in the play and its meaning. They cut themselves off from crucial, external stimuli with which the director and the production team try to help them.

'Rather than let this happen to you, learn to look and see onstage, surrender to the things around you, respond to them. In a word, be able to use all the given stimuli.'

In today's class Tortsov said: 'So far we have gone from stimulus to feeling. But we often have to do things in reverse, go from feeling to stimulus. That's what we do when we have to pin down an experience created by chance. Let me give you an example.

'Here's what happened to me in one of the first performances of Gorki's play The Lower Depths.[9]

'The role of Satin was comparatively easy for me, apart from the long speech "on Man" in the last act. I was asked for the impossible, to convey the general, not to say universal, significance of the scene, the infinite wisdom of the subtext, so that the speech became the key to the whole play. As I reached the danger spot I put the brakes on internally, became very wary and started to strain like a horse with a heavy load faced with a steep mountain. That "mountain" in my role stopped me running freely, spoiled the pleasure of the creative moment. After the speech I felt like a singer who has missed his top C.

'However, quite unexpectedly, this sticky passage came off well on the third and fourth performance quite spontaneously.

'To understand the reason for my chance success, I started to go through everything that had led up to my performance. First I had to go over the whole day from the morning onwards.

'To begin with I had received a large bill from my tailor. That made a dent in my budget, and I was annoyed. Then I lost the key to my desk. And you know what a nuisance that is. I was in a bad mood when I read a review of our production in which everything that was bad was praised and everything that was good was damned. The review depressed me. I thought about the play all day. I analysed it a hundred times over, tried to discover what was most important in it, the gist, recalled every moment of my own experiencing and was so wrapped up in what I was doing that on that evening I wasn't interested in success, wasn't worried about it before I went on, didn't think about the audience, didn't give a fig for the outcome of the show and my own performance in particular. I wasn't playing a part but just logically, sequentially fulfilling the Tasks in the role in words, actions and deeds. Logic and sequence combined set me on the right path and the role played itself and the sticky passage passed by without my even noticing it.

'As a result my performance achieved if not "universal" at least considerable significance for the play, although I hadn't thought about it.

'What did it mean? What was it helped me free myself from my chains? What was it prodded me onto the right track and led me to the goal I was seeking?

'Of course, it wasn't the fact that the tailor had sent a large bill, or that I had lost my key and read a review. All these things together, my daily circumstances, the chance elements, put me in a mood in which the review had a greater effect on me than one would have expected. It called my overall view of the role into question, and obliged me to look at it again. That led me to success.

'I went to a very seasoned actor, and a good psychologist, and asked him to help me fix that chance experience I had had that evening. He said to me:

' "Trying to repeat something you have experienced by chance is like trying to bring a dead flower back to life. Wouldn't it be better to do something else, not try to revive something that's already dead, but to grow something new in exchange? What do we have to do? First, don't think about the flower itself but water its roots, or plant a new seed in the earth and grow a new flower."

'But in the vast majority of cases that is not what actors do. If they happen to have a successful moment in a role and want to repeat it, then they take the direct route to the feeling itself and try and experience it. And that's the same as trying to create a flower without the help of nature. That's impossible, and so there is nothing to do but substitute a prop flower.

'What are we to do?

'Not think about the feeling itself but think about what made it grow, the conditions which led to the experience. They are the soil which you have to water and manure. Meanwhile nature herself will create a new feeling, analogous to the one you experienced before.

'It's the same with you. Never start with the result. It will not come of itself, it is the logical consequence of what has gone before.

'I did just as my wise counsellor told me. I moved down the bloom to its stalk, to its roots, or, in other words, retraced my way through the speech, "on Man", until I came to the basic idea of the play, the reason why it was written. What shall we call this idea? Freedom? Human self-awareness? That, in essence, is what the pilgrim, Luka, talks about the whole time, from the beginning of the play.

'But now, when I went to the roots of my role I realized that they were overgrown with mould and fungus, with every conceivable kind of useless, damaging, actorish Tasks.

'I realized that my "universally meaningful" speech bore no relationship to the speech "on Man" that Gorki had written. The first interpretation was only me overacting heavily, while the second was intended to express the main idea of the play, and be its climax, the major, creative, uplifting moment as experienced by the author and the actor. Earlier, all I had thought about was how to deliver someone else's lines effectively, not to convey my thoughts and experiences, which were parallel to the thoughts and experiences of the character, as clearly and beautifully as possible to my fellow actor. I played the result instead of behaving logically and sequentially and thereby moving quite naturally towards the result, i.e. towards the main idea of the play and of my own creative work as an actor. All the mistakes I had made blocked me off from the main idea like a stone wall.

'What was it helped me break down the wall?

'Questioning the way I had planned the role.

'Who questioned it?

'The review.

'And what gave it such power?

'The tailor's bill, the lost key, and other chance events which put me in a generally bad, jumpy state, which then made me take a critical look at what had happened that day.

'I give you this example so as to illustrate the second way I spoke of the path from feeling to stimulus.

'Once he is familiar with this path an actor can, at will, at any moment, summon up the recurrent experiences he needs.

'So, we go from feelings created by chance to the stimulus so that thereafter we can go from the stimulus to the feeling,' said Tortsov, summing up.

.. .. 19..

Today Tortsov said:

'The more comprehensive Emotion Memory is, the more raw material it has for us to work on, the richer and fuller that work is. That, I think, is self-evident and needs no further clarification.

'But apart from the richness of our emotion memories, we must distinguish between the strength, stability and quality of the material it contains.

'The strength of Emotion Memory is of great importance in our work. The stronger, sharper, more precise it is, the clearer and fuller our ability to experience. A weak Emotion Memory evokes barely perceptible, wraith-like feelings. They aren't suitable for the stage as they don't catch on, they hardly reach the auditorium.'

When he talked further about Emotion Memory it emerged that the degree of its strength, duration and influence varied considerably. Tortsov said this about it:

'Imagine that you have been insulted or have had your face slapped in public and that makes your cheeks burn for the rest of your life thereafter. The psychological shock that incident caused is so great that it has blotted out all the details and external circumstances of the savage attack you had received.

'For some quite trivial reason, or even for no reason at all, the offence you experienced flares up in your Emotion Memory, comes alive with redoubled strength. Then your face turns red or deathly pale, your heart sickens and beats uncontrollably fast.

'If he possesses such keen-edged emotional raw material and he can easily be aroused, all the actor has to do is experience a scene as parallel to the shock stamped on his memory in life. He requires no technique to help him. Everything happens spontaneously. Nature helps the actor.

'That is one of the most powerful, keenest, cleanest, most vital features of emotion memories and recurring feelings.

'Let me give you another example. A friend of mine, who is phenomenally absentminded, after a long break, went to lunch with some people he knew and proposed a toast to the health of the hostess's son, a small child whom his parents adored.

'His good wishes were received in deathly silence, after which the hostess, the child's mother, fainted. Apparently my poor friend had forgotten that the lunch was being given exactly a year after the death of the child whose health he had toasted. "I'll never forget what I experienced at that moment as long as I live," he acknowledged.

'However, this time feeling did not blot out the circumstances, as with the slap of the face, and so not only his emotions but every detail of what had happened were clearly imprinted in my friend's memory. He could vividly remember the horrified faces of the guests sitting opposite him, his neighbour's lowered eyes and the cry that was wrung from the other end of the table.

'Now, after some time has elapsed, the feelings that he had then, during that shocking incident at the table suddenly, spontaneously, come alive again. But sometimes he can't manage all the details at once. He has to recall the circumstances of that unfortunate incident. Then the feeling comes alive again, either all at once or gradually.

'That's an example of a weaker or, so to speak, middling vitality and strength in Emotion Memory, which needs help from our psycho-technique.

'Now I will give you a third example of the same kind. It happened to that same absentminded friend, only not in public but in a private conversation.

'His cousin came to see him after the death of her mother to thank him for the wreath he had sent for the funeral. The cousin had scarcely finished doing what she had come to do than my absentminded, crazy friend politely asked for news of "his dear aunt's health" (the deceased).

'The embarrassment he experienced then was, of course, imprinted on his memory, but considerably less strongly than the earlier example of the toast. So, if my friend wanted to use this material as an actor he had to do a great deal of preparatory work. That's because the traces in his Emotion Memory were not deep or sharp enough to come alive by themselves, without outside help.

'That's an example of weak Emotion Memory and recurrent feelings.

'In cases like these our psychotechnique is called on to do a great deal of complex work.'

.. .. 19..

Tortsov continued with the discussion of the different qualities and strengths of Emotion Memory.

He said:

'Some emotion memories are weak, others are strong, though this is far less frequent.

'Often impressions live on in our memory and continue to grow and deepen there. They become stimuli for new processes which, on the one hand, remind us of the details of a past event which as yet we have been unable to recall and, on the other, stir the imagination which then fills in the details we have forgotten. That is a common occurrence among us actors. Remember the Italian actor on tour whom you met at my home.

'And here's another, more remarkable example from life, which happened to my sister.

'She was going back home to the country from the city and, in her bag, was carrying letters from her dead husband which were very dear to her. Because she was in a hurry, she rushed out of the train as it was arriving and hurried down to the last step of the carriage. This was covered in ice. She missed her footing and to the horror of all those standing round my sister found herself between the moving train and the pillars holding up the edge of the platform. The poor woman gave a desperate cry, but not because she feared for herself but because she had dropped her precious burden, the letters, which might fall under the wheels. Confusion reigned, there were shouts that a woman had fallen under the train and the driver, instead of helping, cursed my sister roundly. A stupid, disgusting scene ensued. The poor woman was so upset by it that she couldn't pull herself together all day and vented her resentment against the driver on everyone at home, completely forgetting her fall and the terrible accident she had barely escaped.

'Night fell. In the dark my sister recalled everything that had happened and had an attack of nerves.

'After that accident she couldn't bring herself to go to the station where she had so narrowly escaped a fatal accident. My sister was afraid that her memories would be made even more intense and she preferred to go an extra two miles by carriage to another station further away.

'So, at the moment of danger people stay calm and only faint when they remember it. That is not an example of strong Emotion Memory but of the fact that recurrent experiences can be stronger than first-time experiences since they continue to develop in our subconscious.

'But apart from the strength and intensity of emotion memories, we must distinguish their particular qualities. For example, imagine that you played no part in the incidents I described about the slap, the aunt and the cousin but were mere spectators.

'It's one thing to be insulted or to experience acute embarrassment and another to observe what is going on, get excited over it and criticize the actions of those who are guilty of the dispute when you have no responsibility for it.

'Of course, there's nothing to prevent the observer having strong feelings. In individual cases they may even be greater than for those taking part. But that's not what interests me for the moment. Right now I will merely comment that the quality of lived experiences as remembered by an observer and by a participant are not the same thing.

'But there are cases when we are not an active participant or even an observer of what happens but only hear or read about it.

'That doesn't prevent us from being strongly influenced by it, from having deep emotion memories. These depend on the power of persuasion of the person writing, or talking and on the receptivity of the person reading or listening.

'I will never forget an eyewitness account of a boat with a crew of young people in training that was shipwrecked when the captain suddenly died in the middle of a storm. Only one person was fortunate enough to survive. The story of this tragedy at sea, which was related to me in vivid detail, shook me and continues to move me now.

'Of course, the emotion memories of a participant, an observer, a listener and a reader are of a different kind.

'Actors have to deal with all aspects of this emotional material, adapt it and reshape to meet the demands of the role.

'For example, let's say you were not a participant but an observer of the electrifying scene with the slap in the face I told you about in the previous class.

'Let's also say the impressions you then received are firmly imprinted in your Emotion Memory. It would be easy for you to repeat onstage those same experiences in the right kind of role. Let's further suppose that such a role was found but that you are not an observer of the scene but the one who really gets slapped. How are you to reshape the Emotion Memory of the observer into the experience of the character in the drama itself?

'The latter feels, the former has fellow-feeling. So we have to turn fellow-feeling into feeling.

'Here's an example of how the fellow-feeling of an observer is reborn as the genuine feeling of the character.

'Let's say you went to see a friend and found him in a terrible state. He was mumbling something, raging, weeping, showing all the signs of total despair. But you were unable to understand the reason, although you were genuinely worried by his state. What is it you experience in moments like that? Fellow-feeling. But your friend takes you into the next room and there you see his wife, stretched out on the floor in a pool of blood.

'The sight of it causes the husband to lose all self-control. He chokes and sobs, he yells something but you can't understand the words although you feel their tragic meaning

'What do you experience at that moment?

'Even stronger fellow-feeling for your friend.

'You manage to calm the poor man down and he begins to talk more intelligibly.

'It emerges that he killed his wife out of jealousy . . . of you.

'With that news everything changes for you. The fellow-feeling you had earlier as an observer is reborn as the feeling of a participant in the tragedy, which you have indeed become.

'A similar process occurs when we are working on a role. From the moment that the same kind of inner transformation takes place, the actor feels that he is an active character in the life of the play, genuine human feeling is born. Sometimes this transformation of the fellow feeling into the feelings of a character occurs spontaneously.

'The former (the human being) may have such a strong grasp of the situation of the latter (the character) and respond to it so that he feels he is in his place.

'In that case he will see what is happening, though unintentionally, as though he were the one who got slapped. He will want to react, get involved in the rumpus, protest against the behaviour of the guilty party as though it were a matter of his own personal honour and he was being insulted.

'In this instance, the experiences of the observer spontaneously transform fellow feeling into direct feeling, i.e. they acquire the same quality and almost the same strength as they have for the character in the play.

'But what if this doesn't happen during the creative act? Then we have to turn to our psychotechnique for help, to the Given Circumstances, magic "if" and other stimuli which evoke a response in our Emotion Memory.

'So, when we are searching for raw material we should use not only our own life experiences but things we have recognized in other people with whom we have felt a natural fellow-feeling.

'A similar process occurs with recollections of reading, or from stories told by other people.

'These impressions also have to be inwardly reshaped, i.e. the fellow-feeling of the person reading or listening has to be transformed into his own, genuine feeling, similar to the feelings of the character in the story.

'Aren't you familiar with this process whereby the writer's feelings become the character's feelings? Isn't that what we do with every new role we play? We become familiar with it through reading plays, which tell us about incidents in which we, the actors, were neither observers nor participants and which we learn about from our reading.

'When we first encounter a dramatist's work, with rare exceptions, only fellow feeling for the characters occurs. It is our job, as we rehearse, to turn this fellow feeling into our own genuine feeling as actors and human beings.'

.. .. 19..

'Do you remember the "madman" or the "crashed plane"?' Tortsov asked us today. 'Do you recall the "ifs", the Given Circumstances, the ideas you had and the other stimuli, all of which helped you reveal the creative material which lay in your Emotion Memory and which you needed? You achieved these same results with the help of external stimuli.

'Do you remember the scene from Brand and how it was divided into Bits and Tasks, and caused a big fight between the male and female halves of the class? That was a new kind of internal stimulus.

'Do you remember the objects of attention, which were illustrated by electric lights which lit up first here then there, onstage and in the auditorium? Now you know that living objects can also act as a stimulus for us.

'Do you remember the physical actions, their logic and sequence, truth and belief in their authenticity? That is also an important stimulus to feeling.

'In the future you will have to learn a whole series of new internal stimuli. The most powerful of them lies in the words and ideas of the play, in the feelings that lie beneath the author's text, in the interaction of the characters.

'You are now acquainted with another whole series of external stimuli: the setting, the lights, the sound and other production effects, which create the onstage illusion of real life and a living atmosphere.

'If we bring together all the stimuli you are already familiar with, and add those you still have to learn about, then you have stored up a hand-some number. That's your capital, your psychotechnique. You have to know how to use it.'

'But how? I'm desperately anxious to learn how to call up recurrent feelings to order and to stimulate my Emotion Memory,' I assured him.

'You must handle Emotion Memory and the feelings it contains in the same way a hunter handles wildfowl,' Tortsov explained. 'If the bird won't fly to him, there's no way of tracking it down in a dense green thicket. There's nothing for it but to entice it out of the woods with the help of special whistles, which we call "decoys".

'Artistic feeling, like the woodfowl, scares easily and it hides in the deep recesses of our mind. If our feelings will not come out into the open there is no way to ambush them. In that case we have to rely on a decoy.

'These decoys are precisely those stimuli to Emotion Memory and recurrent feelings which we have been talking about all this time to lure them out.

'Each successive stage in our studies has brought a new decoy (or stimulus) for our Emotion Memory and recurrent feelings. In fact, the magic "if", the Given Circumstances, our imagination, the Bits and Tasks, the objects of attention, the truth and belief in inner and outer actions, provided us with the appropriate decoys (stimuli).

'So all the work we have done so far in school has led us to these decoys which we need to stimulate our Emotion Memory and stored-up feelings.

'Decoys are the most powerful means at our disposal when it comes to working in the area of our psychotechnique.

'The link between the decoy and feeling can be widely used, the more so since it is natural and normal.

'The actor must be able to respond directly to the decoys (stimuli) and master them, as a virtuoso does a keyboard. You invent a gripping story, or Task, about a madman or a crashed aeroplane, or burning money and immediately some sort of feeling flares up inside you. You invent some-thing else and, lo and behold, other experiences are evoked. You must know which stimulates what, what the right bait is to get a bite. You have to be the gardener, so to speak, of your own heart, one who knows what grows from which seeds. You must not reject any subject, any stimulus to your Emotion Memory.'

The end of the class was devoted to demonstrating that all our work at school, in all its phases leads principally to arousing Emotion Memory and recurrent feelings.

.. .. 19..

In today's class Tortsov said:

'It is clear from everything that has been said what a huge role Emotion Memory and recurrent feelings play in the creative process.

'Next comes the question of our stores of Emotion Memory. These must be continually replenished. How are we to do that? Where are we to find the necessary creative material?

'As you know, first in line are our personal impressions, feelings, experiences. These we obtain from the real world and from our imagination, from our recollections, from books, from science and learning, from travelling, from museums and, most important of all, from our relationships with other people.

'The nature of the material the actor obtains from life varies according to the degree to which the theatre understands the purpose of art, and its own particular responsibility towards the audience. There were periods when the theatre was available to a small number of leisured people who were seeking diversion, and it tried to satisfy the demands of its audience. There were other periods when the material an actor could use lay in the turmoil around him, and so forth.

'In different periods the theatre uses different kinds of material. Superficial observation was sufficient for vaudevilles. A certain actor's temperament together with an external technique and a minimal acquaintance with the heroic style was sufficient for Ozerov's conventional tragedies.[10] To bring the mediocre drama written between 1860 and 1890 (if you discount Ostrovski) to life actors could make do with the knowledge they obtained from their own circle and the strata of society attached to it. But when Chekhov wrote The Seagull, which is shot through with the atmosphere of a new era, earlier material proved inadequate and we had to dig deeper into the life of our society as a whole and humankind, in which more complex, subtle trends appeared.

'The more the lives of individual people and the whole of humanity became more complex, the deeper the actor had to dig into the complexity of that life.

'To do that he had to broaden his horizons. They extend ever wider and, in times of world-shaking events, reach infinity.

'But it is not enough to broaden one's horizons, to encompass all the aspects of life, it is not enough to observe, you must also understand the meaning of the phenomena you observe, you must digest the feelings and impressions in your Emotion Memory, you must penetrate the real meaning of what is happening around you. To create art and portray "the life of the human spirit of a role" onstage, you must not only study life but come into direct communication with it in all its manifestations whenever, wherever and however you can. Otherwise our creative work will wither, turn into clichés. The actor who observes the life from the sidelines, feeling the joy and sorrow of the things that happen but who does not penetrate the complex reasons for them, and does not go beyond to see them as majestic events, full of great drama, great heroism, such an actor is dead to real creative work. If he wants to live for his art, he must dig deep into the life around him, whatever the cost, use his mind to its full extent, fill the gaps in his knowledge and re-examine his opinions. If an actor doesn't want to kill his creative capacity, then he must not see life like a narrow-minded Philistine. A Philistine cannot be an artist worthy of the name. But the majority of actors are precisely that – Philistines, making a career for themselves.

'When searching for emotional material we must also bear in mind that we Russians tend to see the worst in others and in ourselves.

'So, when it comes to negative feelings and recollections, we have a great store of them in our Emotion Memory. Our literature is overflowing with negative characters and very poor in positive ones.

'Of course there are many artistic portrayals of vice (Khlestakov, the Mayor)[11] and darker human attributes contain passions of explosive power (Ivan the Terrible) but they alone do not represent the essence of our art, which is to convey the beauty of "the life of the human spirit". We need different kind of material. Seek it in the brighter corners of our inner world, in the places where ardour and enthusiasm live. Let your Emotion Memory be filled with a mighty store of things which are beautiful and noble.

'It must surely now be clear to you that for a genuine actor to do everything that is required of him, he must lead a rich, interesting, beautiful, diverse, exciting, stimulating life. He should know what is happening not only in the big cities but also in the provinces, the country, in factories and plants, in the cultural centres of the world. The actor should observe and study the life and psychology of peoples both at home and abroad.

'We need endlessly broad horizons since we are performing plays of our own time from countries all over the world and we are called on to convey the "life of the human spirit" of all the peoples of the globe.

'More than that. An actor creates not only the life of his own period but also of the past and the future onstage.

'Our tasks grow more complex. When creating his own period an actor can observe the things that are, what's going on around him. But when creating a past or future life, or one that doesn't exist, he has to restore them or construct them from scratch in his imagination and that, as you have seen, is a complex business.

'Our ideal as actors, in all periods, has been and remains what is eternal in art, that which never ages or dies and which is ever young and dear to people.

'I am talking of the heights of our creative achievement, established for us by classical models, the ideal towards which we should eternally strive.

'Study these models and search for living, emotional, creative material to convey them.

'The actor takes everything he can give to a human being from his real or his imaginary life. But all the impressions, passions, delights, everything others live as themselves are inwardly transformed into material for his creative work.

'Out of what is personal and transient he creates a whole world of poetic images, radiant ideas, which will live eternally for all,

'I've told you everything about Emotion Memory it is possible to tell beginners. The rest you will learn in the future, as you go on studying our programme,' Tortsov concluded.

10

COMMUNICATION

.. .. 19..
A large notice was hanging up in the auditorium. It read:

COMMUNICATION

Tortsov came in, welcomed us to a new phase in our work and turned to Igor.

'With whom or what are you in communication right now?', he asked him.

Igor was lost in his own thoughts, and didn't immediately understand what he was being asked.

'Me? Nobody, nothing,' he replied almost automatically.

'Then you must be one of "nature's wonders"! We'll have to put you in the freak museum if you can live without being in communication with anyone or anything.'

Igor tried to make excuses, assuring us that no one was looking at him or in communication with him. So he couldn't be in communication with anyone.

'Do you really need someone to be looking at you or talking to you to do that?' said Tortsov in astonishment. 'Close your eyes, stop up your ears, say nothing, and find out whom and with what you are mentally in communication. See if you can detect one single moment when you have no object you are in communication with.'

I did the same, closed my eyes, stopped up my ears and started to check on what was going on inside me.

I had a picture of the previous evening's soirée at the theatre at which a famous string quartet appeared and, step by step, began to remember everything that had happened to me. I came into the foyer, said hello to people, sat down and started watching the musicians who were getting ready to play.

They began to play and I listened to them. But I wasn't able to get into the performance, hear it and feel it as I should.

'That's an empty moment, I wasn't in communication at all,' I decided and quickly communicated my thoughts with Tortsov.

'What!' he exclaimed in amazement. 'You consider responding to a work of art an empty moment, when you weren't in communication with anything?'

'Yes, because I was listening without hearing, trying to understand and not understanding. So I maintain that I wasn't yet in communication with the music and so this was a empty moment,' I added.

'You weren't in communication with the music because your attention was still on what had gone before. But, once that was over, you listened, or turned, became interested in something else. So you were in communication all the time.'

'All right,' I said, and continued remembering.

I absentmindedly moved too forcibly, and felt I was attracting people's attention. I had to sit quite still for a while and pretend I was listening to the music whereas in actual fact I wasn't listening at all but checking on what was going on around me.

My gaze wandered over towards Tortsov and I realized he hadn't noticed my fidgeting. Then I looked round for Uncle Pasha, but he wasn't there, neither were the other actors. Then I took a look at everyone else present in turn. By then my concentration was flying off in all directions so that I couldn't control it or direct it where I wanted. The pictures, the thoughts that went through my mind at that time! The music helped these flights of thought and imagination. I thought of the people at home, of my relatives who live far away in other towns and of a dead friend.

Tortsov said that these images came to me not in spite of but because of the need I felt either to surrender to the objects I was thinking about or feeling, or to draw other thoughts from them. Finally my attention was attracted by the small lamps in the chandeliers and I spent a long time looking at their intricate forms.

'Now there's an empty moment,' I decided. 'You can't count looking at stupid lamps as being in communication.'

When I told Tortsov of my new discovery he explained it this way:

'You were trying to understand how it was made, and what it was made of. It conveyed its form, its overall look, and all manner of details. You received all these impressions, inscribed them in your memory and then thought about what you had seen. That is, you took something from the object, and you did it because relating is essential for us actors. You were confused by the fact it was inanimate. Yet pictures, statues, exhibits in museums are also inanimate, but they hold the life of their creator within them. And a lamp can, to a certain degree, be given life by the interest which we take in it.'

'If that's the case,' I argued, 'are we in communication with every article we happen to see?'

'You're hardly likely to be able to take in or surrender a little of yourself to all the things you catch sight of. You can only be in communication when you see something and surrender to what you see. Brief moments of being in communication are created by things to which you give something of yourself, or from which you take something.

'I have told you more than once that onstage you can look and really see, and you can look and see nothing. To be more precise, you can look at, see and feel everything that's happening around you, or you can look and yet really be interested in what is going on in the auditorium or outside the theatre.

'You can look, see and understand what's happening, but you can also look, see and understand nothing.

'In a word, there is an external formalistic, or, so to speak, "token registering with empty eyes", as we say here.

'The theatre has its own tricks of the trade to mask our inner emptiness but they only emphasize the vacancy of the eyes.

'Need I say that this kind of seeing is unnecessary and harmful. The eyes are the mirror of the soul. And empty eyes are the mirror of an empty soul. Don't forget that!

'It is important that an actor's eyes, his gaze, his glance, reflect the size, the depth of his creative mind. So, he needs to have stored up considerable, profound inner content of mind, experiences that are similar to the "life of the human spirit" of a role, which he will need to communicate with the other actors. He must share that content with his partner the whole time he is onstage.

'But the actor is a human being with the usual human weaknesses. When he goes onstage he naturally carries with him his thoughts, personal feelings, his ideas from the real world. His own humdrum, daily life is still there, and takes the first opportunity to slip into the character he is experiencing. The actor only gives himself wholeheartedly to the role when it takes him over. Then he merges with the character, and undergoes a creative transformation. But should he be distracted, he is once again caught up in his own personal life, which carries him away beyond the footlights, into the auditorium or further, outside the theatre, seeking some object with which mentally to communicate. At such moments the role is conveyed externally, mechanically. All these distractions constantly break the lifeline of the character and communication. The gaps are then filled by details from the actor's personal life, which have nothing to do with the role he is playing.

'Imagine a valuable necklace in which three gold rings are followed by a fourth of plain tin, with the next two gold rings tied with string.

'What's the good of a necklace like that? Who needs a broken line? Constantly breaking the line of a role in this way either cripples it, or kills it.

'Yet if we need to be in proper and continuous communication with people or things in life, the need is ten times stronger onstage. This is due to the nature of theatre itself, which is entirely based on the relationships among the characters and of individual characters with themselves. So, imagine that the author has taken it into his head to show his characters while they are asleep or unconscious, that is, in those moments when their inner life is in no way apparent.

'Or imagine that he brings on two characters who don't know each other, who neither wish to introduce themselves, nor exchange their thoughts and feelings but, on the contrary, to hide them, and who sit, silent, in different corners of the stage.

'If that's the case, the audience is wasting its time, since it is not getting what it came for. It doesn't sense the feelings or learn the thoughts of the characters.

'It's quite another matter if they come onstage and one of them wants to tell the other what he is feeling, or to convince him that his opinions are right, while the other meanwhile tries to understand.

'When the audience sees two or more characters exchanging their thoughts and feelings, it becomes involved in their words and actions involuntarily, rather like someone accidentally overhearing a conversation. It participates silently in these exchanges, sees them, understands them and is caught up in other people's experiences.

'It follows that the audience can only understand and indirectly participate in what is happening when the characters in the play are in communication with each another.

'If the actors do not wish to lose their grip on a large audience, they must take great care always to be in unbroken communication with their partner through their own feelings, thoughts and actions, which are similar to the feelings, thoughts and actions of the character. Of course, the inner material they have to communicate must be of interest, attractive to the eyes and ears of the audience. The process of communication is of exceptional importance. We have to pay particular attention to it. That means taking next a more conscientious look at its various aspects which we shall encounter later.'

.. .. 19..

'I'm going to start with solitary communication, or self-communication,' Tortsov explained when he came into class. 'When do we talk out loud to ourselves in real life?

'When we are so upset and angry we can't contain ourselves, or when we are trying to drum a difficult idea into our heads, which our mind cannot grasp quickly, when we use sounds to remind us of something we already know, when we are all alone and express sadness or happiness, just to lighten our mood.

'This occurs very rarely in real life but very often onstage.

'When I have to be in silent communication with myself onstage, I feel good, I quite like it because it is familiar to me. It happens naturally. But when I have to be onstage face to face with myself and deliver long, flowery speeches in verse, I feel lost and don't know what to do.

'How am I to justify onstage something which I am almost never able to justify in life?

'Where am I in that mood to find my *real Self*? A human being is no small thing. Where am I to turn? To my brain, my heart, my imagination, my arms and legs? . . . How do I direct the inner flow of communication – from where to where?

'I need a properly defined subject and object. Where are they inside us? Without two related centres, I cannot keep a firm grip on my power of concentration which is unstable and unfocused. It's hardly surprising if it flies off into the auditorium where an irresistible object is ever lying in wait for us – a big crowd.

'But I was taught how to get out of this situation. I learned there was another centre, apart from the centre of the nervous system in the brain, one located near the heart – the solar plexus.

'I tried to get these two centres talking to each other.

'I marvelled in the fact that not only did I feel they actually existed, but they had started talking to each other.

'I took the centre in my head to represent consciousness and the solar plexus to represent emotion.

'So, my impression was that my head was in communication with my heart.

' "Well then," I said to myself, "let them talk." My subject and object have been found.

'From that moment on my mood when relating to myself onstage felt secure, not only in silent pauses, but also when speaking out loud.

'I have no wish to go into whether what I felt is acceptable to science or not.

'My criterion is the way I felt. It may indeed be purely personal, it may indeed prove to be the product of my own imagination but it helps me, so I make all possible use of it.

'If my practical and unscientific technique is also useful to you, then so much the better. I make no assertions.'

After a short pause Tortsov continued:

'Learning to communicate with another actor is easier. But even there we encounter obstacles which we need to know about, and overcome. For example, we are onstage together, and you are in direct communication with me. I'm a big fellow. Just look at me! I have a nose, a mouth, legs, hands, a torso. Can you really be in communication with every part of my body at the same time?' Tortsov asked me. 'If that's not possible then choose some part of me, some point, through which you can make communication.'

'The eyes!' someone suggested. 'They are the mirror of the soul.'

'As you can see, what you first look for in someone is their soul, their inner world. Look for the living soul in me, my living "I".'

'How are we to do that?' the students asked in bewilderment.

'Hasn't life taught you that?' said Tortsov in amazement, 'Haven't you ever felt out someone else's mind, probed it with your feelings? You don't need to learn how to do that. Watch me closely, try to understand, to sense my inner mood. So. What am I now, would you say?'

'Kindly, warm-hearted, affectionate, lively, interesting,' I said, trying to sense his mood.

'And now?' asked Tortsov.

I prepared myself but suddenly saw, there in front of me, not Tortsov but Famusov[1] with all his usual tics, his naive eyes, thick lips, podgy hands and the soft, senile gestures of a pampered man.

'Who are you in communication with?' Tortsov asked me in Famusov's voice, in the contemptuous tone he uses when speaking to Molchalin.

'With Famusov, of course,' I answered.

'So where is Tortsov?' Tortsov asked, instantly becoming himself again. 'If you weren't in communication with Famusov's nose, nor with his hands which I altered as part of the character I had created, but with my mind, then that mind was still there inside me. I can't drive it out, I can't hire another one from someone else. Does that mean you went wrong this time and were in communication not with a mind but with something else? What was it?'

Yes, what was I in communication with?

With a living mind of course. I remember how when Tortsov was transmuted into Famusov, i.e. when the object changed, my feelings were transformed, too, from the deep respect I have for Tortsov to the gentle, ironic amusement the character of Famusov as played by Tortsov aroused in me. So I couldn't work out who I was in communication with and told Tortsov so.

'You were in communication with a new being, whose name is Famusov/Tortsov or Tortsov/Famusov. In due course you will come to know this marvellous metamorphosis that takes place in a truly creative actor. For the time being, understand that people always try to make communication with the living soul of an object and not with his nose, eyes or buttons as actors do onstage.

'So, as you can see, all two people need is to meet and immediately there is mutual communication.

'For example, just now we met and a form of communication was established between us.

'I was trying to convey my thoughts to you and you listened and made an effort to receive my knowledge and experience.'

'That means it isn't mutual, two-way communication,' interjected Grisha, 'because emitting feelings is something the subject, that is the person speaking, does, and receiving feelings is something we the objects, the people listening, do.

'Tell me please, how was it two-way? Where's the return flow of feeling?'

'What are you doing right now?' Tortsov asked him. 'You're telling me I'm wrong, you're trying to convince me, i.e. you are conveying your doubts to me and I am receiving them. That's the return flow you were speaking of.'

'Now, yes, but what about before, when you were the only one speaking?'

'I don't see any difference,' Tortsov countered. 'We were communicating then and we are still communicating now. Obviously, emitting and receiving alternately. But when I was speaking and you were listening I could already feel the doubts that were creeping into your mind. Your impatience, your astonishment, your animation came across to me.

'Why did that happen? Because you couldn't contain them, because giving and receiving alternated involuntarily. Even when you were saying nothing, the return flow was there. In the end it came out into the open in your final objection. Isn't that an example of continuous, two-way communication?!

'Mutual, unbroken communication is particularly necessary and important for us since the play and the acting consist almost entirely of dialogue, which is mutual communication between two or more characters.

'Unfortunately continuous communication is a rarity onstage. Most actors, if they use it at all, only communicate while they are saying their own lines. As soon as they have nothing to say and someone else is speaking, they don't listen, don't receive their partner's thoughts. They stop acting until it's their next line. This actorish behaviour wrecks the direct communication that the giving and receiving of feelings requires, not only during spoken words, but in moments of silence, when very often it is the eyes that go on speaking.

'Gaps in the words are wrong. But you must learn to speak your thoughts to someone else and then ensure they have reached his consciousness and his feelings. For that you need a short pause. Only when you are convinced that this has happened and you have spoken with your eyes what is not possible to say in words, should you go on to deliver the next part of the speech. In your turn, you must receive your partner's words and thoughts as though they were new, fresh that day, every time. You must pay proper attention to thoughts and words which you know well, which you have heard many times in rehearsal and in the countless performances you have played. The process of continuously giving and receiving feelings and thoughts must be gone through each and every time you recreate the role. That demands great concentration, technique and discipline.'

Tortsov was unable to complete his explanation as the class had to end.

.. .. 19..

Tortsov continued his description of the characteristics of various kinds of communication he had begun last time.

'I shall move on to examine a new kind of relationship – with imaginary, unreal, non-existent objects (for example, the ghost of Hamlet's father). He is not seen either by the actor onstage or the people in the auditorium.

'Faced with such objects, the inexperienced try to delude themselves into thinking they can really see an object which does not actually exist but is only implied. All their energy and concentration goes into it.

'But experienced actors know that it's not the actual "ghost" that matters, but their relationship with it, and so they replace a non-existent object with a magic "if", and try to answer sincerely and honestly what they would do if a "ghost" were to appear in the empty space before them.

'In their turn some actors, particularly students, beginners, when working at home, also resort to an imaginary object in the absence of a living one. They place it mentally before them, then try to see it and communicate with an empty space. A great deal of energy and concentration is invested in an all-out effort to see something that doesn't exist rather than into the Task (which is what is needed for experiencing to happen). This becomes a habit, which they carry over unwittingly onto the stage. In the end they are no longer used to seeing a living object but are used to placing a sham, dead object between them and their fellow actor. This is deadly and is often so deeply ingrained that it lasts a lifetime.

'It is agony to play opposite actors who look at you and see someone else and adapt to him, not you. A wall separates them from those with whom they should be in direct communication. They don't take in your lines, your voice, there isn't any form of communication. Their glazed eyes stare at emptiness as though they were in a trance. Beware of this, it is dangerous, murderous and crippling. It takes root easily and is difficult to eradicate.'

'Yes, but what do we do when there's no living object to make communication with?' I asked.

'Simple. Don't communicate at all until you've found one,' Tortsov responded. 'You have a class in "training and drill". It was created so that you should do exercises not on your own but in twos or in groups. Let me repeat, I absolutely insist that students should not communicate with an empty void but do exercises with living objects, under expert supervision and not with an empty space.

'Communication with a group object, or, in other words, with a huge audience is equally difficult.'

'You must never make communication with them! In no way!' Vanya warned.

'Yes, yes true, direct communication during a show, no, but indirect communication is essential. Both the difficulty and the uniqueness of our form of communication lie in the fact that it occurs with another actor and with the audience simultaneously. Communication with the former is direct, conscious, but with the latter it is indirect, unconscious, through *another actor*. It is evident that, in both cases, the communication is two-way.'

But Pasha protested:

'I can understand that the communication an actor has with other actors can be called two-way, but is the relationship to the audience the same? For that, the audience would have to give something. But what do we actually get from them? Applause, flowers, but not when we are performing, only after the curtain.'

'And laughter, tears, applause or hushing during the act, uproar – and God knows what! Don't you count them?' Tortsov wondered.

'I will give you an instance that perfectly describes the link, the two-way communication between the audience and the stage,' he said continuing his argument. 'During a children's matinée of The Blue Bird in the scene in which the trees and the animals are sitting in appraisal on the children, I felt someone nudge me in the darkness. It was a ten-year-old boy.

'Tell them Cat is eavesdropping. He's hiding but I can se. . .eee him!' he whispered, frightened for Tyltyl and Myltyl.[2]

'I couldn't calm him down, and so he came right up to the stage, and, over the footlights started to whisper to the actors playing the children that they were in danger.

'Isn't that a response from out front?

'If you want a better idea of what you get from the audience, try getting rid of it and playing to a completely empty house. Is that what you want?'

For a moment I put myself in the place of some poor actor performing to an empty house . . . and felt I wouldn't make it through to the end.

'And why is that?' Tortsov asked after I had admitted it. 'Because then there is no connection between actor and audience, and without that, there can be no performance.

'Playing without an audience is like singing in a room with a dead acoustic, full of soft furnishing and carpets. Playing to a packed and sympathetic house is like singing in a space with a good acoustic.

'The audience creates, so to speak, a psychological acoustic. It registers what we do and bounces its own living, human feelings back to us.

'The art of representation and stock-in-trade acting deal with this form of communication very simply. Often the style of the play, the performance, consists entirely of conventions. Thus, for example in old French comedies or farces the actors speak their lines straight out front all the time. The characters go downstage and deliver individual lines or long-winded speeches setting out the plot. This is done confidently, boldly, with great aplomb and is very impressive. And the fact is, if you're going to make communication with the whole house you'd better do it in such a way as to take charge of it.

'In the next kind of group communication – crowd scenes – we also have to deal with a large body of people, only this time not in the auditorium but on the stage itself, and we use not indirect but direct communication with a group object. Sometimes we make communication with individual objects, at other moments we encompass the whole mass of people. That is, so to speak, extended two-way communication.

'The people in crowd scenes are all quite different, and are part of this two-way communication. They bring with them a great variety of thoughts and feelings, and intensify the process. The group fires you, either individually or as part of the whole. That simulates the actors and makes a great impression on the audience.'

After that Tortsov went on to a new kind of communication – the stock-in-trade.

'It is directed straight from the stage to the house, bypassing the other actor, who is a character in the play. It's the line of least resistance. This kind, as you well know, is mere exhibitionism, theatrics. We won't waste any time on it as I've already said enough about stock-in-trade acting in previous classes. We can assume that you don't confuse mere exhibition-ism with a genuine effort to transmit something to your fellow actors, and to receive living, human experiences from them. There is an enormous difference between the creative heights and mere, mechanical functioning. These are two diametrically opposed kinds of communication.

'In our theatre we recognize all of the forms of communication I have indicated except theatrical. But you have to know it and study it so you can fight it.

'In conclusion I will say a few words about the active and dynamic nature of communication.

'Many people think that the visible movements of the hands, legs and body are signs of dynamism whereas invisible actions, mental communi-cation are not true activity.

'That is a mistake, and all the more regrettable since in our kind of acting which creates the "life of the human spirit" of a role, each indication of inner action is especially important and precious.

'Communication through the mind constitutes one of the most import-ant dynamic actions in acting and should be valued. It is absolutely essen-tial in the process of creating and emitting the "life of the human spirit" of a role.'

.. .. 19..

'If you want to communicate, you must have something you wish to communicate, i.e. first and foremost, your own thoughts and feelings, your experiences,' Tortsov said in today's class.

'In the real world, life itself creates them. There the material we com-municate arises spontaneously, depending on our circumstances.

'This is not the case in the theatre, and therein lies a new difficulty. In the theatre we are given someone else's thoughts and feelings in a role which has been created by a writer and appears in cold print on the page. It is difficult to experience that kind of material. It is so much easier to be external, play the appearance of non-existent passions in the role.

'It is the same thing with communication. It is more difficult genuinely to make communication with your fellow actor than to play at being in communication. That's the line of least resistance. Actors love it and so are all too willing to swap genuine communication for mere theatrics. What are we sending to the audience at moments like that?

'That's a question we have to consider. To me it's important that you should not only understand with your intelligence, not only feel, but that you should see with your own eyes what it is, most of the time, we bring onstage with us to communicate to the audience. To show you what I mean, the easiest thing is to go onstage and demonstrate the things you need to know, feel and see.'

Tortsov went onstage and played a whole show for us. It was remarkable for its talent, mastery and technique. He started by reciting some verses, which he delivered very fast, to great effect. But their meaning was unclear so that we didn't understand a thing.

'What was I communicating to you?' he asked us.

The students were stumped for an answer.

'Precisely nothing!' he told us. 'I rattled off a few words, scattered them like peas from a basket without even knowing what I was saying or to whom I was saying it.

'There you have the kind of flimsy nonsense actors often communicate to the audience, rattling off words with no concern for their sense, their Subtext, only for the effect they have.'

After a moment's thought Tortsov explained he was going to read Figaro's speech from the last act of The Marriage of Figaro.[3]

This time his acting was an absolute torrent of prodigious moves, vocal changes, infectious laughs. His diction was crystal-clear, his voice resonant, swift and brilliant. It was so effective, we could hardly stop ourselves applauding. As to its inner content we had no idea what the speech was about.

'What did I communicate to you?' Tortsov asked us once more and once again we couldn't answer, but this time because he had given us too much, and we couldn't immediately grasp the full meaning of what we had seen and heard.

'I showed myself in the role,' Tortsov answered us, 'and exploited Figaro's speech, its words, staging, movements, actions etc., not to demonstrate the role but myself in the role, i.e. my own attributes – body, voice, gestures, poses, mannerisms, movements, walk, voice, diction, speech, intonation, energy, technique – in a word everything except proper feelings and experiences.

'This is not difficult to do for anyone with a good technique. All I had to do was make sure that my voice was resonant, that the tongue rapped out the letters, syllables, words, sentences, that the poses and gestures were expressive and that the whole thing pleased the audience. At the same time, you must not only watch yourself but the people out front. I pre-sented you with parts of myself or the whole, like a cabaret "star", keeping a constant eye on the effect I was having. I felt I was a piece of merchandise and you were the buyers.

'Here's another example of something an actor should never do onstage, although it is a great success with audiences.'

A third experiment followed.

'A moment ago I showed you myself in the role,' he said. 'Now I will show you the role in myself as given by the author and rehearsed by me. That doesn't mean I will experience it. It's not a matter of experiencing it, but rather of giving its outward shape, the lines, the face, the moves, etc. I won't create the role, I will merely dispatch it.'

Tortsov played a scene from Enough Stupidity in Every Wise Man in which an important general who happens to be left at home all alone doesn't know what to do with himself.[4] Out of sheer boredom he lines up the chairs like soldiers on parade. Then he tidies up all the things on the desk, thinks up something amusing and spicy, casts a horrified eye at the official papers, signs a few without reading them, yawns, stretches and starts the whole stupid business all over again.

The whole time he was playing this scene, Tortsov delivered the lines on the nobility of those in high places, and the lack of breeding found in everyone else, with great precision.

Tortsov gave us the dialogue coldly, externally, demonstrated it, showed us the shape, the outward form, without attempting to give it any life or depth. In some passages he rendered the lines technically, in others it was the actions, i.e. sometimes he underlined a pose, moves, business, gestures, sometimes stressed a typical trait in the character, with one eye on the audience the whole time to make sure the picture of the role he had planned was getting across. He would carefully hold a pause when he had to. It was like those actors who play a role they are sick of but which has been well planned, and in the five hundredth performance feel at moments that they are a gramophone, at others a projector endlessly showing the same old reel of film.

'Strange and sad as it may seem, even this external demonstration of a well-rehearsed role is rarely seen in the theatre,' Tortsov noted.

'Now,' he continued, 'I still have to show what you should communicate onstage, i.e. your living feelings, which are similar to the character's, and are fully experienced and physically embodied.

'But you have seen this kind of acting many times, when I managed more or less to complete the process of communication with you. You know, in those performances I try only to have dealings with my fellow actor, so that I can communicate my own human feelings, similar to the character's. The other things which produce a total fusion with the role, and give birth to a new creation, the actor/role, appear subconsciously. In performances of that kind I always feel myself as myself, in the Given Circumstances defined by the play, the director, myself and the whole production team.

'That is a rare form of communication, which, to my great sorrow, has few exponents.

'Need I say,' Tortsov summed up, 'that here we recognize only the last kind of communication with our fellow actor, using feelings we have personally experienced? The other kinds of communication we reject or, with a certain heaviness of heart, tolerate. But every actor must also know what they are so that he can fight against them.

'Now shall we try and see what you communicate with and how? This time you will perform and I will indicate moments when your communication is wrong by ringing a bell. Those will be moments when you lose communication with the object – your fellow actor – or when you are showing the role in yourself or yourself in the role or simply reporting it. I will indicate all these mistakes with the bell.

'Only three kinds of communication will meet an approving silence:

1) direct communication with the object and through it, indirectly, with the audience;
2) self-communication;
3) communication with a non-existent or imaginary object.'

After that the review began.

Leo and I played well rather than badly, but, nonetheless, to our amazement the bell sounded a lot.

The other students took the same test and it was Grisha and Sonya who were last to be called up onstage.

We expected Tortsov would have to keep ringing practically all the time but, to our surprise, though he did ring a lot, it was much less than we had anticipated. What did that mean? What conclusions were we to draw from our experiments?

'That means', Tortsov summed up, after we had expressed our astonishment to him, 'that many of you who pride yourselves on your ability to communicate properly are, in fact, often mistaken, and those whom you criticize so strongly turn out to be capable of doing well. The difference between the two groups is a matter of percentage. With some the incidence of poor communication was high, while with others, it was the incidence of good communication that was high.

'You can draw the following conclusion from these experiments,' said Tortsov at the end of the class, 'there is no absolutely good or bad communication. An actor's career abounds in moments of both kinds, and so good moments are mixed with bad moments.

'If it were possible to analyse communication, you would divide it up so: so many percent communication with your fellow actor, so many percent communication with the audience, so many percent demonstrating the shape of a role, so many percent reportage, so many percent exhibitionism, etc. The combination of all these various percentages defines this or that degree of right communication. Those who have the greatest percentage of communication with their fellow actor, with the imaginary object or with themselves have come nearest to the ideal. Those, on the other hand, who have fewer of these moments are the farthest removed from good communication.

'Moreover, there are degrees of failure in what we consider to be poor communication. For example, demonstrating the role in oneself, its psychological profile, but not experiencing it is better than demonstrating oneself in the role or mere hack reportage.

'The combinations are endless, and it is difficult to itemize them.

'The task for every actor is to get rid of the mixed approach and always to act with truth.

'The best way to go about it is this: on the one hand, learn to fix upon the object, your fellow actor and your communication with him, and, on the other hand, learn to recognize wrong objects and wrong communication, learn to fight them. Pay special attention to the quality of the inner material you are sharing.'

.. .. 19..

'Today I want to examine your means of communication. I need to know how highly you think of them,' Tortsov explained. 'Go up onstage all of you, sit in twos and start an argument of some kind.'

'That's easiest to do with our king of quarrels, Grisha,' I thought to myself.

So I sat next to him. In a minute I had reached my goal.

Tortsov noticed that while I was explaining my ideas to Govorkov I was using my hands and fingers a great deal. So he ordered them to be tied with a napkin.

'Why did you do that?' I asked in amazement.

'As a proof by contradiction, so that you will better understand that we often don't appreciate the things we have and "rue what we have lost". And also to convince you that if the eyes are the mirror of the soul, the fingertips are the mirror of the body,' he said as my hands were being bound.

Deprived of my hands and wrists, I intensified my speech. But Tortsov suggested that I should turn down the heat and speak softly, without raising my voice or colouring my words.

Instead I had to get help from my eyes, facial expression, the movements of the eyebrows, neck, head and torso. They used their combined strength to try and compensate for what had been taken away. But they bound my arms, legs, torso and neck to the armchair and all I had at my disposal were my mouth, ears, face and eyes.

Soon they covered my entire face with a cloth. I started to make noises but that didn't help.

From that moment the outer world was taken from me and all I had left was my inner eye, my inner ear, my imagination, 'the life of the human spirit'.

They left me like that a long time. Finally a voice from outside filled my ear, as from another world.

'Would you like one of your sense organs back? Choose. Which one?' Tortsov shouted at me with all his might.

I tried to respond by a movement which meant: 'Fine, I'll think about it.'

What went on inside me while I was choosing which was the most important, the most essential organ of communication?

First, two candidates disputed primacy of place – sight and speech. Traditionally, the first expresses and conveys feelings, the second thought.

In that case, who are their comrades in arms?

This question produced conflict, wild argument, revolt, muddle, I was at war with myself.

Feeling yelled that the mechanism of speech belonged to it, as the important thing was not the words themselves but the tone which expressed the inner attitude to what was being said.

War also broke out over hearing. Feeling declared that it was the best stimulus for that, and speech insisted that hearing was necessary because without it there could be no communication. Then they squabbled over the wrists and facial expression.

They could not in any way be ranked with speech as they said nothing. Where do they belong then? And the torso? And the legs?

'To hell with it!' I burst out, in complete confusion. 'An actor's not a cripple! Give me all of them! No compromises!'

While my bonds and ties were being removed I explained my 'mutinous' slogan 'all or nothing' to Tortsov. He praised me for it and said:

'You're finally talking like an actor who understands the significance of each of the means of communication! Let today's experiment teach you to appreciate them properly.

'Let's rid the stage forever of empty eyes, static faces, lacklustre voices, flat speech, awkward bodies with rigid spines and necks, wooden hands, wrists, legs through which movements don't flow and an awful gait and mannerisms.

'Let the actor pay the same attention to his creative apparatus as a violinist gives his beloved Stradivarius or his Amati.'

The class had to end early as Tortsov has a show tonight.

.. .. 19..

'So far we have been dealing with the process of *external, visible, bodily communication,*' Tortsov said in today's class. 'But there is another, more important kind: *internal, invisible, mental communication,* and that is what we shall be talking about today.

'The difficulty is that I shall have to talk about things which I sense but don't actually know, things which I have experienced only in practice and for which I have no theoretical formulae, no clear, ready-made words. I can only explain them to you by hints and by trying to make you sense what we are talking about.

He took me by the wrist and held me hard,
Then goes he to the length of all his arm,
And with his hand thus o'er his brow
He falls to such perusal of my face
As he would draw it. Long stay'd he so.
At last, a little shaking of my arm
And thrice his head this waving up and down,
He raised a sigh so piteous and profound
That it did seem to shatter all his bulk

And end his being. That done, he lets me go
And with his head over his shoulder turn'd,
He seem'd to find his way without his eyes,
For out o' doors he went without their help,
And to the last bended their light on me.[5]

'Don't you feel that the subject here is the silent communication between Hamlet and Ophelia? Haven't you ever been aware, in life or onstage, when in communication with other people, of a current emanating from your will, flowing through your eyes, your fingertips, your skin?

'What shall we call this method of communication? *Emitting and receiving rays, signals? Radiating out* and *radiating in?* In the absence of an alternative terminology let us stick with these words, since they illustrate very clearly the kind of communication I have to talk to you about.

'In the near future, when this invisible current has been studied by science, a more appropriate terminology will be established. For the moment let us stick to the names we have developed in our actors' jargon.

'Now we shall try to investigate this invisible method, using our own impressions and we will try to find and note them.

'When our mood is calm the so-called emitting and receiving is barely perceptible. But in moments of intensity, of heightened feeling, they are clearer, for both those involved.

'Perhaps some of you saw them in the good moments in the show, when, for example, you, Marya, first rushed out onstage with the cry, "Help!" or when you, Kostya, played the speech "Blood, Iago, blood!" or during the exercise with the madman, or in life itself, when we are aware of that inner current we are talking about every minute.

'Only yesterday, at the home of one of my relatives, I witnessed a scene between a young fiancée and her future husband. They had quarrelled, weren't speaking to each other and were sitting far apart. The girl was pretending not to notice her fiancé. But she did it in such a way as to gain his maximum attention. (People know this trick: avoid communication so as to make communication.) Then the fiancé, with a hangdog look, motionless, looked at his betrothed imploringly, his eyes boring right into her. He tried to catch her eye from afar so as to feel and understand what was going on in her heart. He fixed his eyes on her, to communicate with her living soul. They probed her. But his angry fiancée avoided communication. Finally he managed to catch one ray from her eyes, which flashed for a second.

'But the poor young man was no happier for it but, on the contrary, became even gloomier. Then, as if by chance, he moved to another place from where he could look her straight in the eyes. He would have liked to have taken her hand but he couldn't because his fiancée was determined not to make communication with him.

'There were no words, no exclamations or cries, no facial expression, movements, actions either.

'But there were the eyes, the looks. That is direct, immediate communication in its pure form, from mind to mind, from eye to eye, or from the fingertips, from the body with no visible physical action.

'It is for men of learning to explain the nature of this invisible process to us. I can only speak about the way I am aware of it inside me and how I use this awareness in my own acting.'

Unfortunately the class was interrupted as Tortsov was urgently called to the theatre.

.. .. 19..

'Let's try and discover in ourselves the invisible rays we emit and receive while we are communicating, so we can recognize them from own personal experience,' Tortsov suggested.

We were divided into pairs and once again I found myself with Grisha.

On the spot we started to emit and receive externally, physically, mechanically, without rhyme or reason.

Tortsov stopped us immediately.

'We already have the kind of tension of which we must be very wary in the delicate, tricky process of emitting and receiving. They cannot occur while there is muscular tension. And there you have Darya and Vanya, deep in each other's eyes, getting nearer to each other as if about to kiss, not for invisible radiating out and radiating in.

'Start by getting rid of tension wherever it appears.

'Lean back,' Tortsov ordered. 'Go on! Go on! Further, much further!! Sit as comfortably and relaxed as possible! That's not enough! Not nearly enough! You really have to be at rest. Now, look at each other. Do you really call that looking? Your eyes are popping out of your head, you're so tense. Do much, much less. No tension in the pupils of the eyes!

'What are you receiving?' Tortsov asked Grisha.

'Well, I want to go on with our argument about art.'

'Do you intend emitting thoughts and words with your eyes? You won't succeed,' Tortsov commented. 'Convey thoughts through the voice and words, and let the eyes supply what can't be transmitted by speech.

'Maybe, while you are arguing, you will feel the process of emitting and receiving rays which occurs in every act of communication.'

We started arguing again.

'Just now, in the pause, I felt you were emitting something.'

Tortsov pointed at me.

'And you, Grisha, were preparing to receive them. Do you remember what was happening in the pause while he was waiting?'

'I wasn't on target,' I explained. 'The example I had advanced to prove my point didn't convince my partner, so I was preparing a new one and tried a second shot.'

'And you, Vanya,' Tortsov suddenly asked, 'did you feel Marya's look at you. That was genuine emitting.'

'And how!!! Ouf! I've been on the receiving end all week, and all for nothing,' Vanya complained.

'Now you're not only listening, you're trying to take in the things the object speaking to you is feeling,' Tortsov said to me.

'Did you feel that, apart from the verbal, conscious argument and intellectual exchange of ideas, another process was happening at the same time, one of mutual probing, a current that was streaming into and out of your eyes?

'That was invisible communication, the emitting and receiving that, like an underwater stream, flows continuously under our words, in silences, and forms the invisible link between objects which creates an inner connection.

'Do you remember how, in a previous class, I told you we can look, see and take in and give out nothing. But you can look, see and receive and send out a stream of rays.

'Now I will make another attempt to get you to transmit. You will make communication with me,' Tortsov decided, sitting in Grisha's place.

'Sit as comfortably as you can, don't be nervous, don't rush and don't strain. Before you convey anything to someone else, you prepare what you have to convey. You can't convey something you don't have. Think of something to communicate mentally,' Tortsov suggested.

'Not so long ago our work, the study of our psychotechnique, seemed complicated to you, now you do it for fun. It will be just the same with emitting and receiving rays,' Tortsov assured us as we were getting ready.

'Convey your feelings to me without words, with the eyes only,' Tortsov ordered me.

'I can't convey the subtleties of what I have to communicate with my eyes only.'

'There's nothing you can do about that, let the finer points go.'

'Then what's left?' I wondered.

Feelings of warmth, respect. You can convey them silently. But without words I can't make someone else understand that I love him because he is clever, active, hard-working, decent.

'What is it I want to convey to you?' I said fixing my eyes on Tortsov.

'I don't know, it's of no interest to me,' Tortsov responded.

'Why?' I said, surprised.

'Because you're giving me a blank stare,' said Tortsov. 'For me to feel the general tone of the feeling you are conveying to me, you must live its inner essence.'

'And now? Do you understand what I am communicating? I can't do it any more clearly,' I said.

'You despise me for some reason, but why we can't know without words. Still, that's not the point. What's important is, were you aware of a voluntary stream issuing from you or not?' Tortsov was interested to know.

'Well . . . in the eyes,' I answered, and tried once more to check on the feelings I'd had.

'No, just now all you were thinking about was how you could force it out of yourself. You tensed your muscles. You stretched your neck and chin, your eyes were popping out of their sockets . . . What I want from you can be transmitted more simply, more easily, more naturally. The muscles don't need to work for you to be able to "shower" someone with the rays of your will. The physical sensation of a stream issuing from us is barely perceptible, while the physical tension you went through just now was enough to bring on a heart attack.'

'In other words, I didn't understand you!' I said, losing all patience.

'Calm down and in the meantime I will try to remind you of the sensation we are seeking, one with which you are perfectly familiar from life.

'One of my students likened it to the "scent of a flower", another added that "a brilliantly flashing diamond must experience the same feeling of emitting rays of light". Can you imagine the sensation a flower has when giving off its scent, or a diamond has when flashing its rays of light?

'I myself recalled the sensation I had of a voluntary stream issuing from me,' Tortsov continued, 'when I watched a magic lantern casting its bright rays on a screen in the darkness, and also when I stood on the edge of a volcano, which was belching out hot air. At that moment I felt the mighty, inner heat of the earth erupting from its bowels, and recalled the sensation of the current that issues from us when we communicate.

'Do these comparisons lead you to the feelings we want?'

'No, they say nothing to me,' I said obstinately.

'In that case I'll try and come at you from another angle,' Tortsov said to me with extraordinary patience. 'Listen to me.

'When I'm at a concert and the music is doing nothing for me, I think of something to amuse me. For example, I select someone in the audience and start to hypnotize them with my gaze. If it's a woman with a pretty face I try and transmit my attraction, if it's a face I don't like, I transmit my aversion.

'For those few moments I make communication with my chosen victim and bombard it with the rays streaming from me. When engaged in this activity, which may be familiar to you, I feel just that physical sensation we are looking for now.'

'When you hypnotize someone else, is there the same feeling?' Pasha asked.

'Of course, if you have practised hypnotism you must know what it is we are looking for,' said Tortsov delightedly.

'So it's a simple sensation we all know well?' I said delighted.

'Did I say it was out of the ordinary?' said Tortsov in amazement.

'But that's what I was looking for, something out of the ordinary.'

'It's always the way,' Tortsov stated. 'All you have to do is talk about art and you all immediately start getting tense and pompous.

'Quick, let's repeat our experiment,' Tortsov ordered.

'What am I emitting?' I asked.

'Disdain again.'

'And now?'

'Now you want to be nice to me.'

'And now?'

'That's a friendly feeling too but with a hint of irony.'

'Almost right,' I said, happy that he had guessed properly.

'Do you understand the feeling of an outward flow we are talking about?'

'Could be,' I said undecided.

'That's what we call emitting rays.

'The term defines the feeling beautifully.

'It is as though our inner feelings and wishes give off rays, which pass through our eyes, our body and engulf other people in their stream,' Tortsov explained, animatedly.

'Receiving is the opposite process, i.e. taking in other people's feelings and impressions. And that term defines the process we are talking about right now. Try it out.'

Thereupon Tortsov and I changed places. He started to transmit his feelings and I was quite successful in guessing them.

'Try and define in words the sensation of receiving,' Tortsov said to me when the experiment was over.

'I'll define it with an example, like the student you mentioned,' I suggested. 'A magnet attracting iron might experience the same sensation of receiving.'

'Right,' Tortsov agreed.

We had to cut this interesting lesson short as we were expected in our fencing class.

.. .. 19..

Tortsov continued where he had left off.

'I hope you felt the inner link which is forged between actors when they are in communication with or without words,' he said.

'It looks like it,' I told him.

'That was an inner bonding. It was created out of fortuitous, separate moments. But if you use a long line of experiences and feelings which are in logical sequence and are interconnected, then that bonding will be strengthened, will grow and finally develop the degree of strength which we call the iron grip and which makes the process of emitting and receiving rays stronger, sharper and more concrete.'

'What kind of iron grip is that?' the students asked with interest.

'The kind a bulldog has in its teeth,' Tortsov explained. 'And we must have an iron grip onstage, in the eyes, the ears, in all five sense organs. If you are listening, then listen and hear. If you are smelling, then smell. If you are looking, then look and see, don't let your eyes slide over the object, without latching on to it, just visually licking it. You must, so to speak, sink your teeth into the object. But that doesn't, of course, mean you should go unnecessarily tense.'

'In *Othello* was there a moment when I had that grip?' I said, going over what I had felt.

'Yes — one or two moments. But that's not enough. The entire role of Othello needs continuous grip. Indeed, if you need iron grip in other plays, in Shakespearean tragedy you need mortal grip. That you didn't have.

'You don't always need continuous grip in life, but onstage, especially in tragedy, it is essential. Indeed. What's the normal run of things? Most of our life is taken up with minor routine. Getting up, sleeping, fulfilling this or that obligation. That doesn't require grip and happens automatically. But there is no place for that onstage. There are other Bits in our lives, when moments of horror, sometimes short, sometimes long, or of great joy, of wild passion and other momentous experiences erupt into our daily routine. They summon us to fight for freedom, for an ideal, for our very existence, for justice. Those are the moments we need onstage. But they require inner grip if we are physically to embody them. So we have to discard ninety-five percent of real life which doesn't require grip and only take onstage the five percent for which it is essential. That's why you can live your lives without grip, but why onstage it is needed almost all the time, in every moment of intense creative activity. And remember, grip doesn't mean extreme physical tension but a great deal of dynamic, inner action.

'Don't forget either that the conditions under which we work, in public, are fraught with difficulty and require to be endlessly and energetically resisted. In life you don't have the black hole, a packed house, the glare of the footlights, the need to be successful, to please the audience whatever the cost. A normal human being would find these conditions unnatural. You must be able to overcome them or ignore them, divert your attention from them with your own creative Tasks. Let them focus all your concentration and creative ability, i.e. create grip.

'Thinking about that, I am reminded of a story: a man who trained monkeys went off to look for wild animals in Africa. Hundreds of samples were gathered together for him to chose from. What did he do to find the one most suitable to be trained? He took each monkey separately and tried to interest it in some item or other: a bright handkerchief, which he waved in front of its eyes, or a trinket which might amuse the monkey by its glitter or the noise it made. Once the animal was attracted to the item the trainer tried to distract its attention with something else – a cigarette, a nut. If he succeeded and the beast easily transferred its attention from the handkerchief to the new item, the trainer would reject it. If, on the other hand, he saw that, despite being momentarily distracted by the new object, its attention persistently returned to the first object, the hand-kerchief, and that the monkey looked for it and tried to take it out of his pocket, the trainer's mind was made up and he bought the monkey who could concentrate. He bought it because the monkey displayed a capacity for bonding or grip.

'We judge our students' concentration and their power to make communication in the same way, by the strength and duration of their grip. So develop it.'

After a moment Tortsov continued with his explanation:

'I happened to read in some book or other, the scientific value of which I won't vouch for, that the face of the murderer is sometimes imprinted in the eye of the victim. If that is so, then judge for yourselves how strong the process of receiving is.

'If only we had some gadget which would enable us to see this process of emitting and receiving, the exchange that takes place between the stage and the auditorium at moments of creative intensity, we would be amazed to see how our nerves bear up under the pressure of the stream of rays which we are emitting to the auditorium and are receiving back from the thousand living organisms sitting out front!

'How are we possibly to fill a huge space like the Bolshoi Theatre with our transmissions? Inconceivable! Poor actor. To conquer the house he must fill it with the invisible stream of his own feelings or will . . .

'Why is it difficult to play in a wide-open space? Not because we have to push our voices or force the action. No! That's simple. That's not difficult for someone who has mastered stage diction. It's emitting which is difficult.'

I think that today, when I was going back home from the school, people must have taken me for a freak. The whole time I was walking I was doing exercises in emitting and receiving. I couldn't bring myself to do experiments with the living people who crossed my path, and so I limited myself to inanimate things. The major objects involved in my exercises were the many stuffed animals in a furrier's window. There was a whole menagerie: a huge bear with a tray in his paws, a fox, a wolf, a squirrel. I developed a close intimate friendship with all of them and tried to penetrate through their hides into their imaginary souls, in an effort to draw something from them and take it into myself. I tried so hard to drag something out of these empty stuffed figures that I leant my neck, head, torso back and in so doing forced the people behind me as I stood there gawping, into a huddle. But then I remembered that Tortsov had recommended me not to try too hard. Then, like an animal tamer, I hypnotized the beasts and said to myself, if this bear came up to me, rearing up on his back paws, would I be able to stop the animal by making him take in my will through his eyes and jaws? I leant so far forward towards the object while emanating from myself that I stuck my nose against the dirty glass of the huge window. I tried to give so much to the object that I thought I was going to be seasick. And my eyes, as happens when one is in that condition, were popping out of their sockets.

'No!' I said, criticizing myself, 'working that hard is more like gagging and guzzling than communicating.'

'Ease up! Ease up!' as Tortsov would say. 'Why so tense?'

But when I started communicating less strongly all physical sensation of something going out of me or, conversely, coming into me, disappeared. I had to cut my experiments short as a crowd was gathering round me. Inside the shop five people, evidently assistants and buyers, were looking at me and smirking. Obviously they had seen my experiments and found them very funny. That didn't stop me trying the same experiment at the next shop.

This time the object was a bust of Tolstoi.

I sat in front of the Gogol Monument and tested out my grip. I wanted to hold the bronze statue with my eyes and use them to pull it towards me so that it would rise from its chair.

But my eyes soon hurt from staring. Besides which, at the critical moment, I caught sight of someone I knew passing by.

'Aren't you feeling all right?' he asked sympathetically.

'No, I've got a terrible migraine,' I said, blushing to the roots of my hair, not knowing how to get out of the situation.

'You should never get to that level of tension!' I decided inwardly.

.. .. 19..

In today's class Tortsov said:

'If emitting and receiving rays is so important, we have to ask are there ways of mastering it technically? Is there a way of doing it at will? Is there a technique, a "decoy" that will stimulate invisible emitting and receiving and thereby intensify our capacity for experiencing?

'If you can't go from the inner to the outer, then go from the outer to the inner. Then we can use the organic link between the body and the mind. The link is so powerful, it could almost raise the dead. Like a drowned man, with no pulse or signs of life who, when put into a certain medically defined position, jerks violently, and so obliges the respiratory organs to inhale and exhale automatically. That is sufficient to stimulate the circulation of the blood and thereafter the working of all parts of the body. And also, because of its indissoluble link with the body, the "life of the human spirit" of a man who had almost drowned is revived.

'We follow this principle when we stimulate emitting and receiving artificially: if inner communication does not occur spontaneously, then approach it from the outside,' Tortsov went on to explain. 'This help from outside is the lure which sets the process in motion and then experiencing itself.

'Fortunately as you will soon see, the new decoy can be developed technically.

'Now I will tell you how to use it.'

It began with Tortsov sitting opposite me and making me think up a Task, an idea to justify it and then communicate what I had done. I could use words, facial expression, gestures, everything that could help me. Tortsov asked me to be aware of the outgoing and incoming flow of emitting and receiving.

Preliminary work took a long time because I couldn't understand what Tortsov wanted.

When I did manage it, communication was established. Tortsov made me make communication intensely with words and actions and pay attention to my physical sensations while I was doing so. Then he took words and actions away from me and suggested I remain in communication by just emanating.

However, I had to struggle quite a lot before I could get physical emitting and receiving going as such. When I did, Tortsov asked me how I felt.

'Like a pump sucking air out of an empty tank,' I quipped. 'I had the feeling of an outgoing current, especially from the pupils of my eyes and, I think, from the side of my body that was turned towards you,' I explained.

'Go on emitting towards me physically and automatically for as long as you are able,' he ordered me.

But it didn't last long and I soon broke off this 'meaningless activity' as I called it.

'Didn't you want to give it some kind of meaning?' Tortsov asked me. 'Didn't your inner feelings cry out to let them step in and help you? Didn't your Emotion Memory do all it could to suggest an experience you could use for physical communication?' Tortsov insisted.

'If you're going to make me go on communicating physically, automatically at any price, then it'll be difficult if I have nothing to help me make sense of my actions. In other words, I need something to transmit and something to receive. Where am I to get it?' I was bewildered.

'Transmit whatever it is you're feeling now to me, i.e. bewilderment, helplessness, or find some other feeling inside you,' Tortsov advised.

That's what I did. When it became impossible for me to go on emitting physically, without any meaning, I tried to convey my vexation and annoyance.

'Leave me alone! What are you after? Why are you making my life pure torture?!' my eyes seemed to say.

'How did you feel?' Tortsov asked me once more.

'Like a pump that's been attached to a barrel of water and can now expel something other than air,' I quipped once again.

'So, your meaningless, physical emitting acquired a meaning and a purpose,' Tortsov commented.

After repeating these exercises he did the same thing with receiving. It was the same process but in reverse. So I won't write it down but merely note a new factor that arose during my experiments.

Before I could receive anything, I had to probe Tortsov's mind with my eyes and find something in it that I would be able to receive.

To do that I had carefully to inspect and, so to speak, take in his state of mind and then try to connect with it.

'As you can see it's not so simple to stimulate the process by technical means when it doesn't arise spontaneously, intuitively, as it does do in life,' Tortsov said. 'However, let me reassure you it is a great deal easier to accomplish in performance than when doing exercises or in class.

'Here's why this happens. Just now we had to find some chance feelings quickly to keep the process of emitting and receiving going, but onstage this process is much easier. In performance all the Given Circumstances have been explained, all the Tasks have been found, all the right feelings have matured and are waiting for an opportunity to surface. All you have to do is give a little push and the feelings flow out in an continuous stream.

'When you use a pipe to draw water from an aquarium, you only have to take one suck of air and the water just flows out. It's the same with emitting. Give it a small push, make an opening and feelings just flow, from within.'

'What exercises can we do for this?' the students asked.

'They develop the same idea as the two exercises you did just now.

'The first exercise consists of using a decoy to arouse some emotion (feeling) or other in yourself and emitting it to someone else. While you're doing it you pay attention to what is happening to you physically. In the same way get used to what it feels like to receive, when it occurs naturally and note what it is when you are communicating with others.

'The second exercise, try and transmit or receive without emotion. It requires a great deal of concentration. Otherwise you could mistake mere muscular tension for communicating. When the physical process has been set in motion, find some feeling or other to be transmitted or received. But, I repeat, you must beware of forcing and physical strain. Communication must always be easy, free, natural, with no waste of physical energy. Let it also be said that this new technique will help you focus your attention firmly on the object, as there can be no emitting without a stable object.

'Only don't do these exercises alone, by yourself or with an imaginary person. Make communication only with living objects, which really exist in life, with someone really standing beside you and really wanting to receive your feelings from you. Communication must be mutual. Don't ever do exercises alone, without Rakhmanov. You need an experienced eye so you don't go astray, and take mere muscular strain for the sense of genuine communication. That's dangerous, like any form of dislocation.'

'God it's so difficult!' I exclaimed.

'Difficult to do something which is a normal part of our nature?' said Tortsov in amazement. 'You're mistaken. What's normal is easy. It's much more difficult to train yourself to go against nature. So recognize its laws and only ask what is right for it. I predict, there will come a time when you will be constitutionally incapable of standing onstage, next to your fellow actor, and not connect with him mind to mind, by a bond or a grip – something which at this moment you find difficult.

'Muscular release, concentration, the Given Circumstances and all the rest of it also seemed difficult for you and now you can't do without them.

'So be happy that you are enriching your technique with a new, very important lure to motivate communication, i.e. emitting and receiving signals.'

11

AN ACTOR'S ADAPTATIONS AND OTHER ELEMENTS, QUALITIES, APTITUDES AND GIFTS

.. .. 19..

Tortsov came in and read the placard, 'Adaptation', which Rakhmanov had hung up, congratulated us on reaching the next phase in our work, then called on Vanya and gave him this Task:

'You have to go out of town to see some friends. You're hoping to have a very good time. The train leaves at two and it's one o'clock already. How are you going to leave school early? The problem is that you've got to fool not just me but your classmates as well. How are you going to do that?'

'Pretend to be sad, moody, depressed, sick,' I advised him. 'Get everyone to say: "What's up?" You can tell some unlikely story in such a way we all believe it. Then we shall have to let the sick man go whether we like it or not.'

'Yes! I get it! I really get it!' beamed Vanya and from sheer joy thrashed his legs about in a kind of dance step it would be impossible to describe.

But . . . after the third or fourth twirl he stumbled, yelled with pain, stood rooted to the spot with one leg raised and face contorted.

For a moment we thought he was trying to fool us and that he was playing a game. But he seemed to be in real pain and I believed him and got up to help the poor fellow but . . . had my doubts. The rest ran onto the stage. Vanya wouldn't let anyone touch his leg, tried to put his weight on it but gave such a yell of pain that Tortsov and I exchanged an enquiring look as to whether what was happening was a hoax or not. Vanya was carried towards the exit very carefully. He hopped on his good leg supported under his armpits on both sides. We moved quietly, solemnly, without a word being spoken.

But suddenly Vanya leaped into a dance and broke into loud laughter.

'That's what I call experiencing! Yes indeed! . . . I was brilliant! Got it to a T! You couldn't tell the difference!' he exclaimed, in broken sentences, helpless with laughter.

His reward was a round of applause and once again I felt how gifted he was.

'Do you know why you applauded him?' Tortsov asked and immediately gave the answer. 'Because he found the right Adaptation and carried it through successfully.

'This word, Adaptation, is the one we shall use in future to designate the ingenuity, both mental and physical, people use to adjust their behaviour and so influence other people, their object.'

'What does "adjust" mean?' the students enquired.

'It means what Vanya did just now. He used his ingenuity so he could leave the class before time,' Tortsov explained.

'I think he just fooled us,' someone interjected.

'Would you have believed him without this practical joke?' Tortsov asked. 'The trick was essential for him to achieve his end, leaving school early. Vanya decided on it, and on deception, to adjust to the situation, the Given Circumstances that were preventing him from ducking out.'

'Does that mean Adaptation is deception?' Grisha asked.

'In some cases, yes, in others it is a visible expression of inner feelings or thoughts. Sometimes Adaptation helps you draw the attention of someone you want to communicate with and whose sympathy you want. Sometimes it conveys things which are invisible and scarcely perceptible to others, things which can't be said in words and so forth.

'As you can see, there are many kinds and many uses for Adaptations.

'For example, let's say that you, Kostya, hold an important official post and I have come to you with a petition. I must have your help. But you don't know me from Adam. So, to achieve my end, I must do something to set myself apart from the general mass of petitioners.

'But how am I to get your attention and hold on it? How am I to develop a scarcely embryonic link between us? How am I to persuade you to look favourably on me? How shall I reach your mind, your feelings, your imagination? How am I to touch the heart of an influential man?

'If he sees the pitiful state of my life with his inner eye, if, in his imagination, he creates a picture, which is anywhere near as awful as reality, then he will take an interest in me, and will open his heart so we can communicate. Then I am saved! But to be able to penetrate someone else's heart, make communication with his life, I need Adaptations.

'We use them to highlight our inner feelings, the state we are in, as much as possible.

'But in other cases we use Adaptation to hide, to mask our feelings and our general state. A vain, proud man tries to be amiable to mask his sense of an affront. An investigator cunningly hides his real attitude towards the criminal he is questioning, using Adaptations.

'Adaptation is one of the most important techniques in communication, even when we are alone, since we need to adapt to ourselves and to our own state of mind if we are to convince ourselves.

'The more complex the Task and the feelings to be conveyed, the more different, various, colourful, the more subtle the Adaptations must be.'

'Look, please, I'm sorry,' Grisha countered, 'but that's what words are for.'

'Do you imagine they can convey every last nuance of feeling? No, when we are communicating with someone, words are not enough, they are too formal, dead. We need feeling to breathe life into them, and we need Adaptations to reveal and communicate that feeling to the object with whom we are in communication. They supplement the words, complete incomplete statements.'

'That means, the more Adaptations there are, the stronger and fuller the communication?' someone asked.

'It's not a matter of the quantity but of the quality of the Adaptations.'

'Which qualities do we need onstage?' I asked.

'They are many and various. Each actor has his own, particular, Adaptations of varied origins and varying effectiveness, which belong to him alone. It's the same thing in life. Men, women, old people, children, the great, the humble, the angry, the kind, the irritable, the calm and so on, have their own particular kinds of Adaptation.

'Every new circumstance in life, in our surroundings, place and time produce corresponding changes in our Adaptations. At night when everyone is asleep, our Adaptations are somehow different from the daytime, in the light, when we are with other people. When we arrive in a foreign country we try to find Adaptations appropriate to local conditions.

'Each feeling we experience requires its own elusive, special Adaptation if it is to be communicated.

'All kinds of communication – two-way, group, with an imaginary or non-existent object and so on – require a corresponding Adaptation.

'People make communication through their five senses, using visible and invisible means, i.e. the eyes, the face, movements of the hands and fingers, the body and also through emitting and receiving. In every case they need the corresponding Adaptations to do this.

'Some actors are masters at Adaptation in drama, but lack them completely in comedy, or, conversely, adapt well in comedy and badly in drama.

'You often have actors who can experience every aspect of human feeling splendidly with fine, truthful Adaptations. But these actors often make their deepest impression in the intimacy of the rehearsal room, when the director and the audience are sitting close by. When they are put onto the stage where greater clarity is required, their Adaptations seem pallid. They don't get beyond the footlights, or, if they do, they are neither clear enough nor dramatic enough.

'We also know actors whose Adaptations are clear but few. They soon lose their strength, their sharpness, their edge.

'But there are a number of actors, on whom fate has not smiled, who have poor, monotonous, vague yet truthful Adaptations. These people will never be in the front rank.'

.. .. 19..

Tortsov went on with the explanation which he had left incomplete in the last class:

'If people in real life need an infinite number of Adaptations, actors need them in even greater measure, since we are continuously in communication with someone or something, and because we are adapting all the time. The quality of the Adaptations plays an important role in this. Their clarity, colour, boldness, subtlety, delicacy of tone, elegance and taste.

'For example, in our last class Vanya's Adaptation was vivid, almost cheeky. But it can be different. Varya, Grisha and Igor, go up onstage and play the "burning money",' Tortsov ordered.

Varya lazily drew herself from her seat and stood waiting with a bored face for her fellow actors to follow her example and stand up too. But they stayed sitting.

An awkward silence ensued.

Unable to endure the sheer inaction, Varya started talking. To tone down her words she used feminine wiles, since she knew from experience that they have an effect on men. She lowered her eyes and carefully picked away at the number plate on her seat to hide her state of mind. Wanting to hide her cheeks which flushed bright red she covered them with a handkerchief.

The pause went on for ever. To fill it, to reduce the awkward feeling the situation had created, Varya tried to put a humorous gloss on the misunderstanding and forced out a laugh which sounded hollow.

'We're bored! Aren't we, very, very bored,' the beautiful creature assured us. 'I don't really know how to say it but please give us a new exercise . . . and then we'll play . . . we'll play . . . it'll be terrific!'

'Bravo! Well done! Splendid! Now we don't need to play the "burning money"! You've shown us everything we need without it,' Tortsov stated.

'What exactly did she show us?' we asked.

'I'll tell you. If Vanya gave us a cheeky, vivid, external Adaptation, Varya showed us something more elegant, subtle, inward. She patiently pulled out all the stops to win me over, and tried to make me feel sorry for her. She made good use of her embarrassment, even her tears. Where she could, she flirted so as to get her way, and fulfil the task. She modified her Adaptations in her wish to communicate with me and make me register every nuance of her feelings.

'If one Adaptation was unsuccessful or palled, she tried a second, a third, in the hope of finally hitting on the one that was most convincing and would pierce the heart of the object.

'We must know how to adapt to circumstances, to time and each person separately.

'If you're dealing with a fool, you must adjust to his mental capacity, find simpler forms of words and Adaptations that are right for the mind and understanding of a fool.

'If, on the other hand, the object of communication is someone sharp-witted, you have to act more carefully, find subtler Adaptations so he doesn't see your cunning and evade communication and so forth.

'You can judge the importance of Adaptation by the fact that many actors who have a mediocre capacity for experiencing but a vivid capacity to adapt make you share their inner "life of the human spirit" better than others who have stronger, deeper feelings but whose Adaptations are colourless.

'The best thing is to observe children's Adaptations. They are more clearly expressed than in adults.

'Take my two nieces for example. The younger is openness, inspiration itself. When she wants to express the height of joy, a kiss is not enough.

That can't convey her pleasure to the full, so to give greater strength to her expression of feeling she has to bite. That is her Adaptation, which she doesn't even notice. It happens spontaneously. That is why when the victim of her pleasure gives a cry of pain, the little girl is truly amazed and asks herself, when did I "bite" you?

'There's a model of subconscious Adaptation for you.

'The older one, on the other hand, quite consciously and deliberately selects her Adaptations. She says hallo and thanks different people according to how much respect she has for them, or how much they have done for her. But these Adaptations can't be considered fully conscious and here's why.

'I see two stages in creating Adaptations: 1) choosing the Adaptation; 2) carrying it out. I agree that my niece chooses her Adaptations consciously. But she carries them out, like most people, for the most part subconsciously. I call these Adaptations semi-conscious.'

'But are there fully conscious Adaptations?' I was interested to know.

'There are, of course but . . . you know, I have never, in real life, been aware of Adaptations that were both selected and carried out in a fully conscious manner.

'Only onstage where, it would seem, subconscious communication has free rein, do I come across totally conscious Adaptations all the time.

'Such things are actors' clichés.'

'Why do you say that in the theatre subconscious communication has complete latitude?' I asked.

'Because when you are performing you need powerful, irresistible ways of influencing people, and most of our biological, subconscious Adaptations are numbered among them. They are vivid, persuasive, immediate, catching. And it's only by using these natural Adaptations that you can convey barely perceptible nuances of feeling from the stage to a packed house. Such Adaptations are of primary importance in the life of great classical figures, with their psychological complexity. Only our organism and our subconscious have the ability to create and convey them. You can't carry out that kind of Adaptation with your intelligence or your technique. They occur spontaneously, subconsciously when feeling reaches its climax.

'How vivid and bright subconscious Adaptations are onstage! They take hold of the people you are in communication with, and print themselves in the audience's memory! Their strength lies in their unexpectedness, their audacity, their effrontery.

'When you are watching an actor, his behaviour, his actions, you expect him, at key moments, to deliver his lines loudly, clearly, with seriousness.

But suddenly, quite unexpectedly, he says them lightheartedly, happily, almost inaudibly instead, and that conveys the originality of his feelings. This surprise is so convincing, so stunning that his interpretation of this particular passage seems the only one possible. "Why didn't I have the sense to see the hidden meaning here?" the audience ask in amazement, completely taken with the unexpected Adaptation.

'We only encounter unexpected Adaptations like these in people of great talent. However, they don't happen all the time, only in moments of inspiration even with these exceptional people. As far as semi-conscious Adaptations are concerned, we encounter them rather more often.

'I won't venture to analyse and define the degree of the subconscious in each of them.

'I will only say that even a minimal dose of the subconscious gives life, a sense of awe when feelings are expressed and transmitted onstage.'

'That means,' I said trying to sum up, 'you don't acknowledge conscious Adaptations onstage?'

'I acknowledge them in cases when they are suggested to me from the outside — by the director, my fellow actors, people who give both solicited and unsolicited advice. But . . . conscious Adaptations of that kind must be treated with caution and wisdom.

'Don't ever think of using them in the form they are given. Don't simply copy them! You must absorb other people's Adaptations and make them your own, personal possession. That needs a lot of work, new Given Circumstances, decoys and so on.

'That's what we should do when an actor sees Adaptations in real life which are typical of the role he is creating and he wants to use them. Beware simply of copying. It always pushes the actor into playacting and the stock-in-trade.

'Once you have devised a conscious Adaptation, give it life by using your psychotechnique which will help you endow it with a small dose of the subconscious.'

.. .. 19..

'Vanya, come up onstage with me and let's play a new version of "getting out of class early",' Tortsov said.

The lively young man leapt onto the stage while Tortsov followed slowly whispering to us:

'Now I'll get him going.' —

'So, you have to get out of class early at any price! That's the major task. Do it.'

Tortsov sat at the table and got on with his own affairs. He drew a letter from his pocket and became absorbed in it. Vanya stood near him, concentrating, trying to think up the most ingenious Adaptation he could to influence Tortsov, or fool him.

He tried a wide variety of tricks, but Tortsov, almost deliberately, paid no attention to him. What didn't our irrepressible young man do to be able to get out of class! He sat motionless for a long time with a tired expression on his face. (If Tortsov had looked at him he would surely have taken pity on him.) Then he suddenly stood up and made a hurried exit into the wings. He stayed there a while and then he returned, looking ill, walking rather shakily, wiping cold sweat from his brow and sank heavily into the chair next to Tortsov, who continued to ignore him. Vanya played truthfully and there was a warm response from the auditorium.

Later on, he almost died from exhaustion; he developed spasms, convulsions; he even slipped off his chair onto the floor and went so far over the top that we all laughed.

But Tortsov did not respond.

Vanya thought up another Adaptation which caused even more laughter. But Tortsov still said nothing and paid no attention to the actor beside him.

Vanya went further and further over the top and the laughter in the auditorium grew louder. This drove the young man to fresh, very funny Adaptations, which finally ended up in clowning which caused great guffaws.

That was what Tortsov was waiting for.

'Do you understand what's just happened?' he asked turning to us when we had calmed down.

'Vanya's basic task was to get out of class. All his actions, words, attempts to pretend he was ill, to get my attention and make me feel sorry for him, were only Adaptations with which to fulfil the major task. At first Vanya performed the right kind of actions. But here's the rub. He heard laughter in the auditorium and immediately switched his object of attention, and started adapting not to me, the person ignoring him, but to you, the people encouraging his antics.

'Now he had a new Task, to amuse the audience. How can that be justified? Where are we to find the Given Circumstances? How are we to test and experience them? You can only overact, which is what Vanya did. That's why it all fell apart.

'As soon as that happened all genuine human experiencing ceased and stock-in-trade came into its own. The major task was broken up into a whole series of gags and stunts, which Vanya is very fond of.

'From that moment on the Adaptations became an end in themselves and took on the primary, not the secondary role assigned to them. They became Adaptation for Adaptation's sake.

'Things often go awry like that. I know quite a few actors who are capable of splendid, vivid Adaptations which they use not to make communication but merely for display, to make the audience laugh. Like Vanya, they transform the Adaptations into a series of stunts, a cabaret act. Odd moments of success turn their heads. They sacrifice the role for the sake of a few laughs and some applause, using words and actions which very often bear no relation to the play. When Adaptations are used like that they lose all sense. They are useless.

'As you can see, good Adaptations can be a dangerous temptation for an actor. There are many reasons for that. There are entire roles that offer constant temptation to an actor. For instance, there's the part of the old man, Mamaev, in Ostrovski's play *Enough Stupidity in Every Wise Man*.[1] Because he has nothing to do, he lectures everyone. He does nothing in the whole play except give advice to anyone he can get hold of. It's not easy to pursue one single Task for five whole acts, to lecture away, and share the same feelings and thoughts with one's fellow actors. It's easy to become monotonous. To avoid that many people concentrate entirely on their Adaptations. They change them minute by minute while fulfilling the same Task (to keep on lecturing). The continuous, non-stop switching of Adaptations introduces some variety. That, of course, is good. But the bad thing is that the Adaptations, unbeknown to the actor, become his main, his sole purpose.

'If you watch what is going on in their minds at moments like these, it will become apparent that the score of their role consists of the following Tasks, "I want to be forbidding" (instead of "I want to achieve my goal by using a forbidding Adaptation") or, "I want to be affable, decisive, abrupt" (instead of "I want to be successful in my appointed Task by using affable, decisive, abrupt Adaptations").

'But you know that you mustn't be forbidding for being forbidding's sake, affable for being affable's sake, decisive and abrupt for being decisive and abrupt's sake.

'Then the Adaptations imperceptibly become ends in themselves and take the place of the major Task in the role of Mamaev (to lecture and go on lecturing).

'This leads to their being overplayed. It distracts you from the Task, and even from the other actors. When that happens living, human feeling and genuine action disappear and theatrics come into their own. As we all know, the typical feature of theatrics is the fact that though the object is the fellow actor up there onstage with you, the person with whom you are supposed to be in communication, you create another object for yourself – in the auditorium, and that's what you adapt to.

'External communication with one object while adapting to another ends in absurdity.

'Let me explain my thoughts through an example.

'Imagine that you live on the upper floor of a house and opposite across quite a wide street she, the one you love, resides. How are you to tell her what you feel? Blow kisses, clasp your hand to your heart, portray a state of ecstasy, represent your sadness, your melancholy, gesture like a ballet dancer to try and ask if you can go and see her. You have to carry out all these external Adaptations in a clear-cut, discernible manner otherwise you won't be understood at all.

'But now imagine a wonderful piece of good luck. There's not a soul in the street, she is standing alone at the window, all the other windows in the house are closed . . . There's nothing to stop you calling out words of love. You have to pitch up your voice to match the considerable distance that separates you.

'After this declaration you go out and meet her – she is walking arm in arm with her forbidding mother. How are you to use this opportunity, so that while you are near to her you can tell her you love her and beg her to meet you?

'Given the circumstances of the encounter, you have to use your hands in ways that are expressive but can scarcely be seen, or just use your eyes. If you have to speak a few words they must be whispered in her ear almost imperceptibly and inaudibly.

'You're getting ready to do just that when suddenly, on the opposite side of the street, your detested rival appears. The blood rushes to your head, you lose all self-control. The desire to boast of your victory is so strong that you forget how near mamma is and shout expressions of love at the top of your voice and start using the balletic gestures which you used earlier when in communication at a distance. All this is done for the benefit of your rival. Poor girl! How she caught it from her mother because of your absurd behaviour!

'Most actors constantly perpetrate this absurdity, which would be inexplicable in any normal human being, and get away with it.

'They stand next to their fellow actors and adapt their facial expression, voice, movements and actions, not with an eye to the actors close by with whom they are supposed to be communicating, but to the empty space which lies between them and the back row of the stalls. Putting it simply, they don't adapt to the actor standing next to them but to the audience out front. Hence a wrongness in which neither cast nor audience can believe.'

'But, look here, please, I'm sorry,' Grisha protested, 'you have to think of the person who can't afford a front seat where everything can be heard.'

'You must in the first instance think of your fellow actor and adapt to him,' Tortsov responded. 'As far as the back row of the stalls is concerned, we have our vocal technique for that, a well-placed voice, good rounded vowels, clear consonants. With that kind of diction you can speak quietly, as in a room, and you will be heard better than if you shouted, especially if you interest the audience in the content of what is being spoken and get them involved in what you are saying. But when you have theatrical bellowing, intimate words, which need a quiet voice, lose their inner meaning. They don't dispose the audience to get involved in nonsense.'

'But, look here, I'm sorry but the audience has to be able to see what's happening,' Grisha persisted.

'And we have long, clear, sequential, logical action for that purpose, especially if we use it to engage the audience and involve them in the action. But if the actor works against the inner sense of what he is saying and waves his arms about without rhyme or reason, adopts poses, even beautiful ones, you can't watch them for very long, first because they're of no use to the audience or the character, and, secondly, because there's a great deal of repetition in these bursts of gesticulation and movement, and it soon palls. It's boring to watch the same old thing endlessly. I'm saying all this to explain how the stage itself and the fact of performing in public can lead you away from natural, genuine, human Adaptations, and push you towards those that are conventional, unnatural, theatrical. But they must be driven from the stage and out of the theatre ruthlessly, by any means possible.'

.. .. 19..

'Next we come to the question of how we produce and reveal Adaptations technically,' Tortsov explained when he came into class.

That told us immediately what today's class was about.

'I'll start with subconscious Adaptations.

'Unfortunately there is no direct route to the subconscious, so we have to be indirect. We have a number of decoys for that purpose which we can use to stimulate the process of experiencing. And where there is experiencing, you inevitably have communication and conscious or subconscious Adaptations.

'What else can we do in an area where the conscious mind cannot penetrate? Not get in nature's way, not infringe or violate the laws inherent in her. When we succeed in bringing ourselves to that normal, human state, the most subtle feelings, which take refuge in the deep, come to light and the creative process happens spontaneously. These are moments of inspiration when Adaptations occur subconsciously and stream up to the surface and dazzle the audience with their brilliance. That is all I can say on this matter.

'Different conditions prevail when it comes to semi-conscious Adaptations. There are some things we can do with the help of our psychotechnique. I say "some things" because there's not a great deal we can do here either. The technique for finding Adaptations isn't very extensive.

'I do have one practical technique, however. An example will explain. Varya! You remember how, a few classes ago, you implored me to alter the exercise with the "burning money" by repeating the same words but with quite different Adaptations.

'Try and play the exercise now, only not with the old Adaptations, which have lost their impact, but find new, fresh ones, consciously or unconsciously.'

Varya couldn't do it and, apart from one or two things she hadn't done before, repeated the old, threadbare Adaptations.

'Where are we to keep finding new Adaptations?' we asked, bewildered, when Tortsov reproached Varya with being monotonous.

Instead of answering us Tortsov turned to me and said:

'You're a stenographer, you keep a record of what we do. So write down what I am going to dictate:

'Calm, excitement, friendliness, irony, mockery, controversy, reproof, caprice, contempt, despair, threat, joy, warm-heartedness, doubt, amazement, warning . . .'

Tortsov named many more states of mind, moods, feelings and so on which made up a long list.

'Put your finger on the list,' he said to Varya, 'and read the word you come on by chance. Let the state of mind indicated by the word be your new Adaptation.'

Varya did as she was told and read out, warm-heartedness.

'Adopt this new tone in exchange for your old Adaptations, justify the change and it will bring freshness to your acting,' Tortsov suggested.

Varya found the justification and the tone fairly easily. But Leo stole her thunder. He started droning away in his bass voice, as though it had been oiled. And at the same time his tubby body and face exuded infinite good humour.

Everyone laughed.

'That's a demonstration of how useful a new tone is in the same task — persuasion,' Tortsov noted.

Varya put her finger on the list again and read out, controversy. She went to work with all the persistence of a woman but this time Grisha stole her thunder. He has no rival when it comes to being controversial.

'That's another demonstration of the truth of my technique,' Tortsov summed up.

The same exercise was then repeated with other students.

'Whatever states of mind, moods you use to fill this list, they are all useful in providing new tones and subtleties of Adaptation, if they are inwardly justified. Sharp contrasts and surprises in Adaptations can only help you influence other people when you are communicating states of mind. So, let's imagine that you've gone back home after a show which had a shattering effect on you . . . Just to say the actor was good, excellent, inimitable, incomparable is not enough. None of these adjectives expresses what you experienced. You have to pretend to be depressed, jaded, exhausted, enraged, in the depths of despair and use the unexpected moods of these Adaptations to express the heights of enthusiasm and joy. In moments like that you say to yourself:

' "Those devils really played well!" or "No, this happiness is too much to bear!"

'This technique is valid when it comes to dramatic, tragic and other experiences. But you can laugh unexpectedly in a tragic moment to strengthen the mood of an Adaptation and say to yourself:

' "It's a joke the way fate pursues and strikes me!"

'Or: "My despair is such I have to laugh, not cry!"

'Think about this. What versatility, what power of expression, what sharpness, discipline of the face, body and voice you need to respond to the almost incommunicable subtleties of an actor's subconscious life.

'Adaptations place the highest demands on an actor's expressive means when he is in communication.

'That places an obligation on you to equip your body, face and voice in the appropriate way. I remind you of that only in passing for the moment, linked with the study of Adaptations. Let it make you more deeply conscious of the work you are doing in gymnastics, dance, fencing, placing the voice, etc.'

The class had ended and Tortsov was getting ready to go when suddenly the curtains opened and onstage we saw 'Marya's sitting room' of which we are so fond. It was full of decorations and placards of various sizes hung everywhere and written on them was:

1. Inner tempo-rhythm.
2. Inner characterization.
3. Stamina and polish.

4. Inner ethics and discipline.
5. Charisma and allure.
6. Logic and sequence.

'There are many placards but for the moment we won't worry much about them,' Tortsov commented, looking at good old Rakhmanov's latest effort. 'The fact is we haven't yet gone into all the Elements, faculties, talents and artistic gifts which the creative process requires. There are still quite a few. But the question is, can I talk to you about them now without upsetting my basic method which is to proceed from the practical, from clear examples, from our own sensations to theory and its creative laws? How, indeed, am I to speak of invisible inner tempo-rhythm or of invisible inner characteristics? And how am I to illustrate my explanations clearly through action?

'Wouldn't it be simpler to put off that phase in our studies until we have moved on to the examination of outer tempo-rhythm and outer characterization which are visible to the eye?

'Then we will be able to study them as clear, external action and at the same time sense them inwardly.

'And more than that, can I talk about stamina when you have neither a play nor a role which requires stamina when putting it across in the theatre? Can I talk about polish when we have nothing to polish?

'Likewise, how can I talk about artistic or any other kind of ethic and discipline onstage, while you are creating, when many of you went up onstage for the first time in your show?

'Finally, how is one to speak about charisma if you have had no experience of its force, its effect on a large audience?

'We are left with logic and sequence.

'It seems to me I have talked about them so much in the course of the present year I have bored you quite enough. Our whole programme has been littered with individual remarks about logic and sequence so I've managed to say quite a bit about them already and will say more in the future.'

'When did you talk about them?' Vanya asked.

'What do you mean, when?' Tortsov asked, amazed. 'All the time, at every available opportunity, when we were working on the magic "if" and the Given Circumstances I required logic and sequence in your imaginative ideas and in the performance of physical actions, as, for example counting money without the actual objects, miming them. I also made sure we had strict logic and sequence in actions and in the continuous exchange of objects of attention. When we were dividing the scene of the abandoned child in *Brand* into Bits, and fixing the Tasks in them and finding names for them, I also demanded the strictest logic and sequence. The same thing happened when we were using lures and so on.

'I have the feeling I told you all you need to know about logic and sequence right at the beginning. The rest will be demonstrated in parts as the course continues. After all I've told you do I really need to set up a separate phase in the programme for logic and sequence? I'm afraid of straying from the practical and making the classes dry and boring by going into theory.

'That's the reason I felt obliged only to give you a passing reminder of the intangible Elements, the aptitudes, talents and gifts acting requires. Rakhmanov has reminded us of the missing elements so as to complete the bouquet. In time, when work itself leads us to all the questions we haven't dealt with, we will first experience and feel practically and then define each of the Elements we have dealt with theoretically.

'That's all I can say to you about them for the moment.

'This list concludes our lengthy study of the inner Elements, the aptitudes, talents and artistic gifts we need for our creative work.'

12

INNER PSYCHOLOGICAL DRIVES

Tortsov said:

'Now that we have looked at the Elements of our psychotechnique, we can take it that our mental apparatus is fit and ready. That's our army and we can go into action.

'We need generals to get it moving. Who are they?'

'We are,' the students answered.

'Who is this "we"? Where is this unknown being to be found?'

'Our imagination, concentration, feeling,' the students spelled out.

'Feeling, that's the most important of all,' Vanya decided.

'I agree with you. All you need do is feel a role and all your mental forces are immediately ready for war.

'So, we have found the first, the most important general, the prime mover, the drive in the creative process. It is feeling,' Tortsov acknowledged but immediately commented, 'the only trouble is that feeling is intractable, it won't take orders. You know that from experience. That's why, if feeling doesn't create spontaneously, we have to turn to another general for help. Who is this "Other"?'

'The imagination! Without that . . . forget it!' Vanya decided.

'In that case imagine something and let's see your whole creative apparatus get on the move right away.'

'What am I to imagine?'

'I don't know.'

'We need a Task, a magic "if" something . . . to . . .' Vanya said.

'Where are you going to get them?'

'His mind will suggest something,' said Grisha.

'If his mind suggests something, then it will be the general, the leader, the drive we are looking for. It launches and justifies what we create.'

'That means the imagination can't be a general?' I asked.

'You can see it is lacking in initiative and leadership.'

'Concentration,' Vanya decided.

'Let's take a look at concentration. What is its function?'

'It helps feeling, the mind, the imagination, the will,' came the list from the students.

'Concentration shines like a floodlight on the chosen object, makes us interested in its ideas, feelings and wishes,' I explained.

'And what designates this object?' Tortsov asked.

'The mind.'

'The imagination.'

'The Given Circumstances.'

'The Tasks,' we recalled.

'That's to say they are the generals, the leaders, the inner drives which get work started. They designate the object, while the power of concentration, if it can't manage that on its own, is limited to an auxiliary role.'

'Fine, so the power of concentration is not a general. In that case who is?' I asked.

'Play the "Madman" and you'll understand who the leader, the drive, the general is.'

The students said nothing, looked at each other, found it hard to stand up. Finally, one after the other, they all rose and reluctantly went up onstage. But Tortsov stopped them:

'It's good that you made an effort. That shows that you have some kind of willpower. But . . .'

'That means it's the general,' Vanya decided in a flash.

'But you were going up onstage like men about to die, against your will, not because of it. That's no basis for being creative. If you are cold inside, your feelings are cold and without warmth of feeling there can be no experiencing, no art. But if you were to rush up onstage as one man, with all the artistic passion you are capable of, then we could talk about will, creative will.'

'Well, there's no way you'll get that with the exercise about the madman. It drives us all mad,' grumbled Grisha.

'I'm going to try anyway! Did you know that while you expected the madman to break in by the main door, he was stealing up the back steps and is breaking in right now. The door is old. It can barely stay on its hinges and if he tears it down you are in for it! What are you going to do now in these new Given Circumstances?' asked Tortsov.

The students began to think, concentrated, considered carefully, focused and finally decided to build another barricade.

Then there was chaos, the place hummed. The young people were all afire, their eyes shone, their hearts beat faster. In a word they did almost the same thing they had done before when we played this exercise, which we now found so boring, for the first time.

'So, I asked you to repeat the "Madman" and you tried to force yourselves, to go up onstage and arouse, so to speak, your will, but forcing didn't help you drum up any excitement for what you were doing.

'Then I suggested a new "if" and Given Circumstances. They were the basis for you to create a new Task, to arouse new wants (will) but this time they were not just ordinary wants, they were creative. You set about things with enthusiasm. Ask yourselves, who the general turned out to be, who was the first to plunge into the fray, dragging the army behind him?'

'It was you!' the students decided.

'My mind, rather,' Tortsov corrected. 'But your minds could do the same and also become generals. So, the second general has been found. The mind (the intellect).

'Now, let's see if there isn't a third general. Let's go through all the Elements.

'Maybe it's the sense of truth and belief? If that were the case, we could just believe and our whole creative apparatus would set to work immediately, as it does when we stimulate feeling.'

'What are we to believe in?' the students asked.

'How should I know . . . that's your affair.'

'First you have to create the "life of the human spirit" and then believe in it,' Pasha commented.

'Which is to say that the sense of truth and belief is not the third general we are looking for. So maybe it's communication and adaptation?' asked Tortsov.

'To communicate, you first have to create the feelings and thoughts you wish to pass on to other people.'

'True. That means they aren't generals either.'

'Bits and Tasks!'

'No, it's not them, but the living wants and deliberate striving which create the Tasks,' Tortsov explained. 'But if these wants and intentions can activate an actor's whole creative apparatus and focus his psychological life onstage . . .'

'Of course they can!'

'If that is the case then we have found the third general. It is the will.

'So, it would seem that we have three generals, namely: . . .'

Tortsov pointed to the placard hanging in front of us and read the first line:

'MIND, WILL AND FEELING.

'These are our "inner psychological drives".'

The class was over; the students were about to disperse when Grisha started to argue:

'Look, please, I'm sorry, but why haven't you talked to us about the mind and the will before, instead of filling our ears with all this talk about feelings?!'

'So you think I should have said the same thing over and over again, in detail, about each of the inner drives, is that it?' Tortsov enquired.

'No, why should it be the same?' Grisha countered.

'How could it be otherwise? The three inner drives are indivisible, and so when you talk about the first of them you inevitably touch on the second and third. When you talk about the second you recall the first and the third and when you talk about the third, you think about the first two. Would you really want to listen to the same thing repeated over and over again?

'Let's say I'm really talking to you about Tasks, how to divide them up, choose them, name them. Doesn't feeling have a part to play when we are doing that?'

'Of course it does,' the rest of the students affirmed.

'And does the will have nothing to do with these Tasks?' Tortsov asked.

'No, it has a direct relationship to them,' we decided.

'If that is so, when I talk about Tasks I would have to repeat almost the same things I said about feeling.

'And doesn't the mind participate in creating Tasks?'

'It takes part in separating them out as it does in the process of naming them,' the students decided.

'In that case, I would have to repeat the same thing about Tasks for the third time. So you should thank me for not trying your patience and wasting time.

'Nonetheless, there is a grain of truth in Grisha's objections. Yes, I do lay too much stress on the emotional side of creative work, but I do so intentionally, as other schools of acting all too often forget about feeling. We have too many intellectual actors, and productions that are all in the mind, while genuine, living, emotional theatre is rarely encountered. And so I feel I have to pay double attention to feeling, somewhat to the detriment of thought.

'Because of the work we have done in this theatre over a long period of time, our actors have grown accustomed to considering the mind, the will and feeling as the psychological inner drives. That now lies deep in our consciousness. Our psychotechniques have been adapted to it. But in recent times science has introduced important changes in the definition of the psychological inner drives. How will we relate to them? What changes do they bring to our psychotechnique?

'I won't attempt to talk about this today. So, until our next class.'

.. .. 19..

Today Tortsov spoke of the new scientific terms for psychological inner drives.

'REPRESENTATION, APPRAISAL AND WILL-FEELING'[1]

he said, reading the second line on the placard.

'These terms are, in essence, the same as the older ones. They merely refine them. When you compare them, the main thing you will note is that representation and appraisal, when combined, fulfil the same inner function as the mind (intellect) in the old definition.

'If you examine the new terms further, you will see that the words "will" and "feeling" have been merged into one — "will-feeling". I shall explain the sense of this term, and the others, by giving you examples.

'Suppose you have a free day and want to spend it in as enjoyable a way as possible. What are you going to do to satisfy your wish?

'If feeling and will are silent, then all you can do is turn to the mind. It's up to it to advise you on what to do. I will assume the role of your mind and suggest:

' "Wouldn't you like to take a stroll through the town to get some exercise and fresh air?"

'The sharpest and most receptive of our five senses — sight — aided by your imagination and what you see with your mind's eye creates an image, a representation of what awaits you, of what might attract you on the walk I have suggested. You see a film on your inner "screen", with all manner of views, familiar streets, places in the suburbs and so forth. So, you have a mental representation of your intended walk.

' "I don't feel like that today," you say to yourself. "Wandering the streets isn't interesting and nature isn't exactly attractive when the weather's bad. Besides, I'm tired."

'Thus you form an appraisal on your representation. "In that case, go to the theatre this evening," your mind advises you.

'At this, your imagination and your inner eye draw a series of vivid pictures of theatres you know. In your mind you go from the box office to the auditorium, watch one or two scenes of the play. Then you can see and appraise your new plan for the day. But this time both the will and feeling suddenly get angry and reject what the mind has suggested (i.e. a representation and an appraisal). You have created inner turmoil and aroused the inner elements. So,' Tortsov summed up, 'having started with the mind (an imaginary picture and an appraisal) you brought will and feeling into play.'

After quite a long pause he continued:

'Where do our observations lead? They illustrate how the mind works. They demonstrate two important factors in the way it functions. First, it represents and second, it passes appraisal.

'My explanation gives you the essence of the first half of the new definition of our psychological inner drives.

'When we investigate the second half, we see, as I told you earlier, that in the new definition will and feeling are hyphenated – will-feeling. Why is that? My reply is another example. Imagine this coincidence. You have fallen passionately in love. She is far away. You are here, and you are pining because you don't know how to calm the disquiets that love creates. Then you get a letter from her. It seems that she too is tormented by loneliness and begs you to come as quickly as possible.

'No sooner have you read your darling's request than your feelings are on fire. But, as luck would have it, just at that moment you are offered a new role – Romeo. Thanks to the similarity between your feelings and the character's, many passages come alive for you easily, quickly. Who in that instance is the general, directing the creative process?' Tortsov asked.

'Feeling, of course!' I replied.

'And what about will? Wasn't it inseparable from feeling, wasn't it too in turmoil, didn't it simultaneously desire, yearn for the beloved in life, and, onstage, for Juliet?'

'Yes, it did,' I had to acknowledge.

'That means they were both leaders, two psychological inner drives coming together in a common effort. Try to divide them. Try, in your spare time, to think of cases when will and feeling are separate, draw the line between them, show me where one ends and the other begins. I don't think you'll be able to do that any more than I did. That's why the most recent scientific terms have united them in one word – will-feeling.

'Those of us who work in the theatre recognize the truth of this new term, and foresee practical applications in the future, but we aren't able to use it fully at the moment. That needs time. Let us use it only partially, in so far as we have seen it in practice, and for the rest, for the moment, will be content with the old, well-tried terms.

'I can see no other way out of our situation for the present. So, I am obliged to use both sets of terms for the psychological inner drives, the old and the new, depending on which one seems easier to master in each individual case. If I find it more convenient at any given moment to make use of the old term, i.e. not dividing off the functions of the mind, not merging will and feeling, I will do so.

'I hope that men of science will pardon me for this liberty. It is justified by the purely practical considerations which govern the work I am doing with you here in school.'

.. .. 19..

'So,' said Tortsov, 'mind, will and feeling, or, according to the new terms, representation, appraisal and will-feeling occupy leading roles in the creative process.

'Their strength is increased by the fact that each of the inner drives serves as a decoy for the others, arousing the other members of the triumvirate to be creative. Mind, will and feeling cannot exist alone, without mutual support. So they always function together, simultaneously, in strict interdependence (mind-will-feeling, feeling-will-mind, will-feeling-mind). This also increases the significance of the inner drives to a considerable degree.

'When we set the mind to work we also involve the will and feeling in the creative process. Or to put it in other terms: the representation of something naturally provokes an appraisal of it.

'Either of them involves will-feeling in the operation.

'Only when all three inner drives are working in a common alliance can we create freely, sincerely, directly, organically, not using someone else's but our own personality, at our own risk, as our conscience dictates within the Given Circumstances of the role.

'When a real actor embarks on Hamlet's soliloquy "To be or not to be" does he merely deliver the author's ideas, which are not his own, as mere words, and merely carry out the moves the director has given him? No, he gives much, much more, and invests the words with something of his own, his personal representation of life, his heart, his living feelings, his will. In such moments an actor naturally evokes memories of things he has experienced in life, which are similar to the life, ideas and feelings of the role.

'He speaks not as the non-existing person, Hamlet, but in his own right, in the Given Circumstances. Other people's thoughts, feelings, representations, appraisals become his own. And he doesn't say the words just so other people can hear the lines and understand them. It is essential that the audience should feel his inner relationship to what is being spoken, so that they desire the same thing as his creative will.

'At that moment all the inner drives unite, they become interdependent. This interdependence, this reciprocity, this close link of one creative force with another is very important in our work, and it would be a mistake not to exploit it for our own practical purposes.

'That demands an appropriate psychotechnique.

'The basic principle is this: to use the complementary workings of the three inner drives and the actor's creative skills to stimulate each of them to action, naturally and organically.

'Sometimes the inner drives set to work immediately, spontaneously, suddenly, subconsciously, bypassing our will. These moments of chance success must be attributed to their creative efforts. But what are we to do when mind, will and feeling don't respond to the actor's creative call?

'Then you have to make use of decoys. Not only are they to be found in every Element but also in each of the inner drives.

'Don't activate them all at once. Choose one of them – let us say, the mind. It's the most compliant of them all, more obedient than the others, it takes orders more readily. The actor then creates a representation which corresponds to the idea in the text and begins to visualize what it is the words say.

'In its turn, this representation provokes an appraisal. Together they produce an idea which is not dry as dust or formal but has been brought to life, and that in its turn stimulates will-feeling.

'You have seen many examples of this in your short career. Remember, for instance, how you breathed life into the "madman", which you found so boring. The mind produced an idea – "if", the Given Circumstances. These produced new, exciting representations, appraisals which, in turn, activated will-feeling. You played the exercise splendidly as a result. This is a good example of how the mind initiates the creative process.

'But we can approach a play, an exercise or a role in other ways, i.e. starting with feeling, despite the fact that it is totally capricious and unstable.

'If emotion immediately responds to the call, that is an enormous piece of luck. Then everything falls into place spontaneously, in a natural way. A representation surfaces, an appraisal on it is formed, and the two together activate the will. In other words, all the psychological inner drives start to work because of feeling.

'But what if this doesn't happen spontaneously, if feeling doesn't respond to the call and remains inert? Then you have to turn to the most available member of the three inner drives – the will.

'What decoy can we use to wake slumbering emotion?

'In time you will come to know that tempo-rhythm is this decoy and stimulus.

'We still have to settle the question: how are we to arouse our slumbering will to be creative?

'How are we to stimulate it to creative action?'

'With a Task,' I recalled. 'It directly affects our creative wants, i.e. our will.'

'That depends on what the Task is. If it's not very compelling, it has no effect. That's the kind of Task you have to slip into the actor's mind by artificial means. You have to hone it, breathe life into it, make it interesting and exciting. On the other hand, a really urgent Task has a powerful, direct, immediate effect. Only . . . not on the will. An urgent Task mainly works on our emotions, not on our wants because it works on feeling directly. In acting you must first feel the urgency, and then want. And so it is essential to realize that the effect a Task has on the will is not direct but indirect.'

'But you were good enough to tell us that according to the new term, the will was indivisible from feeling. That means, if the Task has an effect on the latter, then it follows that it stimulates the former at the same time, surely?' Grisha reminded Tortsov.

'Indeed. Will-feeling are two sides of the same coin. In some instances emotion dominates wants and in others wants, even when pushed somewhat, dominate emotion. And so, some Tasks work better on the will than on feeling, while others strengthen feeling to the detriment of the will.

'But . . . one way or another, directly or indirectly, the Task affects our will, it is a beautiful decoy, we love it, it stimulates our urge to create and we make diligent use of it.

'That means we shall, in the first instance, continue to use Tasks to exert a direct influence on will-feeling.'

After a short pause Tortsov continued:

'Nature itself supports the truth of the statement that the inner drives are the mind (representation, appraisal), will and feeling in that she frequently creates individual actors cast in an emotional, volitional or intellectual mould.

'Actors of the first type – in whom feeling dominates the will and the mind – when they are playing Romeo or Othello – emphasize the emotional side of the given role.

'Actors of the second type – in whom the will dominates feeling and mind – when they are playing Macbeth or Brand – underline their ambitious or religious desires.

'Actors of the third type – in whom the mind dominates feeling and will – when they play Hamlet or Nathan The Wise[2] – unwittingly give the role an overly intellectual, cerebral emphasis.

'However, the dominance of the first, second or third drive should not totally overwhelm the other two. We need a harmonious relationship among the inner drives in our personalities.

'As you can see, art simultaneously acknowledges emotional, volitional and intellectual acting in which feeling, will or mind play the leading role.

'We only reject work which is the result of sterile, theatrical calculation. We call acting like that cold, cerebral.'

After a dignified pause Tortsov concluded the class with the following flourish:

'You are now rich, you have at your disposal a large group of Elements which will help you experience the "life of the human spirit" of a role. They are your mental instruments of war, your army, in performance. You have discovered the three generals who can lead your troops into battle.

'That is a great achievement and I congratulate you!'

13

INNER PSYCHOLOGICAL DRIVES IN ACTION

'The troops are ready for war! The commanders are at their posts! We can advance!'

'Advance how?'

'Imagine that we have decided to put on a marvellous play, and each of you has been promised a dazzling role. What would you do once you got home from the theatre after the first reading?'

'Act!' Vanya explained.

Leo said that he would start thinking about the role. Marya would sit in a corner and try to 'feel'. Having learned from bitter experience at our first show, I would resist such dangerous temptations and start with the magic of other 'ifs', the Given Circumstances, with all the other details. Pasha would start dividing the role into Bits.

'In a word,' said Tortsov, 'each of you, one way or another, would try to get into the brain, the heart, the wants of the role, to stimulate your own emotion memory, create a representation, a personal appraisal of the life of the character, to excite your will-feeling. You would reach into the heart of the role with the feelers of your own heart, striving towards it with your own psychological inner drives.

'In very rare cases an actor's mind, will and feeling grasp the meaning of a new work immediately, are creatively stimulated by it and in a surge of enthusiasm establish the requisite inner state for work.

'Much more often, the lines are only partially assimilated by the intellect (mind), partially grasped by the emotions (feeling) and evoke a vague, intermittent flow of wants (will).

'Or, to use the new term, in the preliminary period when we get to know a writer's work, we form a hazy notion and quite superficial appraisal of it. Will-feeling also responds partially, hesitantly, to first impressions and then an inner feeling for the life of the role is created – "in general".

'You can't expect anything else if the actor only understands the sense of the role in general terms. In most cases the inner meaning can only be fathomed after a great deal of work, after the play has been studied, after you have traced the same creative path the author took.

'But there are times when the first reading of the written text says nothing to an actor, produces no response from the will and feeling, when no representation of the play is created, or any appraisal on it. That often happens with impressionist or symbolist works.

'Then you have to use other people's appraisals and outside help to try to get into the written text. After much hard work a rather tenuous representation is formed, someone else's appraisal which gradually begins to develop. In the end you manage, more or less, to get will-feeling and all the inner drives working.

'In the beginning, when the goal isn't clear, the direction in which they are invisibly moving is embryonic. Individual moments, which the actor grasped on his first acquaintance with the play cause the psychological inner drives into great bursts of purposeful activity.

'Thoughts and wants appear in fits and starts. They are born and die, are then born again and die again.

'If you were to express this in a diagram you would get a broken line, fragments, dashes.

'But as you get to know the role better and deepen your understanding of its goal, its trajectory gradually evens out.

'Then it becomes possible to talk about the first stirrings of creative activity.'

'Why is that so?'

Instead of answering Tortsov quite unexpectedly started to twitch his arms, head and his whole body and then asked us:

'Can you call my movements dance?'

Our response was negative.

Then, in a sitting position, Tortsov executed all manner of movements which flowed into each other and formed an unbroken line.

'And could you make a dance out of that?' he asked.

'You could,' we answered in chorus.

Tortsov started to sing some individual notes, with long gaps between them.

'Could you call that singing?' he asked.

'No.'

'And this?' He sang a few sustained, resounding notes, which flowed into each other.

'You could!'

Tortsov started to scribble individual, random lines, dashes, dots and flourishes on a piece of paper and asked us:

'Could you call that drawing?'

'No.'

'And could you make a drawing out of these lines?' Tortsov drew a few long, beautiful, curved lines.

'You could!'

'So, you see, what any art needs first of all is unbroken lines?!'

'We see that!'

'And acting also needs an unbroken line. That is why I said to you that when the line evens out, i.e. when it is unbroken, you can start talking about creative work.'

'Look, please, I'm sorry, in life and even more so onstage, can you really have a completely unbroken line?' asked Grisha.

'Such a line can exist but not in people who are normal, only in the insane and we call it an *obsession*. As far as healthy people are concerned, a few gaps are normal and obligatory. At least that's how it seems to me. But people don't die during these breaks, they go on living, and so each of their lifelines continues its forward movement,' Tortsov explained.

'What kind of lines are those?'

'You'll have to ask the scientists. But for the future we will agree to consider as normal lines in which a few, obligatory gaps occur in a human being.'

At the end of the class Tortsov explained that we need not just one such line but a whole series of them, i.e. our imagination, concentration, objects, logic and sequence, Bits and Tasks, wants, effort and actions, truth, belief, Emotion Memory, communication, Adaptations and other Elements which are essential to creative activity.

If the line of action is interrupted onstage it means the role, the play, the performance stop dead. If that happens to the forward direction of the inner drives, say, for example, to thought (the mind), then the human being/actor will not be able to create his own representations and his appraisals of them but just say words, which means he will have no idea what he is doing or saying. If the line of will-feeling comes to a halt, the human being/actor and his role will have no motivation, there will be no experiencing.

The human being/actor and the human being/role live all these lines almost continuously. They give life and movement to the character. But, if they are broken, the life of the role is cut short and paralysis or death occurs. When the line is restored the role comes to life again.

This alternation between dying and rebirth is abnormal. A role requires life to go on, and its line to be almost unbroken.

.. .. 19..

'In our last class you acknowledged the fact that in drama, as in any other art, what we need most of all is an unbroken line,' said Tortsov. 'Would you like me to show you how it is created?'

'Of course,' the students said.

'Tell me what you did this morning from the moment you woke up?' he asked Vanya.

The spirited young man made comic efforts to concentrate and thought hard about answering. But he couldn't direct his mind to the earlier part of the day. To help him Tortsov gave him this piece of advice:

'When recalling the past don't go forwards from then towards the present but, conversely, move backwards, from the present to the past you can remember. Moving backwards is easier, especially when you are dealing with the immediate past.'

Vanya couldn't understand right away how that was done, so Tortsov came to his aid. He said:

'We are talking right now in class. What did you do before that?'

'I got changed.'

'Getting changed is a small, independent process. Within it lie individual, small Elements – wishes, efforts, actions, etc. – without which you cannot fulfil the Tasks in turn. Changing clothes traced a short line of your life in your memory. There are as many short lines in a role, as many Tasks and ways of fulfilling them as there are in life. For example:

'What happened earlier, before you got changed?'

'I was at fencing and gymnastics.'

'And before that?'

'I was smoking in the buffet.'

'And before that?'

'Singing class.'

'All these were short lines in your life which left traces in the memory,' Tortsov noted.

So moving further and further backwards Vanya reached the moment he woke up and the beginning of his day.

'So we have now got a long series of short lines, which you lived in the first half of the day, starting with the moment you woke up and ending with now. Traces of them have been retained in your memory.

'To fix them more firmly, repeat what you have done several times in the same order as we have just done,' Tortsov suggested.

After this had been done he acknowledged that Vanya had not only become aware of the earlier part of the day but had fixed it.

'Now repeat the same thing several times over, but in reverse order, i.e. starting with the moment you woke up to the moment you are experiencing now.'

Vanya did so, not once but several times.

'Now tell me,' Tortsov said to him, 'don't you have the impression that your actions and your feelings form some kind of representation of the fairly long line you have lived through today? It is created not only from memories of individual actions which you performed in the immediate past, but also of a series of feelings, thoughts, physical sensations and so on which you experienced.'

It took Vanya a long time to understand what he was being asked. The students, including me, explained it to him:

'Don't you understand that when you look back, you remember a whole series of very familiar, everyday things which form a sequence which is routine for you? If you pay more attention and concentrate hard on the immediate past, then you recall not only the outer but the inner line of your life today. It leaves vague traces, it trails along behind us like a train.'

Vanya said nothing. He looked totally confused. Tortsov left him in peace and turned to me:

'You've understood how to bring the first half of today to life. Do the same thing now with the second half, what you haven't yet lived today,' he suggested.

'How can I know what's going to happen to me in the immediate future?' I said in amazement.

'What do you mean? You know you have other things to do after my class, don't you, that you'll have other classes and be going home to have dinner? Don't you have plans for this evening – visiting friends, the theatre, the cinema, a lecture? Whether or not you will do what you planned, you can't be sure, but you can surmise.'

'Of course,' I agreed.

'If that's the case, that means you have some ideas about the second half of today! Don't you feel a line stretching out into the future with its cares, obligations, joys and worries which, when you think about them, make you feel happier or sadder?

'There's also movement in this future, and, where there is movement, there is an emergent line, your line of life. Can you feel it when you think about what lies ahead of you?'

'Of course I am aware of the things you're talking about.'

'Put this line together with the earlier one and you will get one, large, continuous, through-line – past, present, future – for today, extending from the moment you woke up to the moment you fall asleep. Do you now understand how the individual, small lines in your life have been merged into one, large, continuous line that is the whole of your life?

'Now, imagine,' said Tortsov, 'that you have been told you have to rehearse Othello in a week. Don't you feel that, for that period, your whole life will be reduced to one thing – acquitting this most difficult task with honour? It will take you over for the whole seven days and for that time you will have one overriding concern – to get through this terrifying show.'

'Of course,' I acknowledged.

'Don't you also feel that in the life I have just created for you there lies an even longer line than in the previous example, an unbroken lifeline running through a whole week, devoted to preparing Othello?' Tortsov continued. 'If we have lines for a day, a week, why can't we also have lines for a month, a year, finally for a whole lifetime?

'These long lines are the result of merging many small ones.

'The same thing happens with every play and every role. There too, a long line is made up of small ones. They can occupy various lengths of time, a day, a week, a month, a year, a lifetime, etc.

'In the real world it is life which spins this line and in a play it is the author's true-to-life plot which creates it.

'But the line he has created isn't continuous, unbroken, for the duration of the role. It exists only in parts, with large gaps.'

'Why is that?' I asked.

'We have already discussed the fact that the dramatist doesn't give us the whole life of a play or a role but only those moments which are presented and performed onstage. He doesn't write a great deal about what happens offstage. He is often silent about what happens in the wings, in the gaps in the character which the actor is playing onstage. We have to supply what the author has not created in his printed text, using our own imagination. Otherwise you won't get a continuous "life of the human spirit" in a play from the actor, you'll be dealing with isolated scraps.

'To be able to experience you must have a (relatively) continuous line in a role and a play.

'Jumps and gaps in the line of a role are inadmissible not only onstage but in the wings as well. They break up the life of the character and create dead spots in it. These are then filled with the personal thoughts and feelings of the human being/actor and bear no relation to what he is playing. That pushes him in the wrong direction – into his own private life.

'Let's say, for example, that you are playing the "burning money". You are following the line of the role very well. When your wife calls, you exit to the dining room to admire your son being bathed. But when you get into the wings you meet a friend who has just come a great distance and has managed to pull a few strings to get backstage. From him you learn of something amusing that has happened to one of your relatives. Hardly able to contain your laughter you re-enter for the moment when the money is burning and the pause – "tragic inaction".

'You know that such gaps are of no use to the role and no help to you. That means you must not break the line even in the wings. But many actors are unable to go on playing the role in the wings. So, let them rather think what they would do that day if they found themselves in the situation the character is in. The actor must answer that question and others, in every show. That's the reason why an actor comes to the theatre to perform. If the actor leaves the theatre without having answered the questions he has to ask on that day, he has not done what he should.'

.. .. 19..

Tortsov began the class by telling us all to go up onstage, settle ourselves as comfortably as possible in 'Marya's apartment' and talk about anything we liked.

The students sat at the round table, and against the walls which had electric lamps fixed to them.

Rakhmanov was the busiest of all, from which we concluded he was going to demonstrate his latest brainwave.

During the general conversation lights came up and down in various parts of the stage and then my attention was caught by the fact that they lit either the person speaking or the object being discussed. For example, as soon as Rakhmanov said a word the light came up on him. As soon as he recalled something or other lying on the table, the light shone on that, etc.

But there was one thing I couldn't explain. All the lights were outside our room, in the dining room, the hall and other adjacent spaces. It turned out that the light showed up what was happening outside the sitting room.

So, for example, the lamp in the corridor came up when we recalled the past, the light in the dining room when we talked about things happening now outside our room. The lamp in the hall shone when we dreamed of the future. I also noted that the lighting was continuous. No sooner had one lamp faded than another came up. Tortsov explained that the lighting illustrated the continuous change of objects of attention which occurs in our lives endlessly, logically, sequentially, or even just by chance.

'The same thing should happen in performance,' Tortsov explained. 'It is important that objects of attention should take over from each other without a break and create a continuous line. That line should be on our side of the footlights, and should not extend beyond it to the auditorium.

'The life of a human being or a role is an unbroken sequence of changing objects, circles of attention, be it in the real life around us, or onstage, be it in an imaginary world, or in dreams of the future, as long as it's not in the auditorium. This continuity of line is extremely important for an actor and you should do all you can to make it stronger.

'I will use light and show you how the line should extend unbroken through the entire role.

'Go into the auditorium,' he said to us, 'and Rakhmanov will go up into the lighting box and help me.

'Here's the play I am going to perform. Today there is an auction. Two Rembrandts are being put up. While waiting for the sale, I am sitting at the round table with an expert so that we can agree on the reserve price for the pictures. To do that we have to take a close look first at one then the other.'

(The lights on both sides of the room came up and down one at a time while the lamp in Tortsov's hand went out.)

'We have, at the same time, to make a mental comparison of the pictures we have here with other unique Rembrandts in museums at home and abroad.'

(The light in the lobby, representing the imaginary pictures in the museums, went up and down, alternating with the two lights on the walls which illustrated the imaginary pictures in the sitting room.)

'You see those dim lights that suddenly came up near the exit doors. They are the minor buyers. They caught my attention and I went to meet them but with no great enthusiasm.

' "If they are the only kind of clients who are coming, I won't be able to reach the reserve price," I say to myself. I am so lost in my own thoughts that I don't notice anyone or anything.'

(All the earlier lights go out but above Tortsov's head a follow spot appears, illustrating the small circle of attention. It moves with him as he nervously paces the room.)

'Look, look, the whole stage and back rooms are filled with new lights coming up, big ones this time.

'They represent the buyers from foreign museums. Of course I greet them with particular respect.'

After Tortsov had portrayed their meeting he did the same thing with the auction itself. His concentration was particularly acute when a bitter dispute occurred among the major buyers, culminating in a huge row, which was conveyed by an orgy of lights . . . The big lamps came up and down together or separately which created a beautiful picture like the end of a firework display. Our eyes were dazzled.

'Have I managed to show you how an unbroken line is created onstage?' said Tortsov.

Grisha said, 'If you don't mind my saying so, you showed us the exact opposite. The lights you used didn't give us an unbroken line but endless jumps.'

'I don't see that. An actor's concentration moves from one object to another without a break. This constant change creates an unbroken line. If the actor latches on to one object and sticks to it for a whole act or a whole play, never letting go of it, there would be no movement, and if it did emerge, it would be the line of someone who was mentally ill, and that, as I have said, is called an *obsession*.'

The students sided with Tortsov and insisted that he had succeeded in giving a graphic explanation of his ideas.

'So much the better,' he said. 'I have shown you how this should happen, always. Remember, for the sake of a comparison, what happens to most actors but which ought never happen to you. I illustrated that for you in an earlier class with these same lights. They came up rarely on the stage while they were almost continually alight in the auditorium.

'Do you think it normal for an actor's life and concentration only to be alive for a moment or two and then to go dead for a long time and move out into the auditorium or outside the theatre? And then to return only to disappear again for a long time?

'In acting like that only a few moments of the actor's life onstage belong to the role, for the rest of the time they are a stranger to it. Art has no need of such a hotch-potch of feelings.

'Learn to create a (relatively) unbroken line onstage for each of the psychological inner drives and each of their elements.'

14

THE ACTOR'S INNER CREATIVE STATE

Today's was not a plain class. There was a placard. Tortsov said:

'Where do the inner psychological drives head for once they have been lined up? Where does the pianist head for in moments of excitement so he can release his feeling and give his creative powers full scope? To the piano, his instrument. Where does the painter head for? To his canvas, his brushes and paints, i.e. to the tools with which he creates. Where does the actor head for, or rather, where do his inner drives head for? To what motivates them, i.e. to his mind and body, his mental Elements. Mind, will and feeling sound the alarm and he uses his strength, energy and conviction to mobilize all his creative forces.

'Just as a military camp, deep in slumber, is roused to action by the alarm, so our artistic forces are stirred and swiftly prepare for an artistic sortie.

'The endless number of ideas, objects of attention, communication, Tasks, wishes and actions, moments of truth and belief, emotion memories, Adaptations each form up in ranks.

'The inner drives pass through them, activate the Elements and in so doing are themselves fired with even greater artistic energy.

'Moreover, something of the natural qualities of the Elements rubs off on them. As a result mind, will and feeling grow more dynamic, more active. They are stimulated even more strongly by the imagination, and that gives the play greater credibility and substantiates the Tasks more fully. That helps the inner drives and Elements better to sense the truth of a role, and to believe that what is happening onstage could be possible. All this stimulates the process of experiencing and the need to make communication with the other characters, and for that you must have Adaptations.

'In a word, the inner drives pick up the tones, colours, nuances of the Elements through which they pass. They take on their emotional content.

'In their turn the inner drives infuse the ranks not only with their own energy, force, will, emotion and thought, but also pass on those transitory hints of the role and the play, the things which so excited them on first acquaintance with the script, and which inspired them to creative activity. They graft these first shoots of the emotional life of the role onto the Elements.

'The feelings of the actor/role gradually develop from these shoots in the actor's mind. In that respect they are like a well-ordered army moving forward under the leadership of the inner drives.'

'Where are they going?' the students asked.

'Somewhere far away . . . to a place where the hints and flashes they get from their imagination, the Given Circumstances and the magic "ifs" of the play summon them. They are forging ahead to where the creative tasks lead them, to where the wishes, intentions, actions of the role draw them. They are drawn by objects who wish to enter into communication with them, i.e. the characters in the play. They reach out towards things which are easy to believe in, both onstage and in the script, i.e. towards artistic truth. Note that all these features are to be found on the stage, on our side of the footlights, and not in the auditorium.

'The further the Elements move forwards together, the greater their unity. This coming together of all the elements creates a state of mind which is extremely important for actors, and which in our vocabulary we call . . .' Tortsov indicated the placard hanging in front of us on which was written:

THE ACTOR'S INNER CREATIVE STATE

'What's that?!' exclaimed a terrified Vanya.

'Very simple,' I said. I started to explain to him mostly to convince myself. 'The inner drives, and the Elements combine to form one common goal for the role. See?'

'Yes, but with two provisos. First, that there is one basic, common goal which is still some way off, and that the Elements come together only to investigate it using their combined strength.

'The second proviso is a matter of terminology. Up till now, by agreement, we have simply called our artistic aptitudes, qualities, talents, natural gifts and even some of the methods of our psychotechnique, Elements. That was only a temporary designation. We only used it because it was too early to talk about states of being. Now that we have introduced this word I will state that its real name is:

'ELEMENTS OF THE ACTOR'S CREATIVE STATE IN PERFORMANCE.'

'Elements . . . of the actor's . . . creative . . . state . . . ,' Vanya tried to drum the strange words into his head. 'There's no way of understanding that!' he concluded with a deep sigh, giving up, desperately tugging his hair.

'There's nothing to understand! It is almost a completely normal human state.'

'Almost?!'

'It's better than the normal state in some ways and . . . worse.'

'Why worse?'

'Because we work, we create, in public, which is unnatural, and so there is a lingering trace of theatricality in our minds, and exhibitionism, too, which don't exist in the normal human state. And so we call this state not merely the creative state and add the word *actor's*.'

'And in what way is the actor's creative state in performance better than the normal one?'

'Because there is the feeling of public solitude which is unknown to us in real life. That's a delightful feeling. You remember, earlier, you said that it was boring to play for a long while in an empty theatre or in a room at home, face to face with your fellow actor. We compared that kind of acting to singing in a room filled with carpets and soft furnishings, that deadened the acoustic. But in the theatre with a packed audience, with a thousand hearts beating in unison with the actor's heart a wonderful resonant acoustic is created for our feelings. For every moment genuinely experienced onstage we get back a response from the audience, participation, empathy, invisible currents from a thousand living, emotionally stimulated people who create the performance with us. An audience can not only tyrannize and terrify an actor, it can also arouse genuine creative energy in him. It gives him an inner glow, belief in himself and in his artistic efforts.

'The response from a packed house affords us that great joy which only a human being can know.

'So, on the one hand, creating in public is a hindrance to an actor and, on the other, it is a help.

'Unfortunately this authentic, almost totally natural, human state occurs very, very seldom spontaneously onstage. When, exceptionally, a performance or parts of it are successful, the actor goes back to his dressing room, saying: "Today I was in the mood!"

'That means that he discovered, by chance, an almost normal human state.

'In exceptional moments like these, the actor's whole creative apparatus, all its separate parts, all its, so to speak, internal "springs" and "knobs" and "pedals" function superbly, almost the same as, or better than, in life.

'That's the kind of creative state we need to the maximum when we are onstage, since only then can genuine creative work be done. That is why we place such a special value on it. This is one of those major factors in the creative process and that was why we developed the Elements.

'How fortunate we are to have a psychotechnique which can, at our behest, at our discretion, produce the creative state, which used to come to us by chance, "out of the blue". That is why I am ending the class by congratulating you on having passed through a very important phase in our work at this school, you have learned –'

.. .. 19..

'On those – alas all too frequent – occasions', said Tortsov, 'when the true creative state does not arise, the actor, when he gets back to his dressing room, moans: "I'm not on form, I can't act today."

'This indicates that his mental apparatus isn't working properly or isn't functioning at all, and that mechanical, convention-based playing, clichés, stock-in-trade have come into their own. What brings this about? Perhaps the actor was afraid of the black hole and that confused all his Elements? Or was under-rehearsed, believing neither his words or the actions. Did that produce an uncertainty which shattered his creative state?

'Or it could be the case that the actor was simply too lazy to prepare in the proper manner, didn't breathe new life into a role he already had fully planned. Yet you should do that every time before every performance. But he went onstage and presented the outer form of the role instead. That's all right if it's done using the well-established score and the perfect technique which we find in the art of representation. Performance of that kind can even be recognized as art although it bears no relation to our school of acting.

'But perhaps the actor didn't prepare because he was ill or just lazy, or thoughtless, because he had private worries and troubles which took his mind off his work. Or perhaps he is one of those "actors" who are accustomed to rattle off the role, to posture, to amuse the public because they are incapable of anything else. In all the cases I have mentioned the composition, detail and quality of the Elements of his creative state were, in their different ways, equally untrue. There is nothing to be gained by examining each of these cases separately. It is enough to take a general conclusion.

'You know that when the human being/actor confronts a packed audience, either out of fear, confusion, shyness, a sense of his responsibilities, his personal problems, he loses his self-control. He can't speak, look, listen, think, wish, feel, walk, behave in a human way. He has a nervous compulsion to please the audience, to display himself and to conceal his state of mind by posturing so as to amuse them.

'In such moments the actors' Elements split apart and live their own lives. We have concentration for concentration's sake, objects for the objects' sake, the feeling of truth for the feeling's sake, Adaptations for Adaptations' sake. This, of course, is abnormal. It is normal when the Elements which produce the creative state in the human being/actor, are, as in real life, indivisible.

'These Elements must be indivisible at the creative moment, when you are in the proper inner state, and that state is almost indistinguishable from life. That is what happens when the actor is in the proper creative state. The trouble is that this state, because of the abnormal conditions in which we perform, is unstable. Hardly is it broken than the Elements lose their common link and they begin to live apart from each other, in and for themselves. Then the actor is being active onstage not in the general direction the role needs, but simply to be "active" are there just so that "actions" can be performed. The actor is in communication, not with what the play needs . . . but with the audience, to entertain them. Or he adapts not so as to convey his own thoughts and feelings, which are similar to the role, to his partner more fully, but to dazzle the audience with his own virtuosity and finesse, etc. Then, as the characters move about the stage they lose first one, then another, and finally all the qualities of heart and mind the human being/role needs. Some of these flawed people lack the feeling of truth and belief in what they are doing, others don't possess the necessary human power to concentrate on what they are saying, others still find their object of attention has disappeared and, without that, any meaning or possibility of natural communication vanishes.

'That is why the actions of these freaks onstage are dead, and you have no sense of living human representations inside them, no mental images, wants and yearnings and without these will-feeling cannot come alive.

'What would happen if there were similar physical defects, visible to the eye, and the character we were creating had no ears, hands or teeth?

You would have a hard time getting used to such a freak. But our mental defects aren't visible to the eye. The audience is not conscious of them but only senses them unconsciously. They are only understood by discriminating specialists in our profession.

'That's why the average member of the audience says, "It was fine, but I wasn't gripped by it!" That's why the audience doesn't respond to that kind of playing, doesn't applaud and doesn't come back a second time. All these afflictions, and worse, threaten us onstage and produce instability in our creative state.

'Moreover, the danger is exacerbated by the fact that a wrong state can be created with unusual ease and speed, without our realizing it. All it needs is for one wrong Element to be introduced into the inner state we have created and it immediately becomes unstable. The wrong Element attracts others, which distorts the mental state which makes creative work possible.

'Verify what I say. Establish a creative state in which all the constituent parts are working amicably together, like a well-trained orchestra, then replace one of these Elements by another, which is wrong, and you will see the kind of disharmony you get.

'For example, imagine that one of the cast has come up with an idea which he can't bring himself to believe in. Then you inevitably get self-deception and lying, which disrupts the truth of your own creative state. The same thing happens with other Elements.

'Or, imagine an actor is looking at an object but isn't really seeing it. As a result his concentration is on the object which is essential to the role and the play, no, it brushes the true object that it has taken on sufferance aside and turns to another, wrong object which it finds more interesting and exciting, i.e. the audience or an imaginary life offstage. The actor starts to "look" mechanically and that produces playacting and then our whole creative state is thrown out of joint. Or, try replacing a living Task in the person/role with a dead, actorish Task, or show off to the audience, or use the role so as to flaunt your energy and fire. The moment you introduce some wrong Element or other into a true creative state, all the other Elements are changed, either all together, or gradually. Truth turns to convention and to technical tricks, belief in the real nature of one's experience and action into belief in one's own stock-in-trade, reflex action. Human Tasks, wishes and intentions become actorish, professional; creative ideas are replaced by trivia, i.e. by a convention-based presentation, by playing, by a show, by "theatre" in the pejorative sense.

'Now, add up the result of all these distortions – an object of attention beyond the footlights, a feeling of truth that has been violated, theatrical emotion memories that are not true to life, dead Tasks, and all this happening not where thought and reflection prevail, but in a world of trivia, of unreal conditions, not to mention the increased muscular tension which is unavoidable in such cases.

'All these Elements come together to make a wrong state in which you can neither experience nor be creative but can only make an outward show, pose, amuse, fake, mimic the character.

'Doesn't the same thing happen in music? There, one wrong note ruins the harmony, turns consonance to dissonance and makes all the other notes sound out of tune. Put the wrong note right and the chord sounds once more as it should.

'In all the examples I have given you today there was, inevitably, first distortion and then the actor's wrong creative state, which, in our vocabulary we call the stock-in-trade (actorish) state.

'Actors who are just beginning, or students, like you, who lack experience and technique, often fall under the sway of this wrong state. It brings a whole set of conventions into play. As far as a true, normal, human creative state is concerned, that is something they achieve only by chance, involuntarily.'

'How can we fall into stock-in-trade when we've only ever been onstage once?' I asked, as did other students.

'If I'm not mistaken I can answer that with your own words,' he told me. 'Do you remember the very first class when I made you simply sit onstage among your fellow-students. Instead of sitting you started play-acting, and you said more or less the following: "Strange! I've only been onstage once and the rest of the time I've lived a normal life, but it's infinitely easier for me to make a display onstage than to live naturally." The secret is that lying is implicit in the stage itself, in the very circumstances of a public performance. There can be no compromise, we must wage constant war against it, be able to go round it without noticing it. Theatrical lies wage constant war with truth. How can we defend ourselves against the first and fortify the second? We will look at the answer in our next class.'

.. .. 19..

'Let's try and answer the next question on the agenda. On the one hand, how do we protect ourselves onstage from the wrong, stock-in-trade (actorish) state in which only posturing and playacting are possible? On the other, how do we induce that right, human, mental state in which only genuine creative activity is possible?' said Tortsov, giving us the subject for today's class.

'We can answer these two questions simultaneously since one of them precludes the other. Once a true creative state has been created, it destroys the other which is wrong, and vice versa. The first of these questions is the more important and that's what we'll talk about.

'In life, each mental state occurs spontaneously, naturally. It is always true, per se, if you take the internal and external conditions into account.

'Onstage it's the opposite. Given the unnatural conditions of creating in public, you nearly always get a wrong, actorish state. Only very seldom, by chance, do you find a state which is natural and approximates to one which is normal and human.

'What are we to do when a proper creative state doesn't occur?

'Then you have to use conscious, technical means to create a natural, human state which is almost the same as the one we experience all the time in real life.

'For that you need our psychotechnique.

'It helps us establish the true and destroy the wrong creative state. It helps the actor keep within the atmosphere of a role, it protects him against the black hole and the magnetic pull of the auditorium.

'How does this process work?

'All actors make up and dress before the performance so they can make their outside look something like the character, but they forget the essential – to prepare, so to speak to "make up" and "dress" their hearts and minds, so they can create the "life of the human spirit" of a role, which above all they are called on to experience in every performance.

'Why then do actors display such a particular concern for their bodies? Is the body the most important creative agent onstage? Why doesn't the actor's mind "make up" and "dress"?'

'How could you "make it up"?' the students asked.

'Clearing the mind and preparing for the role consists in the following: not getting to your dressing room at the last moment as most people do, but (if it's a major role) preparing for your first entrance two hours before the show begins. How, though?

'The sculptor kneads the clay before he models, a singer does vocal exercises before he sings, we warm up with games in order, so to speak, to tune our mental strings, to test our mental "springs", "pedals" and "knobs", all the separate Elements and decoys we use to get our apparatus moving.

'You know all this from your class in "training and drill".

'The exercises start with relaxing the muscles as without that no further work is possible.

'And then . . . Here:

'The object is this picture. What does it portray? How big is it? What are its colours? Select a distant object. A small circle that goes no further than your legs or your ribcage. Devise a physical Task! Justify it, give it life first with one then with another idea. Bring the action to a point of truth and belief. Devise a magic "if", Given Circumstances, etc.

'After all these Elements have been separated, communicate with one of them.'

'Which one?'

'The one you feel best about, the Task, the "if", an idea, an object of attention, an action, a small truth and belief, etc.

'If you manage to get one of these working (but not "in general", not approximately or as mere form but true through and through) then all the other Elements will follow after. And all this will happen because of the natural proclivity the inner drives and the Elements have for working in common.

'This happens as it did with the actorish state in which one wrong element drags the others after it. So here. One truthful element that has been fully brought to life stirs all the other truthful Elements to work and so creates a true creative state.

'Pick up one link in the chain and the rest follow. The same applies to the Elements of the creative state.

'What a wonderful piece of work our creative nature is, if it is not abused. How interlocked and interdependent all its parts are!

'We must use this quality with care. And so every time we try to get into the true state, every time we begin to create, be it in rehearsal, or — more important — in performance, we must prepare ourselves properly and carefully, tone up the Elements and establish the right creative state out of them.'

'Every time?!' asked Vanya in amazement.

'That's hard,' said the other students in Vanya's support.

'So you think it's easier to perform actions with Elements that have been misused, do you? With no Bits and Tasks, no feeling of truth and belief? Are true wants, intentions towards a clear, tempting goal, using magic "ifs" that have been justified, and given circumstances you can believe in, really a hindrance to you, and are clichés, playacting and lies, conversely, such a help you are loath to part with them?

'No! It is easier and more natural to unite all the Elements, the more so since that is their inborn inclination.

'We are created in such a way that we need hands and feet and a heart and kidneys and a stomach, all at once, simultaneously. We find it very disagreeable when one of our organs is removed and a substitute put in its place — a glass eye, a false nose, or an artificial leg or arm or wrong teeth.

'Why don't you grant the same privilege to a creative actor, or the role he is playing? He also needs all the constituent Elements of his organism and artificial substitutes — clichés — are a hindrance to it. So let all the constituent parts which create the proper creative state work in friendship, in full co-ordination.

'What use is an object of attention, taken separately, of and for itself, to anyone? It can only live with the rest of our ideas. But where there is life there you find its constituent parts, or bits and where there are bits you find Tasks. A Task that leads you on naturally evokes wants, intentions which culminate in action.

'But a wrong, spurious action is no use to anyone, and so you must have truth, and where there is truth you have belief. All the Elements combined unlock Emotion Memory so that feelings can arise freely and the "truth of passions" be created.

'Can that occur without objects of attention, creative ideas, bits and Tasks, wishes, intentions, actions, truth and belief? We go back to the beginning again, like a children's song that goes round and round, over and over again.

'What nature has joined you should not cast asunder. Don't contradict what is natural, don't cripple yourselves. Nature has its demands, its laws and conditions which must not be denied, but which must be studied, understood and defended.

'So, don't forget to do all your exercises each time, whenever you do creative work.'

'But, look here, I'm sorry,' Grisha began to argue, 'in that case you have to do not one but two shows an evening. The first, for ourselves as we get ready in our dressing room, the second, onstage for the audience.'

'No, you don't have to do that,' Tortsov reassured him. 'When you are getting ready for the performance, all you have to do is touch on individual, basic moments in the role or the exercise, the important moments in the play, you don't have to develop all the Bits and Tasks in full.

'Just ask yourself, can I believe my attitude to this passage in the role — today, now? Do I feel this particular action? Should I alter or expand this or that minor detail with a creative idea? All these preparatory exercises before the performance are only "testing the waters", trying out one's expressive apparatus, fine-tuning one's mental, creative instrument, running through the score and the constituent Elements of an actor's heart and mind.

'If the role has matured, then the preparatory work proceeds easily and comparatively quickly every time, and the performance is recreated every time. The trouble is that far from every role in an actor's repertoire achieves that degree of maturity when he is in total possession of the score, and has become a master of his psychotechnique, and he is the creator of his own art.

'In those circumstances the process of getting ready for a role is difficult. But it becomes all the more necessary, and requires even greater care and attention each time. The actor must tirelessly try to induce the right creative state, not only during the performance but before it, in rehearsal and when working at home. The right, creative state is unstable both early on, when the role is not secure, and subsequently when the role is a little jaded, and has lost its edge.

'The right creative state wavers continuously. It is like a plane hovering in the air, which needs to be piloted. With more experience the pilot's job becomes automatic and doesn't require much attention.

'The same thing happens in our own profession. The Elements of our creative state need constant adjustment which you finally learn to cope with automatically.

'An example will illustrate.

'Let's say that the actor is feeling good. He is such a master of himself that he can test his creative state and its constituent Elements without stepping out of the role. They are all working splendidly, helping one another. But then a slight hitch occurs and the actor immediately "turns his eyes in on himself" to see which of his Elements isn't working properly. Having found the mistake he corrects it. In doing so he has no difficulty in splitting himself in two, i.e. on one hand he corrects something which is wrong and, on the other, continues to live his role.

'The actor lives, weeps, laughs onstage but weeping or laughing he observes his laughter and tears. And it is in that double life, that balance between life and the role that art lies.'[1]

.. .. 19..

'You now know what the creative state is, and how it is made up of the individual inner drives and our Elements.

'Let us try and get right inside an actor at the moment when that state of mind is being established. Let us try and follow what happens in his mind as he creates a role.

'Let's say that you have been invited to work on a most difficult and complex character, Shakespeare's Hamlet.

'What can we compare it to? A huge mountain. To get the measure of the riches that lie in its bowels, we must explore its hidden seams of precious metals, stones, marble, ore deposits. We need to know the composition of the mineral water from its mountain springs, we need to appreciate the beauties of nature. One man alone cannot accomplish such a Task. He needs help from others, a complex organization, financial resources, time, etc.

'At first you view this inaccessible mountain from below, at its base; you circle round it, study it from the outside. Then you cut footholds in the rockface and climb up them.

'You build roads, dig tunnels, bore holes and fill them, sink shafts, set up machines, mobilize skilled labour and after various explorations and soundings are convinced that incalculable riches lie hidden within it.

'The deeper you go, the more abundant the spoils become. The higher you climb, the more you are staggered by the breadth of the horizon and the beauties of nature.

'Standing on the precipice, above a bottomless pit, you can just make out the sunlit plain far below which startles you with the combination and variety of its colours. A watery stream cascades down into it. It winds through the plain and sparkles in the sun. And, further off, there is a thick forested mountain, higher up it is hidden in grass and higher still it turns into a sheer, white rock-face. The sun's rays and patches of light run and play on it. From time to time it is crossed by the shadows of cloud swiftly passing through the sky.

'And higher up there are snowy peaks. They are always hidden in the clouds and you cannot tell what is happening up there, in the space above the earth.

'Suddenly there is a stir among the people on the mountain. Everybody is running about. They are jubilant and shouting: "Gold, gold! We've found the vein!" Work starts in earnest. Holes are bored on all sides of the mountain. But time passes, the picks cease, everything goes quiet, the workmen scatter in silence, depressed and set off somewhere else, a long way off.

'The vein has run out. All that work has been done for nothing. Hopes are dashed, energy flags. The surveyors and prospectors are lost, they don't know what to do.

'But time passes and once again joyful cries are raised to heaven. They clamber to the spot, dig, the whole crowd shouts and sings.

'But once again human effort was vain – no gold was found.

'From the bowels of the earth, like a subterranean rumble, rise the sounds of the picks and the same joyful cries then they too are silent.

'But the mountain cannot conceal its hidden treasure from the diligent. Human endeavour is crowned with success. The vein is found. The picks start up anew, the workers strike up joyful songs, people stream cheerfully across the whole mountain. A short while yet and a vein of the most precious of metals is found.' After a short pause Tortsov continued:

'In *Hamlet*, the greatest work a genius (Shakespeare) wrote, incalculable treasures (psychological Elements) and their ore (the subject of the work) lie hidden, like the mountain with the gold. These precious objects are extremely subtle, complex, elusive. They are more difficult to dig out of the heart of a role and of an actor than a vein of minerals from the earth. When you approach a writer's work you look at it from the outside, as with a mountain full of gold, you study its form. Then you look for ways in, some means of penetrating its secret depths where the riches of the mind are hidden. For that too you need "boreholes", "tunnels" and "shafts" (Tasks, wants, logic, sequence, etc.); you need workmen (creative forces, Elements); you need "engineers" (the inner drives); you need the appropriate "mood" (your creative state).

'The creative process is on the boil for many years in the actor's personality, by day, by night, at home, in rehearsal, in performance. This work can best be characterized by the words: "the joys and sorrows of creation".

'There is also "great jubilation" personally for us as actors when we uncover the vein of gold, the ore, in us.

'Every moment of an actor's work on a role serves to establish a profound, complex, strong, sustained, stable creative state in him as a creative artist. Only in these circumstances can one speak of genuine creative work and art.

'But unfortunately this all-penetrating state is a rare phenomenon – it is to be found in great actors.

'More frequently actors create in a much more shallow mood in which you can only skim the surface. They take a casual stroll round the role, as round the mountain, with no concern for the incalculable riches that lie hidden within it.

'In that shallow, superficial state you cannot reveal the psychological depths of a play, you merely become acquainted with its external beauties.

'Unfortunately, more often than not, it is this kind of actor that we encounter.

'If I ask you to go up onstage and look for a piece of paper that isn't there then you will have to create the Given Circumstances, the "ifs", your ideas, you will have to arouse all the Elements of your creative state. Only with their help will you be able to recall once more, to recognize (feel) once more how the simple Task of looking for a piece of paper is accomplished.

'A minor goal requires a minor creative state, one that is neither deep nor prolonged. In a good technical actor it will be there instantly and the action once accomplished vanishes instantly.

'Each Task and action has its own corresponding inner creative state.'

'We can only draw one conclusion from this, that the quality, strength, stamina, stability, depth, duration, penetration, composition and forms of the actor's creative state are infinitely varied. If you consider that in each of them one or other of the Elements, the inner drives and the individuality of the actor, is predominant, then the variations in the creative state seem endless.

'In other instances, the creative state seeks out the subjects for its creative action on its own, by chance.

'But the opposite can be the case. An interesting Task, a role, a play can stimulate the actor to be creative and so evoke the right state.

'This is what happens in an actor's mind as he is performing and rehearsing.'

15

THE SUPERTASK, THROUGHACTION

'The inner creative state of the actor/role has been established!

'We have studied the play using not only our cold intellect (the mind) but our wishes (the will), emotions (feeling) and all the Elements! The creative army is even better prepared for war!'

'We can advance!'

'Where are we to send it?'

'To the centre, to the capital, to the heart of the play, to the basic goal which caused the writer to write and the actor to act in it.'

'And where are we to find this goal?' said a puzzled Vanya.

'In the writer's work and in the psychology of the actor/role.'

'How is it to be done?'

'Before answering that I have to talk about one or two important moments in the creative process. Listen to me.

'Just as a seed grows into a flower, so a writer's work grows out of an individual thought and feeling.

'These individual thoughts, feelings, living dreams run through the writer's life like a golden thread and guide him when he is creating. He makes them the basis of his play and from this seed he develops a work of literature. All these thoughts, feelings, lifelike dreams, the eternal joys and sorrows the writer has, become the basis of the play. It is because of them he takes up his pen, the main task of the production. The transmission of the writer's feelings and thoughts, his dreams, his sorrows and joys is the main task of the production.

'Let us agree that in future we will call this fundamental goal, which draws together each and every Task, and stimulates the creative efforts of the inner drives and the Elements that comprise the creative state of the actor-role:

THE SUPERTASK OF THE WRITER'S WORK

Tortsov pointed to the inscription on the placard hanging in front of us.

'The Supertask?!' Vanya mused with a tragic expression on his face.

'I'll explain,' said Tortsov to help him. 'All his life Dostoievski looked for God and the Devil in people. That drove him to produce *The Brothers Karamazov*. That is why the search for God is the Supertask in this work.

'Tolstoi strove for self-perfection all his life and many of his works grew from that seed, which formed their Supertasks.

'Chekhov fought against vulgarity and petty-mindedness and dreamed of a better life. This struggle, this striving towards it became the Supertask of many of his works.

'Don't you feel how readily these great, life-giving goals which men of genius set themselves can become stimulating, compelling Tasks for an actor, and how they can pull together all the individual Bits of the play and the role?

'Everything that happens in a play, all its individual Tasks, major or minor, all the actor's creative ideas and actions, which are analogous to the role, strive to fulfil the play's Supertask. Their common link with it, and the sway it holds over everything that happens in the play, is so great that even the most trivial detail, if it is irrelevant to the Supertask, becomes harmful, superfluous, drawing one's attention away from the essential meaning of the work.

'This pursuit of the Supertask must be continuous, unbroken throughout the whole play and the role.

'Apart from its continuity you must discern the quality and origin of that pursuit.

'It can be histrionic, mere form, and only provide a more or less credible, overall direction. Efforts of that kind cannot bring the whole work alive, nor arouse you to dynamic, genuine, productive, purposeful actions. The stage does not need these kinds of creative efforts.

'But there is another kind, which is genuine, human, active, and which tries to achieve the basic goal of the play. This continuous pursuit, like a major artery, feeds the actor's entire organism and the character he is playing and gives it, and the whole play, life.

'Genuine living pursuit stirs the special quality of the Supertask itself and its power to compel.

'A masterly Supertask has great drawing-power, is strong, but when it is ordinary, its pull is weak.'

'And when it's bad?' Vanya asked.

'When it's bad an actor must take pains to give it strength and depth.'

'What are the qualities we need in the Supertask?' I asked.

'Do we need a wrong Supertask which doesn't correspond to the ideas the author expresses in the play, even if it is interesting in itself and to the actor?' Tortsov asked.

'No! We can do without it! Moreover, it is dangerous. The more compelling a wrong Supertask, the further it leads the actor away from the author, the play and the role,' said Tortsov in answer to his own question.

'Do we need a cerebral Supertask? We can do without a cold, cerebral Supertask too. But we do need a *conscious* Supertask, that comes from our intelligence, from an interesting creative idea.

'Do we need an emotional Supertask, that arouses our whole nature? Of course we do, in the highest degree like air and sun.

'Do we need a volitional Supertask, which will draw together all our mental and physical qualities? Yes, very much so.

'And what are we to say about a Supertask which stimulates our creative imagination, which attracts our total attention, satisfies our feeling of truth and stimulates our power to believe as well as the other elements in the actor's state of self-awareness? We need every Supertask, which stimulates the inner drives, the Elements, as we need bread and nourishment.

'So it appears that we need a Supertask which is analogous to the writer's thoughts but which unfailingly evokes a response in the actor's personality. That is what can evoke not formalistic, not cerebral but genuine, living, human, direct experiencing.

'Or, in other words, you must look for the Supertask not only in the role but also in the heart and mind of the actor.

'The same Supertask, which every actor playing the role must accept, has a different resonance for each person. You get a Task which is the same and not the same. For example, take the most real of human aspirations, "I want to live happily". How many different, elusive nuances there are in the same wish and the different ways of achieving it and in the same representation of happiness. There is a great deal which is personal, individual in all of this which we can't always appreciate at a conscious level. If you then take a more complex Task, the individual peculiarities of each human being/actor will be even more pronounced.

'These individual nuances in the personalities of different people playing the same role are of great importance for the Supertask. Without their subjective experiences, it is arid, dead. It is essential to find a response in the actor's personality if the Supertask and the role are to become living, vibrant, resplendent with all the colours of genuine, human life.

'It is important that the actor's attitude to the role should lose nothing of his individual sensibility and at the same time not diverge from the author's ideas. If the actor doesn't invest his own nature as a human being in the role, then what he creates will be dead.

'The actor must find the Supertask for himself and take it to his heart. If it is indicated to him by others, he must filter it through himself and stir it to life emotionally with his own personality and feelings. In other words, he must be able to make each Supertask his own. That means, finding the things in it which have an essential affinity to his own personality.

'What is it that gives the Supertask its special, elusive attraction which stimulates every actor playing the same role? In the majority of cases this special quality gives the Supertask the special something we feel in it, something which is hidden in the subconscious.

'The Supertask should be in the closest affinity with it.

'You see now how long and hard we must look for a Supertask which is substantial, stimulating and profound.

'You see how important it is to feel its presence in the author's work and to discover a response to it in one's own heart and mind.

'How many potential Supertasks we have to reject and then nurture once more. How many times we have to take aim and miss before we achieve our goal.'

.. .. 19..

Today Tortsov said:

'The process of seeking and consolidating the Supertask of a great role is difficult, and choosing a definition plays an important part in it.

'You know well enough that when we are dealing with simple Bits and Tasks, accuracy of definition gives them strength and meaning. Earlier we also said that the substitution of a verb for a noun increases the level of dynamism and the impulse to creative activity.

'This is even more the case when we come to defining the Supertask verbally.

' "It doesn't matter what you call it," the layman says. But it so happens that the line we take and the interpretation we give to the work depend on the accuracy of the name, and the action implicit in that name. Let's say we are playing Griboedov's *Woe from Wit* and that we have defined the Supertask of the work as "I want to strive for Sophie". There are many actions in the play which justify that wording.

'Unfortunately the socially critical aspect of the play is given only incidental significance in such an interpretation. However, you can define the Supertask of *Woe from Wit* with the very same words "I want to strive", not for Sophie, but for my country. In that case Chatski's passionate love for Russia, for his nation, for his people, comes to the fore.

'When that happens the socially critical side of the play looms much larger and the whole work acquires a greater inner meaning.

'But you can give even greater depth to the play if you define its Supertask by the words "I want to strive for freedom!" If that is what the hero is striving for, the force of his criticism becomes even sharper and the whole work takes on not a personal, private meaning, as in the first instance – for the love of Sophie, not a narrowly national meaning, as in the second version, but a meaning which is common to all men.

'The same metamorphosis occurs in the tragedy of *Hamlet* when you change the name of the Supertask. If you call it, "I want to honour my father's memory" you push it towards family drama. If you have the title "I want to understand the secrets of existence" you get a mystical tragedy in which a man, once he has glanced beyond the threshold of life, cannot go on living until he has answered the question of the meaning of existence. Some people want to see a second Messiah in Hamlet who must cleanse the world of all that is base, sword in hand. The Supertask, "I want to save mankind" gives the tragedy even greater breadth and depth.

'One or two examples from my own artistic practice will explain the significance of finding a name for the Supertask more graphically than the examples I have already provided.

'I was playing Argan in Molière's *Imaginary Invalid*. Initially we approached the play in a very simplistic fashion defining the Supertask as "I want to be ill". The harder I tried to be so, the more successful I was, the more a joyous satirical comedy turned into a tragedy about illness, into pathological study.

'But we quickly grasped our error and defined the despot's Supertask as, "I want people to think I am ill".

'With that the comic aspect of the play suddenly came alive and the ground was created for a fool to be exploited by charlatans from the medical world, whom Molière wished to ridicule in his play, and a tragedy was suddenly transformed into a joyous comedy about the petite bourgeoisie.

'In another play, Goldoni's *Mistress of the Inn* we initially called the Supertask "I want to hate women" (misogyny) but then the play could not be seen as either funny or effective. Once I had understood that the hero loved women and did not actually wish to be a misogynist but only appear so, then the Supertask became "I want to woo them secretly" (simulating misogyny) and the play suddenly came to life.

'But that task related more to my own role than to the whole play. But when, after a great deal of work, we understood that the "mistress of the inn" or, to put it another way, "the mistress of our lives" was Woman (Mirandolina) and established an active Supertask on these lines, the whole meaning of the play emerged.

'The examples I have given tell you that the naming of the Supertask is an extremely important factor in our creative work and the technique we use in it and gives sense and direction to all our efforts.

'Very often the Supertask is only defined after the performance has been given. The audience frequently helps the actor discover the right name for it.

'Is it now clear to you that the unbreakable link between the Supertask and the play is an organic one, that the Supertask proceeds from the very heart of the play, from its secret depths?

'The Supertask should be fixed in the actor's personality, his imagination, his thoughts, his feelings, as firmly as possible. The Supertask should remind him ceaselessly of the inner life of the role and the goal of his creative work. The actor must be concerned with it throughout the performance. It should help him contain his sensory attention within the ambit of the role. When this happens then the process of experiencing proceeds normally but if a division occurs onstage between the inner goal of the role and the intentions of the human being/actor performing it, then you have a disastrous mess.

'That is why the actor's first concern is not to lose sight of the Supertask. To forget it means disrupting the lifeline of the play. That is catastrophic for the role, the actor himself and the whole performance. When that happens, the actor's concentration moves in a wrong direction, there is an emptiness at the very heart of the role and its life is cut short. Learn to create normally, biologically onstage what happens easily and spontaneously in real life.

'The author's work was engendered by the Supertask and it is towards that the actor should direct his creative efforts.'

.. .. 19..

'So,' said Tortsov, 'the inner drives, which stem from the actor's intellect (mind), wants (will) and emotions (feeling), move forward, pull all the tiny parts of the role together. This is then permeated by our inner creative Elements of the human being/actor which unite, merge into a planned design, like woven strands, and are drawn into a tight knot.

'All these lines form the creative state, which is the prerequisite for the study of all the parts, all the complex subtleties both of the inner life of the role and, by the same token, of the personal life of the actor himself during the creative act.

'The Supertask, the reason why the play and its characters were created, is distilled out of this multi-faceted study of the role.

'Once the proper goal of your creative intentions has been understood, all the inner drives and Elements speed along the path set by the author towards their common, ultimate goal, the Supertask.

'In our vocabulary we call this the linear thrust of the inner drives throughout the play . . .'

Tortsov pointed to a second inscription on a placard hanging in front of us:

THE THROUGHACTION OF THE ACTOR/ROLE

'So, for an actor, the Throughaction is the direct extension of the dynamic of the inner drives that have their origin in the mind, will and creative feeling of the actor.

'If there were no Throughaction, all the Bits and Tasks in the play, all the Given Circumstances, communication, Adaptations, moments of truth and belief, etc. would vegetate separately from one another, with no hope of coming alive.

'But the Throughaction brings everything together, strings all the elements together, like a thread through unconnected beads, and points them towards the common Supertask.

'After that everything serves it.

'How am I to explain the enormous practical significance of the Throughaction and the Supertask in our creative work to you?

'Concrete examples from real life will best convince you. Let me give you one.

'The actress Z, who was very successful and popular, became interested in the "system". She decided to study all over again and to that end quit the stage for a while. Over the course of a few years she studied the new method with various teachers, did the whole course and then went back to the stage again.

'To her amazement she didn't have the success she'd had before. People found she had lost the things she was most famous for, immediacy, sudden flashes of inspiration. They had been replaced by flatness, natural-istic detail, conventional acting and other faults. You can easily imagine the poor actress's situation. Every entrance onstage turned into another ordeal. This got in the way of her acting, increased her bewilderment which reached the point of despair. She tried herself out in different towns, claiming that in the capital the enemies of the "system" were prejudiced against the new method. But the same thing happened in the provinces. The poor actress cursed the "system" and tried to be free of it. She tried to go back to her old ways but she couldn't. On the one hand she had lost her theatrical facility and belief in her old ways, and on the other had recognized the absurdity of her earlier method of acting in com-parison with the new one to which she was now very attached. She had abandoned the old method but had not caught on to the new and so was betwixt and between. It was said that Z was going to give up the stage and get married. Then there were rumours that she was thinking of putting an end to herself.

'At that time I happened to see her onstage. After the performance, at her request, I went to her dressing room. She greeted me like a guilty schoolgirl. The performance had long been over, cast and audience had departed but she, still in make-up and costume, wouldn't let me out of her dressing room and in a state of agitation so great it bordered on desper-ation, begged to know what had happened to her. We went over every moment in her role, the work that had been done on it, all the techniques of the "system" she had mastered. Everything was as it should be. The actress understood all its parts separately but had not mastered the creative fundamentals of the "system" as a whole.

' "What about the Throughaction and the Supertask?" I asked her.

'She had heard something about them and knew them in general outline, but it was only theory and had not been turned into practice.

'If you play without Throughaction it means that your actions are not in accord with the Given Circumstances and the magic "if", it means you are not bringing your own nature and your subconscious into your creative work, you are not forming the "life of the human spirit" of the role, and that is what the main goal and the fundamentals of our school of acting require. There is no "system" without them. It means that you were not creating onstage but merely doing individual, entirely unrelated exercises according to the "system". They are fine in class, at school, but not in a performance. You forgot that these exercises and everything else about the "system" are needed, first and foremost, for the Throughaction and the Supertask. That is why the individual Bits in your role, beautiful as they were, made no impression and were not satisfying as a whole. You are breaking a statue of Apollo into bits and showing each of them separately. Fragments will hardly capture an audience.

'A rehearsal was arranged for the following day at her home. I explained how she should make the Throughaction run through all the Bits and Tasks she had worked on and then direct them towards a common Supertask.

'She set to work with great enthusiasm, and asked me to give her a few days to master it. I went to see her and checked over the things she had done on her own, and finally made my way to the theatre to see the performance in its new version. There is no need to describe what happened that evening. This talented actress was rewarded for all her sorrows and doubts. She had a staggering success. That is what the miracle-working, remarkable, life-giving Throughaction and the Supertask can do.

'That is, I think, a convincing example of the enormous significance they have for us.

'I'll go a step further,' Tortsov exclaimed after a short pause. 'Imagine an ideal human being/actor who devotes himself to one single great goal in his life, "to inspire and bring joy to people by his high art, to make plain the hidden spiritual beauties which a masterly work of art contains".

'A human being/actor of this kind goes out onstage to show, to make plain his new interpretation of a masterpiece and a role to the audience gathered in the theatre, because, in his creative opinion it is better able to convey the inner essence of the work. This kind of human being/actor can give his life to the elevated, cultural mission of giving enlightenment to his contemporaries. He can use his personal success to purvey ideas and feelings which are dear to his heart and mind, etc. to the masses. Who knows how many inspiring goals great men may have!

'Let us agree for the future to call this vital goal a human being/actor has, the super-Supertask and the super-Throughaction.'

'What's that?'

'Instead of answering that I'll give you an example from my own life which helped me to understand (i.e. feel) the thing we're talking about.

'A long time ago when our theatre was on tour in Petersburg, the day before we opened, I was kept late because of a bad, ill-prepared rehearsal. I came out of the theatre exasperated, angry and tired. Suddenly I was presented with an unexpected sight. I saw a huge camp spread out all over the square in front of the theatre. Fires were burning, thousands of people were sitting, dozing, sleeping in the snow and on benches they had brought with them. This huge crowd was waiting for the box office to open in the morning, so they could get the lowest number and be able to buy tickets.

'I was stunned. To appreciate the full measure of the heroism these people showed, I had to ask myself what event, what tempting prospect, what extraordinary phenomenon, what world genius could make me shiver out in the ice and snow not one night, but several nights running? They were making this sacrifice just so they could get a bit of paper that gave them the right to go to the box office with no guarantee of obtaining a ticket.

'I couldn't answer the question or conceive of any event that would make me risk my health or even my life.

'The theatre means so much to people! How deeply aware we must be of that! What an honour, what great fortune it is to bring supreme joy to an audience of thousands which is ready to risk its life for it. I want to set myself that supreme goal which I have called the super-Supertask and achieve it by means of the super-Throughaction.'

After a short pause Tortsov continued:

'But woe betide the actor if, on the way to a grand, ultimate goal, be it the Supertask of the play or role, or the super-Supertask of his whole life as a creative artist, he pays more attention than he should to something petty or private.'

'What happens then?'

'This. Do you remember, there is a children's game in which they whirl a weight or a stone attached to a long rope above their heads. As it rotates it winds round the stick from which it gains its momentum. When it is rotated faster the rope with the weight attached describes a circle and at the same time gradually winds round the stick the child is holding. In the end the weight comes nearer and nearer to the stick and knocks up against it.

'Now imagine that while the game is in full swing someone else puts his walking stick in the path of rotation. Then, when the rope with the weight comes into communication with it, the rope, by its own inertia, starts to wind round the walking stick and not round the stick from which it gets its momentum. As result the weight gravitates not towards its real master, the child, but to the stranger who caught the rope up with his stick. With that, of course, the child loses all possibility of controlling his game and stays on the sidelines.

'Something similar happens in our profession. Very often when we are intent upon the ultimate Supertask, on the way we come up against a secondary, wrongly theatrical task, of minor importance. All the creative energy of the working actor is given over to it. Need one explain that this exchange of a major goal for a minor one is a dangerous phenomenon which distorts all the work the actor has done?'

.. .. 19..

'I am going to use graphics to make you appreciate the significance of the Supertask and the Throughaction more fully,' said Tortsov going to a large blackboard and taking a piece of chalk.

'Normally all the Tasks and the short lines of life within the role are directed, without exception, in one single direction – i.e. to the Supertask. So:'

Tortsov traced on the blackboard:

'A long series of small, medium and large lines of life in the role all go one way, towards the Supertask. The short lines of life in the role and their tasks, alternate and are linked to each other in logical sequence. Thanks to that, one continuous through line is created, running through the entire play.

'Now, imagine for a moment that the actor has no Supertask, that each of the short lines of life in the role he is playing is moving in a different direction.'

Tortsov once again illustrated his idea with dashes that broke up the unbroken line of the Throughaction:

'Here's a series of large, medium and small tasks and little bits in the life of a role pointed in different directions. Can they create a continuous, straight line?'

We acknowledged they couldn't.

'Then, in that case, the Throughaction is destroyed, the play is broken down into bits, going off in different directions, and each of its parts is obliged to exist on its own account, in the absence of the whole. In that form, beautiful as they may be, the individual parts are of no use to the play.

'I'll give you a third case,' said Tortsov continuing his explanation. 'As I have already told you, in every good play the Supertask and the Throughaction emerge organically from the work itself. That's something you cannot infringe with impunity, without destroying the work itself.

'Imagine there are people who want to introduce an extraneous goal or slant which has nothing to do with the play.

'In that case the organic link between the play and the Supertask and the natural Throughaction which has been created remains in part but is, at moments, deflected by the slant that has been introduced:

'A broken-backed play like that cannot live.'

Grisha protested energetically, as an actor.

'Look here, please, I'm sorry, you're taking away all personal initiative from the director and the actor, all personal creative contribution, his very own *ego*, the possibility of renewing the art of the past and of bringing it closer to the present!'

Tortsov explained calmly:

'You and many others who think like you confuse three words: the eternal, the contemporary and the merely topical.

'What is contemporary can become eternal if it contains questions of substance and ideas which are profound. I have nothing to say against that kind of contemporaneity if the author's work requires it.

'In complete contrast to that, what is exclusively topical can never become eternal. It only lives for today and can be forgotten tomorrow. That is why an eternal work of art is never to be organically combined with mere topicality however ingenious the ideas of the director, the actors or, in part, you yourself, may be.

'When you force topical elements or some other extraneous goal into a monolithic, classical play, it is like a canker on a beautiful body and often deforms it beyond recognition. The crippled Supertask neither allures nor attracts, it only angers and irritates.

'Forcing is a bad method in art and so a Supertask that has been "updated" by using a topical slant means death both to the play and the characters in it.

'But there are times, it is true, when the slant is closely linked with the Supertask. We know that you can graft a lemon onto an orange tree and then grow a new fruit, which is called in America, a grapefruit.

'You can perform a similar grafting in a play. Sometimes you can graft a new idea quite naturally onto a classic and so rejuvenate it. In that case the new idea ceases to exist independently and re-emerges in the Supertask.

'This can be expressed graphically like so: the line of the Throughaction is coextensive with the Supertask and the slant.

 Supertask
slant

'In that case the creative process proceeds normally and the work is organically intact.

'The conclusion to be drawn from all I have said is:

'Above all protect the Supertask and the Throughaction, be wary of forcibly introducing a new slant and other extraneous intentions and goals into the play.

'If, today, I have succeeded in making you understand the totally exceptional, pre-eminent role the Supertask and Throughaction play in creative work I shall be a happy man and consider that I have explained one of the most important elements in the "system" to you.'

After quite a long pause Tortsov continued:

'Every action meets a counter-action and the second evokes and strengthens the first. So, in every play, parallel to the Throughaction, there is an opposing counter-Throughaction coming from the opposite direction to meet it.

'That's good and we should welcome such a phenomenon because a reaction naturally provokes a whole series of new actions. We need this constant clash. It produces struggle, opposition, strife, a whole series of corresponding problems and ways of resolving them. It stimulates our energy, action, which are the fundamentals of acting.

'If there were no counter-Throughaction in the play and everything just worked out, there would be nothing for the cast and the characters to do, and the play itself would be actionless and therefore untheatrical.

'So, if Iago didn't weave his treacherous plot, then Othello would not be jealous of Desdemona, and kill her. But as the Moor yearns for his beloved with all his being, and Iago stands between them with his counter-Throughaction, you get a five-act, highly active tragedy which ends in catastrophe.

'Need we add that the line of the counter-Throughaction is made up of individual moments and the small lines of life in the actor/role. I will try and illustrate what I have said using Brand as an example.

'Let's say we have established Brand's watchword, "all or nothing" as the Supertask (whether that's right or not doesn't matter for the present example). In a fanatic this principle is terrifying. It admits of no compromise, concession or weakening in the fulfilment of his ideal in life.

'Now try and link the individual Bits of the extract "with the abandoned child", which we analysed earlier, to the Supertask of the whole play.'

In my mind I tried to use the abandoned child as the starting point and set my sights on the Supertask, 'all or nothing'. Of course my imagination and my ideas helped me establish the link between them, but I could only do it with a great deal of strain, which is crippling to the play.

It is much more natural if you have resistance instead of compliance from the mother, and so in this Bit Agnes does not follow the Throughaction but the counter-Throughaction, going not towards the Supertask but against it.

When I did the same thing with Brand, and looked for the link between his Tasks – 'to persuade my wife to give up the abandoned child, so as to make a sacrifice' and the Supertask – 'all or nothing' – I was able to find it at once. It was natural for the fanatic to demand everything for the sake of his ideal in life. Agnes' counter-Throughaction provoked stronger action from Brand. Hence the struggle between two basic principles began.

Brand's sense of duty is in conflict with a mother's love. Ideas fight feelings. The fanatical pastor against the grieving mother, the male principle against the female.

So, in this particular scene the line of the Throughaction is in Brand's hands and the counter-Throughaction comes from Agnes.

By way of conclusion Tortsov gave us a brief schematic summary of the things he had said over our whole year of study.

This short overview helped me put all the things I had learned in the first year of study in order.

'Now give me all your attention as what I am going to say is very important,' Tortsov stated. 'All the stages in our programme, from the beginning of our work here in the school, all the investigations of the individual Elements, we have undertaken this year, have been done so that we can achieve the creative state.

'That's what we have been working for the whole winter. That's what demands and always will demand your undivided attention.

'But at this stage in your development, your creative state is not ready to cope with the subtle, intense search for the Supertask and the Throughaction. The creative state we have developed needs one major addition. It holds the great secret of the "system", one which justifies the most important principle of our school of acting: *the subconscious through the conscious*.

'We shall turn to the study of this addition and its principles in our next class.'

* * *

So the first year studying the 'system' is over and 'in my heart', like Gogol, 'I feel so confused, so dreadful.'[1] I had counted on the work we had been doing for almost a year to lead me to 'inspiration' but, unfortunately, in that sense, the 'system' didn't live up to my expectations.

Such were my thoughts as I stood in the foyer of the theatre, mechanically putting on my coat and lazily twisting my scarf about my neck. Suddenly I felt a 'dig' in the ribs. I gave a cry, turned and saw a smiling Tortsov.

Seeing the state I was in, he wanted to know why I was downcast. My answer was evasive but he persisted obstinately and asked me in detail:

'What do you feel when you are onstage?' He wanted to know what it was in the 'system' that bewildered and worried me.

'The trouble is I don't feel anything special. I feel good onstage, I know what I have to do, I don't feel useless, or empty. I believe everything, I am aware of my right to be onstage.'

'What more do you want?! Is it really so bad not to tell lies up there, to believe everything, to feel yourself master of the place? That's a great deal!' Tortsov assured me.

Then I owned up about inspiration.

'So that's it! . . .' he cried. 'Don't come to me about that. The "system" doesn't manufacture inspiration. It just prepares the right soil for it. As to the question whether it arrives or not that you must ask heaven, or your own nature, or chance about. I'm no wizard. I can only show you new lures, techniques for arousing feelings and for experiencing.

'I advise you in the future not to chase after the ghost called inspiration. Leave that question to the enchantress, nature, and concern yourself with what is accessible to human consciousness.

'Shchepkin wrote to his pupil Shumski, "You can sometimes play feebly, sometimes adequately (that often depends on how you feel) but play truly."

'That is the direction in which your artistic aspirations and concerns should be moving.

'Once the role has been put on the right track, it moves forward, broadens, deepens and finally reaches inspiration.

'Until that happens, rest assured that lies, playacting, clichés, posturing never produce inspiration. So do your best to play truly, learn to prepare the right soil for "inspiration from on high" and rest assured that it will be much more in tune with you because of it.

'In any case we shall be talking about inspiration in our next class. We shall take a close look at it,' said Tortsov as he went out.

'Take a close look at inspiration?!' Reason, be 'intellectual' about it? Is that really possible? Did I reason when I pronounced 'Blood, Iago, blood' in the presentation? Was Marya reasoning when she shouted her remarkable 'Help!'? 'Is it really possible that we can gather crumbs, scraps and individual flashes and combine them to form inspiration as we do with physical actions and the small moments of truth and belief they contain?' I wondered as I left the theatre.

16

THE SUBCONSCIOUS AND THE ACTOR'S CREATIVE STATE[1]

.. .. 19..

'Kostya and Vanya, play the first part of the "burning money",' Tortsov told us as he came into class.

'You know that in acting we must always start by relaxing the muscles. So first of all sit comfortably and easily as though you were at home.'

We went onstage and did as we were told.

'No, no! Be more free, more at ease!' Tortsov shouted from the auditorium. 'Ninety-five per cent less tension!

'Perhaps you think I am going too far? No, an actor can try too hard in front of a large audience. And the worst thing of all is that it happens unnoticed, for no cause, an actor's will and common sense have nothing to do with it. So be bold and get rid of it – as much as you can.

'Feel more at home onstage than you actually do in your own home. You must feel more at ease onstage than in real life because in the theatre we are dealing not with just being alone but with "public solitude". It gives us the greatest pleasure.'

But I tried so hard I reached a state of total prostration, lapsed into an enforced state of stillness and could not get out of it. That too is one of the worst kinds of blockage. I had to fight it. So I changed position, moved, tried to get things moving, and finished up at the other extreme, being over-busy. That made me feel uncomfortable. To get away from that I had to exchange a fast, nervous rhythm for a very slow, almost lazy one.

Tortsov not only acknowledged but approved what I had done:

'When an actor works too hard, it is helpful if he adopts an indifferent, almost casual attitude to what he is doing. That's a good antidote to working too hard and overacting.'

But, unfortunately, that didn't bring you the ease you feel in real life, at home, on your own sofa.

The fact was I had forgotten three elements in the process: 1) tension, 2) relaxation, 3) justification. I had to correct my mistake quickly. When I'd done that I felt that I was free inwardly of something superfluous. Something I didn't need seemed to have fallen away and vanished. I sensed the earth's gravity on my whole body, its weight. It just sank into the soft armchair in which I was half-lying. At that moment the enormous pain of muscular tension went. But even that didn't give me the freedom I wanted, the freedom I knew in real life. What was it all about?

When I examined my own mood, I understood that it was not my muscles but my mind which was tense. It was keeping watch on my body and preventing it from resting quietly.

I told Tortsov what I had been thinking.

'You're right. There is a great deal of excess tension in the Elements too. Only you have to deal with inner tightness differently from crude muscles. Psychological Elements are threads of gossamer in comparison with the muscles, which are like cables. Threads of gossamer break easily but if you wind them together they are like cables that not even an axe can cut. But you must handle them with care from the outset.'

'How do you deal with these "gossamer threads"?' the students asked.

'When you are battling against psychological tension, you must remember there are three stages, i.e. tension, relaxation, justification.

'When dealing with the first two, look for the inner tensions, find out their origin and try to get rid them. In the third stage, you justify your new psychological state with the right Given Circumstances.

'In the case in question, use the fact that one of the most important of your Elements (concentration) is centred in you, in your muscles, it isn't spread all over the stage and the auditorium. Focus on something interesting, a more important object in the scene. Direct it towards some goal or action which appeals to you. That brings your work alive.'

I started to recall the Tasks in the scene, the Given Circumstances. Mentally I wandered through the whole apartment. While I was doing that, suddenly a new circumstance came into my head. I came across a room I had never known before, and saw a very old man and woman – my wife's parents, who were living with us in retirement. This unexpected discovery moved me, and, at the same time worried me, since an increase in the size of my family complicated my relationship to them. I had to work very hard to feed five mouths, not counting my own! In those conditions my job, the next day's audit, the general meeting, the work I was doing at present, going through papers and checking the cash, assumed much greater meaning in my life. I sat down in the armchair and nervously wound one of the bands which I happened to have in my hand, round my finger.

'Well done!' said Tortsov approvingly from the stalls. 'There we have really relaxed muscles. Now I believe it all – what you're doing, what you're thinking, even though I don't exactly know what's going on in your mind.'

When I checked my body I found that my muscles were completely free, without any stress or strain on my part. Evidently the third stage, the moment of justifying my sitting down, which I had forgotten about, had happened spontaneously.

'Don't rush, though,' Tortsov whispered to me. 'Use your inner eye to see everything right through. If you need to, bring in a new "if".'

'Well, what if there is a big error in the cash?' the thought suddenly occurred to me. 'Then I'll have to check the books and papers. How awful! Can I manage to do that alone . . . at night?'

I looked at the clock automatically. It was four. Four what? Day or night? For a moment I thought it was night, was worried because of the late hour and instinctively rushed to the table and furiously set to work, forgetting everything else.

'Bravo!' I heard an approving Tortsov say with half an ear.

But I wasn't paying attention to encouragements. I didn't need them. I was living, feeling onstage, I had the right to do anything that seemed appropriate.

But that wasn't enough. I wanted to make my situation even more difficult and make my feelings more intense.

To do that I had to bring in a new Given Circumstance, a large deficit.

'What am I to do?' I asked myself in great turmoil. 'Go to the office,' I decided, rushing into the corridor. 'But the office is closed,' I remembered and went back into the sitting room and walked about a long time to clear my head, smoked a cigarette and sat in a dark corner to get a grip on myself.

I had a vision of some hard-faced people. They were going through the books, the papers, the cashbox. They questioned me, and I didn't know what to answer, I got confused. Stubbornness and despair prevented me from acknowledging my mistakes.

Then the fatal decision was taken. Groups of people whispered in corners, I was alone, apart, in disgrace. Then the trial, the sentence, confiscation of my possessions, eviction from the apartment.

'You see, Kostya isn't doing anything, but we can feel that everything is boiling up inside him,' Tortsov whispered to the students.

At that moment my head started to spin. I lost myself in the role, and didn't know what was me and what was the character. My hands stopped winding the string. I was still, not knowing what to do.

I don't remember what happened after. I only know I was at ease and at home with every impromptu action.

Then I decided to go to the Public Prosecutor and rushed into the corridor and looked through all the cupboards for invoices and did other things I can't remember, but which I learned about after from the people who had been watching. There was a magical transformation inside me, as in a fairy tale. Before I had fumbled my way through the scene, not knowing fully what was happening in it or me. Now it was as though my 'inner eye' was open and I understood everything completely. Every detail onstage and inside me took on a different meaning. I was aware of feelings, representations, appraisals, mental images in the role and in myself. I was, in fact, performing a new play.

'That means you have found yourself in the role and the role in you,' said Tortsov when I explained my feelings to him.

'Before I saw, heard, understood differently. Then there had been the "feelings that seem true" and now there was the "truth of the passions". Before there had been the sincerity of a poor imagination, now there was the sincerity of a rich imagination. Before, my freedom onstage had been limited, bound by conventions, now it was unbounded and bold.

'I feel that in the future I will play the "burning money" differently every time I do it.

'Isn't that what it is to live and be an actor? Isn't that inspiration?'

'I don't know. Ask the psychologists. Science is not my field. I'm a practical man, and can only explain how I experience the creative process at such moments.'

'What is your experience?' the students asked.

'I will tell you with pleasure, only not today as the class is over. You have other classes.'

.. .. 19..

Tortsov didn't forget his promise and began the class as follows:

'A while ago, I was given a spoof operation at a party given by some friends.

'They brought in big tables: one was ostensibly for the surgical instruments, the other – with nothing on it – was for the "operating table". The floor was covered with sheets, they brought bandages, bowls and dishes.

The "doctors" put on gowns and gave me a shirt. They carried me to the "operating table", put on a blindfold or, to put it more simply, bandaged my eyes. The most irritating thing was the fact that the doctors treated me with exaggerated care, like someone badly ill, and that they treated the joke and everything connected with it in a serious and business-like fashion.

'That put me in such a muddle I didn't now how to behave, whether to laugh or cry. I even had the stupid thought, "What if they were really to start cutting me up?" The uncertainty and the waiting were disturbing. I was all ears, I didn't miss a single sound. There were lots of them. There was whispering all round, water was poured, surgical instruments clattered and sometimes the large dish tolled like a funeral bell.

"Let's start," someone whispered, enough for me to hear.

'A strong hand squeezed my skin tight, first of all I felt a dull pain and then three jabs . . . I couldn't stop myself flinching. They scratched the upper part of my wrist with something uncomfortably prickly and hard. My arm was bandaged. There was hustling and bustling. Things fell on the floor.

'Finally, after a long pause . . . they talked out loud, laughed, congratulated me, unbandaged my eyes and . . . lying on my left arm I saw a baby made out of my right arm which was all bound up. A silly child's face had been drawn on the upper part of the wrist.

'Now comes the question, were the experiences I then had really true, accompanied by real belief, or should what I felt more properly be called "feelings that seem true"?

'Of course, it wasn't real truth and belief. There was an constant switch between "I believe" and "I don't believe", between real experience and an illusion of experience, between "true" and "true-seeming". Then I understood that if they had performed an actual operation on me, at certain moments almost the same things would have happened to me in reality as while the joke was being played. The illusion was convincing in the highest degree.

'Among the feelings I then had there were moments of total experiencing during which I felt just as I would in reality. There were even signs I was about to faint, of course, only for a second. They went as quickly as they came. Nonetheless the illusion left its marks. And now it seems to me that the things I felt could have happened in real life. That was the first time I felt a hint of that state of mind in which there is a large measure of the subconscious, with which I am now very familiar onstage,' said Tortsov concluding his story.

'But that's not a line of life but snatches of it.'

'Perhaps you think the subconscious creates in an unbroken line, or that the actor experiences everything just as he does in real life?

'If that were the case, the human organism couldn't bear the strain, mental and physical, that art lays on it.

'As you know, onstage, we live emotion memories of the real world. At moments they seem like real life. Losing oneself in the role totally, continuously, having an unwavering belief in what is happening can occur, but only rarely. We know individual, more or less lengthy moments of such a state. The rest of the time, the true and the true-seeming, the believable and the likely alternate.

'Like me during the spoof operation, Kostya had moments of dizziness when he played the "burning money" the last time round. Both our lives as human beings with our emotion memories were so like the role, so closely intertwined you couldn't tell where one began and the other ended.'

'Then that must be inspiration,' I asserted.

'Yes, there is a great deal of the subconscious in this process,' Tortsov corrected me.

'And where you have the subconscious, you have inspiration.'

'Why should you think that?' said Tortsov in amazement, turning immediately to Leo who was sitting beside him:

'Quick as you can, without thinking, name something that isn't here.'

'A pole!'

'Why a "pole" precisely?'

'No idea!'

'I've "no idea" either and nobody has any "idea". Only the subconscious is aware why it palmed you off with this idea.

'And you, Igor, give me a mental image.'

'A pineapple!'

'Why a pineapple?!'

Apparently, as he was going through the streets at night recently, Leo, without any kind of rhyme or reason, remembered a pineapple. For a moment he thought that this fruit grew on a palm tree. That is no accident since it looks like a palm tree. In fact the leaves in a pineapple recall a pine tree in miniature and the scaly skin of a pineapple is like the bark of a palm tree.

Tortsov vainly tried to discover the reason such an idea came into Leo's head.

'Perhaps you've eaten a pineapple beforehand?'

'No,' he answered.

'Perhaps you've thought about it?'

'No, again.'

'That means all we can do is look for the solution in the subconscious.

'What have you been thinking about?' Tortsov said to Vanya.

Before answering the question our quirky friend pondered deeply. While he was preparing to answer, unawares, he mechanically rubbed the palms of his hands against his trousers. Then he went on thinking hard. And took a piece of paper out of his pocket and began to fold it smaller and smaller.

Tortsov burst out laughing and said:

'Try consciously to repeat the actions Vanya performed before he answered my question. Why did he perform them? Only the subconscious knows the meaning of such nonsense.

'You see,' said Tortsov turning to me. 'Everything Pasha and Leo said, everything Vanya did, occurred without inspiration of any kind, and yet there were elements of the subconscious in their words and acts. That means it appears not only while we are acting, but in the most simple moments of wanting, of communicating, of adapting, of doing, etc.

'The subconscious and we are good friends. We encounter it in real life with every step we take. Every emergent representation, every mental image requires the subconscious in some measure or other. They arise from it. In every physical expression of our inner life, in every Adaptation – in whole or in part – there is an invisible prompting from the subconscious.'

'That doesn't make sense!' said Vanya, irritated.

'And yet it's really very simple. Who prompted the word "pole" to Leo, who created that representation for him? Who suggested that strange movement of the hand, the facial expression, the tone of voice to Igor – in a word all the Adaptations by which he conveyed his amazement at the idea of pineapples growing on palm trees? Who would consciously take it into his head to perform the unusual physical actions Vanya did before he answered my question? Once again the subconscious prompted them.'

'That means', I said, trying hard to understand, 'that each representation, each Adaptation is in some measure or another of subconscious origin?'

'The majority of them,' Tortsov hastened to confirm. 'That is why I maintain that in life the subconscious and we are good friends.

'That makes it all the more tiresome that we rarely find it in the place we most need it – in the theatre, onstage. Try and find the subconscious in a performance that has become a fixed routine, that's rattled off parrot-fashion, when everything's been worked out and planned once and for all. But without the creative power of our nature, mental and physical, our acting is cerebral, wrong, mere convention, arid, lifeless, formalistic.

'Try to give free play to the creative subconscious! Remove the things which hinder it, and make the things which help it stronger. And so the basic task of our psychotechnique is to bring the actor to the state in which his creative subconscious can burgeon.

'How can we consciously approach something which, evidently, by its very nature is not accessible to the conscious mind, which is "subconscious"? Fortunately for us there is no sharp dividing line between conscious and subconscious experience.

'Moreover, the conscious aspect often indicates the direction in which subconscious activity will go. We make use of this in our psychotechnique. It enables us to fulfil one of the most important fundamentals in our school of acting: *to induce an actor's subconscious creative powers through a conscious psychotechnique.*

'So, next on the agenda we have the actor's psychotechnique, which stimulates his natural, subconscious creative powers. But we'll talk of that next time.'

.. .. 19..

'So, today we are going to talk about the way to stimulate our natural, biological, subconscious creative powers through a conscious psychotechnique.

'Kostya can tell you about that. He experienced the process in the class before last when he did the "burning money" again.'

'All I can say is all of a sudden I had a kind of inspiration. I have no idea what I did.'

'You're not drawing the right conclusions. Something much more important happened than you allow. The coming of "inspiration" on which you always count was a mere accident. You can't depend on it. We are talking about something on which we can rely. Inspiration came not by chance, but because you awakened it and prepared the ground for it. That's a much more important result for us as actors, for our psychotechnique, our practical work.'

'I didn't prepare the ground at all and don't know how to do it,' I said, rejecting the idea.

'That means it was I who prepared the ground without your knowing it.'

'How? When? Everything went as it should, as always. My muscles were free, the Given Circumstances had been studied, a series of Tasks had been set up and fulfilled, etc.'

'Absolutely right. In that respect there was nothing new. But you have forgotten one extremely important detail, a new element of great importance. It was just a tiny addition – I made you perform every creative action right through to the end, down to the last drop. That was all.'

'How do you do that?' Vanya asked.

'Very simple. Bring all the Elements, the psychological inner drives, the Throughaction, to the point where they become normal, human – not convention-bound and actorish – activity. Then you will come to know the truth of your own mind and nature. You will come to know the truth of the character. You cannot but believe the truth. And where there is truth and belief the state of "I am being" arises of itself.

'Have you noticed how each time they appear, spontaneously, independent of the actor's will, nature and the subconscious join in?

'That was what happened to Kostya, remember, in the "burning money" and also in the class before last.

'So, it is the actor's conscious psychotechnique pushed to its very limits which creates the ground in which our natural subconscious, creative process can come to life.

'Pushing to the limit, the perfect use of our psychotechnique, constitutes an extremely important addition to what you already know about creative acting

'If you only knew how very important this new addition is!

'The general opinion is that every moment in our acting should unfailingly be grand, complex, exciting. But you know from your previous work that the smallest action or feeling, the smallest aspect of our technique acquires enormous significance if onstage they are pushed to the very limit. There it ends and living, human truth, belief and the "I am being" begin. When that happens, then the actor's mental and physical apparatus starts to work according to the laws of human nature, exactly as it does in life, notwithstanding the artificial situation we find ourselves in, having to be creative in public.

'Things which occur naturally, spontaneously in life have to be prepared for onstage by using the psychotechnique.

'Think about this. The most insignificant physical or mental action, which creates moments of genuine truth and belief, taken to the threshold of "I am being" skilfully involves the actor's own nature and his subconscious in what he is doing. Isn't that something new, isn't that an important addition to what you already know?

'In total opposition to some teachers, it is my view that students, beginners, who, like you, are taking their first steps onstage should, within the limits of the possible, be led immediately towards the subconscious. This should be done in the earliest stages when working on the Elements, on mental states on all the exercises and improvisations.

'Beginners should know at the very start, albeit in isolated moments, that happiest of moods an actor can have as he is being creative. They should know it not just in words and phrases, not as dead and dry terminology which can only frighten them but in their own feelings. They should come to love this creative mood as part of their work, and really strive for it onstage.'

'I understand its importance,' I said to Tortsov, 'but it's not enough. We need to know the right psychotechniques, and be able to use them. So teach us the right ones, give us a more concrete approach.'

'As you wish. You'll hear nothing more from me. I can only be more precise about things you already know. Here's a piece of advice. As soon as you have created the right mental state and feel that the psychotechnique has helped you to put everything in place inwardly for you to be creative, and when you feel that your nature is only waiting for the go-ahead, then give it.'

'How do I do that?'

'In chemistry when the reaction of two solutions is slow or weak, a small amount of a specific third substance is added which acts as the catalyst in a given reaction. It is a kind of seasoning which allows the reaction to reach its limit. And you introduce such a catalyst in the form of something impromptu, a detail, an action, a moment of genuine truth – it doesn't matter if it is mental or physical. This sudden surprise rouses you and nature rushes into the fray.

'That happened the last time the "burning money" was played. Kostya was in the right mental state and, as he then explained, to sharpen his creative mood he introduced, on the spot, an impromptu Given Circumstance – a large deficit in the money. That idea was his "catalyst". The "seasoning" pushed his reaction to the limit, i.e. to the point where his mind, naturally, subconsciously began to create.'

'Where can we find "catalysts"?'

'Everywhere – in representations, in mental images, in appraisals, in feelings, in wants, in tiny mental and physical actions, in new small details created by your imagination, in the objects with which you are in communication, in the passing details of the setting, in the staging, the mise-en-scène. In fact anywhere you can find small, genuine, human, living truth which evokes the kind of belief that can establish the mood of "I am being".'

'And then what happens?'

'Your head spins with the number of moments when the life of the character and your own unexpectedly and totally fuse. You will feel parts of yourself in the role and of the role in you.'

'And after that?'

'What I told you. Truth, belief, "I am being" put you in the control of nature and the subconscious.

'You can do work similar to what Kostya did in the class before last, starting with any of the Elements. Instead of starting, like him, by relaxing the muscles, turn to the imagination and the Given Circumstances, wants and tasks, if they are clear, for help or to the emotions if they are stirred spontaneously, to representations and appraisals. You may subconsciously feel the truth of the writer's work, then belief and the "I am being" will arise spontaneously. The important thing, in every case, is that you should not forget to make the first Element that emerges fully alive. You know that only you have to start with one of the Elements and that all the rest will follow on behind because of the indissoluble link that exists among them.

'This conscious method of stimulating our natural, subconscious creative power is not unique. There is another but I haven't the time to demonstrate it today. So, till next time.'

.. .. 19..

'Pasha and Kostya,' said Tortsov to us as he came into class, 'play the opening of the scene between Iago and Othello, just the first few lines.'

We got ready, played the scene it seems quite well, with good concentration and the right creative state.

'What were you concerned with just now?' Tortsov asked us.

'The immediate Task, that is to get Kostya's attention,' answered Pasha.

'I was concerned to explore what Pasha was saying, and to see the things he was talking about with my inner eye,' I explained.

'So, one of you was attracting attention to himself for the sake of attracting attention to himself, and the other was trying to explore and see what he was being told for the sake of exploring and seeing what he was being told.'

'No! Why . . .?' I protested.

'Because that's all that can happen when there's no Throughaction or Supertask for the play or the role. Without them you can only draw attention to yourself for the sake of drawing attention to yourself and explore and see for the sake of exploring and seeing.

'Now repeat what you've just done and go on to the next scene in which Othello jokes with Iago.'

'What was your Task?' Tortsov asked once more when we had finished.

'The idea of *dolce far niente*,'[2] I answered.

'And where has the earlier Task, "trying to understand the person speaking to you" gone to?'

'Into a new, more important Task. It has been absorbed by it.'

'Remember, while the memory is fresh, how you fulfilled both Tasks and how you spoke the lines in the two Bits,' Tortsov suggested.

'I remember what I did and said in the first Bit but not in the second.'

'That means it played itself and the lines said themselves,' Tortsov asserted.

'It would seem so.'

'Now repeat what you have just done, and go on to the next scene, that is the first bewilderment that will turn to jealousy.'

We did as we were told and defined our Task rather clumsily with the words: 'to laugh at Iago's ridiculous slanders'.

'And where have the previous Tasks "to understand what the other person is saying" and *dolce far niente* disappeared to?'

I would have liked to have said that they too had been swallowed up by a new, stronger task but began to think and said nothing.

'What's wrong? What's troubling you?'

'That, at this point, one line in the role, happiness, stops and a new line, jealousy, begins.'

'It hasn't stopped,' Tortsov corrected me, 'but is gradually taking on a new life because of changing Given Circumstances. First, it went through the brief period of happiness enjoyed by the newly married Othello, his joking with Iago, then bewilderment, bafflement, doubt, repulsion in the face of approaching unhappiness set in. Then jealousy abates, spontaneously, and the earlier mood of blissful happiness returns.

'We know these transitions from one mood to another in the real world. There too life flows happily along and then we are invaded by doubt, disillusion, sorrow and then it all brightens up again.

'Don't be afraid of these transitions, on the contrary, treasure them, bring out the differences between them. It's not difficult in this particular instance. All you have to do is remember the beginning of the love story of Othello and Desdemona, in your mind you have to experience the lovers' past joy and then, in your mind, make the transition to a contrasting mood and compare it with the horror, the hell which Iago predicts for the Moor.'

'What past are we supposed to remember?' said Vanya in a muddle once more.

'The wonderful first meeting of the lovers in Brabantio's house, Othello's beautiful tales, the secret meetings, the abduction of the bride and the marriage, the separation on the wedding night, the reunion in Cyprus under a summer sun, the unforgettable honeymoon. And then the future . . . think what awaits Othello in the future.'

'What about the future? . . .'

'Everything that happens in the fifth act is the result of Iago's diabolical plot.

'When you have established these two extremes, past and future, the premonitions, the bewilderment of the Moor as he grows more and more jealous, become comprehensible. The attitude of the actor towards the fate of his character becomes clear. The more vividly we show the happy period in the Moor's life, the more strongly you will be able to convey the darkness of the end. Now, onward!' Tortsov ordered.

We went through the whole scene in this way, right up to Iago's famous oath to heaven and the stars, 'Iago doth give up / The execution of his wit, hands, heart / To wronged Othello's service'.

'If you work on the role this way,' Tortsov explained, 'the small Tasks hang together and create a series of large ones. There aren't so very many of them. These Tasks are like markers along a channel, and indicate the Throughaction. What is important for us now is to understand, that is to feel, that the process of absorbing the small Tasks into major ones occurs subconsciously.'

We talked about what we should call the first major Task. None of us, not even Tortsov, could settle the question right away. Yet that's not surprising. The true, living, compelling Task, not something cerebral or formalistic, doesn't come spontaneously, just like that. It is established by the life we create onstage, as we are working. We still didn't really know what that life was and so weren't able to define its meaning properly. Nonetheless, someone gave it a rather clumsy name, which we accepted in the absence of anything better, 'I want to worship Desdemona, the ideal among women; I want to serve her and devote my life to her'.

When I thought about this major Task and gave life to it in my own way, I realized that it enabled me to find a personal basis for the whole scene and the individual Bits. I felt that when, at any given moment in the scene, I started to head for the final goal we had established: 'worshipping Desdemona, the ideal among women'.

As I addressed the final goal, starting from the small Tasks I had created, I felt that the name we had given it began to lose all sense or meaning. For example, let's take the first Task – 'to try and understand what Iago is saying'. What's the point of this Task? No one knows.

Why bother when it's perfectly clear? Othello is in love, he thinks of nothing but Desdemona, wants to speak only of her. And so every question, every memory he has concerning his beloved is a necessary comfort to him. Why? Because 'he worships Desdemona, the ideal among women', because 'he wants to serve her and devote his life to her'.

Now for the second Task – dolce far niente. This Task is superfluous, too.

What's more, it's wrong. When he speaks of his beloved, the Moor is doing the thing which is most important to him, something he needs. Why? Because 'he worships Desdemona, the ideal among women', because 'he wants to serve her and devote his life to her'.

After Iago's first allegation, Othello, as I understand him, laughs. It pleases him to think that nothing can besmirch the crystal purity of his goddess. This belief puts the Moor in a good mood and strengthens his admiration for her. Why? Because 'he worships Desdemona, the ideal among women', etc. I realized how slow the birth of his jealousy is, how imperceptibly his belief in her, his ideal, weakens, how the awareness of the perfidy, the depravity, the fact that she is a snake in the grass with an angel's face, grows ever stronger.

'And where have your earlier Tasks disappeared to?' Tortsov enquired.

'They have been swallowed up in a unique concern for a shattered ideal.'

'What conclusion can we draw from today's experiment? What is the result of the class?' asked Tortsov.

'The result is that I obliged the two actors to recognize in practical terms the process by which small Tasks are absorbed into large ones.

'There's nothing new in that. I was only repeating what I had said earlier when we were discussing Bits and Tasks or the Supertask and the Throughaction.

'What's new and important is something else, that Kostya and Pasha realized that the ultimate goal draws attention away from the immediate goal, just as small Tasks disappear from our minds. These Tasks automatically become subconscious. They are no longer separate, they become subordinate and lead us to a large Task. Kostya and Pasha now know that the deeper, the broader, the more meaningful the ultimate goal is, the more attention is drawn to it and the less opportunity there is to succumb to immediate, subordinate, small Tasks. Leave them alone and these small Tasks come under the control of nature and the subconscious in a perfectly normal way.'

'What's that you say?' said Vanya, getting upset.

'I was saying that when an actor commits himself to a major Task, he is totally taken over by it. While that is happening, nothing prevents nature from working freely, at her own discretion, in accordance with her needs and desires. Nature takes control of all the small Tasks and uses them to help the actor reach the ultimate Task into which all his attention, his conscious activity has been sunk.

'The conclusion to be drawn from today's class is that *the major Task is one of the best means we can find for our psychotechnique to influence our minds, bodies and the subconscious.*'

After quite a long pause for reflection Tortsov continued:

'Exactly the same transformation which you have just observed in small Tasks takes place with the large, provided that they are led by an all-embracing Supertask. When they serve it, the large Tasks become subsidiary to it. In their turn, they become steps which lead us up to the basic, all-embracing, ultimate goal. When the actor is totally focused on the Supertask, then the large Tasks are also, to a great extent, fulfilled subconsciously.

'The Throughaction, as you know, is made up of a long line of major Tasks. In each of them there are an enormous number of small Tasks which are fulfilled subconsciously.

'Now, the question arises, how many moments of subconscious creative activity are there in the Throughaction which runs right through the play?

'There are, in fact, an enormous number. The Throughaction is precisely that powerful, stimulating means we have been seeking so we can influence the subconscious.'

After a little thought Tortsov continued:

'But the Throughaction doesn't just happen. Its creative strength is to be found in its direct dependence on a compelling Supertask.

'The Supertask also has a capacity for stimulating moments of subconscious creative activity.

'Add them to the moments which exist, hidden, in the Throughaction and you will understand that the Supertask and the Throughaction are the most powerful lures for arousing our natural, biological subconscious creative powers.

'Every creative actor's greatest dream should be to give them full scope in the deepest and broadest sense of the word each time he performs a role onstage.

'If that happens, then the rest happens subconsciously through the wonder that is nature.

'In those circumstances every time we repeat a performance there will be immediacy, naturalness, truth and most important of all unexpected differences. Only then will you be able to deliver yourself from stock-in-trade, clichés, gimmicks, and from every assault by the kind of theatrics we detest. Only then will living people appear onstage and the life that goes on around them be cleansed of anything that sullies art. That life will emerge almost new each time, every time you repeat whatever it is you have created.

'It remains for me to counsel you to use the Supertask as a guiding star and never to flag. Then the entire Throughaction of the play will be followed with ease, naturally and, in a large measure, subconsciously.'

After another pause Tortsov continued:

'Just as the Supertask and the Throughaction swallow up all the large Tasks and make them subordinate, so the super-Supertask and the super-Throughaction of the life of the human being/actor as a whole swallow up the Supertasks of the plays and the roles in his repertoire. They become the means, steps towards the accomplishment of the major goal in his life.'

'Is that good for the show?' said Pasha in some doubt.

'Not if it tips the scales towards the cerebral, but good when you achieve the effect by using artistic means.

'So now you know what conscious psychotechnique is. It has the capacity to create the practices, the favourable conditions in which the work of nature and the subconscious can take place.

'Think, too, about what stimulates our inner drives, think of the creative state, the Supertask and the Throughaction. With their help learn to create favourable soil for the subconscious. But never consider or try the direct route to the subconscious, because you are looking for inspiration for inspiration's sake. That only leads to muscular tension and the opposite result.'

.. .. 19..

'Apart from a conscious psychotechnique which prepares our minds for subconscious creative activity, there are often pure accidents. We need to know how to use it but for that we need the proper pyschotechnique

'For example, Marya, try and remember your cry of "Save me!" during the first showing and tell us what you felt in the few seconds your emotional outburst lasted.'

Marya said nothing because she probably only had confused memories of her first appearance onstage.

'I'll do my best to remember for you what happened,' said Tortsov coming to her aid. 'The orphan you were portraying had been thrown out into the street and at the same time you, the student Marya, had been thrown onto an expanse of empty stage with the terrible black hole before you. The terror of the emptiness, the loneliness of the orphan and of the student, a beginner, were like enough and close enough to merge into one. Taking the emptiness of the stage for the emptiness of the street and your own loneliness for the loneliness of the orphan, you yelled, "Save me!" with the kind of immediate, natural fear we only know in real life. That was a fortunate accident due to the similarity and closeness of the two situations.

'An experienced actor with the right kind of psychotechnique would make full use of such a happy accident. He would know how to develop the fear of the human being/actor into the fear of the human being/role. But with you, because you are inexperienced and have no psychotechnique, the man overcame the actor. You betrayed your creative powers, stopped acting and took refuge in the wings.'

Then Tortsov turned to me and said:

'Haven't you experienced the mood we've just been talking about? Didn't you feel the same identity between yourself and the role?'

'I think I did in the scene "Blood, Iago, blood!" '

'Yes,' Tortsov agreed. 'Let's recall what happened.'

'First of all I yelled the words not as Othello but as myself,' I recalled. 'But that was a cry of despair from an actor in a mess. My cry came from me but it forced me to remember Othello and Leo's moving story and the Moor's love for Desdemona. I took my despair as a human being/actor as the despair of the human being/role, i.e. Othello. They became one in my mind and I spoke the lines without being aware of them or of what they were actually saying.'

'However, it could well be that on this occasion similarity and closeness produced something like identity,' Tortsov stated.

After a pause Tortsov continued:

'In practice we deal not only with that kind of accident. Frequently a mere accident unconnected to the play, the role or the performance, bursts in from real life into the conventional life of the stage.'

'What kind of accident?' the students asked.

'Well, a chair falling over or a handkerchief that's dropped, which I've already talked to you about.

'If the actor has his wits about him, if he doesn't get confused or try to ignore this accident but, on the contrary, makes it part of the play then it becomes a tuning fork for him. It provides one true living note in the midst of the convention-bound theatrical lies, it recalls the real truth, it draws the whole line of the play to itself and obliges you to believe and to feel the thing we call "I am being". All this leads the actor to his natural, subconscious creative powers.

'You must use accidents, feelings wisely, must not reject but cherish and yet not base your artistic planning on them.

'That's all I can tell you about conscious psychotechnique and accidents which stimulate one's subconscious creative powers. As you see, for the moment the right kind of conscious methods are rare. We still have a great deal of work and research to do in that field. So we should treasure what we have so far discovered all the more.'

.. .. 19..

In today's class I saw the light, I understood everything and became a fervent admirer of the 'system'. I saw how a conscious technique can beget subconscious creative activity, which itself is inspirational. This is what happened:

Darya played the scene with the 'abandoned child' which Marya had played so splendidly earlier.

You need to know why Darya had such a predilection for scenes with children such as the 'abandoned child' from *Brand* and the new scene. She had recently lost her only son whom she adored. I had heard secret rumours about this. But today, seeing her playing the scene, I knew it was true.

While she was acting, floods of tears streamed from her eyes and her motherly affection turned the log of wood, representing the child, into a living being for those of us who were watching. We could feel it under the tablecloth representing the abandoned child. When we came to the moment of the child's death we had to cut the scene short to avoid a disaster. The flood of emotion Darya was experiencing was so turbulent.

We were all shattered. Tortsov was weeping and so were Rakhmanov and the rest of us.

How can you talk about decoys, lines, Bits, Tasks, physical actions when you are faced with real life.

'There's an example of how nature, the subconscious, creates!' said Tortsov who was carried away. 'They create strictly in accordance with the principles of our kind of acting, since those principles have not been invented by us but given by nature itself.

'But such discoveries, such prophetic powers are not sent to us every day. On another occasion they may not arrive and then . . .'

'No, they will come!' cried an ecstatic Darya, who happened to have heard our conversation.

As though fearful that inspiration might abandon her, she rushed to repeat the scene she had just played.

Tortsov wanted to stop her, to spare her young nerves, but she soon stopped of her own accord as nothing happened.

'What now?' Tortsov asked her. 'In the future you will be asked not just to play well in the first performance, but in all the subsequent performances. Otherwise the play which had a successful premiere will flop in the other performances and stop taking money.'

'No! All I need to do is feel and then I can act,' asserted Darya.

'Once I've felt I will act!' laughed Tortsov. 'That's as good as saying, "When I've learned to swim, I'll take a bath."

'I understand your wish to go direct to feeling. Of course that's the best.

How good it would be if we could master the technique of repeating things we have successfully experienced. But feelings can't be fixed. Like water, they slip through your fingers . . . So we have, willy-nilly, to seek more stable methods, influence and stabilize them.

'Take your pick – anyone! The most accessible, the easiest, a physical action, a small truth, small moments of belief.'

But our Ibsenite brushed aside anything physical in art with distaste.

We went through all the means an actor can use – Bits, Tasks, the imagination. But none of them was sufficiently compelling, stable or accessible.

Whichever way she turned, however much she tried to bypass physical actions in the end she had to settle for them as she couldn't suggest anything better. Tortsov soon set her in the right direction. He didn't look for new physical actions. He tried to get her to repeat the things she had just discovered intuitively and had so brilliantly performed.

Darya played well, with truth and belief. But how could it be compared to what she had done the first time?!

Tortsov said to her:

'You played splendidly, but not the scene you were given. You changed the object. I asked you to do a scene with a living foundling but you gave me a scene with a dead log of wood in a tablecloth. You adapted your physical actions to it: you wrapped up the piece of wood with skilful, capable hands. But dealing with a living child requires a host of details which you left out. For example, the first time you swaddled the imaginary child you spread out his arms and legs, you were aware of them, you kissed them lovingly, you murmured something to it with an affectionate smile and tears in your eyes. That was very touching. But this time these details were left out. And that's understandable – a log of wood has no arms or legs.

'The first time, as you wrapped the head of the imaginary infant, you took great care not to squash its cheeks, you carefully smoothed them out. Having swaddled the child you stood over him a long time weeping copious tears of motherly joy and pride.

'Let's correct these mistakes. Do the scene with the child for me again, not the scene with the log of wood.'

After a great deal of work with Tortsov on small physical actions Darya finally saw the point and consciously recalled the things she had done subconsciously the first time she played the scene . . . She was aware of the child and the tears flowed spontaneously from her eyes.

'There you have an example of the effect of our psychotechnique and physical action on feeling!' cried Tortsov when Darya had finished.

'Maybe so,' I said, disappointed, 'but this time Darya didn't feel any kind of turmoil and so neither you nor I shed a tear.'

'No matter!' Tortsov exclaimed. 'When the soil has been prepared and feeling burgeons in an actress, turmoil follows, and all you have to do is find a way in for it – a highly challenging Task, a magic "if" or some other "catalyst". I don't want to fray Darya's young nerves. On the other hand . . .' Then turning to Darya, after a short pause, he said:

'What would you do with this log of wood in the tablecloth if I were to introduce a magic "if" like that? Imagine that you have given birth to a child, a fascinating little girl. You are passionately attached to her . . . But . . . after a few months she dies. The world has no place for you. But fate takes pity on you. You are offered a foundling, also a little girl, even more fascinating than the first.'

He had hit the nail on the head!

Tortsov could hardly finish telling her his idea before Darya burst into tears over the log of wood in the tablecloth and the upheaval recurred with redoubled strength.

I rushed over to Tortsov to explain the secret of what had happened. He had precisely guessed Darya's real tragedy.

Tortsov clasped his head in his hands, ran to the footlights to stop the poor mother, but he was so taken with what she was doing that he decided not to interrupt her performance.

When the scene was over and everything had calmed down and tears had been dried I went up to Tortsov and commented:

'Don't you find that what Darya was experiencing just now was not a figment of her imagination but reality, that is her own personal, human, real-world grief? So, I think that we ought to consider what happened just now as the effect of chance, accident and not as a victory of acting technique, not as something creative, as art.'

'And what she did the first time, was that art?' said Tortsov putting a counter question.

'Yes,' I acknowledged. 'That was art.'

'Why?'

'Because she subconsciously recalled her own grief and took life from it.'

'So the trouble is that I prompted her to recall things that had been retained in her Emotion Memory and that she did not discover them for herself as she did the last time. I can't see any difference between an actor reviving his own living memories on his own or having a reminder from someone else. The important thing is that her memory had retained and then reactivated what had been experienced with the right kind of incentive. You cannot but believe as a human being, with all your very heart and body, the things your own memory holds.'

'All right, let's assume it's as you say. But you must acknowledge that just now Darya wasn't drawing life from physical Tasks, or from truth and belief but from the tiny "if" you suggested to her.'

'Am I denying that?' Tortsov interrupted me. 'It's almost always a question of the imagination and a magic "if". You just have to be able to bring in the "catalyst" at the right moment.'

'When's that?'

'I'll tell you when! Go and ask Darya if she could have drawn life from my magic "if" had I set it in motion earlier, when, the second time she did the scene, she was coldly binding a log of wood in a tablecloth, when she was still not aware of the legs and arms of the foundling child, when she wasn't kissing them; before she had started to swaddle a living, beautiful creature instead of a nasty piece of wood, which she had transformed? I am convinced that before that moment, my comparison of a dirty piece of wood with her beautiful baby would only have inhibited her. Of course, had she been moved by the chance coincidence of my suggestion with the sorrow she had felt in life, she would have shed copious tears. That brought back vivid memories of the death of her son. But they would have been tears for the dead, whereas the tears we need for the scene with the foundling, were tears for the dead mixed with joy for the living.

'Moreover, I am convinced that until the inner transformation of a dead piece of wood into a living being had occurred, she would have rejected it in disgust and gone as far away from it as possible. Then alone with her cherished memories, she would have shed tears. But then they would have been tears for the dead and not the tears we need, the ones she shed the first time she did the exercise. But once she had seen, and, in her imagination, felt the arms and legs of the baby, Darya wept the way she should, the way the scene needed, with tears of joy for the living.

'I guessed the right moment and kindled the spark, suggested the magic "if", which coincided with her deepest and most secret memories. Then we had a genuine emotional upheaval, which, I hope, fully satisfied you.'

'Doesn't that mean that Darya was having delusions while she was playing?'

'No!' said Tortsov, waving his hands. 'The secret is not that she believed the log of wood could become a living being, but that the scene could happen in life and could bring her welcome relief. Onstage she believed in the genuineness of her actions, their progression, logic and truth. Thanks to them she felt the "I am being" and stimulated the creative powers of nature and the subconscious.

'As you can see, approaching feeling through truth and belief in physical actions and the "I am being" is applicable not only to roles you are creating but to roles you have already created.

'The greatest piece of luck is that there are ways of stimulating feelings that have already been created. If that were not so inspiration would only flash for a moment and then disappear for ever.'

I felt wonderful and after the class went up to Darya and thanked her for making me see with my own eyes something that was very important in art, which I had not fully taken into account.

.. .. 19..

'Time to make a check!' Tortsov proposed as he came into class.

'On what?' – the students didn't understand.

'Now, after almost a year's work, each of you has formed some idea of what the creative process is.

'Let's compare this idea with the one you had before, the overacting you remembered from amateur performances, or from your first show when you came to school. For example:

'Marya! Do you recall how in one of the first classes you looked for the valuable brooch on which your fate and your continuing at school depended? Do you remember how you fussed and ran and rushed about and tried to overact despair and found artistic pleasure in it? Would you now be satisfied with this kind of "acting" and the state of mind it entails?'

Marya thought for a moment, remembering the past, and a contemptuous smile spread across her face. She finally shook her head and gave a silent laugh, evidently over the naive overacting she had indulged in earlier.

'You see, you are laughing. What about? About the fact that previously you played "in general", everything at once, going straight for the results. No wonder it was all out of joint, an exaggeration of the character and its passions.

'Now, remember your experiences in the scene with the "abandoned child", how you played tricks and games not with a living child but with a log of wood. Compare that life, which was genuine, and your creative state with the way you overacted earlier and tell me, are you satisfied with the time you have spent at the school?'

Marya thought for a while, her face became serious, then sombre, there was a flicker of alarm in her eyes, without saying anything she gave a meaningful, thoughtful nod of the head.

'You see,' said Tortsov. 'You're not laughing now, you're ready to cry over a single memory. Why should that be?

'Because when you were creating the scene you went about it in a completely different way. You didn't go straight after the final result – to startle, to stagger the audience, play the scene for all it's worth. This time you planted a seed in yourself and gradually produced fruit from its roots. You proceeded according to the creative laws of nature itself.

'Always remember these two different paths, one of which leads inevitably to stock-in-trade and the other to genuine creative acting.'

'And we felt that same mood in the scene with the madman!' the students said, wanting to be praised.

'Agreed,' Tortsov acknowledged.

'And you, Darya, were you aware of that mood during your famous scene with the "abandoned child"?

'And as for Vanya, he took us in with the fake injury to his leg while he was dancing. He believed so sincerely in his own story that for a moment he was caught up in the illusion. Now you know that creative work is not just technical trickery, externally overplaying a character, as many of you thought earlier.

'What is the nature of acting as we understand it?

'It is the conception and birth of a new living being, the human being/role.

'That is a natural creative act, like human birth.

'If you go back carefully over what happens in an actor's mind as he gets into a role you will recognize the truth of this comparison.

'Every character in the theatre is a unique, inimitable, creation, like everything in nature.

'Like the birth of a human being it goes through analogous stages in its development.

'In the creative process there is he, the husband (the author).

'There is she, the wife, (the actor or actress who is pregnant with the role, who receives the author's seed, the kernel of his work).

'There is the fruit, the child (the role as it is being created).

'There is the moment when he and she (the actor and the role) first meet. This is the time of their coming together, of falling in love, quarrelling, disagreeing, being reconciled, of coupling, insemination and pregnancy.

'During this period the director serves as a matchmaker.

'There are, as in pregnancy, various stages in the creative process which are reflected, well or badly, in the actor's private life. For example: it is well known that mothers, at various moments of their pregnancy, have their whims, their capricious ways. The same thing happens to the human being/actor while he is creating. Various periods in the conception and growth of the role have varying effects on the actor's private life.

'I consider that the organic growth of a role needs no less, and in certain cases considerably more time than the conception and growth of a living human being.

'During this period the director participates in the process as a midwife or obstetrician.

'In a normal pregnancy and labour the actor's creation is formed physically in a natural way, is then nursed and raised by the mother (the actor creating it).

'But there are premature births, miscarriages, abortions in our business too. The result is an unfinished, stunted, theatrical monster.

'An analysis of this process persuades us of the well-defined limits within which nature operates, when it brings a new phenomenon into the world, be that a biological phenomenon or the product of the human imagination.

'In a word, the birth of a living theatrical being (the role) is a normal act of the actor's own creative nature.

'How sorely those people who do not understand these truths, who devise their "principles" and the "fundamentals", their own "new art", who have no faith in the creative powers of mature, go astray.

'Why make up your own rules when they already exist, when they have been laid down once and for all by nature itself. Its rules are obligatory for all those people, without exception, who do creative work in the theatre, and woe to those who break them. Transgressors of acting like these do not become creative artists but counterfeits, imitators, mimics.

'Once you have made a deep and intense study of the laws of nature and learn to obey them freely not only in life but onstage, you will create what and how you please, with this one absolute condition, that you observe all the creative laws of your nature strictly and without exception.

'I think that the genius, the outstanding technical master, has not yet been born who would be capable, using our own nature as a basis, of many unnatural, contrived, fashionable new-fangled fads and "isms".'

'Look here, please, I'm sorry, are you rejecting everything new in art?'

'On the contrary. I think that human life is so subtle, complex, multi-faceted that to give it full expression we need an incomparably greater number of new "isms" of which we are not yet aware. But at the same time I am sorry to have to say that our technique is feeble and primitive, and we shall not be able to meet the interesting and justifiable demands of serious innovators all that soon. These people make one big mistake, they forget that there is an enormous difference between ideas, principles, fundamentals, however right they may be, and putting them into practice. For us to come anywhere near them we need to work a long time on our technique, which is still in a primitive state.

'So long as our psychotechnique is incomplete, our greatest fear must be of forcing our own creative, organic nature and its innate, unbreakable laws.

'As you can see, everything makes the absolute demand that each student who wishes to become an actor should in the first instance study the creative laws of nature thoroughly, in detail, not just theoretically but in practice. He is also obliged to study and master, practically, all the methods of our psychotechnique. Without that no one has the right to go onstage. Otherwise we shall create not real masters but amateurs and incompetents. With colleagues like that our theatre cannot grow and flourish. On the contrary it will be condemned to failure.'

* * *

The class ended with goodbyes as today was the last class on the 'system' for this semester.

Tortsov concluded his address to the students with the following words:

'Now you have your psychotechnique. With its help you can stimulate the process of experiencing. Now you can cultivate feelings and give them physical form.

'But for the subtle, often subconscious life of nature to find external expression, you must possess an extremely responsive, wonderfully developed vocal and physical apparatus. They must instantly and precisely convey, with enormous subtlety and immediacy, inner experiences which cannot quite be captured.

'In other words, the dependency of the actor's physical life onstage on his psychological life is extremely important in our school of acting. That is why actors of our kind, much more so than in other kinds of acting, must be concerned not only with our internal apparatus, which creates the process of experiencing, but with our external, physical apparatus which truthfully conveys the results of the creative work done by feeling – its outward form of bodily expression. Our nature and our subconscious have a great influence on this work too and in this field – giving bodily expression – there can be no comparison between them and the most expert actors' technique, however self-sufficient that technique may be or whatever its claims to superiority.

'The process of giving bodily expression is, naturally, next on the agenda. We shall devote the greater part of next year to it.

'That's not all. You have taken in some aspects of our later "work on a role": you have learned to establish that creative state, which is the only way to approach this process. This is also a major trump card for the future of which we shall make full use at the right time when we come to the study of "work on a role".

'So, till we meet again! Get some rest. In a few months we shall assemble again to continue the "work on oneself" and in particular the process of giving bodily expression.'

* * *

I am overjoyed, I am walking on air. Now I know completely, in practice, the meaning of the words:

'*Through the actor's conscious psychotechnique to nature's subconscious creative power!!*'

For me this now means: spend years and years of your life developing that psychotechnique and you will create the soil for inspiration. Then it will come to you of its own accord.

What a wonderful prospect! What great joy it will be!

That's what one should live and work for!

Such were my thoughts and feelings as I put my scarf round my neck in the corridor.

Suddenly, as before, Tortsov appeared out of nowhere. But today he didn't give me a dig in the ribs. On the contrary I flung my arms round him and embraced him warmly. He was stunned and asked me the reason for my outburst.

'You made me understand', I told him, 'that the secret of our art lies in strict observance of the laws of nature and I solemnly vow to study them carefully, in depth! I give a firm undertaking to obey them as only they can indicate the right path to creativeness and art. I vow to develop my psycho-technique and to do it patiently, systematically, tirelessly. In a word I will dedicate myself to everything to learn how to prepare the soil for the subconscious so that inspiration may come to me!'

Tortsov was moved by this outburst. He drew me to one side, took my hand, held it a long time in his and said:

'It is pleasing but also frightening to hear you make these promises.'

'Why frightening?' I said in astonishment.

'There have been far too many disappointments. I have been working in the theatre for a long time, hundreds of students have passed through my hands, but I can only call a handful of them my successors who have understood the essence of the things I have given my life to.'

'Why are there so few?'

'Because far from all of them have had the will and the stamina to work right through to genuine art. It's not enough just *to know* the "system". You must be *able to use* it. For that you need daily training and drill throughout your whole acting career.

'Singers need to vocalize, dancers need to go to class and actors need technical training as set down by the "system". Do this work, want to do it, all your life, learn about your own nature, discipline it and, if you have talent, you will become a great actor.'

Year Two

DRAFTS AND FRAGMENTS
A Reconstruction

17

TRANSITION TO PHYSICAL EMBODIMENT

.. .. 19..

We guessed that today's class was something special first because the entrance to the auditorium, and to the stage, was closed and second because Rakhmanov kept running in and out, carefully closing the doors behind him each time. Something was obviously going on inside. In the third place because, exceptionally, there were unfamiliar faces in the corridor where we had to wait.

Rumours were rife among the students. They were convinced that these were tutors who would teach the most bizarre, non-existent subjects.

Finally the secret doors opened. Rakhmanov emerged and asked us to enter.

The auditorium was more or less decorated in good old Rakhmanov's style.

There was a row of chairs for the guests with new little flags on them. They had the same colour and shape as others hanging on the left wall. The difference lay in what was written on them.

On the new flags we read: 'singing', 'placing the voice', 'diction', 'the laws of speech', 'tempo-rhythm', 'expressive movement', 'dance', 'gymnastics', 'fencing', 'acrobatics'.

'O-ho!' we said. 'We'll have to go through all that!!'

Tortsov came in shortly, greeted the new tutors and turned to us and made a short speech which I have transcribed almost verbatim.

'Our family here at the school', he said, 'has been joined by a group of talented people who have kindly agreed to share our experiments and studies.

'Rakhmanov, tireless as he is, has set up a new display about our teaching so that today may be engraved on your memory as a special one.

'All this means that we have reached a new *stage* in our programme of study.

'Up till now we have been dealing with the inner aspect of our art and its psychotechnique.

'From today on we shall be working on the bodily apparatus we use for physical embodiment and its outward technique. Here in this theatre we assign exceptional importance to its role, which is to make the *invisible* creative life of the actor *visible*.

'Physical embodiment is important in so far as it conveys the "life of the human spirit".

'I have spoken a great deal about experiencing, but I haven't told you the hundredth part of what you need to know when it comes to intuition and the unconscious.

'This is the place from which you will draw your raw material, the technical means of experiencing. It is infinite, and will not succumb to cold calculation.

'The techniques we use to embody unconscious experiences do not respond to cold calculation either. They, too, must often embody our minds unconsciously and intuitively.

'This is beyond the conscious mind. Only nature can do it. Nature is the best creative artist and technical master of all. She alone has the absolute power to control both the inner and outer apparatus of experiencing and of embodiment. Only nature herself is capable of embodying subtle *immaterial* feelings [using] the crude *material* of which our vocal and physical apparatus of embodiment is composed.

'However, in this difficult work we must proceed using our creative powers. They do no harm but, on the contrary, bring what nature has given us to a true state of natural perfection. In other words, we must develop and prepare our physical apparatus with which we embody in such a way that all its parts respond to whatever nature asks of it.

'We must develop our voice and body with nature as a basis. That requires a great deal of long, systematic work, and it is to that work that I sound the call from today onwards. If you do not do it, then your physical apparatus will prove too crude for the work nature assigns to it.

'You can't convey the subtlety of Chopin's music on a trombone and you can't express delicate unconscious feelings with the crude parts of our physical apparatus, especially if it's off key like a badly tuned musical instrument.

'It's impossible to convey the things nature creates unconsciously with an unprepared body, just as it's impossible to play Beethoven's Ninth Symphony on instruments that are out of tune.

'The greater the artist, the more subtle his creative efforts, the more work and technique he requires.

'Develop your body and subordinate it to the inner creative commands nature gives . . .'

After he had spoken Tortsov introduced all the students to the tutors not only by their full name, but as actors, i.e. he made all of us play our extract from the original show.

So I had to do my part of the scene from Othello.

How did I do? Badly, because I was showing *myself* off in the role, i.e. I was only thinking of my voice, my body, my movements. As we all know, the effort to appear beautiful only binds and tenses the muscles and every tension is a barrier. It constricts the voice and binds the muscles.

After we had presented our extracts Tortsov invited all of the new tutors to make us do whatever seemed necessary for them to get to know our artistic pluses and minuses better.

That was the beginning of a real farce which once again made me lose my self-confidence.

As a test of our sense of rhythm we had to walk in different note values and tempi, i.e. on whole notes, quarter notes, eighth notes etc., on dotted notes, triplets and so on.

It was a physical impossibility not to laugh at the sight of Leo's huge, friendly frame and the look of tragic seriousness on his face as he measured out giant steps across the tiny stage, with no furniture on it, neither on the beat, nor in rhythm. He got all his muscles in a tangle and so went off in all directions like a drunkard.

And what about our Ibsenites, Nikolai and Darya? They were totally self-absorbed throughout the exercise. It was very funny.

Then we were all required to enter in turn from the wings, go up to a lady, and, after she had curtsied, kiss the hand she held out to us. It was, on the face of it, a simple task but you should have seen what happened when Paul, Leo and Vanya displayed their social graces. I would never have imagined they could be so clumsy and gauche.

And not just them, but also the specialists in external display, Igor and Grisha, were on the verge of being funny.

I, too . . . caused a few smiles, and that finished me.

It's amazing how the glare of the footlights picks out and magnifies people's faults and silly side. An actor standing at the footlights is seen as under a magnifying glass which blows up things which pass unnoticed in life many times.

That's something we have to understand. And we have to be prepared for it.

Tortsov and the tutors went out and Rakhmanov and we put the flags in their place.

I won't record what we did and said as we did it as writing it down wouldn't add anything new.

I'll end today's notes with a sketch of the way we hung the little flags.

By the way three flags were blank, just like those hanging on the left half of the wall, where the process of experiencing had appeared, we weren't sure when. We hung them up without any ceremony and nobody said anything. And Rakhmanov didn't offer any kind of explanation, merely saying: 'We'll talk about that all in good time, don't you worry!'

18

PHYSICAL EDUCATION

Today they opened a secret room, next to the corridor, which none of us had ever seen. There were rumours it was going to be the *school museum* and it would also serve as a common room for the students. The intention was to put a collection of photographs and reproductions of the finest works of art in the world in it. If we were surrounded by them for the best part of the day, we would become accustomed to beautiful things.

It was also said that besides this classical museum, which an actor needs, they intended, on the other hand, to create a small museum of kitsch. In it, among other things, there was to be a collection of photographs of actors in the most clichéd kind of theatrical costumes, make-up and poses, the kind that must be driven off the stage. This collection would be placed next-door in Rakhmanov's office. Normally it would be hidden behind a curtain and only displayed to students in exceptional circumstances, for teaching purposes, as a demonstration through opposites.

This is all Rakhmanov's idea – he's tireless.

But, evidently, the museum isn't going to happen soon as we found absolute chaos in the secret room. There were fine things, plaster of Paris statues, statuettes, a few pictures, furniture from the period of Alexander I and Nicholas I, cupboards with excellent publications on costume. A lot of photographs, framed and unframed, lay in disorder on chairs, windows, tables, on the piano, on the floor. Some were already hanging on the walls. A whole arsenal of rapiers, daggers, poniards, fencing masks and vests and boxing gloves were stacked in two corners. That was a sign they were preparing to give us a series of new physical training classes.

One other noteworthy detail. There was a notice on the wall with the days and opening times of the Moscow museums and art galleries on it. From the pencil marking on the sheet I concluded that systematic sight-seeing visits all over town were being prepared. These, so it seemed from what was written, were to be conducted by experts who would give us a series of lectures which would be adapted to suit our requirements.

Dear old Rakhmanov! What a lot he does for us, and how little we appreciate him!

.. .. 19..

Today, Tortsov came to our class in Swedish gymnastics almost for the first time and talked to us at length. I took down the most important bits.

Here's what he said:

'People don't know how to use the equipment nature has given them. They can't even keep it in good condition or develop it. Slack muscles, a distorted frame, poor breathing are common occurrences in life. These are all the result of our inability to educate and develop our physical apparatus. No wonder then if the work nature assigns it is performed in an unsatisfactory way.

'For the same reasons we constantly encounter badly-proportioned bodies which have not been properly developed by exercises.

'Many of these faults can be corrected, in whole or in part. But not everybody takes this opportunity. Why? Physical defects pass unnoticed in private life. They become normal, everyday occurrences for us.

'But, once transferred to the stage, many of our faults become unbearable. In the theatre there are a thousand people watching an actor through the magnifying lenses of their binoculars. This means the body on display must be healthy, beautiful and its movements expressive and harmonious. The gymnastics you have been doing for the last six months or so have helped you keep your body healthy and improve it.

'We've done a lot of work already. The daily exercises you have been doing have helped you locate the major centres of your musculature, exercises which life itself provides or, which, up till now, you had not developed. To put it briefly, the work that has been done not only activated the ordinary, crude motor centres but the more refined ones we rarely use. They practically die and atrophy because they don't get the work they need. Once you have activated them you will become aware of new sensations, new movements, new means of expression, greater chances to be subtle than you have known up till now.

'All this makes your body more mobile, supple, expressive, responsive and sensitive in its functions.

'The time has come to start on more important work which will have to be done in the gymnastics class.'

After a moment's pause Tortsov asked us:

'Do you admire the physique of strong men in the circus? Or athletes? Or wrestlers? Personally I can't think of anything more ugly than a man with shoulders like a bullock, with knots of bulging muscles all over his body, that are neither the right size nor in the right place for beauty of proportion. Have you ever seen them in the dress suits they put on after they've done their act and follow the circus master as he leads a beautifully dressed stallion? Don't they remind you of those ludicrous figures who walk in a funeral procession? What would happen if these ill-proportioned bodies were to don a body-hugging medieval Venetian costume or an eighteenth-century riding jacket? How stupid these lumps of meat would look.

'It's not for me to judge how far this kind of physical education is necessary in sport. My duty is to warn you that acquiring this kind of monstrous physique is quite wrong for the stage. We need compact, strong, developed, well-proportioned, well-built bodies with nothing unnatural or overdone. Gymnastics should correct not ruin our bodies.

'You are now at the crossroads. Which way are you to go? Take the line of developing your muscles for sporting purposes or fashion yourselves to the demands of our art? We must, of course, direct you along that second way. And that's why I came here today.

'Look! We place the same demands on the gymnastic class as we do on sculpting. Just as a sculptor looks for correct, beautiful proportions in the constituent parts of the statue he is creating, so the teacher of gymnastics should achieve the same thing with the living body. There is no ideal form. It has to be made. To do that you have to observe the body and understand the proportions of its parts. Once its faults have been understood, you have to correct and develop what nature has left incomplete and preserve what she has done well. So, many people have shoulders which are too narrow and hollow chests. You have to work on them to strengthen the shoulder and chest muscles. Other people, on the other hand, have shoulders which are too broad and barrel chests. Why use exercises to reinforce defects? Wouldn't it be better to leave them in peace and turn our attention to the legs if they are too thin? By developing the leg muscles you can bring them to the desired form. Sporting exercises can help gymnastics achieve a specified end. The rest is done by the designer, the costumier, a good tailor and a shoemaker.

'We must find the body's just proportions and golden mean in the things I have indicated.'

.. .. 19..

A famous clown from the Moscow circus accompanied Tortsov to today's class. Introducing him Tortsov said:

'From today on we shall be introducing acrobatics into our programme of study. However strange it may appear, the actor needs them more for internal than for external use . . . *for moments of great psychological climax . . . for creative inspiration.*

'Does that astonish you? *I need acrobatics to develop decisiveness in you.*

'It's disastrous for an acrobat to have thoughts or doubts before doing a somersault or a risky trick. Death threatens. It's no time for doubts, you have to do, not think, leave things to chance, dive in at the deep end! What will be, will be!

'It's exactly the same for an actor when he comes to moments of climax in a role. In moments like "so let the stricken deer" in *Hamlet* or "Blood, Iago, blood!" in *Othello*, you mustn't think, doubt, reflect, prepare or test yourself. You have to do it, take a running jump at it. Yet most actors have a quite different psychological attitude. They are afraid of big moments and painstakingly prepare for them well in advance. That produces the kind of constrictions that prevent you from opening out in big moments of climax in a role so that you can give yourself completely to them without reserve. At times you may get bumps and bruises on your head. The teacher will see to it they're not too serious. Getting a bit of a bump you "put down to experience" won't kill you. It will make you repeat the experiment without unnecessary thinking next time, without shilly shally-ing, *decisively, like a man, with physical intuition and inspiration.* Once you have developed your will in terms of body movement and action the easier it will be to carry it over into big moments inside. That's when you learn to cross the Rubicon, without thinking but surrendering completely to the power of intuition and inspiration. Moments like this are to be found in every big part so let acrobatics help you get on top of them as far as they are able.

'Besides which, acrobatics can render you another service: they help you to be more agile, work better physically onstage when rising, turning, bending, running and doing other, difficult, rapid movements. You will learn to do things in a quick rhythm and tempo and that can only be achieved by a well-exercised body. I wish you luck.'

As soon as Tortsov had gone we were asked to do somersaults on a bare floor. I was the first to volunteer as Tortsov's words had made a great impression on me. Who was more sorry than me that I couldn't handle tragic moments!

Without much time for thought I did a somersault. Wham!! – a enormous bump on the top of my head. I got mad and did another one. Wham!! – another bump on my head.

.. .. 19..

Today Tortsov continued doing the rounds and came for the first time to the dance class we have been doing since the beginning of the academic year.

He said, among other things, that this class was not basic to the development of the body. Its role, like that of gymnastics, was ancillary, a preparation for other more important exercises.

That, however, was not to deny the great significance Tortsov attached to dance in developing physically.

It not only improves the body but opens movements out, broadens them, gives them definition and finish which is very important as choppy, clipped gestures are no good for the stage.

'I value this dance class because it is excellent for the correct placing of the hands, legs and spinal column,' Tortsov explained.

'Some people, owing to the fact that they have hollow chests and round shoulders, have hands which dangle in front of them and bang against their belly and thighs when they walk. Others, owing to the fact that they have their shoulders and trunk thrown back and their belly sticking out, have their hands dangling behind their spine. Neither of these can be considered correct, as the proper position for the hands is at the sides.

'Elbows are often turned in towards the body. They ought to be turned in the opposite direction, with the elbows in the outside. But this must be done in moderation as exaggeration upsets the "placing" and ruins everything.

'The placing of the legs is no less important. If it is incorrect the whole figure suffers in consequence, becoming awkward, heavy and clumsy.

'In most cases women have their legs turned in from the hips to the knees. The same thing applies to their feet which have the heels turned out and the toes turned in. The ballet barre corrects these faults splendidly. It turns the legs out at the hips and positions them properly. And so they become more shapely. The correct placing of the leg at the hips has its effect on the feet which have their heels joined together and the extremities separated on different sides, as it should be when the leg is properly placed.

'And it's not only barre work that contributes towards this but many other dances and exercises. They are based on different "positions" and "pas" which require the hips to be turned out and the legs and feet properly placed.

'With that end in view, I recommend something else of, so to speak, a more home-grown nature which you can use often, daily. It's extremely simple. Turn your left foot out as hard as you can at the toes. Then place your right foot in front of it, close to, with the toes turned out as hard as you can. The toes of the right foot will touch the heel of the left foot and the toes of the left foot will touch the heel of the right foot. At first you will have to hold on to a chair to stop yourself falling over, bend your knees and your whole body. But you should try, as far as possible, to straighten up the knees and the torso. Straightening up will force your legs to turn out at the hips. The feet will come apart a little at first. Otherwise you won't be able to straighten up. But, with time and as your feet begin to turn out you will be able to achieve the position I have indicated. Once you've got it, do it every day and as often as time, patience and strength allow. The longer you can stand like that the stronger and sooner your hips and feet will turn out.

'Finish in the feet, hands, wrists and toes is of no less significance both for flexibility of movement and for the development of the body.

'Here, too, ballet and dance exercises can be of great service. In dance the finish of the feet is very eloquent and expressive. Gliding over the floor in various "pas" like a sharp pen over a page, they trace elaborate designs. When the toes are "en pointe" they give an impression of flight. They deaden the shocks, give smoothness and grace, mark the rhythm and accents of the dance. Small wonder then if, in the art of the ballet, great attention is paid to the toes and their development. We must make use of the techniques it has evolved.

'Things are not so good, in my opinion, when it comes to the finish of the hands in ballet. I don't like the way dancers' wrists move. It's mannered, conventional, maudlin; there's more beautification than beauty. Many ballerinas dance with dead, immobile wrists and fingers which are tense through strain.

'In this instance we are better off turning to the school of Isadora Duncan.[1] It has better control over the wrists.

'There's another element in ballet training which I value and which is of great significance in all further education of the body: its flexibility of movement, the general placing of the torso and our way of holding ourselves.

'It's this: our spine, which bends in all directions like a coil, must be firmly set on the pelvis. It must be, as it were, screwed in at the place where the first, lowest vertebra begins. If a person feels that the imaginary spiral is firmly set then the upper part of the trunk receives support, has a centre of gravity, stability, it's straight.

'But if, on the other hand, the imaginary spiral is wobbly, the spinal column loses stability, straightness, its correct placing, its harmony and also beauty of motion and flexibility.

'This imaginary spiral, this centre which supports the spinal column, is of great significance in the art of the ballet. They have been able to develop and strengthen it. Profit from it and take over methods of developing, strengthening and placing the spinal column from the dance.

'In this regard I also have an old-fashioned method up my sleeve for, so to speak, daily use at home.

'In the old days French governesses used to make round-shouldered children lie on a hard table or on the floor so that the back of their head and spine were touching it. The children used to lie in that position every day for hours on end, while the patient governess read them interesting books in French.

'Here's another simple means that was used for straightening up round-shouldered children. They were made to draw backs their arms, bent at the elbows while a stick was passed between them and the back. When they tried to stand up normally, the arms, naturally, drew the stick towards the spine. When it touched, the stick obliged the child to straighten up. Children went around in this position for practically the whole day under the eagle eye of their governess, and finally got used to keeping the spine straight.

'While gymnastics produces clear-cut, almost jerky movements with strong accents and almost martial rhythm, dance tries to create smoothness, breadth of gesture, like a cantilena. It develops them, gives them line, form, direction, lift.

'Gymnastic movements go in straight lines.

'But in ballet and dance breadth of movement and refinement of form lead to exaggeration and affectation. That's not good. When a dancer or a ballerina has to indicate through mime the entrance or exit of a character, or an inanimate object, they don't simply extend the arm in the required direction but first of all move it to the opposite side so as to increase the scope and sweep of the gesture. When they perform this disproportionately broad, wide movement, they try to make it more beautiful, more splendid, more ornate than is necessary. That produces balletic affectation, simpering, mawkishness, lies, falseness, often ludicrous exaggeration, caricature.

'If we are to rid the drama of all this I must remind you of something

I've told you many times already, namely: there must be no gestures for the sake of gestures onstage. So try not to make them and so rid yourselves of affectation, simpering, balletic exaggeration and other dangers.

'The trouble is they can creep into action itself. To defend yourself against that you must ensure that your actions onstage are always genuine, productive and purposeful. Actions like that have no need of affectation, mawkishness or balletic exaggeration. They will be forced out by effective, productive action.'

At the end of the class a touching incident occurred which I must describe as it indicates something else which they have decided to bring into the programme. It is also typical of Rakhmanov and demonstrates his tireless dedication to his work.

Here's what happened.

Listing the classes that would assist in the development of the body and our expressive apparatus Tortsov happened to remark that he still hadn't managed to get hold of a teacher who dealt with *facial expression* and then immediately corrected himself:

'Of course,' he remarked, 'you can't teach facial expression as what you get from that is face pulling. Facial expression happens of itself, naturally, through intuition or inner experiencing. Still, you can help it by exercises and by developing the face muscles. But . . . to do that you have to know the musculature of the face. I can't find a teacher for that.'

Rakhmanov responded to this with his usual impulsiveness and promised to learn it as quickly as possible, if necessary by working on corpses in an anatomical theatre so that he could, in time, become this so far non-existent teacher for our class in facial expression.

'Then we shall have the teacher we need to conduct exercises in the development of our facial muscles in the classes in training and drill.'

.. .. 19..

I've just got back from Pasha's uncle's. Pasha practically dragged me there by force. It was because another elderly uncle, the famous actor V . . . had come to visit and he was someone who, according to his nephew, I had to see. He was right. Today I made the acquaintance of a remarkable actor, who speaks with his eyes, mouth, ears, the tip of his nose and fingers in barely perceptible movements and turns.

When describing a person's exterior, the form of an object or the contours of a landscape he gives an external picture, with extraordinary clarity, of *what* he is seeing and *how* he is seeing it. For example, describing the home of a friend even more corpulent than he, the narrator was literally transformed before our very eyes into a swell-bellied chest of drawers, or a large cupboard or a squat chair. But he didn't copy the objects, he conveyed a sense of overcrowding.

When he started, as it were, to force his way, with his corpulent friend, through the furniture you got a splendid picture of two bears in one den.

He didn't even need to get out of his chair to describe the scene. He sat in it, bent slightly, raised his pot belly or lowered it and that was enough to give an illusion of pushing our way forward.

As we listened to another story concerning someone who jumped off a moving trolley-car and hit against a post, we all cried out as one man because he had made us see the awful thing he was describing.

Even more remarkable were the mute responses the guest made while Uncle Shustov was telling the story of how, in their youth, he and his friend had both played court to the same lady.

Paul's uncle boasted amusingly of his own success and even more amusingly of V . . . 's failure.

The latter was silent but at certain points in the story, instead of saying something, he ran his eyes over his neighbour and all of us as much as to say:

'The cheek of the man! He's lying like a mountebank and you idiots listen to him and believe him!'

At one such moment the fat man closed his eyes and in a show of despair and impatience, stayed quite still with his head thrown back and started to wiggle his ears. He seemed to be using them like hands to ward off his friend's tiresome chatter.

When Uncle Shustov made further boastful remarks, the guest wickedly twitched the end of his nose first to the left then to the right. Then he raised one eyebrow, then the other, did something with his forehead, let a smile pass over his thick lips and did more to discredit the attacks made on him with these almost imperceptible movements than with fine-sounding words.

In another comic dispute between the two friends they argued without words, using the fingers only. It was evidently about a trick that had been played in a love affair which they were accusing each other of.

First the guest expressed a highly significant rebuke using his index finger. To this Pasha's uncle made a reply in similar fashion but using the little finger. If the first gesture expressed a threat the second was ironic in tone.

When the fat man finally threatened Pasha's uncle with the fat fingers of his huge paw we felt this gesture was a final warning.

Further discussion was conducted with the hands. They depicted whole episodes from their early life. Someone crept up and hid himself. Then the other found him, went up to him and beat him. After which, the first man took to his heels and the second pursued him and overtook him. It all ended with the same rebukes, irony and warnings as before, expressed with the fingers only.

After the meal, over coffee, Pasha's uncle made his guest, and friend, show the young people and ourselves his famous set piece 'The Storm', which he portrayed wonderfully, not only in outward form but, if one may so express it, psychologically, using only his facial expression and his eyes.

.. .. 19..

Tortsov came to our rhythmics class. Here's what he said:

'From today on we shall be having classes in flexibility of movement which Xenia Sonova will take in parallel with classes in Dalcroze eurhythmics.[2]

'I want you to be fully conscious in your approach to this new subject. So, let's have a few words together before the class begins.'

After a moment's pause he continued:

'I attach great importance to classes in flexibility of movement. It is generally considered that these classes can be taken by any old hack dance teacher and that the art of choreography with its trite methods and "pas" is the same thing as the flexibility of movement a dramatic actor needs.

'Is that really so?

'For example, there are quite a few ballerinas who, when they dance, wring their hands and demonstrate their "poses" and "gestures" to the audience, while observing them from the outside. They require movements and flexibility of movement for their own sake. They study their dances in terms of "pas" which are devoid of inner content and create forms which are lacking in substance.

'Does a dramatic actor need these external, expressive actions which have no content?

'And think of these servants of Terpsichore offstage. Do they walk in the way our art requires. Are their theatrical, artificial airs and graces the right thing for our creative ends?

'We also know some dramatic actors who need expressive movements to quell the hearts of their female admirers. These actors create *poses* by combining the beautiful twists and turns of their bodies; they trace complicated, external lines as they move their arms through the air. These "gestures" originate in the shoulders, hips and the spinal column; they run along the outside of the arms, the legs, the whole body and then return to their starting point, having accomplished no productive action whatsoever, bearing no inner intent to fulfil a Task. Such movements are like a messenger-boy delivering letters when he has no interest in what is in them.

'These gestures may look expressive but they are empty and meaningless, like dancers waving their arms so as to be beautiful. We don't need either balletic techniques, or histrionic poses or theatrical gestures, which follow an external, surface line. They don't give life to Othello, Hamlet, Chatski or Khlestakov as human souls.

'Let us rather try and adapt these actorish conventions, poses and gestures so as to accomplish some living task, so as to reveal inner experiences. Then a gesture ceases to be a gesture and becomes a genuine, productive and purposeful action.

'We need simple, expressive, natural actions which have inner content. Where are we to find them?

'There are dancers and dramatic actors of a different kind from the first. They have developed their own flexibility of movement to last them a whole lifetime and give no further thought to this aspect of physical action.

'Flexibility of movement has become part of them, it's theirs, it's second nature. Ballerinas and actors like these don't dance, don't play, they are what they do, and can't do anything without flexibility of movement.

'If they were to pay genuine attention to the things they are feeling, they would be aware of the energy inside them, stemming from their secret depths, from their heart of hearts. It courses through the whole body, it isn't empty, it is launched by emotions, wishes, Tasks which drive it along an inner line to stimulate a creative response.

'Energy, encouraged by feeling, launched by the will, guided by the mind, moves confidently and proudly like an ambassador on an important mission. This kind of energy emerges in creative, sensitive, fertile, productive action which can't be done just anyhow, mechanically, but in accord with the impulses of the heart.

'As it flows through the network of the muscular system and stimulates the internal motor centres, it elicits external action.

'That's the kind of movement and action, originating in the secret places of the heart, following an inner line, which genuine artists of the drama, the ballet and other theatre and movement arts need.

'Only that kind of movement is right for the artistic embodiment of the life of the human spirit of a role.

'Only through inner awareness of movement can we begin to learn to understand and feel it.

'How are we to achieve this?

'Sonova will help us answer this question.'

Tortsov then handed the class over to her.

'Look,' Sonova said to us, 'there's a drop of mercury in my hand and now, carefully, very carefully, I pour it, see, onto the second, index finger of my right hand. Right on the very tip.'

So saying she pretended to put the imaginary drop on the inside of her fingertip on the motor muscles.

'Let it run all over your body,' she ordered. 'Don't rush it! Gradually! Very gradually! First of all over the finger joints which should straighten out and let the mercury pass over the hand and then on down the arm to the elbow. Is it there? Can you feel it? Good! Very good! Now, don't hurry, feel it happen. Good! Very good! Now, don't rush, carefully, let it go onward, over the arm to the shoulder! Right, good! Wonderful, absolutely wonderful! Now the whole arm is extended and straight, raised, joint by joint, flexion by flexion. Now, let the mercury roll in the opposite direction. No, no, that's not the way at all! Why drop the arm all at once, like a stick? That way the mercury will run down to the tip of your finger and drop onto the floor. You must let it roll gently, gently! First of all from the shoulder to the elbow. Bend the elbow, bend it! Right! But don't drop the rest of the arm. Not on any account or the mercury will run away. Right. Now let's go on! Carefully, carefully! Gently! Let the mercury roll down to the palm of the hand. Not all at once. Do it carefully, carefully. Why are you letting the hand drop? Keep it up or the mercury will run away. Gently, gently, good! Now, let it pass carefully, so it doesn't run away, over the palm of the hand to the adjacent finger joints. That's it, let them drop gradually. Gently! Right. The last flexion. The whole hand has been dropped and the mercury has run away . . . Splendid.

'Now I'll pour the mercury on the crown of your head,' she said to Paul. 'And you let it pass over the neck down the spinal column to the pelvis; let the mercury pass down the right leg to the big toe and then up again to the pelvis. Let the mercury go further down the left leg to the big toe and back again up to the pelvis. Then up the spine to the neck and finally over the neck to the crown of your head.'

We let the imaginary drop of mercury roll to our fingers and toes, shoulders, elbows, knees, nose, chin, the crown of our heads and then let it go.

Did we really feel the movement passing through our muscular system or did we only imagine we could sense the passage of the imaginary drop of mercury inside us?

The tutor didn't give us time to ponder this question but made us do exercises without thinking about them.

'Tortsov will explain everything you need to know,' Sonova told us. 'For the time being let's go on working, with a lot of concentration, over and over and over again. You need time, you have to do many exercises and get used to the feeling without knowing you're doing it, then the habit will be firmly ingrained; whether the drop of mercury, the driving force of energy is real or not doesn't matter,' the tutor stated in a soothing manner, as she did movements with us, correcting the arms, legs and torso of first this then that student.

'Come here, quickly!' Tortsov called to me, 'and tell me frankly, don't you find all your classmates have greater flexibility of movement than before?'

I began to admire Leo, who was so fat. The roundness of his movements amazed me. But then I came to the conclusion that the fullness of his figure was something of a help.

But then there was Darya, who was skinny with angular shoulders, elbows and knees. Where did the smoothness and allusiveness of her movement come from? Could the imaginary mercury with its unbroken motion have produced such a result?

Tortsov took the rest of the class. He said:

'Be aware of the things you have just learned from Xenia Sonova.

'She focused your physical concentration on the movement of energy through the inner network of muscles. We need the same kind of concentration when we are looking for tensions in the process of relaxing the muscles of which we spoke earlier. And what is muscular tension if not blocking the passage of motor energy?

'You also know from your own experience of radiation that energy moves not just internally but passes from us, from the secret places of feeling towards the focal object which is to be found outside ourselves.

'Physical concentration plays a great role in those processes, as it does now in flexibility of movement. It is important that this concentration should move continuously in conjunction with the flow of energy as this helps create an infinite line which is essential in art.

'By the way, such continuity is not only essential in our profession but also in other arts. So, what do you say: is this line of sound essential for music?

'It's quite clear that a violin cannot begin to sing a melody until the bow has passed smoothly and continuously over the strings.

'And what would happen if we took the unbroken line away from the painter when he is drawing?' Tortsov continued. 'Could he even draw a simple outline without it?

'It's impossible, of course, and line is essential for a painter in the highest degree.

'And what would you say of a singer who coughed out broken noises instead of sustaining continuously sounding notes?' Tortsov asked.

'I'd suggest he went to the hospital instead of the theatre,' I quipped.

'Now try to take a sustained line away from the dancer. Can he create a dance without it?' Tortsov went on.

'He can't, of course,' I concurred.

'Dramatic actors also need an unbroken line. Or do you consider we can do without it?' Tortsov enquired.

We agreed that we needed a line of movement.

'So, it is essential in all the arts,' said Tortsov, summing up. 'But that's not all. *Art itself is born at the moment when an unbroken, sustained line, sound, voice, movement is created. While there are only individual sounds, scrapings, notes, cries instead of music or individual short lines and points instead of drawing, or individual, spasmodic jerks instead of movement there can be no question of music or singing, of drawing, of portraiture, of dance, of architecture, of sculpture, or, finally, of the art of the theatre.*

'I want you to examine how an infinite line of movement can be created for yourselves.

'Watch me and do as I do,' Tortsov said to us. 'Now, as you can see, my arm which has an imaginary drop of mercury on it, is lowered. But I want to raise it so let's set the metronome at its slowest speed . . . Each beat equals a quarter note. Four beats make a measure in four/four time, the period I allow for raising my hand.'

Tortsov set the metronome in motion and told us he was starting the session.

'This is the first count, a quarter note, during which one of the constituent actions is performed: raising the arm and the flow of inner energy from the shoulder to the elbow.

'That part of the arm which is not raised should be free of tension and hang like a whiplash. The muscles that are relaxed make the arm flexible and then it unfolds to a straight position like the neck of a swan.

'Note that raising and dropping, as with any other movement of the arm, must be done close to the torso. An arm which is detached from the body is like a stick raised at one end. You must extend your arm and once the movement is complete bring it back again. The gesture goes from the shoulder to the extremities and back again, from the extremities to the shoulder.

'Onward,' Tortsov ordered himself after a moment. 'Two. Here we have the second quarter note in the bar, during which another action, raising the second part of the arm and letting the imaginary drop of mercury roll from the elbow to the hand, is performed in its turn.

'Onward,' Tortsov announced. 'Three! . . . Here we have the next count, which is allotted to the third quarter note, raising the hand and the flow energy through the finger joints.

'And, finally: four! Here we have the last quarter note which is allotted to raising all the fingers.

'I lower the arm in exactly the same way, allotting one quarter note to each joint.

'*Ooone!* . . . *Twooo!* . . . *Threeee!* . . . *Fooour!*'

Tortsov rapped out the commands very sharp and short, military fashion.

Ooone! Pause . . . while waiting for the next count. *Twooo!* Silence once more. *Threeee!* – another pause. *Fooour!* a stop etc.

Given the slowness of the tempo, there were lengthy pauses between the words of command. The beats, alternating with silent inaction, obviated any kind of smoothness. The arm moved jerkily, like a cart going over deep potholes and sticking in each of them.

'Now, let's do the exercise over again but at a different, at double speed with the count split. Let each quarter note comprise not a single *one* but *one-one*, like doublets in music; not just *two* but *two-two*; not just *three* but *three-three*; not just *four* but *four-four*. As a result each beat will retain the earlier four quarter notes but split into eight moments or eighth notes.'

We did the exercise.

'As you can see,' said Tortsov, 'the intervals between the counts were shorter, as there were more of them to the bar and that, to a certain extent, facilitated smoothness of movement.

'Strange! Can the mere fact of pronouncing the number of each count influence the smoothness of raising or lowering the arm? Of course, the secret lies not in the words but in the *concentration* focused on the movement of energy. This rises with each count which must be watched carefully. The smaller the fractions in each count the more are packed into the bar and the more they fill it, the more continuous the line of concentration you need for the movement of energy. If you split the count up even more then the fractions you have to observe will be even more numerous. They completely fill the bar, thanks to which you get an even, more continuous line of concentration and movement of energy and consequently of the arm itself.

'Let's test what I have said in practice.'

After that we did a whole series of tests during which the quarter notes were divided into threes (triplets), fours (quadruplets), sixes (sextuplets) up to twelfths, sixteenths, twenty-fourths and even smaller fractions in every bar. As we did this full continuity of movement was achieved, like the buzzing noise the counting had become:

Oneoneoneoneoneoneoneonetwotwotwotwotwotwotwotwothreethree threethreethreethreethreethreethreefourfourfourfourfourfourfourfourfour.

I couldn't keep up the count as it required a rapidity of diction I don't possess.

The voice was buzzing away, the tongue moved very fast but you couldn't make out the words. During this very fast count the arm moved continuously and slowly while the tempo remained as before.

The result was a wonderful smoothness. The arm bent and unbent.

Tortsov said:

'The comparison with an automobile once again suggests itself. As it starts moving it gives short, sharp bursts but then they become continuous, like the movement itself.

'It was the same when you were counting; at first the command was spat out and now these jerky counts have united to form one continuous buzzing noise and slow, flexible movement. In that respect it was near to art, since you achieved an unbroken cantilena.

'You will be even more aware of this when you perform your actions to music which will replace the buzz of your counting with a beautiful, unbroken line of sound.'

Rakhmanov sat at the piano, played something leisurely and slow and we extended our legs and arms and bent our spines to the music.

'Do you feel', Tortsov said, 'your energy majestically progressing along an infinite, inner line?

'*This line creates the smoothness and flexibility of movement we require.*

'This inner line may emerge from the secret depths and energy may be imbued with the promptings of our feelings, our will, our intellect.

'*Once, with the help of systematic exercises, you have become used to, have grown to love, to relish your actions, not by following the outer but the inner line, then you will know what the art of movement and flexibility of form are.*'

When we had finished the exercises Tortsov said:

'An unbroken, continuous line of movement in our art represents the raw material out of which we can develop flexibility of form.

'Just as ordinary cotton or wool thread is continuously fashioned as it passes through a loom, so, in our art, an unbroken line of movement is subjected to artistic elaboration: in one place we can lighten our movement, in another make it stronger, in a third speed it up, slow it down, sustain it, break it, and finally co-ordinate our movements with the accents in the tempo-rhythm.

'Which instant in the movement we are producing should coincide with the beats in the bar we are counting in our minds?

'These momentary stages are barely perceptible seconds during which energy passes along the individual joints, the parts of the finger or the vertebrae of the spinal column.

'It is just these instants which are noted by our attention. In the earlier exercise as the imaginary drop of mercury passed from one joint to another our concentration noted the moment when it passed over the shoulders, the elbows, the bends in the joints. We shall now do this exercise to music.

'It may be that things don't coincide just when we expect, but later when you are counting the great majority of moments. They may fly past you and leave you behind. It may be you won't count the number of bars properly but only approximately as measures of time. The important thing is that even an action divided up in this way should totally imbue you with tempo-rhythm, that you should be aware of the measures and that your concentration should catch up with the subdivided count which your tongue can't articulate. That should establish an unbroken line of concentration and the continuous line of movement we are seeking.

'How pleasing it is to combine the inner movement of energy with the melody!'

Vanya who was sweating away working beside me found that 'music lubricates movement, so that energy lives in clover'.[3]

Sound and rhythm help smoothness and lightness of movement so that it seems that the arms take flight from the torso of themselves.

We did the same sort of exercises on motor energy not only with the arms but with the spinal column and the neck. The movement along the spinal column was accomplished in just the same way as the exercises we had done previously on 'releasing the muscles'.

When energy slid from the top down it felt as though we were falling into the inferno. But when it moved up through the spinal column you had the feeling you were taking off.

We were also made to stop the movement of energy completely. And that was also done in rhythm and tempo. The result was a fixed pose. That was believable when it was inwardly justified. A pose of that nature is transformed into stationary *action*, a living sculpture. It's good not only to perform actions which are inwardly justified but also to perform no action in tempo-rhythm.

At the end of the class Tortsov said:

'Earlier on, in gymnastics or dance class you were dealing with the external movement of the arms, legs and torso. But today, in the class for flexibility of movement you have learned something else, *the inner line of energy*.

'Now decide which of the two lines, inner or outer, you consider the most suitable for the artistic embodiment onstage of the life of the human spirit.'

We unanimously opted for the *inner line of motor energy.*

'So,' Tortsov concluded, 'it *would appear that you have to establish not outward, visible but inward, invisible energy as the basis for flexibility of movement.*

'*And this must be co-ordinated with the rhythmically accented moments in tempo-rhythm.*

'*We call this inner awareness of the passage of energy through the body a sense of movement.*'

.. .. 19..

Today's work on flexibility of movement was held in the theatre foyer. It was Tortsov who took the class. He said:

'Energy doesn't just move along the arms, spine, neck and legs. It provokes the action of the leg muscles and causes a way of walking, something of extreme importance onstage. Is there a special way of walk- ing for the stage which is not the way we walk in ordinary life? Indeed it is not as in life precisely because none of us walks properly, whereas *walking onstage should be as nature intended in accordance with all her laws.* And that's where the major difficulty lies.

'Those to whom nature has denied a good, natural gait and are unable to develop one, resort to all manner of contrivances, when they go onstage, to conceal their deficiencies. And so they learn to walk in a special, unnatural, grand way, as in a painting. They don't walk, they process across the stage. But this theatrical, grand, artificial way of walking is not to be confused with a *stage walk based on the laws of nature.* That is its problem.

'Let's talk about this and the possibilities of developing it, so that we can rid the stage once and for all of that grand, actorish, theatrical way of walking which is so common in the theatre at the present time.

'In other words, start learning to walk onstage from scratch, just as we do in life.'

Tortsov had hardly finished what he was saying when Varya jumped up and walked past him, flaunting the way she walked which she evidently considered exemplary.

'Well,' said Tortsov meaningfully, looking at her feet. 'The Chinese use tight shoes to turn the human foot into a cow's hoof. But what do modern ladies do, and ruin the best, most complex, most beautiful piece of equipment in our body – the human leg, in which the foot plays such an important role. What a barbarous thing to do, especially for a woman! For an actress! A beautiful walk is one of the most attractive of her charms. And all this is sacrificed to some stupid fashion. In future I must ask our dear ladies to come to movement class in low-heeled shoes or, even better, in pumps. Our wardrobe can supply all the necessary.'

After Varya, Igor walked past, displaying his lightness of step. It would be truer to say he didn't walk but fluttered by.

'If Varya's feet and toes didn't do their job properly yours were far too zealous,' Tortsov said to him. 'But that's no great pity. It's difficult to develop the foot and incomparably easier to keep it within bounds. I'm not worried on your account.'

To Leo who lumbered past him Tortsov said:

'If one of your knees went stiff because of an injury or an illness you would run from one doctor to another and spend a fortune on them just to get back to moving properly. So why when both your knees have practically atrophied are you so indifferent to your shortcomings? Meanwhile when walking the movement of the knees is of great importance. You can't walk with stiff, straight legs.'

In Grisha's case the spine, which is also involved and plays an important part in walking, wasn't sufficiently flexible.

To Pasha, Tortsov suggested 'oiling' the hips as they were rusty and getting jammed. That prevented him from advancing his foot far enough forward and reduced his stride, making it disproportionate to the size of the leg.

Darya was found to have a typical woman's fault. Her legs were turned in from the hips to the knees. Her hips would have to be turned out with barre exercises.

Marya's toes were so turned in they almost collided with each other.

On the other hand Nikolai's feet were too turned out.

Tortsov found the movement of my legs was arrhythmic.

'You walk the way many people from the south speak: some words are spoken too slowly, others, suddenly for some reason or other, like scattered peas. That's the way you walk, one group of steps is even then suddenly you go galloping off in seven league boots. Your walk skips a beat as in valvular heart disease.'

As a result of watching the way we walked we understood our own faults and other people's and realized we had forgotten how to walk.

Like very small children, we had to learn this difficult and important art anew.

To help us do that Tortsov explained the structure of the human leg and the fundamentals of correct walking.

'You have to be not so much an actor as an engineer and a mechanic to understand and appreciate the role and action of our leg as a piece of machinery,' he said by way of introduction.

'Human legs', he went on, 'from the pelvis to the feet remind me of the easy motion of a Pullman car. Because of the large number of springs which absorb and deaden the shocks coming from all sides, the upper part, where the passengers are seated, hardly moves at all, even when the car is travelling at a furious speed with jolts coming from everywhere. That's what should happen when human beings walk or run. Then the upper part of the torso and the ribcage, shoulders, neck and head should not suffer jolts but be at rest completely free in their movements, like a first-class passenger in his comfortable car. The spinal column is, to a large extent, of assistance in this.

'Its job is to bend spirally in all directions, at the slightest movement so as to maintain the equilibrium of the shoulders and the head, which, as far as possible, should remain at rest and not be jolted.

'The role of the spirals is played by the pelvis, the knees, the ankles and all the joints of the toes. Their job is to deaden the jolts that come when walking or running and also when bending forwards, backwards, to the right, to the left, that is, as it were, when pitching and rolling.

'The role of the springs is to move the body, which they support, forwards. This must be done in such a way that the body floats in a horizontal line from prow to stern.

'Speaking of this way of walking I am reminded of an incident which made an impression on me. I was watching some soldiers marching by. Their chests, shoulders and heads were visible above the fence which divided us. It looked as though they were not walking but skating or skiing on a smooth surface. It felt like gliding, not steps jerking up and down.

'That happened because all the right springs in the shoulders, hips, knees, ankles and toes were doing their job splendidly. Thanks to which, the upper part of the torso floats along the fence in a horizontal line.

'So that we can get a clearer idea of the function of the leg and its individual parts I will say a few words about each of them.

'I'll start from the top, that is from the pelvic girdle. It has two jobs: first, like the spinal column, it deadens the effect of lateral jolting and the swaying from left to right that happens when walking, and second, it moves the whole leg forward when taking a step. This movement must be broad and free appropriate to our height, the size of the leg, the length of our stride and the desired speed, tempo and character of our walk.

'The better the leg is swung forward the more freely and easily it will travel back and the better the step and the faster its movement will be. This swing of the leg, forwards and back, should not, from now on, depend upon the torso. Though the torso often tries to participate in our advance by bending forward or back so as to increase the momentum of the forward movement. This movement should only occur in the legs.

'This requires special exercises to develop our stride and to allow the leg to swing forward and back freely and broadly.

'They consist of the following. Stand up and lean your right then your left shoulder and torso against a column or a doorpost or one of the solid double doors. This support is needed for the body to keep its vertical position intact and not lean forward or back, left or right.

'Having thus secured the torso in a vertical position, stand firmly on the leg which is against the post or the door. Raise yourself a little on your toes and then swing the other leg forward then back. Try to do this at a right angle. This exercise should at first be done for short periods and at a slow pace and then for longer and longer periods. Of course, don't go all out at first but gradually, systematically.

'Once this exercise has been done with one, let's say the right, leg turn the other side to the door and do it with the left leg.

'In both cases bear in mind that when you swing your leg out the foot should not be at a right angle but extend in the direction the movement is going.

'When walking, as has already been said, the hips fall and rise. When the right hip rises (when you thrust the right foot forward) the left hip drops as the left leg moves back. Then there is the sensation of a circular, rotatory movement in the hip joints.

'The next springs after the hips are the knees. They, as has been said, also have a double function: on the one hand, they advance the trunk, and, on the other, they deaden the jolts and shocks which occur when you transfer the weight of the torso from one leg to the other. At this point the leg which is taking the weight is slightly bent at the knee, sufficiently to maintain the equilibrium of the shoulders and the head. After which, when the hips have fully done their job of moving the torso forward and regulating its equilibrium, it is the turn of the knees which then straighten out and push the torso onward even further.

'The third group of springs which deaden movement and at the same time move the torso forward, are the ankles, feet and toe joints. This is a very complex, sharp-witted piece of apparatus which is important in walking and I draw your special attention to it.

'The flexing of the leg at the ankles, as at the knees, helps the torso advance further. The feet and especially the toes are not only involved in this operation but have another function. They deaden the jolts while you are moving. Their importance in both the first and second operations is considerable.

'There are three ways of using the apparatus of the foot and toes, which create three types of walk.

'In the first of these you first step onto the heel.

'In the second type, you step on the whole foot.

'In the third, the so-called Greek walk à la Isadora Duncan, you first step into the toes, then the movement rolls over the foot to the heel and back again from the heel to the toes and then up the leg.

'For the moment I'll talk about the first type of walk, which is most used when wearing shoes with heels. When walking in this way, as has already been said, the heel takes the weight of the body and rolls the movement over the length of the foot to the toes. The toes don't bend back but on the contrary, dig into the ground like animals' claws.

'As the weight of the body begins to press down and roll across the toe joints they straighten out and push away from the ground until the movement has finally reached the end of the big toe, on which, as with dancers "en pointe", the whole weight of the body rests for a short while without impeding the forward movement, carried by its own momentum. The lower group of springs – from the ankle to the end of the big toe – plays a large and important role in this. I will give you an example from my own experience.

'When I am going home, or to the theatre, and my toes are doing their job thoroughly, I reach my final destination, at a uniform speed, five or six minutes faster than when my feet and toes are not working as they should. It's important that the toes should, so to speak, "follow through", extend your step right to the end.

'The toes are also of immense, primary importance in cushioning jolts. Their role is particularly important in that most difficult moment in smooth walking when undesirable vertical jolts may occur, as the weight of the body is transferred from one leg to the other. This transitional stage is a danger to smoothness of motion. At that point everything depends on the toes (especially the big toe) which, more than the other springs, are able to cushion the shift of bodyweight through the deadening action of their extremities.

'I have tried to outline the function of all the constituent parts of the leg for you and so divided them into individual actions. But, of course, they don't work in isolation but simultaneously, in total, mutual response and interdependence. Thus, for example, at the point when one transfers the body from one leg to the other, just as in the second stage of moving the body forward and in the third moment of shifting, transmitting the weight to the other leg, all the motor parts of the apparatus of the leg are more or less involved and completely connected. It is impossible to describe their mutual relationships, their mutual assistance in writing. These are things you will have to discover for yourselves while you are in motion, using your own sensations. I can only sketch a general outline of the wonderful, complex work the motor apparatus, our leg, performs.'

After the explanation Tortsov had given us all the students started to walk significantly worse than they had before – neither in the old nor the new way. Still, Tortsov noticed I had some small success but then added:

'Yes, your shoulders and head are protected from being jolted. Yes, you're gliding but only along the ground, you're not flying in the air. Your walk is more like creeping or crawling. You walk like a waiter in a restaurant when he's afraid of spilling a bowl of soup or a dish with food and sauce in it. They protect their body, hands and also their tray from bumps and jolts.

'However, smoothness in movement is only a good thing up to a certain extent. If it goes too far the result is the exaggeration and vulgarity we all notice in waiters. A certain amount of variation, up and down, is needed. Let the shoulders, the head and the torso float through the air not in an absolutely straight but slightly wavy line.

'Our walk should not be creeping but *gliding*.

'I asked myself to explain the difference.

'The fact is that when our walk is a creeping movement, at the moment the body in being transferred from one leg to the other, say from the right to the left, the first leg ceases to function at the same moment the second begins. In other words, the left leg transmits the weight of the body and the right leg receives it simultaneously. So, when our walk is a creeping or crawling movement, there is not a single moment when, as it were, the body is airborne, resting solely on the big toe of one foot which carries its assigned movement through to the end. In a walk that is a floating movement there is a second during which a person is detached from the ground, like a dancer "en pointe". After this momentary lift into the air the smooth, imperceptible, shock-free lowering and transmission of the body from one leg to the other begins.'

Tortsov attaches great importance to both these moments, the lift and smooth passage from one leg to the other, as it is because of them we get lightness, smoothness, continuity, airiness, the quality of floating in a person's walk.

However, floating when you walk is not as simple as it seems.

In the first place, it's difficult to locate the moment when you float. But, fortunately, I managed it. Then Tortsov started taking me to task for bobbing up and down.

'But how are you to "take off" without it?'

'Don't fly straight up but forwards in a horizontal line.'

Tortsov insisted above all that there should be no stops or delays in the forward movement of the body. Forward flight should not be broken for a moment. When you are on the end of the big toe you should prolong your flight through your own momentum in the same tempo in which the step began. A walk of this kind flies over the ground, it doesn't suddenly bob up and down in a vertical line but moves forward and onward horizontally, leaving the ground like an aeroplane at the instant when it takes off and as smoothly as when it lands without bobbing up and down. Horizontal movement forward gives a slightly curved, wavy line on a graph, bobbing up and down when walking gives a crooked, zigzag, angular line.

Had an outsider dropped into today's class he'd have thought he'd ended up in a hospital for paraplegics. All the students were moving their legs, deep in thought, concentrating their attention on their muscles as though absorbed in some puzzling problem. The motor centres in consequence were in a total mess. Things which had previously been done intuitively and automatically now demanded the intervention of conscious thought which proved rather inexperienced when it came to anatomy and the musculatory motor system. In fact we weren't pulling the right strings and so got random movements like a puppet when the lines are tangled.

As a result of paying this increased attention to our movement we came, through our conscious mind, to appreciate all the subtlety and complexity of the mechanism of the leg.

The way everything is connected and co-ordinated!

Tortsov asked us to 'follow our step through' to the very end.

Under Tortsov's direct observation and working under his orders we slowly moved, step by step, attentive to our bodily sensations.

Stick in hand, Tortsov used it to indicate every spot, every moment when muscular tension or a passage of energy occurred in my right leg.

Simultaneously Rakhmanov moved on the other side of me, using another stick to indicate the same movement of muscular tension in my left leg.

'Look,' said Tortsov, 'at the same moment my stick is going up the right leg, which is extended forward and is taking the weight of the body, Rakhmanov's stick is going down your left one which is passing the weight to the right leg and moving the body over to it. And now the sticks are moving in reverse: mine is going down, Rakhmanov's is going up. Have you noticed the way this alternating movement of our sticks, from the toes to the hips and from the hips to the toes, occurs in reverse order and in opposite directions? That is how the pistons work in a steam engine of vertical type. Have you noticed how, at the same time, flexions and relaxation alternate up and down, down and up, in logical order?

'If there were a third stick, we could use it to indicate how part of the energy goes up the spinal column, deadening the jolts and maintaining equilibrium. Once its work is done the tension in the spine again goes downwards to the toes from whence it came.

'Did you notice one further detail?' Tortsov went on.

'When the moving sticks go up to the hips there is a second's pause during which they rotate at the place where the joints are and then go down.'

'Yes, we did notice,' we said. 'What does this rotation of the sticks mean?'

'Didn't you notice the rotatory movement in the hips for yourselves? Something literally doing a full turn before moving downwards?

'I am reminded of the turntable which enables a locomotive at a terminus to turn round so it can go in the opposite direction.

'The same turntable exists in our hips and I can feel its movement.

'Another observation: did you feel how skilfully our hips work as tension passes in and out?

'Like the controls in a steam engine they stabilize, deadening the jolts at moments of danger. At the moment the ship moves up and down, down and up. This sense of rolling comes from the passage of energy through the leg muscles.

'If this occurs smoothly and evenly, our walk is smooth, even and has flexibility of form. If the energy moves in jerks, with hesitations half-way along, in the joints or other motor centres, then our walk can't be even, it is jerky.

'And so, once our walk has an unbroken line of movement, it means we feel it has tempo and rhythm.

'Movement, as in the hands, is divided into separate moments in the passage of energy through the flexions and joints (extension of the leg, forward movement of the body, release, changing legs, deadening of shocks etc.).

'*So, when you go on to do more exercises you must match the accents of the tempo-rhythm when you are walking not to the outer but inner line of movement of energy just as we did with the arms and the spine.*'

When I was going back home today people must have thought I was drunk or crazy.

I was learning to walk.

How hard it is!

So much concentration required to observe the even, rhythmic movement of motor energy.

The slightest hesitation or hitch and you get an unnecessary jolt, continuity of smoothness of movement are destroyed, rhythm ruined.

The moment when the weight of the body is transferred from one leg to the other is particularly difficult.

Even as I was going home, when I got there, I had, as it were, been able, to a certain extent, to eliminate the shocks which occur when transferring the body from one leg to the other, let's say from the toes of the right leg to the heel of the left (after rolling the movement along the whole of the left foot) and then from the toes of the left foot to the heel of the right foot. Above all, I learned from my own experience that evenness and an unbroken, horizontal line of movement depend on the simultaneous action of all the springs in the leg and on the co-operation of hips, knees, ankles, heels and toes.

I paused, as usual, at the Gogol monument. Sitting on the bench and watching the passers-by I checked the way they walked. Not one of the people who went past me 'followed through' to the tips of their toes, not one of them stopped in the air, on one toe, for a hundredth of a second. I only saw flight and not the creeping walk that all the others without exception had in one little girl.

Yes! Tortsov is right when he maintains that people don't know how to use that wonderful apparatus which is the leg.

We must learn. Learn everything from scratch: walking, looking, doing things.

Earlier on, when Tortsov said this to us, I had a little smile, thinking he meant it figuratively. Now I'm beginning to understand the literal sense of his words, as our immediate programme of study for the development of our physical attributes.

That realization is half the battle. But even more important is the fact that if I haven't understood (felt) the significance of motor energy in flexibility of movement, I do have a clear image and sensation of the way it moves during stage action, its flow through the whole body, I can feel that inner unending line and am fully aware that without it there can be no evenness of beauty of movement. Now I despise those illicit, staccato movements, which are all shreds and tatters. I don't yet have the broadness of gesture which reveals inner feeling but it has become a real need for me.

In a word, I don't have genuine flexibility of movement or a feeling of movement but I have a premonition of what they are and I know that outward flexibility of movement is based on an inner sensation of the movement of energy.

19

VOICE AND SPEECH

1.[1]

There was a piano in the middle of the main room. Apparently this is where we shall be having our singing class in future.

Tortsov came in with a singing teacher we know well, Anastasia Zarembo. We've been working with her since the beginning of the academic year. Tortsov said:

'When they asked the great Italian actor Tommaso Salvini what you needed to be a tragic actor he replied: "Voice, voice and still more voice!" For the moment I can't explain and you can't quite grasp the profound, practical sense of that great actor's response. You can only understand (that is, feel) the true meaning of these words through practice and long personal experience. Once you realize the possibilities a well-placed, naturally functioning voice opens up for you, the full import of Tommaso Salvini's sentence will be clear.

' "To be on voice!" – what a blessing for a singer and for a straight actor too! To feel that you can control it, that it obeys you, that it can convey the minutest details, modulations, nuances in your acting with resonance and strength! . . . "Not to be on voice!" – what torture that is for the singer and for the straight actor, when it doesn't obey you, when it doesn't reach a house full of people waiting to hear you! When you can't reveal what your mind is creating clearly, deeply, and invisibly. Only an actor can know what agony this is. Only he can compare what has come to be deeply inside with what appears outside, and how it is conveyed by his voice, his words.

If his voice is out of tune, he feels shame because the experience he created within has been distorted by the outward form he has given it.

'There are actors for whom not being on voice is normal. And so they are hoarse, speaking in sounds which destroy what they are trying to convey. And yet there is beautiful music in their souls.

'Imagine a mute who wants to convey the tender, poetic feelings he has for the woman he loves. But he has a hideous squeak instead of a voice. This warps the beautiful, the exquisite things he feels and that drives him to despair. The same thing happens to the actor who can really feel but whose voice is poor.

'Often actors have good natural voices, with a fine timbre and flexibility of expression but no strength. They don't get beyond the fifth row. The first row can just about enjoy the attractive timbre of the sounds they make, their expressive diction and beautifully trained speech. But what about the people sitting further back? There are a thousand people in the audience who will inevitably be bored. They cough so that other people can't listen and the actors can't speak.

'And they have to push their beautiful voices and this pushing not only ruins their voice production and diction but their inner experiences as well.

'There are also voices which are quite audible in the top or bottom register but which have no middle. Some force their voices up so that they become strained and tight and squeak. Others drone and creak in the bass. Pushing ruins the timbre and you can't be expressive with a range of five notes.

'It is equally distressing to see an actor who is good in all respects – strong, flexible, expressive voice production, with a good range – a voice like that can convey all the subtleties and nuances of your inner picture – but here's the rub: the timbre of the voice is unpleasing and lacking all charm. What's the use of strength, flexibility and expressiveness if the heart and ear reject them?

'Sometimes these vocal deficiencies can't be corrected because of some innate peculiarity or damage due to illness. But mostly they can be removed by centring the voice correctly and eliminating tightness and tension, pushing, faulty breathing and articulation of the lips or, finally – in the case of illness – by treatment.

'And so it is essential to keep a careful check on our breathing and our vocal apparatus.

'When should we start work? Now, in our student days, or later when we are already actors and have a performance every evening and rehearsals during the day?

'Actors must go onstage fully equipped, but the voice is the most important part of their creative ways and means. Besides, when you are professionals, a false sense of pride prevents you learning your ABC like a student. So make the best use of your youth and student days. If you don't do the work now, you won't tackle it later and you'll suffer throughout your whole creative career from this fault from your student days. Your voice will be a hindrance and not a help.

' "Mein Organ ist mein Kapital!"[2] the well-known German actor Ernst Possart said. He was a guest at lunch, and was dipping a pocket thermometer in the soup, the wine and other drinks. In his concern to protect his voice he kept a careful watch on the temperature of the things he ate. That was the extent to which he cared for one of the finest gifts of creative nature – a beautiful, resonant, expressive, strong voice.'

.. .. 19..

Today Tortsov came into class arm in arm with Anastasia Zarembo.

'From today on Anastasia Zarembo will place your vowels and also your consonants. I, or someone else in my place, will at the same time correct your articulation.

'I don't need to do anything about the vowels as they are corrected by singing itself, but by speech.

'As for the consonants, we have to work on them in singing and in speech class as well.

'Unfortunately there are singing teachers who have little interest in words and consonants in particular. But there are teachers of speech who do not always have a clear understanding of sound and how it is placed. As a result in singing the voice is properly placed for vowel sounds but wrong for consonants, while in speech, conversely, it is wrong for vowels and right for consonants.

'And so singing and speech classes can be simultaneously helpful and harmful.

'This is abnormal and the guilt is often due to poor judgement.

'How good it would be if teachers of singing could, at the same time, teach speech, and teachers of speech could teach singing. But since this cannot be, let both kinds of specialists work together hand in hand.

'Anastasia Zarembo and I have decided to make just such an experiment.

'Work on voice mainly consists of developing breathing and producing sustained notes. Very often that means only sung vowels. But can't consonants be sustained notes? Why not make them resonant like vowels?

'I can't bear the usual, declamatory, actorish singsong we get in drama. Only people whose voices do not naturally sing but hammer need it.

'To make it resonant they have to resort to vocal "whirligigs" and theatrical, declamatory "fiorituri", they have to slide their voice down by intervals of a second to appear dignified, or, to break the monotony, screech individual notes an octave higher, and the rest of the time, because of their narrow range, hammer away within a range of three, four, or five notes.

'Would these actors need this trickery if they had a natural singing tone?

'But a good voice is rare in conversational speech. If you do come across one, it lacks strength and range. And you can't express the "life of the human spirit" with a range of five notes.

'The conclusion of all I've said is that even a good natural voice must be trained not only for singing but for speaking as well.

'What does this work consist of? Is it the same as in opera or does drama have quite different demands?

'Quite different, some maintain: you need open sounds for conversational speech. But from my own experience I would say that this opening out of the voice makes it vulgar, pallid, diffuse and finally makes it rise in pitch which is bad for stage speech.

'What nonsense, others protest. In conversation you must have constricted, closed sounds.

'But that, as I have discovered in my own case, makes the tone tight, muffled, with a narrow range, as though it were in a barrel, dropping at the feet of the person who is speaking instead of flying forward.

'What can we do?

'Instead of answering that I will tell you about the work I have done in the course of my acting career on tones and diction.

'When I was young I was 'preparing to become an opera singer,' said Tortsov, beginning his story. 'Because of that I have some idea of the usual methods of placing the breath and sounds in the vocalist's art. But I don't need these for singing but so as to discover the best methods to develop natural, beautiful, inwardly meaningful speech. It must convey in words the sublime feelings of the tragic style just as it does simple, intimate, elegant speech in drama and comedy. My discoveries have been helped by the fact that I have worked in opera in recent years. Coming into contact with singers I talked to them about their art, heard the tones well-produced voices make, came to know the most diverse timbres, learned to distinguish among throat, nose, head, chest, occipital and other shades of tone. All this was imprinted on my aural memory. But the important thing was that I understood the advantage of voices placed "in the mask", where the hard palate, the nasal cavities, the antrum of Highmore and other resonators are situated.

'Singers told me: "A sound which is 'placed on the teeth' or directed 'at the bone', i.e. in the skull, acquires a ring and power." Sounds which fall against the soft palate or the glottis resonate as though they were in cotton wool.

'From my talks with one singer I also learned another important secret in placing the voice. When breathing while singing you must be aware of two streams of air issuing simultaneously from the mouth and the nose. It appears that as they emerge they come together in one common wave of sound in front of the singer's face.

'Another singer told me: "I place the sound when singing just as sick or sleeping people do when they moan, with a closed mouth. I direct the sound to the head and the nasal cavities, I open the mouth and continue the lowing sound as before. But this time the moan is broken into sounds which emerge freely and resonate 'in the mask' and the other true resonators in the head."

'I tested out all these techniques for myself to try and find the kind of sound of which I had a vague inkling.

'My efforts were directed by chance. For example, while I was abroad I met a famous Italian singer. However, on the day of the concert he felt that his voice didn't sound right and he wouldn't be able to sing that evening.

'The poor man asked me to go with him to the concert and tell him how to deal with the situation if things went wrong.

'His hands cold, pale, and much troubled he went onstage and began to sing wonderfully. After the first number he came back into the wings and did an entrechat out of joy, trilling happily:

' "It got there, it got there, it got there!"

' "What came?" I asked in amazement.

' "It! The note!" he repeated picking up his songbook for the next number.

' "Where did it get?" I asked, not understanding.

' "Here," said the singer, pointing to the upper part of the face, to the nose and teeth.

'On another occasion I happened to be at a concert given by the pupils of a well-known singing teacher and was sitting beside her. And so I could observe her anxiety about her pupils closely. The old lady grabbed my hand every minute, nervously poked me with her elbows and knees when the students didn't do what they should. And the poor woman repeated the whole time in a state of terror:

' "Itago, itago!" (i.e. it's gone, it's gone).

'Or, alternatively she whispered joyously:

' "Itadere, itadere" (it's there, it's there).

' "What's gone where?" I said uncomprehendingly.

' "Nota go to de back neck," the terrified teacher said in my ear or, in contrast, she repeated joyously:

' "Itadere, itadere in muscle" (it's in the muzzle, i.e. in the "mask").

'I was reminded of these two incidents with the same words "it's there" and "it's gone", "in the mask" or "in the back of the head" and I started to find out from my own experience why it is so terrible when the note leaves and good when the note returns to the "mask".

'To do that I needed the help of singing. I was afraid to disturb the people living with me so I conducted my experiments *at quarter voice, with my mouth closed.* This sense of tact brought me considerable rewards. *Because initially, when placing the voice, it is best to whisper quietly so as to find the right support for the voice.*

'When I began I sustained only one, two or three notes in the middle register, supporting them in all the resonators of the *facial mask* I could feel from the outside. It was long, difficult searching work. At moments it seemed that the sound had dropped into the right place, at others I observed that "itago".

'Finally as a result of long exercises I got into the habit and with the help of some technical devices learned to place two to three notes properly which sounded in a new way – full, compact, ringing, something I had never noticed before.

'But that wasn't enough. I decided to bring the tone right forward so that the tip of my nose quivered from the vibration.

'And I was, you might say, successful except that my voice became nasal. This made me do more work. This consisted in ridding the tone of its nasal quality. This cost a lot of time and effort although the secret turned out to be quite simple. All I had to do was get rid of the small, barely perceptible tension in the inner part of the nasal area where I could sense pressure.

'I finally got rid of it. The note came much further forward and was more resonant but not with the pleasant timbre I would have liked. There were traces of an undesirable pre-sound which I couldn't eliminate. But, out of stubbornness, I wouldn't take the note backwards and downwards, in the hope that with time I would overcome this new obstacle which had appeared.

'In the next stage of my work I tried to broaden the range I had fixed for my exercises a little. Amazingly the middle notes, like the upper and the lower, sounded well of their own accord, comparable in kind to the ones I had worked on earlier.

'So I gradually tested and evened out the notes within my range which were naturally open. Next on the agenda was work on the most difficult, the notes at the upper limit which demand, as you know, artistically placed closed tone.

'When you're looking for something you don't just sit on the seashore and wait for a discovery to come to you, you have to go on tirelessly looking, looking, looking.

'That's why I spent all my free time at home humming, trying to find new resonators and supports and to come to terms with them.

'While I was conducting my search I noticed, quite by chance, that when you try to bring the tone into the frontal resonators *you lower the head forward and drop the chin. That position helps you bring the note as far forward as you can.*

'Many singers use this method and approve of it.

'In this way a whole scale of high notes was worked out. But for the moment all this was done by humming and not by singing properly with the mouth open.

'It was the beginning of spring. My parents went off to the country. I was alone in the apartment and that allowed me to do my exercises and humming not only with a closed but with an open mouth. On the first day after their departure I came back home for lunch and as ever lay on the sofa. I began humming as usual and after a gap of almost a year decided for the first time to open my mouth once a note had been well established by humming it.

'What then was my amazement when suddenly, unexpectedly an unknown sound, that had long been maturing, just rolled off my nose and mouth and took strong wing, a sound like that I had long been dreaming of, which I had heard from singers and had long been searching in myself.

'As the voice became stronger the sound became firmer, fuller. Up till then I didn't know I had such a sound. It seemed as though I had undergone a miracle. I was so heartened I sang the whole evening and my voice not only did not tire it rang out better and better.

'Previously, until I started working systematically, I quickly went hoarse if I sang loudly for a long time, now, on the other hand, it had a salubrious effect on my throat and cleared it.

'I had another pleasant surprise: I had notes in my range which were not there before. There was a new colour in my voice, another timbre which I found better, more graceful, velvety than the previous one.

'How could all that just happen?! It was clear that quiet humming could not only help develop tone but also even out all notes on vowel sounds. And how important that is!

[How disagreeable voices that are all bits and pieces are, when one vowel comes from the stomach, another from the glottis, another rumbles as in a barrel, and others fall into a hole you can't get them out of.][3]

'With the new placing of the voice which I had developed open vowel sounds were directed to the same place, to the hard palate at the root of the teeth and then rebounded somewhat higher into the nasal cavities at the front of the mask.

'Further experiments showed that the higher the voice goes, moving into artificially closed notes the higher the sound supports moved upward and forward into the mask, the area of the nasal cavities. Moreover, I noted that my naturally open notes found support in the hard palate and bounced off the nasal cavities, but that closed notes which were supported in the nasal cavities bounced off the hard palate.

'I sang for a whole evening in the empty apartment enchanted with my new voice. But I soon became disenchanted. In one opera rehearsal I was witness to a well-known director criticizing a singer for pushing his tone too far forward into the mask so that his singing acquired an unpleasant gypsy quality, a slight nasality. This incident once more knocked me off my feet when I had felt so secure. Yes, I had noticed an undesirable tinge in the voice which appeared in notes placed far forward in the mask.

'I had to begin further study.

'Without casting aside the things I had already done I started looking for new resonators in my skull, at every point in the hard palate, the antrum of Highmore, in the upper part of the skull and even in the occiput which I had been told to be careful of. I found resonators everywhere. They all did their job to a greater or lesser extent and embellished the tone with new colours.

'The experiments made it clear that singing technique is more complex and subtle than I had imagined and that the secret of vocal art doesn't just lie in the "mask".

'There was another secret I was lucky enough to learn.

'In singing classes I was interested by what one tutor often shouted when her students were doing high notes.

' "Yawn," she reminded them.

'It would seem that to release tension on high notes the larynx and pharynx must be placed in the same position as when yawning. When that is done the throat is naturally open and so undesirable tensions are eliminated.

'Thanks to this discovery my top notes were broad and acquired a ring and were freed from strain. I was delighted.

'After all this work I have described I achieved a properly placed voice on vowel sounds. I did vocalizing exercises with them and my voice rang out even, strong and full in all registers. After that I went on to songs with words. But to my amazement they all sounded like vocal exercises as I was only singing the *vowel* sounds of the words. As far as the *consonants* were concerned, not only were they not voiced, they hindered my singing with their dry clatter.

'Then I understood from my own experience S. M. Volkonski's marvellous aphorism – the vowels are the river and the consonants the banks.[4] That is why my singing with slack consonants was like a river with no banks, that overflows and turns into a swamp, a marsh in which words get caught and sink.'

.. .. 19..

'Stime topen updedor tpursnal freem,' Tortsov unexpectedly said to us as he came into class.

We looked at him then at each other in amazement.

'Didn't you understand?' he asked, after a pause.

'Not a word,' we acknowledged. 'What do these antagonistic words mean?'

' "It's time to open up the door to personal freedom." The actor who spoke like that in a play had a fine, big voice that could be heard everywhere; nonetheless it was impossible to understand him and we all thought as you did just now, that he was being antagonistic,' Tortsov told us.

'The result of this trivial and comic episode proved of great import to me and so I will spend some time on it.

'Here's what happened to me.

'After many years as an actor and director I fully realized (came to feel) that all actors should possess excellent diction, pronunciation, that they should feel not only phrases and words but each syllable and each of its letters. The fact is, the simpler the truth the longer it takes to see it.

'I also understood that everyone in life or onstage speaks appallingly and that each of us can only find one person who, in our opinion, speaks well. Oneself. This happens because first, we are used to ourselves, secondly because we hear ourselves differently from the way our speech is received by others. We must study it attentively so as to hear ourselves naturally.

'I studied myself the same way I did others and the final result was that I decided that everyone should go back to school and start with the ABC. [We don't feel our language, phrases, words and letters and so we distort them easily: we substitute one sound for another. Add to that lisping, guttural tone, nasal tone, shrieking, squeaking,[5] creaking and stuttering.]

'A word with a bumbled beginning is like a man with a flattened head. A word where the end isn't pronounced reminds me of a man with one leg.

'The dropping of individual letters and words is the same thing as a squashed nose, a missing eye or tooth, a cauliflower ear or similar kinds of deformity.

'When out of laziness or sloppiness some people's words come out in a formless lump I am reminded of a fly that has fallen into the honey; I have a picture of autumn mist and fog when everything merges into the darkness.

'Arrhythmic speech in which the word or phrase begins slowly and suddenly speeds up in the middle only to slip away unexpectedly, reminds me of a drunk or the babble of a man with St. Vitus dance.

'You have had occasion, of course, to read books and newspapers which were badly printed with missing letters and misprints. Isn't it true, it's agony having to stop, try and guess the answer to the riddle?

'And it's agony too, reading a letter of a notice written in handwriting that just smudges everything. Your guess is someone is inviting you to something but where and when you can't make out. It says, 'You are a w . . . f . . .' So what are you, a waster or a wonder, a friend or a fool? Impossible to make it out.

'However hard it may be to deal with a badly printed book or with poor handwriting with a lot of effort you can guess the sense of what's been written. The paper or the letter is to hand and you find the time to go back over it and decipher what you don't understand.

'But what are you to do when in the theatre, during a performance, the actors deliver the established text like a badly printed book, dropping individual letters, words, phrases which often are of primary, even decisive significance as the whole play is built on them? You can't bring back a spoken text or stop the performance or the play as they quickly unfold so you can decipher the things you haven't understood. Bad speech creates one misunderstanding after another. They accumulate, blur or completely obscure the sense, the essence or even the style of the play. At first the audience strain their ears, attention, minds so as not to miss what's going on onstage; if they don't succeed they start to get restless, cross, to whisper to one another and finally to cough.

'Do you understand how awful that word 'cough' is for an actor? A crowd of a thousand people who have lost patience and contact with what's going on onstage can 'cough away' the actors, the play, the performance. That's a disaster for the play and the performance. An audience that coughs is our worst enemy. One way of guarding against it is beautiful, clear, vivid speech.

'I also came to understand that distortions in conversational speech just about get by in our home surroundings. But when resounding verses on noble subjects, on freedom, on ideals, on pure love are delivered onstage with coarse speech, that coarse declamation is an insult and a hindrance, like a ballgown on a vulgar woman.

'Letters, syllables, words were not invented by man; they were suggested by our instinct, impulses, nature itself, time and place, life itself.

'Pain, cold, joy, fear provoke in everyone, all children the same expressive sounds; so, for instance, the sound A-A-A emerges from within spontaneously out of the fear or joy that grips us.

'All sounds which combine to form words have their soul, their nature, their content which the person speaking must feel. If a word has no connection with life but is said in a formalistic, mechanical, limp, soulless, empty way then it is like a corpse in which no pulse beats. A living word is filled from within. It has its own individual character and must remain as nature created it.

'If a person doesn't feel the soul of a letter he won't feel the soul of a word, won't sense the sound of a phrase or a thought.

'Once I had understood that letters only have an acoustic form to fulfil their content I was naturally faced with the task of studying the aural form of letters so that I could better understand their content.

'I deliberately went back to the alphabet and began to study each of the letters individually.

'It was easier for me to begin with the vowels as they had already been prepared, corrected and made even by singing.'

.. .. 19..

'Do you understand that feeling emerges from our souls through the clear sound A-A-A? This sound is associated with profound, inner experiences which want to get out, to fly freely from within us, from the depths of our souls.

'But there's another kind of A-A-A which is dull and closed and which doesn't tear freely out of us but stays within and rumbles and echoes ominously, as in a cavern or a vault. There is also an insidious A-A-A that worms its way out and drills its way into the person we are talking to. There is also a joyful A-A-A that flies out of our soul like a rocket. There is also a heavy A-A-A which sinks downwards like an iron weight into a well.

'Don't you feel that little bits of our own soul rise and fall because of these vocal waves? They aren't empty but vowel sounds which are full of psychological meaning, which give me the right to say that inside, in their very heart, there is a little bit of the human soul.

'So I came to know (feel) the acoustic form of all letters representing vowels and then went on to a similar study of consonants.

'These letters had not been corrected and prepared through singing and so work on them proved more complex.

'I became strongly aware of the importance of my new task after I had been told that a well-known Italian baritone V . . . sounded weak when vocalizing on vowels. But as soon as he joined them to consonants the strength of his voice increased ten-fold. I began to test this out on myself but my experiment didn't give the desired results. Moreover, it convinced me that my vowels were not sounding by themselves, separately, but in conjunction with consonants. A great deal of work was needed before I understood how to develop resonance in all letters without exception.

'After that my attention was directed only to consonants.

'I watched the way they sounded in myself and in others, went to the opera and concerts, listened to singers. And what happened? It turned out that with the best of them, just as with me, arias and songs turned into pure vocalizing because of the laziness of the consonants or the careless way they were pronounced.

'In The Expressive Word it is said: if the vowels are the river and the consonants the banks we must fortify the latter so we don't get flooding.

'But apart from directive functions consonants are also voiced.

'Consonants of this kind are : V, B, G (hard), D, L, M, N.

'I started with them.

'In these notes you can clearly distinguish a sustained note coming from the larynx which sounds the same as vowels do. The only difference is that the sound does not emerge immediately and unimpeded but is held is various places which give it its articular colouring. When this pressure which holds back the build-up of laryngeal sound bursts the sound emerges. So, for example, B, the build-up of the laryngeal hum is held back by the pressing together of both lips, which give [the sound] its characteristic colouring. With the release of pressure you get an explosion and the sound emerges. It is no surprise therefore that this and similar sounds are called "plosives". When pronouncing the letter V the same thing happens with the pressure of the lower lip and the upper teeth.

'The same thing occurs with the letter G because of the pressure of the back of the tongue and the hard palate.'

[Stanislavsky continues with a discussion of the correct placing of voiced and other consonants in Russian.]

'When letters are joined to make syllables or whole words, phrases, their sound shape, naturally, becomes roomier and so we can put more into them.

'Say, for example the letters A-B.'

'My God,' I thought, 'we're going to have to learn our ABC all over again. We're really living a second childhood – artistically: the *letters A-B!*'

Ba-ba-ba . . . we all began bleating, like a flock of sheep.

'Look, I'll write down on paper the sound you got,' said Tortsov stopping us.

On a piece of paper he had by him, with a blue pencil he drew: *pba*, i.e. initially an indistinct, uncharacteristic little *p* which was either percussive or plosive, but not a totally voiced little *b*. While they were yet undefined they toppled into a large, open, hollow, white-sounding unpleasantly harsh *A* and disappeared.

'It's another sound I need,' Tortsov explained, 'open, clear and broad – *Ba-a* . . . the kind which conveys surprise, joy, a friendly greeting which makes the heart beat faster, happier. Hear for yourselves. *Ba!* You can feel how, within me, in the secret places of my soul a *b* is coming to the boil in the larynx and how my lips are scarce able to hold the sound, and the feeling that accompanies it, in. How finally, when the obstacle was broken, a broad, hospitable, welcoming *A* sound flies from my open lips towards you, like a host greeting a treasured guest. *B-b -- A-a-a!* Can't you feel a bit of my own soul in that exclamation, flying straight to your heart with a joyous sound?

'Now here's the same syllable *ba* of a different kind.'

Tortsov pronounced these letters in a gloomy, lacklustre, depressed manner. This time the humming sound the letter *b* made was like the subterranean rumbling that precedes an earthquake; the lips didn't part as in a friendly welcome, they opened slowly as in doubt. Even the sound *a* had no ring of joy to it but sounded lacklustre, flat and seemed to drop back into the stomach, not having achieved freedom. Instead a whispering breath emerged from the lips, like hot steam coming from a large, open vessel.

'The number of entirely different variations we can think up for syllables of the two letters, *ba!* And in each of them a small bit of the human soul is apparent. It is these kinds of syllables that lived onstage just as those which are the result of slack, soulless, mechanical articulation are like a corpse from which comes no sense of life but of the grave.

'[Now, try and develop syllables of three letters: *bar, bam, bak, bat, bash* . . .[6]] As the mood changes with each new letter so each new sound lures another little bit of our feeling from the various corners of our soul!

'[If you combine two syllables there is even more room for feeling: *baba, bava, baki, bali, batbat, bambam, bambar, barbuf.*[7]]'

We repeated after Tortsov and made up our own syllables. Perhaps for the first time in my life I really listened to the sounds they made and understood how incomplete they are when we do them and how rich they are in Tortsov's mouth, who, like a gourmet, savours every word and letter.

The whole room was filled with varying sounds, which struggled and collided with each other. But the resonance was inadequate despite all our zeal to produce it. Amid our dull croaking vowels and thumping consonants Tortsov's ringing vowels and vibrant consonants seemed bright, reverberant, bouncing off every corner of the room.

'How simple yet how hard the task is,' I thought. 'The more simple, the more natural it is, the harder it is.'

I watched Tortsov's face: it was shining, like a man enjoying something beautiful. I switched my gaze to the faces of my fellow students and could hardly refrain from laughing when I saw the look on their rigid faces which bordered on a grimace.

A delighted Tortsov, who was now riding his hobbyhorse, was revelling in syllables out of which he created words we knew and others he had made up himself.

He started making phrases out of words. He spoke a long speech then went back once more to individual sounds, syllables and words.

While Tortsov was revelling in sounds I watched his lips closely. They reminded me of the finely tooled keys on a wind instrument. Whether open or shut no air filtered through a crack. Thanks to such mathematical precision of sound he achieved exceptional clarity and purity. With the kind of speech apparatus Tortsov had fashioned for himself, the articulation of the lips occurs with incredible lightness, speed and exactness.

Not so with me. Like the keys of a woodwind instrument of poor manufacture my lips didn't shut tight enough. They let air get through; they came unstuck, they were badly tooled. And so my consonants weren't clean and clear enough.

The articulation of my lips is so underdeveloped and so far from total mastery it won't even allow me to speak rapidly. Syllables and words are blurred, trip over each other, slide away, like crumbling riverbanks, and in consequence vowels constantly overflow and the tongue gets tied up in them.

'When you have understood that the way I did you will have the conscious desire to work on and develop the articulatory apparatus of the lips, the tongue and all those parts which form clear, sharp consonants.

'The famous singer and teacher Pauline Viardot said one must sing "avec le bout des lèvres" (the tip of the lips). And so work hard to develop the articulation of the lips. The muscles play a major role in this process and require systematic development and time.

'I won't go into details of this work right now. You're studying that in "training and drill".

'For the moment, at the end of the class, I will warn you against one other widespread fault which we often encounter in people pronouncing words of two or more letters, consonants and vowels, joined together.

'These faults consist in the following. In many people the vowels are formed in one part of the head and the consonants in quite another. And so you have to move the consonants upwards, roll them "along the tracks" from somewhere below to combine with the vowels in a common sound.

'The result is not one sound from two letters: Ba, Va, Da . . . but two, coming from different places. So, for example, instead of Ba you get a rumbling in the larynx, with closed lips: gmmm . . . Then, after it has travelled from the larynx to the lips and these have been opened and after a slack pop, out comes a huge A-a-a . . . gmmm – buA. That is wrong, ugly and vulgar.

'The laryngeal hum of the consonants should gather and resonate in the same place the vowels are formed. And so they mix and mingle with the consonants and after the popping of the lips the sound flies out in two streams from the mouth and nose, resonating in the same resonator as the vowels.

'Just as the mixed character of a voice with vowels coming from different parts of the apparatus of the head is bad, so are consonants travelling from various centres of the sound apparatus.

'A comparison with a typewriter is not inappropriate. There too all the letters of the alphabet jump up and strike the same place they are printed on the paper.'

.. .. 19..

Today Tortsov continued his explanation. He said:

'Having absorbed the principal laws of sounds, diction and articulation, in the evenings I "bellowed" or sang music with words.

'However things didn't go well with all the consonants. Many of them, like, for example, the sibilants, the affricates and fricatives escaped me. Evidently the cause was an innate failing which had to be addressed.

'First I had to understand the positions in which the mouth, lips and tongue are placed to produce the consonants correctly. For that I turned to a "natural", that is, I enlisted one of my students who had good diction. He proved a patient fellow. That gave me the opportunity to watch his mouth for hours on end, to observe what his lips and tongue were doing when articulating those consonants which I had recognized as incorrect.

'Of course, I realized there are two, completely individual ways and techniques of speaking. People must adapt in one way or another to what they have been given. Nonetheless I tried to take on the things I had observed in my "natural".

'But there are limits to anyone's patience. The student I had chosen didn't last. He found various excuses for not coming.

'I had to turn to an experienced lady teacher of diction and work with her.

'It's not part of my task today to repeat what I learned during those lessons. Specialists in the field of diction will tell you all you need to know in good time.

'For the moment I will confine myself to a few comments on what my own practical work brought me.

'Above all I learned that class-time alone isn't enough to place the voice and correct diction. In class you can only establish what needs to be done in "training and drill", first under the watchful eye of a répétiteur then on your own, at home, everywhere, in your daily life.

'Until this new way of speaking has become part of your life, you can't consider it as really your own. We must see to it that we always speak correctly and beautifully onstage and in life. We must put it into practice, create a habit, make what is new part of our lives, make it once and for all second nature. Only in those conditions, when it has become a habit, second nature to us, can we stop paying attention to our diction when we are appearing onstage. If someone playing Chatski or Hamlet has to think about his vocal failings or speech defects while he is performing, this is hardly likely to help him in his main creative purpose. And so I advise you now, in your first two years, to have done with the basic demands of diction and voice production. As for the subtleties of the art of speaking, which will help you express the imperceptible nuances of feeling and thought artistically, beautifully and precisely, you will have to work on them throughout your whole life.

'I was so taken up with singing I forgot the principal purpose of my studies — *stage speech and techniques of declamation*.

'But I did remember them and tried to speak the way I had learned to sing but, to my astonishment, the sounds came out at the nape of the neck and I couldn't haul them into the front of the head. When I finally managed it, both my speaking voice and my singing seemed unnatural.

' "What does this mean?" I asked myself in amazement. "Evidently one should speak differently from the way one sings. That is what professional singers do, and with good reason; they sing differently from the way they speak!"

'My questions and discussions on this subject made it clear that many vocalists do this so as not to ruin the timbre of their singing tone while speaking.

' "But," I decided, "in our business this is an unnecessary precaution because we, in fact, sing so as to be able to speak with timbre."

'I had to spend a lot of time on this problem before I reached the truth. Chance came to my aid. A famous foreign singer, renowned for his voice, diction and declamation, told me: "Once the voice is properly placed, you must speak exactly the way you sing."

'From that moment on my work moved in a different direction and went faster. I alternated singing and speaking: I sang for a quarter of an hour and then spoke for the same period in a predetermined tone. Once again I sang for a while and spoke for a while. This went on for a long time but the results were nil.

' "Hardly surprising," I decided. "What can these few hours of correct speaking begin to do when they are surrounded by hours of incorrect talking! I'll keep a constant eye on myself and on the placing of my voice. I'll transform my life into one long class! That way I'll get out of the way of speaking incorrectly."

'However it wasn't so easy to get used to but I did what I could as long as my concentration held out.

'I finally felt some difference in my conversational speaking. Good individual sounds began to appear, whole phrases, and I noticed that just at such moments things I had discovered in singing were being applied in conversational speech. In those moments I spoke as I sang. The trouble was that this kind of speech didn't last long as the tone was constantly trying to disappear into the soft palate and the throat.

'The same thing happens to me now. I'm not convinced that I'll be able to place the voice for my lifetime in such a way that I'll always be able to speak properly, the way I sing. So, obviously, I have to correct my voice before every performance or rehearsal using warm-up exercises.

'Nonetheless I had an undoubted success. I learned to place the voice into the front of the head quickly, easily, at will at every moment of the performance, not just for singing but for speaking.

2.

. . . . 19

I was doing sound effects today and in the gaps between I heard Tortsov and the actors talking in the Green Room.

Tortsov was giving notes to one of the actors about his performance and one of the scenes he had heard while standing in the wings.

Unfortunately I came in on the middle of what he was saying and missed the beginning.

This is what Tortsov said:

'When delivering verse, I tried to speak as simply as possible, without bombast, without betraying the melody, without emphasizing the metre, following the inner meaning of the work, its essence. This wasn't done out of vulgar primitivism but was still beautiful speech. This was helped by the fact the syllables in the phrase rang out, sang and that lent elegance and musicality to my speech.

'When I started speaking in this new way in the theatre, my fellow actors were amazed at the change in my voice, my diction, and at the new technique for expressing feeling and thought. But I still had further to go, as it turned out. Apart from the pleasure you take in your own voice you must also allow the audience to grasp, to take in things which merit attention. You must slip words and intonations into the listener's ear without his noticing. It's easy to go down the wrong path and start showing your voice off to the audience, flirting with them, flaunting your way of speaking.

'But that's something you should never do; you must only acquire those skills which make your words easy for everyone to understand in a large space. To do that you must articulate more clearly in some passages and hold back in others, or stop speaking, so as to give the listener time to take in what has been said, to admire a beautiful, vivid expression, or realize the full depth of an idea, or appreciate clear examples and comparisons, true and vivid intonations.

'For that an actor must really know which word, phrase or thought to bring out or, conversely, which must be pushed into the background.

'This skill must become reflex, second nature.

'I learned how as we say in our private language "to feel the word".

'Speech is music. Dialogue in a play is a melody, an opera or a symphony. Diction onstage is no less difficult an art than singing and demands preparation and technique at virtuoso level. When [an actor with] a well-trained voice and a virtuoso delivery speaks his lines in good clear tones, he conquers me with his mastery. When he has a sense of rhythm and involuntarily marks the rhythm and the phonetics of his speech he excites me. When an actor goes to the heart of letters, words, phrases, thoughts, he carries me with him into the deep secrets of the author's work and into his own soul. When he uses clear sound to paint and inflexions to outline his inner life, he makes me see the images and pictures his creative imagination has shaped and his words describe, with my inner eye.

'When an actor is master of his movements and uses them to complement what his words and voice are saying, I think I hear a proper accompaniment to fine singing. A good male voice delivering its lines is like a cello or an oboe. An actress's chest notes remind me of a violin or a flute, while the bass rumble of a dramatic actor's [voice] reminds me of a viola, or a viola d'amore coming in. The rich bass voice of a "noble father" sounds like a bassoon, while the villain's voice is a trombone which cracks under its own force and bubbles within because of the saliva that has built up, out of spite.

'How is it actors don't feel a whole orchestra in human speech?'

....

'Words and phrases have such possibilities! What richness there is in language. It is powerful not in its own right but in so far as it contains human heart and thought!'

....

'[Just] as the universe is created out of atoms, so words are put together out of letters, and phrases out of words, and thoughts out of phrases, and whole scenes out of thoughts, and acts out of scenes, and plays of great moment out of acts, plays which contain the tragic life of the human spirit, of Hamlet, Othello, Chatski and others. That is a whole symphony!'

2.[8]

.. .. 19..

1.

Today there was a sign hanging in the auditorium:

STAGE SPEECH

As usual Tortsov congratulated us on reaching this new phase in our work, then said:

'In the previous class I told you that you must feel letters and syllables and be sensitive to their true nature.

'Today, we shall discuss complete words and phrases in the same way.'

....

After a pause for thought, Tortsov continued:

'I have warned you many times that anyone going on the stage has to learn everything from scratch – to look, walk, do, make contact and, finally, to speak. Most people speak badly, poorly in daily life but aren't aware of it. We are used to our faults. I don't think you are an exception to this rule. And so, before you start work on the next phase in our work, you must recognize your own faults, so you can break free of the common actors' habit of referring back to yourself and taking your own, incorrect, daily speech as a model to justify even worse speech onstage.

'Speech is in an even worse state onstage than in life. In the vast majority of cases actors state their lines decently or tolerably well. But their speech is still crude and conventional.

'There are many reasons for this of which the first is:

'In life they usually speak for some purpose, some goal, some need, to perform some genuine, productive, specific verbal action. And even in those rare cases when they gabble the words without thinking about them, they do it for a reason: to make the time go faster, to distract attention, etc.

'But the stage is different. There we speak someone else's, the author's, lines. Often they're not what we need or want to say.

'And, in life, we speak in response to what we see physically or mentally, to what we genuinely feel and think, and actually sense things which really exist. Onstage we have to talk about what our characters live, see, feel, not what we ourselves see, feel and think.

'In life we listen properly because we're interested, or because we have to. Onstage, most times, we only represent being attentive, we make a show of listening. There is no practical necessity for us to get into someone else's mind or take in another actor's lines. We have to force ourselves to do it. But this often results in playacting, stock-in-trade and clichés.

'There are also other tiresome conventions which destroy living human communication. Lines that have been repeated over and over again in rehearsal and frequent performance are rattled off. Then their inner content vanishes and only the mechanics remain. To win the right to be onstage, you must do something positive. One way of filling the dead spots in a role is to rattle off the lines mechanically.

'The result is that actors get used to speaking mechanically onstage, i.e. to mouthing the lines meaninglessly, with no thought for their essence and the more you indulge in this habit, the stronger mechanical memory becomes and the more stubborn the habit of gabbling.

'Gradually a specific stock stage speech develops.

'It is said that we meet the same mechanical mouthing of words in life. For example: "Hallo. How are you?" "Fine, I'm happy to say." "See you soon. Keep well."

'Mechanical speech is particularly apparent in prayers. For example, someone I know in his declining years, thought that "Hail Mary, full of grace" was two words not five.

'What do people think about, what do they feel when they are mechanically mouthing these words? Nothing that has anything to do with their sense. They just come out while we're distracted by other thoughts and feelings. The same thing happens with an acolyte priest in church. While his tongue is mechanically repeating the prayers in praise of God his mind is at home. You see the same thing in school. While the pupil is repeating the lesson he has learned parrot-fashion, he is thinking about the grade he's going to get. It's the same in the theatre. When an actor rattles off his lines, he is thinking about irrelevancies, he speaks full pelt to fill the empty, unfelt gaps in his role, to keep the audience occupied so they don't get bored. Then, he speaks for the sake of speaking, with no concern for the sounds or the sense either, only so that the process of speaking itself is lively and fiery.

'For those actors, the character's ideas and feelings are step-children. The real children are the lines themselves. When they read the play for the first time the dialogue they and their fellow actors have seems interesting, new, important. But once they're used to them, worn threadbare through rehearsal, the lines lose their savour, their sense. They're not even stored in their minds, in their hearts, only in the articulatory muscles. After that, what they, or others, say isn't important. The important thing is to rattle the lines off non-stop without a gap between.

'It is totally senseless when actors don't listen to what's been said to them, or asked of them, or don't give other actors time to speak their most important thoughts, or even cut across the end. Then the key word is fudged, it doesn't reach you. The entire thought loses its meaning and there's nothing to reply to. You feel like asking them to repeat their question but there's no point because they haven't any idea what it was they were asking. All these lies create the conventions, the clichés which destroy the credibility of what is being said or felt. It is even worse when actors deliberately misread their lines. We all know how many of us exploit the lines to show how good our vocal equipment, our diction, our rhetoric, our articulation are. Actors like that have only a very tenuous relationship to art. No better than employees in music shops who throw off flashy trills and runs on every conceivable kind of instrument, not to convey the composer's work and their understanding of it, but to demonstrate the quality of the merchandise.

'Actors, too, use the voice to make ingenious cadences and decorative figures. They sing individual letters and syllables, drag them out, howl them, but not with any idea of genuine action, or of conveying their experiences, only to show off their voices and titillate the audience's eardrums.'

.. .. 19..

Today's class was spent on the Subtext.

'Only when the whole line of the Subtext runs through our feelings, like an underground spring, can we create the Throughaction of the character and the play. This is effected not only through physical movement but through speech. You can take action not only with your body but with sounds and words as well.

'What we call Throughline in action, we call Subtext in speech.

'Need I add that a word that is not filled from within and is taken in isolation is mere sound, little cries?

'Dialogue which is made up of little cries is a sequence of empty sounds.

'Take, for example, the Russian word "lyublyu".[9] This strikes foreigners as comic because of its unusual combination of sounds. For them it is empty, because it is not related to beautiful inner images which lift the heart. But once feeling, thought and imagination have brought empty sounds to life, the attitude towards them changes, the word has content. Then these sounds, "lyublyu", can inspire passion and change lives. When the word "forward" is brought to life by patriotic feelings it can send whole regiments to certain death. The simplest words, which convey complex thoughts, can change our whole outlook on life. It is no accident that words are the most concrete expression of human thought.

'Words can also stimulate our five senses. All you need to do is recall the name of a piece of music or an artist, a dish, a favourite perfume and so on and you revive aural and visual images, the smells, tastes, tactile sensations of which the words speak.

'They can also stimulate painful sensations. For example, there is a case in the book *My Life in Art* when a story about toothache produced toothache in the listener.

'There should be no soulless, emotionless words in the theatre. Neither should there be unthinking, actionless words. Words must excite all manner of feelings, wants, thoughts, intentions, creative ideas, aural and visual images, and other sensory experiences in the actors and their partners and, through them, the audience.

'This means that the words, the dialogue, aren't valuable in and for themselves but for their content, their subtext. We often forget that when we go on.

'Nor should we forget that the published play is not a complete work until it has been performed by actors and brought to life by their living, human feelings, just as a piece of music is not a symphony until it has been performed by an orchestra.

'As soon as musicians and actors bring the subtext to life with their own experiences, the secret hiding places, the essence of the work they are performing, the reason it was created, become apparent both in the subtext itself and in themselves. The meaning of a work of art lies in its Subtext. Without it words are ineffectual onstage. When we create a performance the words are the author's and the subtext is ours. If it were otherwise, the audience wouldn't make an effort to come to the theatre to see the actor. They'd stay at home and read the play instead.

'You can only come to know a dramatic work in all its fullness of meaning in the theatre. Only there can you feel the real, living heart of the play, the subtext that has been created by the actor and is re-experienced in every show.

'Actors must set the play to the music of their own feelings and learn to sing that music through the lines they are given to speak. Only when we listen to the melody of the living heart can we fully appreciate the worth and beauty of the text and what it contains.

'You know from your own first year of study all about the inner line of feeling and its Throughaction, the Supertask, which you create through experiencing. You also know how to draw all these lines together and how to arouse experiences by your psycho-technique when they don't arise spontaneously, intuitively.

'This whole process applies to words and speech but with one important addition. We shall have to spend several classes on it. So, until next time.'

.. .. 19..

'Cloud . . . war . . . kite . . . lilac,' Tortsov pronounced each word flatly with a long pause in between. That was how today's class started.

'What happens when your ear receives these sounds? Let's take "cloud", for example. What memories, feelings, images come to you when I say [this] word?'

I had an image of one huge, smoke-coloured blot in a clear summer sky.

Marya saw a long, white sheet stretched right across the sky.

'Now, let's examine the effect the sentence "Let's go to the station" has when your ear catches it.'

In my mind, I left my house, took a cab, drove along Dmitovka Street, along the boulevards, along Myasitskoi Street, reached Sadovaya Boulevard by some sidestreets and soon found myself at the station. Leo saw himself pacing up and down the platform. As for Varya, she even managed to take a mental trip to Yalta, Alupka and Gursuf. After we had told Tortsov about our mental images he spoke to us once more:

'So, I had barely spoken a few words before you immediately filled out their meaning in your minds. And you described your response to my sentence with such care!

'The way you used sound and inflexions to portray your visual images so we could see them with your eyes! What an effort you made to choose your words and colour them differently. You wanted so much to make your sentences fully rounded.

'The care you took to ensure that the picture you conveyed was close to the original, that is to the mental images which the imaginary trip to the station produced in you.

'If you went through this process onstage, every time, with the same affection and spoke your lines with such deep insight into their meaning, you would soon become great actors.'

After a short pause, Tortsov started to repeat the word 'cloud' in different ways and asked us which kind of cloud he was talking about. We guessed more or less correctly. We saw the cloud as a light haze, a fantastical vision, a frightening thundercloud, etc.

How did Tortsov convey these various images? Through inflexions? Facial expression? His own attitude to the image he was creating? By his eyes, which seemed to be looking for the non-existent object on the ceiling?

'This way, that way, five ways, twenty different ways,' Tortsov told us. 'Ask nature, the subconscious, intuition, anything you like, how they communicate their mental images. I don't like, I am very wary about framing precise questions that lie outside my competence. So, we won't get in the way of the subconscious when it's working but rather learn how to involve our natural mental processes in our creative work, and ensure that our vocal, aural, indeed, all the mechanisms of physical embodiment by which we communicate our feelings, thoughts, mental images, etc., are sensitive and receptive.

'It's not difficult to communicate more or less clearly defined mental pictures such as "kite", "lilac", "cloud" in words. But it's much more difficult with words which express abstractions like "justice" or "right". It's interesting to observe what happens mentally when we speak [these words].'

I started to think about the words we'd been given and made myself examine the sensations they produced.

At first I was confused, not knowing where to concentrate, what to fix on, and so my thoughts and feelings, my imagination and all the other mental elements cast about wildly.

My intellect tried to figure out the subject matter and investigated its meaning. I had a vague awareness of something large, important, bright and noble but these adjectives had blurred edges, too. Then I recalled several commonly accepted definitions the concepts 'justice' and 'right' suggested.

But lifeless definitions aren't enough, they're not exciting. Vague feelings flashed through my mind and then were gone. I grabbed at them but couldn't hold on to them.

I needed something more tangible to pin down this abstract concept. It was my imagination more than all the other psychological elements which, in the middle of all this wild searching, responded by drawing a picture for me.

But how do you represent 'justice' or 'right'? By using symbols, allegory, emblems. Memory sifted through all the hackneyed images that are supposed to personify the idea of justice and right.

They showed a woman with scales in her hand and an open law book with a finger pointing at one of the paragraphs.

But that didn't satisfy my intellect or my feelings either. Then my imagination quickly created new visual images – a life built on the pillars of justice and right. It was easier to believe in a story like that than in a bodiless abstraction. Make-believe about real life is more concrete, more accessible, more tangible. It is easier to see and, once seen, feel. It moves you much more quickly and leads quite naturally to re-experiencing.

Recalling instances from my own life, akin to the picture my imagination had drawn, the [concept] 'justice' took definite shape.

When I told Tortsov about my observation of myself he drew the following conclusion:

'Nature has so ordered things that when we are in verbal communication with someone we first see the things we are talking about with our own inner eye and then say what we have seen. If we are listening, then, first of all, our ears take in what is being said and then we see what we have heard with our eye.

'In our vocabulary to hear means to see what is being talked about, and to speak means to draw visual images.

'For actors, words aren't mere sounds, but stimuli to images. So, when in verbal communication, we speak not so much to the ear as to the eye.

'So, from today's class you have learned that we need an illustrated not a plain subtext for the role and the play.'

'How do we create it?'

'We'll talk about that next time.'

In today's class Tortsov called on Pasha and asked him to speak something. But Pasha is no hack, he doesn't have any audition pieces.

'In that case, go onstage and speak these sentences, or rather, tell the whole story:

'I've just been to see Vanya. He's in a terrible state. His wife has run off. We have to go to [a friend] and ask him to help us calm the poor man down.'

Pasha spoke the sentences but they didn't work. Tortsov said to him:

'I didn't believe a word you said. I didn't feel you needed or even wanted to say words which someone else had given you.

'And no wonder. Can you say them if your creative ideas, magic "ifs" and the Given Circumstances don't create mental images for you? You need to know them, see them with your inner eye. But at the moment you don't know or see what's suggested by what I said about Vanya or his friend. Think about the creative idea, the magic "if", the Given Circumstances that will grant you the right to say these words. And don't just know, but try to see clearly the picture your creative idea produces.

'Once you've done this, the words you've been given will become a necessary part of you. You'll know who this Vanya, whose wife has left him, is, who this friend is, where they live, what the relationship between them and you is. [When you] see them with your own inner eye and picture where, how and with whom they live, Vanya and his friend will become real people in the imaginary life you have created. And remember, take a detailed look with your inner eye at their apartments, the layout of the rooms, the furniture, the small objects and how they are arranged. You will then have to go to Vanya's home, then to his friend's and then to the place where you have to say the words you have been given.

'That means you have to see the streets you go through in your mind, the doors to the houses you have to enter. In a word, you have to create and see on the screen of your inner eye everything you've imagined, all the magic and other "ifs", all the Given Circumstances, the outward situation in which the subtext of Vanya's domestic tragedy unfolds and which the words you have been given describe. Mental images create a mood which evokes corresponding feelings. In life, as you know, all this is set up in advance by life itself, but onstage we have to take care of it for ourselves.

'We don't do this just to be naturalistic or realistic but because our creative nature, our subconscious need it. They need truth, even a fictitious truth which we can believe and live.'

Once he'd found credible ideas Pasha repeated the sentence he'd been given and I thought said it better.

But Tortsov still wasn't satisfied and said that Pasha still didn't have an object to which he wished to communicate his mental images and that without that he couldn't speak the sentence so that both he and the listener believed the words had to be said.

To help him Tortsov sent Marya onstage as his object and said:

'Make certain that your object not only hears and understands the meaning of the sentence, but also sees with her inner eye what you see, or almost, when you speak the words you've been given.'

But Pasha didn't think that was possible.

'Don't start thinking about it, that will block nature. Try to do what you've been asked. It isn't the result that matters. That doesn't depend on you. What matters is your intention to complete the task, what matters is the action, or rather, the attempt to act on Marya, on her inner eye which is what you are dealing with at the moment. What is important is inner activity!'

This is Pasha's explanation of what he felt and experienced during the experiment.

'I'll indicate the typical moments,' he explained.

'Before communicating with the object I first had to select and arrange the matter to be communicated, that is analyse its meaning, recall the facts I had to discuss, the Given Circumstances I had to consider, and establish my own mental images in my mind's eye.

'Once I was fully prepared and wanted to embody them everything started to bubble and seethe inside: mind, feeling, imagination, adaptations, facial expression, eyes, hands, body tried to find the angle from which to approach the Task. They were like a large orchestra tuning up quickly. I kept a close watch.'

'On them, not the object?' Tortsov enquired. 'Evidently it didn't matter to you whether Marya understood you or not, whether she felt your subtext, saw everything that was happening in Vanya's life with your eyes or not. That means when you were in contact you forgot this natural, essential, human task – implanting your mental images in someone else.

'This indicates a lack of dynamism. If you had really been trying to communicate you wouldn't have spoken the lines straight through, like a speech, without looking at the other actor, as you did just now, but would have waited at moments. The object needs these breaks so as to register the subtext you are conveying and your mental images. You can't take them in all at once. The process requires three parts: transmission, pause, reception and, again, transmission, pause, reception, etc. Things which are obvious to you, the person experiencing, are new to the object and require to be decoded and registered. And that takes a certain amount of time. But you didn't do that and thanks to all these mistakes you didn't have a conversation with a living person, as in life, but a speech, as in the theatre.'

Finally Tortsov got Pasha to do what he wanted, i.e. made him convey what he was thinking and feeling to Marya. She understood, or rather, felt his subtext, as did, to some extent, the rest of us.

Pasha was in his seventh heaven and assured us all that today he had not only understood but also felt the practical meaning, the true significance of communicating the mental images of the illustrated Subtext.

'Now you understand what an illustrated Subtext means,' said Tortsov at the end of the class.

All the way home Pasha told me what he had experienced while he was doing the 'Vanya' exercise. Evidently what impressed him most was the fact that the Task of influencing someone else's mind with his own mental images had imperceptibly transformed alien, irritating, boring words into something personal, essential for him.

'You see,' he said, 'if you don't explain the fact that Vanya's wife has deserted him, there's no story. And if there's no story, there's nothing from which to create an illustrated subtext.

'That means mental images are not necessary either and there's no reason to communicate them to someone else.

'But, you see, you can't convey Vanya's sad story just by mental images, emanation, movements or facial expression. You need words.

'That was the moment when the words I'd been given became imperative! That was the moment when I fell in love with them as if they were my own! I grabbed them, relished, treasured every sound, loved every inflexion. Now I needed them, not so I could deliver them mechanically, or show off my voice and diction but for a purpose, so that the listener could understand the importance of what I was saying.

'And, you know, the most wonderful thing of all', he continued enthusiastically, 'is that as soon as the words became my own, I felt at home onstage. And from that sprang calm and control.

'How great it feels to be master of yourself, to win the right to go slow and make other people wait.

'I planted one word after another in the object, one mental image after another. You can appreciate better than anyone how important, how significant the calm and control I felt was because we both are fearful of a gap onstage.'

Pasha's story captivated me. I went home with him and stayed for a meal.

As usual, as we were eating, Old Shustov asked his nephew what had happened in class. Pasha told him what he'd already told me. His uncle listened, smiled, nodded approvingly, accompanying each nod with:

'Yes, yes! That's right.'

Then, after something Pasha said, his uncle suddenly jumped up and, waving his fork in the air, shouted:

'You've hit the nail on the head! Affect the object! "Steal into his very heart."[10] And you'll affect yourself even more. And if you affect yourself, you'll affect others even more. Then your words will be like strong wine. And why is that? It's our grandmother nature, the actress! It's our grandfather, the miracle worker – our subconscious!!!

'They would stir the dead to action! Dynamism in creative work, that's the steam in the engine!

'*Dynamism, genuine, productive, purposeful action is the most important thing in creative work and in speech too!*

'*Speaking is action. Dynamism gives us the task of planting our mental images in someone else. It doesn't matter whether the other person sees them or not. Mother-nature and father-subconscious will take care of that.* Your business is wanting to plant and the wanting generates action.

'It's one thing to go out in front of a respectful audience and reel off "tum-ti-tum", "tum-ti-tum" and exit. It's quite another to get down to business and be active!

'The first way of speaking is "theatrical", the second, human.

'We not only feel these parts of our lives but see them with our mind's eye.'

.. .. 19..

'When we think, picture, remember some event, object, action, moments in our real or imaginary lives, we see them in our mind's eye,' [said Tortsov].

'However, it is essential that all our mental images relate exclusively to the character and not to the actor, because his life won't match the role unless it is actually very similar to it.

'That is why our main concern in performance is that our mind's eye should always reflect mental images which relate to the character. The mental images our imagination creates, the given circumstances, which bring the role alive and justify its actions, intentions, thoughts and feelings and maintain and fix the actor's attention on the inner life of the role. We must use them when concentration wanders, draw it to the "film" and make it follow that line.

'Last time we worked on a little speech about Vanya and his friend,' Tortsov said today. 'But imagine that we have worked on every line, every scene, the whole play in just the same way, as we should when creating illustrated "ifs" and Given Circumstances. Then the whole script is accompanied by mental images in our mind's eye just in the way the actor pictured them. Out of these, as I explained to you earlier, when I was talking about imagination, we create a whole unbroken film that is projected onto the screen of our mind's eye. It guides us while we are saying or doing something onstage.

'Watch it as closely as possible, use your lines to describe what you see, as though you were seeing the illustrations for the first time at every performance. Talk onstage about mental images, we don't [rattle off] the lines.

'For that, you have to dig deep into the meaning of the words you are saying, and feel them. But this is a difficult process and we don't always get it right, first because one of the main elements of the subtext is the memory of previous experiences which are very elusive and capricious and difficult to pin down, and second because constant digging into the meaning of words and the subtext requires a well-disciplined memory.

'Forget about feeling altogether and concentrate solely on mental images. Look at them closely and describe what you see and hear as fully, deeply and clearly as possible.

'This technique is far stronger, more stable in moments of dynamism, of action. The lines aren't spoken for their own sake or for the audience but for the other actors, to implant your mental images. That means actions must be carried right through. They bring the will into play and with it the three psychological motivators, and all the elements of the actor's creative soul.

'Why shouldn't we use the best in our visual memory? A series of mental images is more accessible to us and once we have fixed it firmly in our heads it is easier to maintain concentration on the true line of the *Subtext and the Through-action*. When we stick to that line and only talk about what we see, we stimulate the recurring feelings which are stored in our emotion memory, and which we need for experiencing, in the right way.

'Thus, when we observe our mental images we are thinking about the subtext of the role and are feeling it.

'This technique isn't new. We used similar methods when dealing with movement and action. We used tangible, stable physical actions to stimulate our unstable emotion memory and established the unbroken line of the "life of the human body in a role".

'Now we use the same technique, for the same reason and use an unbroken line of mental images and describe them in words.

'Previously physical action was a decoy for feelings and experiences and now inner mental images are a decoy for feelings and experiences in words and speech.

'Project the film your mind's eye has made as often as you can. Draw what you see like a painter, describe what you see and how you see it like a writer in today's performance. Then you will know, understand the meaning of the words you are to speak.

'There should be variations each time these mental images occur and each time you describe them. That's all to the good because the impromptu and the unexpected are the best stimuli to creative work. Only be sure always to watch the film of your mental images before you talk of them and implant them in the person you are in contact with.

'You have to drum this habit in through long, systematic work. On days when your concentration is weak and the line of the subtext you have established can be easily broken, latch onto the objects in your mind's eye as to a lifebelt.

'And there's another advantage of this technique. As we know, lines can become mere chatter because we have repeated them too often. But visual images, on the other hand, gain in strength and breadth through frequent repetition.

'The imagination doesn't sleep but fills out the mental images with new details, fills out the film in the mind's eye bringing it even more alive. So, repetition is advantageous, not disadvantageous, to our mental images and the whole illustrated subtext.

'Now you not only know how to establish and use the illustrated subtext but also the secret of the psychotechnique I have recommended to you.'

.. .. 19..

'So, one mission words have in the theatre is to communicate our illus-trated subtext to the other actors or to see completely ourselves each time,' Tortsov said at the beginning of the class.

'Let's see if Leo's speech fulfils this mission.

'Go up onstage and speak anything you like.'

'Isweartoyoubelovedthat / Icanonlyliveonearth / withtheealoneand . . . / willdiewhenthouleav'stmefortheshadesof / hellwherewe / shallmeet-again,' Leo declaimed in his usual gabble, with meaningless pauses that broke the prose up into bad verse and the verse into even worse prose.

'I didn't understand a thing and won't if you go on breaking up the lines the way you did just now,' Tortsov said to him. 'When you deliver lines like that we can't talk seriously about a Subtext or even a text. With you it all just rolls off the tongue haphazard. Will and consciousness aren't involved. It depends on the amount of air you have to breathe out.

'So, before you go on, we have to put some order into the lines and put them into proper groups, or families or, as some people put it, speech bars. Only then can we tell which word relates to which and understand the parts which go to make up the sentence, or the whole thought.

'To break speech down into bars you need stops, or, in other words, logical pauses.

'As you doubtless know, they have two opposite but simultaneous functions: to bring words together in groups (or speech bars) and to divide the groups off from one another.

'Do you know that a man's fate can depend on where the logical pauses are placed? For example:

' "Pardon impossible send to Siberia."

'How are we to understand this order before it has been divided up by logical pauses?

'Put them in and then the meaning of the words will become clear.

' "Pardon / Impossible send to Siberia" or "Pardon impossible / Send to Siberia." In the first instance we have mercy, in the second, exile.

'Put the pauses into your speech and do it again. Only then will we understand its content.'

With Tortsov's help Leo divided the sentence into groups of words and started to say it again but Tortsov stopped him after the second bar.

'The text between two logical pauses should be spoken with as few breaks as possible, all together, almost as a single word. You mustn't break up the text and spit it out in bits, as you are doing.

'There are, of course, exceptions, when you have to stop in the middle of a bar. But there are rules for that which I will explain to you at the right moment.'

'We know what they are,' Grisha objected. 'Speech bars are read according to the punctuation. We learned that, if you don't mind my saying so, in primary school.'

'If you know, then speak correctly,' Tortsov responded. 'And speak as well as you possibly can onstage too.

'Pick up a book and a pencil whenever you can, read, and break up what you have read into speech bars. Train your ears, your eyes, your hands. Reading by speech bars has one, major practical advantage: it helps the actual process of experiencing.

'Marking out in speech bars and reading by them is also essential because it makes you analyse sentences and look into their meaning. If you don't look into them, you can't speak them properly.

'The habit of speaking in bars not only gives what you say harmony of form and clarity of expression but depth of content because it makes you think all the time about the meaning of what you are saying. Until you've done that it is pointless your undertaking one of the major Tasks words fulfil, i.e. communicating *the illustrated Subtext of a speech* not even the preliminary work, creating mental images to illustrate the subtext.

'Work on speech and words must always start with dividing up into speech bars, or, in other words, placing the logical pauses.'

.. .. 19..

Today, Tortsov called on me and told me to speak something. I chose a speech from *Othello*:

> Like to the Pontic sea,
> Whose icy current and compulsive course
> Ne'er feels retiring ebb, but keeps due on
> To the Propontic and the Hellespont,
> Even so my bloody thoughts with violent pace
> Shall ne'er look back, ne'er ebb to humble love
> Till that a capable and wide revenge
> Swallow them up.

There's not one full stop and the sentence is so long I had to say it fast. It seemed to me I had to deliver it like a broadside, without a pause for breath. But, of course, I couldn't do it.

Small wonder then that I squashed some bars together, got breathless and red in the face from sheer effort.

'To avoid what's just happened in the future, first get help from logical pauses and divide the lines up into speech bars, because, as you can see, you can't say them in one,' Tortsov suggested after I'd finished.

Here's how I distributed the breaks:

> Like to the Pontic sea\
> Whose icy current and compulsive course\
> Ne'er feels retiring ebb\ but keeps due on
> To the Propontic and the Hellespont\
> Even so my bloody thoughts with violent pace\
> Shall ne'er look back ne'er ebb to humble love\
> Till that a capable and wide revenge
> Swallow them up.

'Fine,' said Tortsov and made me repeat this exceptionally long sentence several times over, following the speech bars I had marked.

After I'd done that, he acknowledged that the lines were a little easier to hear and to understand.

'Pity you still don't feel them though,' he added.

'You're your own worst enemy, because you're in such a hurry you don't give yourself time to get inside what you're saying, you never manage to explore and feel the subtext under the words. And without that, you're stuck.

'That's why the first thing is to stop rushing.'

'I'd be happy to, but how?' I asked, totally bewildered.

'I'll show you one way of doing it.'

After a short pause he continued:

'You have learned to do a speech from *Othello* using logical pauses and speech bars. That's good. Now, speak it for me again using the punctuation.

'The punctuation marks call for special inflexions. The full stop, the comma, the question and exclamation marks, etc. have their own characteristic vocal shapes and cannot function properly without them. If the voice doesn't drop at the full stop, the listener won't understand that the sentence has come to an end. If you don't give the question mark its characteristic phonic "curve", the listener won't understand a question is being asked and requires an answer.

'These inflexions have an effect on the listener and require them to do something: a questioning phonic shape requires an answer, an exclamation mark a sympathetic response, agreement, or protest; a colon requires you to concentrate on what comes after, etc. There is great expressive power in all these inflexions.

'*Words and speech have their own nature which requires a corresponding inflexion for each punctuation mark.* The inherent qualities of the punctuation marks will help calm you down and stop you rushing. That's why I'm spending so much time over them.

'Do Othello's speech for me, using the punctuation marks, the commas and full stops and their natural inflexions.'

When I began to say the speech I felt as though I was reading a foreign language. Before I could say a word I had to weigh it, search around, speculate, mask anything that caused me doubt, and . . . stopped because I just couldn't go on.

'This demonstrates that you don't know the nature of your own language and, in particular, the nature of punctuation marks. Otherwise you could easily have done what I asked.

'Remember what's happened. It should be another reminder of how essential it is to study the laws of speech thoroughly.

'So, right now the punctuation marks are a hindrance to your speaking. Let's try and do the opposite and make them help you!

'I can't [solve] the problem of all the punctuation marks,' Tortsov continued.

'And so, for demonstration purposes, I'll experiment with one of them. If the experiment is successful, I'm sure you'll want to explore the nature of all the other punctuation marks for yourself, in the same way.

'I repeat, my task isn't to teach you, but rather to persuade you to study the laws of speech for yourself. I'll take the comma for your experiment because it is practically the only one at work in the speech you have chosen.

'Do you recall what you instinctively want to do at each comma? First of all, of course, stop. But before that, you want an upward inflexion on the last syllable of the last word (not stressing it if it isn't logically necessary). Then you leave the last note hanging in the air for a while.

'Inflecting the sound upwards is like moving something from a lower to a higher shelf. These upward inflexions can be of different shapes and heights: in intervals of a third, a fifth, or an octave. The rise can be short and steep or broad, smooth and gradual and so on.

'The most remarkable thing about a comma is that it possesses a miraculous quality. Its upward rise is like a hand raised in warning. It forces the listener to wait patiently for the unfinished sentence to continue. Can you see how important that is for nervous people like you, or impetuous people like Leo? If you believe that after an upward inflexion on a comma the listener will wait patiently for you, then you have no reason to be in a hurry. That not only calms you down, it forces you to love the comma and all its natural attributes.

'If you knew the satisfaction when telling a long story or speaking a long sentence, like the one you spoke just now, to make an upward inflexion before the comma and wait confidently, knowing for certain that no one will interrupt or rush you.

'The same thing happens with the other punctuation marks. As with the comma, they place certain demands on the listener. For example, a question requires the listener to answer . . .

'An exclamation mark demands a sympathetic response . . . (once again we waited patiently as before) . . . a colon . . . increases another actor's concentration as he waits for what comes after. This temporary transfer of responsibility to someone else guarantees you stay calm as it is the listener who now needs the pauses, which made you nervous and hasty. Do you agree?'

Tortsov ended his sentence, his question with a sharp upward inflexion and waited for an answer. We tried to find something to say but couldn't and became quite worried but he stayed perfectly calm because it wasn't his problem.

Tortsov laughed all through the pause and then explained why.

'Not long ago, I was trying to explain to a maid where to hang the key to the front door. I told her: "Yesterday evening, passing through the hall, I saw the key in the lock . . ." '

'Having made a huge upward inflexion I forgot what I was going to say, and silently went into my study.

'A good five minutes passed when I heard a knock. The maid's head appeared round the door with an expression of curiosity on her face. "You saw the key in the lock, what then?" she enquired.

'As you can see, the upward inflexion before a comma was operative for five whole minutes. There had to be a drop in the voice at the full stop for the sentence to end. This requirement will not be denied.'

At the end of class, summarizing what we'd done Tortsov prophesied that I would soon stop being afraid of pauses because I had learned the secret of making other people wait for me. And when I understood how to use pauses to increase the clarity, expressiveness and power of my speech and stronger closer contact with others, I would not only stop being afraid of pauses, I would learn to like them and indeed, misuse them.

.. .. 19..

Tortsov entered in high spirits and suddenly, for no reason at all, told us very calmly but quite firmly and categorically:

'If you don't pay proper attention to me, I will not continue to work with you.'

We were stunned. We didn't know what to think. We looked at each other and were about to assure him that we weren't just interested in his classes, we were enthusiastic about them but didn't get the chance. Tortsov burst out laughing.

'Can't you see what a good mood I'm in?' he asked, very lively. 'I couldn't be happier because I've just read in the newspaper that one of my favourite pupils has had a huge success. But I only had to produce the inflexions, words and speech, which, by their very nature, are required to convey decisiveness, firmness, implacability and I turned into a harsh, ill-tempered schoolmaster!!

'There are mandatory inflexions and phonic shapes not only for individual words and punctuation marks but for whole phrases and sentences as well.

'They have a definite, natural form. They have specific names.

'For example, the inflexion I just used is called, in the book *The Expressive Word*,[11] a "double bend sentence". There is a vocal rise to the top and a comma which coincides with the logical pause, then a momentary hiatus, after which the voice drops sharply downward to the lowest point. This diagram shows what I mean.

'This is a mandatory inflexion. There are many other phonetic shapes which govern whole sentences but I won't demonstrate them to you as I am not teaching this subject, merely discussing it.

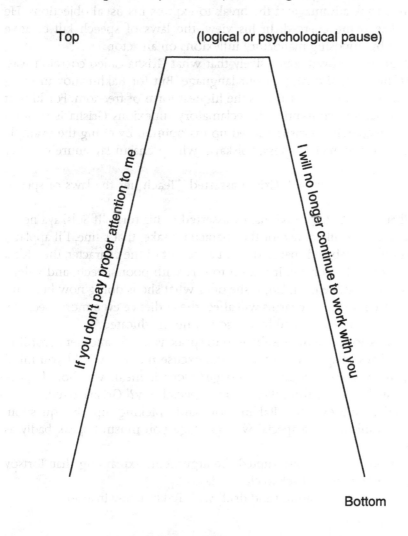

Top   (logical or psychological pause)

If you don't pay proper attention to me

I will no longer continue to work with you

Bottom

'Actors need to know all these phonetic shapes and here's one of many reasons:

'Onstage, when we are feeling self-conscious, often our vocal range shrinks and our speech loses its shape.'

....

'How do we rectify this? There is no way out for people who don't know the mandatory phonic shapes for given phrases.

'The laws of speech can be of help here.

'So, if your inflexions betray you, go from the outer, phonic shape to its justification and thence to the natural process of re-experiencing.'

Just then Tortsov's noisy secretary came in and called him away.

Tortsov left, saying he would be back in ten minutes.

Grisha took advantage of the break to express his usual objections. He didn't like being coerced. In his view, the laws of speech kill creative freedom by imposing mandatory inflexions on an actor.

Rakhmanov proved conclusively that what Grisha called coercion was, in fact, the natural quality of our language. But for Rakhmanov meeting the demands of nature is always the highest form of freedom. For him, it is the unnatural, conventional, declamatory inflexions Grisha is so fond of that are coercion. Grisha backed up his opinion by citing the example of a certain provincial actress, Solskaya, whose charm lay entirely in her wayward speech.

'That's her, you know!' Grisha asserted. 'Teach her the laws of speech and she won't exist.'

'What a good idea!' Rakhmanov asserted in his turn. 'If Solskaya needs to speak in a peculiar way for the character's sake, that's fine. I'll applaud her. But if her debased speech doesn't arise out of the character, then it's a minus, not a plus for her. It is a sin to flirt with poor speech, and vulgar. That's what it is! Tell her, lad, if she does what she is doing now but with good speech, then her charms will affect the audience even more. Because, lad, they won't be devalued by her sounding uneducated.'

'I don't know, one time we're told to speak as in life, another according to some laws of speech or other. Look, excuse me, but would you mind telling us what we should do onstage? Does it mean we should speak somehow differently from life, in some special way?' Grisha asked.

'Exactly, lad, exactly!' Rakhmanov said, picking up the question. 'Not as in life but in a special way. Onstage you mustn't speak badly as in life.'

The busy secretary interrupted the argument, explaining that Tortsov would not be coming back to class today.

There would be 'training and drill' with Rakhmanov instead.

19

Today I had to do Othello's speech for Tortsov several times, with the sound properly inflected before each comma.

At first these upwards inflexions were mechanical, dead. But then, one of them reminded me of a real-life inflexion and immediately something warm and familiar began to stir inside me.

Encouraged by this, I slowly became more venturesome and started, sometimes successfully sometimes not, to make all sorts of inflexions, sometimes with a short, sometimes with a broad upward swing. And each time I hit on the right phonic shape new and very different emotion memories stirred inside me.

'That's the real basis of vocal technique, something real, organic, not contrived. Words, by their very nature, influence emotion memory, feeling and re-experiencing from the outside, by the way they are inflected,' I thought to myself.

Now I was tempted to hold on to the pause after the upward inflexion so that I could understand and feel the stirrings inside me right through.

Then disaster struck. I was so absorbed in all these feelings, thoughts and experiments I forgot my lines, stopped half-way through with thoughts and lines in a jumble and couldn't finish. Nonetheless, Tortsov praised me highly.

'You see!' he said, happily. 'I hardly had time to tell you you would acquire a taste for pauses before you really started enjoying them! You not only marked all the logical pauses, you communicated many of them psychologically. That's very good, really, and quite legitimate but only provided first, that the psychological pause doesn't supplant the logical pause but enhances it, and, second, that the psychological pause at all times fulfils the tasks allotted to it.

'Otherwise what happened to you is inevitable – theatrical muddle.

'You'll only understand my warning after I've explained what psychological pauses are. While logical pauses automatically create bars and whole sentences and so help make the sense clear, psychological pauses bring these ideas, sentences and bars to life and try to communicate the subtext. If speech without logical pauses is illiterate, without psychological pauses it is inanimate.

'Logical pauses are passive, formal, inactive. Psychological pauses are always dynamic and rich in inner content.

'The logical pause serves the head, the psychological pause the heart.

'The Metropolitan Filaret said: "Let thy words be few, thy silence eloquent."

'Psychological pauses are this eloquent silence. They are an extremely important means of communication. Today, you felt you had to use these silently eloquent pauses for creative ends. Words are replaced by looks, facial expression, transmitting, signs, barely perceptible movements and many other conscious and subconscious means of communication.

'They say what words can't, and often their silent action is more intense, more subtle, more irresistible than speech itself. Their non-verbal utterance can be no less interesting, rich and persuasive than verbal utterance.

'Pauses very often communicate that part of the subtext which comes not only from the conscious mind but from the subconscious and can't be expressed concretely in words.

'These experiences and their mode of expression are, as you are aware, greatly prized in our approach to acting.

'Have you any idea how much we prize psychological pauses?

'They are not subject to any laws. All laws are subject to them.

'You can bring in a psychological pause where it is apparently impossible to stop logically, or grammatically. For example: imagine the company is going on tour. All the students are to make the trip except two. "Who are they?" you ask Pasha, in alarm. "Me and . . ." (psychological pause, to soften the blow or, on the contrary, to increase your alarm) ". . . you," Pasha answers.

'Everyone knows, there's no stop after the conjunction "and". But a psychological pause blithely breaks this law and brings in a pause that hasn't been indicated. And a psychological pause has an even greater right to replace a logical one without destroying it.

'A logical pause is more or less well defined, and of short duration. If it is extended then you must quickly transform an inactive, logical pause into a psychological one. The length of a psychological pause isn't defined. It isn't concerned with the time it takes to do its work, it holds up speech for as long as it needs to perform a genuine, productive, specific action. It is aimed at the Supertask, it follows the line of the Subtext and the Throughaction and, therefore, cannot but be interesting.

'Nonetheless, psychological pauses must be aware of the danger of dragging on too long, which is what happens when productive action stops. Rather than let that happen, they must give way to speech and words.

'It's a pity when you miss the right moment because then the psychological pause degenerates into a mere stop and that creates a theatrical mishap that leaves a gaping hole in the play.

'That's just what happened today and why I'm anxious to explain your mistake to you immediately, so you can avoid it in the future.

'Replace the logical pause with a psychological pause but don't do it unnecessarily.

'Now you know what pauses mean for us in our stage speech. Broadly speaking, you are now in a position to use them. The pause is an important element in our speech and one of its best trump cards.'

.. .. 19..

Tortsov settled himself comfortably in an armchair, sat on his hands, assumed a fixed position and delivered the opening of a speech and then some verse with great expression and passion. He spoke them in an unknown but rich-sounding language. He enunciated the incomprehensible words with great drive and energy, lifting the voice for long passages or dropping it right down, or he was silent saying what couldn't be said in words with his eyes. All this was done with enormous inner power and without shouting. He spoke other passages with particular resonance and roundness of tone, painting a complete picture for us. Other phrases were barely audible but he packed them with experiences and inwardly justified feelings. When he did that he was close to tears and even had to make an expressive pause to master his emotion. Then there was another inner change. His voice rang out and we were astonished by his youthful exuberance. But he unexpectedly cut this transitory outburst short and reverted to silent experiencing.

The verse and prose were of his own devising, as was the phonetic language.

'So,' Tortsov summed up, 'I spoke in a language you couldn't understand but you listened to me attentively. I avoided any movement but you watched me closely. I was silent and you tried very hard to guess what my silence meant. I placed images, thoughts, feelings which seemed connected under the sounds. Of course, this connection was only general, not specific. Naturally the resulting impression was of a similar kind. I achieved this on the one hand through sounds and, on the other, through inflexions and pauses. Doesn't the same thing happen when we listen to poems and dramatic speeches in languages we don't know when foreign actors and singers are on tour? They produce an enormous impression on us, create a mood, move us, don't they? And yet we don't understand a word that's being said.

'Here's another example. Not long ago, one of my friends was enthusing about a poem he had heard actor B. recite in a concert.

' "What did he recite?" I asked him.

' "I don't know," he replied. "I couldn't make out the words."

'Evidently actor B. produces an impression not with words but something else.

'What's the secret? It's the sound-colour of the words. Inflexions and eloquent silence influence the listener, filling out what the words didn't say.

'*Inflexions and pauses exercise a strong emotional influence on the listener in their own right, irrespective of the words.* Witness my delivery in an incomprehensible language, today.'

.. .. 19..

Today, after I'd done Othello's speech once again, Tortsov said to me:

'Now we not only understand the speech, we are beginning to feel it. But still not strongly enough.'

The next time through, I tried to achieve power in a 'theatrical' way. I put my foot on the loud pedal and playacted passion for its own sake. The result, of course, was tension and rush so that I jumbled all the bars together.

'What on earth were you doing?' Tortsov said, throwing up his hands. 'You've destroyed all our work in two minutes flat. You've killed the sense, and the logic too.'

'I wanted to make it more vital, more powerful,' I said, in embarrassed self-justification.

'Power lies in logic and sequence, don't you know that? And you destroyed them. Have you, by any chance, ever heard simple, unadorned speech, onstage or off? No special effort, no rise and fall, no exaggerated intervals, no intricate inflexions?

'Despite the lack of rhetorical devices, simple speaking often produces an indelible impression by the persuasiveness, the clarity of the thoughts expressed, the precision and subtlety of the words, their logic and sequence, their close grouping, the construction of the phrases, the restrained delivery.

'Logical pauses are a living part of all such speech. They increase its power to influence and persuade.

'That's what you should use them for, but you destroy them. To achieve the power you are looking for, learn first to speak logically and sequentially, with proper pauses.'

I quickly went back to the speech the way it was, clean and clear but, as before, it was also dry as dust. I felt as though I were in a vicious circle.

'It's clear to both of us that it's still too early for you to be thinking about power. Power is a combination of many factors. We will try and find them.'

'Where? In what?'

'Different actors understand power differently. There are those, for example, who try to find it in physical tension. They clench their fists and puff up their whole body, they almost go into convulsions to intensify the effect they have on the audience. Their voices, in consequence, are squeezed out in a horizontal line, with the same pressure I am pushing out at you right now.

'In our jargon we call this use of pressure to produce power, high-voltage acting. But this method doesn't produce power, only yelling and shouting, constriction and hoarseness within a limited vocal range.

'Try it out for yourself. Speak a sentence like: "I can endure it no longer" in a few notes, in intervals of a second or third with all the inner power you possess.'

I tried it.

'No, more power!' Tortsov ordered.

I tried again, increasing the power as much as I could.

'More power, more power,' Tortsov urged me. 'Don't expand the vocal range!'

I obeyed. Physical tension turned into spasm. My throat constricted, my range was limited to thirds and I still couldn't achieve an impression of power.

Having used up every resource, I had once more, when pressed by Tortsov, to resort to mere shouting.

It was awful. I sounded as though I were being strangled.

'This is what happens when you use "high-voltage" to produce volume, i.e. expelling sound under pressure along a horizontal line,' Tortsov said.

'Now try another, absolutely opposite, experiment. Get rid of "high-voltage", don't playact passion, don't worry about power but speak the same sentence for me with the maximum vocal range and properly justified inflexions. To do that, imagine Given Circumstances which excite you.'

Here's the idea I had.

If I were a teacher, and one of my pupils, like Grisha, was half an hour late for the third time, what would I do to end such sloppiness?!

The sentence was easy to speak on that basis and my vocal range extended spontaneously and naturally.

'You see, the sentence became stronger than your previous shouting which failed earlier, and no pushing was required,' Tortsov explained.

'Now, speak the same words for me with an even greater range, not in fifths, like last time but in whole, justified octaves.'

I had to devise new given circumstances. So, imagine that despite all my demands, reprimands, notes, warnings and reports, Grisha was late again, only not half an hour but a whole hour. I had tried everything. Now there was only one thing left.

'I can't endure this any longer!' The sentence tore out of me spontaneously, but not loudly. I held back, supposing that my feeling still had some way to go.

'You see!' said Tortsov in great delight. 'It came out powerfully, not loudly and with no pushing. That's what the movement of sounds up and down in, so to speak, a vertical line can do. Without the "high-voltage", the thrust along a horizontal line, as happened last time. When you need power in the future, use a wide variety of upward and downward inflexions, like a piece of chalk making shapes on a blackboard.

'Don't take actors who look for power of speech in loudness as your model. Loudness isn't power, it is just loudness, shouting.

'Loud and not loud are forte and piano. We all know that forte isn't forte in itself, forte is just not piano.

'Conversely, piano isn't piano but not forte.

'What does this mean, forte isn't forte in itself but not piano? It means that forte isn't a fixed quantity like a metre or a kilogram.

'Forte is to be understood relatively.

'Let's suppose you begin the speech quietly. If you speak slightly louder after the first line, that won't be the piano you started with.

'You say the next line louder still so that it will be even less piano than the previous line, etc. until you reach forte. If you increase power step by step you will ultimately reach the highest level of loudness, which can only be described as forte-fortissimo. It is this gradual transformation of sound from piano-pianissimo to forte-fortissimo that constitutes the increase in relative loudness. However, we must be sparing in using the voice in this way. We must have a sense of discretion. Otherwise, it's easy to go over the top.

'There are singers with no taste at all who think that sharp dynamic contrasts are chic. For example, they sing the opening words of Tchaikovski's serenade "In distant Alpuchart . . ." forte-fortissimo and drop the following words "the golden lands" to a barely audible piano-pianissimo. Then, once again, they bawl "the enticing sound of the guitar" forte-fortissimo and immediately continue with "come to me, my dearest" piano-pianissimo. Don't you feel how totally banal and tasteless these contrasts are?

'The same thing happens in straight theatre. There is exaggerated shouting and whispering in tragic moments, regardless of inner meaning and common sense.

'But there are other singers and actors I know, with little voice and fire, who can give the illusion that they are ten times more gifted than they really are by using the contrast of piano and forte.

'Many of them have a reputation for possessing great voices. But they are perfectly well aware what technique and skill are needed to get the results they achieve.

'Loudness, as such, is almost never required onstage. In most cases it is only there to split the ears of the ignorant and profane with a lot of noise.[12]

'So, if you want powerful speech, forget about loudness and think of inflexions, the rise and fall along a vertical line, and pauses.

'Only use loudness briefly, for a concluding sentence or word at the end of a speech, a scene or a play, only when you have exhausted every vocal technique in your armoury – progression, logic, sequence, gradation, every conceivable phonic shape and inflexion, and when the meaning of the sentence calls for it.

'When Tommaso Salvini was asked how he managed to shout so powerfully at his advanced age, he answered: "I don't shout. You do the shouting. I just open my mouth. My business is to work up to the climax slowly and then when this is done, let the audience do their own shouting, if that is what they need."

'There are, however, exceptional circumstances when you have to be loud. In crowd scenes, for example or when speaking to music or with background effects.

'But remember, we need relative dynamics, progression, every gradation of sound, and that hanging on to one or two high notes merely upsets the audience.

'So, what are we to conclude from the examples I have given of different notions of powerful sound in speech? This: that it must be sought not in "high-voltage", not in loudness or shouting, but in the rise and fall of the voice, i.e. in inflexions. And in the contrast between high and low pitch, or in the transition from piano to forte and their interrelationship.'

.. .. 19..

'Varya, go onstage and speak something for us,' Tortsov said, at the beginning of today's class.

She went up onstage and gave us the name of the piece she was going to do:

'Á Góodly Pérson.'

'Just listen to that!' Tortsov shouted. 'Three words, all stressed. The title tells us nothing.

'Speech that is all stress or no stress is meaningless, you know that surely? You can't squander stress like that! Wrongly placed stress distorts the sense, cripples the sentence when it should build it up.

'Stress is an index finger, marking the most important word in the bar. The selected word contains the heart, the essentials of the subtext!

'You still don't understand the importance of stress and that's why you have so little respect for it.

'Learn to love it in the same way some of you came to love pauses and inflexions. Stress is our third trump card in speech.

'Your stress is erratic, onstage or off. It wanders through the lines like sheep through a field. Bring some order to it. Say "person".'

'Pér-són,' Varya enunciated.

'You've gone one better!' Tortsov marvelled. 'Now you have two stresses in one word. Can't you say "pér-son" as one word, not two, with the stress on the first syllable: "pérson"?'

'Péeerson,' our beauty said, making a great effort.

'That's not a stress, it's a bang on the head,' Tortsov joked. 'What makes you think a stress is a wallop? You not only hit the word with your voice, your sound, you round it off with a jerk of your chin and your head. That's a bad habit, and very common among actors. The head and nose are thrust forward as though they could bring out the importance and meaning of the words. Nothing could be simpler.

'But, in fact, it's extremely complex. Stress can be a friendly or hostile, respectful or contemptuous, ambiguous or sarcastic delivery of a syllable or word. It serves it up on a platter.

'Besides,' he continued, 'having split the word "person" in two, you hurl the first part at us like a bursting grenade and then treat the second part with such disregard, practically swallowing it. Let's have one word, one idea, one concept. Let's have a series of sounds together in one common line of sound! You can lift it, drop it, bend it here or there!

'Take a length of wire, bend it upwards a little and you'll get quite a beautiful, expressive line, with a high point, which, like a lightning conductor or a dome, will take the stress while the rest of it forms a pattern. Then the line has form, definition, integrity, unity. That's better than bits of wire scattered all over the place. Try to bend the phonic line of "person" in various tones of voice.'

There was such hubbub you couldn't hear a thing.

'You did what I asked mechanically,' said Tortsov, stopping us. 'You pronounced a few dead sounds which only had an external formal connection. Breathe life into them.'

'What are we supposed to do?' we asked in confusion.

'Above all, make sure the words fulfil the function nature has given them, that they convey thoughts, feelings, ideas, concepts, pictures, mental images and don't just bang against the eardrums.

'Shape the word to the thought, to whomever you're thinking and talking about, whatever you see in your mind's eye. Tell the other actors whether the "person" is beautiful or ugly, big or small, nice or nasty, good or evil.

'Do your utmost to convey what you see or feel through sound, using inflexions and other expressive means.'

Varya tried but it didn't work.

'Your mistake was speaking the words first and only trying to understand what you were saying afterwards. You're not drawing from life. Try it this way round instead: first think of someone you know, set him before you, as an artist does a model, then describe, in words, what you see on the screen of your mind's eye.'

Varya made a conscientious effort to do what she'd been asked.

Tortsov encouraged her and said:

'I don't actually feel who this person you are talking about is, but, for the moment, I'm happy that you're trying to introduce me to him, that you're concentrating where you should, that the word forced you to action, to genuine contact and not just mouthing.

'Now say "a goodly person".'

'A góodly pérson,' she enunciated.

'Once again, you're giving me two different perceptions or characters: one of them is "goodly", the other is just a "person".

'Whereas the two together form one being.

'Now, take the difference between "a góodly . . . person" and the three words run together "agoodlypérson". Listen, I'll stick the adjective and the noun firmly together as one so that we get one concept, one idea, not of a "person", just anybody, but of a "goodly-pérson".'

'The adjective characterizes, colours the noun and so marks this "person" off from all other persons.

'But first, be calm, remove all the stresses and then restore them."

Easier said than done.

'That's it!' Tortsov said, having finally got it out of her after a great deal of work.

'Now,' he instructed her, 'place one stress on the penultimate syllable "goodlypérson". Only don't hit it, please, love it, savour it, carefully highlight the stressed syllable in the selected word.

'Listen, here are the two words with the stress removed: "goodly person". Do you hear how long and boring the sound is, flat as a plank. Now, here are these same connected words but with a tiny, barely perceptible inflexion: "goodly person". There's a slight, a gentle rise in sound on the penultimate syllable "per-".

'There are all manner of devices to help you shape "a goodly person" as naive or decisive, gentle or tough.'

After Varya and all the other students had tried what Tortsov asked, he stopped them and said:

'It's no good listening to your own voices. That's narcissism, exhibitionism. It's not question of how you say it but of how other people hear and understand it. "Listening to yourself" is a false task. Influencing other people, conveying mental images to them is an infinitely more important task. So, don't speak to the ear but to the eye. That's the best way to avoid "listening to yourself" which endangers creative work, confuses you and diverts you from the active path.'

.. .. 19..

Tortsov came in, turned to Varya, laughed and asked her:

'How's your "goodly person"?'

Varya replied that the 'goodly person' was fine, and in so doing placed the stress absolutely right.

'Well now, speak the same words but with the stress on the first word,' Tortsov suggested to her. 'But before you do that,' he interrupted himself, 'I must acquaint you with two rules. The first is that *an adjective qualifying a noun is not stressed*. It only defines, complements the noun and merges with it. That's why they are called "qualifiers".

'That would seem to imply that we shouldn't say "góodly person" as I have suggested, with the stress on the first word, the qualifier.

'But there is another, stronger law, which, like the psychological pause, overrides all other laws and rules. That is the law of juxtaposition on the basis of which we must at all costs clearly highlight antithetical words which express thoughts, feelings, images, perceptions, actions and so on. That is especially important in stage speech. Do that, do it *any way you like*. Make one of the juxtaposed parts loud, the other soft, one in the upper, the other in the lower, register, the first in one, the second in another colour, tempo, etc. Just let the difference between the two juxtaposed parts be as clear, indeed as clear as possible. According to this law, to say "góodly-person" with the stress on the *adjective*, means there has to be, either in reality or in fantasy, "another person", an "*evil* person" so you can place a "goodly person" in antithesis to it.

'To make sure you say the words spontaneously, naturally, first imagine you are not talking about an "evil" but . . .'

'A "góodly man",' Varya interjected instinctively.

'You see! Splendid!' Tortsov said, encouragingly.

After this we added one, two, three, four, five, etc. words until there was a whole story.

'*A goodly man was here but you weren't at home so he went away unhappy, saying he would not come back.*'

As the sentence grew, the more stressed words Varya required. Soon she was so bewildered by them all she couldn't string two words together.

Tortsov laughed a lot over her dismay, her worried face and then said to her, serious now:

'You panicked because you needed to place the maximum number of accents and not remove them. But the fewer they are, the clearer the sentence, provided, of course, you only highlight the few most important words. Removing stress is as difficult as placing it. Study both.'

Tortsov has a show tonight and so class ended early. Rakhmanov used the rest of the time for 'training and drill'.

.. .. 19..

'I am coming to the conclusion that you must learn to remove stress before you can place it,' Tortsov said today.

'Beginners try too hard to speak properly. They abuse stress. To counter this, we must learn to remove unnecessary stress. As I've already said, this is an art in itself and very difficult. In the first place it frees your speech from the false stresses life has ingrained in you. Once the ground is cleared it is easier to plant correct stress. Second, knowing how to remove stress will help you in your future work. For instance, when we are conveying complex ideas or detailed facts, for the sake of the clarity you have to remember individual episodes, related to what you are talking about. But we must do it in such a way that we don't distract from the basic storyline. These parenthetical remarks must be lucid but not obtrusive. We must be economical with inflexion and stress. In other cases, in a long heavy sentence we must only highlight certain words and let the others pass clearly but unnoticed. This technique makes it easier to make a difficult text lighter, something we have to do quite often.

'In these circumstances, knowing how to remove stress will be of great help to you every time.'

Tortsov called Pasha up onstage and told him to repeat the story about the 'goodly man' but he was only to highlight one word and remove the stress from all the others. In the last class Varya failed a similar task. Today it took Pasha some time. After he had made one or two fruitless attempts, Tortsov said to him:

'Strange, Varya was obsessed with bringing in stresses and you were obsessed with taking them out. Avoid both extremes. When a sentence is devoid of stress or weight it loses all meaning.

'Varya needed them too much and you too little. That was because neither of you had a clear Subtext. Establish that first so that there is something to communicate and some way of doing it.

'Justify the absence of stress by a creative idea.'

'That's not so easy,' I thought.

But in my opinion Pasha found an excellent way out. He not only justified the absence of stress but also found the Given Circumstances in which it was easy to displace the one available stress from one word to another when Tortsov asked him to do so. Pasha's idea was that all of us in the front rows would cross-question him about the arrival of the 'goodly person'. This questioning, according to Pasha, was caused by the fact that we doubted the reality of the facts he had presented and the truth of his assertion that the 'goodly person' was coming. To justify himself, Pasha had to establish the truth of every word in his story. That's why he highlighted each of them in turn and hammered the stressed word into our heads. A 'góodly person came here and', etc. A 'goodly person, came here and', etc. A 'goodly person cáme here and', etc. Each time he repeated the same sentence right through removing all the stresses except on the one highlighted word. This was done so as not to deprive the stressed word of its meaning and sense. Naturally, taken out of context, with no connection to the story as a whole, it lost all its inner meaning.

When he'd finished the exercise, Tortsov said to him:

'You placed and removed the stress very well. But why the rush? Why squash the part of the sentence you only had to tone down?

'Rushing, nervousness, gabbling, spitting out whole phrases doesn't tone them down, it totally destroys them. But that wasn't your intention. Nervousness in a speaker only irritates the listeners, poor diction angers them because they desperately have to try and guess at what they haven't understood. This focuses attention on the very things you want to tone down. Fidgeting makes speech heavy. Calm and control lighten it. To tone down a phrase you need a very leisurely, flat inflexion, almost no stress at all and exceptional calm and confidence.

'That's what produced calm in your listeners.

'Highlight the important word clearly, then fill in the rest lightly, cleanly, deliberately for the general sense, without emphasis. That's the way to remove stress. Develop control of speech in your classes in "training and drill".'

In another exercise, Tortsov split up the story of the 'goodly person' into a series of episodes, which had to be highlighted and clearly outlined.

Episode One: The goodly person arrives.

Episode Two: He learns why he can't see the person he wants.

Episode Three: He is upset and wonders whether to wait or leave.

Episode Four: He takes offence, decides to leave and never come back again.

This produced four independent sentences with four stressed words, one to a bar.

At first, Tortsov only asked us to convey each fact clearly. To do that we needed a clear mental image of what we were talking about and to place the accents in each bar properly and expressively. We had to create the mental images we needed to convey the object and see them with our mind's eye.

Then Tortsov wanted Pasha not only to see what happened but to make us feel how the goodly person came and went.

Not only the what but the how.

He wanted to see, from Pasha's account, what mood the goodly man was in when he arrived. Happy? Sad? Worried?

That meant that he needed not only a stress but an inflexion to colour it. Moreover, Tortsov wanted to know what offence the man took: great, deep, violent, silent?

Tortsov also wanted to know in what mood the decision to leave was taken: in sorrow or in anger? That called for a corresponding picture to colour not just the stressed moment but the whole episode.

The other students performed similar exercises on placing and removing stress.

.. .. 19..

I needed to check whether I had really taken in what Tortsov had said.

He heard Othello's speech through and found many faults in the ordering and technical placing of the stress.

'A correct stress is a help, an incorrect one a hindrance,' he noted in passing.

To correct my faults he had me redistribute the stresses and do the speech again right there in class.

I started to go back over the speech bar by bar and to indicate which words I thought needed highlighting.

' "Like to the Pontic sea / Whose icy current". Normally', I explained, 'in this bar the stress falls on the word "sea". But now, after giving it a lot of thought, I would transfer it to the word "current" because that's what we're really talking about in this bar.'

'You decide,' said Tortsov turning to the students. 'Is that right?'

Everybody started shouting at once. Some said 'current', others 'icy', others 'Pontic', Vanya yelled with all his might I should hit the word 'like'.

We got bogged down in a welter of stressed and unstressed words during the rest of the speech. In the end, we decided we needed a stress on practically every word.

But Tortsov reminded us that a sentence with a stress on every word is meaningless. It has no sense.

We went over the whole speech in this way but couldn't make a single decision on what was to be highlighted. In fact, I became more and more confused because I could place a stress on any word or remove it and maintain different meanings. Which was nearest the truth? That was the question which put me in a total muddle.

Perhaps that's the result of a personal idiosyncrasy. When there is too much of everything, my eyes are all over the place, in a shop, a baker's, a table of hors d'oeuvres. It's difficult for me to fix on any one dish, cake, or merchandise. There are so many words and stresses in Othello's speech, I got lost.

We stopped, having decided nothing, but Tortsov still obstinately said nothing and smiled wickedly. There was a long, awkward pause which made Tortsov burst out laughing. He said:

'None of this would have happened if you had known the laws of speech. They would have helped you through so you could define the mandatory, and therefore correct, stresses, right away without having to think about it. Very few would have remained in your judgement.

'So what should we have done?' we asked.

'First of all, learn the laws of speech and then . . .

'Imagine you've just moved into a new apartment and all your things are lying about in every room,' said Tortsov by way of illustration. 'How do you create order?

'First you have to collect all the plates in one place, the teacups in another, the chess and chequer pieces in a third and sort out the large items of furniture according to their use, etc.

'When you've done that you'll see where you are going.

'You have to do the same preliminary sorting out with a text before placing the natural stresses. In order to explain this process to you, I have to touch upon one or two of the first, highly relevant, laws which are discussed in the book *The Expressive Word*. Understand that I am not doing this to teach you these laws but only to point out to you what they are needed for and how in time you will come to use them. Once you have learned their purpose and their worth the easier it will be consciously to take the material you have studied away with you.

'Let's suppose you have broken down the text or speech and there is a long series of adjectives – "a nice, goodly, noble, wonderful person".

'Adjectives aren't stressed, you know that. But what if there's an antithesis. That's another matter. But do we really need a stress on every one of them?! Nice, goodly, noble, wonderful are almost the same thing, with the same meaning.

'Fortunately, thanks to the laws of speech, you know with absolute certainty, that adjectives with a common meaning are not stressed. And so, you unhesitatingly remove the stress from all the adjectives and elide the last of them with the stressed noun, thus getting "wonderfulpérson".

'Then you go on. Here's another group of adjectives: a dear, lovely, young, talented, intelligent woman. These adjectives don't have a common but a separate meaning.

'But you know that each of these adjectives without a common meaning must have a stress, and so you automatically place them in such a way they don't kill the principal stress on the noun: "woman".

'Names are stressed on the surname, dates on the year, addresses on the house-number. Pyotr Petrov, July 15 Nineteen Hundred and Eight, Number Twenty Moscow Street.

'These are juxtapositions. Highlight them any way you can, including stress.

'Once words have been grouped, it's easier to find your way around the individual stresses.

'You have two nouns. You know that the stress must fall on the possessive, because the possessive is stronger than the word it qualifies. My brother's book, my father's house, the ocean's current. Don't think about it, stress the possessive and go on.

'You have two repeated words with an increase in energy. Boldly stress the second of them because it's a matter of a rise in energy, as in: "Onward, onward to the Propontic and the Hellespont".

'If, on the other hand, there's a drop in energy, then stressing the first word will convey a decline, as in the lines: "Dreams, dreams where is your sweetness now?"

'You can see for yourselves how many words and stresses fall into place when we use the laws of speech,' Tortsov continued.

'There aren't many stressed words left to sort out and it isn't hard to find your way through them, particularly since the subtext with its innumerable strands, all woven together, the Throughaction and the Supertask guide and help you all the time.

'After that, all you have to do is organize all the marked stresses, some to be given more strongly, others toned down.

'That is difficult and important and we'll talk about it in the next class.'

.. .. 19..

In today's class, as promised, Tortsov talked about organizing the many stresses in individual sentences and paragraphs.

'A sentence with one stressed word is much easier to understand,' he explained. 'For example: "Someone you know well came here." Stress any word you like, and the meaning will come out different every time. Try placing not one but two stresses, for example on "well" and "here".

'That sentence is not only difficult to justify, it's difficult to say. Why? Because you're injecting a new meaning into it: first, that not just anybody but someone "known" came, and second that they didn't come just anywhere, they came "here".

'Put a third stress on "came" and the sentence becomes even more difficult to justify or communicate because a new fact has been added, namely that "someone you know well" didn't drive but "came" on his own two feet.[13] Now, imagine a sentence with everything stressed but no inner justification for any of the words.

'Faced with that, all we can say is that "a sentence with every word stressed is meaningless". However, there are times when you have to justify a sentence in which you stress all the words which add new content. It is easier to break down such sentences into a number of independent sentences rather than try to deliver them as one.

'For example,' Tortsov took a piece of paper from his pocket, 'I'll read you a long speech from Shakespeare's *Antony and Cleopatra*:

> Hearts, tongues, figures, scribes, bards, poets, cannot
> Think, speak, cast, write, sing, number, – ho!
> His love to Antony.

'The eminent scholar Jeavons',[14] Tortsov went on reading, 'states that in the sentence, Shakespeare has joined six subjects and six adjectives, so that, strictly speaking, it has 6 × 6, or 36 sentences.

'Would somebody like to read this sentence so as to bring out all 36 sentences? Any takers?' he said.

Nobody spoke.

'How right you are. I wouldn't try to solve the problem Jeavons set, I wouldn't have the vocal technique for it. But that's not the business in hand. It doesn't interest us, what does is the technique of highlighting and co-ordinating several stresses in one sentence.

'How do we highlight the key word in a long speech and also a series of less important words which are nonetheless essential to the meaning?

'For that we need a complex scale of stresses: strong, medium and weak.

'In painting there are strong, weak, half-, quarter-tones in colour, or light and shade. Similarly, in speech there is a wide scale in the degree of stress.

'Stress must be computed, combined, co-ordinated but in such a way that minor stresses don't detract from, or compete with, the key word but highlight it more strongly. Everything must work together to construct and communicate a difficult sentence. There must be perspective in the individual propositions and in the speech as a whole.

'You know how depth is conveyed in painting, that is, the third dimension. It doesn't really exist. The artist paints on a flat, stretched canvas, within a frame. But painting creates the illusion of several planes. They recede into the canvas but the foreground comes out of the frame at us.

'These planes exist in our own speech and they lend perspective to the sentence. The key word is highlighted most clearly of all and comes right into the foreground of the sound-plane. The less important words create a series of deeper planes.

'In speech we create perspective, mostly, through carefully organized stresses of varying intensity. And it is not only the intensity of the stress which is important but its quality.

'For example, it's important whether the stress comes from above or below, does it land heavily or does it fly up lightly and strike cleanly? Is it hard or soft, obvious or barely perceptible, does it fall suddenly and immediately disappear or does it linger for quite a while?

'There are also what we might call masculine and feminine stresses.

'The first (masculine) are definite, brutal, like a hammer on an anvil. They are brief, short-lived. The second (feminine) are equally definite but don't come to a sudden end, they linger. As an illustration, let us assume that after delivering a sharp blow on the anvil you have to slide the hammer back towards you so it will be easier for you to lift it again.

'We will call this kind of definite, prolonged stress "feminine".

'Or here's another example from speech and movement. When an angry host throws out an unwanted guest, he yells "Out!" and points towards the door energetically. He uses the masculine stress in speech and movement.

'If a more polite man has to do the same thing, then his dismissive "out" and gesture are only decisive and definite for a second, then his voice drops, the movement slows and the sharpness of the first moment is softened. This long, elongated stress is "feminine".

'Besides vocal stress and inflexion there is another element of speech we can use to highlight words: inflexions. Their shape lends greater expressiveness to the highlighted word, and strengthens it. Once again, you can combine inflexion and stress. Then the stress is coloured by many different shades of feeling: cordial (as with "person"), malicious, ironical, contemptuous or respectful, etc.

'Apart from vocal stress and inflexions there are other ways of highlighting words. To strengthen a highlighted stressed word, for example you can turn this or that pause into a psychological pause. You can also highlight the important word by removing the stress from all the unimportant words. Then the stressed word, which is intact, gains strength by comparison.'

.. .. 19..

Today, Tortsov continued his unfinished explanation from last time.

'First, you must choose the key word in the sentence and highlight it by a stress. Then, you must do the same with other highlighted, but less important, words.

'As to the unimportant, unhighlighted words, they are only needed for the general meaning and must fade into the background.

'*We must discover interrelationships, gradations of strength, qualities of stress among all the highlighted and unhighlighted words and create a perspective in sound, that will give the sentence life and movement.*

'This harmonious, balanced relationship of different gradations of stress and individual highlighted words is what we mean when we talk of organization.

'In this way, we create harmony of form and beauty of architecture in a sentence.'

After a moment's reflexion, Tortsov continued:

'Just as words form clauses, so propositions form complete thoughts, narratives and long speeches.

'Then, we not only highlight words in clauses, but whole clauses in narratives and dialogue.

'Everything we said about highlighting and organizing words in clauses applies to individual clauses in narrative or dialogue. We use the same technique as when stressing individual words. You can highlight the key clause by stressing a word and articulating the important sentences with greater emphasis than the secondary clauses. Then the stress on the key word in a highlighted clause should be stronger than in an unhighlighted one.

'You can highlight a stressed clause by placing it between two pauses. You can achieve the same result by using inflexion, by raising or lowering the pitch of a highlighted clause or by making the inflexion phonetically clearer. That lends new colour to the stressed clause.

'You can change the tempo and rhythm of a highlighted clause in comparison with the rest of the dialogue or story. Finally, you can leave the colour and strength of the highlighted clause alone and tone down the stresses in the rest.

'It's not my business to go into every possibility, every subtlety in stressing words or clauses. I can only assure you that these possibilities are many, as are the ways of using them. You can use them to create the most complex arrangements of every kind of highlighted and stressed words and clauses.

'In this way you create a perspective with various planes.

'If they are directed towards the play's Supertask, if they follow the through-action they become critically important because they help us achieve what is fundamental to our art, creating the life of the human spirit of a role or play.

'The degree to which we can use the vocal possibilities is governed by our practical experience, knowledge, taste, sensitivity and talent. Actors with a feeling for language and their native tongue, become virtuosos in organizing and creating perspectives in sound.

'They carry out these processes almost intuitively, subconsciously.

'Less talented people have to work more consciously, they have many things to learn, they have to study their own language, the laws of speech, they need practical experience and art.

'The more extensive the means at our disposal, the more vital, power-ful, expressive, and irresistible our speech will be.

'Learn how to make full use of the laws and techniques of verbal com-munication, and, in particular, of organizing and creating a perspective in sound, with all its planes.'

.. .. 19..

Today I spoke Othello's speech again.

'Your work has paid off,' Tortsov said, encouragingly.

'It's good in detail. Here and there it's even powerful. But the speech as a whole is running on the spot. It doesn't get anywhere. Two bars forward, two bars back, all the time.

'The constant repetition of the same phonetic pattern becomes irritating like the same old design on gaudy wallpaper.

'In the theatre, you must use your expressive gifts differently, not just as God gave them, but knowingly.

'Rather than explain what I mean, I'll do the speech myself, not by any means to show off my skill but to reveal the secrets of my vocal technique, step by step, as I go, and show the kinds of thoughts actors have about the dramatic effect on themselves and the other actors.

'I'll start by defining my task more clearly,' he said, turning to Pasha.

'It's to make you, as Iago, feel Othello's elemental drive towards a terrible revenge. To do that as Shakespeare would have wished, I will juxtapose a vivid picture of the surging waves of the "Pontic Sea" and the mental turmoil of a jealous man. To do that, the best thing is to capture you with my mental images. That's a difficult task but not impossible particularly as I have material ready prepared which is clear, vivid and exciting enough to do the job.'

Tortsov prepared for a moment then fixed his eyes sharply on Pasha as though the faithless Desdemona stood before him.

Like to the Pontic sea. He spoke softly, quite calmly, then added tersely:

'I'm not giving everything out for the moment. I could do more!

'You must save, build up emotion.

'The phrase is incomprehensible.

'You can't see what's being talked about.

'So I finish it in my mind: *Like to the Pontic sea . . . keeps due on to the Propontic and the Hellespont.* I'm careful not to hurry. After the word "sea" I make an upward inflexion. Almost infinitesimal. Two seconds, three, no more.

'I lift the voice at the next inflected comma (there will be many more) but don't reach top yet.

'I move vertically. No horizontal lines from now on!

'No high voltage. Not flat, shaped!

'I must climb, but step by step, not straight up.

'I make the second bar stronger than the first, the third stronger than the second, the fourth stronger than the third. No shouting!

'Shouting isn't strength!

'Strength lies in the crescendo.

Whose icy current and compulsive course . . .

(*. . . Keeps due on to the Propontic and the Hellespont*)

'But if I raise each bar by a third, the fifty-two words in the sentence will require a range of three octaves, which I haven't got!

'Then four notes up and two down.

'Five notes up and two down.

'Total: an interval of only a third.

'But the impression is of a fifth!

'Then again, four notes up, two down!

'Total, a rise of only a second. But the impression is of a fourth.

'And so on, the whole time.

'By economizing my range holds out for all fifty-two words.

'Economy, economy, economy!

'Not only of emotion but of register.

'Later if you don't have enough notes to rise further, inflect more strongly. And enjoy it!

'That gives an impression of increased power.

'The inflexion has been done!

'Wait, don't rush.

'There's nothing to stop you introducing a psychological pause, in addition to the logical one.

'The upward inflexion whets our curiosity.

'The psychological pause has the same effect on your creative nature, your intuition . . . your imagination and your subconscious.

'A break gives me and you time to examine the mental images, to reveal them through action, facial expression and transmitting.

'That doesn't weaken the effect. On the contrary. An active pause increases it and excites us both.

'How am I to avoid falling into mere technique?

'I must think only of the Task, which is to make you see what I see, whatever the cost.

'I shall be dynamic. I must take productive action.

'But . . . don't drag out the pause.

'Onwards!

Ne'er feels retiring ebb . . . (but keeps due on to the Propontic and the Hellespont)

'Why do my eyes grow wider?

'Are they transmitting more strongly?

'And why are the hands slowly, majestically reaching forward?

'And the whole of me, too?!

'In the tempo and rhythm of heavy, rolling waves?!

'Do you think that's a calculated, "theatrical" effect?

'Not at all! I assure you!

'It was spontaneous.

'I played it first and realized afterwards.

'What does this?

'Intuition?

'The subconscious?

'Creative nature herself?

'Maybe.

'All I know is, the *psychological pause* helped.

'The mood has been created!

'Emotion has been aroused!

'It has been drawn onto action!

'If I'd done this with a conscious eye to the effect, you'd have thought it was an act.

'But nature did it, and you believed it.

'Because it was natural.

'Because it was true.

But keeps due on

To the Propontic and the Hellespont.

'Once again, post factum, I realized something malign had grown inside me.

'I didn't know where from, or how.

'That was good. I liked it!'

'I hold on to the psychological pause.

'And the pause becomes more active.'

....

'Once more I prod nature.

'I shall trick the subconscious into working.

'There are many decoys for doing that.

'I reach vocal top: "Hellespont".

'I say it and then let the sound drop.

'For the run up to the end.

Even so my bloody thoughts with violent pace

Shall ne'er look back, ne'er ebb to humble love

'I highlight the upward inflexion more strongly. This is the highest note in the speech.

Ne'er ebb to humble love

'I'm afraid of false emotion.

'I hold on to my task.

'I make sure my mental images are firmly rooted.

'Intuition, the subconscious, nature – it's all yours.

'Total freedom! But I hold back, I tantalize you with pauses.

'The longer I hold, the more it tantalizes.

'The moment has come. Let fly!

'All my expressive means have been mobilized.

'Everyone to the rescue!

'Tempo! Rhythm!

'And . . . I'm afraid to say it – even loudness.

'Not shouting.

'Only on the last two words of the phrase:

Ne'er ebb to humble love . . .

'The final, climax. The final one:

Till that a capable and wide revenge
Swallow them up!
'I hold back the tempo.
'To make it more meaningful.
'And I place the full stop.
'Do you understand what that means?
'The stop in a tragic speech?
'It means death.
'Would you like to feel what I'm talking about?
'Climb the highest peak.
'Above a bottomless chasm.
'Take a heavy stone and . . .
'Throw it into the abyss.
'You will hear, feel how the stone is smashed to smithereens.
'That's the kind of drop you need – in the voice.
'From the top to the bottom of your register.
'The stop, by its nature, requires it.
'Like this.'

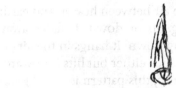

'What!' I exclaimed. 'At a moment like that an actor is living off technical, professional calculation!
'What about inspiration?
'I'm crushed and hurt.'

.. .. 19..

Seeing that many students had found the graphics representing sound clear and convincing in the previous class, Tortsov used them today for scheduled work on *inflexions on punctuation marks*.

Tortsov began this part of the class with a short introduction. He said:

'The real purpose of *punctuation marks* is to group the words in a sentence and indicate the speech rests, or pauses. They differ only in duration and character. Their character depends on the inflexion they carry. In other words, every punctuation mark requires its own corresponding, *characteristic* inflexion and it is this aspect of punctuation marks which we shall now study.

'As you can see, I shall have to speak about them twice, now and later, when we talk about speech rests and pauses, because they have a dual function.

'Don't let this throw you. I am doing it intentionally.

'I'll start with the full *stop*. Imagine a heavy stone hurtling down into an abyss and hitting the bottom. The sound of the last highlighted syllable before the stop hurtles down in just the same way and hits the bottom of the speaker's vocal range. This drop in sound and impact are characteristic of the full stop. The greater the vocal range, the longer the drop, the more headlong and stronger the impact, the more typical the sound pattern is of the full stop, the more conclusively and convincingly the thought you are communicating resounds.

'On the other hand, the shorter the vocal range, the smaller the drop, the speed, the impact, the less clear the communication of thought.

'When we talk in our own particular jargon of "putting the sentence to bed" we mean a well-placed final stop. Judge for yourselves how important it is to have a wide range and a good bass.

'*Suspension points*, as opposed to the stop, don't conclude the sentence but, as it were, launch it into the void where it vanishes like a bird released from a cage, or like smoke, borne on the air between heaven and earth. Float the voice in space, without its going up or down. It fades away, without concluding the sentence, or settling down. It hangs in the air.

'The *comma* doesn't end the sentence either but lifts it upwards, as to the next floor, or a higher shelf. In music, this pattern is called *portamento*.

'This upward inflexion is mandatory with a comma, like a raised index finger it alerts a thousand people to the fact that the sentence isn't over and is about to go on. The listeners know they have to wait, that concentration mustn't slacken but sharpen.

'Most actors are afraid of commas and can't wait to jump over them and end the sentence as soon as possible and reach a point of safety, like a large station where you can rest after a journey, stay overnight and eat before continuing your journey. But we shouldn't be afraid of commas. On the contrary, we should love them, like a brief rest along the way, when it's good to put your head out of the window and get a breath of air and feel refreshed. The comma is my favourite mark.

'The required *portamento* on a comma lends elegance to speech and inflexions. If you aren't afraid of pauses, but use them intelligently, they can help you speak calmly, freely, without rushing, certain that the audience will listen to the thoughts you have to communicate to them. All you have to do is make a clean upward inflexion and hold back further sound for as long as is necessary or as long as you want. Anyone who has mastered this technique knows full well that, when making a *portamento*, calm, control and conviction force an audience to wait patiently even when an actor drags out the pause after an upward inflexion longer than he should.

'It's a wonderful feeling to stand before a packed house and calmly, patiently, pull the complex paragraphs, the structural parts of an idea together and know that the audience is quite still, patiently listening to you.

'The mandatory upward inflexion before a comma, if well done, is a great help in this.

'In terms of inflexion, the *semi-colon* is somewhere half-way between a stop and a comma. The sentence comes to an end but doesn't drop quite so far as with a stop. Indeed, there is a barely perceptible upward inflexion.

'The *colon* requires a short, sharp stress on the final syllable before it. The degree of stress is almost the same as for the stop but whereas the point requires an evident and considerable drop in tone, with a colon the sound can drop or rise a little, or stay on the same level. The most important characteristic of this sign is that it causes a break not to end the sentence or the thought, but to extend it. In this break we should feel what is to come. It is preparatory, it announces what follows, it points the finger at it. The particular forward movement of the sound indicates this.

'The *question mark*. Its trademark is a short quick, or slow, leisurely large or small, upward inflexion, rather like the croaking of a frog, which is either cut short or sustained. You do this by lifting the voice to the top of the register.

'Sometimes this interrogatory high note stays up in the air, at other times it drops a little.

'The height and speed of this upward interrogatory inflexion, the sharpness or broadness of the *inflexion* indicate the degree of urgency in the question. The greater the surprise, the higher the voice rises. The smaller the question, the lower the rise. The keener the astonishment, the higher the loop, the longer the curve of the inflexion, the greater the astonishment it conveys.

'The interrogatory curve can contain *one or many* bends. When the astonishment is keen, this inflexion can be repeated on every word of the interrogatory clause. For example, to strengthen the sentence: "And all this is gone forever?" you can loop on almost every word.

'This sketch will help you understand:

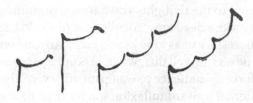

'The *exclamation mark*. Almost everything I've said about the question mark applies here. The only difference is that the loop is missing and is replaced by a short, or somewhat longer, drop after the initial rise. A sketch of this sound shape looks like a flail for threshing corn. The wooden flail can be short or long.

'The higher the voice rises during the inflexion, the lower it falls afterwards and the stronger or weaker the exclamation sounds.

'You can sketch the inflexion like this:

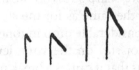

'I have used graphics to explain the mandatory inflexions on punctuation marks. Don't imagine that you'll need to use them in the future, to note down or fix the inflexions in a role permanently. That you must not do. It is harmful and dangerous. Never learn patterns of sound by heart for your roles. They must occur spontaneously, intuitively, subconsciously, only then can your inflexions convey the life of the human spirit of a role exactly.

'Learning sound patterns is arid, mere form, lifeless. I reject and condemn it utterly.

'If the lines I've drawn have explained the mandatory vocal shapes and inflexions at punctuation marks, then forget them, put them out of your head or remind yourself of them at critical moments, when the inflexion your intuition suggests is clearly wrong or it doesn't come spontaneously. Then recalling the sketch can set intuition on the right path.'

In reply to a question: 'Where do inflexions come from?' Tortsov answered:

'And where do words come from and land on our tongue when we are expressing a particular thought? Why is it just the word we need right then? Why do movements, actions occur, in response to an inner summons, without our conscious participation? Why do hands, legs, the torso work on their own? Let's leave that to nature, the miracle worker, to answer. It's no bad thing if something beautiful in the creative process remains shrouded in mystery. That's all to the good, and is useful to intuition, which often suggests the right inflexion.

'Working on inflexions doesn't mean contriving or forcing them. They appear spontaneously if *what* they are supposed to express – feeling, thoughts, the gist – and the *means* by which they can be communicated – words, speech, a rousing, sensitive, broad, expressive vocal tone, good diction – are there.

'They should be your primary concern, then inflexions will come spontaneously, intuitively, as a reflex.

'In other words, learn to master the decoys, develop your voice, the organs of articulation. Note, as you study, that the most important lure, one which intuitively produces an inflexion is *Adaptation*. Why? Because the inflexion itself is a vocal adaptation, designed to stir invisible feelings and experiences. The same lure, Adaptation creates the best intuitive movements and actions physiologically, and the most precise verbal actions and inflexions psychologically.

'So, the purpose of today's and subsequent classes will be to persuade you to work unremittingly on mastering lures, developing the voice, extending its range, perfecting the work of the organs of articulation which reproduce inflexions. These sessions are also intended to prepare you for a new class, "the laws of speech and the art of speaking", to make sure you understand how important this new subject is and will give your full attention to it.

'Have you ever heard simple speech, where the voice doesn't go up or down much, where the range is limited, where there are none of the complexities of shape and sound which are so important in language? Yet, despite the absence of all these elements, simple speech very often makes its effect. Wherein lies the secret of its strength?

'*In the clarity of the spoken thought, the preciseness and definition of the expressions, the logic, the sequence, the structure of the sentence, the grouping and construction of the whole story. The sum total of all these affects the listener.*

'Use this other ability words have. Learn to speak in *logical sequence.*'

'The practice of leaning on every single word (especially when speaking verse) is a common mannerism. But you know that a sentence which is all stress or no stress expresses nothing and is meaningless.

'But there are actors who are less prodigal with stress. They are sparing with it but still put it in the wrong place and so, to a lesser degree, they also distort stage speech. They don't care much for subjects and predicates, nouns and verbs. They prefer adjectives, adverbs, all the "actable" words – *great, small, lovely, ugly, good, evil, special, excessive, or, suddenly, unexpectedly, especially, excessively*. You can illustrate each of these words, you can present them with any inflexion you like. And these "actable" words are preferred to the words around them which convey the essential meaning.

'This arbitrary, indiscriminate placing of stress has become almost normal. Sentences which are spoken quite normally in life calling for a genuine, productive, specific task, are changed out of all recognition onstage by incorrect "actable" stresses. Mangled speech is difficult to follow so all we do is hear it.

'At the other end of the scale there are actors (significantly fewer) whose speech is correct to a fault. You can't take exception to them either in terms of grammar or logical stress. That, of course, is good. Their speech is not only heard, it is *understood*, but, unfortunately it can't be *felt* owing to the absence of *symbolic* or *artistic stress*. Only they can help you transform an arid lump of a word into something living, and literate but formal speech into genuine art which communicates the life of the human spirit of a role.

'It's a difficult problem and I won't go into details but let me give you one valuable piece of advice, drawn from long experience:

'Try, as far as possible, to make only a few highly essential stresses. And make your symbolic stresses coincide, as far as you can, with logical stresses. There will, of course, be exceptions, but don't make them the rule. To ensure that your speech is artistic, with the minimum of stresses, take great care over the subtext. Once that has been established, everything will go smoothly. It may be that you won't have one but many stresses, strong, medium and weak, a whole sliding scale of them, variously related. Intuition places them in such a way that logic, grammar and art are satisfied and the listener is content.'

II.[15]

.. .. 19..

Tortsov reminded us that in our studies so far, we had talked about an unbroken line of sound and its unity whenever the opportunity arose.

'That doesn't mean, of course, that actors should speak the dialogue continuously without a break!

'Talking non-stop would make them look like lunatics. Normal people need breaks, rests, pauses not only in speech but in all their other processes, internal or external – thinking, imagining hearing, seeing, etc.

'We can represent our normal state as a series of alternating long and short lines with big or small pauses, like so:

——————— ——— ————— ——— —————— ——— ——————

The opposite of this is obsession (idée fixe) which we can represent by an unbroken line, like so:

' "Speech without pauses or with overlong, overextended pauses is a senseless muddle," wrote Volkonski in one passage in the book. And in another he exclaims: "You really do not know which is more amazing, how little it (the pause) is used or how much it is misused." "It is difficult to say which is worse: introducing a pause where it is not needed, or omitting a pause when it is needed." (*The Expressive Word*)

'How are we to reconcile these opposites: an unbroken line on the one hand, and the need for rests on the other?

'First by understanding that continuity must not be taken to mean a perpetuum mobile and that breaks and pauses mustn't make mincemeat out of speech, as is so often the case in the theatre.

'In music, which is based on a sustained line of sound, there are pauses which are just as important as continuity, which do not harm the cantilena.

'Pauses are needed to break the music down into its component parts. During these silent breaks, the sound is cut, but flows in an unbroken extended line between the pauses.

'Speech pauses should divide the thought being expressed into its component parts, while preserving the continuity and unity of each of them.

'People who speak well in daily life, instinctively or knowingly adhere to this rule and place the pauses more or less truthfully when they are talking. But as soon as they have to learn someone else's lines and deliver them onstage in most cases they undergo a transformation: they chop up their speech and put the pauses in the wrong places.

'Why does this happen?

'There are internal and external reasons. I'll start with the internal.

'There are many actors whose breath is short and poorly supported. The sounds they make only last as long as their intake of breath and if they have too much they get rid of it anywhere in the speech they like. They also take breaths whenever they feel like it, without asking whether the break is legitimate or not.

'This speech is like asthma. It is neither clear nor educated.

'There is another reason why actors pause in the wrong place.

'They don't know that power isn't loudness, isn't high-voltage, but lies in the rise and fall of sound, or, in other words, inflexions and in logic and sequence.

'Actors who know little of our vocal technique try to intensify verbal communication by using the most naive, "theatrical" methods. In an effort to look more convincing, they drive themselves, pump up their energy, resort to shouting. But all this muscular effort doesn't produce results. They're working on the surface, not inside. Life and experience have nothing in common with all these muscular contractions. Like the pause associated with them, they occur quite arbitrarily, for physical or nervous reasons.

'Can we then see when and where a pause will appear? Evidently wherever the actor considers he can squeeze out "inspiration" (in quotes) more effectively, where he particularly wants to show his "genius". The reasons don't stem from thought, from the true meaning of the role, they arise despite them and often as mere chance dictates.

'As a result, the simplest sentence, for example: "I wish to tell you that your conduct is unspeakable", is transformed and the birth pangs as the words come out are agonizing.

' "I (huge pause, to squeeze out a little inspiration) wísh to tell yóuthatyóur (another spasm, after which some words from the succeeding clause slipped into the first one) cónductisún (fresh pause to pump up energy) – spéakable" (fired off like a bullet, all the remaining breath expelled, followed by another long pause, like postnatal rest).

'This way of speaking is like the judge in Gogol's *Inspector General*, remember? He used to whirr like an old clock for a long time before he said a word.

'You must use singing, and work on breathing and inflexions to help you in the fight against these external reasons.

'But the principal reason isn't external but internal in origin. It lies in a lack of proper sensitivity for words, insufficient love for them, a lack of understanding of our own tongue.

'How can we fight this?

'By a more conscious relationship to words, by digging deeper into their nature. Studying the laws of speech will help, in particular the function of the third important aid in verbal communication (after inflexion and stress) – *rests* (pauses).

'You will study them in detail with specialists in due course. My object is to introduce you to the subject and explain its practical significance in general outline.'

'There are actors who consider it chic to run one sentence into another, or to fill pauses with sound. They claim that this isn't the result of poor speech, it happens because they can't tame the irrepressible nature of their "stormy" temperament which they are unable to control.

'Others do it "on purpose" so they can deliver more words and sounds on a single breath. "Why waste the air you have?"

'But, much more often, the pauses are wrongly placed because they only have a hazy notion of what they're talking about, because they haven't gone deep into the true meaning of the words.

'How are we to avoid these common actors' mistakes? How can we learn to master logical pauses in speech? We must either have an innate sensitivity to words and language, or we need knowledge based on study and, finally, practical experience.

'An innate sensitivity, a feeling for words comes not from you, it is the gift of nature. We can only concentrate our minds and dig deep into the meaning of words and language and that is what I recommend to all actors. Knowledge comes from a study of the laws of speech and practical skill from doing exercises.

'What rules or laws govern speech pauses and in what way do they help?

'Our best help in the placing of the logical (grammatical) pauses is punctuation marks.

'I forewarned you I would be coming back to them. Now that "warning" takes effect.

'Punctuation marks have a double function. The first relates to inflexions, which we've looked at. Now let's talk about the second.

'This consists in the placing and marking of pauses. They divide some words off and, at the same time, group other related words together to form speech bars.

'The length of pauses at punctuation marks depends on the importance, significance, content, depth, finality, the essential meaning of the material between the stops and the commas, on what is foretold by the colon, what is asked by the question mark, what is announced by the exclamation mark, what is left incomplete by the suspension points and completed by the stop. In a word, the length of the pause depends on what calls for a rest and the reason why it happens.

'But the length of the pause isn't only influenced by meaning and purpose, there are other factors. For example, the time your interlocutor needs to assimilate someone's thoughts and for the speaker silently to communicate the unspoken subtext. Or the strength of inner experiencing, the degree of emotional turmoil, the tempo-rhythm of the sentence.

'You cannot precisely calculate the length of the rests which punctuation marks indicate. It is relative. We can only discuss it approximately, comparing a given slowness with a relative quickness, and vice versa.

'As I've already told you, to combat mistakes in logical pauses you need more practical experience and exercises.

'What are they?

'Give me your book,' said Tortsov holding out his hand to me.

I gave him Shchepkin's Memoirs which I'd just bought from a second-hand bookseller.

'Here's a letter from Shchepkin to Shumski. Read these lines in which Shchepkin talks about Shumski's success in Odessa.

Tortsov gave the book to Pasha and he began to read:

'I know that your pains were many, but what is given free? And what would art signify, were it to cost no pain?'

'That will do for the moment,' said Tortsov, stopping him. 'Let's place the pauses in the text we've just heard and group the words to make speech bars. How do we do that? Like this: let's take every two words and see if they bear any direct, immediate relation to each other.

'If they don't, dig into their meaning and make up your mind whether they relate to the word before or the word after.

'Here's the first three: "I know that". Are they together or separate? [There is a brief pause after the first two.]

'Let's take the three words after "I know" – "that your pains".

'Does "that" relate to the "I know" that goes before or "your pains" that follows. With "your pains" of course, because the words "that", "who", "which" are always linked to what comes after.

'Let's now take "were many". These are related to the words "that your pains", so that they all come together as a group, a single bar, which we separate from the clause that comes after.

'It goes on "but". The word "but" contains no thought but the comma before it clearly indicates that it is connected to the succeeding clause.

'I pass on to the new set "what is given". There is a thought here and so we place the word "given" in this group.

'The set "given free" belongs to the same group, it is another member of the family, so we get the speech bar: "but what is given free?" '

Tortsov patiently worked through the rest of the extract from Shchepkin's letter in the same way.

After all the pauses had been placed, Tortsov made Shustov reread the passage we had worked on.

Pasha did so.

'I know / that your pains were many / but what is given free / and what would art signify / were it to cost no pain?'

'There is another equally simple, equally naive practical way of placing the pauses which I will explain to you using the same extract.

'First, place the logical stresses.

"I knów that your pains were mány, but what is given frée? And what would art sígnify, were it to cost no páin?"

'Now, dig into each of the stressed words and try to understand which of the adjacent words they attract.

'For example, the words "I know". They attract the whole sentence, not just individual words. And so, we must mark these words off by a pause and give this stressed moment a special inflexion to put it into closer relation with what follows.

'The second stressed word is "many". Which words does it attract?

' "Pains were many", "were many", "that they were many".

'The next stressed word is "free". Which words does it attract?

' "Is given free", "what is given".

'The stressed word "signify" is closely connected to the words "what would signify" "art signify".

'The next stressed word, "pain", attracts the words "were it to cost".

'Pick up a book as often as you can, read from it and place the pauses.

'If intuition and a feeling for the nature of language get you through, listen to them but when they say nothing, be guided by the rules.

'But don't do the opposite, don't make inwardly unjustified pauses because the rules say so. They are barren and your acting and your reading will be formally correct but dead. Rules should only be a guide, a reminder of the truth, to show you the way.

'The exercises I have recommended will inculcate the habit of grouping words and placing pauses correctly. Make it second nature. Grouping of words, placing pauses correctly is a necessary condition for fine, beautiful speaking, for communicating the nature of the language you speak properly, and for using it intelligently.'

'Psychological pauses are anarchic. While logical pauses are subject to fixed laws, psychological pauses refuse any kind of constraint. You can place them before or after any word, any part of speech (noun, adjective, conjunction, adverb, etc.) or part of a clause (subject, predicate, object, etc.).

'In all the cases I have mentioned, one prime condition must be respected: the pause must be justified. In that, you must be guided by the author's and director's intentions and your own as the creator of the subtext.

'Psychological pauses ride roughshod over all rules.

'In their lawlessness, they are like the arbitrary law of "juxtaposition" which lets nothing stand in its way.

'I'll give you a few examples, to illustrate their anarchy.

'Apparently, we're not supposed to say:

' "This (pause) chair."

' "This (pause) table."

' "I'm (pause) a man."

'Particularly since there is a rule which forbids us to separate these words from whatever they define.

'But psychological pauses have total freedom and so we can say:

' "This (psychological pause, to indicate the chosen object firmly) chair."

' "That (psychological pause to convey indecision in selecting the object) table."

' "I'm (psychological pause to express my delight before another) a man."

'Here's another example of an arbitrary psychological pause.

'We're not supposed to say:

' "He's lying under (pause) the bed."

'But the psychological pause justifies this rest and separates the preposition from the noun.

' "He's lying under (psychological pause to express despair and anger over someone's drunken behaviour) the bed."

'You can place a psychological pause before or after any word you like.

'Psychological pauses can be a double-edged sword. They can be a blessing or a curse. If they are misplaced, and are poorly justified, they have a reverse effect. They are a distraction, they obstruct the expression of important thought and feeling and bring confusion instead. If you place the pause properly, it not only helps communicate the thought, it brings the words alive inwardly.

'Don't abuse either logical or psychological pauses. If you do, speech becomes messy and overextended. Yet this is a common occurrence in the theatre. Actors like to "play about" with everything, including silence. That is why they are prepared to transform the least break into a psychological pause.

'Smolenski[16] advised them only to indulge in a psychological pause when it coincides with a logical one. This would, in his view, reduce the number of rests.

'I think this is to some extent valid. But if it removes the psychological pause altogether stage speech becomes arid.

'It is as harmful to undervalue pauses as it is to overvalue them. We need them in so far as we can use them to organize and vitalize speech.

'Psychological and logical pauses may coincide or they may not. What you must bear in mind is this: when actors have a great deal to offer from within, logical pauses reveal the subtext just as much as psychological ones. They become psychological and bear a dual function.

'If they carry off this dual role, and revitalize speech, then this meta-morphosis is to be welcomed.

'But if this transformation is harmful to the meaning, and the sentence becomes illiterate and confused, then it is not welcome.

'We often find the opposite with actors who have little inside. Not only their logical but their psychological pauses reveal a paucity of subtext. Their speech is arid, formal, lifeless, colourless, which, of course, isn't what we want.

'There are times when logical and psychological pauses don't coincide but exist side by side. Often the psychological pause overrides and obscures the logical pause and so the meaning suffers and confusion enters. This is unwelcome, too.

'Psychological pauses should be placed when they are inwardly motiv-ated but they should not harm logic and sense.

'You know logical pauses are relative in length. But psychological pauses are not subject to the constraints of time. You can extend a silent rest considerably, provided, of course, that you fill it with meaning and dynamic wordless action.'

3.

'Usually, when people talk about "perspective" they have so-called logical perspective in mind. In our own work in the theatre here, we use a rather broader set of terms. We talk about:

1) the perspective of the thought to be conveyed (the logical perspective)
2) the perspective of the feelings to be experienced and
3) the artistic perspective which skilfully deploys the colours which illuminate the story, narrative or speech in the various planes.

'There are all manner of techniques for establishing these perspectives, based on *inflexions* (a rise or fall in sound), highlighting individual words, phrases and sentences (stress), pauses which group and divide the indi-vidual parts, and combinations of tempo and rhythm.

'I'll start with the perspective of the thought to be conveyed (the logical perspective). Logic and sequence play the major role here, developing the ideas and establishing the proper proportions among the parts of the whole.

'We give perspective to ideas as they unfold by using a series of high-lighted, stressed words which confer meaning on the sentence.

'Stresses have varying qualities: strong, not so strong, weak, barely perceptible, short, sharp, light, long, heavy, up-down, down-up, etc.

'Stresses colour a whole sentence. This is one of the best means for laying out the planes and colours and making the play three-dimensional.

' "Needless to say, the overall picture of logical perspective is completed by distributive stresses which . . . are always weaker than logical stresses" (Smolenski).

'The varying degrees of stress on highlighted words are particularly obvious in music. For example, let's take a sentence in Musorgski's *Boris Godunov* (Smolenski's example).

' "Summon the people to the feast, all, from lord to lowly beggar, let all come freely, all are honoured guests."

'The composer gradually intensifies the stress on the repeated word, "all", by raising the pitch and lengthening the notes which also increases their strength.

'The art of the speaker or reader lies in successfully distributing all the degrees of stress throughout the sentence, speech, scene, act, play or role, and putting them in perspective.

'We highlight this or that syllable in a word, this or that word in a sentence, this or that sentence in a complete thought, the key sections in lengthy narratives, soliloquies, dialogue, the key episodes in a long scene, act, etc.

'Besides accenting syllables, we, naturally, highlight words and whole sentences, and whole thoughts, etc. We arrive at a chain of stressed moments which differ in strength and degree of highlighting.'

4.

.. .. 19..

I summoned up my courage and tried to tell Tortsov everything I'd been through in the last few days, since his last class.

'Too late,' he said, stopping me and, turning to the students, explained.

'My job, as far as speech is concerned, is done. I haven't taught you anything and that was never my intention. But I have introduced you to a conscious study of a new and highly important subject.

'By small practical experiments, I have made you understand how many techniques there are for developing the voice, colour, inflexions, sound shapes, all the kinds of stress, logical and psychological pauses, etc. which actors must have and work on if they are to respond to the demands placed on words and speech in the theatre.

'I've told you all I can. Your new teacher, Vladimir Sechenov, will teach you the "laws of speech" better than I.'

Sechenov emerged from the darkness of the auditorium and Tortsov introduced him to us. After a few kind words of welcome, he explained that Vlad would give his first class after a short break.

Tortsov was about to leave but I stopped him.

'Don't go! Please! Don't just go away when you haven't told us the most important thing of all!'

Pasha supported me.

Tortsov was embarrassed, he blushed, took us both to one side and rebuked us for being tactless towards the new teacher and finally added:

'What's the matter? What's happened?'

'It's terrible! I've forgotten how to speak!' I choked on my own words as I tried to unburden myself.

'I've tried very hard to apply the lessons you taught us when I speak or read but I get into such a mess I can't put two words together. I place the stress but it's as though it's laughing at me, it won't stay where the rules say it should be but jumps away. I try to place the mandatory inflexions at punctuation marks but my voice makes such weird shapes I can't believe it's happening. I start speaking an idea and I stop thinking about it because I've got so bogged down in the laws of speech I go through the whole sentence trying to find where to apply them.

'My brains are addled and my mind is in a whirl because of it all!'

'That's because you're impatient,' Tortsov said to me. 'You mustn't be in such a rush! You must follow the programme of study.

'To put your mind at rest I would have to break the sequence and jump ahead and that would confuse all the other students who aren't complaining, or in such a rush as you.'

After a moment's thought Tortsov invited us to his home at 9 o'clock that evening. After that he left and Sechenov began his class.

Is it worth taking down something that is already in print, in The Expressive Word? It's easier to buy it. I decided not to transcribe Sechenov's class.

20

PERSPECTIVE OF THE ACTOR AND THE ROLE

.. .. 19..

We were at Tortsov's house at about nine in the evening.

I told him how offended we were that inspiration had been replaced by conscious calculation on the part of the actor.

'Yes, indeed . . . ,' Tortsov said. 'One half of you is moving towards the Supertask, the Through-action, the Subtext, mental images, the creative state, and the other half is concerned with your psychotechnique and Adaptations as I showed you in earlier classes.

'When he is performing, an actor is divided in two. Salvini said, "When I am acting, I live a double life, I laugh and weep and at the same time analyse my laughter and tears, so that they can touch the hearts of those I wish to move more deeply."

'As you can see, a double life doesn't stop you being inspired. On the contrary! One helps the other.

'We are also split in two in the real world. But that doesn't stop us living or feeling deeply.

'Remember, at the very beginning when I was explaining Tasks and the Through-action to you, I told you of two perspectives, running parallel to each other.

'One of them has to do with the role.

'The other with the actor, his life onstage, his psychotechnique as a performer.

'The path I described to you earlier in the class on *psychotechnique*, the actor's perspective. It is close to the perspective of the role. It is like a small road that runs alongside a highway. But there are moments when they diverge, for some reason that has nothing to do with the play. Happily, that's what our psychotechnique is for, to lure us back to the right path, as the small road always leads us back to the highway.'

We asked Tortsov to explain the two perspectives to which he had previously referred in passing, in greater detail.

He didn't want to depart from our programme of studies, leap ahead and so disrupt its sequence.

'The perspective of the role and the actor belongs to next year, *Work on a Role*,' he explained.

But we pressed him hard with all kinds of questions. He became quite carried away and didn't realize he was talking about something he didn't want to discuss yet.

.. .. 19..

'I was at the theatre recently and saw a five-act play,' Tortsov said in today's class.

'At the end of the first act I felt enthusiastic about the production and the performance. The characters were vivid, the actors had warmth and energy, they had found a style of acting that interested me. I followed the development of the play and the acting sympathetically.

'But the second act was the same as the first. As a result the audience's interest and mine flagged. The third act was the same only more so. The characters hadn't changed an ounce, there was the same kind of energy the audience already knew, and the same style of acting that had lapsed into cliché. They were boring, colourless and at times irritating. In the fifth act I lost interest. I had stopped looking or listening and could only think of one thing, how to escape discreetly.

'How are we to explain this drop in the production and acting of a good play?'

'It was monotonous,' I commented.

'A week ago I was at a concert. There was the same "monotony" in the music. A good orchestra was playing a good symphony. It ended the way it began, scarcely a change in tempo, always the same degree of loudness, with no subtlety at all. This was excruciating for the audience.

'Why did a good play with a good cast and a good symphony with a good orchestra fail?

'Wasn't it because neither the actors nor the musicians knew where they were going, because they had no line, no perspective?

'What we call a "perspective" is the planned, *harmonious relationship and arrangement of the parts of the entire play and the role.*'

'The harmonious relationship and arrangement of the parts . . .,' Vanya tried to drum the words in.

'This is what it means,' said Tortsov, to help him. 'There can be no acting, action, movement, thought, speech, words, feeling, etc., without the right kind of perspective. The simplest entrance or exit, sitting down in any scene, the speaking of a word, a speech, etc., must be in line with an ultimate goal (Supertask).

'Without it you can't even say, "yes", or "no". Large physical actions, the expression of great thoughts, experiencing great feelings and passions which are composed of many small parts, indeed, a scene, an act, a play cannot be carried out without *a perspective, an ultimate goal (Supertask).*

'We can compare the perspective in acting to the perspective, the different grounds of depth in painting. We also have the foreground, mid-ground, background, etc.

'In painting they are conveyed by colours, light, receding and advancing perspectives; onstage, they are conveyed by actions, attitudes, developing thoughts, feeling, experiences, creative acting with the corresponding strength, colour, pace, clarity, definition, expressiveness, etc.

'In painting, the foreground is sharper, more colourful than things further away.

'In acting, the richest colours are placed not according to the physical closeness or distance of an action but because of its significance in relation to the whole play.

'Some major Tasks, wants, thoughts are placed in the foreground and are fundamental while others, medium and small, are subordinate, secondary and are kept in the background.

'Only when an actor has thought about, analysed and lived the entire role and a broad, distant, clear, colourful, alluring perspective opens out before him can his acting, so to speak, take the long view and not the short view as previously. Then he can play not individual tasks, speak not individual phrases but whole thoughts and passages.

'When we read a new book, its overall perspective escapes us. We can only see the immediate actions, words, sentences. Is that kind of reading artistic or right? Of course not.

'An actor playing a role he has not properly studied or analysed, is like someone reading from a difficult book with which he has only a passing acquaintance.

'Actors like that can't see the perspective of the work clearly. They don't basically understand where they should go with the character they are playing. Often when they perform a particular scene they don't know what is hidden in a dark future. As a result, the actor thinks only of the immediate Task, action, feeling and thought. That causes him, at any given moment, merely to think of the immediate Task, action, feeling or thought without relation to the whole and the perspective the play opens out

'For example, some actors playing Luka in *The Lower Depths*, don't even bother to read the last act because they don't appear in it. As a result, they don't have the right perspective and can't play their role. The beginning depends on the end. The last act is the result of the old man's speech. The actor playing Luka must always have the end of the play in view, and lead the other actors, whom he influences, towards it.

'At other times, an actor playing Othello, who has not studied his role properly, is already rolling his eyes and baring his teeth in the first act, foreshadowing the murder in Act V.

'But Salvini was much more careful in planning his roles. In *Othello* for example, he always had a perspective on the play, from the youthful passion of love in the first scene to the final, boundless hatred of a jealous husband and the murder. He planned feelings throughout the play, moment by moment, with mathematical precision and inexorable logic.

'This great actor could do this because he was always aware of the perspective and had not one perspective but two perspectives to follow.'

'Two perspectives? Which ones?' I asked. I was bewildered.

'*The role and himself.*'

'What's the difference between them?' I asked.

'The character knows nothing about perspective, or his future, while the artist must always have it in view, that he must bear in mind the perspective.'

'How can you forget the future when you've played a role a hundred times?'

'You can't and you shouldn't,' Torsov explained. 'Although the character should know nothing about his future, there has to be a perspective on the role so that at any given moment the present mood can be better understood and appreciated so that you can surrender totally to it.'

'Let's say you are playing Hamlet, psychologically one of the most complex of roles. In it we find the bewilderment when faced with the sudden love of a mother who "or eer those shoes were old" has managed to forget her husband. There is the supernatural experience of a man who has a momentary glimpse of the life beyond where his father is in torment. When Hamlet begins to learn the future's secrets, everything in the real world loses any meaning it had before. We also have the desire to understand, and the awareness of an impossible mission that is necessary to save his father in the hereafter. The role demands a son's feeling for his mother, love for a young woman, breaking with her, her death, a feeling of sorrow, and terror at his mother's death, and murder, and his own death after he has done his duty. Try to mix all these feelings into one, with no kind of order and imagine what mix-up results.

'But if you put all these experiences into perspective logically, systematically, as the psychological complexity of the character requires, with its evermore complex development throughout the play, then you achieve a firm structure, a harmonious line in which the leading role is played by all the dependent parts in the tragedy of a great soul as it grows ever deeper.

'Can you play any moment in such a role without giving it perspective? If you don't convey his disturbance and incomprehension at the sight of his frivolous mother at the beginning of the play properly, then the famous scene with her will not be sufficiently prepared. If he is not sufficiently shaken by his knowledge of the afterlife, the impossibility of his earthly mission, his doubts, his urgent search for the meaning of life, his break-up with his beloved, his strange behaviour would be incomprehensible.

'You know from what I have said that the more cautiously the actor playing Hamlet performs the opening scenes, the stronger the passions required of him will be as they develop throughout the play?

'In our particular jargon we call that kind of performance acting with perspective.

'So, as we develop a role we have to bear in mind two perspectives, one belonging to the role, the other to the actor himself. Hamlet must not know his fate and the end of his life, but the artist must see the whole perspective the whole time, otherwise he will not be able to order, colour, shade and shape the different parts.

'The future of a role is its Supertask. The characters in the play must work towards it. There is no harm if for a moment the actor remembers the entire perspective of his role. That only strengthens the meaning of each immediate Bit as he experiences it, and makes him concentrate more strongly on it.

'On the other hand, both perspectives must constantly think towards the future.'

'I'd like to learn through examples of both,' I persisted.

'Fine. Let's start with the role. Let's suppose that you and Pasha are playing the scene between Othello and Iago. It's important for you to remember that you, as the Moor, arrived in Cyprus, were reunited with

Desdemona for ever, that you experienced the best time in your life, your honeymoon.

'Where else are you to find the happy mood you need for the beginning of the scene? It is all the more important since there are few bright moments in the play. It is also important for you to remember that with this scene the happiest period of your life begins to darken, and that you must show this gradually and starkly. There must be a marked contrast between the present and the future. The brighter the former, the darker the latter.

'Only after a rapid glance at the past and the future of the role can you appraise its successive Bits. The better you are aware of its meaning within the whole play, the better you will be able to concentrate your entire self on it.

'That is why you need to have a perspective on the role,' Tortsov said in conclusion.

'And why do we need the second kind of perspective, the actor's?' I asked.

'We need *the actor's perspective, the perspective of the human being playing the role* so that, at any given moment, we keep thinking about the future, that we marshal all our inner creative forces and outer means of expression, so that we can properly order them and see the value of the raw material with some intelligence. For example in Othello's scene with Iago, jealousy creeps into his mind and slowly develops into doubt.

'And so the artist must remember that he has to play many similar, ever mounting moments of passion right through to the end of the play. It is dangerous to play the first scene too intensely, and not hold back for his growing jealousy. Wasting mental energy ruins the entire plan for the role. We need to be economical and sparing and never forget the climax of the play. Artistic emotion is measured in ounces not in pounds.

'Everything I have said applies equally to the voice, diction, movement, facial expression, energy and tempo-rhythm. Here, too, it is dangerous to give everything at once, to be wasteful. We need to be economical, have a true sense of our physical strength and means of expression.

'To keep them all under control we need our own perspective, as we do with our inner forces.

'We must not forget, either, one of the most important qualities of perspective in acting. It gives our experiences room, space, verve and momentum.

'Consider this, you are running a race not all in one go but in stages, stopping each time after twenty paces. Then you will never gather momentum, which is very important for running.

'It's the same for us. If we stop after each Bit and start afresh with another, our efforts, wishes and actions never gather momentum. And we need it, because it fires up our will, our feelings, our ideas, our imagination, etc. You can't build up speed in confined areas. You need space, perspective, distance, a goal that draws you towards it.

'Now that you have a new piece of knowledge, the perspective of the play and the role, tell me, doesn't it remind you of something you know already – Throughaction?

'Of course, perspective is not the Throughaction, but they are very close. It is a close aid. It is the path, the perspective that the Throughaction follows throughout the whole play.

'Finally, I would remark that I have delayed talking about perspective because only now do you know about the necessity for the Supertask and the Throughaction.

'They contain the main ideas of acting, art, the entire "system".'

21

TEMPO-RHYTHM

There was a sign hanging in the auditorium of the school theatre today:

INNER AND OUTER TEMPO-RHYTHM

That meant we had reached a new phase in our programme.

'I should have talked about inner Tempo-rhythm much earlier when we were studying how to achieve *the creative state in performance*, because *inner Tempo-rhythm* is one of its main features,' Tortsov explained today.

'I held back so as to make today's work easier.

'It's much more convenient to talk about inner Tempo-rhythm at the same time as *outer Tempo-rhythm*, because then it is observable in physical actions. At that moment it can be seen as well as sensed, rather like inner experiences which are not visible to the eye. I said nothing about Tempo-rhythm earlier because it was invisible and am only discussing it now when we are talking about *outer, visible Tempo-rhythm*.

'*Tempo* is the rate at which equal, agreed, single length-values follow each other in any given time signature.

'*Rhythm* is the quantitative relationship of active, agreed length-values in any given tempo or time signature.

'*Time signature* is the repetition (or presumed repetition) of a group of agreed length-values, marked by a single stress (length of phonic movement).' Tortsov read from the notes Rakhmanov handed to him.

'Did you understand?' he then asked.

Thoroughly embarrassed, we admitted we hadn't understood a word.

'Without wishing to speak ill of scientific definitions,' Tortsov continued, 'I suggest they aren't of much practical use to you at the moment because as yet you have no personal experience of the significance and effect of Tempo-rhythm onstage.

'They complicate the approach to Tempo-rhythm. They prevent you from enjoying it easily, freely, lightheartedly and playing with it like a toy. And it is precisely that playful attitude that we need especially in our first steps early on.

'It would be harmful for you to try and squeeze Tempo-rhythm out of yourselves, or knit your brow and calculate all its complex combinations, like a mindbending mathematical problem.

'So, let's forget scientific definitions and simply play with rhythm.

'As you can see, we've brought some toys for you to play with. I'll hand over to Rakhmanov. This is his field.'

Tortsov went to the back of the auditorium with his secretary and Rakhmanov placed metronomes a caretaker had brought all over the stage, like sentries. He set the largest in the middle of the round table. He placed three smaller machines on nearby smaller tables. He set the large one in motion. Its tick was clear. (No. 10 on the scale.)

'Listen, everyone!' said Rakhmanov turning to us.

'Now, this large metronome will tick slowly,' he explained.

'Here's how slow it works: one . . . one . . . *andante quasi andantissimo*.

'No. 10 is quite a character.

'If we lower the weight on the pendulum we get a simple *andante* which is a little faster than *quasi andantissimo*.

'It's faster, yes, just a fraction! Listen: one . . . one . . . one.

'But if we push the weight down further . . . this is how it goes: oneoneone . . . This is faster, an *allegro*.

'And here's *presto*.

'And now *presto-prestissimo*.

'These are all indications of *speed*. There are as many different speeds as there are marks on the metronome.

'What a clever contraption!'

Then Rakhmanov rang a handbell marking two, then three, then four, five, six ticks of the metronome.

'One. . . . . two. . . . .

Ring.

'One. . . . . two. . . . .

Ring, Rakhmanov demonstrated duple time.

'Or: one... two... three... Ring. One... two... three... Ring. That's triple time.

'Or: one... two... three... four... Ring. And so forth. That's quadruple time,' Rakhmanov explained enthusiastically.

After that, he started the first small metronome and made it tick twice as fast as the large – two small ticks to one large.

He started the second small metronome four times, and the third eight times faster than the large – four or eight small ticks to one large.

'Pity we haven't a fourth and fifth small metronome. I'd have liked to set them sixteen, thirty-two times faster! That would really be something!' sighed Rakhmanov.

But he soon cheered up because Tortsov came back, with Paul, and the two of them tapped out the missing sixteen and thirty-two ticks on the table with their keys.

The ticking of the metronomes and the tapping of the keys coincided each time the bell marked the start of a bar. The rest of the time the ticks and taps were all over the place and only came together when the bell rang.

There was a whole orchestra of ticks and taps. It was difficult to make sense out of this confused medley. Our heads span.

But there was a moment's harmony in the general disorder when all the beats coincided and that provided momentary satisfaction.

The confusion was increased by the mixture of even and uneven time signatures: two, four, eight time, and three, six, nine to a bar. The result was even greater sub-division and confusion, unbelievable chaos, which Tortsov absolutely adored.

'Listen to that jumble, and yet the order, the harmony of this organized chaos. That's created by the wizard, Tempo-rhythm. Let us investigate this amazing phenomenon and examine each of its component parts.

'Here we have *tempo*,' Tortsov pointed to the large metronome. 'Its function is almost entirely mechanical, and *pedantically regular*.

'Tempo is quickness or slowness. Tempo can curtail or extend an action, shorten or lengthen speech.

'Performing an action, speaking a word demands time.

'Quicken the tempo and there is less time for either. That means I have to act or speak faster.

'Slow down the tempo and you have more time to act and speak and so greater opportunity to do and say what is important.

'Here we have the bar,' Tortsov pointed to the bell Rakhmanov had rung. 'It functions in complete coordination with the large metronome, and with the same mechanical precision.

'The bar is the *timescale*. But there are different kinds of bars. Their duration depends on tempo and speed. If that is so, then it means we also have different timescales.

'The bar is a conventional, relative concept. It is not the same as a yard, by which we measure extension in space.

'A yard is unvarying and unvariable. But bars, which measure time, are different.

'The bar is not an entity, like a yard.

'The *bar* is the same as time.

'*Time is measured by time.*

'What do all these other small metronomes represent? What do Paul and I, tapping in the missing fractions, represent?

'We all create rhythm.

'The small metronomes divide up the time periods, called bars, into different size fractions.

'We combine them in an infinite number of ways and that creates *an infinite number of possible rhythms* within the same bar length.

'The same is true of acting. Actions and speech move through time. We must fill time with a wide variety of movements, interspersed with moments of repose. When we speak we fill time with moments of utterance which have breaks between.

'Here are some very simple formulae, combinations for one bar:

$$1/4 + 2/8 + 4/16 + 8/32 + 1 \text{ bar in } 4/4 \text{ time.}$$

'Or another combination in triple time:

$$4/16 + 1/4 + 2/8 + 1 \text{ bar in } 3/4.$$

'Thus, rhythm is a combination of moments of every possible duration which divide the time we call a bar into a variety of parts. You can create countless combinations and groupings out of them. If you listen carefully to the chaotic rhythms and ticks from the metronomes you may well discover all the fractions you can possibly need for combining and grouping rhythms and for the most diverse, complex formulae.

'You will have to discover, separate out and then group your own personal perspectives as regards tempi, speech bars, movement and experiencing for the role you are playing amid the chaotic Tempo-rhythms onstage, all the actions and words.

'Learn to sort out your own stage rhythm amid the organized chaos created by different tempi and time signatures.'

'Today we're going to play with Tempo-rhythm again,' said Tortsov as he came in.

'Let's clap our hands, like children. You'll see, it can be fun for grown-ups, too.'

Tortsov started with a very slow tick of the metronome.

'One. . . Two. . . Three. . . Four.'

And again.

'One. . . Two. . . Three. . . Four. . .'

And yet again

'One. . . Two. . . Three. . . Four. . .'

And so on ad infinitum.

Clapping on the first beat went on for a minute or two.

We clapped in unison on 'one'.

But this game wasn't any fun at all. It sent us to sleep. It made us feel bored, dull and lazy because of the regularity of the beat. At first we clapped energetically and loudly but the flatter our mood became the quieter the clapping became and our faces expressed growing boredom.

'One. . . Two. . . Three. . . Four. . .'

And once again.

'One. . . Two. . . Three. . . Four. . .'

And again.

'One. . . Two. . . Three. . . Four. . .'

We were practically asleep.

'You don't seem to be having much fun. Soon you'll be snoring,' Tortsov commented and quickly changed the game.

'I'll keep the same slow tempo but put two accents in each bar to wake you up. Clap twice, on "three" as well as "one".

'Like so.

'One. . . Two. . . Three. . . Four.

And again.

'One. . . Two. . . Three. . . Four.

And yet again.

'One. . . Two. . . Three. . . Four.

And again ad infinitum.

It was a little livelier but a long way from being fun.

'If that doesn't work, then accent all four beats in the same slow tempo,' Tortsov decided.

'One. . . Two. . . Three. . . Four.'

We woke up a little and though we still weren't having fun we felt a little livelier.

'Now,' said Tortsov, 'give me two eighth-notes for each quarter-note with the accent on the first eighth-note of each pair, like so:

'One-one, Two- two, Three-three, Four-four.'

That livened us up. The claps were clearer, louder, our faces looked more energetic, happier.

We continued for a few minutes.

When Tortsov went on to sixteenth and thirty-second notes, still with the accent on the first count in each quarter-note, all our energy returned.

But Tortsov didn't stop there. He gradually speeded up the metronome. Soon we were lagging behind. That electrified us.

We wanted to keep up with the beat, in tempo and rhythm. We started to sweat, we went red in the face, we clapped like mad, using legs, body, mouth, grunts to help us. Our arm muscles were tired and cramped. But we were happy. We were even having fun.

'Well, now! Playing happily? Having fun?' Tortsov laughed. 'You see what a wizard I am! I can not only control your muscles but your feelings, your mood as well. I can first lull you to sleep and then whip you up into a frenzy and make you sweat buckets,' he joked.

'But I'm not a wizard. It's Tempo-rhythm that has the magic and affects your inner mood,' Tortsov summarized.

'I think the conclusion you draw arises from a misunderstanding,' Grisha argued. 'Look, excuse me, but we came alive when we were clapping not because of Tempo-rhythm but because we needed ten times the energy to keep up. When a night-watchman stamps his feet and beats his hands against his ribs in icy weather, it's the strength of his movements that warms him, not the Tempo-rhythm.'

Tortsov didn't stop to argue, but suggested another experiment:

'I'll give you a bar in 4/4 time in which there is one half-note, equal to two quarter-notes, then a quarter-note's rest, then finally a quarter-note, which makes 4/4, i.e. a whole bar.

'Clap it for me, accenting the initial half-note:

'One. . . Two. . . hm. . . Four
'One. . . Two. . . hm. . . Four
'One. . . Two. . . hm. . . Four.

'I use "hm" to represent the quarter-note rest. The final quarter-note has a slow sustained accent.'

We clapped for a long time and had to admit that the result was quite a stately, quiet, lingering mood.

Then Tortsov repeated the experiment changing the final quarter-note into an eighth-note rest and an eighth-note, like so:

'One-two (half-note), hm (quarter-note rest), hm (eighth-note rest) and 1/8.

'One. . . Two. . . hm, hm 1/8. One. . . Two. . . hm, hm 1/8. . .

'Have you noticed how the last note seems late and almost to slide over into the next bar? By breaking the barline it upsets the following calm, staid half-note, which shrinks like a nervous woman.'

Even Grisha had to agree that the calm, dignified mood had been altered by an implied, rather than an actual disturbance. Then the half-note was replaced by two quarter-notes, which were later changed to eighth-notes, with rests, and then sixteenth-notes so that the feeling of calm gradually vanished and was replaced by a sense of unease and jumpiness.

We repeated the exercise, adding syncopation, which increased the sense of disturbance.

Then we clapped groups of two, three and four. That produced an ever-increasing sense of alarm. We repeated the experiment in a fast and then a very fast tempo. This resulted in new moods and responses.

We varied the method, style, nature of the claps. At times they were rich and solid, at others sharp and staccato, light or heavy, loud or soft.

The variations of tempo and rhythms produced a wide diversity of moods: *andante maestoso, andante largo, allegro vivo, allegretto, allegro vivace.*

Our experiments were too numerous to count but convinced us that while using rhythm can't actually induce alarm and panic you can get a picture of what they are emotionally.

When we'd finished, Tortsov turned to Grisha and said:

'I hope you won't compare us to the night-watchman, freezing in the ice and snow but recognize that it isn't an action as such but *Tempo-rhythm* which has an *immediate and direct effect* on us.'

Grisha didn't answer and we all supported what Tortsov had said.

'It only remains for me to congratulate you on having made a highly important "discovery", something everyone knows and actors always forget, namely that whatever you do, proper metre in syllables, words, speech and movement and precise rhythms, are crucial to the process of experiencing.

'Don't forget, Tempo-rhythm is a two-edged sword. It can be helpful and harmful in equal measure.

'Choose Tempo-rhythm properly and feelings and experiences arise naturally. But if the Tempo-rhythm is wrong, inappropriate feelings and experiences will arise in precisely the same way, in the same passage, and you won't be able to put things right until you have replaced the wrong Tempo-rhythm.'

Today, Tortsov devised a new game for us.

'Have you done military service?' he asked Leo suddenly.

'Yes,' he answered.

'You learned to bear yourself like a soldier?'

'Of course.'

'Can you remember what that feels like?'

'I expect so.'

'Remember it, then.'

'I'll have to work up to it.'

Tortsov remained seated but started to tap out a military march with his feet. Paul followed his example and Vanya, Marya and all of us joined in. Everything around us began to throb to the beat of the march.

It was as though a whole regiment was passing through the room. To intensify the illusion, Tortsov began to beat rhythmically on the table, like the rat-tat-tat of a drum.

We did too. There was now a whole orchestra. The clear, exact beating of our feet and hands made us straighten up. We felt as though we were being drilled.

Tortsov was thus able to get what he wanted instantly, thanks to Tempo-rhythm.

After a short pause he explained:

'Now I'll tap out something solemn, not a march.'

Tum-tum, tum-tum, tumtumtum, tum tum, tum, tum-tum.

'I know what it is! I've guessed it!' yelled Vanya, at the top of his voice. 'It's a game. Someone taps out a rhythm and someone else guesses what it is. If they don't, they pay a forfeit.'

This time we did not guess the rhythm itself, only its general mood. The first time he'd tapped out a military march, the second, something solemn (the Pilgrim's Chorus from *Tannhäuser* as it turned out). Tortsov then went on to the next experiment.

But this time we couldn't determine what he was tapping out. It was animated, confused, urgent. Actually he was presenting the rattle of an express train.

Vanya, who was next to me, tapped out something romantic for Marya, then something stormy.

'What's this? Listen: tum-tata tumtata-ta-ta.'

'Oh! Great!'

'I don't understand a thing, my darling, absolutely nothing. You're tapping for nothing!'

'But I know what it is. Word of honour. I'm tapping out love and jealousy. Tum-ta-*taaa*! Now, pay your forfeit.'

Meanwhile I tapped out my mood when I get home. I had a clear picture of coming into the room, washing my hands, taking off my jacket, lying down on the sofa and starting to think about Tempo-rhythm. Then the cat came in and lay down beside me. Peace and quiet.

I thought I was conveying this picture of domestic bliss through tempo and rhythm but nobody understood me at all. Pasha detected eternal rest, Igor was reminded of 'Marlborough s'en va-t-en guerre'.[1]

There's no way to count all the other things we tapped out, among others a storm at sea or in the mountains, wind, hail, thunder and lightning, evening bells, alarm bells, a village fire, quacking ducks, dripping taps, gnawing mice, headache, toothache, woe and ecstasy. We tapped and pounded as though we were in the kitchen making meatballs. If anyone had come in, they'd have thought we were drunk or crazy.

Some of the students had clapped their hands till they were so sore they had to convey their experiences and mental images by waving their hands like a conductor. This proved much more convenient and soon everyone was doing it. Thereafter, conducting was 'legal'.

But no one actually guessed what the beats were about. Tortsov's Tempo-rhythm was an obvious failure.

'Well, are you convinced of the power of Tempo-rhythm?' Tortsov asked with a triumphant look.

His question astonished us because we were going to tell him the exact opposite:

'What about your famous Tempo-rhythm? However much we kept beating, no one understood a thing.'

We expressed our bewilderment to Tortsov in somewhat milder terms, to which he answered.

'Do you mean you were beating rhythms for others, not yourselves? The exercise I gave was for the doers not the watchers. I wanted Tempo-rhythm to take you over, and beating time to stimulate your Emotion Memory and involve others. And to involve others you first have to involve yourselves. Listeners pick up the general mood of your rhythm and that is very important when you are trying to influence them.

'As you can see, even Grisha doesn't deny that Tempo-rhythm influences feeling.'

But Grisha did deny it.

'It wasn't Tempo-rhythm, but the Given Circumstances which affected us today,' he argued.

'And what produced them?'

'*Tempo-rhythm*,' we all shouted, rejecting Grisha.

.. .. 19..

Tortsov is inexhaustible. Today he thought up another game.

'Quickly, don't think, show me the Tempo-rhythm of a traveller hearing the first bell to announce the departure of a long-distance train.'

I saw the ticket office in a corner of the station, a long line of people and a window which was still closed.

Then it opened. A long boring advance step by step ensued, then buying the ticket.

Then I visualized another ticket office, with prices written up, luggage piled up on the counter and another long, slow-moving line. Receipts had to be written out and payments made. Then there was the tedious business of my hand luggage. In between, I glanced at the papers and magazines in the kiosk. Then I hurried to the buffet for a snack. I found my train, my carriage, my seat, stowed my things and had a look at my companions. I unfolded my paper and started to read, etc. As the second bell hadn't rung, I had to bring in new Given Circumstances. I'd lost something, so I had to report it. Tortsov still said nothing, so I had to imagine buying cigarettes, sending a telegram, looking for people I knew on the train, etc., etc. In this way I created a long, unbroken series of Tasks which I accomplished quietly, and without rush, because there was still a lot of time before the train left.

'Now, do all that again, only this time you've only arrived in time for the second bell,' Tortsov ordered. 'You don't have a quarter of an hour before the train leaves, as before, but much less time, so you'll have to do all you have to do in five minutes not fifteen. And, unluckily for you, there's a huge crowd. Conduct this new Tempo-rhythm for me.'

That's enough to make anyone's heart beat faster, especially me. I always travel in a complete state of nerves (Reisefieber). My Tempo-rhythm reflected all this. It was no longer regular but jerky and rushed.

'Another change,' Tortsov said after a short pause. 'You arrived just before the third bell, not the second.'

To increase the tension, he imitated the clanging of the bell using a metal lampshade. We had not five, but one minute to do everything we needed. We only had time to think about essentials and forget the rest. We were so worked up we could hardly sit still. Our hands were too clumsy to beat out our inner Tempo-rhythm.

When the experiment was over, Tortsov explained that the exercise was intended to demonstrate that Tempo-rhythm can't be recalled or used without creating the mental images or Given Circumstances to go with it, or without feeling our Tasks and actions. They are so closely linked that each produces the other, i.e. Given Circumstances evoke Tempo-rhythm and Tempo-rhythm reminds us of the relevant Given Circumstances.

'Yes,' Paul affirmed, thinking about the exercise we'd just done. 'We really had to consider and see the *what* and *how* of setting out on a long journey. It was only then that I had some idea of what Tempo-rhythm is.'

'So, Tempo-rhythm not only stimulates Emotion Memory, as we saw by tapping it out in previous classes, but brings our visual memory and mental images alive. That's why it is wrong to think of Tempo-rhythm only in terms of pace and regularity,' Tortsov commented.

'We don't need Tempo-rhythm for its own sake. It must be related to the inner meaning that Tempo-rhythm always hides within it. A military march, walking pace, a funeral procession may have the same Tempo-rhythm but each has quite different *inner content, mood and elusive special features.*

'In a word, Tempo-rhythm possesses not only outward features which affect us, but inner content which nurtures our feelings. It is in that form that memory retains it and makes it available for creative purposes.'

.. .. 19..

'In our last few classes you've had fun with the games I gave you, but today you're going to make your own fun. Now you know what Tempo-rhythm is and you've stopped being afraid of it, there's nothing to prevent you playing with it.

'Go onstage and do anything you like.

'Only make it clear in advance *what* you'll use to mark the strong beats.'

'Move our hands, feet, fingers, our whole body, turn our heads, necks, waists, use facial expression, the sounds we make with letters, syllables and words,' the students shouted, interrupting each other.

'Yes. These are actions any Tempo-rhythm can create,' Tortsov concurred. 'We walk, run, ride a bicycle, speak, work in Tempo-rhythm. But when people aren't moving, when they're resting, waiting, doing nothing, don't they have any tempo or rhythm?'

'Yes, there's tempo and rhythm then, too,' the students acknowledged.

'But it's not outwardly visible, only inwardly sensed,' I added.

'True,' Tortsov agreed. 'We think, dream, grieve in certain Tempo-rhythms because we reveal our lives in all these moments. And where there is *life* there is *action,* and where there is *action* there is *movement,* and where there is *movement* there is *tempo,* and where there is *tempo* there is *rhythm.*

'And transmitting and receiving, don't they have movement?

'If they do, it means that people also work, create, perceive, communicate and persuade in a certain Tempo-rhythm.

'We also talk about flights of ideas and fancy. That means they, too, have movement, and, therefore, tempo and rhythm.

'Listen to the way feelings quiver, throb, seethe and thrill. Each invisible movement has a great variety of implicit time-values and speeds, and so it has tempo and rhythm.

'Every human passion, state of mind, experience has its Tempo-rhythm. Every individual inner and outer character type – sanguine, phlegmatic, the Mayor, Khlestakov, Zemlyanika[2] – has its Tempo-rhythm.

'Every fact, every event inevitably has its own Tempo-rhythm. For example, a declaration of war or peace, a solemn assembly, receiving a delegation, has its own tempo and rhythm.

'If the tempo doesn't correspond to the event, the result is comic. Imagine, for example, a royal couple dashing helter-skelter to their coronation.

'In a word, there is a living Tempo-rhythm in every moment of our existence, mental or physical.

'Now you're clear about what you'll use to show it,' Tortsov concluded, 'let's decide how you'll mark the moments when actions and beats coincide.'

'By performing Tasks and actions, speaking, communicating,' the students stated.

'In music, a melody is made up of bars, and bars of notes of varying length and strength which express the rhythm. Tempo is inward and invisible. Musicians count it in their heads or the conductor marks it with his baton.

'It is the same in acting. Actions are composed of large or small movements of variable length and regularity. Speech is the combination of short and long, stressed and unstressed letters, syllables and words, which mark the rhythm.

'Actions are performed, lines spoken to the tick-tock of our own mental "metronome" hidden as it were inside us.

'Stressed syllables and movements should, consciously or unconsciously, match the mental count.

'If actors feel what they are saying and doing intuitively, properly, then the right Tempo-rhythm will emerge spontaneously from within as they speak, measuring out stresses, matching the word to the beat. If that doesn't happen, all we can do is produce Tempo-rhythm technically, i.e. usually go from the outside in. To do that, conduct the Tempo-rhythm we need. Now you know that this is impossible without mental images, creative ideas, Given Circumstances, etc., which combine to stimulate feeling. Let us verify the link between Tempo-rhythm and feeling by an experiment.

'Let's start with the Tempo-rhythm of action and move on to the Tempo-rhythm of speech.'

Rakhmanov wound up the large metronome and set it ticking very slowly. Tortsov took a large, stiff portfolio, with school papers in it, which happened to be to hand, and put various things on it, like a tray – an ashtray, a box of matches, a paperweight and so on. He then had Leo take them away to the slow, stately beat, remove them from the tray and hand them out to those present, to a count of 4 in the bar.

Leo has no sense of rhythm at all and it didn't work. We had to coach him with a series of exercises. Other students joined in. Here are the exercises they did: they had to fill the long interval between the ticks with one action or movement, no more.

'Just as, in music, one whole note fills a bar,' Tortsov explained.

'How do we justify such slowness and lack of action?'

I justified it by the enormous amount of concentration I needed to examine a smudge I'd noticed on the far wall of the stalls. A side lamp prevented me from seeing it. I had to place the palm of my hand against my temple to shield my eyes. That was the one single action I allowed myself initially. I then re-adapted to the same task in each subsequent bar. That created the need to change the position of my hand, my body, my feet as I leaned forward to see the smudge. These movements filled the other bars.

Then a small metronome was started as well. It beat first 2, then 4, 8, 16 to a bar, like half-notes, quarter-, eighth- and sixteenth-notes in music.

This time we had to fill the bar with 2, then 4, 8, 16 movements.

I justified these rhythmic actions by searching my pockets, slowly or hurriedly for some important notes I'd lost.

I explained the fastest Tempo-rhythm by beating off a swarm of bees.

We gradually got used to Tempo-rhythm and began to play with it. It was splendid when our movements coincided with the tick of the metronome. It made us believe in what we were doing onstage.

But once this mood passed and counting, mathematics took over. We knitted our brows. No more games.

.. .. 19..

Today, Tortsov resumed the exercise with the tray. But this time Leo couldn't do it, so Tortsov passed it over to me.

The metronome was beating at such a slow rate, one whole note to a bar, and therefore one movement, I had to stretch that single action over the entire distance between the beats. This induced a steady, solemn mood which echoed in my head and called for corresponding movements.

I saw myself as the president of a sporting club, giving out prizes and certificates.

At the end of the ceremony, I was ordered to leave the room and then come back in the same stately rhythm, retrieve the prizes and certificates and exit once more.

I did what I was told without bothering to justify my new task. The action itself, and its stately Tempo-rhythm, suggested new Given Circumstances to me.

I felt like a judge, causing unjust pain to the prizewinners. Spontaneously, intuitively, I felt an antipathy towards the objects.

When I had to do the exercise again, in another Tempo-rhythm, with four quarter-notes to the bar, I felt like a flunkey serving champagne at a gala reception. The same actions, performed eight in the bar, turned me into a waiter in a railway buffet, during a short train stop. I rushed about madly, carrying plates of food to everyone present.

'Now change the second and fourth quarter-notes into eighth-notes,' Tortsov ordered.

All solemnity was gone. The unsteady eighth-notes among the quarter-notes created a mood of uncertainty, confusion and clumsiness. It made me feel like Epikhodov in *The Cherry Orchard*, with his 'twenty-two disasters'. When the eighth-notes were changed to sixteenth-notes, the mood was even stronger.

I seemed to drop everything. I had to catch a falling plate by the minute.

'Am I drunk?' I wondered.

Then we all had to do the same exercise with *syncopation*. The atmosphere of nervousness, doubt and hesitation was even stronger and suggested a new story which justified my actions and which I found credible: the champagne was poisoned. This was why I was so jumpy. Igor did the exercise better than I. He conveyed subtle nuances, *largo lento* and *staccato* as Tortsov defined them.

Our one-time dancer had a great success.

I must admit that today's class convinced me that *Tempo-rhythm cannot only prompt the right feelings and experiences intuitively, directly and immediately, it can help create characters.*

Its effect on Emotion Memory and the imagination can be seen even more clearly when we perform rhythmic actions to music. True, we don't just have Tempo-rhythm, as with the ticking of the metronome, but notes, harmonies and melodies as well, which are always very moving.

Tortsov asked Rakhmanov to play something on the piano and us to perform actions to the music. We had to express what the music was saying, what it suggested to our imaginations by moving in the right

Tempo-rhythm. It was a highly interesting experiment and the students were enthusiastic about it.

It feels good to perform actions to a definite Tempo-rhythm.

It creates a mood and affects the way we feel.

Each of us understood the Tempo-rhythm, the music and what Rakhmanov's playing was trying to say in our own particular and often contradictory way. But we were all convinced by our own interpretation.

Sometimes it seemed to me, that the turbulent, pounding rhythm of the accompaniment suggested someone galloping. A Circassian! I was in the mountains, being taken prisoner. I dashed through the furniture and chairs as though they were like rocks and hid behind them, confident the horsemen couldn't reach me there.

Then the melody grew tender, romantic and suggested new rhythms and actions.

It is my beloved. She rushes to meet me. I'm ashamed to have been such a coward. I'm happy, touched by the urgency with which she runs to me. It is a sign of her love. But now the music is ominous. Now all I think and feel is gloom. Tempo-rhythm of the music plays a large part in these techniques.

So, it can not only suggest whole characters but whole scenes as well!

.. .. 19..

Today, Tortsov called everyone up onstage, set three metronomes ticking in different tempi and told us to react however we liked.

We divided into groups, established Tasks, Given Circumstances and started to react, some on whole notes, others on quarter-notes, others on eighth-notes, etc.

But Varya found other people's Tempo-rhythms offputting and wanted to lay down one speed and one beat for everyone.

'Why the regimentation?' asked a puzzled Tortsov. 'People have their own Tempo-rhythm in life as well as onstage. A common Tempo-rhythm is generally an accident. Imagine that you are in a dressing room just before the last act. The first group who responded to the first metronome have finished their performance and are hurriedly taking off their make-up so they can go home. The second group, who responded to the second, faster metronome are putting on new costumes and make-up for the remaining act. You, Varya, are in that group and have five minutes to do your hair and put on a ballgown.'

Our resident beauty surrounded herself with chairs and enthusiastically set about her favourite occupation – making herself appear beautiful, oblivious to other people's Tempo-rhythms.

Suddenly Tortsov started the third metronome at top speed and he and

Rakhmanov started acting in a frenzied, erratic rhythm which they justified by saying that they had a quick change and had to open the following act. Their costumes were littered all over the room and they had to find them among the pile of other clothes.

The new Tempo-rhythm contrasted sharply with the first two and increased the complexity, vividness, jumpiness of the scene. Yet despite the variety of rhythms, Varya continued doing her hair, ignoring the activity around her.

'Why did nothing stop you this time?' Tortsov asked, when the exercise was over.

'Can't say,' our beauty responded. 'I didn't have time to notice.'

'Precisely!' said Tortsov seizing on her answer. 'Earlier on you were doing rhythm for rhythm's sake, but just now you were performing *productive, specific actions in rhythm* and so "didn't have time to notice" what other people were doing.'

Tortsov had this to say about the rhythm of the group as a whole:

'When many people are living and reacting in a single rhythm onstage, like a row of soldiers or the corps de ballet, they create a conventional Tempo-rhythm. Its strength lies in the herd instinct, in mechanical group training.

'Ignoring those exceptional occasions when a crowd succumbs to a common purpose, this single, all-embracing Tempo-rhythm is a rarity in a realistic theatre like ours, which requires all the nuances of life itself.

'We fear pure convention. That leads us to representation and the stock-in-trade. We use Tempo-rhythm but not a single one for all. We mix a great variety of speeds and time signatures which combine to create a Tempo-rhythm resplendent with all the nuances of real life itself.

'Let me illustrate the difference between a basic and a more subtle approach to rhythm in this way. Children use basic colours in their pictures: grass and leaves are green, treetrunks and the earth are brown, the sky is blue. These are basic conventional colours. Real artists create their own colours out of various tints. Blue and yellow produce various shades of [green] . . .

'This produces a very wide palette on their canvas, a combination of shades and hues.

'We treat Tempo-rhythm as painters treat their colours and we combine a wide variety of speeds and time signatures.'

Tortsov further explained that there can not only be different rhythms and tempo simultaneously at work in all the characters in a scene but in one and the same character at one and the same time.

'When major decisions are taken, when a person or the protagonist suffers no doubts or conflicts, one dominant Tempo-rhythm is both possible and necessary. But when, like Hamlet, resolution wrestles with doubt, many various rhythms have to exist side by side. Then a variety of Tempo-rhythms creates an inner conflict, born of many causes. Experiencing is heightened, inner dynamism increased, feeling aroused.'

I wanted to verify this and decided on two different Tempo-rhythms, one very fast and one very slow.

How could I justify combining these two and *with what*?

A very simple idea came into my head.

I was a drunken pharmacist, blundering about the room blindly, shaking up medicines in various bottles. This story enabled me to use very unexpected Tempo-rhythms. The unsteady walk of a drunk justified the slow Tempo-rhythm while shaking the bottles required a fast, mixed rhythm.

First of all, I worked on the walk. I had to increase the degree of intoxication to slow the rhythm down. I sensed the truth of what I was doing and that made me feel good mentally and physically.

Then I worked on the movement of the hands when shaking the medicine bottles. I was looking for meaningless, muddled movements that would fit the state I was portraying.

So two quite opposite rhythms combined spontaneously. Playing the drunkard was fun now and the applause from out front encouraged me further.

The next exercise was to combine three different tempi in one person following three different metronomes.

This is the story I made up:

I was an actor, preparing to go on, running over the lines slowly to the first metronome. At the same time I'm pacing my dressing room, because I'm nervous, to the second metronome, while getting dressed, knotting my tie to the third, fast metronome.

To co-ordinate the different Tempo-rhythms and actions, I did what I'd done before, i.e. first I combined two actions and Tempo-rhythms, dressing and pacing. Once that was automatic, I introduced the third action, running through the lines, in a new Tempo-rhythm.

The next exercise was much more difficult.

'Let's say you're playing Esmeralda, being led away to her execution,' Tortsov said to Varya. 'The procession moves slowly forward to the ominous rolling of the drums. But her heart beats wildly inside her. She feels these are her last moments. At the same time, the hapless criminal recites a prayer for her life to be saved in a third Tempo-rhythm, while rubbing her hands over her heart, slowly in a fourth Tempo-rhythm.'

The exercise was so difficult Varya clasped her hands to her head. Tortsov was concerned and quickly calmed her down.

'The time will come when you'll hold on to the rhythm, not your head, in moments like these, as to a lifeline. But, for the time being, let's try something not quite so difficult.'

.. .. 19..

Today, Tortsov made us repeat all our previous exercises in Tempo-rhythm but without the promptings of the metronome, so to speak, 'dry', with our own 'metronome' or, in other words, by counting in our heads.

Each of us had to choose a speed and a time signature, hold on to it and perform actions so that the strong moments in our movements coincided with the beat of the imaginary metronome.

That raises the question, which line do you follow, the inner or the outer, when looking for the strong moments? The mental images, the imagined Given Circumstances, contact, transmitting, etc.? How can you use inner action to capture and fix the stressed moments when there is no outer action? It's not easy. I started to go through my thoughts, wants, intentions but nothing made sense to me.

Then I began to listen to my own heartbeat and pulse. But that didn't make anything clearer. Where was I to find my 'imaginary metronome' and where was I supposed to beat out the Tempo-rhythm?

Sometimes it seemed to be happening in my head, at others in my hands. I was afraid their movement would be noticed so I transferred it to my toes but their movement was also too obvious so I cut all movement short. Then it transferred of itself to the root of my tongue, which meant I couldn't speak.

Thus, jumping from one place to another, my inner Tempo-rhythm was expressed in a number of physical ways. I told Tortsov about this and he shrugged his shoulders and commented:

'Physical movements are easier to detect and capture, that's why we turn to them. When intuition is dormant and needs rousing, use something physical to tap out the Tempo-rhythm. If that helps, use it, but only now and then, when you need to summon and maintain an unstable rhythm. Use it with a heavy heart because it isn't acceptable as a general method.

'So, once you've tapped out the Tempo-rhythm, justify it as fast as you can with a new idea and Given Circumstances.

'They should maintain the correct speed and pulse, not your hands and feet. And when you feel your inner Tempo-rhythm is faltering, help it with something external, something physical, but only for a moment.

'When your feeling for Tempo-rhythm is stronger, you'll be able to give up this crude device and replace it with a more subtle method – counting in your head.'

What Tortsov had told us was so important that I just had to know first hand what the full implications of this technique were for myself.

Tortsov accepted my request and proposed this task: I was to appear outwardly relaxed, almost languid with a rapid, confused, anxious Tempo-rhythm inside.

First I fixed both the outer and inner speed and time signature, and reinforced them with invisible tension in the fingers and toes.

Then I quickly reinforced and justified them with new ideas and Given Circumstances and asked myself: what would create a very fast, turbulent Tempo-rhythm?

After much searching I decided the cause could be some horrible crime I had committed, which unexpectedly weighed on my conscience. When I tried to picture the horror of such an event, I saw Marya's lifeless body lying on the floor with a huge red stain on her frock. I had murdered her in a fit of jealousy. This put me in a state of turmoil and it seemed to me I had justified and fixed my inner rhythm by my story and the Given Circumstances.

Turning to the relaxed, indolent external Tempo-rhythm once again, I first used tension in the toes to establish it more clearly, then justified and fixed it by thinking up a new idea. I asked myself, what would I do now, here in class, faced with the other students, Tortsov and Rakhmanov, if my terrible story were really true? I not only had to appear calm, I had to look unconcerned, as though I hadn't a care in the world. I couldn't find the right Adaptation right away. I felt I couldn't look people in the eye. That increased the Tempo-rhythm. The more I wanted to appear calm, the less calm I felt inside. Once I believed my own story the more distraught I became.

Then I thought about the Given Circumstances. What would I say to Tortsov and the other students when class was over? Did they know what had happened? Where was I to look when they started talking about this calamity? Where was I to go after class? To see my victim in her coffin?

The more I analysed the situation, the more distraught I became, the more I gave myself away and the more desperately I tried to appear at ease.

Two rhythms had sprung to life, one inner – fast, and one outer – artificial calm. I felt this combination of two extremes was right and that put me in greater turmoil.

Now that I'd found a line of justified Given Circumstances, the Through-action and the Subtext, I stopped thinking about counting tempo and rhythm and lived the Tempo-rhythm naturally. This was confirmed by the fact that Tortsov knew what I was going through although I showed nothing and, indeed, was busy concealing it.

Tortsov understood that I was deliberately hiding my eyes, because they gave me away, that I was finding one pretext after another to switch my attention from object to object, pretending to take a close interest in them.

'Your unquiet quiet revealed your inner turmoil more than anything else,' he said. 'You didn't notice how your eyes, your head, your neck were involuntarily moving in your inner Tempo-rhythm. You gave yourself away because you weren't living a quiet, indolent rhythm but a fast one, which you were desperately trying to conceal from us. You fell into your own trap, got confused and looked at us to see if we'd understood something we weren't supposed to. Then you reverted to your Adaptation, artificial calm. When you took out your handkerchief, when you got up and sat down again to be more comfortable, I knew perfectly well you were doing it to mask your inner turmoil. You kept involuntarily freezing at moments, your attention switched from what was going on around you to something worrying you inside. It was that semblance of unruffled calm, broken by moments of anxiety which gave you away more than anything. That's true of life when we try to hide strong feelings. We sit quite still in a quick, nervous Tempo-rhythm, lost in our own thoughts, tormented by feelings which, for whatever reason, we wish to conceal. If you suddenly speak to them, you'll see them come to, jump up and for a second or two approach you in the fast inner Tempo-rhythm they've been trying to hide. A moment later, they're back in control, they slow down and affect an outward calm.

'If they've no reason to conceal their feelings they will continue walking in the fast, emotional Tempo-rhythm.

'Very often whole plays, whole scenes develop through a series of contradictory Tempo-rhythms. Chekhov builds many plays and characters on this, Uncle Vanya, Astrov, Sonya, the three sisters and others are outwardly calm while in a state of almost constant inner anxiety and unrest.'

Once I'd understood that my slow movements to a quick inner tempo rhythm best communicated the state of mind I needed, I began to make too much of my movements. But Tortsov stopped me.

'We judge another person's state of mind by what we see. Of course, uncontrolled physical movements are visually the most striking. If they are calm and slow we conclude the other person is in a good mood. But if we examine you more closely, look at your eyes, and, so to speak, feel along with you, we perceive the inner [anxiety] you are trying to hide. That means, in the cases I have quoted, you must be able to show the whole audience your eyes. That's not easy. It requires skill and control. It's no easy matter in a show, to see two small dots, the eyes, on a vast open stage, from the auditorium. The person being looked at has to stand still for quite a long while. So, though you can use movement, you must do so with discretion. Acting depends on the eyes and facial expression. Your actions must be such that your eyes can be seen.'

After me Grisha and Varya played a scene they had made up about a wife being questioned by her jealous husband. Before he could openly accuse her he had to trap her. In that situation he had to stay calm, cleverly conceal his state of mind, and not show his eyes.

Tortsov said to Grisha:

'You are completely calm, you're making no attempt to hide your inner turmoil because you have none to hide. Kostya was in a highly emotional state and so had something to conceal. He lived two Tempo-rhythms simultaneously, inner and outer. He just sat down and did nothing and that produced emotion. You just sat, did nothing, but that didn't produce emotion because you only had one Tempo-rhythm, calm, not two to convey the complex, split state of mind you were portraying and that turned the scene into a cosy, family chat.

'I repeat, in complex moods, with contradictory inner lines you must avoid single Tempo-rhythms. You need to combine several.'

.. .. 19..

'So far we've talked about the Tempo-rhythm of particular groups, characters, moments, scenes. But plays, performances have their Tempo-rhythm, too,' Tortsov explained today.

'Does that mean one pace, one time signature should last a whole evening? Of course not. A play or a performance is not a single Tempo-rhythm but a succession of large and small groupings, of divergent and diversified tempi and time signatures brought together in a harmonious whole.

'The sum of these tempi and time signatures creates a mood which can be grandiose and majestic, or light and happy. In some performances the first Tempo-rhythm predominates, in others the second. It is the general tone of the performance as a whole that determines the balance.

'Tempo-rhythm is crucial to the whole performance. Often a fine play, well staged, well acted, fails because it is much too slow or far too fast. Just try and play tragedy in the tempo of farce or farce in the tempo of tragedy.

'Often a mediocre play, in a mediocre performance, succeeds if put across with pace and verve because it is exciting.

'Naturally then, the psychotechniques for establishing the right Tempo-rhythm for a play or a role are of enormous help in a complex, elusive process.

'But we have no psychotechniques in this area and this is what happens in reality, in practice.

'Mostly, finding the Tempo-rhythm of a performance is a matter of pure *chance*. If the actors, for some reason, feel the play and the role as they should, if they are in a good mood, if the audience is responsive, then the right kind of experiencing and, therefore, the right Tempo-rhythm, happen spontaneously. But when that doesn't happen, we are helpless. If we had the right psychotechnique we could use it to establish and justify first the outer, then the inner Tempo-rhythm, which would activate our feelings.

'How lucky musicians, singers and dancers are. They have metronomes, conductors, chorus-masters, ballet masters.

'For them the problem of Tempo-rhythm has been resolved and its importance in creative work recognized. The accuracy of their musical performance is to a certain extent guaranteed and fixed as regards tempo and time signature. This is notated and under the regular control of the conductor.

'Not so with us. We only study *metre* in verse. But for the rest we have no metronome, no notation, no score or conductor, as in music. That is why the same play can be performed in different tempi and different rhythms on different days.

'There is nowhere straight actors can look for help. And we need it badly.

'Let's assume, for example, that a certain actor receives some upsetting news just before a show. As a result his Tempo-rhythm on that particular day increases. He goes on in that heightened mood. A few days later he is robbed and that throws the poor man into a fit of depression. His Tempo-rhythm slows, in life and onstage.

'The performance thus depends on the accidents of daily life, not on our psychotechnique.

'Let us assume, moreover, that this actor calms himself down, or works himself up before his entrance so that his Tempo-rhythm goes from metronome 50 to metronome 100. But that's a long way from the Tempo-rhythm the play needs, which is, say, metronome 200. This error affects the Given Circumstances, the creative Task and the way he fulfils it. But, most important of all, the wrong Tempo-rhythm appears in his feelings and his re-experiencing.

'We often find a disparity between the actor's and the character's Tempo-rhythm.

'For example:

'Remember how you felt in your first show when you were faced with the black hole and an auditorium you thought was full of people?

'Conduct the Tempo-rhythm of that moment.'

We did so but my hand lacked the skill to convey all the thirty-second notes, with their dots, triplets and syncopations, in the Tempo-rhythm of that memorable performance.

Tortsov reckoned I had conducted at metronome 20.

Then he told me to remember the quietest, most boring moments of my life and conduct them.

I thought of my home town and conducted what I felt.

'Now, imagine you're playing Podkilesin in Gogol's *Marriage*, which requires metronome 20 and you, the actor, are at metronome 200 before the curtain rises. How are you to reconcile your own mood and the character's? Let's say you manage to calm yourself down 50 per cent and lower your inner tempo to 100. That seems a lot to you but it's not low enough for Podkilesin who needs metronome 20. How are you to reconcile this discrepancy? How do you bridge the gap without a metronome?

'The best way is to learn to feel Tempo-rhythm as good musicians and conductors do. Give them a metronome marking and they'll conduct it immediately from memory. If only we had a company of actors with an absolute sense of Tempo-rhythm! The things they could do!' Tortsov sighed.

'What, for instance?' we asked.

'I'll tell you,' he replied.

'I recently staged an opera in which there was a big crowd scene for the chorus. Apart from the soloists and the chorus itself, there were extras and walk-ons of varying experience. They were well trained in Tempo-rhythm. If you compared every singer, walk-on and extra individually with the members of our own company they would not bear comparison. They are at a much lower level. But, in the end, opera artists outstripped us, their rivals, stronger though we are, and despite having fewer rehearsals than we do.

'Crowd scenes in opera reach a higher standard dramatically than we can achieve in our theatre although we have a better ensemble and much more careful rehearsal.

'Why should this be?

'Tempo-rhythm coloured, evened out, shaped, unified a rough scene.

'Tempo-rhythm lent clarity, smoothness, finish, flexibility and harmony to the acting.

'Tempo-rhythm helped artists who knew little about psychotechnique to live and control the inner aspect of their roles.'

We tactfully pointed out to Tortsov that his dream of a company of actors with a perfect sense of Tempo-rhythm was hardly practical.

'All right, then I'll compromise,' he declared. 'If I can't rely on all of them, a few members should develop Tempo-rhythm. In the wings we often hear remarks like: "No worries about today's show, such-and-such rock-solid actors are playing." What does that mean? That one or two people can carry the show and the rest of the cast. That's how it was in the old days.

'Tradition has it that our great predecessors like Shchepkin, Sadovski, Shumski and Samarin always went to the wings long before their entrance so they could tune in to the tempo of the performance. That is why they always took life, truth and the right note for the play and the character on with them.

'There is no doubt that they could do this not only because great actors carefully prepare their first entrance but because consciously or unconsciously they were sensitive to Tempo-rhythm and knew what it was. Evidently they could recall the speed, the slowness, the metre of the action in every scene and in the play as a whole.

'Or perhaps they found it afresh, every time, sitting in the wings for a long time before they went on, carefully watching what was happening on-stage. They got into the right Tempo-rhythm intuitively or, perhaps, using certain devices of their own, which, unfortunately, are a mystery to us.

'Try to become that kind of actor, leaders in Tempo-rhythm.'

'What is the psychotechnique for establishing the Tempo-rhythm of a play or a role?' I enquired.

'The Tempo-rhythm of a play is the Tempo-rhythm of its Through-action and Subtext. And you know that when dealing with the Subtext you need a double perspective on the role – the actor's and the character's. Just as paint-ers lay out their colours in their pictures and try to achieve a proper balance among them, so actors try to lay out the Tempo-rhythm of the Through-action.'

'We'll never do it without a conductor,' Vanya decided, deep in thought.

'Rakhmanov will find some sort of stand-in for a conductor,' Tortsov joked as he left.

.. .. 19..

Today I was early for class, as usual. The lights were up, the curtains were open and there was Rakhmanov in his shirt sleeves and the electricians, preparing a new gadget.

I offered to help. That meant Rakhmanov had to reveal his secret prematurely.

Our ingenious inventor has devised an 'electrical time-beat for drama'.

His invention was still in a rough state but here's what it looked like: picture an apparatus with two small lamps, inside the prompter's box. The audience can't see them but the actors can, and they blink silently, replacing the tick of the metronome. The prompter sets the apparatus in motion. He has marked the correct tempo and time signature for each Bit, as agreed in rehearsal, in the prompt copy. By pressing a button on a small switchboard beside him he starts the apparatus which reminds the actors of the agreed tempo. When necessary he stops it.

Tortsov was interested in Rakhmanov's invention and tried it out with him in various scenes as the electrician roughly set whatever rhythms came into his head at random. Both actors have a magnificent control of Tempo-rhythm and a flexible, agile imagination which can justify any rhythm. There could be no argument because both these masters in their own way demonstrated the effectiveness of the electric time-beat.

Paul and I and other students then performed a series of tests. We only managed to match the rhythm accidentally, the rest of the time we came to grief.

'The conclusion is obvious,' said Tortsov. 'The electric time-beat is a great help to us and can regulate a performance. It is both possible and practical but only if all, or some, of the cast are trained in Tempo-rhythm.

'But, unfortunately, such people are rare in the theatre.

'In fact, there is little awareness of the importance of Tempo-rhythm in the straight theatre. All the more need then to pay special attention to the work we are now doing on it.'

The end of the class turned into a general discussion. Many of us had our schemes for replacing a conductor.

Tortsov made a noteworthy remark in this part of the class. In his opinion, actors should gather and do exercises to music before the show and between the acts to get into the flow of the Tempo-rhythm.

'What exercises are these?' we were interested to know.

'All in good time,' Tortsov said. 'Do some more elementary exercises before we talk about them.'

'But what are they?' we insisted.

'We'll talk about them next time,' Tortsov said, and left.

.. .. 19..

'How are you? And good Tempo-rhythm to you!' Tortsov greeted us as he came in. 'Why are you so surprised?' he asked, seeing our astonishment.

'In my opinion it's much more accurate to say "good Tempo-rhythm to you" than "good health". In what way can our health be good or bad? Whereas Tempo-rhythm can be *good* and that is the best indication of good health. That is why I wish you good rhythm and tempo, in other words, health.

'But seriously now, what Tempo-rhythm are you in?'

'I really don't know,' said Paul.

'And you?' Tortsov asked Leo.

'No idea,' he muttered.

'And you?' Tortsov asked all of us in turn.

'What a collection!' Tortsov said, feigning great astonishment. 'It's the first time in my life I've met people like you. Nobody is aware of the rhythm and tempo of their lives. And yet I would have thought all human beings should be aware of the pace, or some other way of measuring their movements, actions, feelings, thoughts, breathing, pulse, heart rate and general state.

'Of course we're aware of them. What we don't understand is, which moments do we elect to observe? When I'm thinking about the good time I'm going to have this evening, which produces a pleasant Tempo-rhythm, or at other times, when I doubt whether the day will be so good or when I'm momentarily bored and my Tempo-rhythm drops?

'Conduct one tempo or other for me,' Tortsov suggested to us. 'You're creating an alternating rhythm. You're living it right now. You could make a mistake. So what? The important thing is that in searching for a Tempo-rhythm you unlock the feeling inside you.

'In which Tempo-rhythm did you wake up this morning?' Tortsov asked us.

We frowned, taking the question very seriously.

'Do you really have to go that tense to answer my question?' Tortsov said, in surprise. 'Our sense of Tempo-rhythm is always, so to speak, available. We always have, or can recall, a rough notion of every moment we have lived.'

I visualized the Given Circumstances this morning and recalled that it was rather a scramble. I was late for school, I had to shave, some money arrived by the mail and I was called to the telephone several times. The result was a restless, rapid Tempo-rhythm which I conducted and relived.

After a short break, Tortsov thought up this game: he beat out a fairly fast, incoherent Tempo-rhythm.

We repeated this Tempo-rhythm several times the better to listen to it and absorb it.

'Now,' Tortsov ordered, 'make up your mind which Given Circumstances and experiences would create this rhythm.'

To do that I had to think up an appropriate story (magic 'if', Given Circumstances). Then, to get my imagination started, I had to ask the usual series of questions: *where, what, why am I here?* Who are all these people? I decided I was in a surgeon's waiting room and that my whole future was being decided. Either I was seriously ill and would have to have an operation and might die, or I was perfectly healthy and would quietly leave the way I came. The story had its effect and I was much more deeply moved by my own suppositions than the Tempo-rhythm we'd been given warranted.

I had to tone down my story and imagine I wasn't at the surgeon's but at the dentist's to have a tooth out.

But this was still too strong for the Tempo-rhythm we'd been given. I had to switch to an ENT doctor to have my ear syringed. That was better suited to the Tempo-rhythm we'd been given.

'So,' Tortsov summed up, 'in the first half of the class you listened to your inner experience and expressed its Tempo-rhythm outwardly by beating time. A moment ago, you accepted someone else's Tempo-rhythm and brought it to life by your own ideas and experiences. Thus, you went from *feeling to Tempo-rhythm* and, vice versa, from *Tempo-rhythm to feeling.*

'Actors should master both techniques.

'At the end of the last class you wanted to know about exercises for developing your Tempo-rhythm.

'Today I have shown you *two important ways to guide you in your choice of exercises.*'

'But where do we find these exercises?' I enquired.

'Remember all the experiments you've performed. Tempo and rhythm are essential in all of them.

'As a result, you have enough material for "training and drill".

'So, today I answered the question I left open last time,' Tortsov said as he departed.

.. .. 19..

'*Following our set plan we first discovered how the Tempo-rhythm of action affects our feelings,*' said Tortsov reminding us of previous classes.

'*Now let's do the same tests with the Tempo-rhythm of speech.*

'*If the effect on our feelings is the same, or stronger, than on your actions, then your pyschotechnique will be enriched by a very important, new working method for using the external to influence the internal, i.e. for the Tempo-rhythm of speech to affect feeling.*

'I'll start with the fact that sounds, speech are a good medium for conveying and expressing the Tempo-rhythm of *the Subtext and the surface text.* As I said earlier, "when we speak we fill time with sounds of varying lengths, with breaks between". Or, in other words, a line of words extends through time but the sound is now broken into letters, syllables and words *grouped in rhythmic sections.*

'The nature of some sounds, syllables and words requires a clipped diction, similar to eighth- and sixteenth-notes in music. Alongside this, others must be spoken with greater length and weight, like whole or half-notes. Some letters and words are strongly or weakly stressed. A third kind, however, are unstressed, a fourth kind, fifth kind, etc., are combined into duplets and triplets, etc.

'In their turn these spoken sounds are broken by pauses and breaths of varying length. All the resources of the spoken word create a continuous, varied Tempo-rhythm, and we can use them to develop metrical speech, which we need to communicate verbally both the sublime emotions of tragedy and the lowly joys of comedy in words.

'If we want to create Tempo-rhythm in speech, we not only have to divide sounds into groups, we have to count the beats and so create *speech bars.*

'The metronome and the bell produced them for actions. What's their equivalent in speech? How do we synchronize this or that letter or syllable with the beat? We have to count in our heads, instead of using the metronome, and never stop listening instinctively to the Tempo-rhythm we hear.

'Metrical, resonant, smooth speech is very much akin to singing and music.

'Letters, syllables and words are the musical notes in speech out of which we create bars, arias and symphonies. Beautiful speech is justly called musical.

'Resonant, metrical speech increases the effective power of words.

'In speech, as in music, speaking in whole, quarter, eighth or sixteenth notes, in quadruplets, triplets, etc., are not the same things. There is a difference between saying:

"I came here (pause) waited a long time (pause) to no purpose (pause) and left"

in measured, flowing, calm whole and half-notes and changing the length and rhythm of the words, using eighth, sixteenth notes in fours, with all kinds of pauses.

"I. . . . . came here. . . . . waited a long time. . . . . to no purpose. . . . . and left."

'In the first instance we have calm, in the second, nervousness, anxiety.

'Talented singers know all about this "by the grace of God". They are afraid of transgressing against rhythm and so, if there are three printed quarter-notes they give them equal value. If the composer puts a whole note, genuine singers will sustain it right through. If the music requires triplets or dotted notes they will give them just as the mathematics of music and rhythm requires. This precision produces an indelible effect. Art requires order, discipline, precision and finish. And even when we have to arrhythmia musically, good, clean finish is still essential. Chaos and disorder also have their own Tempo-rhythm.

'Everything that has been said about music and singing applies to straight actors. But many aren't genuine singers, they are merely people who sing, with or without a voice. They change eighth notes into sixteenth notes, quarter notes in half notes, elide three equal eighth notes into one with astonishing facility.

'As a result their singing lacks the precision, discipline, organization and finish that music needs. It is jumbled, smudged, chaotic. It stops being music and turns into mere vocal display.

'The same thing happens in speech.

'For example, actors like Igor have inconsistent speech-rhythm. It changes not only over a number of clauses but within the same sentence. Often one half of the sentence is spoken in a slow tempo and the second much faster. For example, let's take "Most potent, grave and reverend signiors".[3] This is spoken slowly and solemnly but the words which follow, "My very noble and approved good masters" come out all in a rush, after a long pause. It's the same with individual words. For example, "absolutely" is spoken rapidly but the end is dragged out, "ab . . . so . . . luuuuuute . . . ly".

'Many actors with no feeling for language or concern for words chop the ends off words and sentences because of the meaningless speed of their delivery.

'Changes in Tempo-rhythm are even more apparent in actors of particular national origin.

'This should not happen in correct, good speech or only in exceptional cases, when you change Tempo-rhythm intentionally because it is in character. It follows that the gaps between words should match the swiftness or slowness of your delivery. When you are speaking fast, the stops should be short, when you are speaking slowly, they should be longer.

'Our problem is that many actors haven't developed two important aspects of speech. On the one hand there is *smoothness, slow, resonant flow* and on the other *speed, light, clear, clean articulation*. We rarely hear *slow, resonant,* flowing speech or a genuinely rapid, light delivery on the Russian stage. Mostly the pauses are long and the words between rushed.

'But for slow, stately speech we need a sustained, resonant singing line instead of silences.

'Reading slowly to a metronome while preserving the flow of the words and rhythms and properly justifying them inwardly will help you develop slow, smooth speech.

'It's even rarer to hear a good rapid delivery, that respects the tempo, has clean rhythms, clear diction and articulation and can communicate ideas. We don't dazzle by the speed of our articulation like French and Italian actors. Ours is blurred, heavy, messy, not rapid articulation but gabbling, spitting out, splattering the words. You have to develop rapid articulation by speaking slowly and over-precisely. By repeating the same words over and over you can train the organs of articulation until you can say them very fast. That requires regular exercises and you must do them because stage speech cannot do without pace. So, don't take bad singers as your model, don't distort the rhythm. Learn from good singers, from their precision, regularity of rhythm and their discipline.

'When you are reading, give each letter, syllable and word their proper sound value and rhythm, form sentences into speech bars, organize the phrasing, and treasure good, clean stress, which are typical of lived feelings and passions, and essential when creating a character.

'Precise, clear speech rhythms facilitate clean, rhythmic re-experiencing, and vice versa, rhythmic experiencing helps clear speech. Of course, it only works, if this clarity is inwardly justified by Given Circumstances or a magic "if".'

.. .. 19..

Today, Tortsov had the large metronome started at a slow tempo. Rakhmanov as usual marked the barlines with a bell.

Then they started a small metronome to indicate the speech rhythm.

Tortsov suggested I speak in time to the metronome.

'And say what?' I asked, blankly.

'Whatever you like,' he answered. 'Tell us about something that happened to you, what you did yesterday or what you've been thinking about today.'

I started to recall the film I'd seen yesterday. The metronome marked the beats and the bell rang but were quite unrelated to what I was saying. The machine was working on its own and I was working on my own.

Tortsov laughed and commented:

'When that happens we say, "the band plays but the flag just flaps".'[4]

'I'm not surprised, as I've no idea how to speak to a metronome,' I said, feeling put out and trying to justify myself.

'People can sing, speak verse in tempo and a given time signature, so that the caesura and the metre match certain beats of the metronome. How are we to do this in prose? I have no idea where words and beats should coincide,' I complained.

And indeed, sometimes I was late, sometimes early, sometimes I dragged out the tempo, sometimes pushed it too fast.

Every time there was a disparity between me and the metronome.

Then, suddenly, quite by chance, I found the beat a number of times and felt very good about it.

But my pleasure was short-lived. The Tempo-rhythm I'd chanced on lasted only a few seconds under its own steam and then vanished, and the mismatch recurred.

I did my utmost to find the beat again but the more I tried the more muddled my rhythms became and the more the metronome seemed to get in my way. I had no idea what I was saying any more, and stopped.

'I can't go on! I've no feeling for tempo, or rhythm either!' I decided, scarcely holding back my tears.

'Rubbish! Don't let yourself be intimidated!' said Tortsov encouragingly. 'You expect too much from Tempo-rhythm in prose. It can't give you what you want. Don't forget, prose isn't verse, any more than actions are dance. You can't hit the beat with absolute regularity whereas in poetry and dance you can prepare and construct it in advance.

'People with rhythm find the beat more often and those without less often. That's all.

'I am trying to find out which of you belong to the first category and which to the second.

'But you needn't worry,' he said go me. 'You're one of the students with rhythm. But you still don't know the particular method which will help you control the Tempo-rhythm. Listen carefully and I'll reveal an important secret in vocal technique.

'There is Tempo-rhythm in prose as well as music and verse. But it is quite haphazard in ordinary speech. In prose, Tempo-rhythm is all over the place. One bar is in one rhythm, the next in quite another. One sentence is dragged out, another cut short and each has its own rhythm.

'This leads us to a rather depressing thought, "Can we achieve rhythm in prose?"

'I'll answer that with a question: have you ever heard an opera, an aria or a song which is a setting of prose, not verse? The spoken sounds, syllables, words and phrases govern the notes, pauses, bars, the accompaniment, the melodies and Tempo-rhythm. They all merge to form the rhythmical harmony of musical sounds, the Subtext to the words. When mathematical, metrical rhythm rules, mere prose almost sounds like poetry and acquires a musical structure. Let us try and go down this road when speaking prose.

'Let's recall what happens in music. The voice sings the melody and the words. When there are no sung words, the accompaniment steps in, and rests fill in the missing beats in the bar.

'We do the same in prose. Letters, syllables, words replace notes. Pauses, breaths and counting fill in those rhythmical moments in which there is no spoken text in a speech bar.

'Letters, syllables and words, as you already know, are raw material for the most diverse rhythms.

'Regular matching of syllables and words with the strong beats with spoken prose onstage can have a certain similarity to music and verse.

'We can see this in so-called "prose-poems" and also in the works of new poets which might be called "poetic prose" because they are so close to everyday speech.

'Thus, the Tempo-rhythm of prose is made up of strong and weak utterance and pauses. We may speak, or not speak, be active or inactive in Tempo-rhythm.

'Rests and breaths are very important when speaking verse or prose because they are not only part of the rhythmic line, but because they play a critical and active part of our technique for creating and mastering rhythm itself. Rests and breaths help us match strong moments in speech, action and re-experiencing with identical moments in our mental count.

'Some specialists call this process of filling in missing beats with rests and breaths, "tum-ti-tumming".'

'I'll explain the origin of this expression so you can understand the process better.

'When we sing a song and have forgotten the words, or just don't know them, we replace them with meaningless sounds like "tum-ti-tum-ti-tum", etc.

'When we are mentally counting we also use these sounds to fill in the missing beats and actions in a bar. Hence the name "tum-ti-tumming".

'You were upset because the match between word and beat when speaking prose was a matter of chance. Now you have the assurance that there is a way of combating the element of chance – "tum-ti-tumming".

'*You can use it to make speaking prose rhythmical.*'

Tortsov came in, turned to us and suggested that we speak the opening sentence of Gogol's *Inspector General* in Tempo-rhythm.

'Sirs, I called you here to give unwelcome news – an inspector is on his way.'

We all said the line in turn, but couldn't get the rhythm.

'Let's start with the first half of the sentence,' Tortsov said. 'Can you find a rhythm in it?'

The answers were contradictory.

'Can you turn this sentence into verse and go on from the first line?'

The group began versifying and the result was the following 'work of art':

> <u>Sirs</u>, I *called you <u>here</u> to give*
> <u>At once</u> unwelcome news –
> Someone is on his way
> A government inspector.
> > Who?
> He's coming incognito.
> > What, that too?

'You see,' said a delighted Tortsov, 'it's dreadful, but still verse. That means there is rhythm in a prose text. Now let's experiment with the second half of the sentence: "to give unwelcome news".'

Bad verse was produced in a flash.

> *To give unwelcome news* and so
> To spare you sudden woe.

This new 'work' proved how effective rhythm was in the second half of the sentence. We wrote verses based on the last bar of the speech:

> *An inspector's on his way!*
> That's a stupid thing to say!

'Now I'll set you a new Task,' Tortsov said. 'Combine these three items of verse, in different rhythms, into one "work of art" and recite them one after the other non-stop.'

We tried our best but failed.

The different metres we had forced together recoiled in horror from each other and wouldn't combine at any price. Tortsov had to try.

'I'll speak and you'll listen and you can stop me if the rhythm jars too much,' he stipulated before starting:

> *Sirs, I brought you here today*
> *To give bad news*, to say (ti-tum)
> I'll tell you quickly all I know,
> To spare you (tum-ti) sudden woe (hm).
> Now hear me friends (ti-tum) I pray,
> For I. . . . . (ti-tum)
> have worried many a day (hm)
> *An inspector's on his way.*

'As you didn't stop me, despite my messy verse, I conclude my transition from one metre to another didn't shock you too much.

'I'll go a stage further and shorten the lines to bring them nearer Gogol's text,' Tortsov explained.

> Sirs, I asked you here today (ti-tum)
> To give unwelcome news (ti-tum)
> An inspector's on his way. (ti-tum)

'No one objected. That means a prose sentence can be rhythmical,' Tortsov summed up.

'We are now convinced that "tum-ti-tumming" can help us do our work. It more or less functions like the conductor of an orchestra or choir who has to lead all the musicians and singers, and then all the listeners from one section of a symphony, written, say, in 3/4 to another written in 5/4. That doesn't happen all at once. A large crowd of people who are used to living one tempo and one time signature in one section, can't suddenly switch to a completely different tempo and rhythm in another section.

'Very often the conductor has to help the crowd of performers and listeners to make the transition to another rhythmic pattern. For that he first needs counting, his kind of "tum-ti-tumming", which he marks with his baton. He doesn't achieve his end suddenly, he leads his performers and his listeners through a series of transitional, rhythmic steps which gradually lead them to a new time signature.

'And we have to do the same, to move from one speech rhythm to another, which has a different tempo and time signature. The difference between him and us is that he does it openly, with his baton, whereas we do it secretly, inwardly using mental counting, or "tum-ti-tumming".

'And we actors need these transitions above all so we can move into new Tempo-rhythm cleanly and precisely and confidently carry the object of communication with us, and, through it, the audience, too.

' "Tum-ti-tumming" in prose is the bridge which unites widely differing sentences with widely differing rhythms.'

At the end of the class we talked in time to the metronome in a very simplified way, as we do in life. We only tried to match the strong words or syllables, where necessary, to the metronome.

In between we successively grouped words and phrases so that we could match the stresses to the beats in a way that was logically correct, without altering the sense. We also managed to fill in the missing words in the bar by counting or pausing. Of course, this was still a very haphazard way of speaking but nonetheless it did create harmony and made me feel good.

Tortsov attaches enormous importance to the influence Tempo-rhythm exerts on experiencing.

.. .. 19..

FAMUSOV
What's this? Molchalin, you, boy?
MOLCHALIN
Aye.
FAMUSOV
And at this hour? Pray tell me, why?

Tortsov quoted the first act of Griboiedov's *Woe from Wit*. Then, after a short pause, he repeated:

'What have we here? Is that you, Molchalin, lad?'
'Yes, sir, it is.'
'Where did you spring from at such an hour?'

Tortsov spoke the same sentences but without metre or rhyme.

'The meaning's the same as in the verse, but what a difference! In prose the words spread, they are no longer concise, clear, sharp, unequivocal,' Tortsov explained. 'In verse all the words are essential, none is superfluous. Prose often takes a whole sentence for something that verse can say in two words. And it is as clear as a newly minted coin! "Prose is sluggish, verse is sprightly" a very ordinary person said to me.

'It might be said that the real difference between the two examples I gave is that Griboiedov wrote one and I, unsuccessfully, the other.

'That, of course, is true. But I still maintain that if the greatest poet wrote prose he still couldn't express his meaning with the precision of rhythm and sharpness of rhyme in Griboiedov's verse.

'For example, in his encounter with Famusov in Act One, the panic-stricken Molchalin has only one word with which to express his horror, "Aye". This is matched by the last word of Famusov's line, "why?"

'Do you feel the exactness, the finish of the rhythm, the bite of the rhyme?

'*The actor playing Molchalin must have the same finish, exactness and sharpness in his inner feelings and experiencing and in his external expression of everything hidden behind the words — the horror, embarrassment, the apologetic servility — the whole subtext in fact.*

'We feel verse differently from prose because verse is shaped differently.

'We could reverse this sentence and say, verse is shaped differently because we feel the Subtext differently.

'One of the major distinctions between prose and verse is their Tempo-rhythm, the way in which their different metres affect our Emotion Memory, our memories, feelings and experiences.

'Using that as a premise, we may assert that the more rhythmic verse or prose are, *the more clearly thoughts, feelings and the whole Subtext should be experienced. And, conversely, the more exact and rhythmic the thoughts, feelings and experiences, the more rhythmic their verbal expression should be.*

'*This reveals another aspect of the interaction between Tempo-rhythm and feeling.*

'Do you remember conducting the tempo and rhythm of various moods, actions, even characters you'd created? Then merely marking the beats and their Tempo-rhythm stimulated your Emotion Memory, your feelings and experiences.

'If simply marking the beats could do that, how much easier it is when you use the living sounds of human speech, the tempo-rhythm of letters, syllables and words and the Subtext.

'Even when we don't fully understand the words, the sound of their Tempo-rhythm affects us. For example, I recall one of Corrado's speeches in a melodrama called *A Criminal's Family*[5] as Salvini played it. This speech describes the escape of a galley slave.

'I knew no Italian, I didn't understand a word that was said, but I responded to every nuance of his feeling. This was largely due not only to his wonderful inflexions but exceptionally clear, expressive Tempo-rhythm when speaking.

'In addition, think of all the poems in which Tempo-rhythm creates sound images — ringing bells, galloping horses. For example:

> The evening bell
> The evening bell
> How many dreams
> Its ring can tell.

or

> Wer reitet so spät durch Nacht und Wind
> Das ist der Vater mit seinem Kind.[6]

.. .. 19..

'Speech is a combination of not only sounds but rests,' Tortsov said. 'Both must be imbued with Tempo-rhythm.

'It lives in actors while they are onstage whether they are active or inactive, speaking or silent. It would be interesting now to see how different tempi and rhythms relate during action and inaction, speech and silence. It's a particularly important and difficult problem when speaking verse. It's to that I now turn.

'The difficulty in verse is that there is a limit to how long a rest can last. You cannot overstep the mark with impunity because an over-indulgent pause breaks the line of Tempo-rhythm. Then both speaker and listener forget what the previous tempo and time signature were. They come out of both tempo and rhythm and have to get back into them again.

'That breaks up the verse and creates a hiatus. However, there are times when a prolonged pause is unavoidable because that's the way the play is written, with long periods of silent action between the lines. For example in the opening scene of Act One of *Woe from Wit*, Lisa knocks at Sophie's bedroom door to put an end to the amorous encounter between her mistress and Molchalin before dawn. This is how the scene goes:

LISA
(*at Sophie's door*)
>   They hear me, but pretend they don't
>   Should open wide the shutters, but they won't
(*Pause. She looks at the clock. Thinks*)
>   I'll put the clock on, though I stew,
>   I'll make it chime
(*Pause. Lisa goes over to the clock, opens the glass and pulls or presses a knob. The clock chimes. She does a little dance. Enter Famusov*)
LISA
>   Ah! Master!
FAMUSOV
>   Yes, your master, miss.
(*Pause. Famusov goes to the clock, opens the glass and turns the knob and stops it chiming*)
>   A brazen hussy you are, to be true.
>   So tell me, what tomfoolery is this?

'As you can see, the action creates long pauses in the verse. I must also add that the difficulty of holding onto the rhymes in spoken verse complicates our concern to hold onto the rhythm.

'An overlong pause between "stew" and "true", "miss" and "this" makes us forget the rhyme scheme and that kills rhyme itself. And too short a pause which skimps the action kills our *truth and belief* in them. We have to reconcile time, the gaps between the rhymes and the action. A sequenceofspeech,pauses,silentactionsand"tumm-ti-tumming"maintains the inner rhythm throughout. It creates a mood which evokes feelings that become a natural part of the creative process.

'Many actors playing Lisa and Famusov are afraid of long pauses, they gallop through the actions so they can get back to the words and the broken Tempo-rhythm. The result is a scramble which kills truth and belief in the action, makes a hash of the Subtext, your experiencing and inner and outer Tempo-rhythm, too. Action and speech which are chopped about like that make theatrical nonsense. Both become boring, they don't interest the audience in the play, they kill it. That's why it's wrong for these actors to rush to the clock and make a fuss putting it forward or stopping it. They only reveal their helplessness, their fear of pauses, their senseless scramble, the lack of any *Subtext*. We have to do things differently, perform the actions, calmly, without hurrying, without excessive pauses in the dialogue, counting all the time, guided by our sense of truth and sense of rhythm.

'When you speak after a long pause you must underline the Tempo-rhythm of the verse very strongly for a moment. This helps both actor and audience to get back to the broken, and, perhaps, forgotten tempo and metre. At moments like that "tum-ti-tumming" is of great service to us. First, it fills a long pause with rhythmic mental counting, second it brings it to life, third it maintains the link with the previous broken sentence, fourth it gets you back to the previous Tempo-rhythm.

'Here's what happens when speaking verse with pauses.

	I'll put the clock on
Lisa crosses	Tum-ti-tum-ti-tum-ti-tum
	Tum-ti-tum-ti-tum-ti-tum
	though I'll stew
	(tum)
opens the clock	Tum-ti-tum-ti-tum
	I'll make it chime
	Tum-ti-tum-ti-tum-ti-tum
	Tum-ti-tum-ti-tum-ti-tum

pulls the knob
Clock chimes
Lisa dances
Famusov opens the door,
steals in
Lisa sees him, runs

LISA	*Ah! master?*
FAMUSOV	*Yes, your master, miss*
	Tum-ti-tum-ti-tum
	Tum-ti-tum-ti-tum
Famusov	
stops the chimes	*And you're a brazen hussy to be true*

'As you can see, Tempo-rhythm has a crucial role at every moment be it in speaking, doing or pausing.

'Like the Throughaction and the Subtext it runs like a thread through every action, spoken word, pause and experience.'

.. .. 19..

Today Tortsov said:

'The time has come to sum up a great deal of work. Let's look briefly at everything we've done. Remember how we clapped our hands and how it created a mood to which we automatically responded? Do you remember how we clapped everything that came to mind – a march, a wood in winter, conversations? Clapping our hands created a mood and evoked experiences in ourselves if not in those listening. Do you remember the three bells before the train departed and how really excited you were as passengers? Do you remember how you played with Tempo-rhythm and used an imaginary metronome to stimulate a wide variety of experiences? And the improvisation with the tray and how you were transformed inwardly and outwardly from the president of a sporting club to a drunken waiter in a small railroad station? Do you remember acting to music?

'In all these improvisations and exercises in action Tempo-rhythm created a mood and evoked corresponding feelings every single time.

'We worked in the same way with words. Do you remember how quarter- and eighth-notes, duplets and triplets affected our state of mind?

'Do you remember how we experimented in combining verse-speaking and rhythmic, active pauses? How useful you found the technique of "tum-ti-tumming" every time? How the overall rhythm of spoken verse and precise, metrically regular action brought words and movement together?

'The same thing occurred to one degree or other, one way or other, in all these exercises I have listed – *inner feelings and experiences were created.*

'We are, therefore, justified in asserting that *Tempo-rhythm affects our inner life, our feelings and experiences automatically, intuitively or consciously. The same is true when we are being creative* out onstage.

'Now, give me your full attention because I'm going to discuss an important element not only in our immediate concern, Tempo-rhythm, but *in our creative work as a whole.*

'Here's the new discovery.'

After a long pause, Tortsov soberly began:

'Everything you have learned about Tempo-rhythm leads us to conclude that it is our closest friend and companion because it *is frequently the direct, immediate, at times almost automatic stimulus to Emotion Memory and, consequently to inner experiencing.*

'From that, naturally, it follows:

'First, right feeling is impossible with a wrong Tempo-rhythm.

'[Second], you can't discover the right Tempo-rhythm without simultaneously experiencing the feelings that correspond to it. There is an indissoluble link between Tempo-rhythm and feeling, and conversely between feeling and Tempo-rhythm, they are interconnected, interdependent and interactive.

'Probe a little deeper into what I've been saying and appreciate the full value of our discovery. It is extremely important. We are talking about the *immediate, frequently automatic effect Tempo-rhythm has on wilful, arbitrary, disobedient and apprehensive feelings, which won't take orders, which shy away at the least hint of being forced and hide away where they can't be got at. Hitherto we've only been able to affect it indirectly, using lures, but now we have a technique for direct access.*

'This is indeed a great discovery! And if it is true, then the right Tempo-rhythm for a play or a role can capture our feelings and evoke the right experiences spontaneously, intuitively, subconsciously, almost automatically.'

'That's tremendous!' said Tortsov joyfully.

'Ask singers and actors what it means to sing with a conductor of genius who senses the true, precise, characteristic Tempo-rhythm of a work.

"We didn't recognize ourselves," the singer-actors exclaim carried away by the talent and subtlety of a conductor of genius. But what if the opposite happens and a singer feels and experiences the score correctly and is suddenly confronted with a Tempo-rhythm which is the exact opposite of his own, and wrong. That inevitably kills all experiencing, all feeling, the character and *the creative state*, which is essential in creative work.

'Exactly the same thing happens to us when the Tempo-rhythm doesn't correspond to our feelings and our physical embodiment of them.

'So, what is the end result?'

'An unusual conclusion, which opens up all sorts of possibilities for our psychotechnique: that we possess *direct, immediate stimuli for each of our psychological drives.*

'*Words, lines, thoughts, representations which lead to judgements all directly affect our minds. The Supertask, Tasks, the Throughaction all directly affect our will (wants). Tempo-rhythm directly affects feeling.*

'Isn't this an important addition to our psychotechnique?'

.. .. 19..

Today Tortsov reviewed Tempo-rhythm in speech. First he called on Leo who spoke one of Salieri's speeches and whose Tempo-rhythm was quite satisfactory.

Recalling Leo's failure in an earlier class in the improvisation with the tray, Tortsov said:

'Here you have an example of how arrhythmic action and rhythmic speech can exist side by side in the same person, even if it was somewhat dry and psychologically poor.

Then he tested Igor, who, unlike Leo, had shone in the tray improvisation. But he didn't shine today as a speaker.

'Here we have an example of someone with rhythmic action and arrhythmic speech,' Tortsov said.

Next came Grisha.

Afterwards Tortsov commented that there are actors who have the same Tempo-rhythm for every character, every action, every speech and every pause.

In Tortsov's opinion Grisha was one of them with one pace and one rhythmic pattern.

Their Tempo-rhythm matches their character-type.

The 'heavy' always has a 'heavy' Tempo-rhythm.

The 'ingénue', an innocent young girl, always has a restless, fast rhythm.

The comic, the hero, the heroine, all have fixed Tempo-rhythms.

Grisha, for all his pretensions to be a 'hero', has developed the pace and rhythmic pattern of a 'raisonneur'.[7]

'Pity,' said Tortsov, 'because that deadens everything. It would have been better if he'd kept his own human Tempo-rhythm. At least that wouldn't have stayed the same, it would have lived and changed all the time.'

Tortsov didn't call on me or Paul today, nor Nikolai or Darya either.

Apparently we'd bored him quite enough and shown what we could do as regards Tempo-rhythm in *Othello* and *Brand*.

Marya didn't speak anything because she has no repertoire. Varya is Grisha's *alter ego*.

So, the 'review of Tempo-rhythm' didn't take long.

Tortsov drew no conclusions from the review but stated:

'There are many actors who are only attracted by the externals of speaking verse, the rhythm and the rhyme, and forget all about the Subtext and the *internal Tempo-rhythm of feeling and experiencing*.

'They respect the externals with almost pedantic precision. They carefully highlight the rhymes, the scansion, automatically mark the strong beats and are scared of destroying the mathematical precision of the metre. They're afraid of pausing too, because they feel a hole in the Subtext, but they don't have one, and without a Subtext you can't have any feeling for the words, because words cannot speak to the heart unless brought to life from within. They are only interesting as articulated rhythm and rhyme.

'The result is mechanical babbling, which cannot be accepted as verse-speaking.

'These actors do the same thing with tempo. They adopt a speed and hang on to it all the time they're speaking, forgetting that tempo live, vibrate and to a certain extent change all the time and not stagnate.

'This approach to tempo, the absence of all feeling, is no different from the grinding of a street organ or the mechanical ticking of the metronome. Compare this view of tempo with the attitude of conductors of genius like Nikisch.[8]

'For conductors of refinement like that an *andante* isn't an unremitting *andante*, and *allegro* isn't just an *allegro*. Each makes a fleeting appearance in the other. These fluctuations bring life which is entirely absent in the ticking of the metronome. In a good orchestra tempo is both constant and also subtly changing and blending, like a rainbow.

'All this is entirely relevant to acting. There are stock-in-trade actors and directors and there are also beautiful conductors. The first have boring, monotonous, conventional speech tempi, the second, infinitely varied, living, expressive tempi. Need I say that actors who treat Tempo-rhythm as external form will never master verse-speaking as aesthetic form. We also know other ways of speaking verse onstage in which the Tempo-rhythm is so broken up the verse almost turns into prose.

'This often happens because the Subtext is far too deep and heavy for the lightness of the text itself.

'This kind of experiencing is weighed down with psychological pauses, lumbering inner Tasks and a complex, tangled psychology.'

'The actor is weighed down by heavy psychological pauses, onerous inner tasks and a complex and confused mentality.

'This produces a correspondingly heavy inner Tempo-rhythm and a psychologically confused Subtext which is difficult to marry with words of the verse itself.

'A heavy, powerful, dramatic Wagnerian soprano can't sing feather-weight colloratura arias.

'In just the same way, you mustn't use the light rhythms and rhymes of Griboiedov's verse to express profound, weighty experiences.

'Does that mean verse can't be profound in content and feeling? Of course not. We know how we love to turn to verse to express our highest feelings and tragic emotions.

'I have to add that actors who unnecessarily overload the Subtext have great difficulty mastering verse form.

'A third type of actor finds the happy medium. They treasure both the Subtext, with its inner Tempo-rhythm and its experiences, and the text itself, with its shape, sounds, regular metre and precision. They handle verse quite differently. They enter into the waves of the Tempo-rhythm from the very first reading. It informs everything they do, not only their speech, but their movements, the way they walk. They transmit and receive in Tempo-rhythm. They never abandon it, whether speaking, pausing, marking logical or psychological pauses, whether they are active or inactive.

'Actors who have absorbed the Tempo-rhythm make free use of pauses because the pauses, too, are informed by Tempo-rhythm, given human warmth by feelings and ideas they have justified.

'They carry their own invisible metronome inside them all the time and it mentally accompanies all their actions, words, thoughts and feelings.

'It is only then that verse ceases to be a straitjacket and gives actors total freedom for experiencing and for inner and outer action. Only then can the inner process of experiencing and the outer process of giving it verbal expression produce one Tempo-rhythm and a marriage of text and Subtext.

'How wonderful it is to have a sense of tempo and rhythm. How important it is to develop it when you are young. There are many actors who, unfortunately, have a crude sense of Tempo-rhythm.

'When actors really feel what they are communicating, their words and actions become relatively rhythmic. This is also due to the close link between *rhythm and feeling*. But when feeling doesn't come alive spontaneously, and needs rhythm to help it, they are helpless.'

22

LOGIC AND SEQUENCE[1]

1.

'Inner and outer logic and sequence are crucial for us as actors. That is why we base most of our technique on them.

'You must have noticed this year that I have relied on them throughout, whether dealing with simple, real, outer physical actions or complex, intricate, inner actions and experiencing.

'Logic and sequence in action and feeling comprise one of the most important elements in our current studies.

'How are we to make good use of them?

'I'll begin with external action, because that will make our discussion clearer.

'We perform actions in real life with extraordinary logic and sequence that have been built into our muscles by years of habit. Indeed, we have little choice because many essential actions would be impossible without the right logic and sequence. For example, when we have to fill a glass with water, we first have to remove the stopper from the carafe, place the glass underneath it, take the carafe, tilt it and pour the water into the glass. If we decide to alter this sequence and start pouring the water without placing the glass under it, if we don't remove the glass stopper from the carafe and tilt it over the glass the result is disaster – we either pour water into the tray or on the table on which the carafe is standing or we break the glass when the stopper falls into it from the tilted carafe.

'Sequence is even more important in more complex actions.

'This is all so elementary, so obvious, we don't normally think about it. Logic and sequence come to our aid as a matter of habit.

'But, strange as it may seem, onstage we forget the logic and sequence of even the simplest actions. Do you recall the way singers wave glasses about when they are supposed to be full of wine? Do you recall how they quaff great goblets full but never choke from the huge flow of liquid going down their throats?

'Do that in life and you'll choke and drown, or spill three-quarters of the wine over your collar and clothes. Actors have been performing actions that way for centuries without ever noticing the absence of logic and sequence. That's because we haven't prepared ourselves to drink wine out of an empty cardboard carafe onstage in a natural manner. We don't need logic and sequence for that.

'Normally, we don't even think about them but, nevertheless, our actions are logical and sequential. Why? Because they are essential, we do what we have to out of motor habit, and are unconsciously aware of what we have to.

'Every action we perform subconsciously or automatically in real life has logic and sequence. They are, so to speak, normally part subconsciously of all the actions we need to do to survive.

'But we don't need the actions we perform onstage. We only pretend we need them.

'It is difficult to do something when there's no actual need, no necessity for it. Then we don't perform real actions, we do them "in general" and you know that this leads to theatrical convention, that is, lies.

'What are we to do? We must create a large action out of individual, small actions which fit together logically and sequentially. That was the case with Kostya in the "burning money" when he was counting it.

'But then I took him in hand and directed each of his small, constituent actions. Without me he wouldn't have been able to fulfil the task he'd been assigned.

'Why was that? Because, like the vast majority of people, he pays far too little attention to the finer details of life. He didn't take an active interest in them, he didn't know which individual parts make up our actions: he wasn't interested in their logic and sequence, he was happy just to let them happen.

'But I know from practical experience how much we need logic and sequence in the theatre and I work on them all the time. I observe life. I advise you to do the same. Then it won't be difficult for you to recall small constituent actions onstage, their logic and sequence and to try to put them back together in one large action.

'As soon as you feel the logical line of a stage action, as soon as you have to repeat it several times, in proper sequence, it immediately becomes a living part of your muscular and other forms of memory. Then you feel the genuine truth of your action and truth evokes belief in the reality of what you are doing.

'Once actors know the sequence and logic of their actions, once they recognize and accept them as living organisms, then genuine action becomes part of a role and happens subconsciously, as in real life. Study the logic and sequence of physical actions diligently.'

'How can we study them? How? . . .'

'Take pen and paper and write down what you are doing:

1. I look for paper in the desk.
2. I take hold of the key, turn it in the lock, pull the drawer towards me. I push the chair back to make room for the drawer.
3. I try to remember how and in what order things are arranged in the drawer. I know where to look for the paper. I find it, choose the right sheets and set them out on the desk in order.
4. I close the drawer and pull the chair up to the desk.

'I ought to tell you that I have special notebooks for jotting down things like this, a whole collection of them, and often look up information in them. Notes jog my muscular memory and are a great help to me. I mention this for you to think about.'

'In the last year we have, if you remember, turned to logic and sequence at every step, as we studied each of the Elements. That shows they are needed not only in our actions, or feelings, but in all the other elements of our creative work: thoughts, wants, mental images, ideas, Tasks, the Through-action, contact and Adaptation. Only when there is an unbroken line of logic and sequence running right through our acting can truth arise and convince us that what we are doing is real.

'We can't sincerely believe in something which has no sequence or logic and even when we do [it's] the exception to the rule, a special case. A lack of sequence and logic is, of course, acceptable in such cases but for the rest of the time we must absolutely ensure that everything is logical and sequential otherwise we risk falling into the trap of conveying passions, characters and actions "in general". You know that playing of that kind results in representation, playacting and stock-in-trade.

'In time [you] will learn [how to master the logic and sequence of action]. For the moment let me recommend a little preparatory work to you. I will give you a few pointers.'

'What are they?'

'Train your powers of concentration to observe your inner and outer creative mechanisms.

'Start with what's simplest, with the outer logic and sequence of actions without objects, as we did with "counting the notes" in the opening scene of "burning the money".

'These exercises teach you to explore the logic and sequence of the individual, constituent, small actions, which create one large action.

'You must, as they say, get your hand in, train yourself using regular exercises in a wide variety of actions without objects and scenes which come into your head. When you have analysed them and grasped their linear logic and sequence line and know it well, you will have a feeling of truth. And where there is truth there is belief, and where there is belief you are close to the "threshold of the subconscious".

'Having used these exercises to discipline your power of concentration a little, turn it inwards, into your mind which needs logic and sequence to a very high degree. Don't be intimidated by what I'm saying. It's much easier than it seems.

'Here are the kinds of exercises I recommend.

'Select a mental state, a mood, and ultimately a whole emotion and transform it into a long line of small and large, inner and outer actions. What does this mean?

'Let's suppose you select the mood, *boredom*. An autumn evening, dusk comes early, the countryside, rain, sleet, loneliness, the crackling of dry twigs and leaves. The place of the action, a friend's estate, where you are living or where you might be in your imagination right now. Add, as much as you can, Given Circumstances which are characteristic of the place, time and mood you have chosen.'

'How can I do that?' I asked with interest.

'In exactly the same way you did in earlier classes in "counting the money". You used small moments of truth and belief in the reality of what you were doing (counting the money) and small physical actions and created logically, sequentially, progressively, a large physical action, a large truth, and therefore a belief in what you were doing.

'Remember we compared it to treading down an overgrown path?'

'I remember but can't see how any of it can be an approach to the subconscious,' I commented.

'And what about all your impromptu actions? They were probably suggested by the subconscious.'

'Could be, but they were details,' I argued.

'Those details brought you close to the truth and evoked belief in what you were doing. One large truth called for another larger one.'

'What larger one?' I asked, puzzled.

'You wanted to know about the hunchback's past, your wife's past, your own character's. You had to invent a series of exciting incidents about the past. First, that made your situation more credible, more probable, then brought you closer to truth, belief and the subconscious.'

'Yes, I had to know who I was working for, why I wanted to amuse the hunchback,' I recalled.

'Your story brought you closer to him. It created a family for you, a cosy atmosphere, a serious purpose for your simple, physical actions. It created what we term "I am being".

'Do you really think we can reach that state of mind without being very near the "threshold of the subconscious"?

'You were right in line with it, its waves poured over you. And you achieved all this because of tiny, insignificant, physical actions!'

2.

'Our ubiquitous elements, *logic and sequence*, are present in emotions, too.

'Once again I have to digress for a moment to examine how logic and sequence affect feelings.

'In a word, I will discuss the logic and sequence of feeling in the process of creative re-experiencing.

'An easy thing to say, the logic and sequence of feeling!

'This is a question only scholars can answer. How are we, amateurs and laymen, to deal with it?

'Here's the excuse for our audacity.

'First, there's no other way out. We have to settle this question one way or another. Our kind of acting, which is based on genuine re-experiencing, has to confront the issue of logic and sequence of feelings. Without them there is no truth and, consequently, no belief, no "I am being". Our organism and its subconscious on which our art, our creative endeavours and experiencing are based, cannot function without them.

'Second, I don't approach the question in a scientific way, which is beyond our competence, but in a practical way.'

'As you have probably noticed, whenever science and technology have not been of help, we have turned to our own natural, biological creativity, to our subconscious, to practical experience. And I invite you to do the same now. Let us move out of science into our own lives, which we know, and which provide us with wide experience, practical knowledge and information, rich, inexhaustible emotional material, skills, habits, etc., etc.'

'How are we supposed to do that?' Vanya asked, very worried.

'In just the same way as you did earlier,' said Tortsov, calming him down. 'Ask yourself: *"What would I do, as a human being, if I found myself in the same Circumstances as the character I am portraying?"*

'Don't try to give me any old answer, in terms of outward form. Be serious and sincere. Involve your feeling and will, let them provide the answer not just your intelligence. Don't forget that the tiniest physical action can create truth and produce feeling in a natural way.

'What's more, I want you to give your answer not in words but in *physical actions*.

'Let me remind you that the clearer, more concrete, more precise these actions are, the less you risk weakening your acting.

'So, to recognize and define the logic and sequence of our state of mind and the life of the human spirit, we turn to our body with its precise, accessible, concrete, physical actions, not to our feelings, which are rather unreliable and difficult to pin down, or the complexities of our mind. We recognize, define and fix their logic and sequence not in scientific words and psychological terms but as simple, physical actions.

'If they are genuine, productive and purposeful, if they are inwardly justified by sincere, human experiences, then they forge an unbreakable link between our inner and outer lives. I will use that, too, for my own creative purposes.

'Now you can see how we resolve a complex, impossible question – the logic and sequence of feelings – in a natural, simple and practical way. We use the logic and sequence of doable physical actions which we know from life.

'That means that my simple, non-scientific but practical method leads to the desired result.

'Instead of feelings, which are elusive and unreliable, I turn to easy physical actions, *I look for them in my inner impulses*, I draw the information I need from my own direct, human experience of life. In such moments I let my memories and my own nature take over. It has a nose for organic truth and knows what it can believe. I just have to listen to it. You've realized, of course, that in this method we're not talking about physical actions themselves but the way we justify them inwardly and can truly believe in them.

'When you need to convey some state of mind or other, or a feeling, you have first to ask, "What would I do in similar circumstances?" Write it down, translate it into actions and lay them, like a tracing, over the role. If the play is a good one and its life is real, then you will find the tracing will fit, if not fully, then partly.

'I strongly recommend you to write down questions and answers relating to a new role. This has yet another advantage.

'To write down a question or an answer you have to find exactly the right words. You can't do that without going into the question deeply. That's a very useful way of getting to know the role better. Try not to be vague, define your feelings precisely in words that cannot be altered. That leads to a much wider analysis of feelings.

'There's another advantage. These notes are invaluable, creative material for an actor.

'Imagine that you have gradually noted down every state, every mood you ever experienced in every role and in every play in your career as an actor.

'If our list contained all the individual elements out of which human passions are made, if we experienced each of the constituent parts logically and sequentially, according to our list, we still wouldn't be able to pursue them [so that we could] grasp them with a snap of the fingers, as actors do, we'd have to master them gradually, bit by bit. You cannot master great passions straight off. But that's what most actors try to do.

'A great deal of your Emotion Memory goes into these notes. That's enormous! It is very valuable material when studying the logic of feelings.'

'Take love, for example,' Tortsov began. 'What is it made of, what actions does this human passion provoke?

'Meeting him or her.

'There's an immediate or gradual attraction and much greater intention is paid to the future beloved.

'The lovers relive every moment of their meeting.

'They find an excuse to meet again.

'Second meeting. The wish to forge a link through common interests, activities which will imply more frequent meetings, etc., etc.

'Then:

'The first secret that brings them closer together.

'Friendly advice which requires regular meetings and contact, etc., etc.

'Then:

'The first quarrel, reproaches, doubts.

'Fresh meetings to clear the air.

'Reconciliation. Greater closeness, etc., etc.

'Then:

'Obstacles to meetings.

'Secret correspondence.

'Secret meetings.

'The first gift.

'The first kiss, etc., etc.

'Then:

'Friendship and spontaneity in their relationship.

'A more demanding attitude towards each other.

'Jealousy.

'Separation.

'Parting.

'A further meeting. Forgiveness, etc., etc.

'All these moments have an inner basis. They sum up the inner feelings, passions or states of mind to which we give one name, "love".

'Perform each of these actions correctly in your mind, with a proper foundation, thoughtfully, sincerely and fully and you will come near, first outwardly then inwardly, to states and actions analogous to those of a man in love. If you do this groundwork, it will be easier for you to understand the role and the play in which this human passion features.

'All these elements, or the most important ones, appear, one way or another, to one degree or another, in a good, well-constructed play. Actors look for them in their roles and recognize them. They are landmarks, signposts along the play and the role. We can then perform a series of Tasks and actions which, combined, form the state of mind we call love. We create it bit by bit and not all at once "in general". Then we act, we don't playact, we are human beings, we don't posture like ham actors, we feel, and don't imitate the results of feeling.

'But most actors, who don't think and don't probe the nature of the feelings they are portraying, represent love as one big, "in general" experience. They try to "comprehend the incomprehensible". They forget that major experiences are a combination of numerous separate episodes and moments. You have to know them thoroughly, study them, comprehend and fulfil each of them separately. Otherwise you are doomed to dead clichés and stock-in-trade.

'Unfortunately the logic and sequence of feelings, which are so important for actors, are still not applied onstage. So we can only hope it will happen in the future.

'Perform this task and action for me: lock this door and then go through it into the next room,' Tortsov suggested to us. 'You can't. In that case answer the question: if it were totally dark, how would I switch off this lamp? You can't do that either.

'If you want to convey your most intimate secret to me privately, how can you do it at the top of your voice?

'Because in theatres, in the vast majority of cases, for five acts, he and she do everything possible to get married, suffer every imaginable trial and tribulation, desperately fight against difficulties and when the longed-for moment comes, and after they have kissed fervently, they go cold on each other, as though that was it and the show was over. What a letdown for the audience. Having spent the whole evening believing in their hopes and feelings, how disappointed they are by the coldness the leading actors display and by their poor logic and sequence in planning their roles!

'You see how easily we have resolved the problem of the logic and sequence of feelings. Just ask yourselves, "What would I do if I were in the character's shoes?" Your own personal experience will give you the answer to that question because you have lived in real life and it is organically linked to your own inner nature.

'Of course, that doesn't mean that your experiences and aspirations need be the same as the character's. They can be very different. But it is important that you should judge them not as an actor from the outside but as another human being. You must judge them as one person does another.

'In conclusion I will only say something you already know perfectly well, that logic and sequence are essential in the creative process.

'We need them particularly when it comes to feelings. If their logic and sequence are correct, that will stop us making the huge mistakes we often see in the theatre. If we knew the logical, sequential development of a role we would be aware of its constituent parts. We wouldn't attempt to grasp major emotions at once. We would put them together, logically and sequentially, step by step, bit by bit. A knowledge of the constituent parts and their sequence would enable us to control our inner life.'

23

PHYSICAL CHARACTERISTICS

At the beginning of today's class I told Tortsov that I understand the process of experiencing intellectually, i.e. fostering and nurturing those Elements in an actor's mind which were right for the character. But I was still uncertain about embodying a role. If you don't use your own body, voice, way of speaking, walking and behaving, if you don't find the right features for the character, you can't convey the life of the human spirit.

'True,' Tortsov concurred. 'Without outward forms, the character's particular personality doesn't get across to the audience. Physical features illuminate, illustrate and so put across the invisible, inner shape of a character's mind to the audience.'

'Yes, yes!' Paul and I exclaimed, 'but how and where do we find these external physical features?'

'More often than not, especially in talented actors they appear spontaneously, because the right frame of mind has been created,' Tortsov explained. 'There are many examples of this in My Life in Art.[1] Take, for example, Ibsen's An Enemy of the People. Once the right frame of mind and the right mental characteristics had been created out of Elements similar to Stockman's own, the impetuousness, the gangling walk, the jutting chin, the two thrusting fingers and other features appeared out of nowhere.'

'And what if you're not so lucky?' I asked him, 'What happens then?'

'Do you remember what Pyotr says to Aksusha in Ostrovski's The Forest when he's explaining how they can avoid being recognized when they are running away? "Screw up your face and you'll look as if you've got one eye."

'Disguise isn't in itself difficult. It happened to me. I had a good friend with a rich bass voice, long hair, a long beard and a pointed moustache. Suddenly he shaved off his beard and cut his hair. That revealed a tiny chin and jug ears. I met him in his new look at a family dinner. We sat opposite each other and chatted. "Who does he remind me of?" I kept asking myself, not realizing that he reminded me of himself. This practical joker disguised his bass voice by talking in a falsetto. Half-way through the meal I was still behaving as if I had just met him.

'Here's another example. A very beautiful woman was stung by a bee. Her lip swelled and distorted her mouth. This not only changed her outward appearance out of all recognition, but also her speech. I met her by chance in the corridor and talked to her for several minutes without suspecting she was someone I knew very well.'

While Tortsov was talking, he almost imperceptibly half-closed one eye, as though a sty was forming, and opened the other much wider, raising the eyebrow. It was barely noticeable, even to those close by. These minute changes had a strange effect. He was still Tortsov, of course, but . . . someone else, too, someone untrustworthy. He now had something tricky, sly, vulgar about him, that was not really he. But as soon as he stopped the game with his eye, he was back to good old Tortsov. But when he screwed up his eye again and changed his face, he was once more the swindler.

'Did you notice', Tortsov enquired, 'that mentally I was still Tortsov the whole time, I spoke in my own voice all the time, whether my eye was screwed up or not and whether my eyebrow was raised or not? If I were developing a sty and that made me screw up my eye, I wouldn't have changed mentally, I would still go on living as normal. Why should I change mentally because of a squint? I'm the same person whether my eye is open or shut, whether my eyebrow is raised or not.

'Or let's assume I've been stung by a bee, like a beautiful lady I know, and that my mouth is misshapen.'

With extraordinary technical facility, simplicity and lightness, Tortsov pulled his mouth to the right, which changed his speech and diction.

'Do my personality and my normal experiences', he continued with greatly altered diction, 'have to suffer because my face and speech are distorted? Do I have to stop being me? Neither a bee-sting nor a technical distortion of my face should affect my inner life as a human being. And what about lameness' (Tortsov limped), 'or paralysis of the hands' (for a moment his hands seemed paralysed) 'or round shoulders' (his spine took the appropriate position), 'or turning the heels out or in' (Tortsov walked both ways) 'or wrongly placed arms, either too far forward or too far back, behind the spine?' (he demonstrated both) 'Do all these external details have any relation to experiencing, communicating and physical embodiment?'

The ease, simplicity, naturalness with which Tortsov assumed these physical defects of which he had spoken, on the instant, without any kind of preparation, was amazing.

'But what extraordinary tricks the voice and especially the articulation of the consonants can play, and transform an actor. True the voice has to be properly placed and trained when changing diction. Otherwise you can't speak in the top or bottom register for very long. As regards modifying your diction and especially the articulation of consonants, it is very simple. Draw the tongue back, i.e. shorten it' (he did so) 'and a very particular way of speaking results, rather like the way the English produce their consonants. Or, lengthen the tongue, extend it beyond the teeth and you get the silly lisp, which, if you work on it, is just right for Nedorosl or Belzaminov.[2]

'Or, again, put your mouth in other strange positions and another way of speaking will result. For example, remember the Englishman we all know. He has a very short upper lip and very long teeth like a rabbit. Shorten your upper lip and bare your teeth a far as you can.'

'How do we do that?' I asked trying to do what he had said.

'Easy,' Tortsov replied. He took out a handkerchief, dried his upper teeth and the inside of his top lip. He raised it so we barely noticed and while he was apparently drying his lip, he took his hand away from his mouth and we really did see rabbit's teeth and a short raised upper lip which stayed stuck to the dry teeth above.

This trick hid the Tortsov we all know so well. It was as though we had our familiar Englishman before us. It seemed to us this stupid short lip and rabbit's teeth had transformed Tortsov completely. His voice and speech were different, too. So were his face and eyes, even his way of standing, his walk, his arms and legs. Even his personality seemed to change. But he was doing nothing inside. After a moment he stopped his trickery and spoke as his normal self.

He, too, seemed surprised, because while he was playing tricks with his lip, his body, arms, legs, neck, eyes, even his voice physically changed and took on the character of the rabbit's teeth and the short lip.

Everything was intuitive. He only became aware of it afterwards after he had checked over what had happened. It was we (from the outside), not Tortsov, who explained that the characteristics that had appeared intuitively as a result of a simple trick were the right ones, and filled out the picture of the man with the short lip and rabbit's teeth.

After he had probed his own mind and noted what had happened Tortsov commented that there had been a shift he had not noticed and which he couldn't take in immediately.

There had undoubtedly been a mental change to match the physical appearance and everything that followed from it, because the words he now spoke, as far as we could see, weren't his own, and not in his usual style, although the ideas he expressed were genuine and natural.[3]

.. .. 19..

In today's class Tortsov demonstrated that intuition can produce external physical characteristics and so can pure, mechanical technical trickery.

Where do we get these tricks? Another worrying enigma. Do we have to learn them, invent them, take them from life, chance upon them, find them in books on anatomy?

'In any one of a dozen ways,' Tortsov explained. 'You should draw your external characterization from yourselves, from others, from life (real or imaginary) either intuitively or by observation, from the daily round, friends, pictures, etchings, sketches, books, stories, novels or let chance provide them. It doesn't matter which. Only don't get lost in this outer searching, be yourselves. Yes, that's what we'll do,' Tortsov decided there and then. 'In the next class we'll organize a masquerade.'

?!. . . . . General consternation.

'I want each student to come disguised as a character.'

'Masquerade? An external character? What character?'

'It doesn't matter. Any one you like,' Tortsov explained. 'A business man, a peasant, a soldier, a Spaniard, an aristocrat, a mosquito, a frog, anything that comes to mind. Wardrobe and make-up are at your disposal. Go and choose costumes, wigs, things to stick on.'

This announcement caused first consternation, then a lot of argument and finally interest and excitement.

We all started thinking, planning, making notes and secret sketches so we could decide on costume and make-up for our characters.

Only Grisha, as usual, remained cold and indifferent.

.. .. 19..

Today, the whole class went to the huge wardrobe departments, one which is high up above the foyer and the other which is down in the basement under the stage.

Grisha chose everything he wanted in fifteen minutes and left. Others didn't stay long either. Only Varya and I took a long while to reach a firm decision.

Like most flirtatious women, her eyes were everywhere, her mind was in a whirl from the vast array of beautiful dresses. As for me, I, too, was the same, because I didn't know who I was going to be. I was relying on chance.

I examined everything I was shown carefully, hoping to chance on a costume that would suggest a character to interest me.

My attention lighted on a simple morning coat. It was remarkable for the unusual material from which it was made, a sandy grey-green colour I'd never seen before. It was faded and covered in mildew and dust and ash. I felt anyone in that coat would look like a ghost. As I examined this old jacket I felt something vaguely rotten and repulsive, and at the same time fearful and lethal stirring.

If I could find a matching hat and gloves and dusty, unpolished grey shoes, if I had make-up that was also grey-green-yellowish, and indeterminate like the material then I would have something sinister and yet . . . familiar?! But, for the moment, what it was I couldn't tell.

They set aside the coat for me, and promised to find shoes, gloves and a top hat, as well as wig and beard but I still wasn't satisfied and went on looking until the kindly wardrobe mistress told me they had to get ready for the evening show.

I had to go, although nothing was definite. All I had was the dirty frock coat.

I left the wardrobe, still anxious and puzzled. Who was it I had seen in that mouldy coat?

From then to the masquerade, which was arranged for three days later, something was happening inside. I wasn't the person I knew. Or rather, I wasn't alone. There was someone else inside me I was looking for, but couldn't find. No!

Life went on as usual, but I couldn't feel fully involved, something had changed, something was watering down my normal life. As though I had been brought a [drink] to which something strange had been added, instead of good wine. It only half reminded me of my favourite taste, or a quarter. I had the bouquet of my life but not life itself. And yet, that wasn't it either. I was aware not only of my own life but another life stirring inside me. I was split down the middle. I knew my normal life was there but now it seemed hidden in a fog. And though I tried to look closely at whatever caught my attention, I didn't see it fully, only in broad outline, 'in general' I didn't really see what it was. I was thinking, but only half-thinking, hearing but only half-hearing, smelling but only half-smelling. Half my energy and human faculties had been drained away somewhere else and that sapped and divided my drive and concentration. I couldn't finish what I'd started. It seemed there was still something important I had to do. Yet my conscious mind was in a fog, I couldn't see ahead, I was vague, split in two.

What a wearisome, frustrating state to be in! It went on for days and I still hadn't decided what to play in the masquerade.

Last night, I suddenly woke up and everything was clear. The second life I'd been living in parallel with my own was hidden in the subconscious. That was where the search for the mildewed person whose clothes I had accidentally found was happening.

My moment of insight didn't last long and I was once again plagued by insomnia and doubt.

It was as though I'd forgotten something, lost it and couldn't find it again. It was an agonizing mood to be in, and yet if someone had offered to remove it by magic, I'm not sure I would have said yes.

And here's another strange thing I noted.

I was quite convinced I would find the character I was looking for but I still went on looking. I spent a long time examining all the pictures in photographers' shop windows, trying to work out who the originals were. I was still obviously trying to find what I needed. But then why didn't I go into the shop and look at all the piles of photographs? There were piles of dusty, dirty photos lying about in second-hand bookshops, too. They were material, why didn't I use them? Why didn't I look at them? I took one very small packet and fastidiously avoided the rest, so as not to dirty my hands.

What was it all about? How can I explain this lack of drive, this split personality? I think it came from an unconscious but resolute conviction that sooner or later this dusty, mildewed gentleman would come alive and rescue me. 'No use looking. You won't find anything better than this dusty man,' a hidden voice probably prompted. Then strange things happened two or three times.

I was walking along the street and suddenly everything was clear. I froze in my tracks so I could grasp the full meaning of what had been put in my hands . . . But . . . ten seconds passed and it was gone and I was left with a question mark again.

Another time, I was surprised by my irregular, arrhythmic walk, which wasn't mine at all but which I couldn't shake off.

Lying awake at night, I rubbed my hands together in a strange way. 'Who rubs his palms together like that?' I asked, but couldn't remember. I only know he has small, narrow, cold, clammy hands with red, very red, palms. It's very unpleasant shaking soft boneless hands like that. Who is he? Who is he?

Still divided, still undecided, I went to the students' dressing room next to the school stage. I was very disappointed. They had put us all in the one dressing room and we would all have to make up and dress together not separately as we had for our first show on the big stage. It was difficult to concentrate with all the talk and racket. Besides, I felt that putting on the dusty coat and the yellow-grey wig and beard for the first time was very important. Only they could suggest what I had been unconsciously looking for. I had pinned my last hope on it.

But everything was getting in my way. Grisha, who was sitting next to me, had already made up as Mephistopheles. He had already put on a rich, black Spanish costume and there were 'Ahs' of admiration all round. Others were yelling with laughter at Vanya, who had covered his baby face with every conceivable kind of dots and dashes, like a map, to make himself look old. Paul made me angry because all he could do was put on a very ordinary suit, and the handsome appearance of Skalozub.[4] True, there was an element of surprise in this since no one would have dreamed there was a well-built body, with good straight legs inside his normal baggy appearance. Leo amused me by his efforts to be an aristocrat. He didn't pull it off this time either but you can't deny he had presence. In his make-up, with his well-groomed beard, heels, which gave him height and made him slimmer, he looked impressive. His careful walk, a result, no doubt, of the heels, lent him a suaveness he doesn't possess in life. Igor also amused us all with his unexpected boldness. The athlete, the dancer, the master of rhetoric had decided to hide inside the long frock coat of Tito Titych Bruskov,[5] with baggy trousers, a flowered waistcoat, a pot belly and beard and hair 'à la russe'.

The students' dressing room echoed with people shouting, like the worst kind of amateur show.

'I wouldn't have known you!' 'Is that really you?' 'Wonderful!' 'Well done, I never thought you could do it!' etc.

This shouting made me angry and the questioning, unenthusiastic comments I received made me lose heart completely.

'Something's wrong!' 'I don't know . . . a sort of . . . mystery.' 'Who is he?' 'Who are you playing?'

Who was this person I was playing? Had I known, I'd have been the first to say.

Damn the make-up man, until he arrived and turned me into a standard theatrical blond I felt I was getting somewhere. I began to shake slightly as I slowly put on the old coat, the wig and glued on the beard. Had I been alone, without all the distractions round me, I know I would have found out who this mysterious person was. But the buzz and chatter didn't give me a chance to think and so I couldn't reach the unknown thing coming to life inside me.

Finally they all went out onstage to show themselves to Tortsov. I sat alone in the dressing room, tired and desperate, looking at my standard, theatrical face. I felt it was all a total loss, decided not to go on, but get changed and remove my make-up with a repulsive looking green cream that was next to me. I put some on my fingers and smeared it on my face . . . All the colours ran, as in a watercolour. The result was a grey-green, yellowish face, like an addition to my costume . . . You couldn't tell where my nose, eyes and lips were. I smeared some of the cream into my hair and my moustache and then all over the wig. The hair went lumpy and clotted . . . Then, shaking all over, as though in a delirium, my heart skipping a beat, I eliminated my eyebrows all together. I splattered powder all over . . . I smeared my hands with green and my palms with pink . . . straightened my jacket, adjusted my tie. I did it all quickly and surely because then I knew the kind of man I was portraying.

I tilted my hat at a rakish angle, then became conscious of my once fashionable full-cut trousers, now so thin and worn, shaped my legs to the creases that had formed and turned my toes firmly inwards. The result was silly legs. Have you noticed what silly legs some people have? It's awful! Because of the strange position of my legs, I became shorter and my walk was different. My whole body leaned to the right. I needed a walking stick. There was one nearby so I took it, although it wasn't quite what I had imagined . . . I also needed a quill pen behind my ear or between my teeth. I asked the property master for one and walked about the room, while I waited for his return, becoming aware of how all the parts of the body, my facial lines and features fell permanently into place.

After two or three turns about the room in an irregular, arrhythmic walk, I took a fleeting glance in the mirror and didn't recognize myself. I had been totally transformed since last I looked.

'That's him, that's him!' I exclaimed, unable to contain my pleasure. 'As soon as they bring the pen, I can go onstage.'

I heard footsteps in the corridor. It had to be the props man with the pen so I dashed out to meet him and bumped into Rakhmanov in the doorway.

'What a fright!' he blurted out when he saw me. 'Who's this, lad? What sort of joke is this? Dostoievski? Or the man who couldn't die? Is that you, Kostya? Who are you playing?'

'A snide critic,' I replied in a rather shrill, clipped voice.

'What critic, lad?' Rakhmanov asked me, a little disconcerted by my insolent, piercing stare. I felt like a leech battening on to him.

'Which?' I repeated, with an obvious desire to offend him. 'The critic, Kostya Nazvanov's lodger. I exist to stop him working. It's my greatest pleasure, my noblest ambition of my life.'

I was amazed at my own insolence, the hostility of my tone, my point-blank stare, the cynicism and rudeness with which I treated him. My tone and self-assurance shook him. He couldn't relate differently to me. He didn't know what to say. He was lost.

'Let's go. . .,' he said, uncertainly. 'They started ages ago.'

'Let's go because they started ages ago,' I said, not moving but staring insolently right through him. An uneasy pause ensued. Neither of us moved. It was clear Rakhmanov wanted to end the scene quickly, but he didn't know how. Luckily for him the props man came with the pen at that moment. I grabbed it and stuck it between my teeth.

That narrowed my mouth down to an evil slit and the pointed end on one side and the feather on the other made the expression on my face even more sarcastic.

'Let's go,' Rakhmanov said, quietly, almost timidly.

'Let's go,' I mimicked him, sarcastically and insolently.

We went onstage and Rakhmanov tried not to look me in the eye.

When I went into 'Marya's sitting room' I didn't show myself right away. I hid behind the grey-coloured fireplace, just about showing my profile in the top hat.

Meanwhile Tortsov was watching Leo and Paul as the aristocrat and Skalosub. They'd been introduced and were talking nonsense because that's all their characters can do.

'Who's that over there?' Tortsov suddenly asked, very worried. 'I think there's someone sitting behind the fireplace. Who the devil is it? I've seen everyone. Who is it? Ah, yes, Kostya . . . No, that's not him.

'Who are you?' Tortsov addressed me, very curious.

'A critic,' I said, standing up and introducing myself. With that, to my surprise, my silly leg advanced so that I leaned even more to the right. I removed my hat with exaggerated elegance and bowed politely. Then I sat down behind the fireplace again, almost merging into its colour.

'A critic?' Tortsov repeated, uncertainly.

'Yes. A very personal one,' I explained in a squeaky voice. 'You see the pen . . . I've gnawed it to bits . . . out of sheer fury. I bite it, like this, in the middle . . . it quivers and cracks.'

Then quite unexpectedly, I let out a kind of squeal instead of a laugh. I was taken aback myself. It had quite an impact on Tortsov, too.

'What the devil!' he exclaimed, 'Come over here into the light.'

I went down to the footlights with my silly legs.

'Whose personal critic are you?' staring at me as at a stranger.

'Of the person I live in,' I squealed.

'Which person?'

'Kostya Nazvanov,' I admitted, lowering my eyes modestly like a girl.

'You're inside him?' Tortsov prompted.

'I've moved in.'

'With whom?'

I choked again as I laughed and squealed. I had to calm down before I could say:

'Him. Actors love people who destroy them. And a critic . . .'

Another burst of laughter and squealing stopped me expressing my thoughts. I went down on one knee so I could look Tortsov straight in the eye.

'What can you criticize? You're an ignoramus,' Tortsov said, disparagingly.

'Ignoramuses criticize, too,' I defended myself.

'You know nothing, you can do nothing,' Tortsov continued, provocatively.

'Those who can, do, those who can't, teach,' I said, sitting down by the footlights, opposite Tortsov, in a very affected manner.

'That's not true. You don't criticize, you carp. You're no better than a leech, a slug. They're not dangerous, any more than you are, but they don't give life.'

'I'll drag you through the mud . . . relentlessly . . . tirelessly,' I squealed.

'Vermin!' Tortsov yelled in undisguised fury.

'Oh! What style!' I said, leaning across the footlights, playing games with Tortsov.

'Parasite,' Tortsov almost screamed.

'Good! . . . very, very good.' I was still playing games with Tortsov without the least twinge of conscience. 'You can't wash off a leech. And where there are leeches there's a marsh and where there's a marsh there are devils, and me.'

Looking back on it, I'm amazed at my boldness and insolence. I reached a point where I was flirting with Tortsov as with a good-looking woman and even stretched a greasy finger from my narrow hand, with its red palm, towards my teacher's nose and cheek. I wanted to fondle it but he instinctively knocked it away in disgust and I half-closed my eyes and went on flirting with him through the slits.

After a moment's hesitation, Tortsov affectionately took my cheeks in his hands, drew me to him and embraced me warmly, murmuring:

'Well done! Splendid!'

And then he realized I'd smeared him with the grease that was running from my face and added:

'Oh! look what he's done to me. Water won't wash that off!'

Everyone rushed to clean him up while I, cheeks burning with the mark of his approval, leaped and skipped about and ran offstage, as myself, to applause from everyone.

It seems to me that coming straight out of character, as I had, and showing my own personality, underlined the Critic's special features and the way I became him even more.

Before leaving the stage, I stood still and stepped back into character for a moment and repeated the Critic's affected bow, by way of farewell.

Then I turned towards Tortsov and noticed how, handkerchief in hand, he stopped wiping his face and gave me an affectionate look from a distance.

I was truly happy. But it wasn't the usual sort of happiness. It was a new, artistic, creative happiness.

The performance continued in the dressing room. The students kept prompting me with new lines to which I gave biting answers, in character and didn't once falter. I had the feeling I could go on for ever, could live the role whatever the situation. How wonderful it is to be right on top of a character!

I continued, even after I'd removed make-up and costume, playing the character using my own natural attributes. Face, movements, voice, inflexions, diction, hands, legs adapted so perfectly to the character they replaced the wig, the beard and the grey morning coat. I caught sight of myself in the mirror once or twice and am certain it wasn't me I saw but the mouldy, snide critic. I played him without make-up or costume, using my own face and clothes.

But it still didn't stop there. I couldn't get out of character. On the way home, and going into my room, all the time there were vestiges of the character in the way I moved and behaved.

That's not all. During supper, when I was talking to the landlady and the other residents, I was argumentative, derisive and destructive, like the Critic, not me. The landlady even commented:

'You must have had a bad day! . . .'

I was delighted.

I'm happy because I know what being someone else requires, what *transformation and physical characterization are.*

They are the qualities a talented actor must have.

Today, as I was washing, I recalled that while I was living the Critic I still didn't lose contact with myself, Kostya.

I drew this conclusion because all the time I was acting I took enormous pleasure in observing my own physical transformation.

Half of me was an audience, while the other half was being someone else, the snide Critic.

On the other hand, can you call him someone else?

The Critic came out of me. I, as it were, split down the middle. One half was the actor, the other watched like an audience.

Strange. This sense of being split in two wasn't a hindrance, it fired and encouraged the creative process.

.. .. 19..

We devoted today's class to a thorough-going analysis of the 'masquerade'.

Turning to Varya Tortsov said:

'Some actors, women especially, don't need *physical characterization* or *transformation* because they turn every character into themselves and rely on their own personal *charm*. Their success is built on that. Without it, they are powerless, like Samson without his hair. They are scared of anything that hides their own personality from the audience.

'If their beauty works with an audience, they display it. If their charm is in their eyes, their face, their voice, their particular ways, they show them to the audience, as, for example, Varya does.

'Why transform when it makes you look worse than you do in life? You love *yourself* in the role more than the *role* in you. That's a mistake. You're quite capable not only of showing yourself but the character as well.

'Many actors rely on the charm of their personality. They display it to the audience. For example, Darya and Nikolai believe their attraction lies in their depth of feeling and the intensity of their experiencing. They subject every part to this treatment, filling them with their own most powerful, energetic qualities.

'If Varya is in love with her outside, Darya and Nikolai are not indifferent to their inside.

'Why bother with costume and make-up if they only get in the way?

'That, too, is a mistake. Remove it. Learn to love the *role* in yourselves. You have the creative ability to create it.

'There's another type of actor. No, don't look round for them. There aren't any here. You haven't had time to turn into them yet.

'They are concerned with the originality of their technique, the particular clichés they've so beautifully worked out. That's why they go onstage, to show them. Why bother with transformation? Or physical characterization when it doesn't let them show off their strong points?

'There's a third type of actor, armed with a strong technique and a battery of clichés, except they are not their own but other people's. Their physical characterization and transformation are created according to longstanding rituals. They know how every role, in every play, in every land "is played". Every role has been reduced to a masterplan. Without them, they couldn't play 365 roles a year, with one rehearsal apiece, as in provincial theatres.

'So, those of you who are tempted to take the path of least resistance be warned in time. It's dangerous.

'You, Grisha, for example. Don't imagine your Mephistopheles in the last class was a real characterization just because you showed off his make-up and costume, or that you were transformed, and disappeared behind him. No, not at all. You were still your handsome self, only in a new costume with a new assortment of clichés. This time a "Gothic, mediaeval character" as we term it.

'We saw the same clichés in The Taming of the Shrew only adapted to a comic not tragic role that time.

'We also know your, so to speak, modern-dress clichés for contemporary dramas and comedies in verse and prose. But . . . whatever make-up or costume you put on, whatever mannerisms and habits you adopt, you never get away from "Grisha the actor" while you're onstage. On the contrary, every cliché and trick leads you straight back to him.

'But that is not so. Your clichés don't lead you back to "Grisha the Actor" but "in general" to all the representational actors of all times and countries.

'You imagine you have your gestures, your way of walking, your way of speaking but you haven't. They're commonplace, permanent fixtures for actors who exchange art for stock-in-trade.

'But if you should ever decide to show us something we have never seen before, and show yourself as you are in life, i.e. not "Grisha the actor" but the human being, that would be wonderful because Grisha the person is much more interesting and talented than Grisha the actor. Show him to us because we can see Grisha the actor any time, any place in any theatre.

'I am sure Grisha the human being could produce a generation of character parts. But Grisha the actor will produce nothing because a collection of clichés is so very thin and worn.'

Tortsov then analysed Vanya. He is becoming increasingly tough with him. Possibly to take him in hand because he's so undisciplined. That's all to the good.

'You didn't give us a character but a mishmash. It was neither man, monkey nor chimneysweep. You didn't have a face but a dirty rag to wipe your brushes on.

'And what about your movements, actions, your whole behaviour. What was that supposed to be? St. Vitus' dance? You wanted to hide behind your characterization of an old man, but you didn't. Quite the contrary, the actor, Vanya, came through more obviously than ever. Because your posturing wasn't typical of the character but of you.

'Your tricksy playacting gave you away even more. It had nothing to do with the old man you were trying to play, only with you.

'That kind of physical characterizing doesn't transform you, it's a complete giveaway and provides a pretext for posturing.

'You don't like physical characterization and transformation, you know nothing about them, you don't need them and it's impossible to talk about what you gave us at all seriously. It was something you should never show onstage, under any circumstances.

'Let's hope this failure will bring you to your senses and make you consider your frivolous attitude to what I've been saying and what you've been doing here at school.

'Otherwise, it's trouble!'

Unfortunately, the second half of the class had to be altered because Tortsov had to attend to urgent business. Rakhmanov took over and did 'training and drill'.

.. .. 19..

Tortsov came into 'Marya's apartment' today, with a fatherly arm round Vanya, who looked upset and was red-eyed from crying. Evidently they had talked and were friends again.

As though continuing their discussion, Tortsov said:

'Go and try.'

A moment later Vanya began to hobble round the room, bent over, as though paralysed.

'No,' said Tortsov, stopping him. 'That's not a human being but a cuttlefish, or a ghost. Don't exaggerate.'

The next minute Vanya was young again and hobbling around quite fast like an old man.

'Now you're too energetic!' said Tortsov, stopping him again. 'Your mistake is you take the line of least resistance, you just copy externals. Copying isn't art. It's the wrong path. The best thing is to study old age from scratch. Then you'll know what you have to find in your own nature.

'How is it young people can suddenly jump up, turn, run, stand, sit without preparation and old people can't?'

'They're old . . . that's why!' Vanya said.

'That's no explanation. There are other, purely physiological reasons,' Tortsov explained.

'What are they?'

'Deposits of salts, hardening of the muscles and other reasons, which undermine the human organism over the years. Old people's joints aren't oiled. They creak and jam as though they were rusty.

'That restricts broadness of gesture, sharpens the angles and reduces the degree of flexion in the joints and the rotation of the torso and the head. You have to divide one large movement into many constituent parts and prepare for each of them.

'You may be able to turn at the waist through an angle of 50 or 60 degrees when you're young, but when you're old you can only manage 12 degrees and that has to be carefully done in stages, and you have to stop and get your breath. Otherwise you'll have stabbing pains or be overcome or twisted by lumbago.

'Besides, in old people, the communication between motivating and motor centres is slow, like, so to speak, a freight train, not an express. Your movements will be hesitant and halting. Old people's movements are, therefore, slow and slack.

'These are the "Given Circumstances", the "magic ifs" within which you, the actor, have to operate. Now, observe each of your movements, remembering what an old man can and can't do.'

We couldn't stop ourselves, we all started behaving like old people in the set circumstances Tortsov had described. The room turned into an old folk's home.

It was important for me to feel my actions were human, within the limits prescribed by old people's physiology and that I wasn't just play-acting and mimicking.

Nonetheless, from time to time, Tortsov and Rakhmanov had to stop one of us when we indulged in movements that were too broad or fast or physiologically and logically wrong.

Finally, with intense concentration, we got it more or less right.

'Now you've gone to the other extreme,' Tortsov corrected us. 'You're sticking to the same slow tempo and rhythm as you walk and you're being very careful in your movements all the time. That's not what old people do. I'll illustrate what I mean by telling you something I remember.

'I knew a lady who was a hundred years old. She could still run in a straight line. But she had to get ready for a long time, run on the spot, loosen up her legs and start with small steps. She had the same kind of intense concentration as a one-year-old child learning to walk.

'Once her legs were loosened up and working, and had built up some momentum, she couldn't keep still but moved faster and faster until she was almost running. When she got to the end of the line she even found it difficult to stop. Once there, she halted like an engine that has run out of steam.

'She got her breath back before tackling another very difficult task – coming back. She ran on the spot again for a long time, looking very worried, concentrating hard and taking all manner of precautions. The turnaround was very slow, it took a long, long time, then another pause to get her breath, running on the spot and the start of the return journey.'

We then tested out this story.

Everyone started running in short steps and slowly straightened up as they reached the wall.

I felt that, initially, I wasn't really *behaving* in the Given Circumstances, as an old person, but mimicking, playacting what the 100-year-old woman Tortsov had described would do. However, I finally got started and was so carried away I decided to sit down like an old person who was apparently tired out.

But then Tortsov came down on me and explained that I'd made countless mistakes.

'What are they?' I asked, anxious to know.

'That's how young people sit down,' he explained. 'They want to sit and they do, almost right away, without thinking, without preparing for it.

'And also,' he continued, 'check how many degrees you bend the knees. About 50. As an old person, you can't bend more than an angle of 20. No, you'll have to do less. Much, much less. That's it. Now sit.'

I leaned back and fell into the chair like a sack of potatoes.

'You see,' Tortsov commented, 'your old man has already hurt himself, or has an attack of lumbago.'

I tried to adapt in every possible way to sitting down without bending my knees more than a little. I had to bend in the middle and use my hands to try and find support. I leant them on the arms of the chair, slowly began to bend them at the elbows and lowered myself into the chair.

'Gently, gently, watch it,' Tortsov guided me. 'Don't forget, old people have poor eyesight. They have to look to see what they are leaning on, before they put their hands on the arm of the chair. Now, slower, or you'll set off your lumbago. Don't forget that your joints are rusty and painful. Careful . . . There we are!

'Stop, stop! What are you doing?' Tortsov stopped me because I wanted to lean back against the chair as soon as I had sat down.

'You have to rest,' Tortsov warned me. 'You need time. Old people don't do things quickly. There.'

Now I leaned back a little at a time. Good! First put one hand, then the other on your knees. Rest. Ready.

'Why all the precautions? You've done the most difficult part. Now you can be younger, more agile, more energetic, flexible. Change the tempo, the rhythm. Move more boldly, bend, give your actions the energy of youth. But within a limit of 15–20 degrees of your normal movements. Don't go beyond this limit, or if you do, go very carefully, otherwise you'll get cramps.

'If a young actor, playing an old man, carefully considers and absorbs all the constituent parts of a large and difficult action, if he starts to behave consciously, sincerely and honestly, productively and specifically, within the Given Circumstances of age, without overemphasis or exaggeration, if he does what I have said, by establishing the parts of a major action, he will slip into the old man's tempo and rhythm which are of prime importance when portraying age.

'The Given Circumstances of age are difficult to establish. But once you have found them, it isn't difficult to fix them technically.'

.. .. 19..

Today, Tortsov continued his unfinished critique of the 'masquerade' which had been broken off in the previous class.

He said:

'I talked to you about actors who do their best to avoid physical characterization and personal transformation.

'Today, I want to present another type of actor, who, for various reasons, likes them and pursues them.'

'They do it mainly because they're not very good-looking, and lack charm outside and in. They aren't stage personalities, they have to hide behind a character and so find the charm and attraction they lack.

'That requires great technical refinement and artistry. Unfortunately, this most excellent and precious gift is rare and without it all efforts to characterize can go the wrong way, i.e. towards conventional playacting.

'I'll survey the different varieties of actor to show the right and wrong approach to characterization more clearly. Rather than use examples I'll base my remarks on what you did in the "masquerade".

'You can create character onstage "in general", the merchant, the soldier, the aristocrat, the peasant, etc. Superficial observation provides the more obvious ways, habits and mannerisms of the different social classes into which people used to be divided.[6] For example, "in general" a soldier stands straight, marches rather than walks normally, moves his shoulders to flash his epaulettes. He clicks his heels, jingles his spurs, speaks and clears his throat loudly, to appear gruffer, etc. Peasants spit, blow their noses on the ground, walk heavily, speak uncouthly with the wrong vowels and wipe their mouths on their coat-sleeves.

'Aristocrats always wear top hats and gloves, sport a monocle, speak gutturally and pronounce their "r"s like the French. They like to play with their watchchain or the ribbon of their monocle, etc. All these are clichés "in general" that are supposed to characterize. They are taken from life, they can be encountered in reality. But that's not the point. They aren't typical.

'Igor took this simplistic approach. He gave us everything we could expect from Tito Titych,[7] but that wasn't Bruskov, it wasn't even an ordinary merchant, it was "in general" what we call a "merchant" in quotes in the theatre.

'The same comment applies to Leo. His aristocrat "in general" wasn't a living creation, it was purely theatrical.

'These were all moribund, stock-in-trade traditions. That's the way "you do" merchants and aristocrats in every theatre. These aren't living beings but histrionic, ritual representations.

'Other actors, with stronger and finer powers of concentration can discern particular groups of merchants, soldiers, aristocrats and peasants, i.e. they distinguish infantrymen from guardsmen or cavalrymen, privates from officers and generals. They can tell shopkeepers from tradesmen and industrialists among the merchants. They distinguish aristocrats at court, from those in Petersburg and the country, from Russia and abroad. They endow each group with its own special characteristics.

'That's what Paul did.

'He chose the group of ordinary soldiers out of the military "in general" and endowed them with their typical, basic characteristics.

'He didn't give us a military man "in general" but a private soldier.

'A third type of character actor has even more subtle powers of observation. They select some Ivan Ivanovich Ivanov.[8] Out of the whole military and the group of ordinary soldiers and convey what's unique, what's special to him and no one else. This person is undoubtedly a soldier "in general" but it's also Ivan Ivanovich.

'As regards creating an individual personality, only Nazvanov did that.

'What he gave us was a bold, artistic creation and so we need to talk about it in detail.

'I'm going to ask Kostya to tell us in detail how his snide critic came into being. It would be interesting to know what the creative process was.'

I did as I was asked and went through everything I had written in my diary about the way the mildewed man came to maturity.

When he'd heard everything I recalled, Tortsov put another question to me.

'Try and recall,' he said, 'how you felt when you were really in character.'

'I felt a completely different kind of pleasure. There's nothing I can compare it to,' I replied enthusiastically. 'It was like nothing else, but maybe like what I felt just for a moment in the "Blood, Iago, blood" scene, in our first show – only more so. The same thing occurred during certain exercises.'

'What was that? Try and put it into words.'

'Mostly total belief in what you're doing and feeling,' I said, calling the way I had felt then back to mind. 'Thanks to which, I was satisfied that my character was true and his actions sincere. It wasn't the self-satisfaction of a conceited actor but something of a different order, very close to a conviction of one's own truth.

'When I think of the way I treated you! I have a great deal of affection, respect and admiration for you. In real life they would have inhibited me from opening out and forgetting who I was talking to. I couldn't have thrown off the shackles and let myself go, I couldn't have let go and revealed myself completely. But in someone else's skin my relationship to you was different. I felt it wasn't me communicating with you, but someone else. We were both looking at someone else. That's why your closeness to me, the penetrating look you gave me didn't put me off, they encouraged me. I enjoyed feeling I had every right to stare insolently at you and not be afraid. Would I have dared do that as myself? Never. But as someone else – as much as you like. If I could do that, looking you right in the eye, I could treat the audience out front without shame.'

'And what about the black hole?' someone asked.

'I didn't notice because I was totally absorbed in doing something more interesting.'

'So,' Tortsov summed up, 'Kostya genuinely lived the character of a repulsive snide critic. And note, live it not with someone else's but with its own sensations, feelings and instincts. That means the feelings he gave us as the critic were his own.

'Now, the question is, would he show them the same way as himself, if he couldn't hide behind the character he created? Perhaps there is a seed in his psyche out of which a repulsive person could grow? Let him show this person now, without altering his appearance, without costume and make-up.'

'Would he do that?' Tortsov asked me to declare.

'Why not? I've already played him without make-up,' I answered.

'But with all the right facial expressions, mannerisms, and walk?' Tortsov asked again.

'Of course,' I answered.

'The same as with make-up. But that's not the point. You can create a character to hide behind without make-up. No. Show me your most secret, intimate, innermost self, good or bad, without hiding behind a character.'

'That's embarrassing,' I admitted after some thought.

'But if you hide behind a character?'

'Then I can do it,' I decided.

'You see?' said a delighted Tortsov. 'Now it's like a real masquerade.

'In a masquerade we see how a young man who is shy of women suddenly becomes bold as brass behind a mask, and displays secret desires he wouldn't dare express in life.

'Where does his boldness come from? From the mask and the costume that conceals him. He will do things as someone he's not responsible for that he would never do as himself.

'Characterization is the mask which hides the actor-human being. When we are masked we can reveal the most intimate and spicy details about ourselves.

'This is an important aspect of characterization.

'Have you noticed that actors, women especially, who don't like physical transformation always play themselves like beautiful, noble, kind, romantic roles? And have you noticed how character actors like to play villains, monsters and caricatures because they are sharper, brighter, clearer, more theatrical figures which the audience remembers longer?

'Physical characterization in the process of transformation is something great.

'And since actors have to create a character and not just show themselves to the audience, we all need transformation and physical characterization.

'In other words, all actors, without exception, create characters and transform themselves physically.

'There are no non-character parts.'

24

THE FINISHING TOUCHES

In today's class there was a sign with

INTERNAL AND EXTERNAL CONTROL AND THE FINISHING TOUCHES

written on it.

It had already appeared with other signs but Tortsov had refrained from explaining these new creative elements until the time was right, when it would be possible to talk about their *inner* and *outer* aspects simultaneously. That moment had come.

'I'll start with *control* because there can't be any finishing touches without it and first of all I'll discuss its *outer* aspect because it is more visible and accessible than the *inner* aspect,' Tortsov explained and called Vanya up onstage. He and Igor played a scene we all know between master and servant in an 18th-century play.

Tortsov said:

'I had difficulty understanding what you were doing and saying.'

'Really? But I was feeling it, my actions were genuine!' said Vanya, rather put out.

'I believe you, because certain words and passages came across to me,' said Tortsov calming him down. 'But you rattled away, waving your hands in front of your faces so that I couldn't work out what you were saying, or see what you were feeling in your eyes.

'You have created such insurmountable obstacles you can't communicate as you should, or be theatrically expressive. It's as though you made an artist do a delicate pencil portrait on a grubby piece of paper. The blemishes would merge with the drawing, which would be lost among the chaos and the dirt. The portrait would lose all form.

'If you want to stop that happening, you first have to clean up the paper. The same thing applies to us: gesticulating actors – gesticulations are the same as the blemishes. They blur the shape of a role. Its contours are lost in a welter of unwanted gestures. So eliminate excess and only give us the *movements and gestures* the character needs. Then the audience will see and appreciate them. That's very important for you, Vanya.'

'Why?'

'Because you are a character actor,' Tortsov explained. 'How many of your gestures were typical of the servant you've just played?' Tortsov asked him.

'I don't know. I didn't count.'

'You should have,' Tortsov reproached him. 'I noted three or four, no more.'

'What do you mean, three or four? And the rest?' said the exuberant young man in astonishment.

'They were either your own human, or "actor's" gestures, technical tricks, trite clichés, tics, etc. You gave them their head and they controlled you, not you them. The result was a chaotic jumble of unnecessary gestures. The three or four typical were drowned in them, like a few drops of good wine in a glass full of water, and passed unnoticed.

'Get rid of excess gestures and the really characteristic movements will stand out with much greater meaning and strength, like good wine that hasn't been watered down. Experienced actors know how to select movements and actions which are right for the character, and get rid of harmful ones. But with inexperienced actors, like Vanya and Igor, a flood of personal gestures drowns what the character needs. When that happens, the actors who have their own theatrical personae, step out from behind the mask, stand up tall and block out the real character. If that happens with every role, they inevitably become boring, one-character players. What a shame! Vanya has the capacity to characterize, and thought and variety. When, for whatever reason, his usual gesticulation disappears and his inner life comes to the fore, it expresses the real Vanya in accurate movements and in vivid, bold, not to say audacious adaptations

'The trouble is this only happens by accident. He must take steps to ensure that it happens all the time, consciously and unconsciously. He, like you, like all actors without exception, must not only eliminate *gesticulation* but *gesture itself*.'

'Even when they're essential?' said Grisha, regretfully.

'There's no such thing as essential gestures onstage,' Tortsov corrected him.

'Oh, but excuse me,' Grisha objected, 'suppose I'm playing Narcissus and I'm posing in front of the mirror or parading in front of my partners in the play, how am I supposed to do that without gestures?'

'You don't, because in the example you've just given gestures and poses have become actions and cease to be *gestures*,' Tortsov explained.

'If that's the case, then gesticulation can be useful,' said Grisha, trying to take him literally.

'It is opportune to the extent that it is characteristic of the role,' Tortsov agreed.

'I think ... gesture is also necessary if it helps ... experiencing and physical embodiment ... if it doesn't come easily,' said Igor shyly.

'What?!' Tortsov came down on him. 'Your balletic gestures help you feel properly?! Not at all. They kill all creative effort. They're an open invitation to playacting, representation and exhibitionism. We can't believe in them and where there is no belief there is no experiencing. *I maintain that kind of gesture is not only superfluous, it is positively dangerous onstage.* While really typical *movements and actions* bind actors more closely to a role, *gestures and gesticulation* distance them from it.

'So, either transform gesture and gesticulation into genuine, creative actions or get rid of them altogether!'

'How are we to do that?' I asked, anxiously.

'The best thing is to find the root, the origin, the cause that *produced the gesture*, and eliminate them. They are manifold.'

'Name them,' I exhorted him.

'Nerves, embarrassment, stagefright, a lack of belief in what you are doing, a feeling of helplessness in trying to fulfil an impossible creative task, lost self-control, panic, exhibitionism, showing off to the audience, posing for them, trying to comprehend the incomprehensible, i.e. trying to play the entire role in one go, wanting to give more than you have, etc.,' Tortsov enumerated. 'These are the root causes of gesture and gesticulation.'

'How do we fight them?'

'You know that already: decoys, magic "ifs", Given Circumstances, the Supertask, everything that guides the creative process and produces the creative state. They either eliminate *gesture and gesticulation* entirely or transform them into dynamic movement, genuine, productive, specific actions.

'Another weapon is *technical control*. It eliminates excess gestures and makes room for the *movement and actions* the role needs. Technical control teaches us to use them economically and intelligently. You need to work long and hard to develop technical control.'

'How?'

'Very simple. Don't make gestures or unnecessary movements,' Tortsov said. 'Set yourself the task of conveying the score of a role with the minimum of movement and no gestures at all.'

'That's very difficult,' someone commented.

'You need months, years to master this salutary habit and make outer technical control second nature,' Tortsov warned. 'Once you've disciplined your external mechanism, it will become a "blank sheet of paper" on which you can express the most complex design.

'All great actors go through a period of struggle with gesture as they grow to maturity. They know how useful this can be. The advantage is that removing unnecessary gesticulation automatically calls into play other, more subtle and expressive ways of reflecting our inner life. The face, the eyes, speech, inflexions, transmitting and receiving, etc.'

.. .. 19..

'Today, I'm going to show you a means to develop finish, by which I mean finish in stage actions,' Tortsov said at the beginning of today's class. 'If you can't have control without finish, you can't have finish without control. I'll start with the outside. It's easier to see Kostya go up and light the fire just as you did at the beginning of our studies.'

I went onstage and did as I was asked, having, of course, previously established the Given Circumstances. Tortsov said to me:

'What you did was good enough for life, but it didn't have enough clarity or finish for a large theatre with a big audience.'

'How do I get them?' I asked, anxious to know as soon as possible.

'Very simple,' Tortsov replied. 'You know that large Bits, Tasks, actions are made up of medium Bits, and medium Bits of small Bits, etc. So show me all the parts of the whole, not "in general" as you did just now, but complete.'

I repeated the exercise.

'Not quite,' Tortsov said to me. 'Give each part more finish, more clarity, more polish so that there's only a fine line between them, like a barely perceptible pause. Those of us watching must know where one task ends and another begins.'

I repeated the exercise, trying to do everything I'd been told.

'This time you made me see the parts, but I lost the whole,' Tortsov said. 'That was because you performed the Bits, Tasks and actions for their own sake.'

'I understand. I forgot the Given Circumstances and the Through-action, i.e. Marya's illness and my wish to stop her catching another cold,' I recalled.

I kept this in mind when I did the exercise again and the mistake was put right.

'This time I not only understood, I felt the whole,' Tortsov said approvingly. 'It is so important to give the whole, not destroy it, and yet not blur the parts. Only then can the audience grasp the clear line of the action and not just a general approximation to it.'

To drive the lesson home, Tortsov allowed me to repeat the exercise. Of course I made full use of the solution and so performed all the constituent parts of a large action thoroughly. But Tortsov suddenly stopped me and said:

'Finish requires above all a *sense of truth*. Exaggeration leads to lies, and lies kill truth and feeling. And so, don't indulge in excessive clarity or finish. That can border on playacting. Too much and too little action are equally dangerous. Take the middle way.'

By trying to do that, I once again strayed from the Supertask and the Throughaction. After we'd corrected this mistake, Tortsov said to me:

'I hope you now understand that the most important thing to consider is the finish of the Throughaction and the Supertask and for the small and large bits and parts to them, not be performed for their own sake.'

At the end of the class Tortsov saw Vanya and Darya in their old scene from *Brand*. Tortsov said to Vanya:

'Stretching every Bit and Task and overdoing them doesn't mean you're giving them finish or acting with control. Overdoing control and finish doesn't encourage precision, and clarity of form in acting. On the contrary, if you go too far you break up, undermine the shape and structure of a role or play.'

.. .. 19..

'So far we've discussed *outer technical control and finish*, today we're going to look at *inner* control and finish,' Tortsov said as he came in. 'Pasha, go onstage and do a small Bit from the "burning money", the moment when the hunchback throws the last packet into the flames and you are stunned.'

Pasha went onstage and played the scene. Tortsov said:

'I felt a kind of life and unrest in the silent pauses – on the inside. That's good. But it would have been even better if I understood not your actual thought (which you can't express without words), but at least your overall mood, your mental state, in the pauses, at every point, in each inner Bit, in the logical, sequential transitions from one task to another.

Moreover, I want to know how the inner line of the play and the role develops.

'You didn't allow me to understand, that is feel, that. So, put what you were living and thinking during the pauses into words for us, what you were living and what was happening inside you during the pauses,' Tortsov requested.

'I was mostly trying to understand the circumstances and feel the awfulness of what was happening,' Pasha explained.

'That's why you looked at the blazing fire and the empty table,' Tortsov surmised.

'Yes, precisely,' Pasha replied. 'Then I wanted to see with my inner eye what would happen around us if this were a real-life tragedy.'

'At that moment you inspected every corner of the room.'

'Yes,' Pasha confirmed. 'I remembered the happy life we'd had in this apartment and pictured how appalling life would be in the future now the family home had been destroyed. These mental images helped me get into the criminal's situation and felt I was playing a new role.'

'So, three tasks emerged: you had to register that the documents were no longer on the table, satisfy yourself all the money was burned, remember the past and imagine your future life in this room.'

'Yes,' Pasha confirmed.

'Unfortunately these three clear, precise tasks merged into a single shapeless one. It was impossible to tell which was which.'

'And yet, I felt all three of them in places,' Pasha recalled. 'They burst into flame and then died.'

'If that's so, then the beginnings of real experiencing were stirring inside you. But you didn't show it very well,' Tortsov explained. 'All you needed was one look at the table, the fireplace and the room to realize that a catastrophe had occurred. Had you done that cleanly, with control and finish, I would have understood your outward action and the inner impulses that caused them right away. But instead of that, your head went left and right at least ten times. That's not performing your task thoroughly, but superficially. By endlessly repeating the same movement you reduced its impact, distorted the truth, created a lie, destroyed all credibility. That killed experiencing and confused the audience. The outside hid the inside. None of this, of course, helps bring Emotion Memory or feeling alive. That is why all I can remember of the first half of the silent scene is a mixture of gestures. They stood between me and your mind, stopped me feeling what was going on there, through transmitting and receiving.

'I understood the second half of the pause right away. Why? Because you experienced the Bits and Tasks cleanly and didn't hide them with unnecessary actions. You looked at the door where your wife was bathing the baby. You were confused, you were trying to think and I understood the reason. "Will she forgive me for killing her brother?" You thought, frowned, looked down, covered your eyes and stood very still for a long time. I understood what terrible thoughts you were having. You had compromised your innocent wife, you had made her your accomplice. If the lack of control and finish was a hindrance in the first half, your excellent control and finish in the second helped me greatly. They helped you experience precisely and fully, and to reflect what was going on inside you clearly, and separate out the various Bits and Tasks, layer by layer, and give them clear outlines.'

'That simply happened, it was pure chance and he may never do it again. How can you consciously master control and finish?' I asked, admitting the new doubts I had today.

'You know perfectly well how to do that. Cut down external movements and actions to the minimum to prevent them blocking out the audience from your mind. Replace external movements with the subtleties of your eyes, your face which are more closely connected to the life of the mind. If feeling doesn't come alive spontaneously, don't force it, tantalize it, lure it with mental images. The more precise they are the more precise your experiencing and your Bits and Tasks will be. You must really love them as well as what is happening to you, inside and out, while you're onstage. Don't rush and don't drag out what you do lest you destroy the linear logic and sequence of your mental images. Exaggeration leads to lies. So be logical and sequential in your inner actions to the highest degree. If there is a spontaneous and involuntary lack of logic, leave it alone, if it has sprung from the unconscious. Its particular logic and sequence are beyond your understanding. Make sure you have Tempo-rhythm. You can't have control and finish without it. You must love layers. Carry your Bits and Tasks right through to the end.'

'Yes, but,' said Grisha, 'in real life, you know, we don't have to follow all these rules, we're not expected to have special control and finish, but everyone still understands us.'

'You're quite wrong. Let me give you an example. A few weeks ago an old, respectable, slightly confused friend of my wife's, who had lost a woman close to her, was at our house. She was weeping bitterly, raging on about something . . . and talked and talked. I calmed her down, though I could not understand a thing. A few days later she came back for an answer. What answer? Apparently she had ordered me to enquire whether she could join our company so she could eat. Acting was the only thing she could consider, although she'd never set foot onstage. Why did the misunderstanding arise? Because when people experience a deep personal crisis they can't talk about it coherently. Their thoughts are in a turmoil, tears choke them, their voice breaks and every pitiful look is a distraction and stops us getting to the bottom of what they are saying. But time is the best healer. It smoothes things out and helps them take a more balanced view of past events. They talk about the past logically, sequentially, with control and finish and, therefore, we can understand them. Then the speaker is more or less calm and the listener weeps.

'Actors, too, have to cope with the stormy period when they are experiencing, agonize over a role, go too far at home and in rehearsal, then get rid of inessentials which block their emotions, gain the necessary control and then go onstage and tell the audience with clarity and finish, warmth and inner richness, what they experienced earlier. Then the audience understands everything and is even more moved than the actor.

'The more *control and finish* acting has, the calmer the actor is, the more clearly the shape and form of the character comes across and the more it affects the audience and the greater success the actor has.'

.. .. 19..

'Today, I want to try and get you to feel the strength of control and finish for actor and audience alike.'

2.

'A famous painter was looking over his pupils' work in class and added a brushstroke to one of the endless canvasses and the picture came so alive there was nothing left for the pupil to do. The student was amazed that a miracle had occurred when the professor had "barely" touched the canvas with his brush.

'To this the famous artist responded: ["barely" is everything in art].

'And I, like the famous painter, say that in the theatre, too, we need a "barely" here and there to bring a role alive. Without that "barely" a role has no lustre.

'We see so many roles onstage that lack this "barely". Everything's fine, everything's done, but something very important is missing. A talented director arrives, says one word and the actor bursts into life, the role glows with his full range of colours.

'I recall the conductor of a military band who *waved his arms about* all the time in concerts in the street. At first you were attracted by the sounds and listened but after five minutes you started to watch the regular waving of the conductor's baton and the way his other hand methodically and imperturbably turned over the pages of his score. He wasn't a bad musician and his band was a good one, and famous in the town. Yet his music was bad, unnecessary, because he didn't reveal what was most important, its inner content, and didn't reach the listener. All the constituent parts of the piece seemed stuck together. They were all alike, but the listener wanted to know them, understand them, hear them properly, wanted each of them to have that "barely" that would give finish to each bit and the work as a whole.

'In the theatre we have actors who "wave their arm" in one rhythm throughout the role or the play, with never a thought for that essential "barely" which could provide finish.

'As well as conductors with a waving stick I remember Nikisch,[1] small but great, an eloquent man who could say more with sounds than with words. He could draw an ocean of sounds with the end of his baton and create a vast, musical picture.

'I'll never forget the way Nikisch looked at all the musicians before starting to play, how he raised his baton and waited for the audience to settle down and get ready to listen. His baton said, "Pay attention! Listen! I'm going to begin!"

'There was that intangible "barely" which gives each action such good finish, even in that moment of anticipation. Nikisch loved every whole note, every half-note, every eighth-note, every sixteenth-note, every dot, every mathematically precise triplet, every delicious natural, every dissonance within a harmony. He did all this with relish and calm, without fear of dragging the music out. He used every phrase to the full before letting it go. He drew everything he could out of the instruments, out of the very soul of the players, with the end of his baton. And what a wonderful left hand he had, indicating a *diminuendo* or a *rinforzando*. What ideal control he had, a mathematical precision which encouraged rather than discouraged inspiration. There was the same quality in his tempi. His *lento* wasn't monotonous, boring, dawdling. It didn't set your teeth on edge like my military band, beating time like a metronome. His slow tempi encompassed every possible speed. He never rushed and never lingered. Only when every sentence was complete did Nikisch gather speed or slow down, to compensate for what had been held back or return what he had deliberately taken away by an earlier *accelerando*. He created a new tempo for each phrase. Here it is, don't rush it. Say everything it has to say! Now he's approaching the climax of the phrase. Who can predict how he will shape the top of the phrase?! By a new, even greater *rallentando* or an unexpectedly bold *accelerando*, to emphasize the end?

'How many conductors are like Nikisch, how many can feel and hear all the nuances in a work, and not only draw them out but communicate them clearly?

'Nikisch could because his work not only had control but dazzling finish.

'If my words have given you some idea who Nikisch was, then you know what speech can be in an actor's or reciter's mouth. They will have the same wonderful *lento* as Nikisch. The same richness, the same *piano*, the same infinite range, the same lack of haste, the same precision in giving full value to the words, with all the eighth-notes, the dots, the mathematically precise triplets and the same control and enthusiasm without unnecessary lingering [or] haste. That is control and finish.

' "Demonstration through opposites" is a good way of persuading people. I'll use it now so that you can understand the value of finish in acting more fully. Do you recall actors in a hurry? There are many of them, especially in theatres which specialize in farce, comedies and operettas where you have to be happy, funny and vivacious at any price. But it's difficult to be happy when you are sad. And so you resort to technical tricks. External Tempo-rhythm is by far the best. These actors gabble their lines and whiz through their actions with incredible speed. Everything becomes one chaotic whole which the audience can't sort out.

'One of the finest qualities of great [foreign] touring actors[2] who have consummate technique is their *control and finish*. When you observe them and see how a role develops and grows before the audience's eyes, you feel you are present at a miraculous rebirth, the resurrection of a great work of art. That's how I feel during these remarkable performances. It's easier to explain through an example.

'Imagine you've gone to the studio of a great, a superhuman, almost god-like sculptor. "Show me Venus," you say.

'This genius, knowing the full significance of what must now happen, concentrates his mind and ignores his surroundings. He takes a huge lump of clay and slowly, carefully starts to form it. He sees every line, curve, hollow in the goddess's leg with his inner eye and shapes the formless mass. His swift, strong hands work with extraordinary precision without disrupting the grandeur, the smoothness of the creative act, the process. Very soon his hands create a wonderful woman's leg, the most beautiful, perfect, classical leg that ever existed. There is nothing you could possibly change. It will live forever. Those who see it will never forget it. The sculptor shows you this part of the unfinished statue and you look at it amazed. You, too, begin to feel how beautiful it will be. But the sculptor doesn't care whether you like his work or not. He knows that the work is what it is and cannot be otherwise. If the people who look at the statue are mature enough to understand, they will understand, if not the gates to the kingdom of true aesthetic beauty are closed to them. The sculptor then, with even greater calm and concentration, models a second leg, no less beautiful than the first, and the torso, as though he were performing a religious rite. But then he suddenly gets excited. He feels that the hard mass in his hands is becoming warmer, more malleable. It seems to move, to rise and fall, to breathe. He is totally carried away. He smiles, his eyes are those of a young man in love. Now it seems as though this beautiful female torso could bend gracefully in any direction. You forget it was once dead, lumpen material. He works a long time on Venus' head. He is inspired. He loves, adores her eyes, nose, mouth, her swan-like neck.

'It's finished.

'Here are the legs, the arms, the torso on which the sculptor places the head. Look! Venus to the life! You know her as in your dreams, not in reality. You would never suspect that such beauty could exist in real life, that it could be so simple, natural, light and ethereal.

'Now she's been cast in hard, heavy monumental bronze and yet she is still as before, she is still a god-like dream, although you can feel her, touch her with your hands, although she's so heavy you couldn't lift her. You'd never believe it was possible to create such perfection out of crude, heavy metal.

'Actors of creative genius, like Salvini the Elder, are monumental bronzes. They sculpt one [part of the role] in front of the audience in the first act, and then gradually, quietly, confidently create the other parts during the remaining acts. When all the parts are put together they form an immortal monument to human passion, jealousy, love, horror, revenge and fury. The sculptor creates dreams in bronze, actors create them out of their own bodies. The works actors of genius create are laws, monuments, constant reminders.'

'I saw Salvini for the first time at the Bolshoi Theatre where he played with his Italian company for almost the whole of Lent.

'They played Othello. I don't know what was wrong with me, but owing to absentmindedness, or the lack of attention I paid to other great actors I'd seen earlier, I muddled him up with other celebrities, like Possart[3] for example, who'd played Iago, not Othello. So I paid much more attention to Iago, thinking it was Salvini.

"Yes, he has a good voice," I said to myself. "He has the makings of a good actor, a fine figure, the usual Italian manner of acting and delivering but I don't see anything special about him. Othello is just as good. He has the makings of a good actor, too – a wonderful voice, diction, bearing and

general level." I was unimpressed by the rapture with which the connoisseurs greeted Salvini's first line.

'Apparently the great actor didn't want to be the centre of attention at
the beginning. Had he wanted to be, he could have done so by the masterly pause which he made later, in the Senate scene. There was nothing
new about the opening of that scene, except that I could see Salvini's face,
costume and make-up. I can't say there was anything remarkable about
them. I didn't like his costume either then or later. Make-up? I don't think
he had any. It was his own face and, perhaps, it would have been useless to
make it up.

'He had a large pointed moustache, a wig which was far too obvious, a
broad, heavy, almost plump face, a large, Eastern dagger hanging from his
belt which made him stouter than he really was, especially in a Moorish
robe and head-dress. None of this was very typical of Othello the soldier.

'But . . .

'Othello approached the Doge's throne, gathered his thoughts together
and had the whole Bolshoi audience in his hand before we'd even
noticed. He seemed to do it with a single gesture. He stretched out his
hand, without looking at us, and took us in his palm as though we were
ants or flies. He clenched his fist and we felt death breathing on us. He
opened it and it was bliss. We were in his power and would remain so
for the rest of our lives, forever. Now we knew who this genius was, what
he was and what we could expect. At the beginning his Othello was more
like Romeo. He saw, thought of nothing and no one except Desdemona.
His faith in her was boundless and we were amazed that Iago could
transform Romeo into a jealous Othello.

'How can I make you understand the impact Salvini made?

'Our famous poet, Balmont, once said:

' "We must create for eternity, for ever and always."

'Salvini created for eternity, for ever and always.'

3.

'Now let me ask you, in your opinion, is that kind of acting the result of
inspiration or mere technique and practical experience?'

'Inspiration, of course,' the students stated.

'With ideal outer and inner *control and finish*?' Tortsov asked.

'Of course,' we all agreed.

'Yet neither Salvini, nor any other actor or genius, was inhibited at such
moments. There was no rush, no hysteria, no tension, no forcing the
tempo. On the contrary, they had concentrated, majestic, quiet calm, a

lack of haste which enabled them to do everything thoroughly. Does that mean they weren't moved, or inwardly experiencing with all their might? Of course not. It means that inspiration doesn't come the way it does in bad novels or as bad critics describe it, or the way you think. Inspiration comes in many ways, for the most unexpected reasons, which are often a mystery to the actors themselves.

'More often than not, we don't need some god-like impulse, but an almost insignificant "barely".'

4.

'For you, inspiration means moments of great euphoria. I don't deny that but repeat that inspiration comes in many forms. Calmly probing the depths of your mind can be inspiration. Playing freely, lightly with your feelings can be inspiration. A dark and heavy realization of the secret of life can be inspiration.

'How can I describe it in all its forms, when it hides in the subconscious and is inaccessible to human reason?

'We can only talk about an actor's state of mind, which is good soil for inspiration. That is why a feeling of *control and finish* is so important in acting. It is important to understand that, and to value the new elements not as direct guides to inspiration but as two of the preparatory elements in encouraging it.

'You understand intellectually what control and finish mean in terms of the creative state. Now we have to work in terms of feeling. You have to understand that, too.'

25

CHARISMA

'I'll move on to charisma.

'You know there are actors who only have to make their entrance and the audience loves them? Why? Because they are beautiful? Very often they aren't. Because of their voice? Very often they haven't any. Because of their talent? Often it doesn't merit admiration. Because of what then? Because of that elusive quality we call charisma. It is the inexplicable attraction exercised by the actor's whole being in which even faults are turned to advantage and are copied by his admirers and imitators.

'Everything serves such actors, including playing badly. They just have to make an early entrance and stay onstage long enough to allow the audience to see its idol and fall in love with him.

'Often, meeting these actors in life, even the most fervent theatrical admirer says disappointedly: "Oh! How boring he is offstage!" But it's as though the footlights illuminate virtues which win you over. Not for nothing is this quality called "stage" and not real-life charisma.

'It's a great joy to have it since it guarantees success with the audience in advance and helps the actor convey his creative thoughts which embellish the role and his art to the crowd.

'But how important it is for the actor to use his natural gifts with care, intelligence and discretion! It's a shame if he doesn't understand this and starts to trade in his allure. Backstage actors like that are called gigolos. Like prostitutes they vend their charms, they show them as such, for their own sake, for their own advantage and success, and don't use their charisma to create the character they are playing.

'That's a dangerous mistake. We know quite a few cases when the natural stage gift of charisma brings about an actor's downfall whose sole concern, whose technique is finally reduced to nothing but self-display.

'It is in revenge for foolishly misusing her gift that nature punishes him cruelly, because self-love and self-display deform and destroy that very charisma we speak of. The actors become the victims of their own, beautiful, natural gift.

'Another danger of charisma is that actors endowed with it by nature become monotonous because they always put themselves on show. If they hide behind a character they hear their admirers exclaim: "Oh! what a horror! Why has he made himself ugly like that?" Fear of not pleasing their admirers makes them cling to their dangerous, natural quality and ensures that it is visible through their make-up and costume and the general appearance of the role which frequently doesn't call for the individual qualities of the actor-performer.

'But there are actors with another kind of stage charisma. They shouldn't show themselves as they really are, since they not only lack personal charisma but also have the disadvantage of being deficient in any kind of attraction at all. But all these actors have to do is put on a wig, beard, make-up, which completely conceal their human individuality, and they have "stage magnetism". It is not they, as people, who attract but their artistic, creative charisma.

'There is gentleness, subtlety, grace, or, perhaps, boldness, even daring, sharpness, which are attractive in what they have created.

'I'll say a few words about those unfortunate actors who lack both kinds of charisma. There is something off-putting hidden in their nature. It is often the case that these people are very winning in life. "How sweet he is," people say when they are not in costume. "Why is it we don't take to him onstage?" they add. Yet these actors are often brighter, more gifted, purer in their art and creative work onstage than those who are gifted with irresistible charisma before which everything gives way.

'One must observe and study these actors, so unjustly deprived by nature. Only then can you understand their genuine, artistic merits. Often you need to observe a long time and recognition of their talent is delayed.

'The question arises, isn't there a way on the one hand to cultivate in oneself, even to a limited degree, charisma which nature has not provided and, on the other, is it really not possible to fight against what is off-putting in an actor who is not blessed by fate?

'You can, yes, but only to a certain extent, both as regards creating charisma and eliminating off-putting defects. Of course, the actor himself must, above all, understand them, that is feel them, and, having understood them, learn to fight them. Often that requires great observation, consciousness of self, enormous patience and systematic work to eradicate natural attributes and daily habits.

'As for vaccinating yourself with that unknown something, which draws the audience's attention, that is even more difficult and perhaps impossible.

'One of the best aids in this regard [is] familiarity. An audience can become accustomed to an actor's faults, which acquire a certain attractiveness since habit stops you seeing things you once found shocking. You can, to a certain extent, manufacture "charismatic charms" thanks to technique and good training which are attractive.

'We frequently hear people saying: "How this actor has improved! You wouldn't know him! And he was so unattractive before."

'In response to that one might say:

"Work and a knowledge of his art brought about this change."

'Art makes beautiful and ennobles. And what is beautiful and noble attracts.'

26

ETHICS AND DISCIPLINE

I received a note, asking me to be at the theatre at nine o'clock. Entry by the stage door.

The first person I met in the lobby was our good friend Rakhmanov.

When all the students had gathered, he explained that Tortsov had decided to involve us all in the crowd scenes in Ostrovski's *The Burning Heart*.[1] That would enable him to test our inner performance mode and improve it by appearing in a public show.

However, before sending inexperienced students with no notion of the backstage world out onstage, Rakhmanov thought we should be given some idea of what conditions were like. We ought to learn the layout, the entrances and exits. That was essential in case of fire. Everyone in the show needed to know where the dressing rooms with bathrooms and showers were, where make-up and wardrobe were, the overnight store rooms for props and antiques, where the various craftsmen were located, where the electricians' room was, and the green room.

Newcomers also need to be shown the complexities of the stage itself so they can know where the danger spots are — gaps and traps in the floor you can fall into in the dark, the revolve with all its huge machinery under the stage that can make mincemeat of you, the heavy borders that keep coming in and out, the set drops that can crack your head open and, finally, the places where you can't go during a performance without the risk of the audience seeing you.

Rakhmanov began a detailed tour of the stage and the wings to show us all its secrets, all its parts: the traps, scene docks, workspaces, gantries, flies, the electrical equipment, the control and dimmer rooms, the huge cupboards with electrical items, lamps, etc., in them.

We were taken through the large and small storage rooms where scenery, furniture, props and stage dressing were kept. We went to the orchestra room which had storage for musical instruments.

We were shown the director's and the literary manager's offices, the stage manager's corner, the firemen's posts, the emergency exits, etc.

Then we went through the courtyard and all the buildings where sets are prepared.

It was a whole factory with huge workrooms for set painters, sculptors, carpenters, odd-job men, metal workers, props men, cutters, dyers, launderers. We also went to the garage.

We were also shown the quarters for actors and stage staff, libraries, a hostel for workers, kitchens, dining rooms, cafeterias, etc.

I was staggered by what I saw, as I had never thought a theatre was such a huge, complex organization.

'This "juggernaut" works all day and half the night, my lad, winter, spring, summer, autumn. While actors are away on tour we repair old sets and prepare new ones.

'You can see what organization it takes to make sure all the parts of this "juggernaut" are properly co-ordinated. Otherwise there'd be a disaster.

'There's a problem if the smallest cog isn't working properly. Just one useless cog let me tell you, my lad, and the consequences can be disastrous. Someone can get killed.'

'What kind of disaster could there be?' asked Vanya, very concerned.

'For example, a stagehand is careless, or an old cable snaps, a heavy spotlight or a huge border falls and kills one of the actors. How about that?'

'Wow!'

'Or a cue is mistimed, a trap opens and someone falls down it. Or an electrician has been careless and two cables are touching in an inaccessible spot. The result is a fire, panic, people trampling over each other.

'Other mishaps can occur.

'The curtain comes down too soon and ruins the act, or the end of it. Or it can go up prematurely so that people can see what's going on backstage. That introduces a comic note into the performance. Noise and conversation in the wings create a muddle and demoralize the audience.

'It only needs one small bit-part not to show up after the stage manager has rung the bell for there to be an inevitable hitch. Quite some time elapses while they look for the latecomer in the labyrinthine world backstage. Naturally, he will produce a hundred excuses – he didn't hear the bell, he couldn't get dressed and made up, his costume is torn, etc., etc. But can these excuses make up the time lost, repair the damage, fill the gap?

'Don't forget, there are many people involved in a show and if they don't all pay sufficient attention to their jobs, who can guarantee there won't be any hold-ups between the acts, or that actors won't be late and put the other members of the cast in an impossible position?

'Stagehands, props men and lighting men can cause delay and confusion, too, when they don't set things properly, or take their cue, or give a lighting or sound effect.

'Every member of the team must feel he is a "cog" in a large, complex machine, and be clearly aware of the danger to the whole show if he doesn't do what he should, or if he departs from established procedure.

'All you students are small cogs in a complex machine, the theatre, too, and on you depends the success, fate, well-being of the show, not only while the curtain is up, but when it is down and heavy, physical work is done, changing huge flats, putting up enormous rostrums, and actors are doing quick costume and make-up changes in their dressing rooms. When this is done in a disorderly, disorganized fashion, the audience feels it. The backstage exertions are transmitted out front, and are reflected in the ponderousness of the performance.

'Add to that possible intervals between the acts and the show seems to be in great danger.

'There is one way to avoid that – *iron discipline*. It's essential in all artistic teamwork, be it an orchestra, a choir, or any other kind of ensemble.

'And it applies even more to a complex stage performance.

'There must be organization and model order in our artistic teamwork, so that the mechanics of the show proceed without a hitch.

'Inner creative work demands even greater order, organization and discipline. The mind is subtle, complex and extremely delicate. We must work in strict obedience to the laws of the human mind.

'When we remember that we create in public, with all the difficulties that implies, surrounded as we are by the intricate, cumbersome work backstage, it is clear that the demand for total discipline, inner and outer, is even greater. Without it you cannot fulfil all the requirements of the "system". Everything will be swamped by externals, your performance mode will be destroyed.

'You can only meet this danger by possessing even stricter discipline and placing even greater demands on the teamwork of each tiny cog in a giant theatrical machine.

'But the theatre isn't merely a factory for turning out scenery, it is a factory for human souls. No less!

'In the theatre we nurture the living human creations the actor/role produces.

'The theatre reaches hundreds of thousands, millions of people. Millions, I say! It carries them to the heights of emotion.

'Now you know what a huge machine, a factory the theatre is. To make sure the mechanics function properly we need strict order and iron discipline. But how are we to do that in such a way they don't stifle actors but help them?

'We don't just manufacture sets and staging in the theatre, we create characters, living people, their souls, the life of the human spirit. That is much more difficult than making sure the show, backstage activity, the set and staging are in order.

'Inner work demands even greater inner discipline and ethics.'

2.

.. .. 19..

Class took place in one of the green rooms.

The students had asked to meet long before the rehearsal began. We were afraid we would disgrace ourselves on our first appearance, so we asked Rakhmanov to tell us how we were to behave.

To our amazement and delight Tortsov came to the meeting.

We heard he had been deeply touched by our serious approach to our first appearance.

'You'll know what you have to do and how you have to behave if you think about teamwork,' he told us.

'We all create together, we help each other, we depend on each other. We are all guided by one person, the director.

'Teamwork is pleasant and fruitful if it is properly organized, because then we help each other.

'But without proper order, creative teamwork is torture. People mill about and get in each other's way. Clearly, everyone must, therefore, establish and maintain discipline.'

'How do we do that?'

'First, get to the theatre half or a quarter of an hour before rehearsal starts to assemble all the elements of your creative state.

'If one person is late there's a muddle. If everyone is just a little late then working time is lost in waiting. That leads to a bad atmosphere in which no one can work.

'If, on the other hand, people take their responsibilities to each other seriously and come to rehearsal prepared, that creates a happy atmosphere which encourages you. Then work goes well, because we are all helping each other.

'Imagine for a moment that you've come to the theatre to play a leading role. The show begins in half an hour. You're late because you've had a few minor personal worries and annoyances. Your apartment is in a mess. You've been burgled. The thief took your coat and a new suit. You're also upset because when you got to your dressing room you noticed that the key to the desk where you keep your money is still at home. What if they steal your money, too? You have to pay the rent tomorrow. You can't put it off as you don't get on with your landlady. And then there's a letter from home. Your father's ill and that upsets you. First, because you love him and second, because if anything happens to him you'll be without financial support. And wages at the theatre are low.

'But, worst of all, is the attitude of the other actors and the management towards you. They laugh at everything you do. They spring surprises on you during the show. They deliberately leave out a key line or suddenly change the moves, or whisper something insulting or disagreeable in mid-action. And you're a shy man, so you get into a muddle. That's what they want, they think it's a laugh. They concoct all sorts of silly tricks because they're bored or for the fun of it.

'Let's explore the Given Circumstances I've just outlined a little further and decide, is it easy to prepare the creative state in these conditions?

'We all recognize, of course, how difficult this is, especially in the short space of time you have before curtain up. With any luck you'll be able to make up and dress.

'But don't worry about that,' Tortsov assured us. 'Our hands automatically put on our wig, make-up and spirit-gum. We don't even know we're doing it. At all events you manage to run onstage at the last minute. The curtain has gone up before you can catch your breath. But your tongue reels off scene one out of habit. Then, once you've got your breath, you can think about "the creative state". You think I'm joking, that I'm being ironic?

'No. Unfortunately we have to admit that this abnormal attitude to our artistic responsibilities occurs all too frequently,' Tortsov concluded.

After a short pause he turned to us again.

'Now,' he said, 'I'll paint another picture.

'Your private life is the same as before – you have problems at home, your father's ill, etc. But there's something quite different in store for you at the theatre. All the members of the artistic family understand and believe what is stated in *My Life in Art*, that we actors are lucky people because out of all the immeasurable space in the world fate has given us a few square yards in which to build a beautiful artistic life of our own, where we live creatively, and make our dreams flesh by working with others. We are constantly in contact with writers of genius like Shakespeare, Pushkin, Gogol, Molière and others.

'Isn't that enough to create a beautiful little corner for us here on earth?

'But it is even more important, in practical terms, to live in an atmosphere which is conducive to your creative state.'

'It's clear which version we prefer. What's not so clear is how to do it.'

'Very simple,' Tortsov responded. 'If you protect your theatre against "all pollution", you will automatically establish a good atmosphere, which is favourable to the creative state.

'Here's a piece of practical advice. *My Life in Art* tells us we shouldn't come to the theatre with muddy feet. Clean off the dust and dirt outside, leave your galoshes, your petty cares, squabbles and irritations, which complicate your life and distract you from your art, at the stage door.

'Clean up before you come to the theatre. And once inside, don't spit in corners. Most actors, however, bring all the dirt of their daily lives into the theatre – gossip, intrigue, tittle-tattle, slander, envy, petty vanity. The result is not a temple of art but a spittoon, a rubbish heap, a cesspit.'

'That's inevitable, it's human – success, fame, competition, envy,' said Grisha in defence of the theatre.

'You must rip it all out by the roots!' Tortsov insisted, even more vehemently.

'Is that possible?' Grisha persisted.

'All right. Let's admit you can't get rid of all the dirt in life. But you can, of course, stop thinking about it for a while and turn to something more appealing. You just have to want it deliberately enough and hard enough.'

'An easy thing to say,' said Grisha doubtfully.

'If that's beyond you,' said Tortsov still trying to convince him, 'keep your own dirt at home and don't spoil other people's mood.'

'That's harder still. We all want to get things off our chest,' our argumentative friend persisted.

'I don't understand why Russians think it's their privilege to make a song and dance about their domestic problems and ruin the atmosphere with their whining,' said Tortsov in amazement. 'In all other civilized countries that is considered unseemly, a sign of bad breeding. But we see it as a sign of our profound, sensitive, "Russian soul". How cheap!' said Tortsov, genuinely indignant. 'No, no and no again! We must understand once and for all that washing your dirty linen in public is vulgar, that it reveals a lack of self-control and respect for other people, that it's a bad habit,' said Tortsov hotly. 'We must stop indulging in this self-pity and self-denigration. When you're with other people you must smile, like the Americans. They don't like frowning faces. Weep and wail at home, but when you're with others be warm; happy and pleasant. You must discipline yourselves to do this,' Tortsov insisted.

'We'd be happy to, but how?' the students wondered.

'Think more about other people and less about yourselves. Be concerned for everybody else's mood, everybody else's work and less for your own, then things will go right,' Tortsov advised.

'If all three hundred members of a theatre team brought positive feelings to their work it would cure anybody, even in the blackest mood.

'Which is better, to rummage around in your minds and go over all your grievances, or let the combined strength of three hundred other people help you stop indulging in self-pity and get on with the things you love?

'Who is more free, people who are constantly defending themselves from attack, or people who forget about themselves and are concerned with other people's freedom? If we all behaved this way, in the final analysis, the whole of mankind would defend my freedom.'

'How so?' Vanya asked, puzzled.

'What's so difficult to understand?' asked an astonished Tortsov. 'If ninety-nine people out of a hundred were concerned with their common, that is, my freedom, life would be wonderful for them and me. But if these ninety-nine people are only thinking about their own freedom, and oppress people because of it, and me with them, then I have to fight all the other ninety-nine single-handed to defend my own freedom. Their concern for their own freedom is an unwitting attack on mine. It's the same in the theatre. Not only you, but all the other members of our theatrical family should be able to live happily inside the building. We would create an atmosphere that would overcome bad moods and make you forget your grievances. Then you could work.

'We term this preparation for work, this positive mental disposition, the *pre-work state*. That is the state in which you should always arrive at the theatre.

'As you can see, we need order, discipline, ethics and the rest not only for the overall structure of our affairs but above all for the artistic goal of our creative work.

'The first condition for creating this pre-work state is expressed in the saying, *love the art in yourself, not yourself in art*. So let your major concern be the well-being of your art.

'Another way of creating order and a healthy atmosphere is to bolster the authority of those who, for whatever reason, have to take charge of our affairs.

'We can argue, fight, protest against this or that candidate for the job of director right up to the moment someone has been elected or nominated. Once someone has been put in charge of the theatre, or of the administration, we must support them for the good of the whole enterprise, and our own. And the weaker they are the more we should support them. If the person appointed enjoys no authority, the main motor centre of the whole enterprise is paralysed. Think about it, where can a joint undertaking go if there is no one to take the initiative and guide its common endeavours?

'We should do as the Germans do. When there's no suitable candidate they invent one. They select the best person available at the time, appoint him, then prop him up and protect the authority invested in him. When necessary they give advice in private. Even when the appointment is a total failure, they don't throw someone who hasn't come up to expectation out, but quietly remove him. In humiliating their own appointment, they humiliate themselves. But, on the other hand, if the person appointed becomes conceited and a danger to the theatre, they are unanimous in replacing him. God help anyone who decides to be obstinate and stand out against the rest.

'How very unlike what we do here in Russia. We love to humiliate, discredit, destroy the very people we have chosen. If someone talented other than ourselves occupies a top position, or rises in some way above the common herd, we do our best to join forces, bang him on the head and say: "Don't get above yourself, you upstart!" How many talented, useful people have been brought down this way? But then there are some, who, despite everything, have managed to achieve general recognition and respect but they are crooks, who manipulate and exploit us. We grumble among ourselves and put up with it, because we can't make common cause, and we're afraid to overthrow a despot.

'This, with rare exceptions, is an all too common occurrence in our theatres. The struggle for primacy among actors, actresses and directors, envy of others' success, disputes over salary and casting are everywhere, and they are an iniquity.

'We dress up our vanity, our jealousy, our intrigues in fine words like "honourable competition", but they exude the stench of evil and poison the atmosphere in the theatre.

'From fear, or petty vanity, actors greet new members of the company, knives at the ready. The newcomers are lucky to survive the ordeal. But how many of them take fright, lose their self-confidence and come to grief?

'These actors are like schoolboys who make every new pupil run the gauntlet.

'That's an animal mentality.

'Once, sitting on a balcony in a provincial town, I was able to observe the way dogs behave. They too have their territory and they defend it relentlessly. If a strange dog is bold enough to cross a certain line he is faced with a whole pack of dogs. If he stands up for himself, he is accepted and can stay. If not, he runs away, wounded and maimed, from the territory of living beings, who, like him, have a right to their place on earth.

'It's that animal mentality which we find, with few exceptions, in the theatre. We must destroy it.

'It's not just prevalent among beginners but among old and established actors, too.

'For example, I saw two great leading actresses exchange insults, not only in the wings but onstage, too, which a fishwife would have envied.

'I also saw two very famous actors refuse to enter by the same door or from the same wing.

'I heard about a well-known leading man and a leading lady who hadn't spoken to each other for years but communicated in rehearsals through the director.

' "Tell her", the leading man said, "she's talking nonsense."

' "Tell him", the actress said to the director, "he's an oaf."

'Why did these talented people ruin something beautiful they once created? Because of personal, petty, meaningless insults and quarrels?

'These are the depths of self-destruction to which those who cannot master their baser "theatrical" instincts descend.

'Let this be a warning and a lesson to you.'

'Here's something we often see in the theatre. Those who make the most demands on directors and managers are the young actors who are the least able and knowledgeable.

'They only want to work with the best and cannot forgive the inadequacies or weakness of people who can't work miracles for them.

'You know how ill-founded these demands are.

'It would seem young actors still have a lot to learn, even from someone of limited talent but of mature experience. They could learn a lot from them. For that you have to be discriminating and take what you need.

'And so, don't be fussy, set criticism aside and pay careful attention to what experienced actors can give you, even if they will never be geniuses.

'Learn to take what's useful.

'Faults are easy to copy, good points much harder.'

'Most actors seem to think you only have to work in rehearsal and that you can relax at home.

'That's not the way it is at all. All you learn from rehearsal is what you have to work on at home.

'That's why I mistrust actors who talk a lot in rehearsal. They're convinced they can remember everything without taking notes and planning their work at home.

'Really?! I know perfectly well you can't remember everything, first because the director discusses so many major and minor details, no one could retain them, second because we're not dealing with established facts, but, in most rehearsals, exploring impressions in our Emotion Memory. If you want to understand and recall them, you have to find the right words, expressions, examples, the right written or other kinds of lures so you can evoke and then fix the feeling in question. You must think about it a long time at home before drawing it out of yourself. That's an enormous undertaking and demands great concentration, not only at home but when getting the director's notes.

'We directors know better than most what value to place on an unattentive actor's opinions. We have to remind them of the same note over and over again.

'This attitude towards teamwork is a great obstacle to the common effort. Seven people can't wait for one. So, you have to develop the right *artistic ethics and discipline*.

'That obliges actors to prepare properly for each rehearsal at home. It should be considered shameful and a outrage to the entire cast if the director has to repeat something he has already explained. You mustn't forget the director's notes. You may not be able to take them all in at once, you may have to go back to him to study them further but they shouldn't go in one ear and out the other. That's a crime against everyone working in the theatre.

'So, you must develop an ability to work independently at home, if you want to avoid that. That's not easy, and you must learn to do it properly while you are here at school. I can talk about it slowly and in detail here and now, but I can't turn a rehearsal into a class. The theatre places much more rigorous demands on you than the school. Remember that and prepare for it.'

'Another common fault we often meet in rehearsal comes to mind.

'Many actors are so cavalier in their attitude to their work that they only pay attention to notes which directly concern their own character. They aren't in the least interested in the scenes in which they don't appear.

'Remember, actors should take an active interest not only in their own character but in everything about the play as a whole.

'Besides, much of what the director says about the heart of the play particularly by a good writer, ways of physically embodying it, the style it requires, applies equally to the whole cast. You can't repeat the same thing to each individual.

'Actors should pay attention to comments about the play as a whole and work with others to gain a deeper understanding not only of their own characters but of the entire play.

'*Rehearsals of crowd scenes* require exceptional rigour and discipline. They have to be put, so to speak, on a "war footing". That's understandable. The director has to control a crowd of anything up to a hundred people single-handed. Can there be order without military discipline?

'Just think what would happen if the director couldn't gather up the reins in his hands. Imagine one lateness or absence, one note that hasn't been written down, one of the cast chattering when they should be listening and multiply that by the number of extras, assuming that each one, in rehearsal, makes a mistake that endangers everyone else's work, and you get a very large number of errors. That tries our patience because we have to do the same thing over again and lose time unnecessarily, apart from the fact that it is very wearing for those who are working conscientiously.

'Can you imagine that?

'You must not forget that rehearsing crowd scenes is tiring anyway, for actors and directors alike. So it's best if rehearsals are short but productive. For that you need strict discipline and you have to prepare and train for that in advance. Every mistake when we are on a "war footing" counts several times over, and the punishment should be several times stronger. Otherwise, here's what you get.

'Let's suppose we're staging a rebellion in which everyone has to use their voices full out, sweat, move about a lot and wear themselves out. It's all going well but a few people who missed a rehearsal, or were late, or didn't listen, ruin everything. The whole crowd then has to suffer. Not only should the director explain what he wants, but everyone in the scene should demand that those who've been sloppy come to order and concentrate. Group pressure is much more effective than a dressing down and disciplinary measures from the director.'

'There are a number of actors and actresses who have no creative initiative at all. They come to rehearsals and expect to be spoon-fed. After a great deal of effort the director may manage to strike a spark in these lazy people. Or, once the other actors have found the right line on the play, they follow it passively, picking up other people's experiences and so feel the play themselves. After a series of these creative jolts, if they have any ability at all, they are sparked off by other people's experiencing, feel the role and master it. Only we directors know how much work, inventiveness, patience, nervous energy and time it takes to get lazy actors going. Women flutter their eyelashes and sweetly excuse themselves, saying: "It's the way I am. I can't act a character until I've felt it. Once I've felt it everything will just happen." They offer this boast with pride, convinced that this method of acting is a sign of inspiration and genius.

'You don't need me to tell you what an obstacle these parasites who exploit other people's creative talents, feelings and efforts are to teamwork. We have to postpone the opening for a week because of them. Often they don't only hold up work themselves they encourage others to do the same. So, the rest of the cast has to strain every nerve to get these lazy actors going. That results in forcing, playacting and ruins their own performances which are beginning to come alive but aren't yet firmly established in their minds. When conscientious actors don't get the right cue, they make enormous efforts to get lazy actors going and lose the living quality they have discovered in their own roles. They are in a hopeless position, and, instead of moving the show forward, slow it down or stop it altogether by diverting the director's attention from the team to themselves. Now there's not just one lazy actress introducing lies and playacting in the show instead of life, a genuine re-experiencing, but the rest of the cast as well. Two actors can lead a third astray and those three can muddle a fourth. In the end, because of one person, a show that was going well, goes off the rails and down the slippery slope.

'Poor director! Poor actors! Actors who have a poor creative will, and an inadequate technique ought to be fired from the company. The trouble is, many of them are talented. The less gifted among us would never accept a passive role but talented actors are self-indulgent, knowing they can get away with it. They really believe they have the absolute right to wait for inspiration to come, rather like "waiting for something to turn up".

'Need I add that you can't cash in at other people's expense, that we all have a duty to contribute our own living feelings to "the life of the human spirit" and not take from others. If we all behaved that way, we would not only further our own efforts but everyone else's, too. But if we all rely on someone else, our creative work will lack initiative. Actors aren't puppets.

'It follows from everything I've said that actors must develop their own artistic will and technique. Like everyone else, they must do creative work at home and in rehearsal, and as far as possible, in full voice.

'Is it right for one actor in a well-rehearsed ensemble piece to depart from the true inner line out of sheer laziness, carelessness, or thoughtlessness and turn his performance into mere stock-in-trade?

'Does he have that right? You see, he's not creating the play all by himself. The group work is not his alone. It's all for one and one for all. There has to be a collective guarantee and anyone who breaks it is a traitor.

'For all my admiration for certain very talented individuals I dislike the practice of bringing in guest stars. Teamwork, which is the basis of our acting here, calls for an ensemble, and anyone who disrupts it is guilty of a crime not only against his colleagues but against the art he serves.'

'Many actors (especially guest stars) have the unbearable habit of rehearsing in little more than a whisper. What use is it to anyone to mutter lines inaudibly, without experiencing them or giving them any meaning? First, it is injurious to the role in that it encourages mechanical, meaningless mumbling. Second, it breaks it up so that we get used to stock-in-trade acting. Because the lines we speak are linked to our experiences, which bear no relation to them at all. You know how damaging any breaking up of the line of action can be. What use is a bad cue to your fellow actor? What's he supposed to do with it, how can he respond to words thrown out at random, or woolly ideas and substitutes for feeling? Bad cues, poor experiencing invite bad answers and false feeling in response. What good are rehearsals that are held "for form's sake"? Actors have a duty to play at full voice in every rehearsal and to give and take the right cue along the lines established for the play and the character.

'This rule is binding on all actors because without it rehearsals become meaningless.

'What I am saying doesn't exclude the possibility, if need be, of experiencing and communicating feelings and actions without words.'

'In so far as the mission of the true artist is to create, purvey and propagate beauty, it is a high and noble one, and the stock-in-trade actor, who peddles himself for money, is unworthy and . . .

'The stage, like a book, or a pile of blank pages, can serve the high and the low, depending on *what* is shown, who *plays* it and *how*. *What* is put in the glare of the footlights and *how* it is presented! It can be beautiful, unforgettable performances by Salvini, Ermolova or Duse, or it can be dirty cabaret songs, pornographic farces, or music hall, with a mixture of art, skill, gymnastics, clowning and vulgar display. Where do we draw the line? Where does beauty end and ugliness begin. Wilde was right to say "An actor is either a priest or a clown."[2]

'Try to find the demarcation line as long as you live. Separate the bad from the good in your art. So many of us devote our lives to the bad without knowing it, because we can't gauge the effect it has on the audience. But all that glisters is not gold onstage. A lack of scruple or principles has been the ruination of the theatre at home and abroad. These same reasons have prevented the theatre from enjoying the high position, the significance in social life which is its due.

'I'm no puritan and no . . . in the theatre. No. I take a broad view of what the theatre can do. I like happiness and fun . . .'

'Usually, when people try to create the right atmosphere and good discipline, they want them at once, throughout the company, in every part of a complex theatre organization. They lay down strict rules, regulations, establish fines. The result is external, formal discipline and order. Everyone's happy, everyone boasts about it. But you can't establish what's most unimportant in the theatre by external means. Because it can't be established overnight the organizers lose energy and confidence and attribute their failure to others, they try to justify themselves and transfer their guilt onto the rest of their colleagues. "You can't do anything with these people," they say.

'Try and approach the task from another angle. Don't start with your colleagues but with yourself.

'Try and find everything you want to build into your lives, everything you need to create order and discipline (and you have to decide what that is) first of all in yourself. Persuade by personal example. Then you'll hold a trump card and people will no longer say to you, "Physician, heal thyself" or "Practise what you preach."

'Personal example is the best way to merit authority.

'Personal example is the best proof, not only for others but principally for yourself. When you ask people to do what you do yourself, you can be sure that what you want done can be done. You'll know from personal experience how easy or hard it is.

'If you do, you'll avoid the inevitable consequence of asking people to do something which is either impossible or too difficult. If you know the opposite is true, you'll become excessively demanding, impatient, bad-tempered and severe and to prove you're right will swear that it's perfectly easy to do what you ask.

'That is the best way to undermine your own authority and to make people say: "He doesn't know what he's asking."

'In a word, a good atmosphere, discipline and ethics cannot be established by rules and regulations nor by a stroke of the pen, or draconian measures applied to all. You can't do it, so to speak, "wholesale" as usually happens when you try to influence a whole institution. It has to be done "retail". This isn't *mass production* but *cottage industry.*

'It can never be done right away, as people want, in one fell swoop. Haste and impatience are doomed to failure in advance.

'Go to each person individually. Speak to them and when you know what you're up against, be firm, tenacious, demanding and strict.

'Always remember how children make huge balls and blocks out of fistfuls of snow . . . The same kind of growth should be true of you. First one, *me* alone, then two, me and someone who thinks like me, then four, eight, sixteen, etc., in arithmetical and possibly geometric progression.

'Given time, five members of a company united by a passion for a common ideal can bring a theatre back into line.

'So, if, in the first year, you create a group of only five or six people, who are inseparably bound to one another and understand what they have to do and give their hearts to it, you can be happy because you know victory is already yours.

'Perhaps other, similar groups will form in other parts of the theatre. So much the better. The sooner your ideas will come together. Only not right away.

'In introducing your demands for company and other forms of discipline, in creating the atmosphere you want, you must, above all, be patient, restrained, firm and calm. For that you must first know what you want, recognize the difficulties involved and the time it will take you to overcome them. And you must believe that everyone in their heart of hearts desires the good, but that something prevents them from achieving it. Once they have come near and felt it for themselves they won't want to let it go, because it is much more satisfying than evil. The main difficulty is to recognize what stands between you and someone else's mind and to remove it. You don't need psychological niceties for that, you simply have to be attentive, get close to and observe the person you are dealing with. Then you will see a clear way into their minds, what the blocks are and what stands in the way of our intentions.'

'How do singers, pianists, dancers start their day?

'They get up, wash, dress, have tea and sing or do vocal exercises for a set period. Musicians, pianists, violinists, etc., play scales or do other exercises to maintain or develop their technique. Dancers hurry to the theatre for barre work, etc. This happens every day, winter or summer, and a day missed is a day lost, a step backwards artistically.

'Stanislavski in his book says that Tolstoi, Chekhov and other writers consider that it is essential to write each day for a fixed time, if not a novel, an article or a story, then a diary or notes. The important thing is that the hand that writes or types should not lose the habit of writing, but should daily become more skilful in conveying his spontaneous, subtle, precise feelings, ideas, mental images, intuitive emotion memories, etc.

'Ask a painter and he will tell you the same.

'I also know a surgeon (and surgery is also an art) who spends his free time playing at Japanese or Chinese spillikins. When he drinks tea, or in conversation he will suddenly pull some barely perceptible object out of a pile of things so as, as he puts it, "to keep his hand in".

'Only the actor rushes out in the morning to somewhere familiar or not for his own personal affairs because this is his only free time.

'Fine, but the singer is no less concerned than he, the dancer has his rehearsals, his career, and the musician has rehearsal, classes, concerts! . . .

'Nonetheless actors who have not done their daily exercises at home always say one thing – "no time".

'That's a great pity! Because the actor, more than any other specialist, needs to work at home.

'While the singer is only concerned with his voice and breath, the dancer with his physical apparatus, the musician with his hands, or, as with brass or woodwind players with blowing and his embouchure, etc., the actor has to deal with his hands, legs, eyes, face, flexibility, rhythm, movement and the entire programme we have taught in this school. That doesn't end when the course ends. Its lasts for the whole of an actor's career. And the older you get, the more you need a developed technique, and consequently, a systematic way of working on it.

'But, as the actor has "no time", his art at best comes to a standstill, and, at worst, declines and that random technique which of necessity of bad, false, stock-in-trade rehearsal and poorly prepared performance becomes entrenched.

'But, you know, the actor, and especially, the one most to be pitied is someone who does not play leading, supporting or small roles who, more than in any other profession, wastes his free time.

'Let us look at some figures. Let us take a walk-on in a crowd scene, say in *Tsar Fyodor*. He has to be ready by seven-thirty, to take part in scene two (the reconciliation between Boris and Shumski). After that, there's an interval. Don't imagine that he goes to change his make-up and costume.

No. Most of the nobles keep the same make-up and only remove their furs. And so they gain ten minutes of a fifteen-minute break.

'There's the brief garden scene and then, after a twelve-minute interval a long scene called [Boris' Retreat] which takes not less than half an hour. So that makes thirty-five minutes, including the interval, plus the previous ten minutes – forty-five minutes.

'Then we have the other scenes . . . (check the records and calculate the free time the extras have and work out the overall figure).

'That's what happens to extras in crowd scenes. But there are quite a few actors playing bit parts – servants and messengers – or more important but episodic roles. Once they've made their entrance, they either take the rest of the evening off, or wait for a five-minute entrance in the last act and lounge about in their dressing rooms the whole evening and get bored.

'That's how actors spend their time in a play like *Tsar Fyodor*, which is quite difficult to stage.

'Let's look, by the way, at what the bulk of the company who don't appear in the play, is doing. They're free . . . and complaining. Let's remember that.

'That's the situation of actors working in the evening.

'But what about during the day, in rehearsals?

'In some theatres, ours for example, rehearsals begin at 11 or 12 o'clock. Actors are free till then. And that's right and proper for many reasons, given the special nature of our lives. Performances end late. Actors are wound up and can't get to sleep quickly. While other people are sleeping, or having their third dream, they are playing the last and most powerful act of a tragedy and "dying".

'When they get home, they take advantage of the fact that all is quiet and they can get themselves together, away from people, and work on a new role.

'It's hardly surprising then if, the next day, when everybody else is up and working, tired actors are still sleeping after working long and hard on their nerves all day.

' "They've been hitting the bottle," ordinary people say.

'But there are theatres which keep their actors on a very tight rein because they have "iron discipline and exemplary order" (in quotes). Rehearsals begin at 9 (in their theatre a five-act Shakespearean tragedy ends at 11 incidentally).

'These theatres, which take such pride in their order, don't think about the actors and . . . their rights. These actors "die" three times a day, quite happily, and rehearse three plays in the morning.

' "Bla bla bla, bla bla bla. Bla bla bla," the leading lady whispers to herself. "I cross to the sofa and sit."

'And the hero in reply murmurs in subdued tones . . . "Bla bla bla, bla bla bla. Bla bla bla, etc. . . . I go to the sofa, go down on my knee and kiss your hands."

'Often, when you're on your way to the theatre at 12, you meet an actor from another theatre taking a stroll after rehearsal.

' "Where are you going?" he asks.

' "Rehearsal."

' "What, at 12 o'clock? That's very late," he declares, with a touch of malice, thinking to himself "What a useless layabout. What kind of order do they have in their theatre?"

' "I've been to rehearsal already. We went through the whole play. We start about 9," this hack boasts proudly, with a condescending look towards the latecomer.

'But I don't mind. I know who I'm dealing with and what "art" (in quotes) we're talking about.

'But here's what I don't understand.

'Many managers of good theatres, who are making a great effort, one way or another to create art, consider the order and "iron discipline" of stock-in-trade theatres to be genuine, not to say exemplary!! How can these people run an artistic enterprise or understand how it works, the nervous energy, the sacrifices real artists offer up to something they love in terms of nervous energy and their own finest impulses, when their judgement of actors' efforts and the conditions in which they work is dictated by their accountants and box office managers? These actors "sleep till midday" and disrupt "the work of the casting department".

'How are we to get rid of these shop owners, these bank clerks and small-business men? Where do we find people who understand and, most important, feel what a real actor's work is like, and know how to deal with it?

'Yet, nonetheless, I am still asking more of tired actors regardless of whether they are playing large or small roles. I want them to use what little time they have in the intervals, or in the scenes in which they don't appear, to developing their technique.

'There is time for it, as the figures I have given demonstrate.'

'But you're asking them to exhaust themselves. You're taking away their last moments of rest!'

'No,' I asserted. 'The most exhausting thing for actors is hanging about in the dressing rooms waiting for an entrance.'

'The theatre's task is *to create the inner life of the play and the role and give outward theatrical form to the seed, or thought, that gave rise to the writer's or composer's work.*

'Everyone working in the theatre, from the commissionaire, the cloakroom attendant, the box office assistant, who is the first person people meet when they arrive, to the management, the office staff, the director and the actors, the co-creators with the writer or the composer whom the audiences come to see, are the servants of the basic goal of art and totally subordinate to it. Everyone, without exception, is a co-creator of the performance. Any member of the team who to any degree harms our common effort and stops us achieving our basic artistic purpose, is to be considered dangerous. If the stage doorman, the cloakroom attendant, the usher and the box office assistant don't welcome the audience warmly, they are a danger and our artistic purpose, like the mood of the audience, drops. If the theatre is cold, dirty and untidy, if the curtain goes up late, if the performance lacks proper enthusiasm so that the writer's, composer's, actors', director's basic ideas and feelings don't get across to the audience, there was no point in their coming. The production is ruined and the theatre loses all social, artistic, educative meaning. The writer, composer, the performer create the requisite mood on our, the actors' side of the footlights. Management creates the right mood for the audience out front and for the actors as they get ready in their dressing rooms.

'The audience, like the actors, create the performance and they, like the cast, need to be in the right mood, otherwise they won't take in the impressions, the basic ideas the composer and the writer have to offer.

'The absolute subservience of everyone working in the theatre to the fundamental purpose of art is valid not only during performance but in rehearsal and at other times of day. If, for some reason, a rehearsal is unproductive, anyone who impedes our work is a danger to our basic common goal. We can only work creatively in the right context and anyone who stops us establishing it commits a crime against art and society, both of which we serve. A rotten rehearsal harms a role and a damaged role is a hindrance not a help to our efforts to present the writer's basic idea, which is the principal purpose of art.'

'Antagonism between the administrative and artistic sides, between stage and office, is common enough in the theatre. In Tsarist times that was the ruination of the theatre. "The Office of the Imperial Theatres" was the "name" for bureaucratic red tape, stagnation, routine, etc.

'Administration, clearly, must have its proper place but that place is a subordinate one, since it is the stage, not the office, which gives life to the theatre and to art. It is the stage and not the office that draws an audience or provides popularity and fame. The stage, not the office, creates art. It's the stage, not the office, society loves and the stage which makes the impression and has an educative meaning for society. It's the stage, not the office, that's good for the takings, etc.

'But try saying that to any impresario, theatre manager, inspector or bureaucrat. They will fly into a rage at such heresy. The idea that theatrical success depends on them and their management is rooted in their minds. They decide whether to pay or not to pay, whether to put on this or that production. They accept or reject proposals, fix salaries, levy fines, hold receptions, make speeches, have luxurious offices and a huge staff which eats up most of the budget. They can be happy or unhappy when a show, or an actor, is successful. They give away free seats. Actors have to beg for someone important or an expert to be let in. But these people refuse complimentary tickets to the actors and then give them to their friends. These are the people who swan through the theatre and disdainfully acknowledge the actors' greetings. They are a terrifying evil in the theatre, they are the destroyers and oppressors of art. I can't find words strong enough to vent my bitterness and hate for the bureaucrats we find everywhere in our theatres, who shamelessly exploit our artistic efforts.

'Management has oppressed actors since time immemorial, exploiting all the peculiarities of our nature. Eternally drawn into the world of their own creative imagination, overstretched, living on their nerves from morn till night in rehearsal and performance or when working at home, impressionable, unbalanced, excitable by nature, lacking moral fibre, easily depressed, actors are custom-made for exploitation, the more so because they give everything onstage and have no energy left to defend their own human rights.

'How rare it is to find administrators and accountants who understand their proper role in the theatre. And what a wonderful role it is! Even the most humble employee can and should, to some extent or other, join in the common artistic enterprise, help it along, try and understand what its major tasks are, and carry them out in co-operation with others. It is very important to find the right materials for the production, the sets, the costumes, the effects! Order and harmony, our whole way of life are so important onstage and in the dressing rooms and workshops. The audience, the actors and anyone connected with the theatre must approach it with a special feeling of veneration.

'The audience must be caught up in the right mood as it walks through the doors, to help it respond, not discourage it. The atmosphere backstage and in the auditorium is extremely important for the performance. And so is a liturgical mood backstage. How hugely important they are for an artist! And Order, calm, and the absence of haste in the dressing rooms. They all affect the creation of a *working creative state*.

'The administrative staff are in close touch with the most intimate and important aspects of our creative life and can lend help and support to the actors. If there is calm and good order, that contributes a great deal. It prepares the actor to be creative and the audience to respond. But if there is a moody, unhelpful atmosphere, then you can neither create nor respond, or you need extraordinary courage and technique to fight everything working against you.

'Yet how many theatres there are in which actors have to endure a whole tragedy before curtain up. They have to fight wardrobe, make-up and props for every bit of costume, for the right shoes, clean tights, clothes that fit, and a wig and beard of real hair, not tow. Those in costume and make-up who haven't grasped the crucial role they play in a common artistic enterprise don't care what actors have on when they meet the public. They keep backstage and never see the results of their slovenliness and carelessness. But the actor playing the hero, a noble knight, a passionate lover becomes a laughing stock because of his costume, make-up and wig just when the audience should admire him for his good looks and elegance.

'How often actors' nerves are in shreds, before curtain up or in the intervals so that they go on mentally empty and in tatters and give a bad performance because they haven't the strength for a good one.

'You have to be an actor and have seen this mess for yourself to understand the effect these backstage difficulties have on your *working creative state*. But if there is no discipline or order you feel no better onstage. The chances are you won't find the props you need, something on which the whole scene depends, a pistol or a dagger with which to kill yourself, or your rival.

'How often the lighting man dims the lights and ruins your best scene. Or the props man is busy over in the wings and makes so much noise it ruins your soliloquy or your dialogue. Then, to crown it all the audience, which has sensed the disorder in the theatre, gets restive and behaves so noisily, so badly it creates yet another problem for the actor – fighting them. Worst of all is when the audience makes a lot of noise, talks or moves about or, in particular, coughs during the action. If you want to ensure the audience shows the discipline the performance needs, the theatre itself must be worthy of respect so that the audience senses how it should behave. If the atmosphere in the theatre is not equal to the high calling of our art but invites bad behaviour, then the impossible task of fighting [it] and making the audience forget the distraction, falls to the actor.'

'In view of your making your first appearance, which will be very shortly, I want to explain how actors should prepare for their entrance and establish the creative state.

'Anyone who disrupts the life of the theatre should be fired or neutralized. And we should see to it that we only bring positive, invigorating, happy feelings with us. We should smile in the theatre, because we love our work. The administration and storemen, etc., should remember that, too. They should understand that this is not a warehouse, a shop or a bank where people will cut each other's throats for profit. The humblest clerk and cashier should understand the meaning [of what] they serve.

'People say, "And what about the budget, the outlay, the losses, salaries?!"

'I can only say from my own experience that the financial side gains if the atmosphere is good. An atmosphere reaches an audience, catches them up, without their realizing, cleanses them and creates the need to breathe the artistic air of the theatre. If you knew how aware an audience is of what is going on behind the curtain!

'Disorder, noise, shouts, banging between the acts, stagehands swearing, commotion onstage all get across to an audience and drag a performance down. But order, harmony and quiet give it lightness.

'I'm also asked: "And what about actors' petty jealousy, their intrigues, the craving for good roles, success, wanting to be first?"

'I answer: "Those who scheme, those who are jealous should be fired, without mercy. Actors who have no parts to play also. If they're not happy with the casting they should remember, there are no small roles, only small actors."

'People who love themselves in art, not the art in themselves, should also be fired.

'But what about the schemers and gossips who give the theatre its name?

'You can't fire people because they're difficult or because they stop others feeling good.

'Agreed. You can forgive talented actors anything, but their wings must be clipped by the rest of the cast. When a bacillus attacks the whole organism, you have to develop an antidote, an immunity so that the schemer can't impair the general atmosphere of well-being in the theatre.'

'So we have to assemble a congregation of saints to create the company and the theatre you've been talking about, do we?' Grisha objected.

'And what's your idea?' Tortsov responded hotly. 'Do you want cheapskates and hams to drive human beings, and their noblest, highest thoughts and feelings, off the stage? You want to live your own vulgar little life in the wings and then go on and be on a level with Shakespeare?

'True, we all know actors who have sold out to impresarios and Mammon and amaze us as soon as they walk on.

'But, you see, these actors, men of genius, descend to such coarseness offstage. Their talent is so enormous it makes them forget anything mean when they're acting.

'But can just anyone do that? Actors of genius do it because they are "inspired" but we have to spend our whole lives working at it. Have those actors done everything they should and could?

'So let's agree, once and for all, not to take actors of genius as your model. They are special people and work in a special way.

'There are many cock and bull stories about actors of genius. They are supposed to spend the whole day drinking, like Kean in the French melodrama,[3] and appear in public in the evening . . .

'It's not like that at all. According to those who knew great actors like Shchepkin, Ermolova, Duse, Salvini, Rossi and others close to, they led quite different lives, that those home-grown geniuses who have ruined their own would do well to imitate. Mochalov[4] . . . yes indeed . . . It's said he was different in private life. But why take him as an example in this respect only? He said other things that were much more important, much more valuable, much more interesting.

'The time has come to talk about another Element, or rather precondition for the creative state,' said Tortsov. 'It arises from the atmosphere onstage and in the auditorium. I mean actors' ethics, artistic discipline and a team spirit in our work.

'All this creates artistic cheerfulness, a preparedness for common action. That state of mind is conducive to creative work. I can't think of a name for it.

'It isn't the same as the creative state since it is only one of its elements and helps prepare it.

'In the absence of a right name for it, I call it "*actors*' ethics", which plays a major role in establishing this pre-creative state of mind.

'Actors' ethics and the state of mind they create are very important in our business because of its special nature.

'The writer, the composer, the painter, the sculptor aren't constrained by time. They can work when they feel like it. Their time is free.

'Not so in the theatre. Actors must be prepared to be creative at a definite time, printed on the poster. How can you order yourself to be inspired at a definite time. That's not so easy.'

It so happened that there was nowhere for the students to gather after today's regular rehearsal for Rakhmanov's notes. The green room and the dressing rooms were being cleaned for tonight's performance. We had to meet in the large extras' dressing room.

They were preparing costumes, wigs, make-up and small props in there, too.

The students were interested in everything and caused a great deal of confusion because they just picked things up and didn't put them back in their proper place. I was interested by a belt, examined it, tried it on, and just left it lying on a chair. Rakhmanov reprimanded us very strongly because of it and gave us a whole lecture about it.

'When you've played just one role, it will be clear to you just what a wig, a beard, a costume, a prop means to you and how much you need it for the character you're playing.

'Only someone who has gone down the long, difficult road of not only looking for the soul but the bodily form of a human being/role that has formed in their imagination and then taken shape in their own body, can understand what every feature, detail, object connected with the being they have to bring alive means. How agonizing it is for actors not to find something exciting they saw in their imagination in reality. What pleasure it is when our dreams take physical form.

'A costume or a prop we have found for a character cease to be mere objects and become holy relics.

'It's terrible if it is lost. Worse still if you have to hand it over to another actor, doubling in the same role as you.

'A famous actor, Martynov, said that when he had to play a role wearing the same robe he wore coming to the theatre, he would put it on a peg as soon as he got to his dressing room. And when he had made up and it was time for him to make his entrance, he would put on his coat, which had ceased to be a coat and had become a costume, that is, what the character would wear.

'This is more than just an actor dressing. This the moment when he puts on his *robes*. It is a very important, psychological moment. That is why you can tell real artists by the way they relate to their costume and hand props, the way they love and care for them. No wonder, since they are of endless service to them.

'But there's a quite different attitude to costume and props.

'Many actors have barely finished playing before they remove their wig and beard onstage. Sometimes they even throw them down right there and leave the stage removing the remains of their make-up from their greasy faces, undoing as many buttons as they can and dropping bits of costume anywhere as they turn into themselves again.

'The poor make-up and props men scour the theatre, picking up and looking after things which the actors need but they don't. Talk to them about it. They'll use a flood of swear words to describe these actors. They do that not just because this slovenliness causes them a great deal of trouble but because they were intimately involved in creating the costume or the prop and know its meaning and value to our artistic enterprise.

'These actors should be ashamed. Try not to be like them but to look after and cherish your costumes, jackets, wigs and hand props as holy relics. Each of them should be in its proper place in the dressing room. Take it and put it back properly.

'We mustn't forget that many props are genuine antiques and are irreplaceable. Losing them, or damaging them creates a gap because it isn't easy to imitate an antique. It has the charm of age which is difficult to reproduce. Besides in genuine artists and lovers of rarities, they evoke a special mood. A mere prop lacks this quality.'

'Actors should show even greater love, care and respect for their make-up. You mustn't put it on mechanically but, so to speak, psychologically, thinking about the very life and heart of the character. Then the tiniest wrinkle is based in the life which has etched this trace of human suffering on your features.

'In his book, Stanislavski talks about a mistake actors often make. They make up and dress their body with great care but forget about their minds, which have to be prepared with incomparably greater care before giving a performance.

'So the actor should first think about his mind and start preparing the pre-work state and the creative state. Needless to say this must be your primary concern prior to and after you get to the theatre.

'Real actors, with a show in the evening, have been thinking and worrying about it all day, ever since the morning and sometimes since the day before.'

.. .. 19..

There's been a sensational incident at the theatre over the actor Z. He's been severely reprimanded and warned that if such an intolerable incident occurs again he'll be fired. This provoked a great deal of gossip at the school.

'Look, excuse me,' Grisha sounded off, 'but management has no right to interfere in our private lives.'

We asked Rakhmanov what he thought about it and this is what he said:

'Doesn't it seem senseless to you to create something with one hand and destroy it with the other?

'Yet that's what most actors do. Onstage they try to create an impression of beauty and artistry. But once they come off, they do their level best to disillusion the very people who were admiring them a moment ago as though in mockery. I'll never forget the bitter resentment I felt against a well-known guest star when I was young. I won't tell you his name so as not to sully his memory.

'The performance I saw was unforgettable. It made such a great impression on me I didn't want to go home alone. I had to talk to someone about what I had just experienced in the theatre. I went to a restaurant with a friend. While we were still revelling in our memories, to our great delight our genius came in. We rushed up and poured out our enthusiasm to him. This famous man invited us to supper in a private room where he drank himself into a bestial state. All his human and artistic corruption, hidden by a glossy exterior, was revealed, his repulsive boasting, petty vanity, scheming, gossip, all the attributes of the ham actor. To crown it all he refused to pay for the wine which he had practically demolished single-handed. It took us months to pay off this unexpected debt. After that we had the pleasure of taking our belching, swearing, drunken beast of an idol to his hotel where they wouldn't let him in in such a disgusting state.

'Put all our good and bad impressions of this genius together and what do you get?'

'Something like hiccups after champagne,' Shustov joked.

'So take care the same thing doesn't happen to you when you become famous,' Rakhmanov concluded.

'Actors can only let go in the privacy of their own home or in a very limited circle. They have a duty to be bearers of beauty, even in ordinary life. Otherwise they will create with one hand and destroy with the other. Remember this as you serve art in your early years and prepare yourself for this mission. Develop the necessary self-control, the ethics, the discipline of a public figure who takes the beautiful, the elevated, the noble into the world.'

'Actors, by the nature of the art they serve, are members of a large complex institution – a theatrical company. They appear in its name and under its banner before thousands. Millions read about their work and their activities within that institution almost daily. Their names are inseparable from it, in the same way that Shchepkin, Sadovski, Ermolova are inseparable from the Maly and Lilina, Moskvin, Kachalov and Leonidov from the

Art Theatre. Actors bear the name of the theatre as well as their own. Their private and professional lives are one in people's minds. So, if the actors of the Maly, the Art or any other theatre do something reprehensible, create a scandal, commit a crime, no matter how much they deny it, no matter what excuse or explanation is printed in the press, they can't remove the stain, the shadow they have cast on the theatre they serve. Actors have a duty to conduct themselves decently outside the theatre and to protect its name not only onstage but in their private lives as well.'

27

THE EXTERNAL CREATIVE STATE IN PERFORMANCE

'Imagine,' Tortsov said in today's class. 'You wake up and lie in bed half asleep with your body all stiff. You don't feel like moving or getting up. You feel shivery. But you force yourself out of bed, do your gymnastics, warm, stretch the muscles of your body and face. The blood begins to circulate properly. All your limbs, every finger, every toe is freely filled with energy from head to toe and back again.

'Having put the body in order, you start work on your voice. You sing a little. The sound has good support, it is full, rich, ringing and fills all the resonators in the nasal cavities, the head and the hard palate. The sound flies freely and fills the room. The resonators ring out clearly and the acoustic of the room bounces it back to you as though to encourage your energy, vitality and dynamism.

'Clear diction, clean phrasing, colourful speech try to find thoughts, that will give them even greater clarity, variety and power.

'The unexpected inflexions which come from within give it more relief and expression.

'After that you enter the waves of rhythm and move about in the waves in varied tempi.

'There is order, discipline, harmony throughout your whole physical being.

'Everything is in place and is as nature intended.

'Now all the parts of your physical mechanism which you use for *embodiment* are supple, receptive, expressive, sensitive, agile, like a well-oiled and tuned machine in which all the wheels and rollers are working in perfect harmony.

'It's difficult to keep still. You want to move, take action, fulfil inner impulses, express *the life of the human spirit*.

'You sense a call to action throughout your whole body. You're "all steamed up". Like children, you're not sure what to do with all this excess energy and are quite prepared to squander it on the first thing that comes along.

'You need Tasks, inner commands, psychological material, the life of the human spirit so you can embody them. If they appear, your whole physical mechanism falls on them with a passion and energy as children.

'Actors must learn to produce this physical state onstage, to order all the constituent parts of their physical mechanism of embodiment, limber them and set them to work.

'Our term for this is the *outer creative state*.

'Just like the inner creative state, it is made up of various constituent parts — like facial expression, voice, inflexions, speech, movement, bodily expression, physical action, contact, adaptations.

'All the elements of the outer creative state must be exercised and trained to ensure that your embodiment is as subtle, supple, clear and physically expressive as the capricious feelings, the elusive life of the spirit it is called on to reflect.

'It must not only be superlatively well trained but subservient to the commands of the will. Its link to the inner state and their interaction, must become an instant, unconscious *reflex*.'

28

GENERAL CREATIVE STATE IN PERFORMANCE

1.

Tortsov was in the middle of an [explanation] when the curtains suddenly opened at a signal from Rakhmanov and we saw a large blackboard with a sketch pinned to it in the middle of Marya's apartment. It pictured what happens in an actor's mind in the creative process. Here's a copy of the sketch.

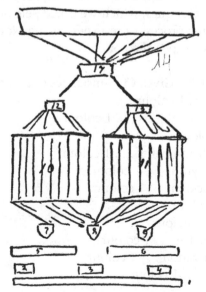

Tortsov explained:

'At the bottom, like the three whales on which the earth rests we place three ideas, the three major foundations of acting. You should base everything you do on them.

'No. 1 is: *The art of the dramatic actor is the art of inner and outer action.*

'No. 2. The second is Pushkin's aphorism, "Truth of the passions, feelings that seem true in the set circumstances."

'No. 3. The third is *the subconscious creation of nature through the conscious psychotechnique of the actor.*

'Two large platforms are constructed on these foundations.

'No. 4. *The process of re-experiencing which we have studied in general outline* and

'No. 5. *The process of embodiment.*

'Three virtuosos are seated at two huge organs on these platforms. Nos 6, 7, 8. The three drives of mental life: *intelligence, will, feeling* (according to the first scientific definition) or *representation, judgement and will-feeling* (according to the more recent definition).

'No. 9. A new play and a new role impregnate our psychological drives, motivators, they plant their seed in them and arouse the urge to create.

'No. 10. The pathways of these psychological drives which bear within them the seeds of the play and the role. At first they are erratic, chaotic but as the fundamental goal of our creative work becomes clearer they acquire continuity, directness and coherence.

'No. 11. Our inner world, our personality, our creative mechanism with all its qualities, possibilities, aptitudes, capabilities, natural gifts, actors' habits, psychotechniques, which we called "elements" earlier on and which we need for the process of re-experiencing. Note that each element has been given its own special colour:

a)   Imagination – ('if', Given Circumstances of a role)
b)   Bits and Tasks . . . 1 colour
c)   Concentration and objects . . . 1 colour
d)   Action . . . 1 colour
e)   A sense of truth and belief . . . 1 colour
f)   Inner Tempo-rhythm . . . 1 colour
g)   Recollected emotion . . . 1 colour
h)   Contact . . . 1 colour
i)   Adaptation . . . 1 colour
j)   Logic and sequence . . . 1 colour
k)   Inner characterization . . . 1 colour
l)   Inner presence . . . 1 colour

m)   Ethics and discipline . . . 1 colour
n)   Finishing touches . . . 1 colour

'All these elements exist in the actor's mind together with the psychological motivators and the mental seeds of the role that have been sown in them.

'You can see how the forward drives go deep and gradually take on the colours of the actor's "elements".

'No. 12 is the same but transformed into the movement of the psychological drives of the actor-role. Compare them before (No. 10) and after (No. 11) when they have entered the mind and you will see the difference. Now the "elements" of the play have absorbed the actor's own "elements", intellect, will, feeling, drives, they are no longer recognizable (No. 12).

'No. 13. This is the nexus in which all the trajectories of psychological motivators come together, the mental state we call the "inner creative state".

'No. 14. This is the rope made of all the trajectories, which move on towards the Supertask. Now that they have been united and transformed we call them the "through-action".

'No. 15. Is the as yet provisional, undefined "Supertask".'

'What's the dotted line on the right of the sketch?' the students asked.

'It shows the second process: *physical embodiment*.'

2.

Tortsov indicated the boxes on the sketch marked 'inner creative state' and 'outer creative state'.

'All that remains is to unite these two creative states to form what we term *the general creative state*.

'As you can see from the blackboard it combines *both inner and outer states*.

'Then every feeling, mood, experience you have created is *reflected* externally. It is easy for actors to respond to all the tasks the play, the author, the director and they themselves have created. All the mental and physical elements of their creative state are on the alert and answer the call immediately.

'The more directly, vividly, precisely the outer reflects the inner, the better, the more broadly, the more fully the audience will understand the life of the human spirit you have created. That was why the play was written, why the theatre exists.

'*The general creative state is the working state.*

'Actors must be in this state, whatever else they do. Whether they are doing the play for the first or the hundredth time, whether they are learning or repeating the lines, whether they are working at home or in rehearsal, whether they are trying to find mental or physical material for their character, whether they are thinking about the life of the human spirit, or its outward shape, about costume and make-up, in other words every time they have the least contact with the role, they must be in the *inner and outer and general creative state in performance.*

'You can't start work without it. It must become a natural, biological part of us – second nature.

'Let us conclude today's class with a rapid review of work on oneself. That will mark the end of the [second]¹ year of your three-year course.

'Now that you've learned how to create the general performance mode, we can pass on, next year, to the second part of the course – work on a role.

'The mass of information you've received over the past year is bubbling and boiling in your heads and hearts. It's hard for you to put all the elements of the performance mode back together in their proper place after we've separated and examined them one by one.

'And yet, the thing we've been studying so painstakingly for a whole year is the most ordinary, human state which we are quite familiar with in life. When we experience a feeling in life, the state we call the general performance mode arises quite naturally.

'It is made up of the same elements we look for in ourselves when we stand in the glare of the footlights. And without that mood you can't surrender to your experience and express and communicate it outwardly in life either.

'It is amazing that something so familiar, so natural, so spontaneous in life, should disappear or go awry as soon as we step onstage. A great deal of work, study, training and technique are needed to put something that is completely normal for every human being onstage.

'The common creative state which is complex in its parts, is in fact the most simple, normal human state. In a dead world of painted flats, wings, colours, glue, papier mâché and props, the performance mode speaks to us of genuine, living, human life and truth.

'How strange that the simplest, most natural feelings and experiences should turn into something complex as soon as we try to analyse them and express them in words. For example:

'Do you want a sweet?' he said offering us a box he was holding. 'Eat it and describe your sensations as you do it.

'You see! It is easier to perform a common action than to describe it. It would take a whole book. If you consciously examine the most common sensations or mechanical actions, you'll be amazed by the complexity, the opaqueness of something we do effortlessly and unconsciously.

'The same thing happens when studying the "system" and, in particular, the performance mode. The state we are examining is, in itself, simple, natural and familiar, but analysing it is complex.

'Now that difficulty is behind you, it will be easy for you to cope with the rest and verse yourself in the proper, natural, living creative state.'[2]

3.

Today, Tortsov came into class with a taciturn stranger, a director, so they say. Class would be devoted once more to reviewing our creative state.

Vanya was called on and asked permission to play the scene in Ostrovksi's *The Forest* between Nestchastlichev and Schastsilev with Pasha. It must be the latest addition to the secret repertoire of set pieces he's been building up.

I openly admit I listened in on Tortsov and Rakhmanov's private conversation quite brazenly. It so happened I was sitting in a seat where I could hear everything. I covered my eavesdropping by writing in my diary with enormous concentration and involvement.

Was it wrong of me to listen in?

'Well done!' Tortsov whispered to Rakhmanov, happy with Vanya. 'Just look how firm his object and how tight his circle of concentration are. That's an absolutely genuine creative state, no doubt of it. A fluke, of course. There's no suspicion Vyuntsov has studied it thoroughly and mastered it. Oh, you young devil! No, that won't do. Now he's acting like one big ham. There he goes again! Not a trace of the creative state left.

'Look, look! Oh, well done! He's put it right. We have truth and belief again. He's even brought in some ideas, and that's his weak point. Oh, he's at it again!' said a pained Tortsov when Vanya pulled a crude stunt, changed the task and lost the 'circle'. 'Now the object's out here, in the auditorium. Here's a fine mess. Congratulations, the elements are uncoordinated, the feeling of truth has gone, he's rigid with tension, and the voice is tight. Memories of actors' emotion creep in and then posturing, gimmicks, clichés and God knows what. Now, of course, it's all beyond redemption.'

Tortsov was right. Vanya was overacting so much he was, as we say in school, 'unwatchable'. For example, to show how Schastsilev rolled then unrolled himself in the carpet because of the cold, Vanya skilfully and even comically rolled himself on the filthy stage floor right down to the footlights.

'He might have spared his clothes,' Tortsov sighed, and turned away.

'What a wonderful piece of work our nature is,' he reflected to the stranger, rather than look at the stage. 'How everything knits together and interlocks. For example, the creative state. If one tiny component is out of place, the whole thing goes wrong. All you have to do is replace one of the right elements and the others, which depend on it, are inevitably altered. A false task or object, a wrong circle of attention, or a disrupted sense of truth, etc., transform our affective memories and feelings, adaptations, etc. All the remaining elements, and our creative state are deformed as a result. It's like music. One wrong note in a chord and it becomes cacophony. Consonance turns to dissonance. Correct the wrong note and the chord sounds right.

'It's the same with us. Replace a false element with a true one and our creative state is like a chord played in tune.

'Every single, proper element has to be there. Only when they are all present can we create the condition we call the *creative state*.'

When the extract was over and the performers came down into the front rows Tortsov said to Vanya:

'I'd like to hug you for the first part and slap you for the second. Your creative state went right down hill. What was it?

'An object this side of the footlights, an inadequate sense of truth, stagey affective memories, not living ones, and the contact, emanation and adaptations of a hackneyed old pro, not a human being. This falseness produced extreme muscular tension which increased and intensified the falseness of your general state.

'These false elements didn't produce a "performance" but a special kind of actor's mode in which you can't be creative, or experience, only *posture* to amuse gawking layabouts.

'This false creative state can't lead to creative work or art, only to the worst kind of stock-in-trade.

'You need to understand how important the right creative state is to you. You can't make an entrance without it, you must keep off the stage. There are two actors inside you. Not only are they different, they are mutually destructive. One is gifted, the other spoiled and hopeless. You have a choice to make. You have to sacrifice one of them. That's something for you to think about. Get a grip on yourself and ask Rakhmanov to drill you in every class and help you create the creative state and make it a habit. All you need for the moment is supervised "training".'

'I really don't understand,' lamented Vanya with tears in his eyes. 'I'd be in paradise. . . . I wasn't up to it. I didn't get started. I don't know what to do.'

'Listen and I'll teach you,' Tortsov said to him affectionately, encouragingly and gently.

'First, learn to tone up all the elements of the creative state, inner and outer. Work on them separately at first and then put them all together. For example combine muscular release with a sense of truth, objects of attention with transmitting, action with physical tasks, etc. You'll notice that when you bring two elements together properly, they create a third and the three of them produce a fourth and a fifth. Then comes a sixth, a tenth, etc.

'But there's one important proviso. You mustn't create the creative state for its own sake. That is unstable and quickly disintegrates into its constituent parts or becomes an *actor's mode*. It all happens very easily, very fast, almost before you have time to notice. If you want to explore all the subtleties of the creative state it must become very much a habit which you can only acquire through exercises and practical experience. And remember you can't create the creative state "cold" but only through a task, or series of tasks, which creates a continuous line of action. This line is, as it were, the core which brings all the elements together in the service of the basic goal of the play.

'This line, and the tasks which create it, must not be dead and mechanical. It must be living, vital, truthful. You need *exciting ideas* (*magic "if", given circumstances*). They, in turn, require *truth and belief, concentration, wants, etc.* They are all interconnected and create one whole "creative state" out of the various elements. Logic and sequence are important, too.'

After this Tortsov turned to Rakhmanov with the following suggestion:

'You saw how I got Nazvanov into the creative state last time, how I gradually built it up. You must do the same thing with Vyuntsov.

'Of course you must make sure he understands his state of mind for himself. He won't get there, of course, for a long time because you need a well-developed, clear-cut sense of truth to control the creative state. But his sense of truth is chaotic. It's the wrong note that ruins the chord. So, you'll have to play the "executor of his sense of truth", by using interesting ideas, or, in other words, set circumstances. His capacity for emotion isn't bad. It's there, no doubt about it. But before you activate it, you must first focus his concentration properly because if he starts to feel something irrelevant that will lead him God knows where, in the opposite direction to truth. So, you must not only train his sense of truth but his feeling for the right Task.

'There are those who are attracted by an audience whether they like it or not. But there are others who love audiences and willingly go out to meet them. Vanya is like that. So, his last hope is a task that will drag him back to the stage. Briefly, when you work with him, fight his *false creative state* which he still can't distinguish from the genuine *creative state*.

'So, if you guide Vanya along the path to truth day after day, he'll get used to it and learn to distinguish true from false. It's hard, laborious, excruciating work.'

'And what about Leo? What shall we do with him? He is in the wrong state? You can be sure of that,' said Rakhmanov, asking Tortsov for orders.

'You can't judge him by Nestchastlichev. The role itself is over emphatic. Let him play Salieri,' said Tortsov.

'If you expect to get genuine experiencing out of Leo, given what we know of him, you'll get nowhere. He isn't an emotional actor, like Marya or Kostya. He experiences with his intellect, he takes the literary line,' Tortsov explained.

'And how are we to establish the creative state?' Rakhmanov persisted.

'For him, at the moment, that is the creative state,' said Tortsov.

'Without experiencing?' said Rakhmanov, amazed.

'With "intellectual" experiencing. Where are you going to get anything else if there isn't anything? We'll see later whether he is capable of the kind of re-experiencing we need, or not,' Tortsov continued. '*The creative state comes in various forms. Sometimes the intellect is dominant, sometimes feeling, sometimes the will.* It acquires its particular colour from them. When one of the elements, say, *the intellect* is at the keyboard you get one type, one aspect of the creative state. But there are other versions, i.e. will or feeling can be the lead voice. That creates two new colourings of the creative state. Leo takes his colouring from reason and literature. Be thankful for that. He really understands and appreciates everything he says. True there's not much warmth or feeling. But what can you do? You can inject feeling. Try to stimulate his magic "ifs", the Given Circumstances. Develop his imagination, devise interesting tasks which will help feeling come alive, defrost it and then he'll warm up. But you won't go very far in that direction. Leo is a typical "intellectual", with a wonderful brain, a fine figure, which, of course, has to be worked on and made to look human. When we've done that, we'll have, I won't say a very good, but a useful actor. He'll be in every production, you'll see. Briefly, this creative state, with its leaning towards the "intellectual" is acceptable for the moment.'

'Poor Leo,' I reflected. 'All that effort just to become "useful". On the other hand, he's not very demanding. Let him be content with that.'

Today the students' creative state was tested again.

Tortsov asked Grisha to perform something. Of course, he had to have Varya with him.

Our super-hacks have a repertoire of pot-boilers known only to them, second-rate plays of poor taste and quality.

Grisha played a public prosecutor interrogating a beautiful suspect he was in love with and was forcing himself upon her.

'Listen,' Tortsov whispered to Rakhmanov. 'This is the stupid dialogue the writer has given to Grisha. "From the burning depths of the people, borne by my power to chastise, millions of hungry, rebellious citizens heap their curses on you." Now, remember how he spoke this trite verbiage.'

'All the high-faluting words in the sentence were pulled out and accented. But the most important word, the reason for the speech, was glossed over.'

'Which word?' Rakhmanov asked.

' "You", of course. The point is that the people are heaping their curses on you.

'Grisha knows nothing of the laws of speech. What has his teacher been doing? Pay serious attention to this [subject]. It's one of the most important. If the tutor's not up to it get rid of him fast. People mustn't be allowed to speak like that.

'My God, what a lot of nonsense!' Tortsov said, feeling sorry for Grisha. 'Better not try and make sense of it, just listen to the voice,' he said to console himself.

'The voice is well supported, with an adequate range, good resonance, free, expressive, quite well placed.

'But can you hear the way he pronounces the consonants:

' "Bbbbbburning dddddddepths . . . bbbbborne by my pppppower to chchchchchastise"!

'Do you think that he's doing that to develop his consonants? Not at all. He thinks his voice sounds better when he hangs on to them. Take away that cheap affectation and his speech, on the whole, is tolerable.

'What can we do with these gifts? Look!' Tortsov suddenly exclaimed. 'If I were a foreigner with no Russian I'd applaud him for that broad gesture which ended with all five fingers outstretched. His voice dropped right down at the same time as his hand to complement it.

'Yes, he speaks beautifully, his voice is well trained and I could forgive him his affectation and theatricality if we were talking about landing or flying a plane. But we're not, we're talking about going down to a place of judgement. The speech is intended to frighten his poor victim and make her agree to what he asks.

'I feel that Grisha was thinking of beautiful gestures and a few effective declamatory flourishes even when he read this stupid play for the first time. He perfected them slowly and painstakingly in the quiet of his room. That's what he calls "work on a role". He studied and rehearsed this cheap script so he could dazzle us with his posing and inflexions.

'What a lot of rubbish! Dear God!

'Let's try and understand what he is going through. Now you know what makes him tick. The elements in his creative state — uneducated speech, a plane coming in to land, and "bbbbburning ddddepths". Put them all together and what do you get? A hodge-podge!

'But ask Grisha and he will swear that this is the real creative state, and that no one has a better "sense of theatre" than he, that this is acting in the grand style not the vulgar naturalism of re-experiencing.'

'Then get rid of both of them. Do it!' Rakhmanov urged. 'Leo and Igor as well. We don't need outsiders. Too right we don't!'

'You think they're useless in the theatre?' Tortsov asked Rakhmanov provocatively.

'Indeed I do!'

'Let's see,' said Tortsov and went to the footlights after our two representationists had finished their scene.

Tortsov asked Grisha to tell him in detail what he was doing, how he understood the role, what the scene was about.

It was incredible.

Neither he, nor she, knew what was important in the scene, why it had been written. To recount the content they first had mechanically to run the lines they had learned parrot-fashion, analyse the ideas and explain the content in their own words.

'Now I'll give you a story,' said Tortsov and sketched out a wonderful story set in the Middle Ages.

He has, as I think I've already said, a remarkable gift for explaining the content of plays. He makes up the most important, most interesting parts, the things the writers forgot to put in, superbly.

Grisha only analysed the content of the scene after he'd played it. There was much more to it, in fact, than Grisha and Varya had shown onstage

Both actors seemed to like Tortsov's interpretation. They willingly corrected the scene following the new inner line without arguing at all.

On his side, Tortsov didn't force them to do anything against their will and did nothing about their acting which was so hammy you'd have thought it needed attention more than anything else. No, Tortsov was only interested in correcting the inner line, the tasks, the magic 'ifs', the given circumstances.

'And clichés, the sense of truth and belief?'

'Where's truth? Why don't you correct all this conventional acting?' Rakhmanov persisted.

'What for?' Tortsov asked calmly.

'What do you mean, what for?' It was Rakhmanov's turn to be surprised.

'Yes, what for?' Tortsov asked once again. 'It won't get us anywhere. They are typical representationists by nature so they should at least represent truthfully. That's all we can expect from them at the moment.'

Finally, after a great deal of work, Grisha and Varya played their scene, helped by promptings from Tortsov.

I have to admit I liked it. It was comprehensible, clear, meaningful, a good sketch of the roles. True, it was far from being what Tortsov had described earlier. But it was undoubtedly better than the first time. True they didn't thrill you, they didn't even make you believe them. You could feel they were 'acting'. They were mannered, affected, declamatory and had all the typical actor's faults. But still . . .

'What was it? Art? Stock-in-trade?'

'Not quite art yet,' Tortsov stated. 'But if you work on the techniques of embodiment, if you get rid of all the outworn actor's clichés, if you develop their acting technique, then even this kind of hamming can come near to art.'

'But that's not our kind of acting,' Rakhmanov said excitedly.

'Of course it's not experiencing. Or, to put it more precisely, they have grasped the shape of the role and perhaps even re-experienced it but the actual embodiment is still full of conventions and clichés. But, with time, they can achieve an acceptable form. The result isn't truth, or even verisimilitude, but a reasonable indication of how the role can be experienced. That's not acting but a picturesque statement of the role, which you can put over if you have a brilliant technique. Quite a few foreign actors come here on tour and are applauded.

'We'll discuss Grisha's suitability to join our theatre once he's graduated. For the moment he's a student and we must turn him into, make him the best actor we can. Perhaps he'll win his laurels in the provinces. Then heaven help him! But he must be educated. We have to put together an acceptable acting technique using what gifts he has and develop what's most essential to combine his talents into a whole, an ensemble, so to speak, or a chord that rings true.'

'And how are we supposed to do that?' Rakhmanov asked nervously.

'First,' Tortsov explained, 'we must help him develop the right creative state. We have to train a more or less acceptable clutch of elements. The right creative state should help him follow the prompter rather than experience properly (though he'll get there at odd moments).'

'But if you want to get the general shape you have to experience, you have to!' said Rakhmanov hotly.

'I already said you can't get anywhere without re-experiencing. But it's one thing to feel a role inside so as to know its shape but another to experience when you are onstage acting. For the time being, teach him to feel the line of the role and communicate it adequately, even if it's all convention. But, of course, you have to do something about his awful clichés and tricks, alter them, improve them or replace them.'

'How am I to do that? What are we to call this "creative state"?' asked Rakhmanov getting more and more heated. 'Actorish?'

'No,' Tortsov defended himself. 'An actorish creative state is based on mechanical, stock-in-trade actions, and even then you find minute traces of experiencing.'

'That's to say, what you showed us,' Rakhmanov commented.

'Possibly,' Tortsov replied. 'This minute bit of experiencing was called "semi-actor's mode" a while ago,' Tortsov reflected.

'Yes, right. To hell with it. Semi-actor's. Fine. Fine,' Rakhmanov replied unhappily.

'But what are we to do with that siren?' he asked worriedly. 'How are we to develop the creative state in her?'

'Give me a moment to find out,' said Tortsov and started watching her closely.

'Oh, that Varya,' Tortsov said sadly. 'All she ever does is show herself off over and over and over again. She can't admire herself enough. Why is she playing this scene? It's clear, someone evidently praised her, or she saw this curved pose, the beautiful line of the torso in the mirror and now the only thought behind her acting is to remember and reproduce a movement she adores, a living tableau.

'You see, she's forgotten what her feet were doing and is using her visual memory to try and find out . . . thank God she's found it . . . No. Not quite. You see, she's pointing her toe even more with her leg in a backward position?

'Now let's listen to her dialogue,' Tortsov half whispered to Rakhmanov. ' "I stand before you as a criminal." I *stand*. But she's lying down. Let's hear some more. "I'm weary. My feet hurt." Does lying down make her feet hurt? Have they gone to sleep because she's stretching them back?

'Try to guess what state she's in, what she's living inside, if her words contradict her actions. An odd kind of psychology. She's putting such concentration on her legs there's nothing left for what her tongue is doing. What contempt for the words and her inner task. What kind of creative state can we call that?

'It's been replaced by the vanity of a siren. She has her own "lady's mode" and she can't get away from it. The elements of which it is composed all have the same "ladylike" origin. What do we call what she is doing? Stock-in-trade? Representation? Ballet? A living picture? None of them. It's "public flirting",' said Tortsov, finding the name at last.

4.

There was a notice on the blackboard summoning us students to a rehearsal at the theatre.

I froze when I read that and my heart beat wildly in anticipation of my debut, in a real theatre with real actors.

In today's class Tortsov explained the purpose and educational meaning of our forthcoming appearance. He said:

'The theatre has called on you not for its own benefit but for yours, not because it needs you, but because you need it.

'Appearing in crowd scenes is only one phase in the school's programme. It's still a class, but in public, in a full-scale production and subject to the conditions of pubic performance.

'What for us actors is a rehearsal, for you is a *preparation for appearing in public*. A show for us is a *public class* for you.

'At school, within our own four walls, with no outside audience, we indicated what you will feel, in time, when you appear in public.

'That moment has now come and you are now to experience onstage what we talked about in school.

'Only when you have done that and you have felt the correct state onstage for yourselves will you be able to appreciate what we have taught you.

'Indeed, where, other than in the theatre, and in public performance, can you learn the practical meaning of the "*magic if*", of concentrating on the stage itself, amid all the distractions of a show? Where, except in front of a packed house, can you feel genuine "public solitude", or the importance of communication with the objects? Where, if not onstage, faced with the black hole, should you create, develop and maintain the correct creative state? So, after a great deal of work, designed to develop the elements of the creative state, we proceed to establish that state onstage and in public performance.

'And that is precisely what all the work we have done has been leading up to.

'I haven't talked about this earlier because I didn't want to summarize things that hadn't been done, and confuse you, but now *post factum* I can explain that *the first year of the syllabus is entirely devoted to establishing the general (or working) creative state and reinforcing it on the stage itself, in front of an audience, in performance.*

'We start with that because any further work is unthinkable without a genuine creative state.

'I congratulate you on reaching this *new phase* in our programme, that is, *appearing in public so you can establish and reinforce the right creative state while onstage.*

'You will go on perfecting and correcting it throughout your career.

'So it is all the more important that now, right at the beginning, your debut, you should point your work in the right direction. But that demands exceptional concentration and honesty from you and an ability to analyse your invisible feelings and actions. We, your teachers, can only guess what they are and if you tell us lies and not what you are feeling, so much the worse for you. You will be the losers in the long run. You will lose the opportunity to judge what's happening to you properly and Ivan Rakhmanov and I won't be able to give you any useful advice.

'So don't hinder us, help us every way you can to understand what's going on invisibly inside you in performance.

'If you really concentrate each and every time to go out under the lights, if you are enquiring, honest, if you approach your creative state not with dead formality, but with conscious enthusiasm, if you give them all you've got, if you apply everything you've learned in school every time you go on, you will gradually master the right creative state.

'We, on our side, will ensure that your public appearances are well organized in the educational sense. But you must understand that in work like this you have to go all the way. You have to see it through to final victory when the right creative state becomes normal, natural, habitual, biological and the wrong state, the actor's state, becomes a total impossibility. Take me, for example. Once I'd discovered and consolidated the right creative state, I couldn't make an entrance without it. Only then could I feel at home. In the actor's mode I was an outsider, unwanted, unnecessary and that was death. It takes a lot of force to get me out of the general, working mode, it is so firm after the enormous amount of work I've done in crowd scenes and long experience as an actor. Now it's almost impossible for me to transfer the object of attention to the other side of the footlights, where the audience sits, and not relate to the actor opposite me. It's even more difficult to stand in front of a thousand people without creative tasks. If that happens, I'm as lost as any novice.

'Try to develop the right *general, working creative state* as soon as you can and make it permanent.'

'In other words try to be permanently creative, be a genius,' Paul commented.

'No. Anyone who knows how to work and finish what they start can develop the right creative state.

'I'm not denying it's difficult but *nature* will help if she is convinced of the biological truth of what you are doing. Then she takes over the creative initiative and, you know, she is incomparable as an artist.

'The creative state that is in harmony with the demands of nature is the most stable, truthful mental state for an actor. Follow the path we've shown you here at the school, go hand in hand with nature and you'll see how quickly you grow as artists.

'If only I had the time and opportunity,' Tortsov mused, 'I'd go back to doing crowd scenes, small parts, I'd be an extra. I got the best part of what I know about my psychotechnique from crowd scenes.'

'Why from them and not leading roles?' I asked.

'Because you can't stumble through a leading part like a student, when it carries the whole play. You have to play them to perfection. They need the accomplishment of a master, not a student's first efforts.

'In a lead role, the responsibility for the whole performance rests on you. You have a duty towards them and they present tasks which are beyond half-trained actors like you. They arouse tensions and strain. And you know where that leads. It's different in crowd scenes or small parts. Your responsibility, your creative tasks are far less important. You perform them in the middle of a large group of people. You can try out a few exercises with impunity, only of course if they don't run counter to the Supertask and the Throughaction of the play.

'These exercises can be done, and are most beneficial when done before an audience. That's why I attach such importance to public classes.

'Besides, what we do in class does not always happen and is not always heard onstage in the theatre. That, too, evokes the necessity to nurture our classes and activities in public.

'What school in the world can provide a situation like that for its students to learn in. Just think: a thousand people out front, the full panoply of a production – décor, furniture, props, stage dressing, lighting, sound effects, costume, make-up, music, dance, the excitement of appearing in public, the backstage code of ethics, discipline, teamwork, an interesting, rich theme for creative work, a compelling Supertask, the Throughaction, the direction, a beautiful script that will teach you to speak beautifully, a building with a good acoustic to which you have to adapt vocally, attractive groupings, staging, moves, living actors and dead objects to make contact with – a whole set of reasons for exercising your sense of truth, etc., all the things that are going through my head right now . . .

'The theatre provides all this so we can use it in school, in our systematic daily classes. What an embarrassment of riches! Do you want to throw this opportunity to become real actors away, or do you prefer the usual actors' search for a "career", "stardom", running after the best parts, the highest salary, their obsession with tawdry success, popularity, cheap glory, publicity and the satisfaction of their own petty, corrupt vanity?

'If you do, get out of the theatre fast because is can ennoble you or it can degrade and poison you. Use what the theatre offers for your own moral growth, not for your moral decline. Actors grow as they come to know more and more what art is, and decline when they exploit it. Get everything you can out of your forthcoming public appearances and first develop the right, general (working) creative state and do it quickly.

'Hurry while there's still time. You won't be able to think about study once you've become professionals. You can't play lead roles without the right creative state. Then you can end up in an impossible situation, which can only lead to stock-in-trade and clichés . . .

'But heaven help you if you treat this new phase in the syllabus, appearing in crowd scenes, as going through the motions, without the sustained, exceptional concentration it requires. You'll get the opposite, undesirable, destructive result. You'll develop an actor's creative state, faster than you can possibly realize it, and that is dangerous and damaging to creative work.

'Appearing in public is a double-edged sword. It can be helpful and harmful in equal measure. And it's more likely to be harmful for the following reason.

'Public appearances have their own ability to secure, fix what happens onstage in the artist's mind.

'Events onstage stick in the mind longer. Every action, every moment of experiencing performed in a state of creative or other excitement is more deeply imprinted in your Emotion Memory than when you are in the intimacy of daily rehearsal or at home. So, both your successes and your mistakes are driven home by the presence of an audience. Stock-in-trade is easier than art, clichés are easier than re-experiencing, so they root themselves in a role more easily in performance.

'It is far more difficult to hold on to and encourage things which lie hidden in the depths of the soul rather than on the surface, or, to put it another way, it is easier to fix the body than the life of the human spirit of a role. But when this life of the spirit sees the glare of the footlights and a vast audience tells an actor by the way it responds which are the true, strong, human, biological moments of experiencing and helps him believe in them, then public appearance is a fixative that locks the successful living passages in an actor's mind for ever . . .'

5.

I've no idea what kind of rehearsal we had today. The actors did a dry run, without make-up or costume.

But we students had to get into costume and make-up as if it were a show. We also had the full décor and props.

The atmosphere backstage was serious, probably as for a show – wonderful order, quiet. Everything on or offstage went like clockwork. The scene changes were done without noise or shouting, by signs and handclaps.

The general air of seriousness was catching and moving. My heart beat wildly.

Rakhmanov brought us to the stage in good time. He made me walk up and down a line he drew like a guard in the provincial prison and stand guard in the places he indicated.

Leo and Igor rehearsed the 'prisoners' walk with barrels of water' from the prison and back several times. They had to do it simply, discreetly so as not to distract attention unnecessarily.

'Remember, you're a background character. So don't put yourself forward, don't stick out! Especially in the big scenes. Your actions should be cautious. Justify that caution. Right!'

It's very difficult to move without drawing attention to yourself. You need to glide. That means you have to focus on your legs. But as soon as I started thinking about them my sense of balance went and I couldn't move properly. It looks as though I'm stumbling. I stumbled like a drunk, I couldn't walk in a straight line, I swayed and I was afraid I'd bump into the fence with the gates in it and knock it over. That made my acting and my movements tense and unnatural. I was so upset I was breathless and had to stand still.

As soon as I stopped observing myself my concentration was shattered. It started looking for new objects. It was drawn to the wings. I watched what was going on there closely.

There were some actors in make-up standing watching me.

'What does he think he is?' they were probably saying.

After talking in whispers and pulling me to pieces, one of them laughed and I went bright red because I thought their laughter and scorn were directed at me.

Rakhmanov arrived and made signs for me to walk up and down the line.

But I couldn't move. My legs seemed paralysed. I had to pretend I hadn't seen him.

Meanwhile Leo and Igor made their entrance from the prison with their barrels. I was supposed to help them through the gate but I forgot. I also hid them from the audience and ruined the scene. They had to push their way through a half-open gate so that Leo almost dragged the set down on him.

What a disgrace!

It was only at the end of the act that I understood that I had failed because I was blocked by muscular tension.

.. .. 19..

I took part in the first performance of the revival of The Burning Heart and tried to rid myself of tension.

I managed to do that quickly and effectively in my dressing room before our scene but as soon as I entered the nervous atmosphere of the wings with all the noise and disturbance, because I was aware of my responsibilities my mind and body tensed. And this happened despite my self-control which was better than before.

After a fierce struggle with tension I managed to focus attention on my body and look for harmful cramps. But focusing isn't enough, you have to maintain concentration on designated objects. That's easy to do in the calm atmosphere of school, but amid the excitement and distractions of the theatre this first, essential phase in the major process of muscular release turns into one long dog-fight between you and the unnatural conditions in which you work. It lasts the whole time you are onstage. You can overcome tensions, discover and release them for a short time. But once you go on to the third phase, consolidation, justifying your creative state, you come up against all the wilfulness of the imagination. As we all know, it should create the set circumstances, the ideas which justify your physical state. But it is difficult to come to terms with the imagination in the nervous atmosphere of a show. It is nervous, difficult and workshy. If you can hold firm and be true to yourself, so well and good. But that doesn't always happen, and if you don't control your imagination, it undermines, confuses your concentration and all the other elements of the creative state.

So, today's performance was entirely taken up with the third phase in the process of muscular release, that is, the inner *justification* of the general physical state.

While working, I recalled how I lay on the sofa last year with Mr Kat and adopted a difficult, stretched position. Once I'd sensed and defined the points of muscular tension, I could release them, but not completely. I needed a 'justification' to complete and consolidate the process, and 'justification' required Given Circumstances, Tasks and actions. I didn't theorize, I thought: 'There's a huge cockroach on the floor. Quick, squash it!'

So saying, I squashed the imaginary bug and justified a difficult pose by my action, automatically freeing my body from excess tension. Had I not done so I couldn't have reached my imaginary victim. Nature and the subconscious did what technique and the conscious mind couldn't.

Today, I decided to repeat this procedure in front of a packed house and started looking for an appropriate action. It had to be dynamic. Where could I find it in the inactive state of a soldier on sentry duty?

I began to think. Think, I ask you, with all the distractions there onstage. For me it was a kind of heroism.

1. I could walk along a straight line and, out of sheer boredom, move my feet in time to music or to the rhythm of poetry I was reciting in my head, I decided.
2. I could walk the line and glance sideways at the entrance to the Mayor's house where all the petitioners were standing in line.
3. I could be totally self-effacing, or march conspicuously, so that everyone could see how well I was doing my duty, and how ready I was to 'grab and hang on to' anyone who fell into my hands, at any minute.
4. I could furtively smoke a pipe round the corner of the prison fence.
5. I could get interested in a beetle crawling up the prison steps. I could play with it, put it under a twig or a blade of grass and make it crawl out from under it, lift it and wait for it to spread its wings and fly away.
6. But, most probably, I would simply lean against the fence, without moving, warm myself in the sun, like a soldier thinking of his village, his home, his family, ploughing and harvesting.

Performing all these actions directly, sincerely, brought nature and the subconscious into play quite normally. They would justify what I did and release the excess tension which was preventing genuine, productive, specific action.

But I had to contain myself and remember Rakhmanov's injunction not to divert attention to myself to the cost of the leading actors by being overactive.

That's why I had to choose a passive task: to stand, warming myself in the sun, thinking about my own affairs. The more so, since I had to consider what I was going to do next. So, I leaned against the fence, basked in the rays of the electric sun and thought.

But I had nothing ready in my head for the role.

How was such a blunder possible?

How could Rakhmanov send me onstage with nothing inside? Unforgivable!

If Tortsov were in Moscow he wouldn't tolerate this hack-work.

I didn't waste time. There and then, onstage, I created the soldier's past, present and future.

'Where did he come from to take up his post?' I asked.

'The barracks.'

'Where are the barracks? Down which street?'

I answered the question immediately, using my knowledge of the streets in the outskirts of Moscow.

Once I had represented the way to the barracks, I started thinking about life in the soldiers' quarters. Then I represented the little soldier's village, his hut, his family. The hot rays of the stage lights warmed and blinded me pleasantly, like the sun. I even had to cover my eyes with the peak of my cap.

I felt good, at peace, comfortable, I forgot about the world outside, about performing in public with all its conventions. I could let my mind wander in front of a thousand people. Up till then, that had been unthinkable!

.. .. 19..

I spent all my free time thinking about my soldier and putting together the Given Circumstances of his life.

Paul and I helped each other because he had a non-speaking role as a petitioner to the Mayor in the same scene.

I got right inside the life of a provincial police officer and mentally performed all his duties: I went with the Mayor to the arcade and the market, carried the wares he'd confiscated from the merchants, took every bribe I could and snaffled whatever was available.

Now I had other, more dynamic wants which I defined as, 'Grab it and hold on to it'.

But I was afraid of altering my earlier actions without permission. Anything new had to be done carefully, discreetly, so as not to distract attention from the other actors.

But that wasn't the only reason for my uncertainty. My problem was that my soldier had split into two opposite characters: on one side a gentle peasant, a family man and, on the other, a policeman whose aim in life was 'grab it and hold it'.

Which was I to choose?

What if I presented both? The gentle peasant in the barracks and the policeman at city hall? That way I killed two birds with one stone. I create two roles and played on two levels. On the second, easier level I get used to the creative state. On the first, more difficult level I work on eliminating the obstacles in public performance.

As I was thinking, leaning against the fence, Khlinov's drunken band burst onto the stage. His comic posturings and pirouettes, his drunken bravado towards the Mayor began.

The actors riveted me with their playing. I stood there open-mouthed. I stared at them, laughed heartily forgetting I was onstage. I felt wonderful and forgot all about my little muscles. They took care of themselves.

Then, once the noisy scene was over and the lovers' lyrical declarations began, I stood for a long time with my back to the audience and really admired the open landscape on the backdrop. And I remembered Tortsov's favourite expression: 'When we concentrate on our side of the footlights we forget the other.' Or, in another version: 'When we're fascinated by what's onstage, we're not fascinated by what's off it.'

I was happy. I felt victorious. I rejoiced that I could forget about myself in front of a packed house in unnatural performance conditions. Even Tortsov says you mustn't lose yourself in the role. That means there's nothing wrong in behaving as yourself.

The only embarrassing thing was that I was playing myself and not the character. But then Tortsov says we must not lose our own self in a role.

So, it's all about interesting objects and tasks on our side of the footlights.

How could I have forgotten an important truth I know so well from school?

It would seem the theatre requires us to re-learn, re-understand, re-experience things we know in life onstage in a public show.

I'm ready to re-learn what I know. Practical work, the stage and the conditions in which I work, the many-headed monster, the audience, the yawning jaws of the black hole, shall be my teachers.

There it is, gaping wide, beyond the forestage.

Yes, there it is! Why didn't I notice it earlier. I recognize the fear, the terrible feeling of disappearing down its bottomless gullet, and its ability to enslave and fascinate an actor. No matter what I do, no matter how I turn away, I can feel its presence. 'I'm here!' it shouts at me all the time, insolently. 'Don't forget me any more than I'll forget you.'

From that moment on, I couldn't concentrate on the backstage world, the background, and everything that was happening onstage. Only the foreground remained, the monster with its gaping, bottomless gullet and I remembered the panic I felt in our first show. I was stunned, I stared into the dark, distant abyss and my muscles went so tight I couldn't move.

If the monster, the proscenium arch overwhelms me when I'm in the background, what would happen if I were in the foreground in the very jaws of the black hole?

At the end of the act, as I was passing the prompt corner an unknown, the stage manager for today's show, fell on me.

'I'll put in the daybook', he said, 'that in future we'll reserve a seat for you in the front row for all performances of The Burning Heart. You can admire the actors better from out front than at your sentry post, upstage. You'll be better off out front.'

'Bravo, bravo,' a pleasant young man said to me. 'Your soldier is an artistic touch in the general picture. Such simplicity and openness.'

'It was good that you were relaxed and felt at home. Very good,' Rakhmanov said to me. 'But where was the "magic if"? Without that, there's no art. So find it, create it and watch everything that's happening onstage not with Kostya's eyes but the eyes of the character in the play.'

? ....

.. .. 19..

Ghastly!

Today I had to replace a sick extra at the last minute and stand guard by the Mayor's house, right downstage, in the jaws of the proscenium arch.

My heart stopped beating when I heard the director's decision. I couldn't refuse. My protector, Rakhmanov, wasn't in the theatre.

I had to obey.

Placed right downstage, in the monster's jaws, by the black hole, once again I felt swamped.

I saw nothing that was happening in the wings and understood nothing of what was happening onstage. All I could do was stand, leaning discreetly against the set and try not to pass out. It was ghastly!

Sometimes I felt as though I were right in the lap of someone in the front row. My hearing became so acute I could hear the odd sentence spoken in the orchestra stalls. My vision became so sharp I could see everything that was happening in the house. I was drawn to the other side of the footlights and had to make an enormous effort not to turn round and look at the audience. Had I done so, I would have lost the last vestige of self-control and stood by the footlights, looking terrified, rigid all over, helpless and on the verge of tears. I didn't turn out front once, but kept in profile, yet I could still see what was happening out there – every moving face, every flash of the binoculars. I felt they were all focusing on me. I had to keep an even closer watch on myself. Once again, I was so conscious of my body it went stiff as a board. I felt pathetic, powerless, ridiculous, inartistic, a blotch on an otherwise beautiful picture.

I was so ashamed! The act seemed to last for ever. I was so tired. I decided to hide discreetly, efface myself, so I used a stratagem and concealed myself behind one of the downstage wing-flats. The black hole seemed less terrifying there.

At the end of the act the stage manager again stopped me at the prompt corner and said:

'It's difficult to see the actors from the wings, too. You really should go out front!'

I got pitying looks onstage. Perhaps I was only imagining it but the fact is no one bothered with a pathetic walk-on like me, which is what I felt like for the whole evening, and still do as I make this entry.

What an insignificant, talentless, so-called actor I am.

.. .. 19..

I went to the theatre today as though I were going to be hanged. The thought of the sheer torture it would be to stand in the monster's jaws, down by the proscenium arch, gave me the horrors.

'What's my best defence?' I asked myself and suddenly remembered the saviour, the 'circle of attention'.

How could I have forgotten it and not used it first of all when I was making my debut?

I felt as though a weight had been lifted from my heart and I'd been given impregnable armour before a bloody battle. While I was making up and dressing I went through all the exercises we'd done in school on circles of attention.

'If I derived indescribable pleasure from public solitude in front of a dozen students, what pleasure it will be in front of a theatre full of people,' I said to myself.

'I shut myself in the circle and try to find a point to concentrate on. Then I open a little window in my impenetrable circle, take a quick look at what is happening onstage and perhaps risk a glance at the audience and come back home fast, into the circle and my solitude,' I thought temptingly . . .

It all happened rather differently. A surprise was in store for me – good in one way, bad in another. The stage manager told me I was to go back to my original position upstage, by the fence.

I was too scared to ask why, and obeyed without question. I was glad, because I'd be more at ease and quieter up there but, at the same time, I regretted it because I felt that the protective circle would help me conquer my fear of the black hole.

I was happy upstage, in the circle, I felt at home. I shut myself in it. Sometimes I enjoyed the feeling of solitude in the presence of an audience, sometimes I watched what was going on outside it. I admired the acting and the distant landscape and boldly looked at the black hole. Today, I had the impression I could even have stood right downstage, in the monster's jaws, thanks to my protective circle.

But I had to control myself and remember Rakhmanov's parting remark that I wasn't supposed to live my own life but that my experiences should be filtered by the 'magic if' and the set circumstances of the role. Without that to occupy me, I would have fallen apart today.

How can I tell where my own life and my other life begins, once I've adapted to the character's circumstances?

For example, I stand there, looking into the distance. Do I do that as myself, as part of my own life, or as the character, as part of the soldier?

First I had to decide whether a peasant would enjoy the view in the same way we do.

'What is there to enjoy?' he'd reply. 'A view's a view.'

A peasant enjoys it, loves it, as he does the whole of nature in all its shapes and forms, without sentimentality. So, the action I'd chosen was wrong for the soldier. He would be more likely to look at the wonderful view with detachment, as something very familiar.

And how would my soldier regard Khlinov's drunken mob, how would he relate to them and their riotous behaviour?

'The nobility are having a good time. Shameful. They're sozzled. My God, they are!' he says disapprovingly, only smiling at the most comic moments. He's seen it all before.

That means my action wasn't right for the soldier or the peasant.

I recalled the advice Tortsov gave us: 'When you play a peasant remember how simple, natural and direct they are. They walk or stand because they need to. And when their leg itches they scratch it, and when they want to blow their nose or cough they do no more than they have to, then drop their hands and wait, quite still, for the next essential action.'

So, my little peasant soldier should only do as much as he has to. That means the role needs great control and restraint. Inaction is typical of my peasant soldier. If he has to stand, he stands, if the sun shines, he pulls his cap down. And that's all, nothing else.

But is this stillness, this total absence of action, theatrical? Theatre requires dynamism.

If that is so, I have to find action in inaction, standing at my post, when playing this soldier and that's difficult.

It's even more difficult not to lose myself in the character but to find me in him and him in me.

All I can do in that case is be myself in the given circumstances.

I try to create these circumstances and put myself in them.

Stillness, immobility, is one of them, I realize, and take it on board. As far as possible I will stand still.

But that's not me, Kostya. I can't just think about nothing. There's nothing to say my little soldier can't daydream while he's standing still. He's human like me. The question is, must I have the same thoughts and dreams as he?

No. That would be like a straitjacket and would create a lie and destroy truth. I'll dream my own dreams. I'll limit myself to the general character of his thoughts. They must be quiet, undisturbed, very private.

.. .. 19..

I wasn't myself today, I couldn't focus properly. Still, I did manage to concentrate and didn't fall victim to the black hole. True, I wasn't concentrating on what the role needed but on what I needed. I was experimenting on myself the whole time. I worked on establishing the right creative state. I wasn't acting in a show, I was doing exercises in public.

I was happy that despite being off-colour I didn't succumb to the bogey-man, the black hole.

That's an undoubted success and a small step forward.

.. .. 19..

'Should I give up the theatre? I'm hopeless. I can't have any talent,' I thought after today's bad performance. A whole year of study, a whole row of performances as an insignificant walk-on and the result is practically nil!

'So far, I've only applied a fraction of what I've learned in school. I forgot the rest as soon as I walked onstage.

'What have I used in *The Burning Heart*? – muscular release, objects of attention, tasks and physical actions and, just recently, circles of attention and public solitude . . . and then what?'

And there's still the question whether I really mastered the little I did try out onstage. Did I use my psychotechnique to reach the crucial creative moment, when our biological nature and subconscious are brought into play? If not, all my work and, indeed the 'system' has no rhyme or reason.

Even if I did, what I've managed so far is only the most insignificant, elementary part of what we've done in school and I still have to master it in practice, in difficult performance conditions.

When I think about it, I lose all energy and faith in myself.

Emotion Memory, communication, Adaptation, the action of the psychological drives, the inner line of a role, the Through-action, the Supertask, the inner creative state, bringing our biological nature and the subconscious into play.

All these are much more difficult and complex than anything I've done so far. Worst of all, I'm taking my first steps alone, with no help at all. Recently, when I complained about this to Rakhmanov, he said: 'My job was to throw you into the water. Now swim and get out of it as best you can.'

No, that's wrong! That's an improper use of force. Tortsov wouldn't approve.

There's another, better way, which is to turn the performance into a public class for us students. It won't harm the ensemble. On the contrary, it will be a help, because the students will work better, closer to the spirit of the play, under the supervision of a teacher.

Why are our tutors so unconcerned with our public appearances? Why don't they use the abundant opportunities to create an entire school in front of a theatre full of people, in a show.

We have all kinds of ways of doing that. Just think what an embarrassment of riches we have – a class in make-up and costume, with a complete set and props, in a well-organized performance with model order backstage, that can be taken by the best directors and supervised by the best teachers. I know, I feel that only in such public 'classes' can we develop the right inner creative state. It can't be done in the intimacy of the school with a dozen fellow students present, whom you don't think of as an audience at all.

I also maintain you can't develop the right inner creative state away from the gaping jaws of the monster, the black hole. We can't call what we achieve in our apartments or in class the creative state but a *home*, a *school* state.

It's obvious to me now that to achieve the creative state, you need a *performance*, the black hole and all the trials of appearing in public. We need a special psychotechnique to help us overcome the innumerable obstacles inherent in public performances. We need to confront these difficulties every day, twice a day, in every scene, every act, every evening. Briefly, we need a long public class every day. Once all the difficulties of appearing in public have become familiar, habitual, normal, they are part of my life, when I can't make an entrance without bringing in the right creative state, when 'difficulties are a habit, and habit is easy and what's easy is beautiful', then I can say I have created the right creative state and use it to my advantage.

All I want to know is: how many public classes do I need for this and to achieve the 'I am being' and bring my own biological nature and subconscious into play?

.. .. 19..

Today I had an appointment with Rakhmanov. Pasha and I went to his home, where we had a long talk. I explained all my ideas and plans.

'That's very commendable,' Rakhmanov said, very touched, 'but . . .'

He frowned, pulled a face and after a pause said:

'There's always a negative side to everything, unfortunately. Yes, negative. There are many moments of danger in public shows.

'No doubt about it, it would be very useful for you to meet audiences and extend what you've learned in school in practice. If a conscientious, talented student has worked a whole year, day after day, according to biological law, then the right creative state becomes second nature. That's wonderful. I shout bravo and I applaud. The more often you appear onstage in the right creative state, the stronger it becomes.'

After a pause and a mysterious look at both of us, Rakhmanov leaned forward and, as though in secret, asked:

'But what if that's not the case? What if, night after night, you create the wrong state the whole time? That would be something! . . . A talented student turns into an unattractive poseur. Then, the more you appear in public the more dangerous and destructive it is. Because it's not a school but a public show. And do you know what a public show is? It's something!

'When you're acting for your family or at school for the other students and you're successful, that's fine. If you flop, that's bad. Success is fine. A flop is bad. Yes! It takes five, six days, a month to get over it. That's when you're acting at home or at school for your mother, your father and your fellow students!

'But have you any idea what it's like to succeed or flop before a packed house in a real show . . . You'll remember it to the day you die! . . . Ask me about it . . . Go on . . . I know. The secret, the one thing to note in all this, is that every good performance with real experiencing or bad with clichéd posturing, is fixed in the mind. The lights, the house fix emotion memories, the Given Circumstances, right and wrong Tasks and Adaptations.

'The bad makes a deeper impression than the good. It's easy to be bad, so the bad is stronger, tougher. The good is more difficult, unattainable, and takes more time and trouble to fix.

'This is how I sum it up.

'You acted well, truthfully today because all the elements were working properly and you were able to apply them onstage as in life. Give yourself a plus point. Only one, mind you!

'Tomorrow, you won't be in control of the elements. They'll do just what they want, your technique will be weak, so give yourself ten minus points immediately. Ten!'

'So many?'

'Yes, that many! Because bad acting habits are stronger. They eat you away like rust. You bet! They don't fight the conditions in which we work, no, they fall in with them. They teach you to surrender to clichés. That's easier than fighting them, uprooting them, swimming against the tide as we do in our theatre. It's so easy to give in to clichés, to let yourself be carried along. That's why you have to give ten good performances after one bad one. Ten, at least! You bet! Only then can you get your creative nature back to what it was before that appalling hammy performance.'

After a short break he continued:

'There's another "but" as regards students appearing daily.'

'What is it?'

'Something bad. Very bad. The backstage world is a bad influence on students. Success, applause, vanity, conceit, bohemianism, hamming, self-importance, bragging, gossip, scandal-mongering, plotting are all danger-ous temptations, very dangerous, for young, green novices.

'We must immunize you in every way possible before we expose you to our infection. We must inoculate you.'

'How do you do that?'

'Creative, artistic principles, a true love of the art in yourself not your-self in art, personal awareness, strong beliefs, good habits, and under-standing of what teamwork implies, a sense of loyalty, these are all power-ful antidotes. We need them, lads, otherwise we get infected.'

'Where do we find them?'

'In school. Take them as you train. It's important . . . Or here, in the theatre, in the business, in practice . . . Teach the young to defend them-selves against danger.'

'Do it then. We're ready!'

'You need an organization, people, teachers onstage, in the dressing rooms and in the green room.'

'But we can try it without all that. We know what we are doing, that's why we came to you. We're not children, we're adults, we made up our own minds. Tell us what to do and we promise to do it, without question. The stage and our dressing room and nowhere else. Trust us.'

'That's right, the stage, the dressing room and nowhere else. I like that, I applaud. Why? I'll tell you . . .

'The most dangerous moment backstage is the long wait before we go on and the periods of idleness between entrances. You can't leave the theatre or do anything. Actors often appear in the first and last acts only, with a couple of lines in each. Hours of waiting for a few moments onstage. You just sit and wait. The hours offstage mount up. Right up. The time isn't empty. It's spent in empty chatter, gossip, scandal, telling stories. And so, day after day. That's terrible. It's the ruin of back-stage life.

'The strangest thing is that these unwilling idlers always complain they haven't any time, that they're terribly busy and can't work on their craft. They should use the time they're waiting in the wings.'

'Maybe working on your craft would distract you from the perform-ance?' I commented.

'And aren't gossip and stories a distraction? Aren't they?' Rakhmanov said, leaning towards me. 'When can you work on your technique if not between acts and entrances? Singers vocalize, musicians tune their instru-ments and actors should do exercises. Our creative instrument is more complex than a violin. We have hands, feet, a body, a face, wants, feelings, imagination, contact, adaptation – a whole orchestra! We have more than enough to tune.

'Actors don't have time to train in the mornings, so they should correct the elements of their creative state – concentration, imagination, a sense of truth, contact, etc. – in their dressing rooms, singly or in groups. They should work on speech. They should perform actions without objects logically, sequentially, truthfully. They should pursue these activities to the point where nature and the subconscious come into play.

'Briefly, they should go through the whole first year of study. They should continue to grow and develop every day of their career.

'And here's something else. You are appearing in your own free time, after working at school. When are you going to study? I ask you, when?'

'Between entrances,' Paul and I said in unison.

'Too tiring. Yes, indeed! It would be reflected in your school work,' said Rakhmanov doubtfully.

'No. We're young.'

'You don't get paid for it, you know.'

'We should be paying for this luxury, a public class, no less!'

'Congratulations, boys,' said Rakhmanov, touched once more by our enthusiasm.

'But what will the other students say?' He was suddenly pensive.

'They're as free to sacrifice their time as we are, if they want to,' we replied.

'Not all of them,' Rakhmanov countered. 'They're not committed enough. And if you two don't behave intelligently, that's it! That would be a great disappointment.

'I'll get it in the neck from Tortsov because of you,' he sighed. 'He'll ask me why I'm using students as walk-ons. He'll say that first you have to work through the entire programme intelligently and then put it into practice. You can't combine work and study. Learning comes first. Walk-ons don't have time to complete the whole programme. Walk-ons can only be half-educated, journeymen players. And we need fully educated, trained actors. Practical work should be done at the right time and they'll have ample time for that later, the rest of their lives, but our time is limited to a full four-year course. That's complex.

'That's what Tortsov will say. He'll give it to me,' Rakhmanov sighed again.

Following today's discussion, it was agreed that:

1. Rakhmanov will obtain permission from the stage manager for Paul and me to alternate the roles of the soldier and the beggar in *The Burning Heart*.
2. He will oversee our work and take us to the stage.
3. He will obtain permission for us to appear in other acts of the play.
4. Paul and I promise to do our school exercises on the 'system' between acts and entrances.
5. We promise not to go anywhere outside out dressing room and the stage.

With that our discussion ended.

29

THE 'SYSTEM'

It is customary to call what we have been studying 'the Stanislavski system'. That is a mistake. The strength of this method lies precisely in the fact that no one conceived it, no one invented it.

We are born with this creative capacity, this 'system' inside us. Creativity is a natural need and you would think we would be incapable of creating other than correctly according to the 'system'. But, astonishingly, we lose what nature has given us the moment we walk onstage and instead of creating we posture, counterfeit, playact and represent.

The sense of being forced, subjected to something alien can only disappear when actors have made something other than themselves. The 'system' helps this process. Its magic 'ifs', Given Circumstances, inventiveness, lures make the other its own. The 'system' can make you believe in things that do not exist. And where there is truth and belief you have genuine, productive, specific action, experiencing, the subconscious, creativity and art. Things that are thrust on an actor, or suggested to him must not only be absorbed by him but made his own. It was only then that Stanislavski suggested it was possible to speak about acting as a valuable art, only then, for him, was the existence of theatre justified.

The 'system' is a guide. Open it and read. The 'system' is a reference book, not a philosophy.

The 'system' ends when philosophy begins.

Work on the 'system' at home. Onstage put it to one side.

You cannot act the 'system'.

There is no 'system'. There is nature.

My concern throughout my life has been to find ways to get nearer what we call the 'system', that is, to the nature of the creative act.

The laws of nature are the laws of nature. The birth of a child, the growing of a tree are manifestations of a single order. It was essential to establish a 'system', i.e. the laws of nature, because in performance conditions nature is violated and her laws broken. The 'system' re-establishes them, brings human nature back to normal. Embarrassment, stagefright, false traditions destroy nature.

On one side the technique of getting the subconscious to start working. On the other, the ability not to get in its way once it does.

The 'system' is not a cookery book. When you want to prepare a particular dish, you merely look in the contents, look up the appropriate page and that is that. But that is not that. The 'system' is not an all-purpose reference book but a whole culture which must be cultivated and nurtured over many long years. An actor cannot learn it parrot-fashion, he can make it part of his own flesh and blood, make it second nature, become one with it forever so it transforms him for the stage. The 'system' has to be studied in its separate parts and then grasped as a whole, so as to understand its overall structure and fundamentals. Only when it fans out before you can you come to an initial understanding of it. This does not happen in a day . . .

Appendices

ADDITIONAL MATERIAL

ADDITIONAL MATERIAL FOR THE CHAPTER 'ACTION, 'IF', 'GIVEN CIRCUMSTANCES'

'The failure in the last class of the "madman" when it was repeated occurred not only because you didn't set yourself any new tasks for that day and repeated old procedures. Another mistake crept in. There was neither sequence nor logic in your actions.

'To understand what I mean, remember how you built the barricade.

'The first time you did the improvisation you dragged a huge bookcase right across the door. One couldn't even open up a crack and get a stick through to push the bookcase away.

'Today you did the improvisation differently. You didn't push the bookcase right up against the door but some distance from it. There was nothing to prevent the madman from half-opening the door and slipping through the gap.

'The rest of the heavy furniture wasn't packed close together, there were gaps between. That weakened the barricade.

'Consequently you couldn't believe your efforts, your actions, were purposeful. Without belief what you are doing onstage cannot come alive.

'Varya gave us another example of purposeless, illogical action. Why did she need the lampshade? Was it really to defend herself against the madman? Why did she drop this wretched shade and make such a thing about picking it up?

'And you, Kostya, why did you need the album with the plush cover. That, too, is a hopeless means of defence. You must agree that your actions were purposeless, *illogical*, they had no credibility.

'I can recall quite a few moments when your actions the second time *lacked sequence*. These had no credibility either. They didn't enable you to have truthful feelings while you were acting either. Quite the contrary, they were a block to spontaneous re-experiencing.'

'I don't understand a thing,' sighed Vanya.

'Yet it's quite simple. Imagine you want something to drink and you pour some water from a carafe into a glass. You take the carafe and tilt it over the glass and the heavy stopper falls out, smashes the glass to smithereens and the water runs all over table instead of down your throat. That is the result of a *lack of sequence* in your actions.'

'Oh!' said Vanya thoughtfully.

'Now let's take another example. You go to see an enemy, to effect a reconciliation with him and have a quarrel which ends in your coming to blows.

'That is the result of a *lack of logic* in your actions.'

'I see! I really do see!' Vanya cried joyfully.

'So we know the next question is, *the role of logic and sequence in the process of psychological and physical action*.

'This is all the more important because logic and sequence are [not] *independent Elements in the creative process*.

'They are constantly interacting with all the other Elements.

'It is easier for me to discuss this each time it occurs. That means I have to split up questions of the way logic and sequence influence the other Elements across the whole study programme, as we study the constituent parts of the actor's creative psychology.

'Now, in our work on action, first we have to deal with its interaction with logic and sequence and I shall spend some time on them so that we can examine them attentively.

'In everyday life, either consciously or out of habit, people's outer and inner actions are logical and sequential. For the most part we are guided by our goal in life, our present necessities and human requirements. We respond to them instinctively, without thinking. But onstage, in a role, life stems not from reality, but from a fiction. When rehearsals start, our own human demands, vital goals, analogous to the character's aren't there already in our minds. We don't create them in one fell swoop but appear gradually after a great deal of work.

'You must be able to make imagined goals real, urgent. Actors who have not mastered the requisite inner technique find naive, primitive solutions to this problem. They give the impression that they are working with all their might towards the play's high purpose and that all their actions are performed to that end. In fact they are only "playacting the passions in the play". But you can't function or feel "as if" when you believe such self-delusion.

'If they don't believe their own intentions are genuine, in the end actors lose control of their vital, human skills, habits, experience, the workings of their subconscious, the logic and sequence of their human wants, ambitions and actions.

'Instead you find a special, specific actors' state of mind which has nothing in common with real life.

'When they have no control over their human needs actors fall apart and take the line of least resistance. They are at the mercy of the cliché and stock-in-trade acting.

'Fortunately for us we have our psychotechnique, which helps us fight the dangers I have indicated and makes us follow the path of nature.

'One of our techniques is based on the logic and sequence of psychological and physical actions. To master it you must study the nature of these actions both in yourself and in other people.'

'That means, with respect, we have to go around the whole time, notebook in hand, and put down the logical, sequential actions we've observed in ourselves and other people?!' said Grisha sarcastically.

'No, I'm suggesting a simpler, more practical method which will make you examine your own and other people's actions,' Tortsov commented.

'Which?' said Vanya impatiently.

'Calm down! I'll give you an example,' Tortsov stated. 'Kostya and Vanya, go up onstage and start some physical action.'

'What?' – I didn't understand.

'Count money, put business papers in order. Throw the ones you don't want on the fire and put the others to one side.'

'And what shall I do?' – Vanya didn't understand either.

'Watch Kostya working, take an interest in what he is doing, try to a smaller or greater extent to participate in it,' Tortsov explained.

We went up onstage and pulled the table over to the fire.

'Please give me some prop money,' I said to a stagehand standing in the wings.

'You don't need it. Play with "nothing",' ordered Tortsov.

I started counting non-existent money.

'I don't believe you!' said Tortsov stopping me as soon as I stretched out to take the imaginary packet.

'What don't you believe?'

'You didn't even look at what you were touching.'

I looked where the imaginary packet was, saw nothing, stretched out my hand and pulled it back again.

'Make it look as though you're pressing your fingers together so you don't drop it. Don't throw it down, put it down. It only takes a second. If you want to justify and physically believe what you are doing don't skimp. Is that the way to untie it? Find the end of the string. Not like that! You can't do it in one go. Usually, the ends are tied together and tucked under the string, so the packet can't come undone. It's not so easy to straighten out the ends. That's it,' Tortsov said approvingly. 'Now count each packet.

'Oof! That was quick. The best cashier in the world couldn't count old, crumpled notes that fast.

'You see the amount of realistic detail, the number of small truths we have to go into, for our nature to believe in the physical truth of what we are doing?'

Tortsov guided me physically, action by action, second by second, logically, in sequence. As I was counting the imaginary money, I gradually remembered how we normally do it, in what order and sequence.

The logical actions Tortsov suggested changed my attitude towards 'nothing'. It replaced the imaginary money perfectly, or rather, it enabled me to focus on an imaginary object. Waving your fingers about meaninglessly and counting the dirty, imaginary, used rouble notes are two different things.

As soon as I felt the truth of physical action, I felt at ease onstage.

I improvised a lot. I rolled up the string very carefully, and put it on the table beside me. This insignificant little action warmed my sense of truth and produced more improvisation. For example, before counting the packets I tapped them on the table for a long time to tidy up the edges. Vanya, who was beside me, understood what I was doing and laughed.

'What is it?' I asked him.

'That was really good,' he explained.

'That's what we call a totally justified physical action in which an actor can biologically believe!' Tortsov shouted from out front.

'So,' he summed up, 'you started with crude playacting. To escape from it you had carefully to check the sequence of the actions you were performing.

'Having repeated them a number of times you gradually recalled the sensations you have in real life, you recognized these sensations, believed in them and in the truth of your actions onstage.

'In real life all these feelings appear natural, accessible, simple, familiar to us. But onstage they are transformed into the conventions of a public performance and appear strange, distant, complex.

'Even the normal logic and coherence of the most elementary, human, physical actions betray us and abandon us. We must recognize this worrisome transformation once and for all as being regrettably unavoidable. We must fight it.

'To do that we need our psychotechnique and a certain elementary knowledge of the nature of our physical and psychological actions. That in its turn demands a detailed study of its constituent Elements.

'When actions come to life spontaneously we have to use the principle of going from the outside in. We put the constituent Elements in logical, coherent sequence and create action out of them. The logic and coherence of the parts reminds us of the truth of life. Familiar motor sensations reinforce this truth and evoke belief in the truthfulness of the actions we are performing.

'Once the actor believes in them, he comes alive. You can go through this whole process today when working on the "burning money".

'I must strongly emphasize that when moving from external technique to living, vital truth, the *logic* and *coherence* of the sequence of the constituent parts which form the action have great significance.

'You must study them, particularly since in the future we shall have to make wide use of the method I have recommended for bringing the whole to life through a fusion of its parts.'

'How are we to study them?' asked a worried Vanya.

'Very simple, put yourself in a situation in which such "study" becomes unavoidable.'

'What situation is that?' I insisted.

'The one you were in today when you were working on "counting the money". It was the situation created by working with "nothing", i.e. with imaginary things.

'In our jargon we call it *"actions without objects"*.

'So you can deal with it quite consciously, I will do my best to explain the secret or practical meaning of this work to you by a very clear example. I shall have to resort to a paradox.

'Kostya and Vanya! Repeat "counting the money" only this time don't do it using "nothing" but with real things which the props man will bring you.'

We repeated the improvisation.

When we had finished Tortsov turned to the students who were watching in the auditorium and said:

'Did you notice, can you remember how Kostya took bundles of notes one after the other from the table, separated them, counted them and laid them out, etc.?'

'More or less,' the students answered lazily.

'Only more or less? Is there much you forgot?' Tortsov pressed them.

'It's not that we forgot, we just had to try really hard to remember,' some of them explained.

'It was hard to follow,' others said.

'And you, the two actors, can you remember all the individual moments in the actions you have just performed using real things?' Tortsov asked Vanya and me.

I had to acknowledge that we didn't think about each physical action, or about each individual moment but that they just happened, automatically.

Then Tortsov turned to the students watching in the auditorium again with the question:

'Now try and remember and tell me: what form do your memories of the previous performance of "counting the money" – *without real things, with "imagined things"* or, in other words, with "nothing" – take?'

It was apparent that 'actions without objects' got through to the house and stuck in the memory more cleanly, clearly, vividly.

'And you, the actors, what have you to say?' said Tortsov turning to Vanya and me once again. 'What memories do you retain of counting the money using "actions without objects"?'

The line of concentration we had established during the exercise on physical actions had stuck in our minds with greater clarity, logic and coherence.

'What conclusion can you draw from the experiments with or without real things?' Tortsov asked us.

We couldn't answer.

'This,' Tortsov explained, 'that in exercises using real objects many of the constituent moments in the proposed action escape our attention without our knowing, there are lapses of concentration. They are carried out mechanically, as habit, without thought. These lapses prevent us learning the nature of the action we are investigating. There is no possibility of placing the constituent parts of the action in logical, coherent order. It also complicates the work of establishing a line of concentration which we should always observe and be guided by.

'When using "actions without objects" things are quite different. Then momentary lapses, when concentration is impossible, simply disappear.'

'Oh! Why is that?'

'Because in exercises with real things, mechanical actions, habits, skills, and the regrettable tendency to lapses of concentration, which is associated with them, disappear. Freeing yourself from this tendency to rush allows you to establish a continuous line, logically, coherently, one which is whole, filled with memories of the individual, constituent moments out of which the action is constructed.

'In other words, imagined objects force us to be fully aware of things which are done mechanically in life.

'What, finally, is the secret of the technique of "actions without objects"?

'In the logic and coherence of its constituent parts. By remembering and combining them you establish true actions and the familiar sensations associated with them. They are credible because they are close to the truth. You recognize them from memories of your own life, from familiar physical sensations. All this gives life to an action that has been created in parts.'

At the end of the class Tortsov urged us strongly to pay full attention to the exercise with 'actions without objects'. He charged Rakhmanov to keep a watchful eye on these classes and to report on how they were going.

'You know, these exercises are to the dramatic actor what vocalizing is to the singer. That focuses the sounds and "actions without objects" focuses the actor's concentration,' Tortsov assured us.

'I have been on the stage for many years but I still work on "actions without objects" for 15–20 minutes a day even now and I know their nature and their constituent parts. I perform these actions in a variety of set circumstances.

'Judge for yourselves the technique I have developed in this area. If only you knew how much an actor needs it, how much it helps him.

'It is too soon to explain what this help is. For the moment you understand me with your intelligence, but understanding of that kind overloads the brain. Let us wait for the time when you will understand what I am saying with the whole of your psychological and physical being.

'For the moment, take me, so to speak, on credit and work full out on "actions without objects" but under Rakhmanov's personal supervision.'

.. .. 19..

Today Tortsov said:

'In the experiments on action with and without things which we conducted in the last class, you noticed that work with "nothing" achieved much greater clarity, finish, logic and sequence than the same actions performed with real things.

'In life, mostly, the constituent parts of an action are muddled and blurred. Should we not therefore conclude from that, that the clarity of which we are speaking contradicts what happens in real life?

'Instead of answering that, I will share with you one of my most precious aesthetic memories, which I have borne with me for more than forty years.

'When Eleonora Duse came to Moscow for the first time I saw her in *La Dame aux Camélias*. There was a long pause in which she wrote a letter to Armand. I can remember that famous improvisation not "in general" but in all its constituent moments. They have stuck in my memory with unusual clarity, brilliance, in all their perfection: I loved that improvisation as a whole and in its parts, as one loves a magnificent example of the goldsmith's art.

'It is a great pleasure, to relish a work of genius in this way. But it doesn't happen in life! Grisha will object.

'Not so. It does, but rarely. I have more than once admired the neat way a peasant woman performs her chores. I have admired the finish a hand gives to his work in a factory, how the black maids clean a room in America . . .'

Additional Material for the Chapter 'Communication'

Tortsov said:

'When a dog comes into a room it observes those present to see what mood they are in. Once it knows, it selects an object with which to communicate, goes to it, rubs against its legs or puts a paw on its knee, to draw attention to itself. When it has got what it wants, it goes down on all fours and fixes its eyes on the person it has chosen with the goal of establishing communication.

'I pass on. A similar process can be observed among insects or sea animals. Living creatures creep out of their holes and study the world of nature around them for a long time. They use their feelers to identify the things and living beings that cross their path. Only after careful investigation do they undertake some kind of action.

'And don't people do the same? When we go into a room we observe the people in it, try to understand their mood. We select an object, go to it, attract its attention, start to probe with our eye, to understand its mood. Using transmitting and receiving, we, as subject, on our arrival, establish contact with the object we have selected.

'In different circumstances the same creatures – dog, sea creature, man – suddenly appear, capture the attention of those present and establish some form of contact.

'As you can see, there are various phases in this process, which all living beings must respect. They are created out of Elements which always follow in the same logical and sequential order.

'Actors are the only exception. They want nothing to do with nature's laws. They are not interested in the prevailing mood when they make an entrance. They do not select an object with which to communicate. They do not look for its eyes, feel its heart, nor sense its proximity.

'The stock-in-trade actor has decided once and for all that his object is *the audience*, out there in the stalls. He knows in advance where he should stand and what he is supposed to do and say. They do all this not out of personal human need, but under duress, in obedience to the author of the play or the director. They are incapable of making someone else's feelings, impulses, thoughts, words, actions, their own.

'That is why stock-in-trade actors do not walk into a set but strut "the boards" and use them to show themselves off to a packed house.

'How are we to avoid this distortion of human nature, which we find in theatres right across the world?! How are we to escape from the crude artifice, the stock-in-trade acting and clichés, which these actors try to substitute for nature's own spontaneous, subconscious creation in accordance with her own laws?

'We have one of the means to hand – our psychotechnique.

'Things which happen spontaneously in life, onstage often need the help of our psychotechnique which teaches us to perform all the moments, phases in our organic processes, including *communicating*, consciously. When this process does not begin spontaneously, subconsciously, we must construct it consciously out of separate moments, in logical and coherent order. If we do that not as form, externally, but by using inner promptings, transmitting and receiving, we are on our way towards the truth.

'But woe to you if you go counter to natural law. That will inevitably lead you down the path to lies, playacting and the stock-in-trade. We shall continue to study the laws of nature diligently and will be vigilant to see they are being obeyed. This injunction is equally relevant to the process of communicating when it does not occur spontaneously, subconsciously.

'So far we have been studying the individual moments of the process of communicating. Now we have to look at making longer phases out of these moments and the process of turning these longer phases into actual organic contact.

'The moments in which an actor enters a room, a set, examines those present, *finds his bearings, selects an object*, constitute the first stage of the organic process of communicating.

'The moments when he approaches the object with which he wishes to communicate, *attracts its attention* using very obvious actions and unexpected intonations, etc., constitute the second stage in the organic process with which we are concerned.

'The moments of *delving into the soul* of the object with the antennae of the eyes, preparing the other person's soul to receive the thoughts, feelings and eidetic images of the subject in the easiest freest possible way, constitute the *third phase* of organic contact.

'The moments of *transmitting one's mental images to the object* using irradiation, the voice, words, intonations, adaptations: the desire and intention to oblige the object not only to hear and understand but to see with the inner eye what the communicating subject is transmitting, and how he is doing it, constitute the *fourth phase* in the organic process of communicating.

'The moments in which *the object responds and there is a mutual exchange of transmitting and receiving* constitute the fifth *phase* in the organic process of communicating.

'All five phases must be respected every time communicating occurs onstage.'

'A difficult task,' I commented.

'I will show you that isn't so. Begin with the fact that the organic processes leading up to communicating are extremely logical and sequential. And logic and sequence, as you already know, lead to truth, and truth to belief and that the two together create the "I am being", stimulate the creative powers, organic nature and its subconscious.'

'It's easy to talk about the five phases in the organic process but just try and master them!' the students said.

'Let's try it out then!' Tortsov proposed. 'Kostya, go into the corridor, come back after a minute and guess what mood you think we are in.'

I was told afterwards that I was hardly out of the room before Tortsov secretly confided to everyone:

'Kostya, poor chap! He doesn't yet know he's got to leave the school because he's being called out of Moscow.'

'What? Kostya's leaving the school?' said the students, rushing up to Tortsov.

He didn't have time to answer because I had already returned to the auditorium.

There was an awkward silence during which some of the students, believing the imaginary news, avoiding meeting me directly, others, having understood Tortsov's trick, smiled and gave me broad looks.

'What the hell! What's happened here I don't know,' I said, staring at each of those present.

'Bravo! The moments of *finding one's bearings, seeking an object with which to communicate* emerged spontaneously and created the *first phase* in the process. You made strong efforts to probe the people present with the antennae of your eyes, because you wanted to know their mood. It doesn't matter whether you understood our mood or not, what matters is that you did your utmost to feel it,' said Tortsov, explaining the meaning of his trick.

'As far as *phase two, attracting the attention of the object* is concerned, I will help you do it. I am your object and you already have my attention. So, come up to me, look into my eyes and try and understand my mood,' Tortsov ordered.

I did what he asked quite easily.

'Bravo! *Phase three, delving into the mind of the object*, that's been done too,' cried Tortsov when I stared into his eyes.

'Not quite, as I can't define your inner mood,' I commented.

'That doesn't matter, what matters is that you caused an inner link with me of your own will and prepared the ground for communicating.

'Of course none of these things was as difficult as they appeared earlier and you didn't have to stimulate the vague feelings which precede communicating. That means you are quite up to this task,' Tortsov stated.

'I'm not up to it onstage, standing in front of the black hole and a packed house.'

'That's a matter of practice, time and concentration. They will help you cope with it. Once you've formed the right habit, I assure you that you, like me, will face a packed house in the way you face an object onstage, and make contact as you should, organically, with mental images, transmitting and receiving – that way and no other. Our psychotechnique will help us artificially to stimulate the normal process of communicating.'

'Yes, but what about the fourth and fifth phases?' I interrupted.

'We'll talk about the transmission of your mental images to the object and the establishment of mutual contact in the next class.'

.. .. 19..

Class began with objections from Grisha, which, surprisingly, were timely for once, as they led us to the main theme of today's class.

'Look, excuse me,' he began critically, 'you were pleased to say that when playing a role you must go through the logical and sequential stages of communicating. But look here! Before you can communicate you must have something to communicate with! Don't we have, first of all, I mean, to start this process and then create something to transmit?'

'That could be so. Let's put the question to a practical test. Let's all go up onstage into "Marya's sitting room".'

We did as we were asked.

'What improvisation shall we play? Let us do a normal class, here, in "Marya's sitting room", the same as we normally do. The only change will be that this time an "Inspector" will unexpectedly arrive. Grisha will play him for us. So, he should go into the wings and the rest of us should get busy with some exercises. Then the inspector arrives. The actor should start by going through all the stages of communicating, according to all the laws of nature, but without any defined Tasks, without having prepared any material.'

Grisha went off into the wings. Tortsov slipped down into the stalls and hid in a dark corner while we students started doing exercises in muscular relaxation.

After a long wait Grisha came on as the inspector. As required by the laws of nature he stood in the doorway, looked at all of us (*got his bearings. Phase One*) looked for Tortsov. When he couldn't find him, he reflected as to which of the students he would speak to and took a long time to select an object. Finally he went up to Vanya (*selecting the object*).

'I need to speak to the director of the school,' Grisha said to him.

'Can't be done! He's not here. He's busy.'

For a moment Grisha was disconcerted by Vanya's unfriendly tone but then sharply changed his own tone and that obliged Vanya to pay more attention to him (*getting the object's attention. Phase Two*).

This time it was Vanya who was disconcerted. There was quite a long pause during which both stared at each other (*delving into the mind of the object. Phase Three*).

'Be kind enough to inform the director', Grisha insisted, 'that I have arrived at the behest of a congress which is now in session. Inform him we have been made aware of some irregularities in your school.'

The 'Inspector' tried to describe as graphically as possible what had occurred in the imaginary meeting, in which Tortsov had apparently been condemned for his teaching methods, which were an assault on the will of the student (*transmission of mental images. Phase Four*).

Vanya refused to budge. A quarrel ensued (*Communication. Phase Five*).

The student's behaviour enraged the 'Inspector' and he asked Vanya who he was, how he came to be at the school, by what right he spoke so rudely to a person in authority, who his parents were.

At that moment Tortsov shouted to Grisha:

'He's your son. He ran away from you and from your tyranny when he was young.'

After some moments' confusion, Grisha continued questioning but at the same time prepared to deal with the new idea that had been imposed on him.

He played it splendidly. Taking this unexpected encounter with his son into his calculations as an actor, Grisha began a flowery sermon on caring attitudes towards young people and children. He spoke of parental duty with much false sentiment. The more lofty his pompous speech, the more ludicrous his situation became afterwards when it was revealed that he was the despotic father and Vanya the victim of his paternal tyranny.

The 'inspector' comically extricated himself from his difficult situation and, to general laughter, fled from the class and from his own son whom he had just recommended should be loved and cared for.

When the improvisation was over Tortsov said:

'You must acknowledge that Grisha and Vanya initiated and completed the process of communicating according to all the laws of nature and that this was done without the prior preparation of inner, psychological material which is necessary for communicating.

'Grisha started to look for this material at the end, after the process was complete. Just remember, the actor playing the inspector came onstage with the sole intention of establishing communication with one of the people who were there. He was given no storyline, no Tasks, if you ignore one "if", i.e. the title and function of the inspector.

'Having chosen Vanya as his object, Grisha established contact with him. As soon as the bond had been created, inner and other kinds of material were needed to keep the process going.

'At that critical moment I stopped to see what was going on in the minds of the people in the improvisation.

'Do you realize that initiating contact is a powerful spur to an actor's creative powers? It seeks help from its inner elements and sets them working one after the other or all at once.'

'Why?' asked an agitated Vanya.

'Because there can be no contact without the participation of all the Elements. Can you communicate with a living person without inner and outer actions, without creative ideas and Given Circumstances, mental images, without focusing your concentration properly, without an object onstage, without the feeling of truth, without belief in that truth, without the state of "I am being", etc.?

'Communicating onstage, bonding, linking requires the participation of the whole of the actor's inner and outer mechanism.

'That's what happened with Grisha. His creative mechanism, stirred by the process of communicating, naturally, spontaneously set to work. Imagination suggested new material to him, new set circumstances, tasks, emotion memories. Impulses to action appeared spontaneously. All this happened logically and sequentially. The section with the quarrel between Vanya and the "inspector" and the questioning, emerged in this way, spontaneously, out of the creative momentum. This section helped develop the storyline of the improvisation.

'Doesn't all we have seen demonstrate the fact that actors can begin their creative work directly with communicating, without prior preparation of inner and outer material which is essential to this organic process?

'If actors manage to complete all the moments leading up to communicating logically and sequentially, in accordance with the laws of nature, if they feel the truth of what they are living and doing, if they believe in the genuineness of what is happening, if they succeed in creating the state of "I am being", then their creative nature and the subconscious set to work. Creative momentum, logic, sequence, create new imposed circumstances, tasks and actions and, out of them, the storyline of the improvisation to be played.

'That's not all. Our experiment showed that when we start the creative process directly with communicating, without a fixed theme we can not only create this theme but we can justify, bring alive, a storyline given to us by someone else.

'That's what happened to Grisha.

'At a moment when his creative powers were in full flight, when he thought of questioning Vanya to keep contact going, I suggested my own version of the continuing development of the improvisation to him. He gratefully accepted my suggestion about his son's running away from the family home. My story helped Grisha to extend the process of communicating which had already begun.

'As an author, I suggested my variation to him at the very moment when his creative psychological mechanism was particularly receptive to any new tasks and set circumstances because he had included all his inner elements in his work.

'This is another demonstration of the fact that creative work can begin with communicating and can even, thereafter, create psychological material to be transmitted to others.'

.. .. 19..

Grisha's intervention in today's class didn't create confusion either but on the contrary introduced questions to which Tortsov gave detailed answers.

This is what happened.

Grisha persisted in his worried objections.

'Even the writer often doesn't leave room in the script to prepare for the process of communicating. He goes straight to final stage,' he explained.

'You are evidently talking about bad writers. No need to waste time on them.'

'No, Griboedov, you know, isn't a bad dramatist, but he makes the same kind of mistake. For example, Chatski's entrance in the first act of Woe from Wit. He rushes in and without first finding his bearings, without using the antennae of his eyes, starts to communicate.'

'Yes. That's what bad actors do. They rush onto the stage as if it were a bullring. They don't give Sofya a single glance, don't find their bearings, but throw themselves on one knee, like a ballet dancer, emote theatrically and declaim:

' "It's daybreak! And you're up! I'm at your feet!"[1]

'But good actors don't do that. They stop in the doorway, find their bearings in a flash, aim at their object, i.e. Sofya, go quickly up to her, as so as to capture the beloved girl's attention even more strongly, go down on one knee and probe her eyes with their own.

'After this all the stages of the process of communicating are gone through, all of them justified by the text. For example:

> Happy? No. Yet look me in the face.
> Surprised. No more. What a reception!
> As though I hadn't been a week away,
> As we both had met but yesterday
> And bored each other to distraction.
> No hint of love. A fine one you!

'These words are written so that Chatski can explore Sofya's heart,

> A hundred leagues I've rushed, for five
> And forty sleepless hours, scarce alive
> Without a soul to keep me company,
> Fall after fall, through storm and snow
> And this is the reward for my brave show!

'These words describe Chatski's mental images, which he conveys to Sofya.

'Later on, according to the text, the process of communicating begins.

'So, you wrongly blame a fine author for breaking the laws of nature and, in particular, of the process of communicating.

'All great poets, dramatists, men of letters, like Griboedov, take full account of the demands of human nature.'

'Look, excuse me, but I can show you good plays in which, when the curtain goes up, the process of communicating isn't in the preparatory stages but is fully developed,' Grisha persisted.

'Because preparation occurs with the curtain down.'

'But that isn't in the play, you know.'

'And that's why the nature of the human being/actor, its laws, logic and sequence, our psychotechnique require it. You can't bring up the curtain until the preparatory process has been gone through. Actors cannot possibly start to act.'

'And what about Nemirovich-Danchenko's play *The Value of Life* which starts at the end, i.e. with the suicide?' Grisha persisted.

'In a play like that the actors must not only prepare to communicate but write down and experience the whole play, before the curtain goes up.'

We had to finish the class early as Tortsov had a show that night.

The Actor–Audience Relationship[2]

1.
IN THE WARDROBE DURING AN INTERVAL

ACTOR: What does it mean? I was weeping and the audience was stone cold?

DIRECTOR: And the other actors who were with you onstage, were they weeping, too?

A: I don't know. I didn't notice.

D: You mean you weren't aware whether you were conveying your feelings to them or not?

A: I was so worried about the audience I didn't notice the other actors. I promise you, I was acting with such fire all I thought of was me and the audience.

D: So why were you onstage?

A: What do you mean, why was I onstage?

D: You went onstage to communicate with the characters the author had given you. What other reason could an actor have for going onstage?

A: What about the audience?

D: If you convey your feeling to the other actors, and move them, you can rest assured that the audience will be gripped and will not miss the slightest iota of your feelings, but if you don't even convey them to your fellow actor, standing next to you, how can you expect an inattentive and noisy crowd sitting twenty rows away from you to feel anything? Think less about the audience and more about the other characters standing next to you.

A: I think the actor is there first and foremost to perform for the audience and not for his fellow actors who have already had enough of him in rehearsal. Authors give us their works so that we can convey them to the people.

D: Don't demean our art. Are we mere go-betweens, intermediaries between the writer and the audience?

We, too are creators.

Does acting mean saying the lines and conversing with the audience?

We live our lives onstage mainly for ourselves because we want to live the character's feelings and are able to convey them to those living onstage with us, while the audience is a bystander. Speak loudly so they can hear you and stand where they can see you but for the rest forget them and only think about the characters in the play.

Actors should not try to take interest in the audience but the audience should take interest in the characters.

The best way to communicate with the audience is through contact with the other characters.

2.
THE LIVING *OBJECT*

'But look here, please, I'm sorry, you can't treat the audience with total disregard,' Grisha protested.

'Why do you assume that I do?' Tortsov wondered.

'You tell us not to look at them or take notice of them. So, in the end, you know, the actor forgets he is onstage, and says the words, you know, wrongly, or behaves in such a way that is only proper in the privacy of his own home. I'm sorry, you just can't do it!'

'Do you think that's possible?' asked Tortsov, instead of giving an answer.

'What is possible?'

'To stand in the full gaze of a thousand people and forget they are there?' Tortsov asked. 'That's just a fable for amateurs and irresponsible theorists. So, don't worry. You don't forget a thousand people. They remind you they are there. You can't get away from the auditorium. It's a powerful magnet. And, however hard you try to get away from it, you'll keep thinking about it. Much more than you should.

'Do you know what your fears remind me of? My eight-year-old niece who is mother to a whole family of dolls. She's very much afraid that her lessons with her governess will distract her from her duties as a mother.

'I also heard a story about a person who had lost his mind and was so afraid he would fly away up into the sky that he roped himself to the earth.

'And you are afraid to give yourself fully to your role and fly off into the creative spheres, and so try in every conceivable way to strengthen your ties with the audience. Rest assured, they are strong enough already. Just as the force of gravity prevents you from flying off into the skies and keeps you on the earth, the audience will never let you out of its power but will always lure you to it however hard you try to break free and give yourself to the role.

'Why be so worried about something that just can't happen?

'Better take a ballerina or an acrobat as an example. They're not afraid of flying up to heaven, on the contrary they know the laws of gravity. They spend their whole lives learning how to get off the ground even if it's just for a minute and fly into the air. And you, too, should learn how to get away from the audience, even for an instant. After long, hard work you might succeed to give yourself fully to your role, but only for moments here and there.

'So stop worrying uselessly about something that is as inevitable as the law of gravity.

'To conquer the audience and capture their interest, Stanislavski in his book *My Life in Art* recommends a totally different method, the opposite of yours. He says:

' "The less attention an actor pays to the audience, the more they will be interested in him.

' "And, on the other hand, the more an actor tries to entertain an audience, the less notice they take of him.

' "By breaking free of the audience to live a role, the actor forces them to pay full attention to the stage." '

6.
ON THE ACTOR'S NAIVETÉ[3]

For the chapter on Belief and the sense of truth

Today Tortsov asked Paul to play something.

Paul wanted to test out his naiveté and so asked if he could be allowed to play a scene with a child, similar to one that had been played by an extra in one of Tortsov's productions.

'I admire your courage,' Tortsov commented and gave Paul permission to try the experiment.

He went up onstage, took the cloth from the table, which caused a cloud of dust, took the nearest piece of wood, the size of a log, and began to wrap the cloth around it as though it were a baby.

'Why are you letting it dangle and not holding it close to you?' Tortsov asked.

'So as not to rumple the cloth,' Paul explained. 'Besides it's full of dust.'

'Ah!' Tortsov said. 'Your naiveté is very calculated. You're not "fool" enough to be as naive as a child when you are being creative,' Tortsov concluded.

'Fool,' we all wondered. 'Does an actor have to be stupid?'

'Yes, if you consider Simple Simon in the folktale is a fool because of his naiveté, innocence and generosity. It is a great thing to be as generous, trustworthy, wise, calm, self-sacrificing as we know Simon is. He got his name not because he has no brains but because he is *naive*.

'Be the same, if not in life, then on the stage. It's a golden gift for an actor.

'Not for nothing did Pushkin say, "Poetry, forgive me God, must be a little foolish." '

'How are we to make ourselves naive?' I asked, bewildered.

'You mustn't, because the result would be nothing but false naiveté, the worst of an actor's faults. And so be naive in so far as it is useful to you. Every actor is naive to a certain degree. But in life he is ashamed of it and hides his natural trait. Don't ever do that onstage.'

'I'm not shamed of being naive. On the contrary, I want to reveal it any way I can, but don't know how,' Paul regretted.

'To become naive, you mustn't be concerned with naiveté itself but, on the one hand with what hinders it, and on the other, what helps it.

'It is hindered by its bitterest enemy, called the *nit-picker*. To be naive you mustn't carp and overanalyse the ideas your imagination gives you.

'Naiveté is helped by its two best friends – *truth and belief*. And so in the first instance, get rid of the *nit-picker* and then create truth and belief through your own exciting ideas.

'When you have done that, don't tear yourself apart with the thought that you have to *create* something and perform it. No. Ask yourself a completely different question; you don't have to create anything but you only have in all sincerity to make a decision and answer the question: what would you do if what you had imagined were really true? When you verify your decision, naiveté emerges spontaneously.

'So first of all find out what you can believe and exclude what you can't, and don't be too carping as was the case a while ago with the tablecloth that you thought was so full of dust you mustn't crumple it. If it's dusty, shake it, if you mustn't crumple it, find something else.'

'But what if I'm not naive by nature?' Paul asked.

'People who are not naive in life can be naive onstage during the creative process. We have to distinguish between natural naiveté and theatrical naiveté, although, truth to tell, they often go together,' Tortsov explained to the young man.

'So,' he continued after a short pause, turning to Paul, 'concentrate the rays of your attention inwards, observe what is happening in your heart, and identify what you believed in the scene you have just played.'

'I didn't believe anything, feel anything, I just postured, without any kind of thought,' Paul acknowledged.

'If that is the case, then justify what you can, believe what you can, so that you will be better able to do, with what it is easier to establish or discover the truth,' Tortsov advised him.

'I don't know where to start,' said Paul looking for somewhere to aim.

'Of course, it is better to start from the inside, without thinking about it,' Tortsov said. 'If you can't get to feeling the direct way, try an indirect approach. We have the *decoys* our imagination creates for that, and Tasks and Objects. We should always start with them.'

Paul tried to discover something inside, to cling on to something that evidently was vague. Naturally that led to forcing, and so to overacting and lies.

'When decoying feeling doesn't give results, don't force. You know that ends in clichés and stock-in-trade,' Tortsov stopped him. 'So there is nothing left but to approach feeling in another way.

'Start by observing closely everything around you and try to understand (feel) what there is you can believe, what you have to concentrate on and what you have to leave aside, in the shadows.

'For example, can you believe "Marya's apartment" is your home?' Tortsov asked.

'Oh yes! I'm so used to it, it's like my own room,' Paul answered without hesitation.

'Fine!' said Tortsov, very pleased. 'Let's press on. Can you believe that a piece of wood is a living being? Can you, and must you, believe in such a delusion?' Tortsov asked.

'Of course not,' he answered without a moment's thought.

'Good,' Tortsov concurred. 'Now, so as you don't have to think about a piece of wood any more, replace it with your *magic* "if ".

'And at the same time say to yourself: if there were not a log inside [the tablecloth] but a living child, what would I *do*?

'Let's push on. Can you believe that the tablecloth has turned into a blanket?'

'Of course,' Paul acknowledged.

'Fine,' said Tortsov happily. 'So you believe it. The tablecloth has become a blanket and, above all, wrapping the child up properly is a real-life truth in which we can believe.'

Paul began to wrap the log of wood in the tablecloth but it didn't work.

'I don't believe you,' said Tortsov. 'If that were a real-life child, you would behave appropriately, you would wrap it up, however badly, so that the baby didn't fall out of it on all sides as it is doing now and that the light didn't prevent it from sleeping.'

Paul worked away for a long time and finally produced a huge, clumsy bundle.

Then Tortsov, as he had done with me, turned his attention to every tiny detail in the physical actions, bringing them to a state of complete, biological *truth and belief*.

Finally Paul got the newborn baby to sleep.

'Why are you hiding the baby's face with the corner of the tablecloth so carefully?' Tortsov asked.

'So that first I don't see the log, that destroys the illusion, and second so that the light "as it were" can't shine in the baby's eyes,' Paul answered.

'Excellent,' said Tortsov, pleased. 'You covered a lie with a truth: out of concern for the baby's eyes, you distracted your attention from something you didn't want to see.

'In other words, you transferred your attention from something that was a hindrance to something that was a help.

'That was truthful, that was good.'

'But there's one thing I don't understand,' Tortsov continued after a minute. 'You're shushing so loudly and rocking the baby so hard it can hardly help it get to sleep. On the contrary. You're waking it up.

'There must be considerable *logical progression and intelligence* in every genuine action. Try to work in that way. It will bring you nearer to *truth* and *belief* in what you are doing onstage while illogical behaviour will distance you from both.

'Now that the baby's settled, you should either lie it down in the cot or sit quietly on the sofa and hold it in your arms.'

Paul settled himself down on the sofa and made a serious effort not to disturb it. He did it so truthfully that no one in the audience laughed.

'Why the miserable face?' Tortsov asked. 'Do you think what you are doing is a small thing? Don't be embarrassed. What you did may be modest but two "modest" things are even better and ten "modest" things are even good, and a hundred of them is excellent.

'When you perform ten simple actions onstage and really believe them to be genuine, you will be very happy.'

'Happy . . . about what . . . how?' Paul tried hard to understand, stumbling in his confusion.

'Happy in the physical feeling of truth that the actor has onstage, and the audience out front,' Tortsov explained.

'If you want to give yourself and me pleasure perform simple physical actions right through with total justification. That is infinitely more interesting than hamming up passions and squeezing feelings out of yourself.

'I can tell from out here in the auditorium that you feel good onstage. You are aware of the line of the human body and the line of the human mind. What more could you wish for you to start with?'

'All right, but it doesn't stir me,' said Paul, playing up.

'That's hardly surprising, you've made no effort to understand who you have swaddled and are putting to bed, and why,' said Tortsov. 'Use the fact that you are sitting on the sofa with the child in your arms and whisper to us (don't lose your head) who the child is, how it came to you. Without an imaginative story, your physical actions will be unmotivated, lifeless and so unable to arouse your creative powers.'

'It's a foundling,' was Paul's sudden answer. 'I found it just now outside the front door to "Marya's apartment".'

'You see,' said a delighted Tortsov. 'What you couldn't do before comes to life spontaneously. Before you couldn't think up an imaginative story, now all you have to do is justify something that exists already and feel the "life of the human body" of the role.

'So, you have established two "magic ifs".

'The first is: if it were not a log of wood but a living child.

'The second is: if the child had been abandoned.

'Is there any consideration or circumstance that makes your situation difficult?' Tortsov asked.

'Yes, there is,' said Paul, catching on. 'My wife isn't at home. I can't decide what to do with the child without her. I wonder whether or not to leave it outside a neighbour's door but that would be a dreadful pity. How am I not to appear a criminal? Prove I'm not the father, that it was not I who abandoned the newborn child, but I who was left with it?'

'Yes,' Tortsov agreed. 'These are weighty circumstances which complicate your magic if. Are there any more difficulties?' he enquired further.

'Yes and a very important one.' Paul went on digging successively deeper and deeper into the situation he had created. 'The fact is', he explained, 'that I have never held a newborn baby in my arms and frankly speaking, they scare me. They can slip out of your hands like an eel. True I decided to pick the baby up but now I'm afraid – what if it should wake up and start to wail? What would the neighbours think?

'What a hullabaloo the appearance of a newborn baby could cause in our home.

'But worst of all what if it should have the usual "accident"? I haven't the slightest idea how to change a baby.'

'Yes, yes,' Tortsov encouraged him, 'these are all serious matters, even if at the same time they are amusing *circumstances* which you must take into account.

'Nonetheless, they are details. There is something far more important.'

'What?' asked Paul, all ears.

'Did you know', Tortsov explained solemnly, 'that when you carefully covered the baby's face with a corner of the tablecloth, it suffocated and died?

'Even I as an innocent bystander in the audience feel my heart shrink at such an unexpected occurrence and feel an inner jolt. Small wonder then, that for Paul, who was part of the action, it was an even greater shock.'

'A dramatic scene occurred spontaneously. Because the human situation of a man who finds himself by chance with an unknown child in his arms is dramatic. It suggests something criminal.'

'Ah!' Tortsov reminded him. 'You've gone pale knowing that the block of wood has stifled in the tablecloth. You believed total nonsense. Do you still need *naiveté*?!'

Indeed, I thought, isn't it naive for a grown man to carefully swaddle a piece of wood, rock it, sit motionless for a long time, because he's afraid of disturbing it and turn white because he knows that the piece of wood has stifled, and believes in the truth of a nonsense and doesn't recognize it's all a story? And he does all this seriously, aware of the importance of what he is doing.

'So,' Tortsov summed up, 'this new, randomly created scene "The Innocent Criminal or the Log in the Tablecloth" should tell us that you possess sufficient *naiveté* for an actor.

'You also convinced yourself onstage that it can be invoked gradually, be made up of Bits, when it doesn't happen spontaneously, as was the case today. This process is made much easier when the seed of what you have imagined falls into the previously prepared soil of the "life of the human body".

'So,' Tortsov summed up, 'in the previous class Kostya prepared rich inner and outer soil to be sowed, but forgot to provide the seeds of the *magic ifs and the Given Circumstances*.

'Today you not only ploughed and fertilized the soil with small physical actions, truths and belief, but sowed the seeds that gave you a rich crop of experiences.'

Drafts and Fragments

TRAINING AND DRILL

Today, as usual, we spent three and a half hours on training and drill with singing and dancing in between.

As we were doing our old exercises, I felt my imagination and concentration had become more flexible and responsive.

If that's the case, then Rakhmanov's motto 'Practice makes perfect'[4] is justified.

In the last half hour initially we tried to *maintain a focal object and extend our attention span with the lights up* but not with lamps as before but *without them, i.e. with the things* in 'Marya's apartment'.

Rakhmanov would indicate something, a chandelier, perhaps. We all tried to focus on it. If the object itself couldn't hold our attention, as usual in these cases, we examined its form, line and colour. But as this isn't a very engaging activity and doesn't last long, we had to use our intelligence, imagination and powers of invention.

I said to myself:

'This chandelier lived through the reigns of Alexander I and Napoleon. Perhaps it shone on one of them during a glittering reception or a government meeting when history was made. Perhaps its fate was more modest and it served mere dignitaries, not emperors. How many beautiful ladies and gentlemen it illumined! How many brilliant, flowery phrases, sentimental verses and tearful songs it heard, accompanied by a clavichord or an old piano. How many lovers' meetings, lively scenes it witnessed.

'Then came the harsh period of Nicolas I. Who knows, this chandelier might have been burning during the secret meetings of the Decembrists[5] and then hung long forgotten in an empty house while its owners suffered far away in the snow, the north, underground, in shackles with their hands chained to a barrow.

'Time flew by and, who knows, maybe the chandelier was auctioned off to a nouveau riche merchant, who hung it up in his shop. How shocked the poor, elegant aristocratic chandelier was by the vulgarity of the society into which it had fallen.

'Was the merchant an embezzler? Did the magnificent chandelier hang for a long time in an antique shop? Its aristocratic beauty wasn't appreciated. It waited for a connoisseur. Tortsov came along and, with great respect, took it to his theatre.

'But once there it was out of his hands. It was handed over to Roubliov, Polushkin[6] and other property makers. Look what they've done to it! How its splendid shape has been ruined. Here's a bent candlestick. The bronze is tarnished. Isn't that ample witness to the tragic fate that has befallen this delicate, aristocrat amid the chaos, the Bohemianism of the theatre?

'Poor, elegant old chandelier, what awaits you in the future?

'Will they junk you? Will they melt you down to make door hinges or pot-bellied samovars?'

I was so lost in my reverie I didn't notice a new object had been indicated.

Everyone else was already concentrating on a tasteless plush album with metal corners and a chiselled nameplate.

Try to open it and you'll see a jumble of photographs the props department has pasted in. Up top, the picture of a self-employed man from the Rozgov district. The young merchant has put his uniform on for the first time and run off to have his picture taken for his descendants. How can he show his daring? He grasps his sabre, half draws it from the scabbard and turns with a fierce look towards the camera as though he were going to kill an invisible enemy. Next to him there is a photo of the Austrian emperor Franz-Josef in a striking pose. Underneath there's a man-fish with unpleasant white eyes in an aquarium. And next to the fish, the portrait of the venerable prioress of a convent. What company this holy woman has fallen into!

How do a rarity like the Alexander I chandelier and flea-market trash like the plush album fare onstage? Take a look from out here, in the auditorium and I'm not sure you wouldn't say, like Grisha:

'Get rid of the chandelier, it looks like trash. Give the album pride of place, because it looks good.'

That's what the stage does. All that glisters is not gold in the footlights. This time I forgot to switch my attention to another object.

'That's good,' I thought. 'If I haven't developed grip at least I've developed a bond.'

After the third object, Rakhmanov asked us to relate the content of our free, carefree private musings as Tortsov calls them.

On the whole, Rakhmanov praised the quality of our imaginations, merely commenting that the observers should define why, i.e. for what inner motive they are looking at the object. In other words, they need an inner task and a 'magic if' to justify it. That we didn't have.

Today we had 'training and drill' with Rakhmanov again.

'Today,' he said, 'Tortsov has a pleasant surprise in store for us. You're going to do all your old exercises to music and do them well because F. . . . . . will be at the piano.

'Stand up, all of you, and thank him for the honour he is showing small fry like you.'

We all stood up and bowed very low very sincerely.

I was so moved I decided to ask the reason for this honour. I wanted to know so I could pay more conscious attention to the exercises and do them better.

Rakhmanov's answer was brief. 'I'm not in a position to give you an answer. My job is to do what I've been told.'

Suddenly we heard someone playing Beethoven's 'Moonlight' sonata in the wings quite splendidly and a blue lamp of semi-circular frosted glass came alight in the middle of the room. It was as though it was trying to be the moon. Beautiful music and the half-light produced their effect and put us in the mood for sad reveries and thoughts . . .

.. .. 19..

'Let's go to church,' Tortsov suggested as he came in.

'Church?! What for?' We were amazed. 'And what about class?'

'That's our class, to go first to church, then to a furniture store, then to a government office, a railroad station and a market.'

Vanya got up, ready to go, but Tortsov stopped him.

'We are actors, we don't need a cab to get to these places. Sit quietly and let your imagination do the travelling. That is the world in which we artists really live, not real life.'

It took only a few seconds for most of us to feel we were in church.

'Which one?' Tortsov asked Varya who had already had time to cross herself, pray and flutter her eyelashes at some imaginary icon of Nicholas the Miraculous as he kissed his hands.

Our beauty couldn't specify which church she was in.

'In general – in a church.'

'No, "in general" has no meaning in art,' Tortsov said to her. 'You are going to church to revere some saint, not going to church in general.'

'I don't know how to do that,' Varya said coquettishly.

'We'll soon learn,' said Tortsov, calming her. 'Give me your hand,' he said amiably. She quickly did as she was asked and extended her beautiful hand to him. But Tortsov pushed it back onto her lap and said:

'Only in your mind . . . give me your hand in your mind and I will take it and we will go. Down which street?' he asked her.

'Prokovaya Street,' she replied.

'Let's go,' Tortsov said firmly, without moving. 'Don't forget to tell me when you get there.'

.. .. 19..

'Right now you're in Moscow, in school.

'I bring in a *magic* "If" and ask you: "What would you do if you weren't here but on a large liner going to America during a violent storm?" '

'What would I do?' thought Paul.

'First you'd have to bear in mind this room would be going up and down,' Tortsov said, prompting our imagination. 'We wouldn't be able to sit on these flimsy chairs . . . They would roll from one end to the other . . . We couldn't stand up either as the floor would pitch and toss . . .'

'In that case, the best thing is to get back to the cabin fast and lie down,' Paul decided.

'Where is my cabin?' he reflected.

'Let's suppose it's right down below and that to get to it you have to go through the door and down the stairs leading to the wardrobe,' Tortsov suggested.

'Right now, the floor is tilted towards the door,' Paul reflected. 'That means . . . I'm sliding towards this wall.'

'How are you going to stay there? What can you hold on to? The bed?'

'No, it's sliding down with me because of the ship's movement . . . Better sit on the floor,' Paul decided. 'You have to admit, life on board ship isn't a picnic, it's all pretty scary.'

'What would you call what you are doing now?' Tortsov continued.

'Imagining the circumstances of getting to my cabin,' Paul replied.

.. .. 19..

Tortsov was barely in the room before he turned to me and asked:

'Where are you right now?'

'In class,' I replied.

'But if you were at home,' he asked me again, 'what would you be doing?'

Before I could answer I had to feel I was in my room, remember what had happened in the morning and what would happen in the evening, all the things that had piled up and were waiting their turn, deal with my own wants and wishes, take other circumstances into account and finally decide what I should do – in this instance, visit my uncle and my cousin, Koka.

'Look!' Tortsov took a ticket from his waistcoat pocket and said: 'Here's a box for tonight's dress rehearsal at the Maly. Imagine I've given it to you . . . the whole class can go. But the trouble is Kostya has to go and see his uncle. If that were so, what would you do?' he asked, turning to me once more.

'That's easy! Go to the theatre,' I acknowledged.

'Then I'll bring in another *magic "if"* ', Tortsov reflected. 'Your uncle needs you on urgent business. He writes that if you don't go at once there'll be trouble.'

'Nonsense. That's just scaremongering,' I refused.

'In real life, perhaps, but acting is different.

'The "if" I've brought in is categorical, so the danger is certain.'

'Oh, that uncle of mine!' I burst out.

'That's enough for me,' Tortsov said. 'That exclamation demonstrates the strength, the power of the *magic "if"* over you better than any kind of reasoning.

'Now, I'll bring in one more *magic "if"* and tell you a secret – it so happens the famous Petersburg actor V. . . . . . will appear in today's rehearsal. He only has one more performance and it's sold out. So, it's now or never, today's your only chance. Make up your mind quickly. It's 7.15 already and the show starts in fifteen minutes.'

'That's cruel!' I exclaimed, no less sincerely than before.

'Remember, your uncle telephoned a second time. He wants you to go as quickly as possible.'

'I'm not playing that game,' I said decisively. 'It puts me on edge.'

'Because of your refusal you recognize *the power of the magic "if" to influence your heart and feelings,*' Tortsov said.

I have to admit that for me there was no doubt about it . . .

At the end of class, Tortsov examined our work in *training and drill*. Having looked at our exercises in *muscular release* he said:

'Now you're beginning to justify chance poses and give them meaning. They become *real actions* for you. Vanya, for example. At first, as usual, there was a certain amount of posturing but now he's beginning to pick grapes or something else.

'He gave meaning to the pose and justified it through action.'

.. .. 19..

Today, Tortsov handed us over to Rakhmanov. He demonstrated exercises for developing a physical sense of truth which we would thereafter include in our 'training and drill'.

First Tortsov drew our attention to the fact that he attached exceptional importance to these exercises. As was clear from our previous classes, our inner world is intuitively illuminated by a feeling of truth and belief. If that doesn't happen, it is achieved from without through external reflex, truthful, justified physical actions, and logical, sequential Tasks which are prompted by probable magic 'ifs', etc.

'It seems easy enough to influence our inner world using physical tasks, but we must remember that physical Tasks or actions that aren't properly justified are just as attractive and irresistible as those that are, and can have dire consequences . . .'

.. .. 19..

Tortsov gave us a series of exercises which Rakhmanov was to do with us in his 'training and drill' classes. He explained that he wasn't doing exercises on the feeling of truth for its own sake (an und für sich).[7] Truth and belief don't exist in and for themselves with no connection to the thing they justify. They are part of all our creative experiences and actions – movement, walk, outward action, voice, speech, thought, tasks, creative ideas, magic 'if'. The outer material world – painted canvas, a prop dagger – must be imbued with truth and belief in what is happening.

That's why the exercises we were given were a repeat of episodes we'd played earlier, the difference being that inner justification wasn't as strong earlier as it is now. We've always rejected any kind of playacting but not to the extent we do in our new exercises. Now we pay more attention to outer action. The feeling of truth of a physical action must be absolute.

As Tortsov said, we know that any stage action contains a certain measure of superfluous effort and affectation. That's why that tiny extra must be eliminated from all our movements and actions.

We had to repeat everything we'd done with Tortsov a hundred times with Rakhmanov. I'll discuss these exercises in detail in the section 'training and drill'.

What I'm writing today isn't concerned with the exercises themselves but with what Tortsov said about them.

First Tortsov suggested we arrange the furniture onstage as 'Marya's room'. We set about it with no precise idea. As soon as some students had put a chair somewhere others came and put it anywhere their fancy took them.

Naturally, to move the chair each of us did what was physically essential, logically and sequentially, to shift it from one place to another, i.e. we all extended our arms, closed our fingers, tensed the right muscles to pick up the object and carry it. In brief, our actions were all normal, not as in a few classes back, not the way I counted the money using thin air in similar exercises. Yet when we examined our stage actions carefully, there were an enormous number of unnecessary extras which ruined our mood and our creative state.

.. .. 19..

'I think I've told you everything I can about the feeling of truth.

'The time has come to think about ways to develop and verify it.

'There is ample opportunity for that. We shall encounter them every step of the way, since the feeling of truth appears every moment we are engaged in creative work, be it at home, onstage, in rehearsal or in performance. What the actor does and the audience sees must be filled with a feeling of truth and approved by it.

'Even the most insignificant exercise connected with the inner or outer line must be tested and sanctioned by the feeling of truth. It is clear from what I've said that every moment we are working, in school, in the theatre or at home, can be useful for developing that feeling. All we have to do is ensure that these moments are helpful, not harmful, and that they help develop and consolidate the feeling of truth, but not lies, falsity and playacting.

'That's a difficult task since it is easier to lie and sham than to speak and behave truthfully. A great deal of close concentration is required and supervision from your teachers for you to develop a solid feeling of truth.

'Get rid of lies, anything you can't yet manage, anything that runs counter to your nature, logic and common sense. They can only throw you out of joint and produce forcing, playacting and lies.

'The more frequently you allow them onstage, the worse it is for your feeling of truth which will be supplanted by lies.

'Being false and lying must not grow into a habit at the expense of truth.'

For fear of leading students into lies, Tortsov was very careful in defining the practical exercises we were to do in Rakhmanov's class, 'training and drill'. At first, Tortsov was content with the simplest, most elementary physical tasks which were familiar to us from life and from our earlier classes. For instance, he made us sit quite still, measure out the room in steps, find a object, tidy the room, examine the carpet, the ceiling, the objects, tidy up our clothes and ourselves, inspect our hands, go up and say hallo to each other, etc. Each of these very simple tasks had to be brought to life by a justifying thought. This process, as always, was accomplished by the omnipresent magic 'if'.

Tortsov was extremely exacting and demanding (but not nit-picking) as regards small and large truth. Every instant, every hint of movement and action had to be justified. Tortsov paid close attention to the strict logic and sequence of each physical task we performed.

He also demanded that the small constituent parts of the largest physical tasks should be performed clearly and not slide into each other. However, when I began to overdo the precision of my movements and actions, Tortsov stopped me, saying that smudging and excessive finish were equally harmful onstage since they create falsity.

Initially, we went through all these exercises in the neighbouring rooms – the dining room, the hall, the corridor – that is in places where we were surrounded by four walls. Of course, in those circumstances, we performed our actions simply, naturally with no playacting because we didn't feel the presence of an audience of strangers. But when we had to do the same exercises in the sitting room, with the fourth wall open to the audience, we felt the artificiality, the staginess of our situation, the need to show off and playact which is so difficult to resist.

We performed many exercises with and without objects. Tortsov attached great importance to work without objects.

Further work on the feeling of truth was handed over to Rakhmanov and his class in 'training and drill'.

.. .. 19..

Today Tortsov continued demonstrating exercises for Rakhmanov's class, 'training and drill' to develop and consolidate the feeling of truth.

He began by taking us into the dining room of 'Marya's apartment' and telling us to set the table for five people. Everything we needed – table-cloth, crockery, napkins – was ready waiting in the cupboard. We had to find them, take them out and set them. We were disorganized, so we got in each other's way. Nonetheless, after various mishaps, the table was laid. Then we were told to clear the table and put the crockery back in the sideboard in its proper place.

There was no question of lies and playacting while we did it because there was no reason to try too hard. We were in a room with no fourth wall open to reveal our actions to the audience. In a word, we behaved as in real life, where everything is true.

On the other hand, in what sense is setting the table for its own sake true? In real life, everything is done for a purpose and our actions had neither justification nor motivation. Tortsov quickly filled this gap and so the next exercise consisted of our setting the table again, justifying it with a *creative idea or a magic* 'if '.

This last was the fact that many relatives had gathered in 'Marya's apartment'. The single maid the imaginary hostess had couldn't cope with all the guests, so we had to look after them. That explained why all the students were setting the table.

Now that the task was set within a creative idea, it was more complex than before when it had merely been an exercise and so required preparation. We had to be clear as to who represented whom and how they were related to Marya, the supposed hostess, and when and why the relatives had gathered, etc. I won't describe our acting in detail, that would be to repeat familiar feelings which I've spoken about in the scenes with the damp fireplace and the mad dog[8] which we did with the curtain up and down. The difference is that this time Tortsov was much stricter as regards a sense of truth than in previous exercises. Nonetheless, he didn't have to stop us very often because, as I've said, we had no one to act to within four walls. We behaved naturally.

The exercise was then transferred to the 'sitting room', that is, to a room with one wall open for the audience to see. The task was much harder, the more so because, this time, Tortsov was extremely demanding as regards justifying every movement of the stage action. He had to stop us every minute and curb the tendency to playacting and lies which crept into our work against our will.

'I don't believe you,' Tortsov said to Igor. 'You're setting the knives and forks with unjustified haste and with a display of polish and obsequiousness which is meant for the people out front, not for us here onstage. Besides, I don't think in real life you'd be so exquisitely courteous to your sister, played by Varya. You wouldn't start bowing and scraping if you trod on her foot. And if she happened to meet you in the street when you were on business you wouldn't let her pass like a gentleman.'

We then repeated the same exercise in the 'dining room' and 'sitting room', only with this difference – we set the table without using objects at all. They were replaced by '*nothing*'.

Tortsov insisted on the same precision, logic and sequence as with counting the money using nothing. We weren't able to do the exercise satisfactorily and justify all the physical actions he gave us sufficiently. However, he didn't think we would and was only showing us work we would complete at length in Rakhmanov's classes in 'training and drill'. Tortsov handed us over to him and once again reminded us that *he considered the exercises he had demonstrated on small and large physical actions, and truth, to be extremely important, if we justified them 'thoroughly'.* We had to master physical actions and small truth completely and practise doing them simply and naturally all the time.

For the first few seconds, work on these exercises seemed stupid. Besides, I reacted badly to the pressure. Not me exactly but a 'theatrical' stranger who'd set up home in me uninvited. Personally, I really wanted to try and do the exercises but my lodger put up defensive buffers against my will and that stopped me coming to grips with my object.

My obstinate lodger obstructed my work with criminal ill-will. Like Grisha, he criticized everything and didn't give me a chance to believe naively and sincerely in the importance of what I was doing. He discredited my work. So, I see-sawed between the poles of belief and disbelief: *I believe, I don't believe.*

There were times when belief tipped the scales but then my insufferable critic secretly tipped them the other way and *I believe* evaporated.

Finally, we achieved a kind of equilibrium. Not because I sincerely believed in what I was doing, but because I got used to the struggle between *I believe* and *I don't believe.* It was boring, wearisome, but it didn't distract me.

Then Tortsov suggested an exercise on truth:

'Suppose', he said, 'you're going home with some friends on a trolley-car. It's crowded and there are strangers all round you. In their presence you start to speak dialogue quite loudly, enunciating it simply and naturally so as not to upset the people around you and make them think it's a normal conversation.'

After class today Paul and I tried this out on the trolley-car and almost pulled it off. But there were passages we couldn't justify and so we got funny looks from our neighbours. That was embarrassing. That's why we have to justify words and actions 'thoroughly'.

How awful it is when you're 'theatrical' in real life. Acting conventions seem pretentious and abnormal. You have to be absolutely natural if you don't want to appear mad.

Truth is arbitrary.

'Let's try another experiment on the effect *the truth of physical action* has on feeling,' Tortsov suggested. 'Right now, you don't want to cry, so we'll get you to remember a state in which it's easy to weep. So, I'll give you this task with the following "if".

'Tell me, what would you do if your eyes filled with tears and you were ashamed to let us see the state you were in?'

I started to rub my forehead hard as though it were the problem, not my eyes. This action allowed me to cover them with my hand.

But you can't keep that up for long without giving yourself away.

I had to find another means of concealment. I leaned against the back of a chair, covered one cheek with my hand, thus hiding one half of my face from the people sitting on the right, then took my handkerchief with my other hand and started to blow my nose, to hide from the people on the left. I had to wipe the tears from my eyes and cheeks unnoticed. But that action couldn't take long, either. I had to think of something else.

What I did was take a piece of paper from my pocket and start to read it attentively. That enabled me to hide from everyone and justify my silence by my great interest in the letter.

There were other actions of a similar kind but there's no need to go into them because my interest was aroused by something else.

My external Adaptation that hid my face from curious eyes reminded me (by analogy or association) of other, subtler, living actions related to my present task. They spontaneously helped me out. I began to blink, swallow my saliva frequently, move my tongue nervously, open my mouth to breathe more deeply as we do when our nose is blocked and we can't inhale properly. These spontaneous small actions and truth set off many other small and thereafter large truths and actions which gave me a feeling of real life and familiar sensations. I tried to interpret my state of mind and asked myself: 'In what Given Circumstances could I experience these sensations?'

My imagination ran riot, trying to find a suitable story. It tried one justification after another.

First, I imagined that the letter hiding my face, and which I was ostensibly reading, concerned the death of a dear friend. That reminded me of the shock you feel at times like that.

Using that mood as a background, my imagination painted one idea after another. For example, someone had told me that Marya had said my 'fatherly' (in quotes) attitude towards her was difficult to bear. That added fuel to the flames.

I was even more upset by the fact that Tortsov had apparently cast Paul as Othello and Grisha as Iago, thus keeping me out of the tragic repertoire.

I felt very sorry for myself. But I didn't weep over all these imaginary woes. Nonetheless they still affected and consolidated my truth and belief in my physical actions. I believed that if everything happened as in my story I wouldn't have to *behave* as I was now and that *belief* moved me to sincere emotion.

At the end Tortsov drew the following conclusion:

'*The best way to stimulate experiences of any kind is to hide your non-existent feelings from others. The truth of your adaptations and physical actions reminds you of non-existent feelings as you hide them, and they spring alive as you recall them.*

'But most actors handle things quite differently. They try to demonstrate non-existent feelings and not the physical actions which give rise to them. This is an invitation for you to lie, to force your emotions, which leads you to the stock-in-trade and to rely on clichés at the critical moment.'

.. .. 19..

Today was a disaster. Poor Rakhmanov was in tears. I would never have thought Tortsov could be so implacable. Here's what happened. We were doing 'actions without objects' during 'training and drill'.

In one of the rooms in 'Marya's apartment' Paul was reviewing what I was doing and correcting my mistakes. Grisha was doing the same thing in another room with Darya and Marya was reviewing Nikolai in another.

As for Rakhmanov, as usual he was doing the rounds, observing every one in turn. 'You learn by teaching others,' he said. So he made the students work together.

I painted a portrait of my uncle 'without objects', from memory, using imaginary paper and canvas, an imaginary pencil, charcoal and colours.

'You picked up the pencil without looking for it,' Paul said critically. 'You did it too fast. You pressed you fingers too tightly together. You can still do less . . . less. You didn't roll up your sleeves and cuffs before painting. Didn't look at the pencil, sharpen it, etc.,' Paul said to me.

.. .. 19..

Everything went wrong in Tortsov's next class. I attributed my failure to the fact that the exercise was unbelievably boring.

'How many times have you played it?' Tortsov asked in amazement.

'Twenty times, maybe more,' I complained.

'Yes, that's really a lot,' Tortsov said ironically. 'Salvini said that he was just beginning to understand how Othello should be played after the two hundredth performance. But you've not only managed to create a role in ten rehearsals you managed to make a mess of it as well.'

I blushed and said nothing.

'Study what's difficult, what isn't handed to you on a plate, not what comes easy,' Tortsov concluded.

EXERCISES AND CLASSWORK[9]

ACTING EXERCISES ON THE MEMORY OF PHYSICAL ACTIONS

1. I polish the floor.
2. I use a sewing machine.
3. I garden.
4. I wash the floor.
5. I am on sentry duty.
6. I am going to my country home.
7. I rinse linen.
8. I tidy the room.
9. I take water from the ice-hole.
10. I train the goat.
11. I catch a fish.
12. I am making a sketch and change a burnt-out lamp.
13. I water flowers and draw.
14. I am the woods in summer.
15. I reap rye.
16. I dine, take medicine for stomach ache.
17. I erase.
18. I drink morning tea.
19. I climb over a fence, shake down apples and steal them.
20. I play the violin.
21. I guard a melon patch, kindle a fire, cook a meal.
22. I work at a machine.
23. I catch birds in the woods.
24. I iron.
25. I sweep the floor.
26. I write a letter.
27. I stoke the oven.
28. I clean boots.
29. I wash the window.
30. I chop wood.
31. I paint the window in winter.
32. In summer I pick flowers in the garden, read a book, it's hot, a bee is troublesome.

33. I feed the chicken.
34. I wash.
35. I play with the cat.
36. I keep to the road.
37. I wash the dog and play with it.
38. I play the piano.
39. I draw water from the well.
40. I work in the kitchen garden.
41. I take a laxative.
42. I paddle in the water.
43. I set the samovar, wash dishes.
44. I change the flowers.
45. I cover my clothes.
46. I sharpen and clean knives.
47. I put up posters.
48. I make a garland of wild flowers.
49. We play doubles at tennis.
50. A 10-piece orchestra.

ON CONCENTRATION

Vision
1. I observe an object and discuss it.
2. I show a group of objects to the students, cover them, ask them to tell me the order.
3. I ask students to remember the place of objects in a part of the room; I ask them not to look. I change the arrangement, I ask them to explain.
4. I observe two objects, looking for similarities, differences between them.
5. I observe two people, also looking for similarities and differences.
6. I observe someone, I want to know his character for a role I'm playing.

Sound
1. I only listen to what's in the room.
2. I only listen to what's on the other side of the wall or the door, etc.
3. Two people read aloud simultaneously, some listen to one, some to the other.

Touch
1. I am absorbed in touching an object.
2. I compare the feel of two objects.

Taste

1. Define the taste in your mouth.
2. Recall the taste of a lemon, etc.

Smell

1. Sense the smell of a room.
2. Sense the smell of an object, see whether it's the same all over.
3. Compare the smell of two objects.

1. Concentrate on an idea, make a decision.
2. Become lost in memories.
3. Mirror: repeat your partner's actions, facial expression, etc.

ON IMAGINATION

1. The teacher says a few words, everyone combines them into a harmonious picture, filling it out with their imagination.
2. There are a few objects, create an imaginary picture and events about them.
3. Use your imagination in previously determined circumstances; stipulate the time, place and quality of the characters in the play.
4. Create an imaginary picture with given objects, move or change the picture, changing your ideas accordingly.

RELATING TO OBJECTS
(MUNDANE OBJECTS)

1. We take a chair and use it as a weight.
2. Change the relationship to the object as the teacher indicates: for example, my book is Ermolova's book, etc.
3. Change the relationship to the room: my own room, a museum, a factory with noisy machinery, a club, a forest, etc.
4. We buy a piano, a couch or something else, we use it and freeze in a definite pose, characteristic of the task we've been given.

ON MUSCULAR RELEASE

1. Gradually tense the body, for example from the feet to the knees, then release it.
2. Suddenly tense and release the hand, etc.

3. On cue change the position of the body, monitor tension, release and justify.
4. Tense some part of the body and while tense try to observe and listen, etc. Feel what a hindrance tension is.
5. Concentrate all your energy in your fist and try to hit the person next to you.

ON MOVEMENT

1. Walk with springy legs.
2. Sit and stand with springy legs.
3. Transfer the body from one position to another, gradually and suddenly.
4. Define a series of movements – for example, stand up, walk, pick something up, make the transitions light and clean.

ON JUSTIFYING MOVEMENT

1. On cue from the teacher suddenly alter your pose and justify it.
2. Justify a given pose in the exercise.
3. Justify a given movement in the exercise.

ON PUBLIC SOLITUDE

1. I receive a telegram about the death of my mother.
2. I wait for my brother after an examination.
3. I make a costume for a drama club.
4. I am studying my lesson, a telephone call disturbs me, a knock at the door.
5. I steal a delicacy.
6. I get a present ready for my sister before she comes.
7. I wake up, detect the smell of smoke, I discover a fire.
8. I am studying a role, my nextdoor neighbours disturb me.
    ....
10. I sew, I receive a letter about my husband who is ill on a business trip.
11. I nurse a sick friend.
12. I go home after duties have been curtailed.
13. I breakfast on the boulevard, I wait for someone I love.
14. I urgently finish work and take it to the management.
15. I search for a paper with a telephone number I need.
16. I overhear a conversation.

17. I read about the death of a friend in the paper.
18. I wait for a friend at home so that we can go to the theatre.
19. I look for a rail ticket, I'm late for the train.
20. I look for a theatre ticket.
21. I break with the past.
22. I go home: excluded from the studio.
23. I write a letter, seal it and forget to write what's most important.
24. I wait for the trolley-car in 40 degrees of frost.
25. I settle an important and urgent question.
26. I tidy the room, I am expecting visitors.
27. I go home tired after a very heavy day, I find a long-awaited letter.
28. I go to a friend's room, wait for him, read, accidentally find a letter in the book.
29. A woman alone in a room, remembering a song for a role.
30. A woman alone in a room, learning to dance.
31. Evening, as day fades, I read an interesting book, eat delicious things, a mouse scratches, I frighten it away.
32. I am bored, I look for something to do, everything slips through my fingers.
33. Holidays soon, I think about a trip and my financial possibilities.
34. I climb through the window of someone else's apartment and steal.
35. I want to take a gold chain to Togsin[10] but don't find it.
36. I go to the doctor with an imaginary heart disease, I need a day off.
37. I go to the theatre where I meet a dear friend.
38. I work but I am terribly sleepy.
39. I wait for someone whom I haven't seen for a long time and who is terribly late.
40. I go into the room where I used to live as a child and where friends live now.
41. I wait for my husband to come home from work and am anxious, I telephone.
42. I run away from my brother who is on my heels, barricade the door, hide, then sit down to work.
43. A woman buys a knitted jacket, I look it over, go and show the neighbours.
44. I become engrossed, I am late for class.
45. I wait for the bus, I go to Kilovodsk.
46. 1905, I wait for a search.
47. I am lost, I knock at the cabin, no one there, I spend the night.
48. After a concert, I dress to go home and discover that my purse and gloves have been stolen.

49. I go home and see that my ration book and money have disappeared from my bag.
50. I go home and accidentally find someone else's things in my trouser pocket. In my haste I've put someone else's trousers on.
51. I get a new suit from the tailor, which is no good.
52. I am a delegate at a formal dinner, I tidy up my one worn-out suit.
53. I knock at an apartment to deliver an urgent package, no one answers so I push it through the door and discover it's the wrong number.

ON NATURAL SILENCE FOR TWO PEOPLE

1. Two people at a newspaper stand. A looks at B ands tries to remember where he met him.
2. A has to tell B something very serious but can't bring himself to do it, B sees that A is avoiding something but can't start a conversation either.
3. A blind person at home, a burglar climbs in.
4. A communist's funeral. Outside they are singing or playing a march. A runs behind the funeral banner. B and C tidy the room. D — the communist's wife — lost in thoughts of her husband.
5. A and B, who knew each other somewhere, meet at the doctor's. Neither wants to acknowledge he knows the other and is afraid the other is aware of it.
6. In the reading room. A wants to know B, thinking he is a famous author. B is convinced A is a nuisance.
7. A has just learned something bad about B. B knows it and wonders how to justify himself. Each waits for the other to speak.
8. After a violent quarrel: A is guilty and doesn't want to approach B who wants to be reconciled.
9. A is sitting on the boulevard, the weather is good, B — a petty thief — wants to steal something from him.
10. B is sitting in the park of culture and rest, he is supposed to be meeting D. A sits on the bench, reads a paper, B wants him to leave soon.
11. Two neighbours in a room. One is studying for a mathematics exam, the other for a singing exam. This is very disturbing for the first neighbour.
12. In a railway carriage. A is going to Moscow to study, B wants to know him.
13. Two people want the same job, they know only one will get it and wait for a decision.

ON PHYSICAL CHARACTERISTICS

1. Everyone is an animal.
2. Everyone is French, English, etc.
3. Everyone is a flower in a flowerbed.
4. Everyone is a bird.
5. Everyone is a statue, for example in a museum of antiquities.
6. Recall the striking characteristics of someone you know and convey them.

ON NATURAL SILENCE FOR SEVERAL PEOPLE

1. At the dentist's.
2. At the doctor's.
3. I await the arrival of the train at the station in summer.
4. I await the departure of the train in winter.
5. A trolley-car stop, in winter, spring, summer, autumn.
6. The deck of an ocean-going liner, pitching heavily.
7. Eating a meal with friends. Everyone knows there is a mentally ill person present and would like to know who it is.
8. Everyone arrives for the first time for class at the studio. No one knows anyone, they've just taken the examination and await the results.
9. Examination at the second level.
10. A carriage in a summer train.
11. An open space with benches in the park.
12. In a second-hand shop.

WITH MUSIC

1. Isadora Duncan gymnastics (hands, feet).
2. Developing a light walk.
3. We sit, we walk.
4. We carry objects, we play with them.
5. We pass objects lightly round the circle, we pick them up.
6. We justify the music, is it at a reception, in the cinema, in a neighbour's room, we work to it.
7. Run through the whole room trying not to make the least sound. Going through the door is our object of attention.
8. Going through the whole room to conceal things from someone.
9. Use a cheerful rhythm to carry all the furniture to one corner of the

room and start to move among the piled up things as lightly and quickly as possible.

10. A crowd, try to move through it without touching one another.

ON CONTACT

(The circumstances are given, the participants find the appropriate tasks)

....

2. Two sisters. The older is giving a lesson in elementary politics to the younger.
3. Milliners at home, a customer arrives with an appropriate order.
4. The arrest of a worker in 1905.
6. Clear a room. Someone else puts it in order.
7. A rendezvous on the boulevard with passers by.
8. A quarrel between husband and wife in 1933 and, as a parallel, in 1910.
9. The reading room of the Lenin Library.
10. A general meeting on topical themes.
11. Today's trolley-car.
12. Knock at somebody's room. They are scared and don't answer.
13. An exhibition of paintings. All visitors, one manager.
14. Work as a maid or get a job.
15. 1905. A gymnast waits to meet a woman gymnast.
16. A is waiting for B at home, C arrives inopportunely.
17. Two people don't get their passports, they sell their furniture, buyers arrive.
18. Information bureau, providing answers to all citizens' questions.
19. Big argument between friends.
20. Something is lost at home. The mistress blames the maid.
21. A dress-maker, customers arrive.
22. A goes to B, delivers a letter and waits for an answer, the two don't know each other.
23. A is a well-known actor, he is invited to a concert at a workers' club.
24. A goes to B for money. B refuses.
25. Customers arrive. An ad in the paper says 'room-share available'.
26. A is reading the paper, sees a favourable opportunity to change his room for another, telephones, makes an appointment.

....

30. The office of a factory manager. They fire A and transfer B to other work.

31. A informs B of the sudden death of someone close who was ruined.
32. A goes into his friend's room but next door and makes himself at home, the woman who occupies the room arrives.
33. The student takes his work to the professor. He has absentmindedly taken half of another piece of work.
34. A is in the street. B and C suddenly grab him from behind. He thinks they are robbers but in fact they are friends.
35. Standing in line for a theatre ticket.
36. Standing in line for the dining room.
37. A famous writer in the provinces. The following people come to see him: A, about a literary evening, the essayist B, the young writers C and D, etc.
38. A daughter who is hopelessly ill surrounded by her family.
39. A goes to B and asks her to marry him, she refuses.
40. A colleague on duty asks an overworked telegraphist to give priority to an official telegram, he refuses and a quarrel ensues.
41. A male and female cook communicate in lyric feelings when work is urgent.
42. A is jealous of B and C who gave her a sweater.
43. A factory worker is informed by telegram that he has a son. He asks leave to go and rushes off.
44. Two people gossip about their lodgers.
45. Preparing a report, several knocks at the door: a telegram, newspaper, a beggar, a dairymaid, etc.

....

47. The local doctor visits a very sick patient.
48. Beginning of rehearsals: people are late, don't turn up, tell stories, madness, etc.
49. Discussion about a bonus.
50. Theatre foyer, several people are late.

....

52. Argument with the paperman who doesn't bring the papers you ordered or doesn't come at all.
53. Preparations for 8 March.
54. Studying current affairs.
55. Workers' club, preparations for the October celebrations.
56. Class for illiterates.

EXERCISE No. 1

1) Sit. 2) Go to the door. 3) Greet everyone. 4) Stand. 5) Walk. 6) Stand up, sit down. 7) Look out of the window. 8) Lie down and stand up. 9) Lie down. 10) Go to the door and open it. 11) The same, to shut it. 12) The same, to see who's there, go back and sit down. 13) Come through the door, sit, stay there for a while, go out again. 14) Go to the table, take a book, take it to the chair and sit. 15) Sit, stand up, go to the table, put the book down, go back and sit down. 16) Take this chair over there and that one over here. 17) Go up to pupils X, Y, Z. Stand or sit by Z for a while (one minute), go back. 18) Change places with pupil X. 19) Sit down with him for five minutes and talk about your work. 20) Go and pour a glass of water, drink it, go back and sit. 21) The same, only give the glass to pupil Y, replace the glass and sit. 22) Rub your face with your hand- kerchief and put it back. 23) Take out your watch, look at the time and put the watch back. 24) Hide this pencil and make other people look for it . . .

Conclusion: action for its own sake.

EXERCISE No. 2

Action for a purpose

1. Sit: a) to rest; b) to hide so no one can find you; c) to hear what's happening in the next room; d) to see what's happening outside the window, or the passing clouds; e) to wait your turn at the doctor's; f) to keep watch over a sick person or a sleeping child; g) to smoke a good cigar or cigarette; h) to read a book, a magazine or clean your finger- nails; i) to see what's going on around you; j) to multiply 373 by 15, or recall a forgotten melody, or mentally speak or remember a poem or a role.

2. *Enter through the door*: a) to visit family and friends; b) to get to know and introduce a stranger; c) to be alone; d) to hide and avoid an unpleasant encounter; e) to see and cheer someone up by your unexpected arrival; f) to scare someone; g) to see what is happening in the room unobserved; h) to meet a woman you love or a friend; i) to let an unpleasant or dangerous person in (an enemy, an evil-doer, a stranger who has knocked); j) to see if there is someone at the door or not.

3. *To greet people*: a) to greet them cordially; b) to show your superiority; c) to show you feel insulted; d) to win their good will and suck up to them; e) to draw as little attention to yourself as possible; f) on the contrary to show yourself off and draw attention to yourself; g) to show how close and intimate, what a good fellow you are; h) to cheer people up, amuse

them, liven them up by your appearance; i) to express your silent condolence; j) to get down to business as soon as possible.

4. *Stand up:* a) to hide and not draw attention to yourself; b) to wait your turn; c) to make yourself noticed; d) to stop anyone passing (a guard); e) to see better; f) to be photographed; g) to observe; h) to give your seat to someone else; i) to stop someone of lower rank sitting down; j) to express a protest or an insult.

5. *To walk:* a) to think up or remember something; b) to pass the time; to get a little exercise while a train is waiting in a station; c) to count steps, or measure out the dimensions of a room; d) to be on guard duty; e) to stop your neighbour and the people downstairs sleeping peacefully; f) to get over your impatience, rage, anxiety and calm down; g) to warm yourself up; h) to stay awake; i) to learn to march.

6. *To stand up and sit down:* a) to greet people of good standing or a lady; b) to draw attention to yourself; c) to vote in an election; d) to go out and then, after some thought, stay; e) to show your agility and style; f) to show your indolence and apathy; g) to flatter by your exaggerated attentions; h) to give a previously arranged signal in this way; i) to protest; j) to remind the guests or the hostess how late it is and it is time to go.

My relationship to the object changes according to the circumstances I and it are in. My actions arise from that.

A white shirt: 1) I am ill: I put a shirt somewhere close by so I can change into it when I perspire; 2) a white shirt I have to wear to go to a ball or the theatre; 3) I get dressed before my wedding; 4) it is hanging on the wall, I take it for a ghost (Hermann in *The Queen of Spades*[11]); 5) a magic shirt: anyone who puts it on can travel to any period in time (like Hans Christian Andersen's *Shoes of Happiness*); 6) the shirt in which Cleopatra died; 7) the shirt in which Pushkin fought a duel.

The mirror: 1) I look at myself, I think up the make-up for a role; 2) I tidy myself up before going out; 3) I look at the mirror: in it I should see what awaits me; 4) I look and see that I have aged or that I am young and in good shape; 5) a valuable antique, I want to buy it or give it as a present; 6) an inheritance, a mirror dug up in Pompeii and stolen; 7) the magic mirror from *Snow White*; 8) a large mirror in the sitting room, I am a chambermaid and tidy the room; 9) a very old mirror on which is written in invisible ink clues in Chinese characters as to the hidden treasure of the mandarins. I learned this from old Chinese books in which the characters on the mirror appear. I find the mirror in a collector's house, who didn't know the secret and didn't wish to sell it, as it was very old. The characters appear when the mirror is strongly heated;. . . .

A knife: 1) kitchen knife, table knife, paper knife, surgeon's knife, hunting knife; 2) a dagger used to kill a great man in the past or which killed many men. It is in my room and now serves as a paper knife. I bought it in an antique dealer's who obtained it after a murder; 3) a dagger which I will use to kill myself (harakiri) immediately, tomorrow, in a few days' time should a misfortune befall me (a conspiracy, a love affair, expulsion from the stock exchange, a theatrical debut) or when I've put my affairs in order (finished my memoirs, paid my debts, arranged my finances, made my will); 4) I polish it, smear it with poison, sharpen it, practise throwing it.

A letter: I am a husband, a lover, a spy, a swindler; the letter is a love letter, an anonymous letter, an i.o.u. letter of credit, a rich inheritance, a denunciation, a death threat, menaces, etc.

SIMPLE UNCOMPLICATED ACTIONS AND STATES

I wait: what does it mean to wait — for a wife, a friend, a child? They are late home. Has something happened to them? In town, in the country (they have to cross a thick wood), in the train, in car races, in a duel, in a storm at sea.

I clean my tail coat: the only one I have. I am poor and the coat is very old but is precious to me. I want to put it on to go to a gala performance. I have used my savings to buy a very expensive ticket because a young woman I am in love with will be there. Maybe I'll get a chance to meet her in her box. But the coat has stains all over (explain why, I remember where the stains come from). My white shirt is dirty or I haven't got one at all. Today's a public holiday, all the shops are shut, etc., etc.; 2) I look for a tail coat to get married in. I don't have a white tie or cufflinks; 3) I look for my coat to sell it. I need it to appear in a concert but I'm broke and have nothing else to sell and I have to eat; 4) I clean my coat and put it on and wonder how I am to steal important documents my government needs from the ambassador's (or war minister's) house where the ball is being held, or how to make the host's daughter, wife or mistress fall in love with me so that I can get the documents through them.

[*I take off and put on my overcoat*]: I take off my coat, I have just lost my job or, 2) I put my coat on to go and find a place; 3) I take my coat off in my boss's hall; 4) I go to my lover's birthday with a bouquet of flowers; 5) I go to invite a celebrity to take part in a concert or I am in Tolstoi's hall; 6) I take off and put on my coat. I am Akaky Akakevich[12]; 7) I put on my coat, put my hand in my pocket for my cigar case but don't find it; there's a newspaper there instead. I look in the other pocket and find a wallet and some letters which aren't mine. I examine the overcoat and it isn't mine. I start wondering where I could have changed it; 8) I take the coat off and look for somewhere to put it. It's a fine coat, I've wanted to have one like it for a long time but in my friend's dirty apartment which I'm visiting there's nowhere to hang it, there's dust all over the place. 9) I leave the meeting; a lot of coats hanging up but I can't find my own. Has someone taken it? I look for it.

[BY ANALOGY WITH THE PREVIOUS EXAMPLES, IN DIFFERENT CIRCUMSTANCES]

Drink coffee.
Look for my wallet.
Look for something in the room.
Tidy the room.
Get dressed.
Put papers in order.
Make the bed.
Pack a case.
Sweep.
Lie in bed.
Manicure.
Sketch something.
Sew, mend a hole.
Erase an ink blot.
Sketch, draw, throw away.
Move furniture around.
Clean clothes, shoes.
Whistle or sing.
Remember and write down expenses.
Sharpen a pencil.
Clean gloves or a belt with cleaning fluid.
Write a letter.
Look at a room which I rent.
Dilute alcohol or prepare a beverage.
Use a thermometer.
Paint walls or furniture.
Polish the floor.
Stoke the oven or the fireplace.
Warm up tongs.
Light a primus stove.

Warm up tea or a meal.
Hang up a picture or a curtain.
Prepare a room for disinfection.
Do gymnastics, expressive movement, voice exercises, diction.
Read a book.
Rehearse a role.
Arrange the room for a production.
Look at a stain.
Design a new car or plane, etc.
Close door, a window, shut, barricade yourself in.
Look for a flea, a bug, a cockroach, a mouse.
Inspect your purchases.
Wait for the landlady.
Find other people's things in your room, your pocket.
Study lessons.
Prepare a lecture or speech.
Water flowers.
Make a bouquet.
Play the guitar.
Play with a dog, a cat, a child.
Look after a child, change, wash and feed it.
Look out of the window, the door.
Overhear, listen.
Hide.
Ransack drawers, steal.
Look at a picture.
Read a letter.
Read the future in the cards.
Cut pictures from a newspaper.
Devise a menu.
Give someone a complicated multiplication.
Let someone crib from me.
Make an inventory.
Calculate your income and expenses.
Make a sketch of your room, the theatre, the street.
Sketch a plan for arranging your room for different purposes – as a sitting room, a cafe, a shop, a library, a bedroom, etc.
Sit.
Take a few steps across the stage.
Move a chair.
Read the ads in the newspapers.

Play charades, solve riddles.

I am in a hotel that was once an old castle. There are ghosts.

Arrive at the hotel; unknown town or unknown people (decide which).

You come on business or on vacation, in the night, by day, etc.

Go home. In the town or the country, to work or rest, etc.

Make a visit – in town, in the country, abroad, etc.

(In the last three exercises the actions are the same: take your bearings, make steps in different moods.)

Go through lonely places – a wood, a sudden rustling – a bear, a suspicious person, a pair of lovers. Stand still, don't move.

Find treasure in a wood.

A thief climbs through a window or over a balcony into an apartment. He is in the dark. He doesn't know which apartment he's fallen into.

Take a play, a story or tale and divide it into simple actions.

'Sleeping Beauty'

A young princess asks the wicked fairy to teach her to spin. She is bored with her toys and she is wandering secretly through her palace. She finds the fairy in a distant, half-dark room. At first she is afraid but the fairy speaks kindly. They start talking. The princess goes to her trustingly and asks to learn to spin. She begs her. She pricks herself. There is blood on her finger, the fairy disappears. The princess is afraid and runs as fast as her legs will carry her, shouting and weeping. She reaches her room and faints.

The prince is out hunting. He and his groom get lost in a thick wood. He sees rocks overgrown with moss and bushes and coming closer sees it is a palace wall. He finds a gate, unearths an entrance, he meets a soldier asleep standing up, equally covered in moss, mould and fungus. He pushes on, etc.

('The Sleeping Beauty' is an exercise in muscular release.)

'Bluebeard'.

'The Frog-Princess'.

LITTLE SCENES

1. The wrong train.
2. Going abroad, can't find the right carriage.
3. Thieves come in the night. The owners are asleep. They wake up early. There's nothing left, the thieves have taken everything.
4. Siamese twins.

5. An Egyptian mummy lies in eternal rest. Suddenly a scraping, knocking, light breaks in. People enter, etc.
6. A flood (the play The Flood).[13]
7. A smithy in England. The blacksmith, by ancient custom, has the right to marry people, and the knots he ties have the force of law. On the anvil are a veil, a cross and a testament and the young people go round it, saying prayers and singing psalms.
8. From Maupassant. An old woman is dying. A nurse is engaged for a low fee because the old woman is going to die soon. But the days pass and she is still alive. The nurse is annoyed she has been bought so cheap because she has a great deal of work at home. She decides to frighten the old woman to death. She dresses up as the devil. The old woman dies.
9. 'The Queen of Spades'.

ACTIONS (ON A PERSONAL BASIS)

1. Take chairs, a table, different objects from one place to another.
2. Look for the jewel which I secretly hid from you.
3. Count the amount of furniture and the number of small objects.
4. Clean the last speck of dust from all the table and objects.
5. Arrange the furniture and objects in perfect order in the old way, the modern way, to your own taste, so that it matches the purpose of the room.
6. Draw a plan of the room, measuring it out in steps.
7. Pour water and give a glass to a lady.
8. Water flowers and cut dead leaves.
9. Play ball. Throw an object to someone and catch it back.
10. Give a chair to a lady. Seat other people or sit down comfortably yourself.
11. Come in and greet everyone. Take your leave individually and collectively and go.
12. A knock at the door. Go and open it and, if no one is there, try to understand the mystery. If there is someone there, let them in and shut the door.
13. Close the shutters so that no light can get in.
14. Shut your eyes, turn round several times to disorient yourself and find the way out of the room or the chair you were sitting on.
15. Name the noises and smells you perceive.
16. Blindfold your partner, bring him several objects to touch so he can guess what they are and name them.

Do all these exercises not physically but mentally. Mentally transfer the action to another room you know well, either your own or a friend's.

Do all the exercises given above only for the physical task they contain, so to speak, in pure form.

As you make your entrance onstage, against your will, you are aware of other, irrelevant tasks: pleasing the teacher, wanting to carry out his orders, wanting to show off, to shine. Wanting to fulfil the task particularly well, precisely, beautifully, adroitly. Perhaps you try to exercise too tight a control which restricts your freedom and everything is forced and contrived. Or, to the contrary, you feel that today you can fulfil the task particularly successfully and that makes you pleased with yourself.

'All these irrelevant, additional tasks are superfluous, unnecessary. You have to free your physical actions from them if you wish to establish them in their pure form . . .'

'No. That's not right. You moved the chair without irrelevant, additional feelings, you carried out the actions to stop me pestering you. That was action for its own sake. That wasn't genuine action. Put the chair somewhere else *because it will be better there or to make room*. Close the curtains *so there isn't a crack showing*. Those won't be actions for their own sake but actions to some purpose. Genuine, physical actions — small, unappealing and uninteresting.

'These actions can't attract you for very long, do them once and that's enough for you. So, to embellish them, put the actions in a story, bring in "magic ifs" and then set circumstances.

'*Perform all these actions according to the following "ifs" and the set circumstances* which logically flow from them:

When?
1. If it happens *by day* (sunny, cloudy), *by night* (darkness, moonlight), *dawn, daybreak* (ditto), *evening, sunset* (ditto).
2. If it happens in *winter* (hard not moderate frost), *summer* (bright, rainy), autumn (bright, rainy).
3. If it happens in *our own time, in the 20s–60s of the last century, in the 18th century, in the Middle Ages, classical times, in prehistoric times.*
(Don't bother about what you don't know or know very little. Do this in your own person, as you imagine it.)

Where?

1. If it happens *at sea, on a lake, a river* (in the north, the polar regions, the south, the tropics). On a ship, on deck, down below, in the captain's cabin. On a big ship, a small ship, a warship, a passenger ship, a yacht, a submarine, a sailing boat, a raft.
2. If it happens in the *air* (a warplane, a passenger plane, an airship).
3. If it happens on *land,* in Russia, Germany, France, England, Italy, etc., in town, in the country, at home, in different rooms, in a hut, a barn, a cellar, at relatives or friends, strangers, in a hotel, at the theatre (onstage, in the auditorium, the dressing room), in prison, a shop, in court, a factory, a barracks, the police station, a canteen, an exhibition, a picture gallery, in the street, a square, a boulevard, in the woods, a grotto, on a crag, at the foot of a mountain, at a rail station, in a railway carriage, at the customs, at the aerodrome.

What for?

If I had to frighten, please, sorrow, tempt, tease, enrage, end, finish, entrance, enamour, evoke sympathy, win friendship, participation, indulgence, take in hand, master, send into ecstasy, interest, draw into conversation, bring nearer, approach, intrigue, grow cold, discard, put in place, merit respect, plot, teach, advise, influence, calm, entertain, amuse, make happy, take revenge, explain, threaten, annihilate, embarrass, shame, call to account, avoid, hide, sham, trick, try to understand, get at the truth.

Why (past)?

If I had duties in the past, retained pleasant, happy memories, had hopes, lost them, felt, believed, asked pardon, forgot, kept unpleasant feelings, was resentful, loved, envied.

Shut the door because it is windy.

Shut the door because there is someone unpleasant I don't wish to meet.

Shut the door to guard against intruders.

Shut the door to be alone with her.

1. Go into the room, greet people and leave, making excuses (in different Given Circumstances).
2. Give a stick or something hollow to someone and say: 'Here's a dagger, stab yourself.'

What actions and tasks make up stabbing?
a) I place the dagger in various spots. (I'm uncertain where it should

go; I consider whether to fall on it and 'I want, don't want' to stab myself); b) I imagine how my wife and children will feel when they see me dead; c) I see myself lying in the coffin.

Let's suppose I believed all these [actions]. All combined they seem truthful.

How can I get nearer the truth? By using the magic 'if', the set circumstances. They will bring what seems true alive and justify it. Create a line of physical life for a day out of many physical actions and the result is scenes and out of scenes come acts.

What is theatrical truth?

1. Close your eyes. I secretly place a coin in one of your pockets. Look for it! You find it. Once again I put a coin in the same pocket. Look for it as though you didn't know where it was. Turn the repeated action into a first action. You need a new magic 'if' and set circumstances.
2. I come in, sit and start talking to the same person I did earlier when I came into class (Samoilov).
3. Repeat what I just did casually in life: lift something, look out of the window, etc.

I want to talk to someone. I need to:

1. Attract attention prior to the conversation. To do that place myself in the circle of attention, the line and field of vision of the object.
2. Astonish, predispose, greet, convey goodwill, inner kindness (all depending on whom you greet, a creditor or a granddaughter), gratitude, wonder, enthusiasm, sympathy, love, pity, compassion, warning, concern, humour, belief, cheerfulness, thankfulness, approval, enthusiasm, ecstasy, wonder. Attract, repel, stop, push, reconcile, teach, entreat, reward, respect, bow, demean oneself, curry favour, despise, curse, slander, hate, avenge, torment, teach, reveal a secret, put in a difficult situation, swear, offend, humiliate, corrupt, seduce, flirt, win love, be jealous, envy, bewilder, calm, deride, hurry, fear, be anxious, be silent, embroil, pretend indifference, deceive, conceal, beg, demean oneself, debase oneself, boast, lie, be overmodest, shame, confuse, curse, mock, murmur, betray, censure, justify, defend, attack.

Start the metronome and undress in rhythm and tempo:

a) fast tempo of the metronome is the inner tempo-rhythm.
But do your actions to whole, half and quarter notes, etc.

Inverse:
b)   Slow tempo of experiencing to fast tempo of actions (this is to 1/8, 1/16, 1/32 notes).
c)   Varying tempo-rhythm (first this then that).

Live in a very fast inner rhythm. Live with pauses, sitting still, with slow exterior actions (not to give yourself away), during a similar slow conversation (overture to *Tannhäuser*).

Learn to maintain the rhythm with invisible movements of two fingers and toes, etc. Take your cue and behave in rhythm but then come to your senses and change externally to a slow rhythm.

Set an imaginary metronome working to various markings and tempi.

Work with a metronome. Mentally justify each metronome mark.

I'm not sitting comfortably – improve my position but in rhythm.
Write a letter, open it, close it also in various rhythms.
Drink tea.
Catch fish.
Eat.
Do your hair, greet people.
Bow.
Everything in rhythm, to music.

Go onstage. When and how to turn without unnecessary curves and turning on one's own axis.

Grouping a crowd onstage. Everyone stops on cue. They all retreat to arms' length, like a chessboard.

Keep at arms' length. Do all kinds of exercises at arms' length. Learn to make groups and fill the empty space.

'Stick' to the floor and do all kinds of expressive movements from the smallest to the largest without becoming 'unstuck'.

1.   *Eyes.* Left, right, up, down, straight ahead (justify).
2.   *Neck.* Help the eyes, left, right, straight ahead (in the distance), up, down.
3.   *Ears.* Add the ears to the eyes and neck.
      [Do] all these exercises to whole, 1/2, 1/4, 1/8, 1/16 notes.
4.   *Fingers.* Small gestures, indicating the line of vision, hearing, as additions to the eyes, ears and neck.

5. *Arm.* Ditto. The movement of the arms up to the elbows to help the foregoing.
6. *Arm.* Ditto, up to the shoulder.
7. *Spinal column.* Added help for the foregoing. First the upper part (to help the neck) then the lower part.
8. *Legs.* Stretch towards the foregoing, to help them.
   Do all this to whole, 1/2, 1/4, 1/8 notes.

Do all this particularly, in various colourings: threatening mood, desperation, affection, joy, love, hate, supplication, horror (justify).

Two people playing a duet or appearing in a play. They should be their own directors, and set moves so that their voices reach the audience naturally and their eyes and facial expressions are automatically seen.
  If the individual recitatives, arias or lines (in a play) are directed so that the person speaking is naturally positioned for the audience, or, when silent, his face is naturally visible when the other begins to speak.

1. Write down physical and other actions in different moments, moods, states, passions. The *nature* of these states.
2. For certain roles, plays, scores.
3. Warm up different approaches for each moment, bit or task and ways of fulfilling each action.
4. Several connected, chance, physical actions. Understand their nature, develop them and create the through-action and move it towards the Supertask.
5. Chess board arrangement.
6. Groups. Their structure.
7. Marble statues.
8. Exhibition of sketches for successful productions.
9. Reading [a play] role by role (history of literature).
10. Costume sketches of various periods. Select them ([and hang them] on the walls).
11. Ditto with architecture.
12. a) Contemporary soirée (reception).
    b) Ditto in [time] of war (post 1905).
    c) Pre-1905. Ditto.
    d) The 1860s. Ditto.
    e) The 1840s–50s. Ditto.
    f) The 1820s–30s. Ditto.
    g) *Incroyable*[14] The Empire.

    h) 18th c. An assembly in the time of Peter the Great.

    i) 17th c.

    j) 16th c.

    k) 15th c.

    l) 14th, 13th, 12th, 11th c.

    m) 10th c, etc.

13. Outlines for scenes, roles, plays and 'gates'.[15]

14. Describe all possible states, feelings, passions in terms of action (physical and psychological). *The logic and sequence of feeling.*

15. Ditto with physical tasks and actions. Create one major action out of small physical ones. *The logic and sequence of physical actions.*

16. *Physical characterization.* Inner, outer (behaviour, its logic, aims, and tasks).

Old age. The nature of old age. Signs and their origin (reduced movement, tempo-rhythm and the reason for it). Logically flowing actions and behaviour.

Youth. (Ditto).

Childhood. (Ditto).

Nationality. (Ditto).

Inner line – don't lose your human 'I'.

Outer [line] – show how to change your walk, gestures, speech, voice, arms, hands, the position of the legs, the torso, tempo-rhythm. Phlegmatic. Sanguine.

ENDNOTES

An Actor's Work

1 Nizhni-Novogorod, where Vakhtangov was born. He first came to Stanislavski's attention because he was a stenographer.

1 Amateurism

1 Nikolai Vasilevich Gogol (1809–1852); Aleksandr Nikolaevich Ostrovski (1823–1886), one of the few Russian writers who wrote exclusively plays; and Anton Pavlovich Chekhov (1860–1904). *Mozart and Salieri* by Aleksandr Pushkin (1799–1837), one of his four 'Little Tragedies' (1836). *Don Carlos* (1787) by the German Romantic playwright, Johann Christoph Friedrich von Schiller (1759–1805). Nazvanov chooses Act III, Scene 4 from Shakespeare's *Othello*.
2 Stanislavski uses a French word, denoting staging, to denote the overall stage action intended to express the characters' intentions.
3 It was practice, as in modern opera, for the prompter's box to be placed down-stage centre, slightly raised, and for the prompter to read the text continuously during the performance,

2 The stage as art and stock-in-trade

1 The Italian actor, Tommaso Salvini (1829–1915), toured Russia in the late 19th century.
2 *L'Art du Comédien*, Paris 1898.
3 Vera Fyodorovna Komissarzhevskaya (1864–1910) was one of the great dramatic actresses of Russia. She founded The Dramatic Theatre (1904–1909) in St. Petersburg, where she actively promoted Symbolist drama and gave

professional starts to many leading Russian directors and designers, including Stanislavski's student Vsevolod Meyerhold.

4 Nikola Vasilevich Gogol's most famous play, first staged in 1836. Stanislavski draws many of his examples from this play.

3 Action, 'if', 'Given Circumstances'

1 A tragedy in verse by Henrick Ibsen first published in 1866 and first performed complete in Stockholm in 1885.

2 Ivan Mikhailovich Moskvin (1874–1946), Vasily Ivanovich Kachalov (1875–1948), and Leonid Mironovich Leonidov (1873–1941) were leading actors at the Moscow Art Theatre.

3 Stanislavski directed the first production of The Bluebird by Maurice Maeterlinck in 1908. (Maeterlinck had written the play in 1905.) In Act I, when the magic diamond is rotated, the children in the play see inanimate objects as alive.

4 This essay by Pushkin (1799–1837) dates from 1830 and concerns a play by M. P. Pogodin from 1808.

5 Concentration and attention

1 Alexander 1 (1775–1825), who became Tsar in 1801.

2 Opera by Anton Rubinstein (1829–1894), first performed in St. Petersburg in 1885. It is based on the poem of the same name by Mikhail Lermontov (1814–1841).

3 Diogenes of Sinope (412–323 BC). Greek Cynic philosopher who lived in a barrel.

4 The oldest residential district in Moscow, near the Kremlin and Red Square.

5 Frédéric Chopin (1810–1849). Second Piano Sonata in B flat minor (1837), 3rd movement. Normally played in an orchestral version on public occasions.

6 Work by Ivan Ivanovich Lapshin (1870–1950), published in Petrograd in 1923.

6 Muscular Release

1 Opera by Charles Gounod (1818–1893), produced in Paris in 1859.

2 Jerome K. Jerome (1859–1927), English novelist, humourist and dramatist. Famous for his comic novel Three Men in a Boat.

7 Bits and Tasks

1 The names given to the children are all from classic works of Russian literature – Pushkin, Gogol, Ostrovski.

2 The reference is to the extreme Left, the avant-garde, who were particularly opposed to Stanislavski.

3 Pavel Stepanovich Mochalov (1800–1848), sometimes called the Russian Kean. He relied mainly on the inspiration of the moment. Tommaso Salvini (1829–1915), quoted earlier.

8 Belief and the sense of truth

1 A town south of Moscow.
2 Act V scene ii. Stanislavski must mean Duncan. Although Banquo is mentioned, her memories are of Duncan's murder and it is his blood that is on her hands.
3 Eleonora Duse (1858–1924), legendary Italian actress who first achieved international fame when she played *La Dame aux Camélias* in St. Petersburg in 1898. The play was written by Alexandre Dumas fils (1824–1895) in 1848.
4 Pushkin's poem 'The Hero'.
5 Puskin's poem 'Elegy'.
6 Gerhardt Hauptmann (1862–1946), German dramatist. *Hanneles Himmelfahrt* (*The Assumption of Hannele*) was written in 1893. Stanislavski directed the play for his Society of Art and Literature in 1896.

9 Emotion Memory

1 Vasili Vasilievich Samoilov (1812–1887), actor at the Aleksandrinski Theatre, St. Petersburg, who had a remarkable gift for self-transformation and was a master of make-up.
2 Théodule Ribot (1839–1916) French psychologist, whose work Stanislavski encountered in 1908.
3 Dulcinea, a character in *Don Quixote* (Part 1,1605; Part 2, 1615), by Miguel de Cervantes (1547–1616). Dulcinea is the beloved of Don Quixote.
4 Streshnovo, a small town near Moscow where Stanislavski worked, in a clinic, on the final version of this book in 1935.
5 Arkashka (Arkardy Schastsilev) and Gennady Nestchastlichev are characters in *The Forest* (1871), by Aleksandr Nikolaevich Ostrovski (1823–1886). Their names mean 'Fortunate' and 'Unfortunate' respectively.
6 At the beginning of the nineteenth century, actors were classified, by imperial decree, into specific types: Leading Man, Juvenile, Heavy, Character Old Man, etc.
7 In Goethe's *Faust*.
8 Goethe's play.
9 Maksim Gorki (1868–1936). *The Lower Depths* was his first play to be produced. It had its première at the Moscow Art Theatre in 1902.
10 Vladislav Aleksandrovich Ozerov (1769–1816), author of pseudo-classical tragedies such as *Oedipus in Athens, Fingal, Polyxenes*.
11 In Gogol's *The Inspector General*.

10 Communication

1 A character in *Woe from Wit* (1824) by Aleksandr Sergeevich Griboedov, one of Stanislavski's major roles. Molchalin is Famusov's secretary.
2 Act III scene ii from *The Bluebird* (1908) by the Belgian dramatist Maurice Maeterlinck (1862–1949). Myltyl and Tyltyl are the heroes of the play.
3 Play by Beaumarchais (1732–1797), written in 1784. Figaro has a long speech on Woman in Act V.

4   The character is General Krutitski in *Enough Stupidity in Every Wise Man* (1868) by Ostrovski (see note 3). This was one of Stanislavski's most famous roles.
5   Ophelia in Act I scene v of *Hamlet*. Stanislavski used a translation by A. I. Kronenberg.

11 An actor's adaptations and other elements, qualities, aptitudes and gifts

1   See Chapter 10, note 4, in Endnotes on Ostrovski's play.

12 Psychological inner drives

1   This is Stanislavski's attempt to bring his ideas into line with Soviet psychology.
2   Eponymous hero of the play (1779) by Gotthold Ephraim Lessing (1729–1781).

14 The actor's inner creative state

1   Tommaso Salvini, *Qualche Pensiero Sull'arte Teatrale* in *Artist* No. 14, 1891.

15 The Supertask, Throughaction

1   In a letter written by Gogol after the first performance of *The Inspector General*.

16 The subconscious and the actor's creative state

1   For the status of this chapter see the *Foreword*.
2   'Idleness is pleasing.'

18 Physical education

1   Isadora Duncan (1877–1927), one of the founders of modern dance, whom Stanislavski met when she was on tour in Moscow.
2   Emile-Jaques Dalcroze (1865–1950), who developed a system of rhythmic movement to develop the co-ordination between mind and body.
3   Stanislavski put a question mark in the margin against this sentence.

19 Voice and Speech

1   In the Russian original *Singing and Diction*.
2   'My voice is my capital.'
3   Square brackets in the text here indicate a paraphrase of a passage where specific Russian sounds are referred to. In each case the original text is given in the footnote. In the original, this passage runs:

How disagreeable voices that are all bits and pieces are, when *A* emerges from the stomach, *E* from the glottis, *O* rumbles as in a barrel, and *U, Y, YOU* fall into a hole you can't get them out of.

4 Stanislavski is telescoping history. The exercises he is describing were done in the 1880s. Volkonski's book on speech was not published until 1913.

5 See note 3. In the original this passage runs:

We don't feel our language, phrases, words and letters and so we distort them easily: instead of the letter *SH* we pronounce *PFA* instead of *L* we say *WA*. The consonant *S* sounds like *TS* and some people change *G* to *GKHA*. Add to that unstressed O and A, lisping, guttural tone, nasal tone, shrieking, squeaking, creaking and stuttering.

6 See note 3. In the original this passage runs:

Now, try and develop syllables of three letters: *bar, bam, bakh, bats, bashch* . . .

7 See note 3. In the original this passage runs:

If you combine two syllables there is even more room for feeling: *baba, bava, baki, bali, bayou, bai, batsbats, bambar, barbuf.*

8 In the original Russian, *Speech and its Laws.*

9 'I love.'

10 Quotation from Schepkin's letter to S. V. Shumski, 27 March 1848.

11 S. M. Volkonski, *The Expressive Word* (1913).

12 Stanislavski is alluding to Hamlet's speech to the players, *Hamlet*, Act III scene ii.

13 In Russian there are specific verbs for indicating motion on foot and by vehicle.

14 W. S. Jeavons, *A Textbook of Logic*. Russian translation appeared in St. Petersburg in 1887; Stanislavski refers to page 87. The manuscript of the following section contains marginalia with alternative versions written at the suggestion of Stanislavski's brother, Vladimir, mainly for reasons of clarity.

15 This section and section 3 are variants of an earlier section but contain new material.

16 I. L. Smolenski in *Textbook of Declamation. On Logical Stress*, published Odessa 1907.

21 Tempo-rhythm

1 A famous French popular song of the eighteenth century.

2 Characters in Gogol's *The Inspector General.*

3 *Othello*, Act I scene i.

4 Quote from the Postmaster in Gogol's *The Inspector General*, Act I scene ii.

5 In the second act of a play by Paolo Giacometti (1816–1882), *La Morte Civile*, translated into Russian as *A Criminal's Family* by Ostrovski.

6 Poem by Goethe, 'The Erl King', best known in the setting by Franz Schubert.
7 A character type from neo-classical French comedy. The *raisonneur* is the man of sense and reason who tries to persuade others to take a middle path and avoid extremes.
8 Arthur Nikisch (1855–1922), Hungarian conductor.

22 Logic and sequence

1 Three manuscripts exist of this section. A number of drafts were gathered together by Stanislavski shortly before his death, so that he could rework them. Many pages are unnumbered. A second, earlier manuscript, entitled *The Logic of Feelings*, is dated November 1937. Stanislavski also considered including a section, *Logic and Sequence*, in a chapter entitled *Other Elements*.

23 Physical characteristics

1 In the section *The Socio-political line*.
2 Nedorosl in *Mother's Darling* by Fonvizin (1745–1792), Balzaminov in Ostrovski's *The Marriage of Balzaminov*.
3 There is a gap here in the manuscript with a note by Stanislavski: *The Outside affects the Inside*. The gap was apparently to be filled by a passage preserved in the archives. See Appendices.
4 Character in Griboedov's *Woe from Wit*.
5 Character in Ostrovski's play *Difficult Times*.
6 Stanislavski is writing during the Soviet period. In Tsarist society, social class was defined by law. These distinctions were abolished after the 1917 revolution.
7 See note 5 in this chapter.
8 The Russian equivalent of John Smith/John Doe.

24 The finishing touches

1 See Chapter 21, note 8.
2 In pre-revolutionary Russia, theatres were closed during Lent. Performances were given by foreign touring companies.
3 Ernst Possart, well-known German actor.

26 Ethics and discipline

1 The production referred to took place in 1926.
2 Oscar Wilde (1854–1900).
3 *Kean*, a play by Alexandre Dumas fils (1802–1870). The play, written in 1836, is subtitled *Disorder and Genius*.
4 Mochalov (see Chapter 7, note 3) was sometimes known as the Russian Kean.

28 General creative state in performance

1 The text speaks of the *first* year of the course, but the first year deals with the inner creative state. This section, like section 1, may originally have been intended to be included in Chapter 15 of Part One Year One, which Stanislavski continually revised.
2 See additional material in the Appendices.

Appendices

1 From Act I scene vii of Griboedov's *Woe from Wit*, translated by J. Benedetti.
2 These first of two articles was written in 1933 at the end of a text called *Physical Characterization* with a note in Stanislavski's hand, 'transfer, but where?'
3 An early version of *Belief and the sense of truth*.
4 Literally, 'Sew the deed, reap the habit'.
5 The Decembrists were a group of officers who had absorbed Western ideas about democracy. Their planned *coup* against the Tsar on 12 December 1825 was a failure.
6 Members of the technical staff at the Moscow Art Theatre.
7 'In and for itself.'
8 No such exercise is ever described. Stanislavski evidently means the scene with the madman.
9 Certain exercises relating to specific aspects of Soviet life in the 1930s have been omitted.
10 Togsin was an early hard currency shop where vouchers could be exchanged for goods not otherwise obtainable.
11 A short story by Pushkin.
12 The main character in Gogol's story *The Coat*.
13 The play *The Flood*, by Berger, was produced at the First Studio of the Moscow Art Theatre in 1915.
14 French. 'Incredible.'
15 By this term Stanislavski means a turning point in a play where an actor passes from one major action to another.

Afterword by Anatoly Smeliansky

1 Trans. Jean Benedetti.

GLOSSARY OF KEY TERMS: A COMPARISON OF TRANSLATIONS

RUSSIAN	AN ACTOR'S WORK	AN ACTOR PREPARES
Deistvie	**Action** In an Aristotelian sense, the play itself in which the actor must be an active participant. In a more restricted sense, anything an actor does purposefully in order to fulfil a **Task**. These actions are an integral part of the overall action.	Action
Prisposoblenie	**Adaptation** A modification of behavour in response to a reaction so as to fulfil an appointed task.	Adaptation
Vnimanie	**Attention** The ability to focus on a thing or a person to the exclusion of everything else.	Concentration of attention
Kusok	**Bit** A section of the total action of the play that can be explored separately. **Bits** can be large, medium or small. The definition of the Bit depends entirely on what the actor can understand and improvise	Unit

(Continued over)

RUSSIAN	AN ACTOR'S WORK	AN ACTOR PREPARES
	immediately in the early stages of rehearsal. Elsewhere, Stanislavski defined bits as episodes, events and facts.	
Krug Bvimaniya	**Circle of attention** The circle (small, medium, large) within which attention is focused.	Circle of attention
Obshchenie	**Communication** The act of being in contact with an object or in communcation with another person, verbally or non-verbally.	Communion
Stsenicheskoe Samochustvie	**Creative state** The creative state appears when the actor is fully prepared to be creative. There are three forms: a) The inner creative state when he is mentally ready b) The outer creative state when he is physically ready c) The general creative state when the two come together.	
Emotsional'nya Pamyat'	**Emotion Memory** The actor's personal memories which arise spontaneously as he explores the dramatic situation, or which are consciously evoked to strengthen the natural reactions.	Emotion Memory
Perezhivanie	**Experiencing** The process by which an actor experiences the character's emotions afresh in each performance.	Living
Predlagamemye Obstoyal'stva	**Given Circumstances** The dramatic situation created by the playwright which the actor has to accept as real. He will also need to accept the director's ideas, the set, costumes, lighting and sound as part of that reality.	Given Circumstances

(Continued over)

RUSSIAN	AN ACTOR'S WORK	AN ACTOR PREPARES
Ya Esm'	**'I am being'** The state of mind when the actor's personality and the written character come together and subconscious creation takes place.	
'Esli B'	**'If'** The actor must ask what he would do 'if' the Given Circumstances were really true.	If
Vnutrenij Zrenie	**Inner eye** The eye with which mental images are percived mentally.	
Vldenie	**Mental image** The picture the actor sees in his mind which relates to what he is saying or hearing.	
Podtext	**Subtext** The thoughts and mental images that occur in the actor's mind during the action.	Subtext
Sverkhzadacha	**Supertask** The theme or subject of the play. The reason why it was written.	Superobjective
Skvoznoe Deistivie	**Throughaction** The logical sequence of all the actions in the play that gives coherence to the performance.	Through line of action

AFTERWORD BY ANATOLY SMELIANSKY

A FEW WORDS ABOUT STANISLAVSKI'S 'MAJOR BOOK' AND THE MAN HIMSELF[1]

The world of the theatre knows Stanislavski's book *An Actor Prepares* very well. It appeared in 1936 and since then has often been published in many languages and many lands. Paradoxically, it is least known in the author's own country. That requires some explanation. K.S. (that was what his friends called him behind his back at the Art Theatre) wrote his book at the behest of an American publisher and gave his translator, Elizabeth Hapgood, a totally free hand. The manuscript was cut and adapted to suit the tastes of the American reader, who wanted a kind of 'Beginners' Manual'. The translator accomplished her mission. The book found its place in the English-speaking world. It appeared in Russian two years later, after K.S.'s death but not in the form in which Elizabeth Hapgood had presented it. A great deal had been rewritten, expanded, rethought in as much as K.S. continued to work on his system in those two final years and many thoroughgoing decisions were taken, yet again. The idea of the Method of Physical Actions emerged. It painted the grammar of acting in a new light. Besides which, K.S. was fully aware that his book would come out in the Soviet Union of 1938, and that had to be taken seriously into account.

The Russian version evolved in an atmosphere of extremes. In August 1934 K.S. returned from France to Moscow after lengthy treatment, passing through Germany where the Nazis were already in overall control. Hitler in Berlin, Stalin in Moscow: this was the choice which K.S. faced, as did most European artists. Publicly, K.S. preferred Stalin. In reality his choice was not so unambiguous. From the summer of 1934 to the end of his life, i.e. prior to 1938, K.S. did not set foot inside the Art Theatre he had founded, the Art Theatre, which now thought of him not in terms of his artistry but of his 'efficacy', i.e. as having nothing to do with major questions of art or of the development of that art. He worked at home with young actors and singers in the last of his studios, the Opera-Dramatic Studio. In reply to a question from Elizabeth Hapgood, he answered somewhat enigmatically, 'There is a rumour that I have quit the Art Theatre. It's a lie. The rumour stems from the fact that since my illness I have not been to the theatre, that is the reason. In winter, when there is ice and cold I can't leave the house. I have cardiac spasms (angina pectoris). In spring when I might be able to go and see my own and other people's productions, theatres like the Moscow Art Theatre and the opera are on tour. In the autumn, when performances begin again, I have to take a holiday. My work is conducted (for the all the theatres and the studios) only in my home in Leontievski Lane.'

Nature knows no such weather in which he could visit the Art Theatre of which he was head. But, of course, it was not a matter of ice and cold. Stanislavski did not set foot inside the theatre he ran for four years, it was a mark of general opposition, a voluntary rejection of it, which for various reasons served everyone. Condemned to a kind of house arrest, he made good use of it. He took no part in Soviet life, did not sign any group letters supporting the murder and torture of dissidents, did not stage propaganda plays. As far as was possible, he preserved his autonomy.

The period in which the Russian version of the book on acting was completed was the transition from 'vegetarianism' (as Anna Akhmatova put it) to 'the age of blood'. It should not be thought that Stanislavski was sheltered from the terror in his home as on a kind of island retreat. As early as June 1930 one of his favourite nephews had been arrested. Neither his status as a 'sacred cow' nor his pleas to the head of the secret police Heinrich Yagoda were of any help. Mikhaïl Alekseev died in jail. The only gesture of kindness that was made by the authorities was to hand his dead body over to his relatives. Other close relatives were arrested and K.S. took charge of their children. The word 'concentration camp' appears for the first time in his letters to mean imminent death.

Confined in his comfortable jail house in Leontievski Lane (the name was changed to Stanislavski Street in his lifetime), he decided to complete his 'great book', which, in Russian, would be called *The Actor's Work on Himself in the Creative Process of Experiencing*. The key word in this title is 'experiencing' which, like many of K.S.'s terms, defies adequate translation. This actor-teacher's slang was adopted by Stanislavski's pupils but was obscure for those unacquainted with the general spirit of his understanding of acting. An edited version appeared in America. K.S. prepared a book for his contemporaries with its meaning uncut. This book is now being offered to the English-speaking reader. The problem of translation is the problem of a general understanding of the Stanislavski system. And so we must be mindful of the circumstances in which K.S. decided on two versions – one for the world at large and one for Russia – and that what we in Russia call the *system* in the English-speaking world is often called mistakenly the *method*.

2.

For many years the system existed in oral form, as a kind of theatrical folklore. It changed according to those who taught it, to those who 'narrated' it. Repeated attempts to set forth Stanislavski's teaching in his place produced resistance from the author. This was even the case when the system was expounded by as intelligent a pupil as Michael Chekhov. That was the case when, let us say, the Art Theatre director Ilya Sudakov did the same (at the beginning of the 30s). In this last case K.S. went into a fury: 'It is not a matter of an author's pride,' he wrote to Tamantsova on 1 February 1934, 'but the fact that the thing I love most, to which I have dedicated my life, has been cynically violated and given over to the judgement of the crowd in mutilated form.'

We need to understand not only the emotional but the substantive reason why he was unwilling for so long to start a book on 'his precious creation' – the system – and generally pin it down in words. In his letters to Elizabeth Hapgood in 1936 he partially reveals the secret of his actor-writer laboratory. 'What does it mean, writing a book about the system? It does not mean writing down something that is already cut and dried. The system lives in me but it has no form. It is only when you try to find a form for it that the real system is created and defined. In other words, the system is created in the very process of being written down.'

The book had been written for America but K.S. was worried by a possible reaction in Russia. The views of his editor, Lyubov Gurievich, who had been one of the first to read the manuscript, confirmed his worst forebodings. His friend as well as his editor, whom he trusted absolutely, explained clearly and directly to him that his book with all its examples and ideals that stemmed from a pre-revolutionary view of an actor's life were doomed in the new Russia. She suggested that K.S. was completely out of touch with the new historical situation, that his favourite examples about precious jewels would be wide of the mark and even offensive. 'Dear Konstantin Sergeevich don't talk to the poor and starving about jewels and investments because it will only provoke bitter irritation in some and a brooding sense of resentment in others,' she admonished this white-haired child of a prophet on 1 April 1929.

Mrs Gurievich was not just speaking for herself but for 95 per cent of the 'ordinary, underprivileged intellectuals'. She suggested that he bring his book into line with contemporary life and adapt it to the needs of new post-revolutionary generations. She used basic concepts of the system as arguments, ' "Contact" with life and "adaptation" to his times – adaptation in the purest, noblest sense of the word, not some tawdry camouflage or compromise, is an artist's duty if he wishes to be effective. This "adaptation" requires great mental effort which you, given your way of life, have never had an opportunity to follow through. Almost every page of your book is revelatory in that regard.'

Broken in spirit, this woman soon wrote a special 'Memo' in which she presented Stanislavski with a plan for completing the system and 'adapting' it to contemporary life, both Soviet and American. The greatest difficulty in completing the manuscript, in the editor's opinion, was the fact that the tastes, ideas, moods of Russian and foreign society had never been further apart than at the present moment. Two worlds stood opposite each other as though prepared for armed conflict. The life, habits, domestic customs of our own pre-revolutionary life and the present Western way of life were inimical to the 'Soviet people' . . . as belonging to the capitalist system. And so, everything in the book that dated from an earlier life, literary descriptions, modes, examples that would draw a Western reader to it would be greeted with hostility by the Soviet people. The demands of home and abroad are irreconcilable.

In her second point, Mrs Gurievich sets out a list of ideological postulates that could not but frighten an author living, as it were, in another period. She knew his weak spots. The most dangerous offence was his beloved 'neutrality' which, she reminded him, 'would be equated by the party as being reactionary or counter-revolutionary'. She warned K.S. that he must be prepared for 'massive accusations of a similar kind' and so he had to address the burning questions of a new era. Not to do so would have 'fateful consequences for the book'.

This was the programme for 'conforming to the contemporary situation' of which K.S. ticked every point with a Yes. Had he followed all these points through it would undoubtedly have meant the death of his forthcoming book and of his life's work.

The agonising years of 'work on himself' began. But he just could not adapt. His genius would not allow it. Broken in spirit and law-abiding he started to baulk. 'If I work in even one of the examples you have found for our young contemporaries,' he wrote in a draft letter to Mrs Gurievich, 'I can say in all confidence that not only will my book never be published but I will never be allowed into America.' That was not included in the letter he sent. What was included was much more forthright in its expression. 'The book . . . speaks of the art of an older era, which was not created under the Bolsheviks. That is why the examples are bourgeois.'

Despite his usual display of political naivety, as he started work he could define absolutely precisely points that could be censored. 'To my mind, the greatest danger of the book is "the creation of the life of the human spirit" (you are not allowed to speak about the spirit). Another danger: the subconscious, transmission and reception, the word *soul*. Wouldn't that be a reason to ban the book.'

Historic change swept through the life of the Art Theatre. It was canonized. It was decided to create an academy alongside it, 'a forge for a creative workforce'. Model 'socialist' textbooks were required. The system took on a new direction. It ceased to be an actor's personal work and exploits. K.S. followed the government's superedicts. A special committee was set up to verify Stanislavski's writings from the point of view of the latest scientific advances. Particular alarm was caused by the draft of the final and most difficult chapter, 'On the Threshold of the Subconscious', which quintessentially defined his conception of the actor's art. The correspondence with a party official Aleksei Angarov reveals the direction in which they tried to steer Stanislavski in this matter, in an attempt, in exactly the same spirit as the 'black séance' in Bulgakov's *Master and Marguerita*, to unmask 'his mystical terminology'. (The irony of this story is that the official who kindly allowed K.S. to use his favourite concepts was very soon arrested and liquidated.)

Lyubov Gurievich stopped work as his editor. She could not endure K.S.'s endless corrections, changes, and obstinacy. 'An old friend was not unfaithful but forced by fate was invalided out like a wounded soldier' (from one of her valedictory letters to K.S.).

In the Russian version he was reaching out to the future. *An Actor's Work on Himself* came out a few weeks after Stanislavski's death.

The pressure of the given circumstances can be felt in his last book. There is not the same freedom with which he wrote *My Life in Art*. The first book is a book of major questions. The second is a book of answers. *My Life in Art* is confessional, *An Actor's Work on Himself* is professional. The attitude of an omniscient teacher and a genuflecting pupil are the principal 'psychological gestures' of the book and unconsciously reflect the dominant 'gesture' of the time. The majority of the omissions in the book are concerned with matters that he would not explicitly declare or explain. But he did not renounce the heart of the system, that is, his own heart. Fundamentally, his 'grammar' of acting is full of heroic acts of rejection. Antiquated in its machinery, Stanislavski's book managed to evoke the spirit 'not of contemporary but of the old, eternal, immutable art of the actor-craftsman and not of the actor-activist.

He did not allow the actor-activist in his home. Within the confines of his 'great book' as in his house in Leontievski Lane, there was not the least hint of the real Soviet world within which it was completed and refined. In both there was an almost museum-like clinical purity. Evidently, as far as possible, the book preserved what Osip Mandelstam described as 'stolen air', that is the air of another culture and other beliefs.

3.

And, finally, a few comments relating to the daily life of the system in contemporary Russian theatre. There the problem is not to translate from Russian into English but the equally complex problem of translating from Russian into Russian. The approach to the system and the way it is inter-preted changed endlessly after K.S.'s death, countries changed and the understanding of the actor's art changed. With the rehabilitation and reinstatement of K.S.'s major opponents, who had been liquidated by the Soviet regime, it became clear that the system had to be placed within the broad context of Russian and world theatre. Account had to be taken of the changes made by Meyerhold and Brecht, Michael Chekhov, Vakhtangov, Taïrov and Grotowski. New generations of Russian actors and directors undertook the enormous labour, often unbeknown to those abroad, of talking through the system and its basic terms. They tried to understand the system beyond the barriers to understanding. I will give just a few examples.

A few years ago, the actor Oleg Borisov's diaries were published post-humously. Borisov was probably one of the most important actors of post-Stalinist Russia. He graduated from the Studio-School of the Moscow Art Theatre, having imbibed the Stanislavski system with his mother's milk, he worked with Tostonogov, played in Dostoievski's *Krotkii* directed by Lev Dodin, spent many years at the Art Theatre. If we are to look for an actor to symbolize the Russian school of acting and what we understand by the system, that man is Oleg Borisov, as in his time was Michael Chekhov, possibly one of the first candidates for that vacancy.

In his diaries, the actor recounts how he adapted K.S.'s system to his own 'immune system'. He started from the fact that much had changed since K.S. had died and his system had been introduced into Russian schools 'blood boiled, overflowed and how they drank it!' Highly significant ideas underwent revision. The actor knows that the most important element in the system is to discover a conscious path to the unconscious, 'to switch off the brain entirely, to become a blank sheet of paper and move into the unconscious in a neutral state'. The problem is to know which technique will work. It all begins with the script. The actor removes all the punctuation marks ('once the first sign of life appears then you can feel a pulse – then you can draw the first line'). He followed K.S. in not trusting words, only deeds, but he refused to deal with them according to the system. He, essentially, rejected the 'throughaction', at least in the way that it was taught in school. 'First, set up a series of complete actions, then choose the most important of them. A mosaic is formed with no "threads", no through-action or the usual transitions. These must then be conveyed to the audience . . . Let everything in man's character be unexpected. The unexpected is the most precious feature in art. But what are we to do in the pauses, in other scenes? Disappear into the shadows. Give a breather. Only shoot at the right moment. Arrhythmia, unpredictability, that is what it is for. Of course, even unpredictability has to be structured, to avoid being meaningless. The actor makes friends with the eminent coaches and football-players of his time and he derives the idea of arrhythmia from new unexpected ways of playing football.' I offer this example so that the reader may understand how the Stanislavski system changed and survived in Russian theatre.

In his book, Valery Galendeev, a well-known teacher and comrade-in-arms of Lev Dodin, comes across, like Dodin, as one of the most powerful of Stanislavski's successors in contemporary Russian theatre, adapting K.S.'s system to himself. He invented his own slang in parallel to Stanislavski's. Dodin did not use the word 'concept' but replaced it with the idea of an *agreement*, as in *to come to an agreement*. These cautious words mean a level of mutual understanding between the participants, to counterbalance the director's own individual ideas as he approaches the other members of the rehearsal with his 'concept'. Dodin did not use the term through-action, fearing, like Borisov, to coarsen the very material the actor was using, and to lose the unforeseen in what he did onstage. 'I use the idea of action and counteraction instead,' the director said to me, 'that stops the actor from creating one line for a role out of one through-concept, that oversimplifies the acting.'

Anatoly Efros, another outstanding director and teacher of the post-Stalinist period, developed the so-called improvisatory method. Efros (following in the footsteps of his teacher, Marya Knebbel, a direct pupil of Stanislavski) tried once more to discover a basis which would enable the actor to use the improvisatory method of rehearsal, i.e. an endless attempt to test out and get into the play. This method has its origins in Stanislavski's final ideas but places the actor's improvisations at the centre of a given play. Efros invented his own slang, in which the unwelcome notion of throughaction was close to a cardiogram, in which there was a flat line (indicating death). For Efros the proper way to build a role recalled a 'curve', a real cardiogram, with its proper peaks and troughs and arrhythmia, etc.

Oleg Efreimov, with whom I was fortunate enough to work for many years at the Art Theatre (he ran it for thirty years), attempted to translate from Russian into Russian Stanislavski's highly important notion of the term *perezhivanie*, 'experiencing', which we now find highly obscure. In his mouth it almost always seemed to sound like 'living in' by which was understood the actor's ability to penetrate and fill every moment of his life onstage with vibrant material at times to create life, at others to complete an action. Living in means remaining alive in every second of the stage action, which moves ahead as a non-stop, complex *process*. This living process (*experiencing* for K.S.) is confronted each time by another kind of acting, which K.S. called *representation* and which Grotowski called the art of composition.

I had the occasion to hear another modification to the Stanislavski system from another director and teacher, Piotr Fomenko. The actor, Stanislavski suggested, must first of all understand what the character wants at any given moment, what drives his behaviour. But, Fomenko objects, quite often the actor, like anyone, does not know what he wants and in strict terms his action consists of trying to figure out what it is he really wants (incidentally, this mood is highly characteristic of many of Chekhov's heroes).

Anatoly Vasiliev, in the 80s, was involved in a sharp polemic with a French Stanislavski scholar (in Paris at a symposium devoted to Stanislavski). The well-known Russian director was aghast at the primitive interpretation (in fact a straight translation) of K.S.'s classroom slang as rigid formulae, a terminology that had lost all living sense. There is a whole section in the system called 'bits and tasks'. So the word *task* which K.S. used, means in the theatre not so much the process of setting ultimate goals for the actor, as the process of planting a seed, teasing the actor with something emotionally enticing, subtleties that provoke him into action, into the creative act. If you translate the word task literally, the director suggested at this symposium, it means you reduce it to something primitive, you kill the actor's living soul along with the living soul of the system.

I have mentioned one or two modifications to the system by contemporary Russian teachers and directors which stand alongside the classic modifications to it in the course of the last century made to it by Stanislavski's contemporaries and pupils and his major opponents. We should not forget that even when the Russian version of *An Actor's Work on Himself* was completed, Stanislavski asked Meyerhold to teach Biomechanics in the last of his studios. When Meyerhold's theatre was destroyed, he was unemployed but K.S. not only stretched out a helping hand to the condemned man, he set up a meeting between creative minds. He compared their coming together to digging a tunnel from opposite ends so that they should finally meet in the middle.

The meeting did not last long. In August 1938 Stanislavski died. Within a year Meyerhold was arrested, tortured in the cellars of the Lubyanka and shot. Discussions on the system were cut short for decades.

This discussion has come alive again at another level. The 'great book', its Russian version, remains, in its thinking, a significant and provocative monument in the culture of world theatre. It is fought with, it is modified in all sorts of ways, but no one seriously concerned with teaching theatre across the world can refuse to acknowledge K.S.'s work, just as no one interested in chemistry can refuse to acknowledge the periodic table created by Dmitri Mendeleiev. The comparison may not be entirely appropriate, but it seems to me essentially true.

Anatoly Smeliansky, PhD,
Rector of the Studio-School of the Moscow Art Theatre,
editor-in-chief of the new Russian edition of Stanislavski's *Collected Works* in ten volumes